Defining Crime

# Defining Creole

John H. McWhorter

UNIVERSITY PRESS

2005

# OXFORD

UNIVERSITY PRESS

Oxford   New York
Auckland   Bangkok   Buenos Aires   Cape Town   Chennai
Dar es Salaam   Delhi   Hong Kong   Istanbul   Karachi   Kolkata
Kuala Lumpur   Madrid   Melbourne   Mexico City   Mumbai   Nairobi
São Paulo   Shanghai   Singapore   Taipei   Tokyo   Toronto

Copyright © 2005 by Oxford University Press, Inc.

Published by Oxford University Press, Inc.
198 Madison Avenue, New York, New York 10016

www.oup.com

Oxford is a registered trademark of Oxford University Press

Library of Congress Cataloging-in-Publication Data
McWhorter, John H.
Defining creole / John H. McWhorter.
p. cm.
Includes bibliographical references and index.
ISBN-13 978-0-19-516670-5; 978-0-19-516669-9 (pbk.)
ISBN 0-19-516670-1; 0-19-516669-8 (pbk.)
1. Creole dialects—Grammar.   2. Creole dialects—Lexicology.
3. Creole dialects—Inflection.   4. Linguistic change.   I. Title.
PM7831.M365 2004
417'.22—dc22      2003061045

1  3  5  7  9  8  6  4  2

Printed in the United States of America
on acid-free paper

# PREFACE

This volume gathers thirteen of my articles over the past decade on creole languages. I have chosen those pieces that demonstrate several related general points that have most concerned me in my work: the definition of creoles as a synchronic, rather than solely sociohistorical, type of language; the grammar-internal diachrony that creoles have undergone apart from contact-related processes; and the fact that structural reduction, far beyond mere inflectional loss, can play as significant a role in language contact as calquing.

Overall, I believe that in much work in creole studies over the past few decades, sociopolitical persuasions have had a way of channeling and even distorting empirical engagement. The themes I treat in this volume are an attempt to identify this tendency for the purposes of pointing the way beyond it, which I believe will benefit creole studies, as well as linguistics as a whole.

All of the papers have been dusted off as thoroughly as possible. New data and sources are included wherever possible. Bibliographical citations are updated. Small errors that have come to my attention over the years are corrected. In many cases, I have even altered or revised observations or argumentation to reflect progress in my own thinking or in scholarly consensus. Some of the chapters are considerably abbreviated versions of the articles they were based on, my aim having been to fashion them as much as possible for the purposes of this anthology.

While I have assembled the papers to illustrate general themes, and have provided section introductions in support of that goal, obviously I did not originally write the papers for the purpose of later including them in a single volume. As such, there are inevitable overlaps between many of the chapters—for example, in terms of data adduced for particular points. I have tried to minimize this as much as possible. However, the fact is that very few readers will have occasion to read the anthology in its entirety, and for that reason, there are various cases where I decided that allowing the overlaps was the best choice.

# CONTENTS

# Defining Creole

# PART I

# IS THERE SUCH A THING
# AS A CREOLE?

When I was teaching a general linguistics class in 1996 and giving an overview of pidgins and creoles, an undergraduate asked me whether creole languages were identifiable as creoles from a synchronic point of view, rather than from a sociohistorical one.

I gave him the conventionally accepted answer for a creolist: "Yes, *creole* is strictly a sociohistorical term. If you looked at a grammar of a creole language without knowing its history, there would be nothing distinguishing that grammar in any way from an older language. For example, remember that Chinese doesn't have inflections."

Yet in the back of my head, I felt vaguely dirty having said that, because I knew that in my heart of hearts, I did have a strong feeling—at this point only that—that there indeed was something "different" about the grammars of the languages I had by then been studying for several years.

The particular work I had concentrated on had required an intensely cross-creole perspective, such that I had had occasion to acquire a basic familiarity with the grammars of almost all of the creoles for which grammars or a fair number of articles had been written. I also started studying creoles when it was still easy to have read every issue of the *Journal of Pidgin and Creole Languages,* since only six issues of it existed when I began studying creoles in 1989.

My experience had lent me a sense that, taken together, creole languages were indeed a "type" of language—although the obvious fact that this was a gradient "type" was clear from the differences between "creole" and "semi-creole" varieties or between basilectal and mesolectal varieties of continuum creoles such as the English-based ones of the Caribbean.

However, common consensus in the field, flagged by countless authors in their work, was that creoles were synchronically indistinguishable in any qualitative sense from older languages. Moreover, there has even been a certain sociopolitical flavor to the assertion: since its inception as an institutionalized subfield in the late 1960s, a tacit assumption in creole studies has always been that our job is partly to show the linguistics community and the world beyond that creoles are "real languages." Obviously, the assertion that they are indistinguishable from older languages is commensurate with that impulse. But then it must be acknowledged that, given the sad history of creoles' dismissal as "baby talk," an implication that creoles are "different" can be taken as tempting a return to framing the languages as "lesser." This is especially so, given the common misimpression throughout history and among laymen that inflectional morphology is the essence of "grammar" and structural sophistication.

In a particularly clear demonstration that creolist investigation is colored by advocacy as well as curiosity, one article (Adamson and Smith 2003: 83) notes: "Firstly, it must be *admitted* that Creole languages are not noted for the possession of inflectional morphology." The italics are mine: note that this is considered something to "admit," whereas a Sinologist would consider it a mere neutral observation. Afterward, the same authors note that "when it comes to derivational morphology, Creoles perform better"—"better," as if there were some kind of competition at stake. The authors themselves seem almost to have internalized the very "inflection envy" that so much creolist work is aimed at dispelling.

While I did not enter creole studies with sociopolitical intentions, I could barely help being passively imprinted by this Zeitgeist in the field. As such, for years I assumed that the truism "creole is not a synchronic term" was valid—actually, I avoided thinking about it very much. When a graduate student colleague asked me, "So, *are* creoles different from other languages in any identifiable way?" I told her, "From what I see, no." But it happened that we did not have occasion to continue the conversation, so I did not have to justify the claim. I made a note to myself to think about it harder in the future. Unsurprisingly, I never did—until that day in 1996, when actually mouthing out loud to an auditorium full of students an assumption that did not square gracefully with my empirical experience made me so uncomfortable that I decided to look further into the issue.

My intention was to be as unbiased going into my investigation as possible. My initial assumption was that I was going to find older languages that would have struck me as "creole-like" if I hadn't known that they weren't creoles, and that my task was simply to smoke out some languages like this and make a small contribution to the field by calling them to attention, given that the truism had always been asserted rather than demonstrated.

Of course, some writers considered the case closed by noting that, for example, Chinese has no inflections (and has serial verbs, free markers of tense and aspect, etc.) and is not a creole. But it always seemed to me that a ready riposte here was that Chinese languages also make use of lexical tone in a far more functionally central fashion than any creole does, and they also have more tones than any creole (e.g., four in Mandarin, nine in Cantonese). Thus the first question I developed for my investigation was simply, "What non-creole language has neither inflectional morphology nor lexically or grammatically contrastive tone?"

That question alone stumped a great many linguists I asked, but, luckily, I worked in a department with a typological bent, and my colleague Jim Matisoff informed me that there were plenty of such languages in Southeast Asia, such as Khmer. As time went by, it occurred to me that Polynesian languages also fit this description.

So my next task was to examine grammars of languages like these and honestly assess whether they struck me as qualitatively indistinguishable from the creole grammars I had dwelled on over the years. I was quite ready to find that grammars like Khmer and Maori did fit this description, and I would have considered this alone a useful discovery.

But quite early in my investigation, there was clearly no question. Perusing any grammar of these older languages, even the briefer ones, it was impossible to pretend that there was nothing saliently different from the grammars of Sranan, São Tomense Creole Portuguese, and Mauritian Creole, for example. One was struck overall by a vaster degree of elaboration in the grammars—richer vowel inventories, or vast batteries of numeral classifiers, or paradigms of conventionalized particles marking pragmatic shadings à la German's modal particles, or particles marking distinctions in possession, or any number of other things absent in Haitian, Cape Verdean, Negerhollands, and others.

What I sought, however, was a feature that cut across all of these older languages that was absent or starkly less common in the creole "type" that haunted me. Clearly, for example, numeral classifiers would not do, as these are present only in a subset of the inflectionless, toneless languages in question. Was there any feature in all of these languages that marked them apart from the creole "type" that I could not help but perceive?

That feature was noncompositional derivational morphology, along the lines of English's *understand*. This is especially obvious in grammars of Mon-Khmer and Tibeto-Burman languages, which so often flag the feature as a challenge to the learner or analyst, but it is also readily observed in grammars of Polynesian languages. And I was struck by the fact that this feature plus inflection and contrastive tone did not constitute a random set. All three are the kinds of feature regularly eliminated in rapid, untutored second-language acquisition (as opposed to, for example, adpositions or markers of tense or aspect), and then all three only emerge in grammars via gradual reinterpretation of other material. Thus the absence or paucity of these features in creoles, the world's newest languages, passes from observation to prediction.

This struck me as an observation worth sharing, and at this point I ventured the Creole Prototype hypothesis: that the only natural languages in the world that lack, or all but lack, all three of the above features will be creole languages—that is, the result of rapid untutored acquisition by adults (that is, pidginization) followed by conventionalization of their version of the language as a natural language.

After that, however, I was still nagged by a sense that this was not the full story: the "elaboration" aspect appeared to constitute a further distinction between creoles and older languages. Even a brief description of an older language, inflectional or not, regularly reveals a degree of *overspecification*—marking of distinctions that natural languages lack as often as they display, and thus ornamental to nuanced communication—of phonological, semantic, or syntactic distinctions that descriptions of creoles, whether brief or detailed, do to a starkly lesser degree. To wit, no creole has four tones, evidential marker paradigms, or ergativity. In later papers, I explored this distinction, presenting a metric of complexity that reveals even older analytic grammars as "busier" than creole ones, and demonstrating that creoles, rather than solely "relexifying" their source language grammars or merely shaving their lexifier grammars of inflectional morphology, consistently reflect less elaborated versions of their source languages' grammars.

*Après ça, le déluge.* My work in this vein has predictably been, as they say, controversial.

Claims that I am tagging creoles as "baby talk" in the vein of nineteenth-century thinkers and casting doubt upon the intelligence of creole speakers are, of course, a kind of willfully uncomprehending street theatre, which an element of modern academic tradition and educated Western sociopolitics encourages.

Beyond this, however, some have misinterpreted me as having claimed that creoles have "no morphology" and presented isolated examples of creole inflection and lists of derivational affixes in creoles—when, in fact, my claim is that creoles have little or no *inflectional* morphology while their *derivational* morphology, while obviously present, tends strongly to be semantically compositional. Meanwhile, the very nature of creole genesis entailed that some creoles had more contact with source languages over time than others, or that some creoles' source languages were more closely related than others' and allowed the retention of more "quirky" features than a context in which speakers spoke widely divergent languages, and so on. But some writers, constrained partly by the binary parametrical alternations of modern syntactic theory and partly by a natural human discomfort with gray zones, labor under the misimpression that the fact that some creoles display the Prototype less robustly than others, and somewhat more "elaborification" than others, refutes my conception. Because of the same discomfort with gradience, some address my hypothesis as claiming that creoles are maximally "simple," thereby assuming that the presentation of a "complex" feature or two in a creole language bodes ill for my model.

Yet the fact is that some of this misinterpretation is my fault in the end. I first introduced my idea in a paper in the journal *Language* that presented the core Prototype idea rather briefly, and whose main intent was to question the superstratist paradigm of Francophone creolists led by Robert Chaudenson and its Anglophone rendition presented by Salikoko Mufwene. As it happens, I initially did not expect the Prototype idea to occasion any particular controversy—given that no one until then had presented me with an older language contradicting it (nor has anyone to date). However, in real life, the Prototype section of the article attracted the most attention, while my impression is that what I considered the heart of the paper—the address of the superstratist school—has happened to elicit little interest over the years.

I unhesitatingly acknowledge that the outline of the Prototype idea in the *Language* paper was, in itself, an unsuitably brief and underargued presentation for a claim that has attracted so much examination. For this reason, I have since written a more detailed outline of the Prototype hypothesis, for a creole conference anthology, which also addresses the criticisms of the idea that had come to my attention by the time of its writing. That is chapter 1 in this volume, and it, rather than the *Language* paper, is what I consider the "official" statement of my thinking on the Prototype idea. Inevitably, a paper published in *Language* would always come more readily to the attention of creolists and other linguists than one tucked away in one of a now lengthy series of anthologies. As such, I present the anthology paper here in a more accessible venue.

Overall, the fact is that the sum of my thesis on what distinguishes creoles from older languages has at present been scattered across three journals plus the anthology. This is awkward, because I believe that it is impossible to completely engage the thesis without reading all or most of the papers in question. The Prototype hypothesis alone is but a fraction of the claim. I outlined the broader complexity issue in *Linguistic Typology* (reproduced here as chapter 2). But then the cross-creole nature of the article understandably may leave a reader seeking a close engagement with a small set of creoles and their source languages—that is chapter 3. A reader might also seek an even closer demonstration entailing just one creole and its source language—and chapter 4 gets down to cases with a detailed comparison of Saramaccan and its main substrate language, Fongbe, using new informant data from Saramaccan and Claire Lefebvre's recently published Fongbe grammar.

The final chapter in Part I, chapter 5, is a recast version of the paper that appeared in *Language*. The Prototype section is removed. I assume that the reader will take the first paper in the section as representative of that argument, and within this anthology, a reproduction of its preliminary rendition would serve only archival rather than demonstrative purpose. As such, the argument of what is here chapter 5 better represents its core intention. Given Robert Chaudenson's three decades of superstratist work and, more immediately to most Anglophone readers, Salikoko Mufwene's twenty-year run of articles taking the same perspective as unrefuted, it will be natural for many to assume that the superstratist conception is less hypothesis than fact, and to therefore suppose that a hypothesis assuming that creoles begin with pidginization neglects established canon. My goal in this final paper in the section is to demonstrate that the superstratist "top-down" creole genesis scenario is unsupportable, not only in view of the Creole Prototype observation but also in view of synchronic, diachronic, documentational, and sociohistorical fact.

I believe that engagement with the totality of these papers will make it difficult for most readers to misinterpret my argumentation in the ways that have been common since 1998. Certainly, I remain open to criticisms, and significant ones. But hopefully, these can address the actuality of my thinking rather than misimpressions inevitable from engaging only a subset of it—something so difficult to avoid given the mayfly life cycle of the academic journal article, quickly consigned to the oblivion of bound fascicles on university library shelves, or the anthology article, hidden between the covers of a book constituting but one more spine in a long series, usually read closely only by reviewers.

# Defining "Creole"
# as a Synchronic Term

## 1. Introduction

It has often been claimed that there are no synchronic features distinguishing creole languages from other ones, such that the term *creole* is in the strict sense solely a sociohistorical one, referring to certain languages born as lingua francas amidst heavy contact between two or more languages (Kihm 1980a: 212, Mufwene 1986a, Chaudenson 1992: 135, Corne 1995a: 121).

This idea, however, has rarely been subjected to close scrutiny from a typological perspective. In this paper, I will explore the hypothesis of what I have called the Creole Prototype more closely.

## 2. Epistemology of the Creole Prototype

Markey (1982) proposed a definition of creole based on a list of features such as lack of gender distinctions, SVO word order, lack of overtly marked passive, tense-aspect markers indicating the three basic distinctions (anterior, nonpunctual, and irrealis), and "semantic repartitions" of lexifier features, such as the use of a locative copula as a nonpunctual marker. This approach has been found insufficient, partly because many creole languages lack a few or even many of these features, and partly because there are non-creole languages that combine many of them. Indeed, Markey's checklist can be considered in large part a typology of analytic languages in general rather than creole ones.

Yet the inadequacy of Markey's approach does not rule out the logical possibility that creoles may be synchronically defined in another way, especially since Markey was concerned more with evaluating whether Afrikaans is a creole language than developing a theoretically self-standing definition of *creole* itself. In fact, since creoles are indisputably new languages, we are faced with a crucial question: since grammars are dynamic rather than static systems, why would we not expect there to be definable signs of youth in the structure of a new grammar? It would seem logical, in fact, that if a grammar is new, then it might be distinguishable from older grammars in terms of particular grammatical features *which are known to arise only over time.* Three such features include:

> *Inflectional affixation.* Over time, one possible fate of a free morpheme is to become a piece of bound inflectional morphology, having been gradually reanalyzed as grammatical rather than lexical. The development in Vulgar Latin, for example, of forms of the verb *habēre* into future and conditional marking inflections in many Romance languages is well known. (It must be clear that we refer not to inflection as an abstract feature of Universal Grammar, but to inflectional affixation.)

> *Tone.* Over time, one result of ongoing phonetic erosion is the development of tonal contrasts beyond the phonological level, such as distinguishing monosyllabic lexical items as in the Chinese varieties, or encoding morphosyntactic distinctions as in Bantu. (This is not the only source of tonogenesis but is one possible one.)

> *Derivational noncompositionality.* Over time, semantic drift leads some combinations of a derivational particle or affix with a root to become idiosyncratically noncompositional. For example, the Russian directional prefix *na-* signifies, compositionally, direction toward, as in *dvigat'sja* "to move" versus *nadvigat'sja*, "to move toward." However, there are many combinations of *na-* and a verb in which this semantic contribution is abstract to the point of lexicalization: *idti* "to go" versus *najti*, which compositionally would be "to go at" but in fact means "to find," or *kazat'* "to show" versus *nakazat'* "to punish."

The pathway from here to a proposed synchronic Creole Prototype begins with the very reason that these three particular features appear only over time. For example, whether or not it has tone, each language spoken by human beings is an expression of natural language generated via the principles of Universal Grammar (UG). Because of this, we can assume that tone is not a sine qua non of natural language but merely a possible manifestation thereof. More specifically, because tonal contrasts beyond the phonological level usually arise via phonetic change and suprasegmental reinterpretations of stress-based systems, we can specify that the tone traceable to this kind of change is ultimately but a by-product of the operations of such change, quite unconnected to any functional necessity inherent to UG. Similarly, inflectional affixation and noncompositional derivation are demonstrably unnecessary to natural language itself; they are frequently encountered permutations of natural language, which arise only because of the erosional processes that continually shape syntax and semantics.

The fact that these traits are epiphenomenal to effective communication is important, because there is a communication strategy typically used between groups speaking different languages but seeking transitory, perfunctory exchange: namely, the creation of a makeshift speech variety encoding only those concepts fundamental to basic communication. This strategy is the *pidgin*. For example, while the Native American languages spoken by their creators are highly inflectional, inflectional affixation is completely absent in Eskimo Pidgin (Van der Voort 1995: 145–47) and Delaware Jargon (Goddard 1997: 57); Chinook Jargon had none except for a tendency for some latter-day speakers to borrow English plural -*s* for a few nouns (Thomason and Kaufman 1988: 30); Mobilian Jargon had only a negator inflection (Drechsel 1997: 103–4). Fanakalo Pidgin Zulu has no tone despite Zulu's complex tonal system, while Chinese Pidgin Russian has no tone despite Chinese's (Neumann 1966, Nichols 1980). Derivational morphemes (free and bound) can be found to a small degree in pidgins, but what is important is that their usages are *compositional*: for example, there are no examples of the use of -*man* in the Russenorsk corpus which stray beyond indicating nationality or group, such as *russman* "Russian" (Broch and Jahr 1984: 156–66), and I am unaware of any description of a pidgin that mentions noncompositional uses of derivational apparatus. Pidgins, serving as useful, but merely utilitarian, vehicles of communication, certainly require, for example, nouns, verbs, predication, and interrogative lexemes, but inflection, tone, and derivational noncompositionality—features marginal even to nuanced communication (witness the myriad natural languages that lack a subset, or in the case of many creoles, all of them)—tend naturally to be severely reduced or eliminated entirely by pidgin creators.

Few would disagree with my statements thus far; however, there are implications to be drawn from them which are, at this writing, a departure from common creolist consensus. To wit, in reference to a thesis that *creole* is a synchronic concept, it is important that pidgins tend strongly to have few or no such features, because creoles often stem from pidgins. Specifically, the birth of many creoles as pidgins leads us to a hypothesis: that the *natural* languages of the world (which do not include pidgins) displaying the three particular traits above will be creole languages, and that conversely, no older natural languages will display them.

Significantly, it is indeed the case that these three traits are combined not only in pidgins but in several of the languages traditionally called *creoles*—that is, documented to have been born in the middle of the second millennium amid displaced multiethnic populations and their descendants, with limited opportunity or motivation to acquire a dominant language fully. Moreover, as of this writing, I have not encountered an older language that *combines* these three traits. It is my claim that the combination of these three traits is an indication that creoles are *new* grammars and, as such, constitute a *predictable* synchronic delineation of creoles from older languages.

It is important to realize that there is no claim that such features cannot be found individually, or even in a pair, in older languages. Because creoles are natural languages, we would not expect them to harbor any individual features unknown in older languages. The claim is that creoles are unique in *combining* these three particular traits. It is indeed plausible that natural languages differ according to this *combination* of features: some natural languages are new while most are ancient, and correspondingly, this particular combination is predictable in a grammar without a lengthy diachrony, as we will see in this chapter.

## 3. Specifying the three traits of the Creole Prototype

### 3.1. Inflectional affixation

Diachronically, inflectional affixes usually arise via the reanalysis of free lexical morphemes, which become bound grammatical ones via gradual phonetic erosion and semantic bleaching, with cliticization often being an intermittent stage in this process (Hopper and Traugott 1993: 6–10). As noted, pidgins tend strongly to have few or no inflectional affixes, because the functions they serve tend to be incidental to the utilitarian level of communication that pidgins typically serve (cf. Mühlhäusler 1997: 142–44). Therefore, we would predict that if a language fulfilled the following two criteria—(1) descending directly from a pidgin and (2) having existed for a relatively short time—that it would have developed few or no inflectional affixes.

This is indeed what was found in McWhorter (1998a) in a sample of eight languages traditionally called *creoles*, this term here taken sociohistorically to avoid circularity of argumentation—that is, all were developed via rapid adoption of a target language as a lingua franca by multiethnic populations in contexts discouraging the full acquisition of that target. Ndjuka English Creole, Saramaccan English Creole, Mauritian French Creole, St. Lucian French Creole, Angolar Portuguese Creole, Haitian French Creole (DeGraff 1999a)[1] and Negerhollands Dutch Creole[2] have no inflectional affixes. Tok Pisin English Creole has one, the adjectival marker -*pela* (the transitive marker -*im* is derivational).[3]

### 3.2. Tone

The use of tone to contrast monosyllables, like inflectional affixation, arises as the result of long-term change, often via consonantal erosion leaving formerly allophonic tonal contrasts to encode meaning contrast once indicated by the consonants themselves. Haudricourt (1954, cited in Matisoff 1973a) reconstructs, for example, the origin of three of the six tones in Vietnamese:

| Vietnamese (beginning of Christian era) | Vietnamese (sixth century) |
|---|---|
| pa | pa |
| pah | pà |
| pa' | pá |

Similarly, the use of tone to encode morphosyntactic distinctions is a diachronic development, generally resulting from the erosion of a vowel, leaving behind its tone as the sole marker of a function (termed "cheshirization" by Matisoff [1991: 443], in reference to the disappearance of the body of the eponymous cat leaving behind only its smile).

Pidgins developed by speakers of tonal languages tend strongly to reduce or eliminate tone *in these particular uses*. Kituba, for instance, was developed by West Africans and speakers of varieties of Kikongo, with the latter playing the dominant role in its stabilization and conventionalization. Despite the fact that Kikongo varieties are tonal, Mufwene (1997b: 176) notes that "Kituba has a predominantly phonological tone or accent system, instead of the lexical and/or grammatical tone system attested in ethnic Kikongo and in most Bantu languages" and that, "moreover, unlike in ethnic Kikongo, tone alone may not be used for tense/mood/aspect distinctions." When a smaller proportion of a pidgin's originators speak tonal languages, tone can disappear altogether, as it has in the pidginized Zulu, Fanakalo, which has been adopted by many South African Indians and whites.

Thus we predict that if a language is descended from a pidgin and is young, then it will make little or no use of tone to distinguish monosyllabic lexical items or to encode morphosyntactic distinctions. Again, this is the case: of all eight of our sample creoles, only Saramaccan makes marginal use of tone in these functions (and on this, see 4.2).

The claim here is certainly not that "creoles have no tone," because tone plays a role in a great many creole grammars. However, the roles it plays tend to be phonological ones, which there is no reason to suppose would be eschewed even in a makeshift, reduced variety like a pidgin. For example, Atlantic English creoles like Guyanese Creole English and West African Pidgin English use tone in various suprasegmental functions,[4] but native phonology, being the aspect of language most difficult to shed in second-language acquisition, often influences individual speakers' rendition of a pidgin. For example, Hiri Motu phonology differs according to speakers' native language (Dutton 1997: 26–27), and similar effects have been observed in Tok Pisin (Romaine 1992: 178–79, Muhlhäusler 1997: 139–40). Some creoles' originators have also substituted tone for a lexifier's stress, a fundamentally phonological process that leads epiphenomenally to some lexical pairs distinguished by tone: Papiamentu *papá* "father" vs. *pápa* "the pope" (Munteanu 1996: 185) and Saramaccan *kái* "call" from English *call*, *kaí* "to fall" from Portuguese *cair*.

Thus an originator of a pidgin can easily carry native *phonological* tone to even the most phonologically, not to mention grammatically, reduced pidgin, and in the case of segmentally identical bisyllabic words, this can extend to some *lexical* contrasts. However, to transfer tonal contrasts of *monosyllabic lexical items* would be formally impossible, given that the target language will have either polysyllabic words or monosyllabic words distinguishable by segmental contrasts. Even if the target did have monosyllabic words distinguished by tone, the correspondence between tone and meaning is so language-specific that the chances that any one syllable in the target would encode the particular range of tonally distinguished meanings that it did in the speaker's native language would be negligible. Meanwhile, transfer of tonally marked morphosyntactic contrasts would be blocked by the strong tendencies for pidgins to eschew inflectional affixation, and to the extent to which a speaker might be inclined to transfer a tonally marked derivational contrast, the opacity of the given contrast to the speakers of other languages in the context would discourage this, just as it does the transfer of individual native language inflections.

Therefore a creole can reveal itself as young even with tone playing a vital role in its *phonology:* it is the absence or marginality of *monosyllabic lexical* and *morpho-syntactic* tonal functions in creole grammars which is significant in the delineation of a creole prototype.

## 3.3. Noncompositional derivation

### 3.3.1. Metaphorical inference versus semantic drift

Preliminary responses to my observations on derivation have often been founded on a confusion between *institutionalization* and *lexicalization* (Matthews 1974: 193–94). Metaphorical and metonymic extensions, fundamental to human mental capacity, quite commonly distort the interpretation of derivation-root combinations from purely isomorphic interpretation. Unlike the long-term gradual process of *drift* yielding Russian's *najti* "to find," these extensions are easily *created spontaneously* by individuals, often on the basis of culturally contingent conceptions, without requiring long periods to develop. Aronoff (1976: 19) notes, for example, the use of *transmission* to refer to the engine component rather than the action: an engineer hardly required eons to apply the word *transmission* to the mechanism.

Because institutionalizations like these stem not from gradual, imperceptible drift but from synchronic human conceptual capacities, there is no motivation to hypothesize that they would be absent or even rare in creoles. For instance, the Saramaccan word for "supporter" is *báka-ma*, from behind-man, based on the expression *wáka a wã sɛmbɛ báka* "to walk behind a person" (Norval Smith, pers. comm.). While one certainly could only derive the meaning of *bákama* via explanation or context, as in *transmission*, the denotational relationship between the word's morphemes and its meaning is readily processible via the very powers of metaphorical inference that created the usage.

The type of noncompositional derivation-root combinations important in identifying a language as old are not these kinds of creative, culturally rooted institutionalizations of the sort that are rife in all natural languages, creoles as well as non-creoles. Our diagnostic is derivation-root combinations whose meanings are not only unpredictable from their parts by the first-time hearer, but where the semantic connection between the morphemes and their referent remains obscure even when the meaning of the word is known. In other words, our interest is in cases in which *the metaphorical connection between the synchronic interpretation and the original compositional one has become either completely unrecoverable or only gleanable to the etymologist or historical semanticist.*

Thus the Creole Prototype hypothesis does not entail a claim that creoles lack idioms and culturally embedded semantic extensions, for the simple reason that no natural language spoken by human beings does. As such, lists of such institutionalizations and idioms in a creole I have cited as fitting the Prototype cannot constitute refutations of my hypothesis, which was constructed in full awareness of such cases. *Transmission* and Saramaccan *bákama* contrast with a case like Russian's *najti* "to find" and *nakazat'* "to punish." The use of "go at" as "to find," or "show at" as "to punish," finds elucidation neither in cultural context nor in metaphorical inference except of the most highly tenuous nature. These are cases not of dynamic idiomatization but of opacification due to inexorable semantic drift.

### 3.3.2. Productivity versus noncompositionality

Contrary to some responses to McWhorter (1998a), the issue of importance regarding the role of derivation in the Creole Prototype is not the *productivity* of a language's derivational morphemes but the extent to which combinations of a given derivational morpheme and a root are predictable or not, or, in the terms of Aronoff (1976: 38), the extent to which they display "semantic coherence."

Productivity is a misleading focus for our purposes, first because its equation with compositionality is quite partial. The prefix *re-* in English is quite productive, and yet there are many uses of it that have drifted semantically into noncompositionality (having actually done so within the European languages they were borrowed from), such as *represent* and *repose*. In contrast, *-ity* is only fitfully productive (*credulous–credulity* but *spurious–*spuriosity*), and the nominalizer *-th* is not productive (*warmth–*coolth*), and yet their combinations with adjectives are generally compositional.

Productivity is also inappropriate as a diagnostic for these purposes because productive processes are, properly speaking, but a subset of the derivation in a language. The criterion for treatment as morphology in the Creole Prototype hypothesis is not productivity but *analyzability* (cf. Bauer 1988: 61), whether or not speakers process the item as morphology. Because productive derivation is naturally of central interest in the study of the rules generating grammars synchronically, theoretical morphologists often discuss derivation under a shorthand assumption that, for the purposes at hand, *derivation* refers to *productive* derivation. This is natural and unexceptionable; however, the Creole Prototype hypothesis examines not synchronic generation but the results of semantic drift. As such, its proper domain is not just productive morphology but this plus all diachronic layers of morphology still synchronically perceptible as such regardless of semantic drift or loss of productivity—that is, *analyzable* morphology.

Thus here we are concerned not with the productivity of a derivational morpheme but with the combinations of such a morpheme with a root that have semantically drifted from compositionality to the point that they must now be stored in the lexicon rather than generated.[5]

Despite its cruciality to my thesis, noncompositional derivation only occasionally requires sustained attention in the context of linguistic research. Thus it will be useful to examine the phenomenon across various languages in the next section.

### 3.3.3. Noncompositional derivation in older languages

In Tok Pisin, there are no noncompositional derivation-root combinations (Peter Mühlhäusler, pers. comm.). For example, the abstract nominalizer *-pasin* is compositional in all of its uses (from Mühlhäusler 1985: 625):

| | |
|---|---|
| *gut* "good" | *gutpasin* "virtue" |
| *isi* "slow" | *isipasin* "slowness" |

| | |
|---|---|
| *prout* "proud" | *proutpasin* "pride" |
| *pait* "fight" | *paitpasin* "warfare" |

By contrast, in an older language like German, the semantic contribution of the prefix *ver-* is often quite obscure. One usage conveys the notion of "away": *jagen* "to hunt," *verjagen* "to chase away." There are several extended meanings from this one: error ("away" from the right path), as in *führen* "to lead," *verführen* "to lead astray"; consumption or waste, as in *hungern* "to be hungry," *verhungern* "to starve"; and antonymy, as in *lernen* "to learn," *verlernen* "to forget." Furthermore, there are usages unconnected (synchronically) with these, such as union (*schmelzen* "to melt," *verschmelzen* "to fuse") and as a simple verbalizer of other parts of speech (*Gott* "God," *vergöttern* "to deify"). All of these usages occur in several cases in the lexicon (and it is significant that there is no derivational affix or particle in the eight creoles in question with this extended a range of connotations). Most important, however, there are a great many uses of *ver-* that are unattributable to any of these meanings: *nehmen* "to take," *vernehmen* "to perceive"; *schaffen* "to manage to do, pull off," *verschaffen* "to obtain"; *mögen* "may, to be able," *vermögen* "to enable" (transitive), "to be able to" (intransitive). This prefix bedevils the second-language learner because its usages throughout the lexicon are so varied and unpredictable.

A similar case is the Russian prefix *ras/z*. The prefix has three basic and productive meanings: separation (*kuporit'* "to cork," *razkuporit'* "to uncork"), dissemination (*razbegat'sja* "to run off in various directions"), and inception (*smejat'sja* "to laugh," *rassmejat'sja* "to burst out laughing"). The Russian speaker easily perceives these core meanings. However, with many verbs, the combination of its meaning with the noun or verb is no longer, in Aronoff's terminology, "semantically coherent," and must be stored in the lexicon: *pisat'* "to write," *raspisat'* "to paint"; *plata* "pay," *rasplata* "retribution," *vedenie* "leading," *razvedenie* "animal breeding."

We see similar examples in Mande varieties such as Mandinka and Bambara. In the latter, the prefix *la-* often encodes causativity: *bo* "to leave," *labò* "to make leave" (Bazin 1965: 351). However, quite often, roots affixed with *la* have become compositionally opaque (Bailleul 1981; orthography follows that source in these and above examples):

| | |
|---|---|
| *bi*ₙ "to fall" | *labi*ₙ "to help" |
| *gǫsi* "to hit" | *lagǫsi* "to criticize" |
| *bạto* "to respect" | *labạto* "to effect a law" |
| *sǫrò* "to get, receive" | *lasǫrò* "to have time for" |

Importantly, noncompositional derivation is also quite common in languages of Southeast Asia, and this is particularly important because some of these languages have neither inflectional affixation nor tone, such that the derivation is the pivotal feature distinguishing them from older languages. An example is the derivational affixes in Chrau, a Mon-Khmer language of Vietnam, which clearly show the effects of semantic drift over time (comments on the noncompositionality of derivational morphemes in languages of this region are particularly common in their grammars[6]). The core meaning of the affix *ta-* is causative (*chuq* "to wear," *tachuq* "to dress"), extended into passive meaning (*ănh rung daq* "I pour water," *daq tarung* "the water got spilled") and unintentionality (*tapăng* "to close unintentionally"). However, there are also opaque lexicalizations with *ta-*: *dâp* "to dam up," *tadâp* "to fold or hem a shirt"; *chĕq* "to put, set," *tachĕq* "to slam down"; *trŏh* "drop," *tatrŏh* "jump down" (Thomas 1969: 102). Meanwhile, the prefix *pa-* has drifted so far from its original meaning that no synchronic meaning is perceivable (Thomas 1969: 103, Thomas 1971: 153):

| | |
|---|---|
| *găn* "go across" | *pagăn* "crosswise" |
| *le* "dodge" | *pale* "roll over" |
| *lôm* "lure" | *palôm* "mislead" |
| *lăm* "set, point" | *palăm* "roll" |
| *jŏq* "long" | *pajŏq* "how long?" |

There is also a prefix *n-* whose meaning is similarly uncoverable (ibid.):

| | |
|---|---|
| *hao* "to ascend" | *n'hao* "up" |
| *ta-ŭm* "to make bathe" | *ta-n-ŭm* "to make bathe" |
| *pajwăch* "to crumple something light" | *pa-n-jwăch* "to crumple something stiff" |

Importantly, speakers perceive these morphemes as affixes (Thomas 1969: 90–91): in other words, while no longer *productive*, they are *analyzable*.

In the preface to the most extensive dictionary of the Mon-Khmer language Khasi, Singh (1983: iii) specifies that examples with derivational prefixes will not be given, "excepting the case where the derivatives so formed bear a special meaning from that of the radicals." In modern terms, Singh meant that only institutionalizations and lexicalizations would be listed, and Khasi has many examples of both. For instance, *ia-* is an associative or reciprocal prefix, used compositionally in cases like *lekhai* "to play," *ia-lekhai* "to play together." There are some conventionalized institutionalizations like *ia-mai* "to quarrel" from *mai* "to scold." Quite common, however, are uses where no associative or reciprocal connotation holds any longer (*ia-lam* "to lead"). In many cases such as the previous one, the prefixed version coexists with a bare reflex of the verb with the same meaning. In others, however, there no longer exists any readily perceivable relationship between the root and the derived reflex: *poi* "to reach, arrive," *iapoi* "to cohabit."[7]

Noncompositional derivation is also found in Oceanic languages, many of which also have low or absent inflectional affixation and no tone. For example, in Fijian, the most productive use of the prefix *va'a* is as a causative prefix, as in *vuli-ca* "to learn" and *va'a-vuli-ca* "to teach" (Dixon 1988: 50). However, with intransitive verbs, its contribution becomes more idiosyncratic: *taro-ga* "to ask," *va'a-taro-ga* "to ask many times," but *muri-a* "to follow," *va'a-muri-a* "to follow where there is difficulty" (ibid. 51). *Va'a* can also be affixed to nouns, but in these cases the meanings not only depart from any conceivable metaphorical extension of causativity but are quite difficult to characterize as representing any single unified meaning: *mavoa* "wound," *va'a-mavoa* "harmful" (ibid. 182), *gauna* "time," *va'a-gauna* "occasionally," *mata'a* "morning," *va'a-mata'a* "breakfast" (ibid. 184).

Indeed, cognates of the Fijian *va'a* in its close relatives the Polynesian languages have typically drifted into noncompositional uses, a phenomenon characterized by

Neffgen (1918: 35) on Samoan: "In a great many cases these words formed with *fa'a* have lost their original signification, and in others they have come to bear quite a different one." In Samoan the prefix, besides its causative use, creates denominal verbs as in *ta'ita'i* "guide," *fa'ata'ita'i* "to convey"; however, there are also examples like *tau* "wages," *fa'atau* "trade, buy, sell" (ibid. 35–36). In Rapanui we find examples like *roŋo* "message," *hakaroŋo* "to obey" (Du Feu 1996: 179).

Finally, there are other noncompositional derivation-root combinations in Polynesian languages. In Rapanui, the abstract nominalizing suffix -*Vŋa* is used compositionally in cases like *mate* "death," *mateiŋa* "dying" but also in cases like *papaku* "corpse" versus *papakuiŋa* "low tide" (ibid). In Tokelauan, the reciprocal circumfix is *fe- -il-aki*, as in *hogi* "to kiss," *feahogi* "to kiss each other"; the compositional uses occur alongside cases like *ilo* "to perceive," *feiloaki* "to meet" and *olo* "to rub, file," *feoloolo* "to be better" (reduplication signifies iteration or diminutivization) (Hovdhaugen, Hoëm, Iosefo, and Vonen 1989: 108).

Like productivity, noncompositionality is a gradient rather than a binary phenomenon, which arises via the accreted effect of small steps in reinterpretation over centuries. Aronoff and Anshen (1998: 242), for example, note slight departures from predictability like *immeasurable*, whose composition encodes "unable to be measured" but whose core meaning in practice is "very large." As such, the compositionality of words with Russian *ras/z-* manifests itself not according to the binary degree of contrast represented by the compositionally transparent *razkuporit'* and the opaque *rasplata*, but in intermediate cases such as *vraščhat'* "to turn" versus *razvraščhat,'* whose literal meaning of "to turn away" has an obvious metaphorical connection to its actual meaning "to corrupt." Another example would be the Bambara *fasa* "to toughen, thicken" versus *lafasa* "to encourage." As such, only a subset of the uses of German *ver-*, Russian *raz*, Bambara *la-*, or the Polynesian causative marker are completely noncompositional, a typical situation with derivational morphemes in old grammars. What is important to the hypothesis proposed is whether or not there is a strong tendency for creoles' derivational morphemes to *not* include such a subset of noncompositional, lexicalized usages.

Finally, it must be clear that I refer not solely to derivational *affixes* but to derivational *morphemes* in general, including both free and bound forms: affixation is not a necessary condition for lexicalization of derivation-root combinations. For example, the Lahu verb *te* "to do" has grammaticalized into a causativizer, but there are concatenations that have lost compositionality, such as its use with *tâʔ* "to carry," in which case it means "to carry along" (Matisoff 1991: 432). There are also institutionalized uses such as with *câ* "to cook," where compositionality has not been lost altogether, but the meaning is not "to make cook" or even "to feed" but "to make it so that people can eat" (Matisoff 1973b: 246).

Derivation is regularly compositional (with allowance made for the institutionalizations inherent to any natural language) in Ndjuka, Saramaccan, Tok Pisin, Angolar, and Negerhollands (confirmed for all five via reference to grammars, available glossaries and dictionaries, and personal communication with experienced researchers on each). There is a degree of noncompositional derivation in the French creoles—Haitian, Mauritian, and St. Lucian—but as we will see in section 5 in this chapter, this is easily accountable for under my hypothesis and, in fact, provides a useful illustration of certain aspects of it.

It is perhaps tempting to interpret these three features as an arbitrary set, the validity of my approach invalidated by a possibility that the conjunction of features is either accidental, or epiphenomenal to a broader factor, which could also be shown to operate on various subsets of older languages. For this reason, I must reiterate that these three features share something uniquely pertinent to my thesis: they are all symptoms of the aging of a natural language, in syntax, phonology, and semantics, respectively. In other words, my hypothesis is that these three traits will *not* be found to apply to any subset of older languages.

Linguistic argumentation does not typically occasion that three topics as particular and seemingly unconnected as inflectional affixation, monosyllabic lexical and morphosyntactic tone, and noncompositional derivation be treated as the central components of a unified thesis. Yet what is of concern to synchronic analysis can sometimes contrast strikingly with what is of concern to a diachronic one. The three features of the Creole Prototype, in this light, are analogous to proportions of decayed radioactive atoms in rocks: of no interest to the petroleum geologist, but all-important to the paleontologists interested in dating the rocks.

## 4. The gradience of the prototype

The hypothesis that creole is a synchronic concept is not based on an attempt to draw a binary distinction between creoles and older languages. Creole genesis was constrained by ratios of speaker to learner, how quickly the latter outnumbered the former, degree of homogeneity of the languages spoken by the learners, and how long source languages continued to be spoken. Because all of these are inherently gradient processes, it is the task of any language contact theorist to approach gradience as an unremarkable yet vital factor. A theory about language contact must be neither created nor evaluated on the misleading notion that the binary contrasts typical of quantum physics are appropriate to the subject matter.

As such, I propose not that every creole language has the above mentioned three traits. This claim would be false. Rather, I propose that as products of gradient language contact phenomena, creoles conform to the hypothesized prototype in degrees: some hew to it, while others fall away from it to varying extents.

To be sure, used inappropriately, an appeal to gradience can serve as a mere fig leaf for sweeping unruly data under the rug. As such, in reference to a hypothesis that there is a creole prototype, gradience can only be appropriately appealed to in an empirically falsifiable manner.

In this vein, there are precisely four factors that determine how closely a given creole will conform to the prototype.

### 4.1. Typological similarity of source languages

Most creoles were developed by people speaking typologically disparate languages, the usual situation being Romance or Germanic Indo-European speakers encountering speakers of various Niger-Congo and Austronesian languages. But in larger view, this was a by-product of the fact that so many creoles were born during a period when a few Western European powers were drawn to fertile subequatorial regions in pursuit of profit and subjugated the peoples who happened to live there. There have arisen some creoles whose lexifier and substrates were all closely related languages. The similarity of the languages involved allowed speakers to retain structural idiosyncrasies particular to that language group which, in a more ethnically heterogeneous setting, would have impeded communication and thus not have entered the contact language.

Our hypothesis proposes that the three prototypical traits in question are due to the roots of a creole in a pidgin, the crucial traits of the pidgin being its virtual or complete lack of affixation or monosyllabic lexical and morphosyntactic tone. As such, this would lead us to predict that creoles descended from lingua francas with ample affixation and/or lexical and morphosyntactic tone would not conform to the Creole Prototype, and this is indeed the case.

Sango, for example, was developed and stabilized largely by speakers of a dialect continuum of Ubangian Niger-Congo languages. Although it is much more analytic than any of these languages, Sango nevertheless retains some inflectional affixes and lexical and morphosyntactic tonal contrasts, unlike creoles like Ndjuka or Angolar (Pasch 1997: 223–30). In these sentences we see two inflections, and in addition, they happen to be distinguished by tone (CONN = connective, SM = subject marker):

(1)   (a)  Lò fá  á-kongba tí      yá      tí      dà      kíríkìrì.
           he cut PL-good  CONN interior CONN house messily
           "He destroyed the things in the house left and right." (Samarin 1967: 80)

      (b)  Zò      kíríkìrì à-língbì tí      mú yɔrɔ      pɛpè.
           person any      SM-can CONN take medicine NEG
           "Not just anybody can take the medicine." (ibid. 81)

Lingala and Kituba, both largely developed by speakers of Bantu languages, fall quite far from the Prototype as well, the written variety of the former being morphologically elaborated to the point that many are surprised that it is even classified as a pidgin or creole language.

## 4.2. Diachronic drift

The Creole Prototype hypothesis stipulates that creoles tend to have the three traits in question because not enough time has passed for the diachronic processes in question to have had significant effect. However, since most creoles have already existed for several centuries, we would predict that at least some of them would already show signs of such processes having taken place to some small extent.

This is indeed what we find, and as such, some creoles depart slightly from the Prototype. However, these cases do not speak against the hypothesis itself *when it can be firmly reconstructed that at its genesis, the creole lacked the nonprototypical traits in question.* (There can thus be no valid appeal to diachronic drift based merely on unconstrained speculation.)

For example, Tok Pisin is arguably developing a habitual inflection from the erstwhile free marker *save: mi save kaikai banana* "I eat bananas" is pronounced [mi sakaikai banana] in rapid speech (Mühlhäusler 1985: 638–39). Meanwhile, Saramaccan has a few uses of tone to encode morphosyntactic contrasts, but they are relatively recent innovations, empirically traceable to diachronic evolution of original constructions in which tone was of no contrastive import (i.e., these features are absent in earliest documentation of the language). For example, *a* is the third-person pronoun while *á*, with high tone, is the predicate negator (*Kófi á wáka* "Kofi does not walk"). However, historical analysis reveals that in the original grammar, the negator was *ná*, with no high-tone *á* contrasting with the low-tone pronoun *a*. The negator *á* resulted from the fusion of a preceding pronoun *a* and a following negator *ná* in topic-comment constructions (see chapter 7 for details):

| *Stage 1* | *Stage 2* | *Stage 3* |
|---|---|---|
| Kófi, **a ná** wáka | Kófi, **á** waka | Kófi **á** wáka. |
| "Kofi, he doesn't walk" | "Kofi, he doesn't walk" | "Kofi doesn't walk." |
| a wáka | a wáka | a wáka |
| "he walks" | "he walks" | "he walks" |

Thus the modern tonal contrast between the pronoun *a* and the negator *á* is a recent development, in a grammar within which monosyllabic lexical and morpho-syntactic tone is distinctly marginal; there are no such contrasts that are not readily analyzable as internal developments rather than original endowments. This is demon-strable not just through historical documentation and internal reconstruction but in synchronic fact. Saramaccan is one of several closely related Surinam creoles, and in its sister Ndjuka, the more conservative distinction between pronominal *a* and the negator *ná* survives (although *á* is also optional as a negator): *A **ná** abi mati* "He didn't have any friends" (Shanks 1994: 136).

## 4.3. Heavy substrate contact

Another factor that can draw a creole away from the prototype is strong influence on its development by an older language, with all of its historical accretions. For ex-ample, there are creoles whose current form was considerably shaped by contact with one or more of the languages spoken natively in its genesis context. This phenom-enon can have effect either at the time of genesis or over the course of the creole's subsequent existence.

### 4.3.1. Substrate influence at genesis: Berbice Dutch Creole

Historical reconstruction suggests that speakers of the Nigerian Niger-Congo lan-guage Ijo predominated on the early plantations in the Berbice colony of present-day Guyana (Smith, Robertson, and Williamson 1987), and indeed this is the only possible explanation for the singularly heavy influence of the Eastern variety of Ijo on Berbice Dutch Creole's structure. It contains some inflectional affixes (as well as grammatical items) from the language, such as the plural marker *-apu* and a perfec-tive marker *–tɛ*.[8]

### 4.3.2. Substrate influence after genesis: Sri Lankan Portuguese Creole

Sri Lanka Portuguese Creole was one creolization of a makeshift pidgin that the Portuguese used in their interracial contacts in Southern Asia (cf. Ferraz 1987); others include various Portuguese-lexicon creoles in India, Malaysia, Indonesia, and Macao. The Sri Lankan variety has been spoken alongside Tamil and Sinhala since its birth in the sixteenth century. As a result, it has recruited Portuguese items to create many nominal and verbal inflections functionally modeled on these two substrate languages (Sinhala, though genetically Indo-Aryan, has converged structurally with the Dravidian Tamil to a considerable degree) (Smith 1984):

(2)  "E:w te:n  dizey ta:l pesa:m-**pə**     **pə**-kəza:," fəla:-**tu**.
     I     have  desire such person-ACC INF-marry QUOTE-PERF
     "I want to marry such-and-such a person." (Smith pers. comm., cited in Holm 1989: 290)

### 4.4. Heavy superstrate contact

Many creoles have arisen and survived in contexts where the lexifier language has continued to be spoken, the usual result being that the lexifier and the creole coexist in a diglossic relationship. Diglossic relationships are inherently porous, with varieties intermediate between the two speech varieties often occurring, such as Greek *mixti* between the "high" *katharévousa* and the "low" *dhimotikí*, and Arabic *al-lugah al-wusṭā* (Ferguson 1972 [1959]: 240). As such, contexts like these tend to pull a creole away from the prototype I propose.

Even though in many cases, only a minority of the creolophone population speaks the lexifier itself, low levels of bilingualism are well known for having a disproportionate effect, even on casual spoken language. Only a minority of English speakers were at any point bilingual in French during the Norman occupation of England, and yet the well-known predominance of French-derived words in even casual English speech traces directly to that bilingualism; the effect of Chinese on Japanese is a similar case among many (Miller 1967: 245).

Again, this lexifier influence can occur either at genesis or afterward.

### 4.4.1. Superstrate contact at genesis: Réunionnais

Réunionnais French is often termed a semi-creole because it is closer in structure to French itself than are creoles like Haitian or Mauritian. Baker and Corne (1982) show that this is because in Réunion there was a long period of several decades when the French coexisted with Malagasies and Indians (the initial servant class) in small-scale, intimate social contexts in relatively equal numbers. These settings conditioned less distance between the contact language and French than was the case in many other French plantation colonies.

For example, Réunionnais retains feminine gender inflection on some nouns, plural inflection in some (Corne 1999: 78), and various inflected forms of the verb "to be" (ibid. 81). In some varieties, such inflections are retained on verbs in general: *mi i mañz* "I am eating," *mi i mañze* "I ate," *mi i mañzre* "I would eat," *mi i mañzra pa* "I will not eat" (the latter inflection used only with negation) (ibid. 80–83). Only the variety closest to French has verbal inflection to this extent, while the others restrict this to *et* "to be," *awar* "to have," and *fo* "to be necessary" (ibid. 81), but even this contrasts significantly with the markedly lower degree of verbal inflection even in acrolectal varieties of other continuum creoles like Cape Verdean Portuguese Creole or, more pointedly, the French creole of Louisiana (Neumann 1985: 52–68; see 4.4.2 in this chapter). The following passage demonstrates the relative closeness of Réunionnais to French, including its inflectional affixation:

(3)  Li voud**ré**     bien qu'elle y    rogarde in pé   band' fim' dokimentaire . . .
     he want:COND well that-she VM look.at a little PL    film documentary
     "He would like [for her] to be able to watch some of the documentaries . . ."

     Elle y    pou**ra**   kiltive    a elle in pé.
     she  VM can:FUT cultivate to she a little
     "She could improve her mind a bit." (Corne 1999: 77) (orthography based on French;
     VM = verb marker)

### 4.4.2. Superstrate contact after genesis:
### Louisiana French Creole

The French creole of Louisiana has coexisted alongside Cajun French for over 250 years, with contact increasing especially after the end of slavery. As a result, this creole is unique among French plantation creoles in having developed a "mesolect" variety that includes some inflection from (Cajun) French. This includes gender marking, albeit highly variable in occurrence, of indefinite and possessive determiners and adjectives (*ẽ gro ŝjẽ* "a big dog," *en gros ŝaʳ* "a big car" [Neumann 1985: 138]), and an alternation in verbs between a short form (using the finite Cajun forms) expressing habituality and a long form (using the Cajun infinitive form) expressing accomplished aspect:

(4)  (a)  Mo **res** isi   ondõ la  mezõ mo tu sel.
          I    stay here inside the house me all alone
          "I live alone in this house." (Neumann 1985: 195)

     (b)  Mo **reste** a    Teksas trwas-õ.
          I    stay   LOC Texas  three-year
          "I have lived in Texas for three years." (ibid.)

The evidence that this creole has moved toward French over time, rather than having originated as a mesolectal variety as Réunionnais did, includes documentary evidence (cf. Neumann 1985: 44–70) and distributional facts such as that the variety of the creole which has been most isolated from Cajun French (the St. Tammany Parish variety) lacks the long-stem verbs described above (Marshall 1997: 344–45).

## 4.5. Implications for the Creole Prototype hypothesis

Because of the operations of these sociohistorical and diachronic factors, it would plainly be false to state that "all creole languages display these three states in their purest form." The falsity of that statement, however, signifies not that there is no synchronic result unique to creole genesis but, instead, that this synchronic result will be a *gradient* one, more evident in some creoles than others. Specifically, I predict (1) that one of the aforementioned four factors will apply to all creoles departing from the Prototype, and (2) that none of those four factors will apply to a creole conforming to the Prototype.

Thus our claim will not be "all creoles have these three features" but, rather, a bipartite claim that appears to account for the typological facts:

a. A *subset* of creole languages will display the three prototypical features
b. Any natural language that displays the three prototypical features is a new language that emerged as a pidgin spoken by adults and was transformed into a natural language: namely, a creole.

## 5. Situating gradience within the model: Demonstration case—Haitian Creole

DeGraff (1999a) observes that Haitian Creole has some nominal inflection and a degree of semantically opaque derivation. This observation is important to creole studies for myriad reasons, but contrary to DeGraff's implication that it constitutes a contradiction to the Creole Prototype hypothesis, in fact it is useful in lending a closer view to how this model accounts in a falsifiable fashion for gradience. Thus, Haitian Creole can be used to explain a language contact phenomenon as it has manifested itself in the real world, rather than a schematic abstraction thereof.

## 5.1. Haitian "inflection"?

DeGraff's claim that Haitian has gender inflection is mistaken. DeGraff usefully points out that Haitian has feminine allomorphs for various suffixes denoting origin, occupation, role, or quality, such as *Ameriken/Amerikèn, radotè/radòtèz* (< Fr. *radoteur/radoteuse*) "person who talks nonsense." Yet this is not grammatical gender but natural gender, which, in changing the denotation of the root and applying to only a subset of the nominal and adjectival classes, is traditionally treated not as inflection but as derivation (Matthews 1974: 47–48, Beard 1998: 57–58). In this light, our claim is not that creoles lack derivation but that its applications be compositional, and all of the examples DeGraff presents quite clearly denote a male/female gender distinction. These must be contrasted with noncompositional occurrences of natural gender marking in older languages, such as the masculine marking of the word for "daughter-in-law" in Latin *nurus*, traceable to a similarly marked Proto-Indo-European form *snusós* (Watkins 1985: xiii–xiv).[9]

## 5.2. Noncompositional derivation

The data DeGraff presents that is pertinent to the Creole Prototype hypothesis is noncompositional derived roots. Again, the data of interest in evaluating this hypothesis constitute a smaller set than DeGraff presents. For one, since I do not claim that creoles lack derivational affixes (McWhorter 1998a), DeGraff's ample listing of various Haitian derivational affixes and words containing them serves as a response to previous broader claims that creoles lack affixation as a whole (e.g., Seuren and Wekker 1986: 61), but not my own.[10]

In the meantime, the use of the derivational prefix *de-* in Haitian is much less semantically irregular than DeGraff implies. In my brief mention of the item in McWhorter (1998a: 797), I characterize its function as inversive, based on pairs like *grese* "to gain weight"/*degrese* "to lose weight," following Brousseau, Filipovich and Lefebvre (1989: 9). However, there is a second reflex of *de-* that is closely related semantically to the inversive one, which can be characterized as encoding "away from." This is its function in a great many of the examples that DeGraff lists, by virtue of not instantiating my particular "inversive" designation, as "noncompositional":

| | |
|---|---|
| *koupe* "to cut" | *dekoupe* "to cut off" |
| *tire* "to pull" | *detire* "to stretch" |
| *vire* "to stroll, drive" | *devire* "to detour, go on an errand" |
| *vide* "to empty" | *devide* "to empty out" |

Importantly, this usage has a semantic relationship to the inversive one, and this relationship is so intimate and readily perceived as to readily suggest a single semantic space rather than two separate ones. It is likely that this secondary usage evolved from the inversive one via intermediate cases like *mare* "to tie" and *demare* "to untie," which encodes not only the undoing of a knot but the freeing of the person or object tied "away from" what it was bound to; *dekoupe* would be a similar case. The Russian prefix *raz-* is again useful to us for two reasons. The first is that the semantic range of the "separative" use of this prefix covers that of both reflexes of Haitian's *de-*, demonstrating the essential unity of the two semantic uses of the latter:

| | "to tie" | "to untie" | "to pull" | "to stretch" |
|---|---|---|---|---|
| Haitian | *de-[1]mare* | *demare* | *de-tire[2]* | *detire* |
| Russian | *vjazat'* | *razvjazat'* | *tjanut'* | *rastjanut'* |

Second, as we have seen, the polysemy of *raz-* beyond this usage is of a degree quite foreign to any Haitian affix, also incorporating dispersal and inceptivity (see 3.3.1).

Meanwhile, some of the words DeGraff presents as "noncompositional" are actually institutionalizations of the sort discussed in 3.3.2: one cannot predict that *debabouye* means "to wash one's face or clean one's self up" based on the meaning of *babouye*, "to smear." However, the semantic connection between "to unsmear" and the actual meaning is easily processible via metaphorical inference. *Debarase* "to straighten out" from *barase* "clumsy" is a similar case.

In other examples, *de-* has been extended redundantly to verb roots whose meanings inherently include the notion of separation:

| | |
|---|---|
| *grennen* "to shell, scatter" | *degrennen* "to shell, separate one by one" |
| *kale* "to peel, scrape" | *dekale* "to chip off, to peel off" |
| *libere* "to free" | *delibere* "to free" |
| *pase* "to pass" | *depase* "to exceed, overtake" |

Yet even in these cases, although we have clearly passed the boundaries of strict compositionality, the connection between the morphemes in these combinations and the meaning of the word is clear, including the semantic motivation for the affixation of *de-*, despite its redundancy.

The cases that DeGraff presents of truly opaquely noncompositional uses of *de-* —where the semantic contribution of the prefix is unrecoverable—are few, including *deperi* "to perish" (*peri* "to perish"), *demefyan* "mistrustful, skeptical" (*mefyan* "mistrustful, suspicious"), and *demegri* "to lose weight" (*megri* "to lose weight" [emphatic]).

DeGraff also judges various uses of the prefix *en-* (*desan* "decent"/*endesan* "indecent") as "noncompositional" based on the fact that their roots are no longer, or in Haitian never were, used alone, such as *enkyè* "anxious" (*\*kyè*) and *enkòmòde* "to disturb" (*\*kòmòde*). However, the motivation for classifying a morpheme as opaque simply because the root it is combined with does not always occur alone is unclear. There are certainly cross-linguistic cases in which derivational morphemes lose compositionality in combination with roots which no longer occur alone, such as the notorious case of derived words based on *-ceive* and *-mit* in which sometimes the meaning of the prefix is no longer apparent (*receive, permit*) (Aronoff 1976: 12). But Haitian's *en-* is not this kind of case: every example DeGraff gives clearly has a negative or inversive meaning in which the core semantics of the prefix are quite salient, with the exception of *entatad* "senile" and *enbesil* "imbecile," in the latter of which cases it is questionable that *en-* is actually perceived as a prefix.

DeGraff presents a more substantial body of indisputably noncompositional derivation in the case of *re-*, which usually encodes repetition, but makes an opaque contribution in a number of combinations such as these and others:

| | |
|---|---|
| *jete* "to throw away" | *rejete* "to reject" |
| *konpanse* "to compensate" | *rekonpanse* "to reward" |
| *pare* "to prepare" | *repare* "to repair" |
| *poze* "to pause, ask" | *repoze* "to rest" |
| *tire* "to pull" | *retire* "to remove" |

## 5.3. Haitian within the Creole Prototype model

Thus the subset of the material in DeGraff (1999a) pertinent to evaluating the Creole Prototype hypothesis is neither the lists of derivational affixes (since my hypothesis does not predict that creoles will lack derivational morphemes) nor the claim that Haitian has gender inflection (because what it has is compositional natural gender *derivation*, again, incidental to my model). The pertinent issue is the body of noncompositional words derived by the prefixes *de-* and *re-*, which is much smaller than DeGraff (1999a) claims but important nonetheless.

### 5.3.1. Import of Haitian derivation

As those familiar with French will note, the compositional and noncompositional uses of *re-* and *de-* in Haitian are derived from the French source words. I have stipulated that the lexifier pulled creoles significantly away from the Prototype only in situations in which speakers of the creole had high levels of contact with lexifier speakers, as they did in Réunion. However, DeGraff observes that the rich derivational inheritance from French in Haitian speaks against the Prototype model in that, unlike in Réunion, in colonial Haiti slaves vastly outnumbered whites and had mostly distant social relations with them. He thus interprets the coexistence of French-derived opaque derivation and radical demographic disproportion as counterevidence to my claim that Haitian, and by extension other creoles, emerged as radically reduced pidgins. Since the Creole Prototype is proposed as a direct descendant of a pidgin grammar, it follows that if pidgin ancestry for creoles is disproved, then there is no motivation for creoles to display a synchronic prototype.

At the same time, however, DeGraff's counteranalysis requires that Haitian Creole *emerged* with this noncompositional derivation, as opposed to having adopted these words as Gallicisms from contact with French over the centuries. In the latter case, we would simply have another example of the sort discussed in 4.4.2, in which contact with the lexifier over the centuries pulled the creole away from the Prototype to which it hewed at its genesis.

As it happens, DeGraff's thesis founders on this point: Goyette (2000) demonstrates through painstaking historical linguistic analysis that the derivational markers in modern Haitian Creole (including the natural gender markers) cannot have been incorporated into the creole at its birth and, in fact, were borrowed from French in later periods. There is not a single point on Haitian Creole in DeGraff (1999a) that this finding does not readily account for.

Meanwhile, DeGraff's (2001) response to Goyette founders. First, the response is caricature—assuming that a lexical item Goyette uses as an example of a general phenomenon is intended as a lone, isolated example. Second, the response is a miscomprehension. *If* Haitian almost always displays a rendition of a French derivational marker that is only phonetically derivable from a French allomorph that only became categorical long after Haitian jelled— *-eur* as opposed to earlier *-eux*— *then* this strong tendency renders irrelevant that French *-eur* was not utterly unknown in French before it became the default allomorph, having long been a marginal and/or a marked variant. If the slaves who created Haitian were readily processing *-eux*, then we would expect a reflex of it in Haitian—and that is the case. If they were by chance also processing the then-marked allomorphic alternate *-eur*, then by DeGraff's own stipulation elsewhere (1999b: 525) that creole creators eliminated "stochastically marked" features rarely encountered, we would predict that *-eur* would fail to be incorporated. Thus, under both Goyette's and DeGraff's scenarios,

we must assume that a reflex of the latterly triumphing -*eur* was incorporated later—
à la section 4.4.2.

### 5.3.2. Accounting for gradience: Predictions from other perspectives

Even though Haitian Creole did conform to the Creole Prototype at its genesis, the
very fashion in which contact with French has pulled it away from the Prototype
usefully demonstrates that this model accounts for gradience in a constrained fashion commensurate with findings in other subfields. Specifically, the fact that Haitian
would have borrowed French derivation but not its inflection is predictable from a
variety of linguistic perspectives:

> *Language contact.* For example, on their scale charting typical effects of
> borrowing at five levels of intensity, Thomason and Kaufman (1988: 74–
> 75) note that cross-linguistically, derivational affixes are borrowed at
> their Stage Three, with the borrowing of inflection typical of the next
> stage of contact intensity, Stage Four. The authors illustrate this with
> examples of the influence of Spanish on dialects of Nahuatl, Slavic
> languages on Yiddish, and Sanskrit on high registers of Dravidian
> languages like Kannada (ibid. 79–82).
>
> *Theoretical morphology.* Lexicon is, obviously, the first level of language
> to be acquired in second-language acquisition and borrowing. In this
> light, it is significant that many theoretical treatments of derivation have
> located the process as a lexical one (Selkirk 1982, Scalise 1984), with
> inflection located in the syntactic module. Because borrowing of inflec-
> tion occurs at a higher intensity of contact than does borrowing of
> lexicon, the theories accounting for derivation in the lexicon would lead
> us to predict that one possible stage of a creole's borrowing from a
> lexifier would be to have borrowed its derivation (as a component of
> borrowing its lexicon) but not its inflection. This is what we see in
> Haitian Creole, which contrasts with the result of more intense contact in
> Louisiana, where the creole contains both French derivation and some
> reflections of its inflections.
>
> *Cross-creole comparison.* If the borrowing of derivation before inflection
> is predictable, then we would expect that no creole would exist which had
> incorporated its lexifiers' inflection without its derivation. This is exactly
> what we find. Papiamentu Spanish Creole has inherited several derivational
> markers from Ibero-Romance, such as the adverbializer -*mentu*, agentive
> -*dó* (< -*dor*), a past participial from Iberian -*ado* (*duna* "to give," *duná*
> "given [here, accent = stress]), and a gerundive -*ando* (Maurer 1998: 169,
> 181–82). Inflectional affixation, however, is absent. (Interestingly, like
> Haitian, Papiamentu has some natural gender derivation; for example,
> *kolombiano/kolombiana* [ibid. 155]). Jamaican patois has some deriva-
> tional markers from English (derived from comparative and agentive -*er*,

diminutive -*y*, nominalizer -*ness*, et al. [Bailey 1966: 16–17]); English inflection, however, is typically absent, a marker of acrolectal varieties (Sebba 1997: 209).[11] I am not aware of any creole language that has inherited inflection from its lexifier without its derivation.

### 5.3.3. Accounting for gradience: Specifying sociohistorical conditions for the prototype

The Haitian derivational inheritance is finally illuminating in that all of the other French plantation creoles in the world have similarly incorporated French derived roots, including the lexicalized ones. Opaquely noncompositional verbs with *de-* and *re-* of the sort discussed in 5.2 are found not only in Louisiana (cf. the dictionary Valdman, Klingler, Marshall, and Rottet 1998), where the intensity of borrowing would lead us to expect it, but also in French Guyanais (cf. Barthelemi 1995), Mauritian (cf. Baker and Hookoomsing 1987), Guadeloupean (cf. Poullet, Telchid, and Montbriand 1984), St. Lucian (cf. examples in Garrett 2000), Seychellois (Susanne Michaelis, pers. comm.), and others. This corresponds with a general observation that there exists no French plantation creole as removed from French as there exist creoles removed from English or Portuguese (Muysken 1994, Alleyne 1998, Parkvall 1999, McWhorter and Parkvall 2002). Compared to basilectal creoles like Ndjuka, Angolar, and Tok Pisin, French creoles stand out in that:

1. They lack a tendency toward CV phonotactics[12]
2. There is relatively little reanalysis of superstrate lexical items as grammatical (along the lines of the reanalysis of *there* as an imperfective marker in Sranan and Ndjuka)
3. Verb serialization is possible with fewer verbs and is less grammaticalized
4. There is less substratal transfer in general on all levels

At first glance, this situation appears to suggest something anomalous: that diglossic situations in French colonies for some reason pulled the creole away from the Prototype and toward the lexifier, while the same situation did not do so elsewhere. Yet in truth, the lexifier influence is not the only factor distinguishing the French creoles: a sociohistorical factor, corresponding causally with the linguistic difference, cuts across these creoles.

What distinguishes creoles that remain most basilectal today is that they are spoken in contexts where either speakers of the lexifier withdrew after a short period from the genesis context and did not return in significant numbers, or lexifier speakers were never a significant presence at all during the stabilization of the language. In Surinam, the English occupied the colony for only sixteen years, from 1651 to 1667; the Dutch ran it from then until Surinam's independence in 1975. After establishing plantations on the islands in the Gulf of Guinea in the early 1500s, the Portuguese began departing at the end of that century and never returned (Ferraz 1979). Portuguese has remained the official language of most of these islands, but there has existed no class of Portuguese-dominant "colonials" with a prestigious diglossic competence exerting an acrolectal pull on the creole over time. Tok Pisin expanded and stabilized in use between people indigenous to New Guinea, many of whom until recently lived in remote areas in pre-literate cultural contexts, rarely encountering English itself in any form.

Crucially, no French creolophone contexts of this type happen to have arisen. In most of these contexts, French has been usually the official, and in any case always the sociologically dominant, language continuously since the birth of the creole (even in cases such as Haiti, where the French relinquished official control for a period in the 1800s, French remained the prestige language). In the cases where a French creole has survived in contexts in which English is now the politically and sociologically dominant European language, this latter situation arose only after the French creole had coexisted with French for an extended period (St. Lucia, St. Barthélemy, Trinidad). There exists no case of a French plantation creole that stabilized in a colony run by speakers of a European language other than French, or in one which the French abandoned shortly after the creole emerged.

The French colonies indicate, then, that even when a large percentage of a creolophone population does not control the lexifier language, the influence of the bilingual elite (as little as 10% in Haiti) on the creole is massive, particularly in the area of the lexicon. As noted previously, this is not an ad hoc proposition, but one founded on long-observed and well-documented diglossic contexts, as well as cases of borrowing, worldwide.[13]

As the historical work on Haitian by Goyette helps to show, even in French colonies, plantation colonization strongly tended to produce creoles close to the Prototype *at genesis*. However, in terms of *diachronic* development, the uniformity of the lexifier influence among the various French creoles suggests that in the present day, creoles closest to the Prototype will be found in particular conditions. This means that there were two possible diachronic fates for a creole that emerged honing to the Prototype.

5.3.3.1. ISOLATION AND PRESERVATION    A creole honing to the Prototype today is most likely to be found in situations that offer two crucial conditions. First, the initial social context so limited learners' ability or desire to acquire the lexifier that a pidgin variety of that lexifier developed (unlike, for example, Réunion). Second, the lexifier was withdrawn, such that the expansion of the pidgin into a natural language did not include borrowing from the lexifier but, instead, occurred mostly or entirely via the recruitment of language-internal resources.

This second condition was vital to the development and preservation of a creole conforming to the Prototype because it allowed a creole to develop without "interference" from the lexifier. By definition, pidgin languages tend to have (among other features of less pertinence here) small lexicons and little or no inflectional or derivational affixation. One component of the transformation of a pidgin into a natural language is expansion of the lexicon (Mühlhäusler 1980). Because a pidgin lexicon is small, the pidgin that expands into a natural language while removed from lexifier influence necessarily expands its lexicon not via borrowing but via new uses of the lexical resources it has. One aspect of this expansion is the development of derivational mechanisms. As we have seen, it is natural to language change in general that derivational morphemes develop gradually via the grammaticalization of lexical items. As such, a creole that began as a pidgin with little or no derivation, and subsequently changes system-internally, will recruit derivational morphemes from its stock of free lexical items, as Tok Pisin has done with -*pasin* (< *fashion*) as an abstract nominalizer (see 3.3.1). But since the opacification via lexicalization of derived roots is a very gradual process, we would predict that after a mere few hundred years little such opacification would have had a chance to occur. Similarly, if a creole changing system-internally develops inflection, this will not be via borrowing from the lexifier as in Louisiana but via (among occasional other processes) grammaticalization of lexical items, a gradual process that we would expect to have rarely proceeded very far in a language born as a pidgin (significantly, in creoles we do find ample *cliticization*, a phase often intermediate between free lexical item and affix). A similar argument applies to monosyllabic lexical and morphosyntactic (but not phonological) tone.

This conception is well demonstrated in Surinam. The English were in Surinam for but sixteen years, and there are only roughly 600 English words in the Sranan lexicon (Koefoed and Tarenskeen 1996: 120),[14] and of these, many are compounds such as *fesi ede* "forehead" from "face-head," lowering the number of actual borrowings from English even more. Thus the transformation into a full language of the material slaves had available to them after the English departed required system-internal expansion rather than borrowing from the lexifier. As a result, the creole has yet to develop inflectional affixes internally because this takes time; it is not a tonal language; and it has developed a few derivational affixes from lexical items, but, predictably, these have yet to drift with the words they affix to into noncompositionality.

5.3.3.2. DIGLOSSIA AND BORROWING   In those colonies in which the speakers of the lexifier stayed on site and imposed their language as the top pole in a diglossic continuum, as they did in the French colonies, we can expect that the creole will have been drawn away from the Prototype to a degree, even if conditions at genesis produced a more prototypical creole.

This is the case, for example, with the Caribbean English–based continuum creoles. Jamaican patois, for instance, has some English-derived derivational morphology. Evidence suggests, however, that this creole originated as a variety much further from English, specifically as Sranan in Surinam. Sranan shares with Jamaican and other Atlantic English–based creoles idiosyncratic correspondences in the etymology of grammatical items that reveal their common ancestry in one original contact language (cf. chapter 8). Various lines of evidence indicate that this ancestor was early Sranan, the most indicative being that Jamaican maroons (descendants of slaves who escaped plantations and founded communities in the mountains) speak a ceremonial variety that parallels Sranan closely enough to reveal a direct historical relationship (McWhorter 2000a: 83–86). This historical relationship is not only linguistically but also historically confirmed: when the Dutch took over Surinam from the English in 1667, English planters brought about 900 slaves to the new colony Jamaica (Bilby 1983: 60).

Significantly, Sranan lacks all of the English-derived derivational morphology of Jamaican, with the exception of agentive -*man*; even here, however, while Jamaican also has the agentive -*er*, Sranan does not. Jamaican has the comparative -*er*; Sranan uses *more* or a serial construction with *pass*; Jamaican has the diminutive -*y*

(-*i*), Sranan encodes the diminutive with reduplication and preposing of *piki* "small"; Jamaican has -*ness* (-*nis*), Sranan makes use of zero-derivation to nominalize (Adamson and Smith 1995: 222–23); and so on. In general, Sranan indeed conforms to the Creole Prototype, with no inflectional affixes, no tone, and no noncompositional derivation. This, then, was the nature of Jamaican patois at its origin in Surinam. In Jamaica the creole was in constant contact with English and thus moved closer to it on all levels, including the borrowing of English morphology. From the perspective of Jamaica alone, it is plausible to suppose that this morphology was in the language at its origins: but the roots of the creole in Sranan indicate that there was an initial stage in the development of Jamaican patois' grammar when this English derivation did not exist. This classifies Jamaican patois, then, as another example of the phenomenon described in 4.4.2 in which a creole beginning at the prototype is brought away from it over time by lexifier contact.

The creoles that have both emerged as prototypical creoles and remained so (except for slight and empirically documented movement away over the past few centuries in a few cases) include Sranan, Saramaccan, Ndjuka, São Tomense, Principense, Fa D'Ambu, Angolar, Tok Pisin, Bislama, Solomon Islands Pijin, Torres Strait Broken, Aboriginal English Kriol, Baba Malay, and Negerhollands (the latter now extinct).

5.3.3.3. PIDGIN, APPROXIMATION, AND SECOND-LANGUAGE ACQUISITION: DIFFERENT PATHS TO THE SAME MOUNTAINTOP    Though this might seem surprising to those outside of creole studies, the claim that creoles arise from pidgins arouses discomfort from some creolists, particularly those of the Francophone school. Reconstructing creoles as having developed "top-down" via successive approximations of a lexifier by adult non-native speakers, authors such as Chaudenson (1992) see no break in transmission of the lexifier as having occurred at any particular point. They instead classify creoles as essentially varieties of their lexifiers, their development mediated by a leaning toward analyticity by second-language learners.

Yet Chaudenson does not consider the modern creoles to have been the immediate result of this approximation process. He considers the initial stage to have been utilitarian, non-native reductions of French offering a variable body of materials from which slaves selected features to "autonomize" into new functions in constructing a natural language (136). While I have reservations about the extent of Chaudenson's skepticism regarding substrate influence in creoles (McWhorter and Parkvall 2002), it is unclear that his conception differs significantly from the general definition of pidgin in linguistic terms. His emphasis on elimination of inflection, omission of overt copula morphemes, and generalization of tonic pronouns parallels innumerable characterizations of the pidgin (e.g., Foley 1988: 165, Romaine 1988: 25–31, Sebba 1997: 39–47), and one's assessment of the degree of substrate influence on such a variety is largely immaterial to this particular issue since substratal contributions to creoles are reduced just as superstratal ones are (Keesing 1988: 89–104, McWhorter 1997a: 155–59). The French creolist tradition tends to restrict the term *pidgin* to varieties used by adults for utilitarian communication while retaining their native languages, and it refrains from extending this term to the initial stage in the birth of plantation creoles. This, however, is essentially an issue of terminology and differing scholarly traditions. For all intents and purposes, what most creolists refer to as *pidgin* while

Chaudenson and his followers refer to it as "approximative varieties" is the same type of language variety in the linguistic sense.

Meanwhile, DeGraff (1999a) urges that the essence of creole genesis be sought in second-language acquisition. Again, however, the issue is one of overlapping terminologies. The observation that pidginization—acquisition of a language by adult learners—is a form of second-language acquisition has been made often, having even inspired a volume of articles (Andersen 1983). Regarding the thesis of this paper, it is significant that second-language acquisition is well known to entail reduction or elimination of affixes; DeGraff himself makes this observation (1999b: 517, 525), citing, for example, Zobl and Liceras (1994). While DeGraff emphasizes the elimination only of inflectional morphology (perhaps in view of the ample derivational morphology on view in modern Haitian), derivational morphology is also often reduced or eliminated in second-language acquisition (Dittmar 1984: 262, Broeder, Extra, Van Hout, and Voionmaa 1993: 56). The essential isomorphy of pidginization, second-language acquisition, and the French creolist school's "approximation" conception is finally underlined by the fact that Chaudenson (1992) makes frequent reference to second-language acquisition as an analog to the "approximated" French on colonial plantations.

The phenomena designated *second-language acquisition* and *pidginization* do not overlap perfectly, of course; more properly, pidgins are qualitatively equivalent to an *early* stage of second-language acquisition. Yet the fact of this very equivalence is indicative: it would be difficult to argue that the native-language influenced, structurally minimal, inflection-free Hawaiian Pidgin English described by Bickerton (1984) and Roberts (1998) differs in any theoretically significant way from the Guest Worker's German (Gastarbeiterdeutsch) often cited as a case of second-language acquisition:

Hawaiian Pidgin English:

(5)   Gud, dis wan. Kaukau enikain dis wan. Pilipin ailaen no gud. No mo mani.
      "It's better here than in the Philippines—here you can get all kinds of food—but over there isn't any money." (Bickerton 1984: 175)

Gastarbeiterdeutsch:

(6)   Un dan E. täläfoniiə kliinik, klinik haidälbärk. Ambulants un  dan foət in kliinik.
      and then E. call      clinic   clinic Heidelberg ambulance and then off   in clinic
      "And then E. called the clinic, the Heidelberg clinic. An ambulance came and then they took him away to the clinic." (Heidelberger Forschungsprojekt "Pidgin Deutsch" 1975: 141)

Second-language acquisition, to be sure, manifests itself along a cline, upon which the Gastarbeiterdeutsch passage falls quite far from full German. Yet pidginization expresses itself along the same cline depending on access to the target, motivation to acquire it, and typological closeness of lexifier and substrates. The Nagas who developed Naga Pidgin Assamese had enough access to Assamese and Bengali to incorporate some markers of case and tense (Bhattachariya 1994), and Sango, developed by people speaking closely related Ubangian languages, has retained enough inflections and tonal distinctions that some analysts prefer to classify it as a koine rather than as a pidgin or creole (Morrill 1997).

Thus the pidgin source, which I refer to as crucial to the development of a creole displaying the three features in question, is formally homologous to what in other frameworks is referred to as "approximation," or second-language acquisition.

Some scholars have questioned whether creoles were preceded by pidgins, given the lack of clear attestation of the pidgin stage of the plantation creoles (e.g., Alleyne 1980: 126); indeed, this perspective informs much of the preference of various creolists over the last twenty years to focus on "approximations of approximations" and second-language acquisition as the essence of creole genesis. In this light, it is important to realize that in addition to the vastly unclear difference between pidginization and second-language acquisition, there are clear signs in plantation creoles' grammars of pidgin ancestry (McWhorter 1998a: 805, McWhorter 2000a, McWhorter and Parkvall 2002), of a sort which, if "approximation" is expanded to encompass them, render "approximation" and pidginization—once again—synonymous.

In the meantime, it must also be clear that while documentation of the pidgin stages of plantation creoles is lost to us, there are indeed several *documented* cases of pidgins developing into natural languages (i.e., creoles) more recently, such as Hawaiian Pidgin English (Bickerton 1981, Roberts 1998), Sango (Samarin 1980), Chinook Jargon (Grant 1996a), Tok Pisin (Mühlhäusler 1980, 1997; Romaine 1992), and Solomon Islands Pijin (Jourdan and Keesing 1997). Few would argue that anything significantly distinguishes Hawaiian Creole English, Sango, or creolized Tok Pisin qualitatively from other creoles; on the contrary, all three of these creoles have been discussed alongside all of the others with no objection for forty years. Those deriving creoles from pidgins, then, are hypothesizing based not only on synchronic traces of pidginization but also on the fact that multiethnic contact languages of like grammatical and sociohistorical profile are *concretely* documented to have developed from pidgins.

## 6. Older languages conforming to the prototype?

A final possible refutation would be the identification of an older language, with no history of radical reduction by non-natives, followed by reconstitution into a natural language, which combines the three features I have cited. One might expect that such a language would be an impossibility, given how readily inflection, monosyllabic lexical and morphosyntactic tone, and semantic drift of derivation-root combinations emerge in grammars. However, since inflectional affixes and tonally-marked contrasts also wear away to be replaced by analytic constructions, myriad languages have replaced tone with phonational or vocalic contrasts, and derivational affixes can gradually lose phonetic form and be replaced cyclically by new ones, there is also nothing ruling out a priori that a given grammar might reach a stage at which all inflectional affixation had been lost, there now was or never had been any tone, and all derivational affixation was new and thus consistently compositional. Indeed, when I first began investigating the Creole Prototype question, my intention was to identify just such a language, in order to give concrete support to the claim that creole is solely a sociohistorical term. The Creole Prototype hypothesis resulted from my not encountering such a language.

Obviously, most of the world's languages are disqualified from the Prototype either by being inflected or using tone to encode monosyllabic lexical and morphosyntactic contrasts. Most linguists draw a blank on identifying an older language with neither of these features unless they happen to be specialists in languages of Southeast Asia or Austronesia. Yet the languages of these groups that I have examined nevertheless have ample noncompositional derivation.

Eric Pederson (pers. comm.) once suggested to me that this suggests that the derivation feature alone could serve as the diagnostic of creolization. Yet there apparently exist older languages whose derivation-root combinations are consistently transparent—but the one that has come to my attention (Soninke, of the Mande subgroup of Niger-Congo) contains inflectional affixation and lexical and/or morphosyntactic tone. Judging from available sources, the derivation-root combinations in this language, while predictably displaying institutionalizations and idiomaticizations (see 3.3.2), present no opacities of the *understand* type. Yet Soninke displays signs of its age with several inflectional affixes:

1. Three plural affixes[15]
2. Two singular nominal inflections (Diagana 1995: 48–49)
3. A marker -*n*V of unrealization (*inaccompli*): *à ró* "he came in, *à róonó* "he will come in" (ibid. 254)
4. A marker of unrealization via gemination: *nà wùtú* "to take," *à w[á] á wùttú* "he will take it" (ibid. 256)

Soninke also has some lexical and morphosyntactic uses of tone:

5. There are a few tonally distinguished monosyllables: *ro* "to enter" or "to put," *ña* "to become" or "to make," *te* "field" or "oil" (Girier 1996: 127–28)
6. The definite marker -*n* with low tone can in some contexts be omitted, leaving behind only low tone on the preceding syllable as a marker of definiteness (Diagana 1995: 45–46)
7. Third-person pronouns *à* (sing.) and *ì* (pl.) are rendered possessive by the addition of a high tone (ibid. 180–81).[16]

If it is true that older languages conforming to the Creole Prototype do not exist, then this nonexistence may be accidental, or it is possible that it is ruled out by laws of probability. Specifically, it is already clear on typological grounds that the chance that one grammar might at any time display neither inflections or lexical/morphosyntactic tone is extremely small. It also appears to be the quite extremely marked case that an old grammar has no noncompositional derivation (and given that Soninke has as yet no comprehensive dictionary, even this one case may prove to be a false alarm). Grammars in which most derivation has become affixed and begun to erode away, thus receding from analyzability by speakers, tend to have maintained at least a derivational affix or two, since there is no reason that all affixes would erode at the same rate, or that all of their semantic functions would be equally susceptible to bleaching and ambiguation. Furthermore, even if a grammar has shed all of its derivational affixes, then given the centrality of derivation to natural language, it develops new derivational morphemes (e.g., Lahu formerly had a bound causative affix *s-, which now exists only as phonetic remnants and has been replaced by the grammaticalized use of the verb *te* "to do" [Matisoff 1973b: 243]).

This means that finding an older language with no noncompositional derivation involves first the small chance that all of the derivational morphemes in the grammar will have either worn away or been bleached of all regular meaning, combined with the equally small chance that we encounter the grammar at a stage when the new derivational morphemes are still so young that noncompositional uses have yet to arise. As such, while it is certainly possible that an older language may have no inflection and no tone (Chrau), or that an older language may have these but no noncompositional derivation (perhaps Soninke), the chance that these two states *coincide* in an older language may be rendered unlikely or perhaps impossible by sheer probability.

## 7. Conclusion

I have argued that creole languages cluster around a prototype comprising three features symptomatic of a language having emerged recently from a pidgin, and that we would predict that this confluence of features would not occur in an older language, thus rendering *creole* a synchronic, as well as sociohistorical, term.

> The *weak version* of the hypothesis appears well-supported on empirical grounds: that older languages exhibiting these three traits are extremely rare (given that none have come to the attention of this author at this writing), and that therefore creoles quite often display a confluence of features that older languages display only rarely and fortuitously.

> The *strong version* of this hypothesis remains at this writing a speculation that will hopefully inspire further research: that *no* older language exists which combines these three features.

If proven valid, this hypothesis will contribute usefully to the development of useful typologies of language contact, as our insights into phenomena such as code-switching, language "intertwining," clines of contact-induced interference, as well as pidginization and creolization, continue to deepen. Furthermore, in calling attention to the crucial role of the semantic drift of derivation in determining whether or not a language has a creole history, the Creole Prototype hypothesis complements various studies that have appeared in the 1990s, suggesting that the essence of creolization lies in the grammar-wide syntactic results of the loss of inflectional morphology (cf. Veenstra 1996, Roberts 1999). This idea is both ingenious and highly promising, but the derivational evidence I have presented suggests that there is a significant body of data distinguishing creole grammars from older ones which are unlikely to yield to an analysis based on universal parameters, and lend themselves instead to explanations based on predictable results of the pidgin ancestry of most creole languages combined with their short life spans since their origin.

After three decades of institutionalized creole studies, there remains a gaping lack of consensus in the subfield as to what a *creole* even is. For various reasons, in creole studies today this topic is generally felt to be a "touchy" issue best left alone, and in general of little importance. I cannot disagree that the issue is volatile, as is clear from the title of DeGraff (1999a): "Morphology in creole genesis: a 20-minute (?*!Δ%$¡?‡!?) prolegomenon." However, unimportant it is not. If there is truly no linguistic difference between creoles and other languages, and creoles are distinct only in terms of the social history of their speakers, then it follows that creole studies ought be the exclusive province of anthropologists, historians, and sociologists, with a grammatical study of Papiamentu tense and aspect no more pertinent to the field than an equivalent one on Hungarian. I highly suspect that few creolists, regardless of their perspectives on the Prototype issue, could sincerely countenance this scenario. Thus, a fundamental sense animating most people studying these languages would seem to be that *creole* is indeed on some level a linguistically valid term. The Creole Prototype hypothesis is simply an attempt to render this guiding intuition more precise.

# The World's Simplest Grammars
# Are Creole Grammars

## 1. Introduction

It has long been a truism in creole studies that creoles are formally distinguishable from other languages only on the basis of their sociohistory and that there is no logically possible synchronic distinction between creole grammars and older grammars. In chapter 1 I argued that, in fact, a large subset of creole languages display a confluence of traits, predictable from the history of creoles in pidginization, which is unknown in any older language grammar and that creole creators strongly tend to eschew nonessential traits from their native languages when developing a creole.[1]

This research program dovetails with Bickerton's Language Bioprogram Hypothesis (1981 and other works), which also proposes that creoles represent an underlying "layer" of language resulting from their roots in pidgins. Bickerton's main focus, however, was on the implications of his hypothesis for generative syntactic and acquisition theory, and as such he had little occasion to examine creoles from a cross-linguistic or typological perspective. My intention is a sustained investigation of creoles from the perspective of cross-linguistic configurational possibilities, beyond the Western European lexifier languages that have served as the primary focus of creolists' attempts to define the term *creole*. The goal of the chapter is to render more precisely my grounds for the claim that creole grammars constitute a synchronically identifiable class.

## 2. Are all natural grammars equally complex?

Just as it is a truism in creole studies that *creole* is strictly a sociohistorical term, it is a truism in linguistics in general that all languages are equally complex (e.g., Edwards

1994: 90; Bickerton 1995: 67; O'Grady, Dobrovolsky, and Aronoff 1997: 6). The claim is generally made in reference to varying conceptions of the meaning of complexity, all broader than the constrained definition to be outlined later in this chapter. However, there is a strong implication underlying such statements that anything "simple" in a given language will be "compensated for" by a "complex" feature, a typical example being Crystal's (1987: 6–7) provisional observation that "all languages have a complex grammar: there may be relative simplicity in one respect (e.g. no word endings), but there seems always to be relative complexity in another (e.g. word-position)."

This must be designated a truism because, like the creole studies truism, it has long been asserted without having been subjected to systematic verification.

## 2.1. Complexity and subsets of grammar

Our first indication that the question is a richer one than generally assumed begins with something all linguists presumably agree upon: that one language can be more complex than another in terms of a particular area of grammar. For example, Kikongo distinguishes between four kinds of past tense, including a completive (Welmers 1973: 350), while Japanese has only one overt marker of past tense and has no grammaticalized indicator of completiveness exclusively:

| (1) | Kikongo | English | Japanese |
|---|---|---|---|
| | *Nsuumbidingí nkóombo.* | "I bought a goat (today)." | *Yagi o katta.* |
| | *Yásuumbidi nkóombo.* | "I bought a goat (yesterday)" | *Yagi o katta.* |
| | *Yasáumba nkóombo.* | "I bought a goat (earlier)." | *Yagi o katta.* |
| | *Nsuumbidi nkóombo.* | "I have bought a goat." | *Yagi o katta.* |
| | | | (goat ACC bought) |

It would certainly be mistaken to characterize the Japanese expression of past tense as "primordial" or unnuanced. For example, Japanese uses the past to describe events that have just come into perception, where European languages (and probably most other languages) use the present: upon seeing a bus coming into view, the Japanese person says *Basu ga kimashita* "The bus came" rather than *Basu ga kimasu* "The bus is coming." It cannot be overemphasized that complexity is a difficult notion, and we will shortly outline a principled characterization of complexity upon which the heart of the chapter's argument will be founded. Nevertheless, under the assumption that despite its difficulties, complexity is not a concept of no epistemological validity whatsoever, we can most likely agree that Kikongo, in happening to have evolved as fine-grained an overt subdivision of pastness as in (1), has a more complex past-marking system than Japanese.[2]

Similarly, with verbs of motion, Russian and most other Slavic languages distinguish not only between imperfective and perfective, as they do with almost all verbs, but make a further subdivision within the imperfective of what grammarians have called "determinate" versus "indeterminate." The "indeterminate" is expressed with a separate verb root. In the case of "to go," a separate pair of verb roots is used for going somewhere in a vehicle (or on a horse), such that where English uses a single verb "to go," Russian uses no fewer than four:

| (2) | | Russian | English |
|---|---|---|---|
| | Indeterminate imperfective | *Ja xožu v kino.* | I go to the cinema (often). |
| | | *Ja ezžu v kino.* | I go to the cinema (often) (in a car). |
| | Determinate imperfective | *Ja idu v kino.* | I am going to the cinema (now). |
| | | *Ja edu v kino.* | I am going to the cinema (now) (in a car). |
| | Perfective | *Pojdjom v kino.* | Let's go to the cinema. |
| | | *Poedem v kino.* | Let's go to the cinema (in a car). |

Again, it is obvious that in the particular case of subdividing the semantic space of movement, Slavic languages are more complex than English and many other languages.

While I could be accused of belaboring the obvious in showing that languages can differ in terms of complexity in particular areas, it is often assumed that overall, languages "balance out" in terms of complexity (cf. Crystal 1987 cited above), such that if Slavic has its aspect-determined motion verb pairs, English has a subtle system of articles overtly marking determination and referentiality that bedevil Slavic learners, or that where Kikongo has its past markers, Japanese has its paradigms of numeral classifiers, et cetera. Yet in the strict sense, there is no a priori reason to assume that all languages ultimately "tally" in terms of areas of typologically unusual complexity.

## 2.2. Complexity and contingency

On the contrary, one suggestion speaks specifically against such an assumption— namely, the very source of much of a grammar's complexity. Many features commonly found in grammars are the product of a gradual evolution of a sort that proceeded independently of communicative necessity and therefore must be adjudged "happenstance" accretion.

A particularly useful example is the set of affixes that mark grammatical gender. Obviously, grammatical gender marking is unnecessary to human communication, given how very many human languages lack it. Grammatical gender affixes, beyond the extent to which they distinguish natural (biological) gender, do not mark any real-world entity or category or serve any communicative need (see Trudgill 1999 for a useful discussion of this point). To be sure, the free classifier morphemes (Greenberg 1978) or former pronouns that gender markers usually arise from did mark real-world categories. However, as affixes, they no longer do, or at best correspond to perceivable categories only very approximately, their fundamental superfluity to communication illuminated further by the fact that they sometimes even arise from happenstance phonetic correspondences (Nichols 1992: 141–42). The result, in requiring the classification of nouns according to two and often more classes (and, as often as not, requiring the control of associated morphophonemic rules and exceptions), gender marking is inherently more complex than its absence. Crucially, this added complexity emerges via chance, not necessity.

Grammatical gender affixes are so starkly devoid of semantic substance or syntactic function that their fundamentally happenstance essence is particularly clear, and they are useful in illuminating the similarly contingent nature of other features often found in grammars. The four Kikongo past markers, in finely subdividing the semantic space of pastness, clearly serve a function within the grammar, as do Slavic motion verbs in theirs. Yet like gender affixes, both of these features emerged from grammars that lacked this particular complexity: Kikongo's Bantu relative LoNkundo has just two past markers (Welmers 1973: 348), as do many other Bantu languages; the determinate/indeterminate distinction in verbs of motion in Slavic languages has no analog in the closely related Indo-European languages in the Germanic branch; et cetera. As such, despite their functional usefulness once having evolved, these features' emergence was at root a chance elaboration.

Lass (1997: 367–68) is particularly illustrative on this underacknowledged but crucial point about human grammars:

> Not only does a language have by definition a sufficient set of structures and categories available for doing anything that a speaker "needs" to do; it will also have a lot of material that simply makes speakers do things, whether or not there is any (functional, discourse, pragmatic) "need" to do them. (English forces a speaker to mark durative aspect every time he utters a sentence in the present tense; German, Afrikaans, French and Swedish don't, but they have machinery for doing it if necessary.) We live perpetually with "decisions" of past generations. Somebody, somewhere (as it were) decided in the eighteenth century or thereabouts that the expression of progressive aspect should be obligatory in English, and as an English speaker I'm simply stuck with it.

If we acknowledge the contingent nature of such developments, then a question arises: Why, precisely, would such chance developments have occurred to an equal extent in all 6,000 or so natural languages on earth? If Kikongo has four past tenses and LoNkundo has just two, then according to the conventional wisdom that all languages are equally complex, we are forced to assume that LoNkundo not just may, but must, have developed some quirky degree of complexity in some other area of grammar where Kikongo has honed to a more cross-linguistically unremarkable pattern (perhaps evolving two more noun classes, or a paradigm of evidential markers). However, what sustained linguistic investigation has been devoted to ascertaining that this is true in LoNkundo—or, indeed, among any conceivable subset of the world's languages? And more to the point, precisely what mechanism would we hypothesize as the source of this purported equalizer of complexity among the world's languages?

Surely the mechanism could not entail that grammars somehow calibrate themselves according to comparison with one another, which thus requires that this equalization would respond to some imperative internal to the *individual* language competence (or I-language, in theoretical syntactic terms). Yet this would require, in turn, that the evolution of needless linguistic complexity was somehow advantageous to the evolution of our species, or, to wit, the passing on of genetic material. The growing current of linguistic thought comparing language change to natural selection might at this point suggest an analogy to cases such as the male peacock's tail: although it is heavy and awkward to an extent that hinders mobility. Yet, the disadvantages of this burden are outweighed by the advantage conferred by its status as a sexual advertisement; meanwhile, however, it is unclear how elaborated verbs of motion or fine shades of pastness could have acquired men or women extra sexual partners. Furthermore, it would be extremely problematic to conceptualize a model of innate grammar that could specifically generate all of the innumerable possible random complexifications of particular areas of natural language grammar while also suppressing most of them in any one grammar.

If we accept that Kikongo's past-marker paradigm and Slavic's unusually elaborated verbs of motion are traceable ultimately to chance elaboration, then we must also accept that we can conceive logically of neither a genetically selected neural linguistic blueprint nor a cognitively or functionally determined mechanism, which would ensure that chance occurrences operate to a precisely equal degree on every natural language grammar on earth. In other words, nothing in modern linguistic theory entails that all natural languages be equally complex, so any assertion or even underlying assumption to this effect qualifies as a truism yet to be tested rather than as an established fact.

## 2.3. Complexity and Creoles

There is, however, one conception under which it could be coherently proposed that all natural language grammars are equally complex. One might stipulate that after countless millennia of usage and drift, we might expect that by a certain point all grammars had, by the sheer dictates of chance, developed various random complexities in parts of their grammars. This might follow from the mounting evidence of natural systems' inherent tendency to complexify with the passage of time according to apparently universal principles of self-organization (cf. Lightfoot 1999: 250). We might propose that the volume of such excrescence in each grammar eventually reached the limit of humans' propensity to process it (e.g., there are no grammars with a different suppletive form of every basic verb for every person/number combination). Under this scenario all natural languages would be equally complex by virtue of having all come to rest at a certain "surplus complexity quotient."

One crucial aspect of this scenario would be that all of the grammars in question trace back tens of millennia. This is unproblematic regarding all of the world's natural languages with one exception, which brings us back to the focus of this chapter: creole languages. Creole languages, by definition, have existed only for several centuries at the most. The oldest known creoles today are the Portuguese-based creoles of Cape Verde and Guinea-Bissau, which trace back to the late fifteenth century; the Caribbean creoles mostly date to the late seventeenth and early eighteenth centuries; the English creoles of the Pacific trace to late eighteenth century interactions at the very earliest; Hawaiian Creole English and most of the creoles and expanded pidgins based on African languages emerged in the decades surrounding the turn of the twentieth century.

This leads us to a hypothesis. Let us assume for these purposes that tens of millennia of drift would leave all grammars existing during that time span equal in terms of the amount of complexity accreted beyond the bounds of the genetic specification for language. This stipulation predicts, then, that one subset of the world's natural languages, creoles, would differ from the rest of the world's natural languages in displaying less of this kind of needless complexity. Specifically, creoles are the world's only instantiation of spoken language having been "born again," when speakers expanded pidgins—universally agreed to be rudimentary codes not fulfilling the needs of full language—into natural language grammars.[3]

It is perhaps possible to assume at first glance that even a language "born again" would, by virtue of being generated by the same innate linguistic competence as all other languages, be immediately indistinguishable from older ones in any qualititative aspect.[4] This presupposes that older grammars' structures are completely, or even mostly, specified by, as opposed to merely compatible with, Universal Grammar, and as I have argued, this is not the case. Creoles, in being recently borne of communication vehicles deliberately designed to eschew all but the functionally central (pidgins), are unique examples of natural languages with much less contingent accumulation of "ornamental" elaboration than older grammars drag along with them. As I will argue later, it would be empirically inaccurate to claim that creoles represent anything approaching the "ground zero" of human language—that is, a perfect or "optimal" matching of irreducible semantic atoms with the simplest conceivable morphosyntactic realizations (cf. Kihm 2000, which is in agreement). Nevertheless, in contrast, Kihm's (1980a) early claim that "creoles can display any degree of complexity compatible with UG" does not correspond with the data set that the world's creoles actually constitute: on the contrary, because so much of a grammar's complexity results from the operations of random accretion over time, creoles display less complexity than the rest of the world's natural grammars.[5]

## 2.4. Measuring complexity

There is no conventionally agreed-on metric for measuring complexity in grammars. This is partly because of the reign of the truism that all languages are equally complex, partly because the construction of a comprehensive diagnostic for precisely ranking any human language on a scale of complexity is a daunting task, and perhaps most of all because the construction of such a diagnostic would be of little relevance or usefulness within most frames of reference in modern linguistic inquiry. Yet the issue of relative complexity is an important one in investigating the nature of creole languages and creolization.

### 2.4.1. Complexity: Difficult but not
### epistemologically vacuous

Complexity is certainly an ambiguous and malleable concept. For example, which plural marking strategy is more "complex": English, which marks plural only on the noun but with a marker that has three allomorphic variants; Swahili, which marks plurality redundantly on adjectives and nouns with a marker that varies according to several noun classes (*vitabu vizuri* "beautiful books," *miti mizuri* "beautiful trees"); or French, which (allowing for simplification of the full range of the facts) marks plural via a plural allomorph of the determiner and redundantly on adjective and noun via a proclitic which is, however, expressed only when the root is vowel-initial (*les arbres verts* [le zarbʁ vɛʁ] "the green trees")? Rankings of complexity here obviously will differ according to acquisitional or structural framework and whether one approaches the data from a first-language or a second-language perspective; it is unlikely that any single ranking could be constructed that would stand as incontestable.

That areas of inherent ambiguity of this kind exist does not, in any logical sense, render the entire notion of linguistic complexity a vacuous one. Indeed, the truism that languages cannot be compared in terms of complexity conflicts with the fact that linguists readily rank grammars in terms of complexity in terms of phonology and, to a lesser but considerable extent, morphology (e.g., Nichols 1992: 64–69). For example, in their work on phonology and morphology in isolated communities, scholars such as Andersen (1988) and Trudgill (1989, 1996) have designated dialects in these communities as having more complex phonologies, allophonies, allomorphies, and derivational pathways from the phonemic to the phonetic than those of varieties spoken in a wider context. These authors have made these observations with no criticism of their assumption that complexity is gradient. This author is unaware of any precise arguments as to why syntax and semantics would be, in contrast, inherently unamenable to complexity rankings. It is much less likely that any such unamenability exists than that the issue, its difficulties acknowledged, simply has not had occasion to receive much attention from modern linguists (cf. Comrie 1992).

In this light, there are ample cases in which complexity differentials are stark enough that most or all linguists' judgments could reasonably be assumed to concur regardless of frame of reference. It is complexity differentials of this degree with which I will be concerned in this paper, and from which my hypothesis will derive its support (and not subtler issues such as whether redundant marking is more or less complex than marking once, etc., which require article-length analysis in themselves).

### 2.4.2. Aims of this presentation

Because linguistic investigation so rarely occasions sustained grappling with the complexity issue, there are various misconceptions that my treatment may foster in the reader.

*My aim in this chapter is not to construct a metric for ranking the world's languages on a scale of complexity*, a goal whose ultimate intellectual benefit would be unclear in any case. My aim is a more constrained one: to provide a metric of complexity that will serve the purposes of elucidating and rendering falsifiable my specific claim that creole languages in general strongly tend to be less complex than older languages. I believe that the difference in degree of complexity between older grammars and a subset of creole grammars is distinct enough that a complexity metric so fine-grained as to, for example, allow us to rank Romanian, Hausa, and Korean in terms of some general complexity quotient would be unnecessary to our project.

*This metric does not stipulate that complexity is indexed with relative difficulty of production or processing*. To wit, the model is not intended to imply that languages more complex according to its dictates are more difficult for the speaker to produce, or that such languages are more difficult for the hearer to process; moreover, this metric takes as a given that all languages are acquired with ease by native learners. Our assumption is that human cognition is capable of processing great degrees of *overspecification* in language, and that possible differentials in ease of production or processing would be of importance more to applied linguistic concerns than to academic and theoretical concerns; as such, this issue will not be explored here. Our object of inquiry is differentials between grammars in degree of overspecification (as we will see, all grammars including creoles can be argued to be overspecified to some degree), to the extent that some grammars might be seen to require lengthier descriptions than others, in order to characterize even the basics of their grammar.[6] (However, it bears mentioning that a highly elaborated grammar could be argued to be easier rather than harder to process, in making distinctions more clearly than a less elaborated grammar, and thus leaving less to context.)

*The metric as presented in this chapter will not suggest what the most "optimal" language would be.* This question, which will occasion different answers according to whether we are concerned with speaker or hearer, is obviously a rich one, and it echoes throughout a great deal of phonological, syntactic, and acquisitional work. Obviously, however, the topic is much too large to be addressed gracefully here and would be tangential to its core argument. (However, the issue will be touched on briefly near the end of section 4.3.)

### 2.4.3. A metric of complexity

With the aims of my project thus delineated, I propose the following four diagnostics of grammatical complexity, chosen to arouse the least possible controversy from as wide a spectrum as possible of linguists. The guiding intuition is that an area of grammar is more complex than the same area in another grammar to the extent that it encompasses more overt distinctions and/or rules than another grammar (this is not meant to subsume redundancy, which involves manipulation of the same form, not contrasting forms).

Specifically:

(a) A phonemic inventory is more complex to the extent that it has more marked members. Markedness is here intended strictly in reference to cross-linguistic distribution: marked phonemes are those encountered less frequently in the world's languages than others conventionally deemed unmarked for example: ejectives, clicks, and labialized consonants vs. stops, rounded back vowels, and glides.

The motivation for treating such sounds as metrics of complexity is not a claim that these are more articulatorily complex in the sense explored by Trubetskoy (1931); determining the precise measurement of articulatory complexity has proven too controversial to serve adequately as a foundation for the project in this paper. Rather, the motivation for using these sounds as a metric is implicational, in the Greenbergian (1966a, 1966b) sense: an inventory with a great many marked sounds (e.g., a click language) is more complex than one with all or almost all unmarked sounds (e.g., a Polynesian language) because *the former type of inventory has marked members in addition to unmarked ones*—the marked sounds *imply* the concurrent existence of unmarked ones (there exist no phonemic inventories with only cross-linguistically marked phonemes). A larger phonemic inventory requires maintaining finer intersegmental distinctions within the bounds of the human vocal apparatus. There is obviously no claim that marked phonemic inventories are more difficult to acquire natively; our reference is solely to the number of distinctions entailed by such inventories in comparison to others.[7]

Similarly, a tonal system is more complex than another one when it has more tones, because this phonology requires mastery and processing of a larger set of contrasts and requires maintaining finer intertonal distinctions within the bounds of the human vocal apparatus.

    (b) A syntax is more complex than another to the extent that it requires the processing of more rules, such as asymmetries between matrix and subordinate clauses (e.g. Germanic V2 rules), or containing two kinds of alignment rather than one (i.e., ergative/absolutive and nominative/accusative). (cf. Henry 1995, Henry and Tangney 1999)

    (c) A grammar is more complex than another to the extent that it gives overt and grammaticalized expression to more fine-grained semantic and/or pragmatic distinctions than another. For example, the Muskogean Native American language Koasati uses different existential verbs for five types of object, depending on their shape (with each verb varying suppletively for plurality):

(3)  Nofó-k      mat-haccá:1
birch-SUBJ afar-stand
"There's a birch over there." (Kimball 1991: 453)

(4)  Ó:la-k      tallá:k.
town-SUBJ lie
"There's a town." (ibid. 458)

In subdividing the semantic space of existentiality more finely than English does, Koasati marks existentiality in a more complex fashion than English does. Here is another sentence in Koasati (SR = switch reference to different subject; weSTAT = first-person plural prefix used for stative verbs; SS = switch reference to same subject):

(5)  Kom-mikkó-k  cikkí:li-t    kom-tohnó:ci-fó:k-on
our-chief-SUBJ keep-CONN to us-send off-when-SR/FOC
mán tokná:wa st-im-ako-yókpa-k            immá:ya-k.
also money    INST-3SOBJ-weSTAT-love-SS to it-be more-SS
"When our chief took care of it and sent off for things for us, we then grew to love money more." (Kimball 1991: 491)

In requiring overt specification of reference tracking where English requires none, and in having particular pronominal affixes used only with stative verbs where English has no separate set of pronouns used according to verbal Aktionsart, according to our metric, Koasati is a more complex grammar (in these areas) than English.

    (d) Inflectional morphology renders a grammar more complex than another one in most cases.

This last point requires discussion. The reader may justifiably object that there is no a priori reason to assume that inflectional encoding is inherently more complex than encoding the same feature with a free morpheme. This is, in itself, true. "I wanted" is *ni-li-taka* (I-PAST-want) in Swahili but *wǒ yào le* (I want PERF) in Mandarin Chinese. There are no empirical grounds for assuming that Swahili is more complex in encoding "I" and pastness with morphemes more phonetically incorporated with the head of the phrase than those in Mandarin Chinese are.

However, inflection more often than not has wider repercussions in a grammar than this, which are complexifying factors in terms of exerting a load upon processing:

*Morphophonemics and Suppletions.* While some languages are as neatly agglutinative as Swahili, as often as not, inflection leads to the development of morphophonological processes, which constitute an added component of a grammar to be learned. It can be argued that these processes have perceptible phonetic motivations and as such can be seen as a relatively minor addition to the processing component. Yet morpho-phonology also often leads to less-phonetically predictable processes, such as Celtic consonant mutation (Welsh *ei gath* "his cat" versus *ei chath* "her cat"), whose rules fall outside of the realm of phonology, or Germanic umlaut (Proto-Germanic [\*foːt] "foot" / [føːt-i] "feet," with the plural form > [føːt-i] > English [føːt] > [fiːt]); in German, umlaut rules also occur variably in certain contexts, such as before the plural morpheme -*e* (*Kuh/ Kühe* "cow/cows" but *Schuh/Schuhe* "shoe/shoes," etc.).

Meanwhile, suppletion also complexifies an area of grammar according to our metric. The various suppletive forms of "to be" in English (or in most Indo-European languages) (*am, are, is, was, were, been*) render these languages more complex in this area than languages where the copula is invariable across person and number in the present (i.e., Modern Swahili's *ni*) or is conjugated relatively predictably in the present and the past (i.e., Finnish *olla*).

*Declensional and Arbitrary Allomorphy.* Inflection also complexifies a grammar when it encodes distinctions between noun classes or verb classes. English is not less complex than Latin in having "to the boy" rather than *puero*. However, English expression of case is simpler overall than Latin's because Latin nouns could belong to any of five classes, each differing significantly in their case paradigms (on top of inflecting for singular and plural).

Similar are cases where a given alternation is expressed via a number of inflectional strategies, each of which must be learned and stored with the root. Russian imperfective *pisat'* "to write" is rendered perfective via the addition of a prefix (*napisat'*), while *pit'* "to drink" is rendered perfective via the addition of a different prefix for no synchronically perceptible reason (*vypit'*); meanwhile, imperfective *načinat'* "to begin" is rendered perfective via the subtraction of a suffix (*načat'*), while the imperfective *klast'* "to put" can only be rendered perfective via a different root altogether, *položit'*.

*Agreement: Useful versus Useless.* As we have seen, a grammar with agreement-marking inflection is also inherently more complex than a grammar like English in that, unlike in the case of Swahili *nilitaka* versus Chinese *wǒ yào le*, agreement marking is not a different way of expressing a category marked in another fashion in English but, instead, marks a category not expressed in any fashion in English.

Thus my claim that inflection almost always complexifies a grammar is based not on an Anglophone's romanticization of Latin declensional paradigms, but on (1) the effects that inflection typically has on a grammar over time; and (2) the fact that some inflection, such as gender marking and declensional noun classes, does not correspond to concepts expressed by all grammars but is, instead, purely supplemental to a grammar's machinery.

## 3. Comparing complexity: An older grammar and a Creole grammar

Based on the preceding definitions of complexity, I now compare the grammar of the Nakh-Daghestanian (Northeast Caucasian) language Tsez (data from Comrie, Polinsky, and Rajabov 2000) and the creole language Saramaccan, which emerged in the late seventeenth century and is thus approximately three centuries old (data collected by the author unless otherwise cited).

### 3.1. Tsez versus Saramaccan

(*a*)

The Tsez phonemic inventory of some forty-two segments includes uvulars, pharyngeals, and a separate series of pharygealized uvulars; most stops and affricates have phonemic ejective alternants. Most consonants have labialized phonemic alternants. A long *a* is phonemic.

    The only marked sounds in the Saramaccan phonemic inventory of thirty are three prenasalized stops and two prevelarized ones, entering into phonemic contrasts only occasionally. There are no uvulars, ejectives, or labialized consonants. There are some minimal pair distinctions for tense and lax mid vowels ([e]/[ɛ], [o]/[ɔ]).

(*b*)

Tsez has four noun classes, marked by agreement prefixes on most vowel-initial adjectives and verbs, as well as elsewhere in the grammar (although vowel-initial adjectives and verbs are a minority in the lexicon). The classes are only about as semantically predictable as those determining gender in German. Tsez verbs fall into four classes, determined by the final segment of the stem. Agreement is marked on both verbs and nouns, but with the stipulation that it is marked only on (most) vowel-initial stems. Matrix verbs are normally marked for agreement with a complement clause, with the gender marker for "other," while focus on an absolutive nominal inside the complement clause is marked via agreement with that nominal (CL3 = noun class 3, CL = noun class 4 ("other"), PP = past participle, NOM = nominalizer) (data from Polinsky 1999):

(6)  (a)  eni-r       [už-ā      magalu       b-āc-ru-λi]      r-iy-xo.
          mother-DAT boy-ERG bread.CL3.ABS CL3-eat-PP-NOM **CL4**-know-PRES
          "The mother knows that the boy ate the bread."

     (b)  eni-r       [už-ā      magalu       b-āc-ru-λi]      **b**-iy-xo.
          mother-DAT boy-ERG bread.CL3.ABS **CL3**-eat-PP-NOM **CL3**-know-PRES
          "The mother knows that the boy ate the *bread*."

Saramaccan has neither inflectional morphology nor free equivalents such as noun classifiers.

*(c)*

A large number of Tsez nouns occur in an alternate stem form before certain inflectional suffixes. The changes are partially determined morphophonologically, but nouns differ as to exactly which suffixes the alternate occurs before, and some occur in different alternate forms for different suffixes. The generation of the alternate stem from the basic one is not a regular process but, instead, follows various rules of thumb, which are about as irregular as those determining plural marking in German: *giri* "pole," *girimo-s* "of the pole" vs. *mec* "tongue," *mecr-ebi* "tongues," illustrating two segments used frequently to form alternate stems.

Saramaccan noun roots do not change according to case.

*(d)*

Tsez has a large number of derivational affixes for deriving nouns, verbs, and adjectives, including markers of evaluative names ("coward"), both denominal and deverbal abstract nominalizers, a marker of enveloping objects, a marker designating residents of a place, a marker meaning "possessing X" (*kot'u* "beard," *kot'u-r-yo* "bearded man"), two denominal adjectival markers with an alienable/inalienable semantic distinction, a caritive suffix, and suffixes to derive transitive and intransitive verbs (from adjectives and adverbs) (14–15).

Saramaccan has two derivational suffixes and one derivational prefix, and reduplication derives attributive adjectives and resultatives from transitive verbs (*mi lái dí gbóto* "I loaded the boat," *dí láilái gbóto* "the loaded boat," *dí gbóto dé láilái* "the boat is loaded"). Reduplication also nonproductively generates nouns from verbs (*síbi* "to sweep," *sísíbi* "broom") (Bakker 1987: 21). One might reasonably surmise that Saramaccan might have analytic derivational strategies for all of the functions covered by the Tsez markers, in which case there would be no grounds for designating Tsez derivation more "complex." Saramaccan indeed marks, for example, causativity with a serial verb construction. However, in most cases—such as all of those listed in the previous paragraph—Saramaccan has no overt derivational strategy corresponding to the Tsez ones.

(*e*)

Word order behavior of wh-words in Tsez depends on the adjunct/argument distinction:

(7)   (a)  Neti obiy          kidir-ā-ɤor   ø-ik'i-x?
          when father:ABS Kidero-in-to AGR-go-PRES
          "When is father leaving for Kidero?"

      (b)  Kidb-ā    **šebi**        t'et'erxo?
          girl-ERG  what:ABS read-PRES
          "What is the girl reading?" (Comrie, Polinsky, and Rajabov 2000: 22)

Wh-movement in Saramaccan is straightforward: wh-words generated after the verb are regularly fronted.

(*f*)

Tsez has an evidential distinction in past tense marking.
    Saramaccan has no grammaticalized evidential markers.

(*g*)

Tsez has some suppletive plurals and some suppletive transitive/intransitive pairs.
    There are two instances of suppletion in Saramaccan: (1) before the verb *gó* "to go," the imperfective marker *tá* is expressed as *nan: mi tá wáka* "I am walking," but *mi nángó* "I am going"; (2) in a portmanteau morpheme with oblique third-person pronoun *ɛ̃*, locative *a* becomes *n-*, as in *nɛ̃ɛ̃* "at/in it." In entailing more suppletive plurals and lexically distinct transitive/intransitive pairs than Saramaccan, Tsez marks certain semantic distinctions overtly where Saramaccan does not.

3.2.  Implications of the comparison

On the basis of the complexity evaluation guidelines proposed in 2.4, Tsez's grammar is indisputably a more complex one than Saramaccan's. The reader may justifiably wonder whether I have "stacked the deck" by highlighting aspects in which Tsez grammar happens to be more complex than Saramaccan's. Certainly there is no intention to imply that Saramaccan does not have its share of morphophonological processes:

- The third-person pronoun causes the assimilation of a preceding [a] with high tone such that *tapá ɛ̃* "cover it" is phonetically [tapɛ̃ɛ̃])
- An epenthetic [m] surfaces morphophonologically between a few verbs and a following third-person singular pronoun: *fɔ̃* "to beat," *a fɔ̃ ɛ̃* ([a fɔmɛ̃ɛ̃]) "he beat him"
- There are some portmanteau morphemes in Saramaccan created by morphophonemic processes: for example, before a pronoun beginning with a vowel, the vowel in *fu* becomes homorganic with the following

one, and over the history of the creole the preposition has fused with the following word: *fu i > fii* "your" (lit. "for you"), *fu ɛ̃ > fɛ̃ɛ̃* "his, her, its" (lit. "for him/her/it")

In addition, there are indeed some features in Saramaccan that would qualify as elaborated quirks. Saramaccan has overt and categorical marking of determination (via articles), whereas Tsez marks definiteness only on nouns with an attributive adjective (Bernard Comrie, pers. comm.). Over its 300 years in existence, Saramaccan has evolved a new negator, such that today one is used to negate verbal predicates and the other is used elsewhere (*Dí wómi á tá wáka* "the man isn't walking"; *Dí wómi ná mi tatá* "the man is not my father") (cf. chapter 7 on this development). There are a handful of lexical distinctions encoded only by tone for example, *dá* "to give" vs. *da* "to be" (cf. McWhorter 1997a: 87–121 on the diachrony). Features of this kind multiply in creoles as time passes, since they are natural languages subject to the same forces as all others.

The crucial point is that creoles have not existed long enough for there to have arisen the sheer weight and depth of such features as in older languages like Tsez. Saramaccan features such as the negator allomorph and the epenthetic [m] are scattered ones of highly local import, and the fact remains that, in all areas, with the single exception of determination marking, according to what is currently known of both Tsez and Saramaccan, Tsez grammar is more complex (according to our metric) than Saramaccan's. For example, morphophonological processes are richer and deeper in Tsez than in Saramaccan. Comrie, Polinsky, and Rajabov describe four main rules, which are applicable across the grammar or to general word classes, and allude to other "more sporadic" ones; in contrast, all morpho-phonemic rules documented to date in Saramaccan are relatively "sporadic," ap-plying, for example, to the single preposition *fu*, to the pronoun *ɛ̃*, or to a subset of the pronouns.

Furthermore, we must note that gender marking is not the only function served by inflection in Tsez which is not marked at all in Saramaccan. For example, with experiencer verbs, Tsez uses a lative marker:

(8)  Aħo-**r**        meši      b-esu-s.
     shepherd-LAT calf:ABS AGR-find-EVID
     "The shepherd found the calf." (Comrie, Polinsky, and Rajabov 2000: 19)

In contrast, Saramaccan does not mark experiencer verbs with any overt marker or strategy on a grammaticalized basis. Importantly, experiencer subject marking is not unique to inflected languages. It is common in Mande languages (Reh and Simon 1998), as well as Polynesian, as demonstrated in Maori where a group of experiencer verbs take the preposition *ki*:

Maori (TS = tense):

(9)  Ka piirangi ia **ki**     ngaa mea katoa.
     TS want      he PREP PL   thing all
     "He wants all the things." (Bauer 1993: 270)

Thus the absence of overt delineation of experiencer verbs in Saramaccan is not a mere epiphenomenon of its analytic structure.

The facts are similar with evidential marking, which, like experiencer verb marking, is indeed compatible with analytic structure, as we see in the Tibeto-Burman Lahu:
Lahu:

(10)  Yɔ̂ šɔ́-pɔ̄    gà    la tù    cê.
he tomorrow come to FUT HEARSAY
"They say that he'll arrive tomorrow." (Matisoff 1973b: 469)

Finally, while Tsez overtly expresses many concepts that Saramaccan does not, the converse does not apply: Saramaccan does not require its speakers to attend to any but the very occasional concept that Tsez does not (e.g., it marks definiteness more widely), lacking, for instance, obviative marking, inverse marking, tracking of referentiality as in languages of the Philippines, switch-reference marking, consonant mutations, clitic movement, subjunctive marking, dummy verbs, and so on.

In other words, the fact that Saramaccan is hardly devoid of marked or complex features does not entail that a complexity gradient between grammars is an empirically invalid concept. With this acknowledged, it appears evident that Tsez is a more complex grammar than Saramaccan.

It must finally be observed that my observations about Saramaccan all apply as well, with minor modifications irrelevant to the basic thrust of the thesis, to the other creoles that I have designated as closest to the Creole Prototype in previous papers: Sranan, Ndjuka, Tok Pisin, Bislama, Solomon Islands Pijin, Torres Strait "Broken," Aboriginal Pidgin English, São Tomense Creole Portuguese, Principense Creole Portuguese, Annobonese Creole Portuguese, Angolar Creole Portuguese, Negerhollands Creole Dutch, Baba Malay, and Papia Kristang Creole Portuguese. The French plantation creoles (e.g., Haitian, Louisiana, Mauritian, Seychellois, Martiniquan, French Guyanais), due to contact over the centuries with French, have borrowed many French lexicalized derivation-root combinations and thus· do not exemplify the Creole Prototype in the purest possible form. However, overall their grammars contrast with Tsez in the same ways as Saramaccan and the above creoles.

The Northwest Caucasian language Kabardian is even more fearsomely elaborated than Tsez (Colarusso 1992: xix):

There are forty-eight consonants in most dialects. . . . Unusual contrasts and complex clusters abound. The phonological rules are complex and highly ordered. The result is that many Kabardian surface forms appear far removed from their underlying sources . . . the morphology of the language is highly complex . . . the verb can inflect for every noun in the sentence as well as for a range of subtle geometrical, aspectual, temporal and pragmatical features. The complex verbal use of several distinct temporal and adverbial positions, as well as the intermixing of personal indices with geometrical and pragmatical ones, strongly suggests that multiple layers of morphology and distinct morphological processes are at work. Such complexity is not restricted to the verb, but appears in word formation in general.

This sort of description is inconceivable of any creole language, and Colarusso refers to Kabardian and Caucasian languages in general as "extraordinarily complex by any linguistic standard" (1992: 2). Any thesis that all natural languages are equally complex automatically renders Colarusso's statement false and underinformed, when in fact it is unclear that a viable case that Mauritian Creole French or creolized Tok Pisin equal Kabardian in overall complexity would be possible.

## 4. Analytical grammars old and new

As discussed here, much of the complexity difference between Tsez and Saramaccan is an outgrowth of the effects of inflection. Although there are also complexity differences independent of this factor, one might reasonably suppose at this point that the complexity difference between creoles and analytic languages would be less than that between them and inflected languages. Nevertheless, when we actually compare an older analytic grammar with a creole, we find a similar difference in complexity.

A comparison of this type is particularly urgent, given a hypothesis in some current creolist work that the traits commonly found in creoles are predictable manifestations of a general analytic grammar, which implies that creoles are not synchronically delineable in any qualitative way from Sinitic, Mon-Khmer, Kwa, Polynesian, or other older analytic languages. DeGraff, for example (1997, 1999b), argues that the differences between a creole grammar and its source languages' are due to certain syntactic results following from loss of inflection during second-language acquisition (such as lack of verb movement to I), with subsidiary results due to the filtering out of low-frequency features, and the ellipsis of certain functional categories, with the qualification that the effect of the latter two was no more marked than that upon other languages with heavy contact in their histories, such as Yiddish (DeGraff 2000). DeGraff considers the association of creoles with pidgins unmotivated, and the exploration of a synchronic delineation of creoles an empirically unmotivated essentialization.

This provocative suggestion does not square with an actual comparison of older analytic grammars with creole grammars, in which case it becomes clear that creole genesis entailed a transformation of source language structures which far bypassed the relatively nondisruptive processes that Proto-Germanic dialects underwent in becoming Swedish. Namely, creoles are natural languages reborn from a radical reduction of their source languages into makeshift jargons. Here I will present a direct comparison of a well-described analytic grammar, the Tibeto-Burman language Lahu (data from Matisoff 1973b; indicated page numbers from this source), with Saramaccan.

### 4.2. Lahu·and Saramaccan

(a)

The Lahu inventory of thirty-three segments includes palatal and postvelar stops, as well as the typical bilabial, alveolar, and velar, with both aspirated and unaspirated phonemic alternants in all five places of articulation; a voiced velar spirant; a central high unrounded vowel and schwa are also phonemic (p. 1).

As noted above, Saramaccan's phonemic inventory is somewhat smaller and less marked overall.

(*b*)

Lahu has seven lexically contrastive tones: *ca* "look for," *cà* "fierce," *câ* "eat," *cā* "feed," *cá* "boil," *câʔ* "string," *càʔ* "machine" (22). Tone also often encodes causativity, as in *câ* "eat," *ca* "feed." There are various other unsystematic tone-based distinctions between closely related words, such as *mû* "heaven, sky," *mu* "be high, tall"; *phu* "silver, money," *phû* "price, cost" (29).

Saramaccan has a high-low tone contrast which is lexically contrastive in less than a dozen cases (*bigí* "to begin," *bígi* "big"; *á* "not," *a* "he, she, it"). (Among creoles, Saramaccan is unusual in displaying lexically or morphosyntactically contrastive tone even to this extent.) There are no semantic relationships between words encoded with tone, either in productive or fossilized fashion.

(*c*)

Lahu has about ten derivational markers occupying a continuum of productivity and semantic transparency. This includes agentive markers distinguished by sex (454–55); two others distinguished by sex to denote ownership or mastership, which can also be used to nominalize clauses (457); two causative markers (244–46); and a marker transforming verbs into corresponding nouns for example, *u* "hatch," *ɔ-u* "egg"; *cā* "to sprout," *ɔ-cā* "a shoot" (68).[8]

As noted above, Saramaccan has only a few derivational markers; it has a single, gender-neutral agentive marker.

(*d*)

Like many Southeast Asian languages, Lahu has several numeral classifiers, for people, animals, shapes, and more general purposes (89–92); in the absence of these the noun can be replicated itself as a classifier: *yὲ tê yὲ* "one house" (89).

Saramaccan has no classifiers of any kind.

(*e*)

Lahu has an accusative marker, *thàʔ* (155–58). In itself, marking patienthood is not necessarily more "complex" than leaving it unmarked. However, Lahu's marker is only very approximately characterized as an accusative marker, in fact occupying a wider and more idiosyncratic semantic space. For one, it is used with patients only to encode certain shades of emphasis. Furthermore, in many uses it marks not patients but other thematic roles (NOM = nominalizer):

(11)  Yɔ qɔʔ   la   ve   ha-pa qhà   ve   **thàʔ** le?
      he repeat come NOM month which NOM ACC INT
      "In which month will he come back?" (157)

(12)  ɔ-qā   chi hê-pā   **thàʔ** vì       ā   ve   lâ?
      buffalo this Chinese ACC buy-from PERF NOM INT
      "Did you buy this buffalo from a Chinese?" (158)

Saramaccan does not have overt markers of nominativity or accusativity. Regarding complexity as opposed to overspecification, it is not clear that overt expression of accusativity is more complex than not expressing it, but under the analysis of complexity adopted in this paper, the overt expression of a form that covers an arbitrary space partly occupied by transitivity and partly by intransitivity is more complex than both a purely accusative marker and thus, by extension, more complex than no overt expression of grammatical relations of any form.

(f)

Lahu has a number of modal and pragmatic particles central to basic expression which are conventionalized into highly particular and idiosyncratic subdivisions of semantic and pragmatic space, reminiscent in both proliferation and in particularity of meaning to those in German and Dutch. Here is one sentence exemplifying the use of just some of them, with the translations provided by myself according to the grammar and checked with the author:

(13)   Kɔ́lɔ́ cɛ            tí  tɛ    qo   ɔ̄,  te  mâ  pɔ̀  tù  hé.
       Thai to-the-extent-that just EMPH as for TOP do NEG finish FUT probably
       "If it's really only the Thai (who are doing it), they'll probably never get it finished!"
       (181)

It may be useful to note that this is a thoroughly *ordinary* sentence of Lahu, not an unusually "expressive" one, and, more important, there is no attempt in the glossing to "exotify" this sentence for the sake of my argument. To give the reader even a preliminary grasp of the actual semantic space filled by each of these particles would require more space than this chapter allows (the interested reader should consult Matisoff's magnificent grammar). However, for example, *cɛ* does not in any sense translate simply as "if," but in its other uses clearly makes a semantic contribution leading Matisoff to term it an "extentive" particle (170–71); *tɛ̀* is not merely a focus particle, but one with the specific pragmatic purpose of averring the truth of a proposition in forceful observation or argument in a "See, there you go!" sense (171).

Saramaccan can certainly convey all of the meanings encoded by the Lahu particles, but importantly, has not grammaticalized nearly as many items for such pragmatic uses, such that (1) pragmatic space is not overtly divided up so finely; (2) the markers that do exist are mostly less conventionalized and less, in Lehmann's (1985: 307–9) term, obligatorified, than those in Lahu; and thus (3) since concatenations of several overt pragmatic indicators are not typical of Saramaccan speech, the grammar does not require control of their specific possibilities of combinability.[9]

(g)

Lahu, like Saramaccan and many other creoles, makes great use of verb serialization and concatenation to express concepts that are usually expressed with prepositions and adverbs in English. However, within this grammatical tendency, Lahu has tightly grammaticalized many more verbs than Saramaccan (Matisoff lists fifty-seven verbs that have evolved such conventionalized usages [212–13, 222–30, 237]), with many of their functions being more specific and more deeply abstract than those in Saramaccan.

For example, one use of the verb *là* "to come" indicates that the verbal action is for the benefit of either first- or second-person but not third- *chɔ là*, "chop for me/ us/you" (324–30); *e* from "to go" expresses not only concrete movement away (*lò? e* "enter into") but also extremely figurative senses of movement away, such as with the verb "to finish" to mean "all used up": *pɜ̀ e* (318–19). *Gu* "to fix" has grammatical- ized into indicating that an action is done better than before, and from here to simple repetition: *gu chi?* "retie" (213). There are many grammaticalized particles used with verbs where a lexical progenitor is no longer in use; whether or not these are derived from verbs, they add often highly specific meanings to verb complexes. For example, the particle *šē* is an "anticipatory inchoative," implying that something implied be- yond the utterance is just about to occur: *Ei-kâ? hé šē* (water bath PART) "Take a bath first (and then we'll eat)" (337).

Furthermore, grammaticalized serial verbs in Lahu vary as to where they occur in relation to the head verb, or within a concatenation of more than two verbs.

In Saramaccan, the serial verbs with especially grammaticalized usages consti- tute about a dozen usually relatively shallow instances of metaphorical extension such as *téi* "to take" (instrumental); *gó* "to go" (direction away), *kó* "to come" (direction toward / becoming), *dá* "to give" (benefactive), *kabá* "to finish" (completive), *tooná* "to return" (repetition), and *táki* "to say" (complementizer) (see Veenstra 1996: 73– 103 for the most comprehensive and insightful treatment to date). Some verbs have moved somewhat further along the grammaticalization cline for example, *dá* "to give" also expresses causation and source: *Dí móni lási dá mi* "The money got lost because of me" (Veenstra 1996: 165); *túwɛ* "to throw" marks an object's reaching the end of a trajectory: *De sɑ̃ ɛ̃ túwɛ a goó.* "They sawed it to the ground." Yet on the whole, the body of grammaticalized serials in Lahu exhibits a greater degree of metaphori- cal extension than Saramaccan's, along with a tendency toward finer subdivision of semantic space: for example, Lahu's "come" verb *là* is restricted in its grammatical- ized use as a benefactive marker to first and second person, while Saramaccan *kó* "to come" applies to all persons in all of its grammaticalized usages. Nor does Saramaccan limit any grammaticalized serial to particular persons. Finally, all of Saramaccan's serial verbs except causative *mbéi* "to make," *hópo* "to arise" (for abrupt inceptivity), and (only partially grammaticalized) instrumental *téi* (instrumental) come after the head verb, and thus the use of a serial verb in this grammar does not regularly entail knowledge as to which of several possible placement patterns applies to the intended meaning.[10]

*(h)*

In Lahu, certain verbs occur only in concatenation with a specific other verb to con- vey completion. Thus *tò?* "catch fire" only occurs after *tú* "to kindle": *tú tò?* "to catch fire; *kì* "be melted" only appears after *lɔ* "cause to melt." The negator *mâ*, which usually precedes verbs and verb compounds, intervenes between the two verbs: *tú mâ tò?* "does not catch fire" (207–8).

There are no verbs with such lexically and syntactically restricted occurrence to my knowledge in Saramaccan, and no verbs that condition exceptional negator placement.

## 4.3. Implications of the comparison

Even factoring out the fact that Lahu is SOV, and despite these two grammars sharing analytic structure and various traits often found in analytic languages like verb serialization, short word length, and tone, there is a clear qualitative difference between these two languages. That difference is that Lahu is "busier," an impression which, translated into linguistic terms, comprises three main observations. One is that Lahu has developed a more elaborate tonal system than Saramaccan's, much of this obviously traceable to segmental erosions during its long history (such as tonally encoded causativized verbs [32–34]). The second is that it shows evidence of the development, erosion, and subsequent regeneration of derivational morphology, another process that requires more time than creoles have yet existed in. The third, and most germane to this chapter, is that Lahu has developed more fine-grained overt expressions of underlying semantic and pragmatic distinctions in many areas, as a result of having been used continuously over countless millennia.

Some readers might observe that English is also less complex than Lahu in all but one of the features cited (derivation) and thus may question whether creoles are unique among natural languages in the degree to which they are less complex than Lahu and similar languages. The important point is that English is more complex, according to our metric, than Lahu in a great many aspects other than those covered in section 4.1. First, of course, English has eight inflections, as well as irregular marking of past in strong verbs and various suppletive verb forms (*was, went,* etc.). English inverts subject and verb to form questions and combines this with *do*-support; this *do*-support is required not simply with negation in general, but it is also necessary in particular kinds of negated constructions (i.e., there is no *do*-support in *I'm not going*). English has overt markers of definiteness and indefiniteness, whose occurrence is determined by referentiality as well: *I saw a movie last night*, where *movie* is marked with *a* despite being presupposed to the speaker, because which movie is not yet known to the hearer. Neither definiteness nor referentiality is marked overtly in any grammaticalized fashion in Lahu. The subtle distinction maintained in English between the *will* future and the *going to* future is another feature, which gives fine-grained and grammaticalized manifestation to a distinction lacking in Lahu, as well as a great many other languages.

I believe that it would be impossible to present an eight-point comparison of Saramaccan and Lahu in which Lahu appeared the less complex according to my definition of complexity, and I speculate that this would be true under any alternate definition of complexity as well.

Again, there is no claim here that Saramaccan, or any creole, is the "ground zero" of human expression, to the extent that such a language could be conceived. There are certainly elaborated features in Saramaccan that Lahu lacks. Tone sandhi is relatively weak in Lahu (27, passim) but rather elaborated and conventionalized in Saramaccan—for example, breaking at the juncture of a verb and a following object, and in shared object serials skipping the object and continuing on the second verb (Rountree 1972):

(14)  underlying:                        surface: (bold indicates spread tones):
      Mi wási koósu butá a dí sónu.   Mi wásí koósu bútá a dí sónu.
      I    wash clothes put   in the sun
      "I washed my clothes and put them in the sun."

Along the lines of the array of pragmatic particles in Lahu, Saramaccan has conventionalized the word *seéi*, from *self*, into a highly versatile particle with a quite idiosyncratic domain of application cutting across emphasis, intensification, continuation, and delimitation (Rountree and Glock 1977: 131–35):

| | |
|---|---|
| *Mi seéi mbéi ɛ̃.* | "I did it myself." |
| *Má kísi seéi.* | "I didn't catch a single one." |
| *A hánse seéi.* | "She's beautiful." |
| *Dóu seéi de dóu.* | "They just got here." |
| *De gó a Fóto seéi.* | "They went all the way to F." |
| *Mi gó ku mi seéi nɔ́ɔ.* | "I'm going by myself." |
| *A tá-kái mi seéi.* | "He keeps calling me." |
| *Mi seéi o gó.* | "I'm going, too." |
| *Gó seéi de gó.* | "They're gone for good." |

Saramaccan also differs from Lahu, as it does from Tsez, in having definite and indefinite markers (although their expression of referentiality is less grammaticalized than in English). The situation is similar in all creoles. For example, grammaticalization has proceeded faster in general in Angolar Creole Portuguese (and its sister creoles in the Gulf of Guinea) than in any other creoles I am aware of (this may possibly be due to the fact that these creoles are about 150 years older than New World creoles like Saramaccan). The subdivision of semantic space between the tense and aspect markers is highly complex and subtle (Maurer 1995: 67–89), with only the barest outline of the tidy form-meaning correspondences in the "prototypical creole TMA system" identified by Bickerton (1981 and later works). In serial constructions, some verbs have drifted into meanings as metaphorically removed from their root meanings as is common in Lahu (often specifically reminiscent of the depth of drift evidenced by "light" verbs in Indo-Aryan [cf. Hook 1991). A combination of "cut" and "put" is one way of conveying inchoativity, while "throw" conveys completion:

(15)  Ane **kota** ona    **pê**.
      they cut   murmur put
      "They started to murmur." (Maurer 1995: 105)

(16)  A baga    kampu ce    **ta**.
      3S ravage field   DEM throw
      "The field was completely ravaged." (ibid. 109)[11]

It is also relevant here, contrary to what most humans might quite reasonably suppose, that not all natural languages even have overt marking of categories as seemingly inextricable to human expression as tense and aspect (e.g., the Papuan language Maybrat [Dol 1999]); many do not have relativization strategies overtly distinct from general subordination (e.g., many Native American languages, cf. Kalmár 1985); various languages of Southeast Asia have been argued to evidence no underlying distinction between basic constituent categories (Gil 1994). All known creoles have all of these traits and a few others not as universal in language as one might suppose, and as such they regularly depart from "the heart of language" in terms of functionally central features unmarked in some older grammars. It also bears mention that many older languages have smaller phonemic inventories than any known creole (Polynesian ones being the most obvious example).

Thus our stipulation is neither that creoles were born devoid of complexity nor that they have not evolved more complexity over the centuries of their existence. Because this is not the stipulation, the identification of scattered exceptions in various creoles to the general tendency I have identified does not constitute a refutation of my argument. The argument refers not to binary opposition but to degree: the crucial point is whether or not creoles tend to exhibit *as much* complexity as older grammars do overall. I suggest that they do not and, more to the point, that creoles are *much* less complex than all but a very few older languages. For example, Saramaccan is more complex than Lahu in terms of tone sandhi, but it is not accidental that, in comparison to its (analytic) substrate languages' tone sandhi,

> all of the major differences between sandhi patterns in Anlo [a Gbe variety] and Saramaccan suggest that, where the choice has presented itself, Saramaccan has taken the easier road—four surface tones reduced to two, elimination of an environmental trigger, and a general capacity for left edges to block sandhi, not requiring any information about the syntactic function of the projection. (Ham 1999: 87–88)[12]

Finally, it must be clear that Lahu is not a special case as analytic grammars compared to creoles go. Examining a grammar of an analytic language, the linguist familiar with a wide range of creole grammars typically encounters a number of semantic distinctions virtually or completely unknown in creoles, and a tendency for case assignment, derivational processes, or syntactic configurations to vary according to factors such as transitivity, definiteness, experientiality, interrogativity, and focus, in contrast to the strong tendency in creoles to display much less particularity and variation in the expression of these underlying oppositions.

## 4.4. A replicable result

It would belabor the point and tax the reader for me to present additional such cases with the detail allotted Lahu above. However, even a brief look at one more example will be useful. Maori not only lacks inflection, but unlike Lahu, also lacks even tone. Nevertheless, Maori grammar presents one feature after another whose expression is more semantically or syntactically complex than the equivalent in any creole grammar according to the metric proposed in this chapter. A Polynesian language is particularly useful for our purposes in showing that these languages' grammars do not parallel their phonologies in simplicity and placing them perceptibly higher on the complexity scale than typical creoles.

Just a few examples, by no means an exhaustive list of such features in Maori, will suffice to illustrate (examples from Bauer 1993):

(*a*)

Maori has several different interrogative constructions according to the grammatical status of the constituent questioned; the following is but a subset of the available strategies:

(17)  (a)  subject—topic-particle fronting:
           **Ko  wai** kua hoki  ki te  kaainga?
           TOP who T/A return to the home
           "Who has gone home?" (7)
           (Saramaccan: **Ambé** bi gó a wósu?)

      (b)  object—marked for genitive and relativized (NEARH = near hearer):
           He **aha  taa**  teeraa wahine e    horoi naa?
           a   what GEN that   woman T/A clean NEARH
           "What is that woman cleaning?" (8)
           (Saramaccan: **Andí** dí mujéɛ-dé tá limbá?)

      (c)  indirect object—no movement:
           I    paatai te  maahita ki a    **wai**?
           T/A ask    the teacher  to ANIM who
           "Who did the teacher ask?" (10)
           (Saramaccan: **Ambé** dí mésítɛ bi hákisi?)

I do not know of any creole in which interrogation strategies vary to anything approaching this extent according to grammatical relation.

(*b*)

Maori has the notorious Polynesian feature of a subtle possessive distinction between marking with *oo* or *aa*, reminiscent of an alienable/inalienable distinction, but basically contingent on dominance of possessor over possessee (209–16). In addition, in marking specific possession, a prefix marks a distinction between future (*m-*) and non-future (*n-*). I do not know of any creole that makes a fully grammaticalized alienable/inalienable possessive distinction[13] (NEARS = near speaker):

(18)  (a)  **N-aa**      Hone te  kii  nei.
           PRES-POSS John  the key NEARS
           "This key belongs to John."

   (b) **M-oo**     Hone te  hooiho raa.
       FUT-POSS John the horse  that
       "That horse is for John." (208)


(*c*)

In subordinate and nonfinite clauses, subjects of intransitive verbs are marked as possessives, while the verb itself is nominalized (NOM=nominalizer):

(19)  (a)  A te  **tae-nga**      mai   o   ngaa  moni,
           at the  **arrive-NOM** to-here GEN the:PL money
           ka  hoko mai  ahau i     te  koha maa-u.
           T/A buy  hither I    ACC the gift  for-you
           "When the money arrives, I'll buy you a present." (278)

      (b)  Saramaccan:
          Té    dí móni kó,  hế  mi o    bái wấ soní paká dá  i.
          when the money come then I   FUT buy one thing pay  give you

(Moreover, the initial preposition *a* in the Maori sentence varies according to tense; it would be *i* in the past.)

     Once again, we see that analyticity alone does not explain the body of features regularly found in creoles. More precisely, analyticity does not provide an explanation for what is regularly *not* found in creoles—specifically, the high degree of elaboration inevitable in grammars tens of thousands of years old, but impossible in a grammar just a few centuries old.


4.4.  Simplification in language change versus
      the Creole Prototype

Certainly, some older languages have evolved into states approaching the relatively low complexity level of creoles. However, evidence suggests that it would be formally impossible for an older language to actually attain the state of, for example, Saramaccan or Tok Pisin. Simplification is an ongoing process in older languages, as phonetic erosion and analogy exert their effects over time. Of course, this simplification is complemented by emerging complexifications as well the very process that prevents a language from eroding into a mouthful of dust. A classic example is the erosion of Latin's future suffixes and their replacement by new ones grammaticalized from forms of *habēre* "to have" in most of the Romance languages. A less familiar example is in Lahu, where an erstwhile causative prefix *s-* eroded long ago, leaving devoicing of initial consonants and tonal disturbances on about a dozen verbs, including *dɔ̀* "drink" and *tɔ* "give to drink." Meanwhile, lexical verbs such as *te* "do, make" have been recruited into a new causative construction, which may well develop into affixes over time (Matisoff 1973b: 243–44). Moreover, at all times, the complexified results of other long-ago accretions remain alongside the emerging new complexifications, since features often persist in a grammar for long periods before being "brought down" by erosions and analogies.

Because this complexification is always "working against" the simplification, and at any given time only a subset of a grammar's complexifications are eroding, an older language retains at all times a degree of complexity alongside the simplifications it is undergoing. Creole languages are unique in having emerged under conditions that occasioned the especial circumstance of stripping away virtually all of a language's complexity (as defined in this chapter), such that the complexity emerging in a creole is arising essentially from ground zero, rather than alongside the results of tens of thousands of years of other accretions. As such, creoles strongly tend to encompass a lesser total degree of complexity than any older grammar. As language change is a nondiscrete and in many facets a contingent process, quite expectedly some older languages fall closer to the "creole" end of the complexity cline than others, such as some Southeast Asian languages and Polynesian languages.

## 5. Complexity and previous investigations of Creole markedness

This essay is by no means the first treatment to suggest that creoles represent a fundamental layer of natural language, unobscured by the results of millennia of phonological, syntactic, and semantic drift that make Universal Grammar such a challenge to glean in older languages (Kay and Sankoff 1974, Bickerton 1981, Seuren and Wekker 1986). However, the complexity metric proposed here designates creoles as "fundamental" for reasons generally independent from these previous treatments, and it will be useful to make this as clear as possible for the purposes of future discussion.

### 5.1. Semantic transparency?

In the semantic area, the "one form–one meaning" constraint often attributed to creoles (e.g., Kay and Sankoff 1974, Seuren and Wekker 1986) is upon examination a treacherous one. Kihm (2000: 167) notes that the concept of *fetch* is potentially reducible to the three semantic atoms GO TAKE COME, which is how it is expressed in the Papuan language Kalam as the serial *am d ap*. Creoles do, as a legacy of their pidgin heritage, have some tendency to use compounds in place of unitary equivalents in their lexifiers. However, a crucial point here, which Kihm does not happen to pursue but with which I presume he would agree, is that it is unclear that creoles map semantics onto lexical items to any appreciably more atomistic degree than many older languages. Vietnamese, for instance, makes heavy use of concatenations of basic verbs where both "Standard Average European" and creoles would use a single one, and forms plural pronouns via combining singular ones with a plural morpheme. As such, we find a contrast such as:

(20)  (a)  Vietnamese:
          Chúng tôi bắt đầu làm bài.
          PL    I   take start do  lesson
          "We began to do lessons." (Finegan 1999: 54)

(b) Saramaccan:
    U  bi    bigí  lési.
    we PAST begin read
    "We began to read."

Moreover, this is not even a tendency restricted to analytic languages; Colarusso (1992: 141) notes that the Caucasian language Kabardian, for example, has relatively few lexical roots, such that "one may see the lexical semantics component at work in a way matched by few other languages and exceeded by none."[14]

Certainly no scholar has made the brute claim that creoles are semantically transparent to the ultimate possible degree (e.g., Seuren and Wekker describe this as a "tendency" [64]). Yet the extent to which creoles depart from this ultimate degree is nevertheless significant, because at the end of the day it is unclear that creoles are "semantically transparent" overall to any greater extent than certain older languages. Certainly, creoles' roots in pidginization leave creoles somewhat higher on the semantic transparency scale than their source languages often are; for example, as Kihm (2000: 186) notes:

> The more I look into linguistic diversity, the more I am convinced that creole languages rank distinctively high on the isomorphism scale, despite occasional departures. . . . The fact that a language group we know to be distinguished by the special way it came into being is characterized by these features must be significant.

However, older grammars can apparently develop similar degrees of semantic transparency in the course of diachronic development without the intermediation of any detectable break in transmission. As such, it is unlikely that any claim could stand that creoles are the world's most semantically transparent grammars, and therefore the one form–one meaning conception will be of little use in a principled synchronic distinction between creoles and older languages.

## 5.2. Markedness versus complexity

In the realm of syntax, the hypothesis that creoles are closer to an ontogenetic foundation than many other languages appears promising. Bickerton (most recently and summarily, 1999) has long maintained that creoles represent unmarked syntactic and semantic settings. In recent statements he has stressed the semantic aspects, but Roberts (1999) reanimates the syntactic aspect of the hypothesis with his argument that creoles exhibit various unmarked parameter settings, specifically weak feature specifications with epiphenomena such as lack of verb movement to INFL, SVO order, preverbal tense-mood-aspect particles, absence of pro-drop, and absence of complement clitic movement.

Lightfoot (1999: 167) is skeptical that parameter settings vary in terms of markedness, asking why a human grammar would tolerate a setting that was not optimal. One might indeed argue that no parameter setting is more cognitively ungainly than another, or that the added movement processes (such as V to I movement) required by some parameters considered "marked" do not constitute significant enough of a mental exertion to be any riper for elimination than unmarked settings.

Yet there are deducibly reconstructable aspects of the first human language, and if we agree that Universal Grammar was set on the basis of this first grammar, then some parameter settings are indeed "derived" in relation to what our innate linguistic endowment would presumably specify, this operating quite independently of whether or not the "derived" setting is cognitively disfavored once it emerges.

For example, observed and documented processes of language change make it clear that the main source of affixes is erstwhile free morphemes. Certainly there are cases where affixation arises via other processes, such as the reinterpretation of fortuitous homophonies or patterns exhibited by certain segments in members of a constituent class (e.g., Nichols 1992: 139–42 on the origin of some noun class markers). Even here, however, the universal principle would appear to be that affixation is not simply created out of the blue: it emerges from the grammaticalization, reanalysis, or reinterpretation of material that was not originally inflectional. It follows logically that *the first language had no affixes* (cf. Comrie 1992). From this, it subsequently follows that, if verb movement to I is conditioned by a manifestation of rich inflectional affixation, then the first human language had no such verb movement.

We could only escape this conclusion by identifying an inherent aspect of Universal Grammar determining that, even before the existence of a grammar with an evolved rich morphology, once that morphology had emerged, the specific result would predictably and inevitably be the specific one of verbs moving to acquire tense. This proposed mechanism would also require *ruling out* the possibility that the verb stay in place and acquire its tense from afar (this latter being particularly urgent if grammars exist where verbs do not move to I despite strong inflection, a possibility which it is unclear those researching this phenomenon have exhaustively investigated). Short of this, it would appear that parameters contingent upon affixation are indeed "derived" in relation to Universal Grammar—compatible with it, but less direct manifestations of its makeup than the alternate parameters. This gains further support in the fact that children do not venture spontaneous affixes during language acquisition; instead, their first attempts at language tend to lack affixation. Moreover, when language "begins anew" amid pidginization, the linguistic vehicle consistently lacks affixation entirely or exhibits it only minimally, with affixes developing only slowly even when the pidgin is creolized.[15]

Thus the controversy over whether parameters can be ranked according to markedness in terms of relative cognitive infelicity does not in itself belie that some parameters may be ontogenetically primary in relation to others. Indeed, in cases of language genesis, if certain Universal Grammar parameters tend to be expressed over others, then this would appear to be strong evidence that parameters exist in this kind of relationship.

Nevertheless, returning to my specific analysis, the fact is that if creoles do reflect the "default" settings of Universal Grammar, this does not in the logical sense entail that they are simpler in the overall sense than older grammars. In fact, upon examination it becomes clear that the question of whether or not creole grammars are less complex than older ones as I have posed it (i.e., according to the metric of complexity outlined in 2.4), is essentially independent of markedness of parameter

settings. This becomes clear when we note that (1) a grammar could have only parameter settings considered unmarked and yet be immensely complex according
to our metric, while (2) a grammar could have all marked parameter settings and yet
be quite simple according to our metric.

For example, a grammar could have no inflection, categorically overt subject
pronouns, and SVO word order (to take three parameters or manifestations thereof
whose markedness ranking appears to be a matter of general agreement) and nevertheless have a large number of noun class morphemes, a plethora of pragmatic particles
central to basic expression, five lexically contrastive tones, deep morphophonemic
processes, various dummy verbs, and movement rule asymmetries between matrix
and subordinate clauses—all factors quite independent of the aforementioned parameter settings (in other words, basically a hypothetical but plausible Southeast Asian
language). By our metric this would be a highly complex language, despite a syntax
that a theoretical syntactician might analyze as "unmarked"—and this would remain
true even if we added any number of other "unmarked" parameter settings. Conversely, a grammar could be inflectional, have pro-drop, and be OVS, but with agglutinative morphology (and thus none of the complexification that can follow from
inflection), an unmarked phonology, relatively broad tense-aspect distinctions, relatively little exceptional case marking, no evidential or switch-reference markers, and
no overt markers of determination (in other words, a kind of object-first Swahili
without noun class markers). This would be a much simpler language than the first
one by our metric, despite its "marked" morphosyntax.[16]

Thus while the hypothesis that creoles display unmarked UG parameter settings
and my own hypothesis preliminarily give the appearance of pursuing the same or
highly similar questions, in fact, the validity of either hypothesis is independent of
that of the other one, because what distinguishes grammars in terms of complexity
according to my definition is largely independent of the syntactician's conceptions
of markedness or optimality. Thus my claim that creoles are less complex than older
ones does not address whether or not creoles display unmarked parameter settings—
because a maximally unmarked grammar could also be a massively complex one by
my metric—and cannot be evaluated according to whether or not the weak-param-
eter hypothesis proves true.

## 5.3. Greenbergian markedness and complexity

A traditional conception of markedness that complexity (as defined in this paper)
does correspond to is one of more direct application to typological studies: implicational markedness as defined by Greenberg (1966a, 1966b). The further a feature
falls on the right in a typical hierarchy, as designated by the Greenbergian framework (e.g., marking of singular/plural/dual/trial, or masculine/feminine/neuter), the
more complex it can be considered to render a grammar. This is because its presence
implies the presence of the features to the left, thus lending the grammar more overt
distinctions. The Greenbergian markedness framework also accounts for my claim
that larger phonemic inventories are more complex, in that the rarer sounds imply
the presence in the inventory of the more common ones (e.g., non-nasal/nasal).
Creoles, as less complex overall than older grammars, tend strongly to hone to the

left sides of the various implicational hierarchies outlined in Greenberg's work; indeed, if one devised a system to quantify a "score" for a grammar according to how many steps on each of these hierarchies were overtly marked in a given grammar, creoles would generally have lower numbers than almost all older languages, both analytic and synthetic.

## 6. Evaluation

The observations I have made are couched in a view of older natural language grammars as vastly *overspecified* systems in comparison to the requirements of Universal Grammar. Certainly the random complexities of any older grammar—Kikongo's four past tenses, Russian's verbs of motion, Maori's nominalized intransitives—are compatible with Universal Grammar and in many ways illuminate its structure. Kikongo's past marking gives usefully overt manifestation to interactions between completivity, perfectivity, and pastness; Slavic motion verbs grammaticalize overt marking of telicity; Maori's treatment of intransitives is one of many ways (such as ergativity) that a grammar may overtly mark valence differences.

Our point is that for every grammar that does give overt, grammaticalized marking to the above distinctions, there are several others that neither have the same marking nor any equivalent mechanism: for example, English does not have past endings to distinguish an action performed yesterday from one performed the day before that; three ways of saying "go" depending on whether there is a destination and whether it is a habitual activity; or specify intransitives to nominalize. Yet languages lacking such things nevertheless fulfill the needs of human speech. It follows from this that all four of the strategies in question are, in the strict sense, incidental to what is necessary to human communication. In other words, not just the occasional marginal or fossilized feature, but a *great deal* of any older language "came into being for a reason, but with no purpose," as Trudgill puts it (1999: 149). Having arisen for locally driven reasons unconnected to outcome in the sense Keller (1994) describes as the operations of "the invisible hand," gender marking, multiple past tenses, nominalized intransitives in subordinate clauses, and, for that matter, evidential markers, subjunctive marking, and subjects marked as experiencers, are all what Lass (1997: 13) deftly terms "linguistic male nipples."

A claim of this sort may appear to smack of "linguocentrism," but in fact the analysis applies to all older grammars, including the one I am writing in. An example of overspecification in English is the overt and categorical marking of definiteness and indefiniteness on singular nouns in English, which, for example, goes beyond the needs of a human grammar as far as encoding definiteness is concerned. This is clear from the thousands of grammars without such overt marking. The highest estimate known to me of the percentage of the world's languages that have grammaticalized articles (free or bound) at all is roughly half (Plank and Moravcsik 1996: 204), and Moravcsik (1969: 87, 93–98) estimates that only 39% of that subset have both definite and indefinite markers, and thus roughly one in five of the world's languages.[17] Typically word order and intonation play a role in encoding the distinction, but not as categorically as in English, the distinction often left to context (e.g., Chinese and Russian).

Once more, our claim is not that creoles are devoid of this kind of random accretion. In Seychellois Creole, past marker *ti* and completive marker *fin* interact in a highly delicate interplay; Angolar Creole Portuguese has one verb, *ba* "to go," which surfaces as an allomorph *be* in contexts of unbounded trajectory; Saramaccan restricts its reduplication of verbs to create attributive adjectives to transitive verbs (*Dí gógó wómi* "the goed man," as in "the man who went away"), and so on. However, it is also true that where creoles display overt marking of such grammatical fundamentals, it is almost always in fashions less complex overall, as defined earlier in this chapter, than in older languages: thus, Seychellois has two past markers, not four; Angolar has two allomorphs of one verb, not three forms each of a set of sixteen motion verbs; while intransitiveness can condition verb nominalization in Maori, Saramaccan to my knowledge only nominalizes verbs at the syntactic level in one affective construction: *Dí woóko mi woóko!* (the working I work) "Boy, I worked hard!"; and so on. To wit, in terms of accreted complexity (according to our metric) incidental to the core requirements of effective and even nuanced human communication, *the least complex grammars in the world are all creoles.*

To be precise, the claim is not that all creoles fall further toward the "simplicity" pole than any older language, since there are creoles whose social histories have lent them moderate inflection and various other elaborations (as discussed in chapter 1). However, my claim is indeed that if all of the world's languages could be ranked on a scale of complexity, there would be a delineable subset beginning at the "simplicity" end and continuing toward the "complexity," all of which were creoles. Following creoles would be semi-creoles like Réunionnais Creole French and creoles highly affected by substrate transfer such as Sri Lanka Creole Portuguese; some older languages that happen to fall especially toward the "simplicity" end of the cline might fall within this band as well. However, in the final analysis, there would be a healthy band of languages beginning at the "simplicity" pole that would all be creoles. This is not a function of syntactic parameter settings, and certainly not a function of culture or psychology: it is a predictable and, in the end, rather unremarkable result of creole languages' recent origins.

Certainly, further grammatical work on creoles will add to our stock of knowledge about their structures. However, I do not believe that the reason creoles appear at this writing to be less complex overall than older grammars is merely because of the paucity of thorough reference grammars of creole languages. For one, there are many more such grammars today than there were twenty years ago, several more on the way, a wealth of extended studies of several others, and a representative number of articles on most. The situation is hardly ideal, but the fact remains that for the modern creolist, the creoles for which there is little useful data available are very much the exception, rather than the rule as it was thirty years ago. In addition, while certainly briefer grammars miss various features, it is also important that even briefer grammars of older languages readily display the kinds of accreted complexities that are strikingly rarer in creoles.

I hope this hypothesis will stimulate further thought on this issue. New data and revisions of my definition of complexity are to be expected. Perhaps there will prove to be a conception of complexity other than mine under which creoles could be considered more complex than older languages. Examination of this issue, however, will ideally proceed within a constant awareness of the following observation, which has motivated this paper. Here is a group of natural languages:

Sranan, Saramaccan, Ndjuka, Tok Pisin, Bislama, Solomon Islands Pijin, Torres Strait "Broken," Aboriginal Pidgin English, São Tomense Creole Portuguese, Principense Creole Portuguese, Annobonese Creole Portuguese, Angolar Creole Portuguese, Negerhollands Creole Dutch, Baba Malay, Haitian Creole, Mauritian Creole, Seychellois Creole, Martiniquan Creole, French Guianese Creole.

Among these nineteen languages, according to the grammatical descriptions known to me and consultation with experts on many of them, there is neither ergativity, grammaticalized evidential marking, fully grammaticalized inalienable possessive marking, switch-reference marking, inverse marking, obviative marking, "dummy" verbs, syntactic asymmetries between matrix and subordinate clauses, grammaticalized subjunctive marking, V2, clitic movement, any pragmatically neutral word order but SVO, noun class or grammatical gender marking (analytic or affixal), or lexically contrastive or morphosyntactic tone beyond a few isolated cases (subtract Saramaccan and there is none at all).[18] None of these factors requires inflectional morphology for its occurrence in a grammar, and thus the absence of these factors is not an epiphenomenon of isolating typology.

Crucially:

1. One would find a great many of the above features in the lexifier and substrate languages that were spoken by the creators of these creoles
2. One would find it impossible to present nineteen of the world's 6,000-odd older (i.e., non-creole) languages which lacked all of the above features.

The hypothesis I have presented suggests an explanation for this observation, which I consider to be one meriting examination and explanation.

## Appendix

The paper that this article is based on appeared in *Linguistic Typology* with responses from several linguists, to which I published a reply article. Out of all of the responses, I considered David Gil's (2001) the most interesting, and here I reproduce the section of my reply article (McWhorter 2001) in which I addressed his arguments.

Ironically, when I first began investigating the creole prototype issue, my aim was to find older languages qualitatively indistinguishable from creoles, in a quest to provide some concrete demonstration of the oft-repeated claim that *creole* is solely a sociohistorical term. It was when I could not find such a language that I changed my tack and took creoles' status as a synchronic category as a given, and began investigating just why there should exist such languages.

For all of the controversy that my work in this vein has engendered, almost never over five years has any writer taken the seemingly obvious tack of proposing an older language with the features I identify as distinguishing creoles. To date, there have been but two exceptions: one scholar's reference to the Mande language Soninke in an exchange on the CreoLIST [but this argument ultimately does not hold up; cf. chapter 1 for details], and a proposal by two of the other respondents in the Linguistic Typology issue that Mandarin Chinese represents my prototype, an argument I find equally flawed (cf. McWhorter 2001: 402–4).

David Gil finally comes through with Riau Indonesian. I fully acknowledge that this language displays no more complexity (according to my metric) than Saramaccan or many other creoles, and that the facts are apparently similar for any number of vernacular Malay dialects. Gil's acknowledgment that no creole is as complex as, for example, a Tsez is also welcome. This is, in my opinion, better supported by our current state of cross-linguistic knowledge and grammatical analysis than claims such as Arends's that further work will somehow show Sranan to be equal to Navajo in complexity.

The more fruitful question will be whether any older language is as simple as many creoles. Gil proposes on the basis of his presentation that older languages can pass through stages of simplicity equal to creoles without undergoing the radical reduction occasioned by pidginization.

In that light, I think it is crucial that Riau Indonesian is a variety of Malay, a language that has served as a lingua franca for innumerable ethnic groups for almost two millennia. Malay was used as an interethnic vehicle in various kingdoms in southeastern Sumatra for over a thousand years starting in the 600s; Malay loanwords in Old Javanese, Tagalog, and even Malagasy are ample testimony to this (Adelaar, Alexander, and Prentice 1996; Grimes 1996). Today Malay (often under the name of Indonesian) continues to serve as a common coin for peoples across an area home to hundreds of minority languages. Along these lines, as Gil notes, Riau Indonesian was born amidst a great deal of non-native acquisition.

Gil proposes that this kind of usage cannot have been the source of Riau Indonesian's simplicity, referring to the fact that Russian as spoken by Daghestanians retains the bulk of that language's complexities. However, Daghestanians have traditionally been taught Russian in school, which presumably assures that most speakers attain a high level of acquisition. On the contrary, until a few decades ago, the way most Southeast Asians acquired Malay was "on the fly" through casual, oral contact.

Thus the relevant contrast is between the full varieties of French that many Africans, taught in the language in school, use as a lingua franca, versus the various reduced varieties—often termed "pidgin" (viz. Heine 1973)—of African languages such as Fula often spoken by the very same people who have learned full English or French in school. Gil is correct that widespread acquisition by adults alone does not necessarily disrupt language transmission. More precisely, it is widespread acquisition by adults *in untutored, nonprescriptive fashion* that creates the disruption.

Along these lines, then, as Gil describes, standard Indonesian is largely a utilitarian, official code taught in school; in earlier times, its equivalent was the literary Malay that was used for writing in the old Sumatran kingdoms. But meanwhile, since time immemorial, the Malay/Indonesian most people have actually spoken has been vernacular Malays much less elaborated than the Malay and Indonesian in textbooks. The crucial distinction here, then, is between written varieties of considerable elaboration on the one hand, and on the other hand strictly spoken varieties much less elaborated, developed, and used by multiethnic populations.

In this light, my honest response to the fascinating data Gil presents is that, in paralleling Saramaccan and other creoles so closely in relative lack of overspecification, Riau Indonesian is a creole.

Gil considers this analysis unsuitable in that there is no evidence of a "pidgin" having given birth to Riau Indonesian. However, it is not necessary to the birth of a creole that a pidgin ancestor have been spoken across several generations before being transformed into a natural language. The weight of attention devoted to Tok Pisin and its relatives understandably gives the impression that the life cycle of these creoles was somehow the prototypical genesis scenario for creoles. But in many other situations, the "pidgin" stage was extremely brief. In most plantation situations, for example, all evidence suggests that an initial pidgin was expanded into a full language not by children, and not by new arrivals long afterward, but by the early adult slaves themselves, as the result of using the pidgin as their primary language day in and day out (see McWhorter 2000a). Acquisition as a first language obviously "streamlined" this "expanded pidgin" somewhat, but only to minor extent: the adults themselves had already created what was essentially a full language (cf. Sankoff and Laberge 1980). Even in the Tok Pisin case, what is often termed a "pidgin" stage because few children were yet acquiring it as a first language, was, in the qualitative sense, quite close in degree of elaboration to a natural language.

"Pidginization," then, refers not necessarily to the development of a pidgin used over a long period of time but simply to a particularly extreme degree of reduction, unknown in language change uninterrupted by a break in transmission. The nature of language contact is such that there are no discrete metrics to strictly designate "pidginization" from slighter degrees of reduction. Yet most will agree that when a variety of English emerges with no inflection whatsoever, no English-derived copula, most pronouns invariant according to gender and case, almost none of English's derivational apparatus, and so on—a disruption has occurred of such an extreme degree that a taxonomic distinction appears natural and useful. Reduction this extreme is unheard of in any vernacular British variety, for instance, despite the obvious simplifications that these dialects have always undergone. This issue of degree is the diagnostic *re* "pidginization," not whether or not there was time for the pidgin to "gel" at that stage and be used over a long period of time.

Gil, however, argues that Indonesian itself is a rather "simple" language—implying that the simplicity of the Riau variety traces all the way back to the "natural" language change that created even the "highest" registers of Malay. But while Indonesian is definitely less overspecified than Cree or Fula, I have a hard time seeing a "simple" language in one with fairly extensive and non-transparent morphophonemics; a good dozen derivational affixes (1) whose functions often overlap, with this (2) often rendering it unpredictable which affix a given root will take, and (3) the particular semantic contribution to the root often being relatively unpredictable and (4), these affixes lending extensive overt marking of passivity and valence oppositions.

In larger view, the idea that Riau Indonesian is just an ordinary development would require that various other related languages be equally or at least approximately as underspecified. Yet this is not the case. Malay's close relatives Javanese, Madurese, and Sundanese are more complexified than Malay; Minangkabau varieties are similar. Nor is there unusual underspecification in more distant relatives, such as languages of Sulawesi like Buginese or Tukang Besi, the latter with, for example, paradigms of pronouns whose usage is conditioned in part by distinctions in mood or valence.

For these reasons, I now quite unhesitatingly view the vernacular Malay varieties as creole languages. I see Gil's papers on Riau Indonesian here and elsewhere, with their insightful observations about the nature of underspecification and its implications for conceptions of Universal Grammar, as some of the best *creolist* work I have ever read.

Because creole studies happens to have been initiated in countries with a history of plantation slavery, our "default" sense of what a creole is has been those that developed among Africans and South Pacific indigenes on plantations. However, it has long been known in a technical sense that creoles have also developed in other contexts, such as armies (Nubi Creole Arabic), orphanages (Unserdeutsch), missions (Tayo Creole French), and island marronage (Pitcairnese). I submit that the extensive untutored acquisition of Malay by multiethnic populations in Southeast Asia has accordingly created creole Malays. One useful comparison would be the pidgin and (semi-)creole Swahilis in East Africa. Another one more pointed would be Baba Malay, rather uncontroversially accepted into the "creole" canon. Since there seems to be little to distinguish Baba Malay from other vernacular Malays in terms of underspecification, there would seem to be no theoretical argument against classing Riau Indonesian and similar Malays in the same fashion.

I sincerely hope not to appear to be "bending the rules" to accommodate inconvenient data. I thoroughly understand that at this point, some readers will be inclined to grouse, "If you give him a language that does look like a creole, he'll just say it's a creole too!" But actually, my conception is eminently refutable. If I were presented with a language whose history did *not* involve acquisition being more often by adults outside of a school setting than by children, and this language were nevertheless as underspecified as Riau Indonesian, then I would readily concede that even an older language can attain a level of relative simplicity akin to Angolar's.

However, I suspect that this language is going to be extremely difficult to find, and that Peter Trudgill is on the right track in supposing that older languages always accrete a great deal of "historical baggage." Erosion and simplification are always at work as well, but a language never sheds all of its "baggage" at once: at any given time a large degree always remains, and the only thing that can reduce this baggage to the extent we see in many creoles is extensive exposure to, as Trudgill (2001: 372) has it, the "lousy language-learning abilities of the human adult."

# The Rest of the Story

## Restoring Pidginization to Creole Genesis Theory

## 1. Introduction

The traditional conception of the life cycle of creole languages has been that they are born as pidgins and subsequently expanded into creoles. This fundamental notion was most explicitly outlined in Hall (1966), followed most explicitly by Bickerton (1981 and later works) and Mühlhäusler (1980 and later works) (see also Samarin 1980 and later works).

While the developmental relationship between pidgins and creoles is assumed outside of creole studies, within the subfield, one trend in thought seeks to dissociate creoles from pidgins. Work in this vein instead proposes that the difference between a creole and its lexifier is determined principally by differences in syntactic parameter settings and their manifestations, resulting from widespread second-language acquisition.

This position is most explicitly argued by DeGraff, who proposes this approach as an advance over those stressing pidginization, the latter characterized as epistemologically superficial analyses incompatible with modern linguistic theory:[1]

> The outcome of [pidginization and creolization] as in [Haitian] can be explained from a fairly well-constrained perspective internal to morphosyntax, with an eye on candidate source constructions in ancestor languages. Indeed, within the adopted theoretical framework, [Haitian] verb syntax could not have been otherwise given the morphological loss independently known to occur in [pidginization and creolization]. (DeGraff 1997: 84)

> There seems to be *absolutely no need* to draw a fundamental divide between creole/creolization patterns and larger developmental/synchronic [*sic*] patterns. (DeGraff 1999a; italics in text of handout for presentation)

Beyond the broad tendencies toward various degrees of inflectional erosion cum semantic transparency (as noticed by, e.g., Meillet 1919 and Weinreich 1953 with regard to *general* language-contact phenomena . . .), no set of exclusively Creole prototypical features have thus far received robust empirical confirmation. (DeGraff 2000)

A primary focus of this school of thought is loss of inflection as the cause for a range of syntactic configurations commonly found in creoles. For example, historical syntacticians (e.g., Roberts 1992, 1999; Platzack 1987) have argued that in languages with verbal inflectional morphology, the verb moves to I, whereas in languages without verbal inflectional morphology, the verb tends to remain in place (although there do exist languages without verbal inflectional morphology in which the verb moves [Roberts 1999: 291–92]):

(1)    a. Jean embrasse souvent Marie. (*Jean souvent embrasse Marie.)
       b. John often kisses Mary. (*John kisses often Mary.) (Roberts 1999: 287)

DeGraff (1994: 42 and later works) notes that as do languages that often have little or no inflection, creoles often pattern like English:

(2)    French: Jacques ne dit jamais bonjour.
       Haitian Creole: Jak pa janm di bonjou.

Veenstra (1996: 145–48, 193) meanwhile argues that verb serialization is predictable of a grammar in which the verb does not move to I, while Déprez (1999) argues that differences in negative concord between French and Haitian can be traced to Haitian's lack of inflection as well. In a similar vein, Roberts (1999: 307–17) attributes creoles' SVO word order, lack of complement clitic movement, and TMA particles preposed to the verb to other unmarked syntactic parameter settings.

DeGraff (1999b: 525) makes the contribution of casting this observation into a preliminary general model of creole genesis. Loss of lexifier inflection is not the totality of this model; most importantly, DeGraff incorporates what he designates *stochastic* (i.e., probability) factors, which refers to observations that second-language acquisition often involves the "weeding out" of features of a grammar that require particularly heavy exposure to master due to relatively low frequency of occurrence. He makes special reference to Henry and Tangney's (1999) observation that second-language learners of Irish Gaelic typically do not acquire a certain copular construction which involves "quirky" accusative case marking. DeGraff also briefly acknowledges Lumsden's (1999) observation that in pidgins, more functional categories lack phonetic expression than in their source languages, which conditions a similar situation in the creoles that develop from them.

All three of the factors in DeGraff's model converge on a conception of the path from source language to creole as fundamentally a *syntax-internal* transformation of the lexifier. Obviously, all three of the cited factors are central components in creole genesis, and the integration of creole genesis scholarship into the frameworks and findings of theoretical syntax is nothing less than urgent.

It is less clear, however, that the syntax-internal model constitutes a corrective to those focusing on pidginization. In this chapter, I demonstrate that a strictly syntax-internal characterization of creole genesis is only possible on the pain of neglecting a large body of creole data which will only yield to explanations founded upon the birth of many creoles as pidgins. This is important because pidginization entails a degree of reduction of a grammar far beyond the relatively nondisruptive processes emphasized in the syntax-internal conception: inflectional loss, the elimination of low-frequency "quirky" constructions, and zero-realization of some functional categories.

To wit, an empirically complete account of creole genesis is impossible without the incorporation of both the syntax-internal and the pidginization-based frameworks of analysis.


## 2. Grammaticalization and reanalysis are blind

My argument is founded on certain crucial aspects of the nature of grammaticalization and reanalysis. The role of these processes in the development of pidgins into creoles is well known (cf. Sankoff and Laberge 1980). However, a lesser-acknowledged aspect of grammaticalization and reanalysis, which also plays a crucial role in distinguishing creoles from older languages, is the following fact: grammaticalization and reanalysis are no less, but no more, contingent on fulfilling functional necessity than is sound change.

This seemingly inconsequential point is in fact crucial to understanding the synchronic difference between old grammars and creoles, which are new grammars, most having existed as natural languages for only a few centuries. The cases of grammaticalization and reanalysis referred to most often are those that create markers of fundamental aspects of grammar, such as the development of future suffixes in many Romance languages from free forms of *habēre* in Vulgar Latin, or the development of nouns into spatial markers as in the development in Ewe of the noun *megbé* "back" into the spatial deictic "behind" (Heine, Claudi, and Hünnemeyer 1991: 123–47). This tendency follows from a natural interest in the origins of functionally central features, such as Roberts's (1993: 219) focus on the emergence of functional categories, leading him to designate the origin of the Romance future "the paradigm case of grammaticalization."

However, much grammaticalization and reanalysis simply gives overt manifestation to underlying semantic distinctions which, while compatible with Universal Grammar and human language processing abilities, are not specified by it. As such, these features are ornamental, rather than fundamental, to human language.

This brand of ornamentality is most graphically illustrated by noun class and gender markers, which typically evolve via grammaticalization through the phonetic erosion and desemanticization of free classifier morphemes or pronouns, or via reanalysis in the reinterpretation of erstwhile happenstance phonetic correspondences (Greenberg 1978, Nichols 1992: 141–42). While these markers typically emerge as indicators of real-world taxonomies within a culture, after millennia of phonetic and semantic drift and cultural changes, the result tends strongly to be an inflectional system with at best tenuous connections to any naturally perceivable categories (German *der Löffel* "the spoon," *die Gabel* "the fork," *das Messer* "the knife"), and importantly, the taxonomy serves no communicative purpose. This kind of marking is obviously not specified by Universal Grammar, something made clear by the fact that so very many of the world's languages lack it: it is merely the fossilized remainder of diachronic drift. As such, it is ornamental to a natural language.

Older grammars contain a great many other features which, while retaining more semantic substance than noun class and gender markers, are in the final analysis ornamental to natural language as well. The Northern Californian American Indian language Karok has grammaticalized different verbal suffixes for various containment mediums: *pa:θ-kírih* "throw into fire," *pa:θ-kúrih* "throw into water," *pa:θ-rúprih* "throw in through a solid" (Bright 1957: 98, 102). (These morphemes are not perceivable reflexes of the words for *fire*, *water*, or *solid*, respectively.) Certainly, unlike noun class and gender markers, these suffixes directly express a concrete, synchronically processible semantic distinction, and thus they render this grammar more overtly expressive in this area than many. However, most of the world's grammars do not happen to have grammaticalized such fine-grained overt expressions of containment mediums, and it would be impossible to argue that Universal Grammar specifies such. On the contrary, as useful as these suffixes are in Karok grammar, their emergence was due to a chance elaboration within a particular semantic area rather than to communicative necessity.

The ornamentality analysis applies even to historical developments encountered more frequently cross-linguistically. In the Tibeto-Burman language Lahu, the verb *là* "to come" has evolved into various uses, one of which is a benefactive particle indicating that the verbal action is for the benefit of either first or second person but not third—*chɔ là* "chop for me/us/you" (Matisoff 1991: 396); the verb *pî* "to give" is used in the third person. This grammaticalization splits according to the distinction between speaker, interlocutor, and referent, and there are corresponding examples in other languages: in Japanese, "to give" is *ageru* in the first person but *kureru* in the second and third. Like the Karok containment medium suffixes, these grammaticalizations reflect a perceptible cognitive distinction. However, lexical (as opposed to pronominal) reflections of this particular distinction, which do not occur in most of the world's grammars, reveal themselves as chance occurrences. The distinction between first-, second-, and third-person *pronouns* is a distinction along this same axis, which is indeed apparently fundamental to human language. However, over time, a language may well develop reflections of this distinction elsewhere in its lexicon or grammar via grammaticalization, and these occurrences, in their cross-linguistic idiosyncrasy, are ornamental to human communication rather than fundamental to it.

The same line of logic extends even to features that are relatively common cross-linguistically. Distinction between alienable and inalienable possession (as in Mandinka *i faamaa* "your father," *i la koloŋo* "your well"; Lück and Henderson 1993: 23) is frequently encountered in the world's languages: for example, in her survey of 402 languages Nichols (1992: 294–301) found it in 81. Almost always, inalienable possession is encoded in a more tightly grammaticalized configuration than alienable, such as juxtaposition of pronoun and possessum, as in Mandinka, or affixation of pronoun to possessum; this results either from conventionalization of the more frequent use of possessive markers with body parts and family members that discourse exerts (Nichols 1992: 116–22) or from the grammaticalization of erstwhile lexical items into possessive particles, such as happened in the Gur language Kabiye with the noun *tɛ* "home" (Heine 1997: 172–83). Once evolved, inalienable possessive marking certainly indexes a perceptible semantic distinction, and can even give overt expression to a shading of possessiveness that must be inferred from context in other grammars, such as in Navajo: inalienable *bi-be'* "her (breast) milk" vs. inalienable *be-'a-be'* "her (store-bought) milk" (Young and Morgan 1980: 7, cited in Nichols 1992: 120–21). Yet at the end of the day, inalienable possession is ornamental to human communication, not fundamental to it: we know this for the simple reason that so many natural languages do so well without it.

Examples of grammaticalization and reanalysis like this are commonplace. The prevalence of references to cases like the Romance future suffixes and West African spatial markers is due to predictable interest in the source of constructions that are central to most human grammars—not to any inherently functional orientation in grammaticalization and reanalysis per se. Obviously all humans perceptually distinguish mediums of containment, speech act participants versus speech act referents, and degrees of possession. However, the chance grammaticalization or reanalyzing of an item to overtly and obligatorily mark such distinctions is driven by no more functional necessity than the fact that French has developed a word describing a person who tends to feel chilly (*frilleux*) whereas English has not. Indo-European developed gender markers, Karok developed *kírih*, Lahu developed its benefactive *là*, and Mandinka restricted its possessive *la* to alienable possession for the same reason that French developed *frilleux:* because the semantic space happened to exist into which an item could evolve, not because natural language required that space to be filled.

The question naturally arises here as to how we might distinguish between features that are ornamental to human language versus those that are fundamental. I would like to venture the simple but strong claim that ornamental features are encountered in only a subset of the world's grammars rather than in all of them. What, then, are the fundamental features? Bickerton (1988: 278) anticipates me on this question, listing "certain minimal grammatical functions that must be discharged" in a natural language. His list is derived from traits common in creoles, but these purposes require a modification of the list to accommodate a typologically broad perspective, as well as a considerable expansion to attempt as full as possible an account of what is necessary to a natural language. This list is composed with an agnostic view toward what features may be genetically specified by Universal Grammar versus those that are universal to language for cognitive reasons:

a.  Definite/indefinite opposition (possibly via zero marking of one)
b.  Nouns
c.  Adjectives (although in many languages the class is very small, with most property items being verbs)
d.  Verbs (claims that certain Native American or Southeast Asian languages have no distinction between nouns and verbs is at present controversial)
e.  A dative/benefactive marking strategy

  f.  An oblique case marking strategy
  g.  A plural marking strategy (although only used emphatically in many grammars)
  h.  Pronouns for three persons (certain languages do not distinguish number in pronouns)
  i.  A proximal and a distal demonstrative
  j.  Spatial deictics (or nominals used in this function)
  k.  One general locative preposition
  1.  One modality marker of obligation and one of probability
  m.  Causative marking
  n.  A subordination strategy (not all languages have a distinct relativization strategy)
  o.  Adverbs
  p.  A focus marking strategy
  q.  A topic marking strategy
  r.  Question words
  s.  A conjunction *and* (or a word with a broader usage subsuming the domain of *and*)
  t.  Interjections

Particularly noticeable may be the absence of tense or aspect marking; I omit these because there do exist languages with no such overt markers, nor any sign of any items grammaticalizing as such (e.g., the Papuan language Maybrat [Dol 1999]). Neither are overt reflexive pronouns universals; many languages use unmarked pronouns reflexively and a nominal such as "body" to express explicit reflexiveness; reciprocals are similarly optional cross-linguistically.

This preliminary list is obviously rather underspecified in places but is designed to serve as a rough but useful outline of what all natural languages have in common in terms of overtly manifested concepts.

This list highlights that older grammars, because they have been subject to countless millennia of the inexorable and fundamentally contingent operations of grammaticalization and reanalysis, are vastly *overspecified* in relation to the genetic endowment for natural language, or if one prefers, the needs of human communication even of all the nuance, metaphorical richness, and sociological layeredness that are associated with all natural languages. Lahu not only marks benefactivity but, unlike most other grammars, does so with two items used according to speech act membership: this is an elaboration upon what is strictly necessary to human expression. English not only marks definiteness but, unlike many other grammars (especially outside of Romance and Germanic), does so in a subtle interaction between definiteness and referentiality (*I saw a movie last night*, where the indefinite article is used even though the movie is familiar to the speaker, to mark that the movie is not yet familiar to the addressee). This is an elaboration upon what is indispensable to human communication.[2]

This basic, although often disregarded, fact about older grammars is crucial because much of what distinguishes creoles from older grammars is that, as recent descendants of pidgins, their grammars are less accreted with such "grammaticalizational overkill." In the next section we will see that the distinction between fundamental and ornamental in natural language is not parasitic upon syntax-internal factors, and distinguishes creole genesis as a taxonomically distinct language change phenomenon.

## 3. Differences between Creoles and source languages unexplainable via a syntax-internal model

### 3.1. Feature one: Ergativity

There is no documented creole language that exhibits ergativity.[3] This finds no explanation under the syntax-internal approach.

#### 3.1.1. There are analytic ergative languages

This is not because ergativity inherently depends on inflectional processes. Although most ergative languages are inflectional (Nichols 1992: 108), some are not, as is predictable from the fact that case relations can be encoded by particles, as well as by affixes, cross-linguistically:[4]

Tongan:

(3)  a. 'oku 'alu **'a**   e  tangatá.
     PRES go  ABS the man
     "The man goes."

  b. 'oku tamate **'e**   he fefine **'a**   e  tangatá.
     PRES kill    ERG the woman ABS the man
     "The woman kills the man." (Tchekhoff 1979)

Akha (Sino-Tibetan):

(4) Àsjhaŋ sjháŋ **nɛ** shḿ-thö nɛ    bzö sèq ŋà   djé   nà-bɔ́ áŋ   nɛ.
    A.   S.    ERG awl     INST hole kill EVID QUOT ear   LOC INST
    "Asjhang Sjhang killed her with an awl through her ear." (Hansson 1976: 16)

#### 3.1.2. The absence of ergativity in creoles is not due to low frequency rendering it a "marked" construction

While a case can be made that ergativity itself is usually marked in a grammar in comparison to nominative/accusative alignment (see 3.1.5), that case cannot be one which appeals to frequency: clearly, ergative constructions are generally too central to a grammar in which they appear to be plausibly viewed as occurring too infrequently to be readily perceived by any but native speakers.

#### 3.1.3. The absence of ergativity in creoles is not due to any conception of functional category ellipsis

Ergative/absolutive alignment involves a different linking of case marking to grammatical relations than nominative/accusative alignment, but such alignment entails no elimination of case markings per se. Ergativity can even entail more overt and categorical expression of case relations and semantic roles: in languages where ergativity develops via reinterpretation of oblique or instrumental-marked nouns as subjects (cf. Garrett 1990), the very reanalysis entails the conventionalization of the marking in question.

### 3.1.4. Ergative languages have been spoken in creole genesis contexts

Korlai Portuguese Creole, for example, was developed by Marathi speakers. Marathi is ergative, and yet the creole displays no sign of ergativity:
Marathi:

(5)  a. Ram-**ne**    kam kelə
Ram-ERG work did
"Ram did the work."

Korlai Creole Portuguese:

b. Ram-ø sirwis hedzew.
Ram   work did
"Ram did the work." (J. C. Clements, pers. comm.)

This cannot be attributed to the creole having incorporated no inflectional affixation. Korlai was developed not by slaves but in a context in which face-to-face religious instruction was a principal conduit of exposure to Portuguese. As such, it has a progressive, past, and perfective inflection derived from Portuguese (Clements 1992: 46, 55).

Nor can we attribute the absence of ergativity to Portuguese influence having presumably pulled the creole too far from Marathi for such influence to reasonably be expected. On the contrary, Korlai is profoundly influenced by Marathi on all levels, including its SOV word order (quite rare among creoles), and even features such as experiencer subjects, as well as a Marathi verbal suffix -u (Clements 1991: 644):

(6)  **Pari** sitin    elo lə   vi    pərət.
to.me feeling they FUT come back
"I think they'll come back." (J. C. Clements, pers. comm.)

This creole is quite richly influenced by both of its source languages to the extent of even retaining many inflections—and yet eschewing ergativity.

Finally, this is not merely a fluke: Daman Creole Portuguese was created by speakers of Gujarati, which is ergative to a degree similar to Marathi; nevertheless, it, too, lacks ergativity.[5]

### 3.1.5. The absence of ergativity in pidgins is predictable

Nevertheless, under an analysis highlighting pidginization and recent emergence, the absence of ergativity in creoles is predictable. I know of no pidgin language with ergative marking. Far from a possible accident of history, this is predictable. Ergativity inherently requires marking of dependents, be this via affix, clitic, or particle (all syntactically ergative languages are also morphologically ergative [Trask 1979: 385]). Pidgins, however, are almost invariably head-marking to the extent that they have any morphology (the Mediterranean lingua franca Sabir, as well as Indo-Portuguese creoles, have an accusative marker *per*, but it is used only with pronominals [Ferraz 1987: 353]). Moreover, most ergative languages are only partially ergative, and split ergativity can be argued to be a mentally marked configuration in comparison to nominative/accusative alignment or fully ergative/absolutive alignment, requiring the speaker to control grammatical operations founded on two alignments rather than one, a more "costly" and thus marked choice in terms of learnability (cf. Henry 1995, Henry and Tangney 1999).[6]

### 3.1.6. In a grammar lacking it, ergativity develops via gradual change

In turn, referring to a pidgin ancestry explains why creoles lack ergativity: pidgins lack it, and ergativity only emerges via the gradual reinterpretation of nominative/accusative constructions, generally passive or nominalized deverbal (Trask 1979, Harris and Campbell 1995: 240–81) or instrumental (Garrett 1990). Thus it follows that the appearance of ergativity in (presumably, a subset of) today's creole languages will be a matter of time. As a corollary, its absence in today's creoles is predictable— but not from an analysis characterizing creolization as a process of only moderately disruptive syntax-internal adjustments.

### 3.2. Feature two: Inalienable possessive marking

The distinction of alienable from inalienable possession is a grammatical feature any linguist learns about quite early in their studies and subsequently encounters regularly in fieldwork or at linguistic presentations (cf. Nichols 1992: 32 for their wide distribution). Yet I do not know of any creole with an obligatory, tightly grammaticalized distinction between alienable and inalienable possession. This is particularly striking given that the strategy is quite commonly marked in many languages spoken natively by creole creators, such as West African and Oceanic ones.

The absence of inalienable possessive marking finds no explanation under the syntax-internal approach. It can be argued that the distinction itself is semantic rather than syntactic, but this cannot be treated as excluding inalienable possessive marking from the purview of the syntax-internal hypothesis, for the distinction is encoded via morphosyntactically distinct constructions.

### 3.2.1. There are analytic languages that distinguish inalienable possession

The reason creoles eschew this distinction is not because it is incommensurate with analytic structure. Mandinka, for example, is one of a great many languages that distinguish inalienable possession via a particle: *i faamaa* "your father," *i la koloŋo* "your well" (Lück and Henderson 1993: 23).

### 3.2.2. The absence of inalienable possessive marking in a creole is not due to low frequency rendering it a "marked" construction in the source languages

It is unclear by what metric we could designate either alienable or inalienable possessive marking as of significantly lower frequency than the other, and it is particularly unlikely that either is encountered with a lesser enough frequency to render it unlikely to be perceived by learners or transferred by speakers.

### 3.2.3. The absence of inalienable possessive marking in a creole cannot be attributed to functional category ellipsis

Inalienable and alienable possessive marking are subsets of genitivity. I am not aware of any creole that marks genitive case (and thus possession) covertly; they all have overt means to do so. As such, the elimination of inalienable possessive marking takes place despite the retention of the expression of the functional category of which it constitutes one possible expression. A syntax-internal hypothesis lacks an explanation as to why creolization so consistently eliminates a particular *manifestation* of genitivity.

### 3.2.4. Languages with analytic inalienable possessive marking have been spoken in creole genesis contexts

The absence of inalienable possessive marking in Melanesian Pidgin English, despite its predominance in its Oceanic substrate (cf. Goulden 1990), can be attributed to the tendency for the distinction to be expressed in these languages via inflection. This explanation, however, does not cover many other contexts of creole genesis.

The influence of Fongbe on the Surinam creoles, for instance, is notoriously profound. The creoles reflect many of its syntactic and semantic features quite closely, such as its syntactic, semantic, and etymological manifestations of verb serialization and its generation of property items (Migge 1998, 2000), with Saramaccan even borrowing some grammatical items wholesale, such as two question words and the focus marker *we*. Yet this fidelity to Fongbe disappears in the realm of possessive marking. Fongbe distinguishes alienable from inalienable possession in that alienables must be expressed with the genitive marker, whereas inalienables can be expressed with either the genitive or the objective marker. The distinction between the two constructions is analytic:

(7)  a. àwà nyè **tɔ̀n**
        arm my  GEN "my arm"

     b. nyɛ **sín**  àsɔ́n / àsɔ́n nyɛ **tɔ̀n**
        my  OBJ crab  crab  my  GEN "my crab" [OBJ = "objective"]; Lefebvre 1998: 101–10)

Yet neither Sranan, Saramaccan, nor Ndjuka—despite being gravid with close and direct Fongbe inheritances—have conventionalized any such semantic distinction beyond an incipient, variable degree. In Saramaccan, there is a tendency for inalienable possession to be expressed with preposed pronouns (*mi wósu* "my house") and alienable possession with a postposed "for" + pronoun (*dí wósu u de* [the house for them] "their house"). But the distinction is only variably maintained; floutings are thoroughly grammatical and often produced spontaneously by speakers, and the distinction is canceled out in various contexts such as the definite-marked plural (cf. chapter 4 in this volume). In addition, the syntactic configuration of possession here obviously departs completely from Fongbe's and gives no indication of being modeled on it; note also that Fongbe uses its genitive marker for inalienable possession, whereas Saramaccan uses *fu* for alienable. The distinction in Saramaccan is a grammar-internal emergent one. Also, Lumsden's (1999) observation that creoles often leave functional categories phonetically unexpressed is a useful one, but here it must be noted that Saramaccan does retain an overt genitive marker, *fu*. The question is why it did not submit it to a Fongbe template as it did so very much else in its grammar.

Similarly, Haitian Creole lacks the alienable/inalienable distinction even though its creators spoke not only Fongbe but also Mande languages (Singler 1993). Mande languages, like Fongbe, make this distinction quite commonly and via particles, not inflection (cf. the Mandinka example above). Sango is another example, making no alienability distinction (*lì tí mbi* "my head," *dà tí Pídà* "Pida's house" [Pasch 1997: 246]), even though its lexifier, Ngbandi, does so (*to ø mbi* "my father," *yé té zò* "a person's possession" [Samarin 2000: 316–17]), again with particles rather than inflection. Importantly, Sango's creators spoke languages that are closely related to this lexifier, and at least some of them made the alienability distinction as well (ibid.).

Under an analysis highlighting pidginization and recent emergence, these facts find a ready explanation.

### 3.2.5. The absence of inalienable possessive marking in pidgins is predictable

As discussed in section 2, the overt distinction of inalienable and alienable possession is an "ornamental" grammatical feature, quite possible within a natural language but by no means necessary to it. This is demonstrated quite clearly by how very well so very many languages get along without any mechanism for expressing such a distinction over millennia's time (such as English). Because pidgins are expressly designed for only basic communication, the eschewal of functionally expendable features is inherent to them, and as such we would expect that pidgins would not overtly mark inalienable possession—and I do not know of a single pidgin that does.

### 3.2.6. In a grammar lacking it, inalienable possessive marking develops via gradual change

Like so many aspects of grammar, this strategy is traceable to gradual reinterpretation of originally lexical materials: recall, for example, the Kabiye example mentioned in section 2. The absence of this distinction in creoles is contingent upon neither inflection, low frequency, nor elimination of a functional category. It is absent because it has not yet had time to emerge from grammars that reveal their pidgin ancestry in having developed much less "grammaticalizational overkill" than older languages have.

## 3.3. Feature three: Overt marking of inherent reflexivity

Many languages in the world overtly mark what is often called "inherent reflexives." These differ from literal reflexives in that while the latter refer to an event that involves two participants of which, contrary to general expectation, both happen to be the same entity (*He shot himself*), inherent reflexives entail a perception of one participant performing upon itself an action whose reflexivity is the expected case rather than an anomaly (*He bathed*) (Haiman 1983, Kemmer 1993).[7]

Russian is a useful demonstration case, distinguishing literal reflexives marked with *sebja* from inherent reflexives marked with *-sja*; *On utomil sebja* "He exhausted himself" versus *On utomilsja* "He tired, got tired" (Haiman 1983: 796). Some languages mark literal and inherent reflexives with the same marker (French *il s'est fatigué* "He got tired"), but in both the "Russian"- and "French"-type cases, inherent reflexive marking is typically found with verbs that denote motion, emotive states, grooming, and other concepts lending themselves to what Kemmer calls "low distinguishability of participants" in a nominally two-participant event. The cline of abstractness culminates in inherent reflexivity-marking effect upon a subject not initiated by the subject itself, as in the Spanish *Se quebró la ventana* "the window broke."

Significantly, the only creoles that have inherent reflexive marking have borrowed it from their lexifiers over time as the result of contact; creoles that emerged as pidgins and have since had little contact with their lexifiers lack inherent reflexive marking. For example, the French creoles have all existed in contexts in which French was the prestige language (cf. McWhorter 2000a). While it is demonstrable that Haitian Creole was further removed from French at its origin (Goyette 2000), over the centuries it has moved somewhat closer to French in some respects. Corresponding to this, Haitian has some inherent reflexive marking (*Robè ap degaje-l Nuyòk* "Robert is doing well in New York [Carden and Stewart 1988: 22]), but there is evidence that this was not the case when the creole was born and that later French influence led to the current situation; for example, one of the earliest sources in the language marks inherent reflexivity only optionally, with non-marking the usual case (ibid. 60). Mauritian Creole French marks inherent reflexives optionally, with contrasts like *Aloñze!* "Lie down" (Corne 1988: 74) and:

(8)  Mo pu  aloñz   mwa ler   mo fatige.
     I   FUT lie.down me  when I  tired
     "I shall lie down when I'm tired." (Corne 1988: 73)

The historical documentation makes it particularly clear in the Mauritian case that this was a development over time toward French (ibid.), and in turn makes it even more likely that this was also the case in Haiti, lending a principled explanation for its difference on this score from Ndjuka or Saramaccan, which have been isolated from their lexifiers for centuries and in which there is no sign of inherent reflexive marking.[8]

The source of creole inherent reflexive marking in superstrate contact is confirmed by other cases. Negerhollands Creole Dutch was particularly illustrative: it only displayed inherent reflexive marking (with *sie* derived from Dutch's *zich*) in the acrolectal Hoogkreols variety spoken by whites (Van der Voort and Muysken 1995: 34–36), and even then only variably (ibid. 32); in the slaves' basilectal Laagkreols variety, *sie* is absent. Along these lines we would predict that inherent reflexive marking would occur in Papiamentu, a highly mesolectal creole with rich structural influence from Spanish (cf. 5.3.2.), and indeed it does (*Mi ta sinti mi un tiki tristo* "I feel a bit sad"[Muysken and Smith 1994: 56]).

The syntax-internal approach cannot explain these facts.

### 3.3.1. Inherent reflexivity is not always marked by inflection

This absence of inherent reflexive marking (either today or before long-term contact with the lexifier) is not due to inherent incompatibility with analytic syntax, because inherent reflexive marking does not require affixation; Mojave, for example, encodes it with a particle: *mat icho* "to become, change into" (cf. French *se transformer en*), *mat iθa:v* "to be angry (cf. French *se fâcher*) (Munro 1976: 45–47).

### 3.3.2. The absence of inherent reflexive marking in a creole is not due to low frequency rendering it a "marked" construction in the lexifier

Inherent reflexive marking applies to a large subset of as central a constituent class as the verb. As such, inherent reflexive marking is encountered with too overwhelming a frequency in a language which marks it for its elimination by creoles to be attributed to stochastic factors—that is, to its elimination by creole speakers as due to their encountering it too infrequently to incorporate it into their mental representation of the grammar.

### 3.3.3. The absence of inherent reflexive marking in a creole cannot be attributed to the ellipsis of a particular functional category

It is doubtful that inherent reflexive marking is a mere manifestation of any discrete syntactic phenomenon to be "ellipsed." For example, the claim that inherent reflexive verbs are simply intransitive reflexes of transitive equivalents (e.g., Babby 1975) seriously undergenerates the actual set of such verbs in a given grammar. For one, languages that mark inherent reflexivity contain many deponent verbs, which have a reflexive marker despite a transitive equivalent neither existing nor even being logically plausible, such as French (*s'évanouir* "to faint"). Also, there are inherent reflexives whose unmarked equivalents are intransitive as well, such as Old Norse *ganga-sk* "to go" (Kemmer 1993: 28–39). In any case, valences, such as transitivity, do not constitute functional categories.

### 3.3.4. Languages with inherent reflexive marking have been spoken in creole genesis contexts

Furthermore, creoles lack inherent reflexive marking even when their source languages contain it. French, Spanish, Portuguese, and Dutch all have inherent reflexive marking. Roberts (1999: 313) refers to arguments that creoles lack complement clitics preposed to the verb because the movement of such clitics is driven by certain "strong" parameter settings; since French, Spanish, and Portuguese encode inherent reflexivity with such a clitic, this would explain creole creators' having not incorporated this aspect of those languages. Dutch, however, marks its inherent reflexives with a clitic that does not move up in the clause: *hij vergist zich vaak* "he makes mistakes often." Yet Berbice Dutch Creole did not mark inherent reflexivity (Kouwenberg 1994: 182), and we have seen that Negerhollands only did so in the "high" variety used with whites, eschewing it in the basilectal variety.

In view of the traditional emphasis in creole studies on transfer from substrate languages rather than lexifiers, the reader may object here that we would not expect Atlantic creoles to inherit features from their superstrate. For one, however, lexifier influence has been underacknowledged by many creolists (despite my reservations about the extremes of the superstratist school; see McWhorter and Parkvall 2002). In general, however, the syntax-internal hypothesis is fundamentally a superstratist framework focusing on the lexifier, and as such lexifier inherent reflexive marking falls under its purview.

### 3.3.5. The absence of inherent reflexive marking in pidgins is predictable, and in a grammar lacking it, it develops via gradual change

An analysis highlighting pidginization and recent emergence explains the scarcity of inherent reflexive marking in creoles. Inherent reflexive marking marks an underlying semantic composition particular to one subclass of verb. The fact that so many languages, such as English, simply leave this composition unmarked overtly (*The cat washes herself* vs. *John washes*) indicates that its overt marking is less a functional necessity than an ornament, a bit of "grammaticalizational overkill" typical of grammars as they age. Overt marking of inherent reflexivity obviously occurs more frequently cross-linguistically than, say, grammaticalized markers of medium of containment (although it is much more common in Europe than elsewhere). However, how variably it does occur nonetheless makes it clear that it is incidental to, not fundamental to, human expression.

It is demonstrable that inherent reflexives emerge via grammaticalization (e.g. Croft 2000: 132–33). Many inherent reflexive markers are clearly the product of phonetic erosion of literal reflexive markers; the Russian *-sja* is a phonetically eroded, affixed descendant of the free reflexive *sebja*, a distinction between literal and inherent reflexive markers also found in other languages (Kemmer 1993: 25), while the Mojave marker *mat* evolved from *imat* "his body." Obviously detransitivization, a syntactic process, is central to the generation of many inherent reflexive–marked verbs in a synchronic mental representation. However, as we saw, the only partial overlap between what detransitivization alone would accomplish and the actual body of inherent reflexive–marked verbs in a grammar demonstrates that the motivation for the appearance of the marking is the semantic nature of certain verbs. "Grammaticalizational overkill" forces the overt expression of an aspect of these verbs' composition that in most languages goes unexpressed.

It follows from this that in a natural language which was transformed from a pidgin, if inherent reflexive marking arose, it would be through gradual change, usually via a literal reflexive marker being extended to inherently reflexive verbs. As such, creoles tend to lack the overt marking of this feature because they have not existed for a long enough period for an item to be grammaticalized in the function as of yet.

### 3.4. Feature four: Evidential markers

Many of the world's languages have paradigms of grammaticalized markers indicating the speaker's attitude toward the truth of a statement. Here is a range of evidential markers in the Amazonian language Tuyuca:

(9)  Kiti-gï tii-      gí     "He is chopping trees" (I hear him)
                       í     "He is chopping trees" (I see him)
                       hòi    "Apparently he is chopping trees" (I can't tell)
                       yigï   "They say he chopped trees" (Barnes 1990)
     chop.trees-he    AUX

There is no creole language known to this author with a paradigm of evidential markers. This cannot be explained under the syntax-internal creole genesis hypothesis.

### 3.4.1. There are analytic languages with evidential marker paradigms

Evidentiality is not contingent on rich inflection: evidential markers can be free forms, and they also occur in analytic languages:
    Hixkaryana:

(10)  Ton **hati**      Waraka.
      he-go HEARSAY Waraka
      "They say that Waraka has gone." (Derbyshire 1985: 128–29)

    Lahu:

(11)  Yɔ šɔ́-pɔ̄     gà   la tù   **cê**.
      he tomorrow come to FUT HEARSAY
      "They say that he'll arrive tomorrow." (Matisoff 1973b: 469)

### 3.4.2. The absence of evidential marker paradigms in a creole is not due to low frequency rendering them "marked" constructions in the source languages

In a language that makes use of such markers, they are required components of even basic utterances, such that they occur with the same frequency as the various markers of tense and aspect. Their elimination in creoles cannot be attributed to low rates of exposure to creole creators.

### 3.4.3. The absence of evidential markers in creoles is not due to functional category ellipsis

Evidential marking, as a semantic feature, is not a functional category. It could be argued that semantic features fall outside of the purview of the syntax-internal hypothesis. This and other differences between creoles and their source languages, however, only underscore that the syntax-internal approach can serve as only a partial account of creole genesis.

Importantly, evidential markers do fall within the purview of a hypothesis appealing to pidginization and the youth of creole grammars.

### 3.4.4. Languages with evidential marker paradigms have been spoken in creole genesis contexts

Chinook Jargon was created by Native Americans of the Pacific Northwest, speaking Penutian languages like Lower Chinook, Takelma, Tsimshian, and Kalapuya, as well as Nootka, Coast Salish, Haida, and Chemakuan (Thomason 1982, Grant 1996a). Evidentials are an areal feature in this region, found in all of the languages mentioned (albeit data on Chinook and Kalapuya is not copious enough for absolute certainty) (Sherzer 1976: 77–78).

Despite its name, Chinook Jargon was a relatively stable pidgin, with broad norms of usage (despite predictable variability across speakers and regions), and was even transformed into a natural language on at least one reservation in the late nineteenth century. Yet while this creolized Chinook Jargon developed auxiliaries, tense and aspect marking, cliticized subject pronouns, a definite article, and a relativizer, (Grant 1996a) it is not documented as having developed evidentials, despite these being a central part of the grammars of most of the adults in the speech community (as well as of the children to whom Native American languages were passed down) and rather salient features to a fieldworker in the languages in which they occur.

To be sure, evidentiality was encoded with inflections in the source languages, and the V-to-I component of the syntax-internal hypothesis would thus predict that these inflections would be lost. However, *this hypothesis does not predict that evidentiality would remain unexpressed in the creole*: on the contrary, it allows that often creoles have replaced what was expressed inflectionally in the lexifier with a free form in the same function. For example, the V-to-I hypothesis certainly explains why Haitian does not have the inflections that French has to mark gender, tense, and aspect. What this hypothesis cannot explain, however, is why Haitian has replaced French inflections for tense and aspect with free morphemes, but did not do so for the gender-marking inflections. Gender marking is not incompatible with analytic grammars; for example, the free noun classifiers in Southeast Asian languages are semantically analogous to inflectional gender markers and could easily evolve over time into inflections. Furthermore, it is obvious both that loss of gender cannot be attributed to low frequency of its manifestation in French (!) and that gender is not a functional category. (The same argument applies to the Melanesian Pidgin English's failure to create free markers distinguishing alienable and inalienable possession.)

Thus the question remains: Why did creolized Chinook Jargon not develop free evidential markers to express the distinctions encoded inflectionally in its source languages?

In fact, I know of only one pidgin or creole that has retained any evidential marking from a source language is one dialect of Chinese Pidgin Russian, which has not a paradigm of markers but a single one:

(12)  A-a!  Ljudi  pomiraj est.'
      EXCL person die      INFERENTIAL
      "Oh! The man must have died." (Nichols 1986: 247)

Significantly, given other strong parallels in this dialect with the Tungusic languages such as Nanai, Udehe, and Uroch native to the speakers cited, Nichols argues that this marker is calqued on the evidentials common in Tungusic. Thus we find only an evidential marker (and then, just one) in the speech of one speaker of one dialect of a makeshift pidgin, who is less speaking a language than constructing one piecemeal via superimposing Russian words upon a grammar reflecting a fragmentary grasp of Russian's but largely filtered through his native one. Even here, the transfer of only one of the Tungusic evidential markers is significant, as is the fact that we find no evidential paradigms in creoles, even though they, unlike pidgins, are natural languages used to express nuanced concepts.[9]

### 3.4.5. The absence of evidential markers in pidgins is predictable, and in grammars lacking them, they develop via gradual change

One might propose that this is merely accidental, but given how common evidential marking is worldwide, another explanation is more attractive. Evidentials are a paradigm example of grammaticalization leading to ornaments on natural language. This is just the kind of feature one would expect to be rare to absent in pidgins—recall that Chinook Jargon eschewed evidentials even when most of its speakers controlled the strategy natively—as well to only evolve over time in a natural language that was born as a pidgin.

### 3.5. Feature five: Grammaticalized referential marking

In many Western Austronesian languages such as Tagalog, when one argument of the clause is new information, it must be marked simultaneously with a verbal affix and a trigger particle (in the terminology of Schachter 1990: 939–40), the latter replacing the free case-marking particle used when the argument is given information. Here is this process illustrated in Tagalog (Schachter 1990: 941) (AT = agent trigger, PT = patient trigger, DT = dative trigger, TG = trigger marker, AC = actor, DR = directional):

(13)  a. **Mag**-aalis          **ang** tindero      ng bigas sa  sako para sa babae.
          AT.PROG-take out TG  storekeeper PT rice    DR sack BEN    woman
          "The storekeeper will take some rice out of a/the sack for a/the woman."

      b. Aalisi-**n**           ng tindero      **ang** bigas sa  sako para sa babae.
          PROG.take out-PT AC storekeeper TG  rice    DR sack BEN    woman
          "A/the storekeeper will take the rice out of a/the sack for a/the woman."

      c. Aalis-**an**           ng tindero      ng bigas **ang** sako para sa babae.
          PROG.take out-DT AC storekeeper PT rice    TG sack BEN    woman
          "A/the storekeeper will take some rice out of the sack for a/the woman."

## 3.5.1.  There are analytic languages with analogues to trigger marking

While Tagalog's trigger marking is accomplished through both a free particle and a corresponding inflection, it would be difficult to conceive of a reason that, cross-linguistically speaking, grammaticalized trigger particles would be *necessarily* contingent on the presence of corresponding inflections of redundant function. Significantly, there are analytic languages in which focus markers have grammaticalized from contrastive function to obligatory appearance with certain arguments in simple declarative sentences. Important here is that the marking of new information is a central and cross-linguistically common manifestation of focus marking.

In the Austronesian language Nalik of Papua New Guinea, a focus particle (a) parallels the Philippines trigger markers in two ways. First, when used with an object, instead of encoding contrastive focus, like the trigger markers it renders an object referential (b) (just as Tagalog *ang* does); second, its appearance in this function is obligatory in certain patient constructions (c) (it also shares the phonetic form of the Tagalog trigger, *ang* [with an allomorph *yang*]):
Nalik:

(14)  a. **Yang** nanga 1-a        raan Mista  Hancock ka wut.
          FOC just    LOC-ART time Mister Hancock he come
          "It was just at the time when Mr. Hancock came." (Volker 1998: 179)

      b. Di   yot  **ang**/ø a      marang.
          they pick FOC/ø ART dry.coconuts.
          "They're picking the/ø dry coconuts." (ibid. 176)

      c. Ga wut   kun  a      vaanong *(**ang**) a      vaal.
          I    come LOC ART finish    FOC   ART house
          "I'm coming in order to finish the house." (ibid.)

The focus marker *nò* in the Niger-Congo language of Cameroon Aghem can mark the verb or any of its complements for contrastive focus (a, b), but in the absence of such complements or any other focus strategy, it is required to accompany the verb (c), in which case no focus is implied:

Aghem:

(15)  a. Fú kɨ   mɔ̀   ñíŋ **nô**   á kí-'bé.
          rat SM PAST run FOC in compound
          "The rat *ran* in the compound."

      b. Fú kɨ   mɔ̀   ñíŋ á kí-'bé   **nò**.
          rat SM PAST run in compound FOC
          "The rat ran in the *compound*." (Watters 1979: 167)

      c. Énáʔ mɔ̀   ñíŋ **nô**.
          Inah PAST run FOC
          "Inah ran." (*Inah *ran*.) (ibid. 144)

This demonstrates a movement of the particle from pragmatic to grammatical function, a development pathway found in other languages as well, such as the evolution of a semantic focus-marking (augment) prefix in Luganda into a syntactically conditioned marker of no semantic content which essentially appears only in the case of the *absence* of overt indicators of contrastive focus (Hyman and Katamba 1993). The development of the Philippines trigger system was a related process, in a movement from topic marking to a grammatical one overlapping considerably with subject marking (Shibatani 1991).

These examples show that there are analytic languages in which focus particles can manifest behaviors and functions similar to that of the referential trigger markers in languages like Tagalog. However, in creoles no such markers have evolved from encoding contrastive focus to becoming obligatory markers of new information, or have moved from pragmatic to grammatical function to indicate, for example, referentiality instead of contrastive focus.[10]

### 3.5.2. The absence of grammaticalized trigger marking in a creole is not due to low frequency rendering it a "marked" construction in the source languages

As is clear from the preceding examples, referential marking in languages of the Philippines is nothing less than central to basic expression in the languages and is thus implausibly analyzed as a "marked" manifestation of a hypothetical "basic" equivalent. On the contrary, the marking system itself is basic in these grammars.

### 3.5.3. The absence of grammaticalized trigger marking in a creole is not due to functional category ellipsis

Referentiality is not a functional category, but a pragmatic feature.

### 3.5.6. Languages with grammaticalized trigger marking have been spoken in creole genesis contexts

It could be argued that it is inappropriate to expect referentiality tracking of the Philippines variety to appear in creoles given that it is not a cross-linguistically common feature. Yet I have included it in this essay for a particular reason: it happens that several creoles have been created by people who spoke languages that had this strategy. Several varieties of Spanish creole have been created by speakers of Tagalog and related languages, but they show no sign of this trigger marking. This lack of marking is especially crucial for our purposes, given that this marking was not part of the creole creators' target language but, instead, was central to their native languages—and yet did not survive creolization. While the nature of creole genesis makes it unlikely that the Philippines Spanish Creoles would have borrowed the trigger *affixes*, the trigger *particle* is a free and salient form.

It is even possible to hypothesize just how such a feature could have been "translated" amid creolization. In Fongbe, the verb "to say" has evolved in a serial construction from introducing complements after *verba dicendi* to (a) introducing complements after verbs of perception and cognition to (b) serving as a simple purposive complementizer devoid of any vestige of perceptual reportage:

Fongbe:

(16)  a. Kɔkú ɖì     ɖɔ     Bàyí wá
         Koku believe COMP Bayi come
         "Koku believed that Bayi came." (Lefebvre and Brousseau 2002: 115)

      b. É  gbɛ  ɖɔ     émì kún ná        bló ó.
         He refuse COMP LOG NEG DEF.FUT do INS
         "He refused to do it (emphatically)." (Éléments de recherche 1983: X, 3, cited in ibid. 544) (LOG = logophoric pronoun; INS = insistence)

Fongbe exerted a dominant influence on the Surinam creoles on all levels of grammar, including a highly grammaticalized reflex of the verb "to say." However, in Saramaccan, the most grammaticalized use of *táa*, the grammaticalized reflex of *táki*, is with verbs of perception and cognition (Veenstra 1996: 154–57); the purposive complementizer is *fu* (< for).[11]

This exemplifies a strong tendency for creoles to incorporate grammaticalized usages of a given form to a less abstract degree than its equivalent in the source language. The Philippines languages are cross-linguistically unusual in having grammaticalized an erstwhile topic-marking strategy to the extent of it being virtually required that a sentence mark some constituent as a trigger, this being symptomatic of the gradual development of the strategy into one overlapping considerably with subject marking (Shibatani 1991: 105–16). Along these lines, it is quite plausible—or, more pointedly, the syntax-internal hypothesis does not systematically rule out—that the creators of Philippines Spanish Creole would have incorporated a trigger-marking strategy in some way, but just to a less deeply grammaticalized extent. One might suppose, for example, that the creole creators would have recruited a form, either from Spanish or Central

Philippines languages, to serve as a grammaticalized topic marker along the lines of Japanese *wa*, or as a grammaticalized focus marker used regularly with certain constituents to encode, for example, referentiality, as in Nalik.

Yet this is *not* what happened. The most important substrate language for the Zamboangueño variety of Philippines Spanish Creole was Hiligaynon, with its very close relatives Tagalog and Cebuano also important (Frake 1971: 228–30). Hiligaynon has a trigger-marking system quite similar to Tagalog's:

Hiligaynon:

(17)  a. Bayuhon       ko      sang hal-o ang humay.
         FUT.pound-PT by.me GEN pestle TG rice
         "The rice is what I will pound with the pestle."

      b. Ibayo       ko      ang hal-o sang humay.
         IT-pound by.me TG pestle GEN rice
         "The pestle is what I'll use to pound rice." (Wolfenden 1975: 98) (IT = instrumental particle; glossing terminology altered to correspond with Tagalog example above)

Cebuano has the same trigger mechanism as well (Shibatani 1991). Yet there is no such thing in Zamboangueño Philippines Spanish Creole—all the more striking given that the creole does have a reflex of one of the Central Philippines verbal affixes (albeit bleached into simply marking verbs borrowed from other languages) and various direct borrowings of grammatical items like pronouns from these languages (Central Philippines borrowings in italics):

(18)  *Hindi? kitá* ay-*man*-enkwentro el   *mana* muher.
       NEG   we FUT-V-meet       the PL   woman
       "We will not meet the women." (M. Ong, John Wolff, pers. comm.) (V = verbalizer)

Thus Philippines Spanish Creole was created by speakers of closely related languages, who thus transferred a great deal of their native-language structural machinery, and even phonetic strings, into the creole they created. Yet there is no hint of trigger marking. Significantly, this is the case in all of the dialects of this creole, which diverge considerably. In other words, trigger marking failed to materialize not just once, but in several cases.

### 3.5.4. The absence of grammaticalized trigger marking in pidgins is predictable

This discrepancy, and the fact that we find no pragmatic (i.e., topic) markers having developed into grammatical ones (i.e., referentiality markers) in any creole language, does not find an explanation under the syntax-internal hypothesis. The reason that no creole has a categorical trigger marker, or even a less grammaticalized but functionally similar marker of new information or referentiality, begins with the fact that creoles begin as pidgins, in which features inessential to basic communication are generally not given phonetic form.

### 3.5.5. In a grammar lacking it, grammaticalized trigger marking evolves via gradual change

Overt topic particles evolve from lexical items over time, with the development of a categorical triggering system such as those found in the Philippines languages requiring especially long periods of gradual reanalysis of topic-marking strategies into subject-marking ones. Creoles lack such items because they are young languages.

## 3.6. Feature six: Consonant mutation

In many languages, affixes or particles induce phonological changes on the initial or final consonant of their base, and, over time, the changes cease to be predictable on the basis of the phonology and thus become morphologized. For example, in Finnish this diachronic process has led to a synchronic one in which some suffixes trigger degemination of consonants whereas others do not: *katto* "roof," *kato-lle* "onto the roof," but *katto-mme* "my roof." In other languages, diachronic development has led such consonant mutations to be triggered by specific lexical items and even grammatical functions. A classic example is Celtic languages like Welsh (Ball and Müller 1992: 195–96):

(19)   a. lexically triggered:

      fy nghath "my cat"    eu cath "their cat"
      ei gath "his cat"     ei chath "her cat"

    b. grammatically triggered (by objecthood):

      i. gwelodd Alun / ef / ø gi.

         saw     Alun he  he dog

         "Alun / he saw a dog"

      ii. gwelodd ci

         saw     dog

         "The dog saw"

There are similar phenomena in, for example, the Oceanic language Erromangan (Crowley 1998), the Siberian language isolate Nivkh, the Nilotic language Luo, and many West Atlantic and Mande languages of the Niger-Congo group.

    While morphophonemic processes are commonly found in creoles, they are virtually never opaque from the point of view of readily predictable processes of incremental phonetic change, and it is unknown in creoles for these processes to effect the stem to the point of being a sole marker of morphologization.

### 3.6.1. Consonant mutation is not contingent on inflectional affixation

This cannot be attributed to creoles' low affixation, because the Celtic data show that consonant mutation can develop functional loads within the context of cliticization or even simple juxtaposition (and in this light, various studies have revealed cliticization in creoles—e.g., Veenstra 1996: 34–40, Kouwenberg 1993—in which there is no consonant mutation to be found).

It is also obvious that consonant mutation is neither stochastically marked nor a functional category.

### 3.6.2. Languages with some consonant mutation have been spoken in creole genesis contexts

Speakers of the Bak cluster of West Atlantic languages were well represented among the creators of Guinea-Bissau Portuguese Creole. Their influence was strong enough that various grammatical items' phonetic form and syntactic behaviors can be responsibly traced to their influence (Kihm 1989). West Atlantic languages are known for often having rich consonant mutation that has taken on functional loads. The Bak cluster, including Manjaku, Papel, and Mankanya, has shed a great deal of this but shows clear signs that its consonant mutation was once as vigorous as in other West Atlantic languages (Sapir 1971: 82).

The Portuguese creole of Guinea-Bissau, however, has no consonant mutation, nor does Cape Verdean Portuguese Creole, which was created mainly by slaves from the same populations that developed the Guinea-Bissau variety on the mainland. (This is even more significant in light of the possibility that the Bak cluster may have still retained its full consonantal mutation system, or something closer to it than today, in the sixteenth century when these creoles arose.)

### 3.6.3. The absence of consonant mutation in pidgins is predictable

Consonant mutation is agreed to result from gradual phonetic evolution forcing reallotments of functional load over time (cf. Jackson 1953, Thomas 1990, Spencer 1998). It has been observed that pidgins are extremely low in morphophonemic processes, partly because they tend to be spoken at a lower tempo than natural languages (Sankoff and Laberge 1980: 198–89, Labov 1990, Mühlhäusler 1997; cf. also Jourdan and Keesing 1997: 414). As such, pidgin versions of languages with consonant mutation typically eschew it, as Heine (1973: 172) notes, exemplifying this via Adamawa Pidgin Fula:

(20)   Fula      Pidgin Fula
       'o wari   o wari       "he came"
       ɓe ŋgari  be wari      "they came"

Indeed, the development of morphophonology is an integral and diagnostic aspect of the transformation of a pidgin into a natural language, that is, not of a pidgin itself (Sankoff and Laberge 1980: 199, Samarin 1997).

### 3.6.4. In a grammar lacking it, consonantal mutation develops via gradual change

Obviously, however, the process creating lexically or grammatically triggered consonant mutations is a lengthy one, requiring first the very development of morphophonology (a step most creoles are well into), followed by the complete erosion of various segments such that contrastive load falls onto other levels of grammar. Given the typical rate of sound change in a language (Spanish, German, or Mandarin Chinese speakers of today could make themselves understood to ancestors from 1600 with relatively minor adjustment), it is hardly unsurprising that a language born from a pidgin just a few centuries ago would never display consonant mutations.

The relative scarcity of consonant mutation cross-linguistically does not render it irrelevant to demonstrating that pidginization and youth are crucial factors in characterizing creole languages. According to the thesis that there is no synchronic distinction between creoles and older languages, we certainly would not expect that *many* creoles would have consonant mutation; however, we might well expect that, for example, one or two would. They do not, and pidginization and recent emergence as natural languages account for this.

## 4. Implications

What I have shown demonstrates that the claim that a syntax-internal model of creole genesis is, by itself, inadequate to explain creole genesis, even with the addition of stipulations based on frequency of occurrence:

1. The evidential and ergativity cases show that the syntax-internal hypothesis cannot explain which inflectionally encoded functions will be replaced with analytic ones rather than simply eliminated.
2. The inalienable possession, referentiality, and inherent reflexive cases reveal that creole grammars often entirely eliminate functions encoded analytically in the source languages, even when of high frequency of occurrence.
3. The consonant mutation case, like the others, shows that youth has synchronic correlates which distinguish creoles from older grammars.

Loss of inflection is clearly of central importance in creole genesis. Frequency-based markedness considerations are equally important, explaining why, for example, Tayo Creole French has inherited a great many syntactic constructions from its creators' closely related Melanesian languages Cèmuhî and Drubéa but consistently in less-elaborated form (Corne 1995a). It is also true that in comparison to its source languages, a creole leaves more functional categories unexpressed phonetically, as Lumsden (1999) elegantly demonstrates in Haitian Creole. However, taken alone, these approaches severely undergenerate the data set in question.

Thus the syntax-internal hypothesis is ingenious and useful, but it is only one part of the picture. Taken alone, it predicts in the strict sense that if Africans had been brought to plantations run by speakers of Khmer, a highly analytic language with neither inflectional affixes nor tone, they would have acquired a second-language variety recognizable as, essentially, full Khmer, distinguishable from native Khmer only via accent, elimination of certain subtler aspects of the grammar of relatively low occurrence (such as some suppletions and the shadings of pragmatic particles), and command of idioms. In its relation to its target, this is reminiscent of the English spoken by first-generation Jewish immigrants in large American cities at the turn of the twentieth century.

Few would see this Khmer scenario as plausible, and the reason is because inflectional morphology, marginal exceptions to and elaborations on general rules, and phonetic expression of basic functional categories are but a subset of the structural features of a grammar that is typically lost during pidginization and is not reconstituted in creolization. Perhaps most important, much of this body of lost elements is unlikely to trace to any of the mechanisms appealed to under the syntax-internal hypothesis to date. The burden of proof is on those in disagreement to present a principled explanation as to how any such explanation squares with the fact that extant pidgins and creoles worldwide have all lost so very many more aspects of their lexifier's and substrate languages' grammars than the syntax-internal approach predicts.

My argument relates to that of Bickerton (1987: 233), who asked:

> Which creole has a. clitic pronouns, b. clitic climbing, c. clitic doubling, d. scrambling rules, e. heavy NP shift, f. noun classifiers, g. impersonal passives, h. case inflections, i. nontopic markers, j. participial phrases, k. VP-fronting, l. case-matching, m. long WH-movement, n. subject-aux inversion, o. "verb-second" rules, p. number-person agreement on verbs, q. gender agreement on NP constituents, r. structural assymetries between matrix and embedded S, s. OV word order, t. agents in nonsubject position [?].

Many of these features, based on recent work such as Roberts (1999), have been argued to trace to weak parameter settings (clitic climbing, scrambling rules, number-person agreement on verbs)—although see chapter 12 for my skepticism regarding this framework. Others have been found in creoles since Bickerton wrote.[12] However, many of the remaining features (such as noun classifiers, subject-aux inversion, verb-second rules, structural assymetries between matrix and embedded clauses) are quite plausibly absent in creoles simply because of their origin as pidgins, followed by a life span too brief for features of these kinds to emerge. To Bickerton's list I would add ergativity, Philippines languages' grammaticalized "trigger" marking, inherent reflexive marking, evidentials, inalienable possessive marking, and consonant mutation triggered beyond the phonological level, as well as many other phenomena lending themselves to the same analysis, such as switch-reference marking, inverse marking, obviative marking, overt markers of both perfectivity and imperfectivity in the same grammar, "dummy" verbs, and other features either extremely marginal or nonexistent in any known creole grammar while quite often encountered in older languages—including analytic ones—worldwide.[13]

At this point, I do not intend to propose the absence of these features as an additional component of the Creole Prototype. It would be beyond the scope of this chapter to specify which of all features encountered in natural grammars are innate from those that are excrescences resulting from nonteleological accretion over time. My purpose here has been to show that where we at present can show a grammatical feature to be one of the latter sort, and thus unlikely to be retained in a pidgin, then there is a very strong tendency for creoles to eschew that feature—even one well represented in the source languages or expressed analytically.

As such, I propose not that the syntax-internal factors are anything less than central to creole genesis but that their operation is ordered after the initial filtering of source language input, via a more general tendency for pidginization to eliminate ornamental features of a grammar regardless of the mechanism by which they are encoded. Because creolization operates in degrees, a comparative perspective on creoles empirically demonstrates this ordering of application. In retaining tense and aspect inflections but having eliminated gender and ergative ones, Korlai Creole Portuguese is a useful instantiation of the general tendency for certain types of construction to be eliminated before others—a point refutable only by the identification of a creole that retains gender and ergativity inflections (or some other conglomeration of ornamental features) but eliminates those encoding tense and aspect. Similarly, Sango, in having retained enough of Ngbandi's grammar to be potentially classifiable as merely a conventionalized second-language variety thereof (Morrill 1997) (*véhicularisé*, in French terms) and yet eschewing ornamental features such as inalienable possessive marking (as well as many others such as lexical and morpho-syntactic tone; see Pasch 1997, Samarin 2000), demonstrates that, regardless of inflection or frequency of occurrence, a fundamental process of reduction of overt grammatical apparatus is a crucial component in the genesis of a creole language.

As is common between contrasting analyses of data, the distance between the syntax-internal hypothesis as it has been stated and my own is eminently bridgeable. DeGraff's explicit statement (1999b: 525), for example, is that "adults shed various *nonessential/marked* properties from the contact languages, such as inflectional morphology (relevant here are Bickerton's pidgin ellipsis, Lumsden's functional category ellipsis, and aspects of Mufwene's scenario)." (By "contact languages" I presume that DeGraff means "languages in contact.") I have italicized "nonessential/marked" because this is a locus that could potentially contain the ornamental features I have discussed. With the wording here and in the surrounding discussion, DeGraff implies that the "nonessential" is largely limited to inflection, stochastically marked features, and the phonetic elision of functional categories that lend themselves to encoding via juxtaposition or zero-marking (recall, for instance, his stipulation cited earlier that creoles exhibit only "the broad tendencies towards various degrees of inflectional erosion cum semantic transparency . . . with regard to *general* language contact phenomena" [DeGraff 2000; italics in original]). My argument, then, serves to elucidate that the "nonessential" includes a larger component of an older language on all levels than DeGraff implies.

## 5. The Creole Prototype and sociopolitics

While my hypothesis, regardless of its ultimate viability, is constructed solely upon empirical observation, it is difficult not to observe that the subjective plays a significant role in the reception of a thesis arguing that creoles are a structurally delineable class of language. Skepticism is a welcome and necessary part of scholarly exchange, but some of the response to McWhorter (1998a) has stemmed less from empirically based cross-creole data in contradiction than upon a certain sense of the very investigation as subjectively distateful.[14]

The "rub" here is, at heart, a supposition that those delineating a Creole Proto-type are designating creoles as "primitive" languages or "baby talk," most explicitly asserted by DeGraff (1999 and later works). Certainly there are concrete historical precedents inspiring this discomfort. Even in the recent past, it was not uncommon to encounter descriptions like this one of Louisiana French Creole—and in a guide to the language (!):

> It would be impossible to describe here, for it would take an entire volume, all the myriad ways in which the tongues of African slaves mutilated and amputated the French language. . . . It may be taken as axiomatic that they all, without exception, made for simplification, for the Negro was as lazy of brain as he was of brawn. . . . His bulbous lips and thick tongue made it impossible for him to pronounce certain French vowel sounds. In his mouth *juge* became *jige*, *tortue*—*torti*, *nuit*—*nouitte*, and the rolled French *r* was quite beyond his powers, so he just "paid it no never-mind," said *neg'* instead of *nègre* and *vend'* for *vendre*. . . . Whenever he could make himself understood without it, the Negro omitted the verb entirely and, like a child who whimpers "me sick," he said *"mo malade."* (Tinker 1936: 8–9)

It must be said in this light that this presentation entails no claim that creoles are functionally primordial compared to other languages. The sense that such an impli-cation lurks behind arguments such as mine traces to the focus on what creoles lack rather than what they have. However, what creoles have less of than older grammars do is not the set of features that comprise the natural language competence in all of its complexity, nuance, and layer but the ornaments on this endowment that emerge randomly as a grammar ages. It is painfully clear that evidentiality and inalienable possession are inherent to the cognitive representations underlying creole speakers' mental grammars, just as they are to those of all human beings. It is also clear, how-ever, that only a subset of even the world's older languages mark either of these dis-tinctions overtly. When only older languages are considered, this obvious fact is not seen to lead to the conclusion that, for example, English is "primitive" in lacking a paradigm of grammaticalized evidential markers. Indeed, such a claim would be vacuous, since "primitiveness" is a measure of functional adequacy, a metric to which an ornamental feature is logically irrelevant. Any argument otherwise would be analo-gous to designating a car with gaudy tail fins and a showy hood ornament to be a more sophisticated machine than one identical to it except for lacking such frills.

The crucial point follows ineluctably from this: even a language piled high with such "ornament" cannot be deemed, on any logical basis, more "advanced" than one with relatively little of it—because both languages fulfill all of the functional needs of human language.

In the real world, however, language is a social as well as biological phenom-enon, and it is not accidental that this thesis has attracted its most piqued responses from linguists of African heritage, most of them creolophone. This is understand-able—because a definition of the creole will, because of the languages' youth, by definition hinge on absences rather than presences, the very endeavor can seem to some to smack of being yet another in the dismayingly long tradition of debasement of people of African heritage.

Yet in addition to the fact that what creoles tend to "lack" in comparison to older grammars is mere randomly accumulated frills superimposed on a universal human endowment of complex and nuanced language, the fact that most creoles are spoken by dark-skinned people is a mere epiphenomenon of certain mundane contingencies: namely, it happened to be the lightest-skinned people in the world who—largely because of the effect that accidents of geography had on the development of particular human societies (Diamond 1997)—sailed across oceans and subjugated other peoples, such that European languages were the ones pidginized and reconstituted by people of color. We can be quite sure that if West Africans had sailed to Europe and subjugated whites, then whites would be the ones who speak creoles, because creolization is a human, not a black, phenomenon. The hopelessness of any thesis otherwise is resoundingly demonstrated by the fact creoles have also been developed by Indians, Pacific Islanders, Aborigines, Chinese, and Native Americans, and today many creoles are spoken by whites as well as blacks, such as on St. Barthélemy, where an overseas French dialect and a creole share space based not on a racial but on geographical distinction.

Finally, it must be noted that the Creole Prototype model hardly claims that creoles are any more diachronically static than older languages are. On the contrary, because it is inherent to natural language to change, this model predicts that creoles ought be in the process of drifting away from the Prototype to the extent that they honed to it, as well as in the process of developing the "ornamental" features discussed in this chapter. This is indeed the case. Saramaccan's subject pronouns are clitics rather than free forms, and there is no reason that after several more centuries or even sooner they might not become prefixes. The verb "to go" in São Tomense Portuguese Creole has one form used with specified goals (*E ba ke* "he went home") and another (morphemically indivisible) used with unspecified goal (*E be d'ai* "He went from here") (Hagemeijer 1999); this is reminiscent of the distinction between "determinate" and "indeterminate" verbs of motion in Russian and may represent a development in that direction. São Tomense's sister creole Angolar has a similar construction (Maurer 1995: 97–98), and its verb "to go" is marked with a third-person object pronoun *rê* to mean "to leave": *Ê bê rê* "He left" (ibid. 145). This is the only verb marked for inherent reflexivity obligatorily, however; such marking occurs optionally with some other verbs but is used to connote emphasis on the action (ibid. 145–46). Nevertheless, as the emphasis connoted by such usages bleaches, regular inherent reflexive marking could quite likely emerge in this creole. Papia Kristang, a Portuguese creole of Malaysia, has developed one evidential marker of reportage *diski* (< "says that"), which reveals its status as an internal innovation in having no analogue in Malay itself (Alan Baxter, pers. comm.).

Nor can it be said that creoles represent the language competence in anything approaching an ontogenetically primary state. Recall, for instance, that it can be argued that even a feature as cross-linguistically common and functionally central as tense and aspect marking is not strictly necessary to human communication, given its absence in some languages. As is well known, all creoles robustly reflect tense and aspect, one of several indications that they have gone a long way in filling semantic spaces not strictly indispensable to a natural language (this being also the case in their expressing relativization with strategies distinct from subordinating ones, having separate monomorphemic pronouns in the plural, etc.).

In a sense, however, to even elaborate on the fact that creoles will eventually be synchronically indistinguishable from older languages is a rather vacuous detour. The discussion has an air about it of implying that this transformation will constitute "progress," as if my proposition were roughly "creoles are natural languages but only older languages are 'real' natural languages." On the contrary, because so many natural languages lack inflections, inherent reflexivity, and so on, not a single one of these phenomena can be classified as "developments" in the strict sense; rather, they are simply faceless changes that all grammars undergo. Saramaccan, like all creoles, achieved par with older languages in terms of "development" as soon as it was transformed into a natural language by its first native speakers. Everything since then has been, and everything henceforth will be, random drift, accumulation, and reshufflings of the deck—as in all natural languages' grammars. The sole difference is that Saramaccan, like so many other creoles, is unique in having undergone so many centuries' less of this *bouleversement*, the result of which is, quite unsurprisingly, identifiable today.

## 6. Conclusion

If creoles can indeed be shown to constitute natural language with a uniquely low degree of the chance accretions that result from long-term elaboration and drift, then this could reanimate the investigation of the possibility that creole languages are unusually and thus usefully clear manifestations of the human language competence. Certainly research since Bickerton's (1981) introduction of this idea has revised some of its specifics. It has been demonstrated beyond any reasonable doubt by various researchers that substrate transfer played a significant role in the configurations of most creole grammars (e.g., Kihm 1989, McWhorter 1997a, Migge 1998, Lumsden 1999, Singler 2000). Research since Bickerton wrote has shown that creole grammars do not display the features of his bioprogram as consistently as it seemed in the late 1970s (e.g. Singler 1990, Winford 2000). It has also been shown that the children who created Hawaiian Creole English did this not as an emergency measure in the face of inadequate linguistic input but while having acquired their parents' languages natively (Roberts 2000).

Yet none of these revisions belies Bickerton's focal point that creoles are in some fashion more directly reflective of the heart of language than older ones. While substrate transfer was central to creoles' emergence, the idea that creoles represent unmarked syntactic parameters remains promising: this unmarkedness would have simply been determined not only by partial acquisition of the lexifier but also by a similarly partial transfer of natively controlled grammars. Regarding the fact that creoles reflect the bioprogram in degrees, Bickerton himself incorporated the fundamental component of gradience into his model early on (1984). Though Hawaiian Creole English was not created as a linguistic "emergency," the fact remains that its structure resembles that of other creoles in some ways unattributable to any of its substrate languages.

In the meantime, the burgeoning of the study of grammaticalization over the past two decades provides a constrained framework for addressing what Bickerton (1984: 188) termed older languages' "bric-a-brac." What Bickerton referred to was the painfully obvious difference in degree of ornamentation, as I have defined it in this essay, visible via comparison of even a substantial grammar of any creole language and that of an older highly analytic language like Vietnamese, Khmer, or Tongan.

The claim that, instead, creole languages from the synchronic perspective are simply a subset of grammars with a particular complex of syntactic parameter settings, and are the product of a diachronic process qualitatively undifferentiable in any empirically valid fashion from that which produced Romanian (with its Slavic influence) or Amharic (with its Cushitic influence), is one which implies that the very existence of creole studies from a linguistic perspective is a needless essentialization that ought be discontinued. As Lightfoot (1999: 148), a historical linguist commenting from outside of creole studies, notes:

> If creolization for the most part mirrors adult second language learning and is not abrupt and instantiated by children, then there is little reason for theoreticians to be interested in the phenomenon. Our data about the early stages of creole languages are generally not very rich, and if one is interested in adult second language learning, one is probably better off refining theories in the light of better data sources.[15]

I suggest that the eclipse of creole studies as a subfield in linguistics would only be possible if a crucial body of pertinent data in both creoles and older languages is neglected. The validity of the characterization of creoles as a delineable synchronic class will be judged by subsequent research. However, it has been constructed on as broad as possible a sample of creoles and a cross-linguistically typological perspective. It will be most fruitfully evaluated on the same basis.

# Saramaccan and Haitian
# as Young Grammars

## The Pitfalls of Syntactocentrism
## in Creole Genesis Research

## 1. Introduction

In the previous three chapters I have argued that creoles are a synchronically identifiable class of grammar (chapter 1), are delineable as less complex than older languages because of their youth (chapter 2), and tend very strongly to reproduce their source languages' structures in less complex renditions (chapter 3).

Predictably, this framework has elicited rebuttals. Lefebvre (2001) considers her Relexificationist model to account for the contrast between creoles and their lexifiers better than my hypothesis does. DeGraff (1999b, 2001) argues that creoles differ from their lexifiers mostly in predictable structural concomitants of loss of inflection and that to propose any contrast in complexity between older languages and creoles is epistemologically flawed and even sociologically suspect. Arends (2001) supposes that creoles only appear "simpler" than older languages because of a lack of detailed grammatical work on them to date.[1]

A guiding theme or implication of these counterproposals is that my demonstrations might neglect counterevidence that is only apparent from a more comprehensive comparison of a single creole with its substrate. This suspicion is both valid and unfounded. Here I show that a detailed comparison of Saramaccan and Fongbe, based on newly available data from both, clearly reveals the former as a younger grammar and that the comparison of Haitian and Fongbe yields a similar result.

## 2. Assumptions

### 2.1. Saramaccan is not a "simple" language

All linguists are aware that all natural language grammars are complex. As such, I must state at the outset that my argument is not that Saramaccan is a "simple" language. Neither is my argument that Saramaccan represents the simplest possible grammar conceivable. As I have discussed at some length in chapter 2, this language contains any number of features which, viewed cross-linguistically, are "frills," such as syntax-sensitive tone sandhi, and even features that seem essential to European language speakers such as definite and indefinite articles (present in only about one-fifth of the world's languages [Plank and Moravcsik 1996: 204], with any kind of overt marking of definiteness and indefiniteness present in only about half [Moravcsik 1969: 87, 93–98]).

I do claim, however, that while all grammars are complex, it is an unexamined truism that all grammars are *equally* complex. An examination of Saramaccan reveals that grammars do differ—and sharply—in complexity, and that social history is a key factor in this difference.

### 2.2. Signs of age in a grammar

#### *2.2.1. The nature of complexity*

I refer the reader to my outline of a metric of complexity in chapter 2 (section 2.4.3), which this chapter uses as a frame of reference. Throughout this chapter, where I refer to *complexity, overspecification,* and *elaboration,* I refer to these concepts as specified in this metric.

#### *2.2.2. Noncompositional derivation*

As noted in chapter 1, over time semantic drift leads some combinations of a derivational particle or affix with a root to become idiosyncratically noncompositional. For example, the Russian directional prefix *na-* signifies, compositionally, direction toward, as in *dvigat'sja* "to move" versus *nadvigat'sja,* "to move toward." However, there are many combinations of *na-* and a verb in which this semantic contribution is abstract to the point of lexicalization: *idti* "to go" versus *najti,* which compositionally would be "to go at" but in fact means "to find," or *kazat'* "to show" versus *nakazat'* "to punish." This trait is found in all older languages known to me,[2] and I analyze it as an unremarkable result of grammatical aging which we would, therefore, not expect to find in creoles. In this chapter we will see noncompositionality beyond the derivational serving just as usefully as an age metric for a grammar.

Importantly, this feature does not qualify as "complex" or "overspecified" by my metric. Words like *understand* are processed as unitary lexicalizations by the speaker, and thus they do not entail more morphosyntactic rules for production than compositional items (and in fact presumably require less). Nor can they be seen as filling in a finer grade of semantic space than an etymologically monomorphemic word for *understand*.

The importance of noncompositionality to this thesis lies solely in the fact that its sheer existence indexes that a grammar has existed for a very long time, during which the morphemes' semantic contributions could drift gradually beyond their core denotation.

## 3. Brief excursus: Saramaccan source languages

I will assume that the primary substrate language for Saramaccan was Fongbe, one of several members of the Gbe complex of Togo, Benin, and Nigeria. This is justified first by the robust representation of Fongbe speakers among slaves brought to Surinam in the late seventeenth century, as demonstrated by Arends (1995a) and Smith (1987a, 2001). The second justification is that Saramaccan grammar parallels that of Gbe in general too idiosyncratically to be accidental (McWhorter 1996a); moreover, since like Ndjuka, Saramaccan is a sister offshoot of early Sranan (Smith 1987a, McWhorter 1996a), Migge's (1998) demonstration of the Gbe roots of Ndjuka are also relevant. In addition, Saramaccan contains grammatical items borrowed complete with their phonetic form from Fongbe specifically (e.g., *andí* "what," *ambέ* "who," the focus marker *wε*), as well as a large number of core lexical items such as *awá* "shoulder" (Smith 1987b). As such, I consider earlier arguments that Saramaccan is a compromise between speakers of several different languages of the Upper Guinea Coast, such as Byrne's (1987) and even my own (McWhorter 1997a), superseded.

The wealth of lexical items in Saramaccan from Kikongo is obvious (Daeleman 1972), but these are largely confined to "cultural" vocabulary, including ideophones. I view these as ordinary results of Kikongo speakers encountering a grammar already formed, with their contribution largely restricted to lexical items along the same lines as French's contribution to English. Saramaccan does not parallel Kikongo or general Bantu grammar in any respect. Because this thesis addresses structural rather than lexical issues, I consider Kikongo irrelevant to it.

Meanwhile, I consider English to be the primary lexifier of Saramaccan, with Portuguese having made a lexical contribution analogous to that of Kikongo. The occasional derivation of progressive marker *tá* from Portuguese *está* is tempting but mistaken: early documents (e.g., Schumann's dictionary of 1778 in Schuchardt 1914) reveal the source as an earlier *tan* from *stand*. Overall, the vast majority of Saramaccan's grammatical items are from English, and there are no specific parallels between Saramaccan grammar and Portuguese's (or Portuguese creoles'). This is predictable if early Sranan was partially relexified but not grammatically restructured by Portuguese, and thus I assume this scenario along with Goodman (1987) and Smith (1987a).

## 4. Saramaccan and Fongbe: Creole simpler than substrate

This chapter takes advantage of the publication of a full-length grammar of Fongbe (Lefebvre and Brousseau 2002), which at last allows detailed comparison of Saramaccan with precisely the language it was based on, rather than related languages for which grammars happen to have long existed such as Ewe, Twi, or Yoruba, as has been common in the past (including in my own work).

In the vast majority of cases, where Saramaccan has a structural inheritance from Fongbe, the Saramaccan rendition is simpler—according to the metric outlined in chapter 2—than the Fongbe one. Here I present three examples, meant to serve as demonstrations of a larger trend I have identified (cf. chapter 3), in which creole languages incorporate substrate features in simplified form. This observation corresponds to similar ones made by various writers regarding other creoles (e.g., Keesing 1988, Corne 2000).

(All Saramaccan sentences were elicited by myself and students in the linguistics department at the University of California, Berkeley.)

## 4.1. Reduplication

In Saramaccan, unusually among creoles, reduplication of verbs serves morphosyntactic functions. Reduplication of verbs denotes resultativity, in both predicative and attributive uses:

(2)  Dí  bóto dé  láilái.
     DEF boat be.at load.load
     "The boat is loaded."

(3)  dí  jabíjabí mánda
     "the opened basket"

This feature is inherited from Fongbe:

(4)  Wɔ́  ɔ́  ɖɔ̀  bìbɔ̀ (< /bɔ̀bɔ̀/)
     dough DEF be.at softened
     "The bread is softened." (Lefebvre and Brousseau 2002: 354)

(5)  xàsùn hùnhùn   ɔ́
     basket open.open DEF
     "the open basket" (ibid. 353)

However, the superficial similarity masks significant differences. In Fongbe, verbs are also reduplicated to create nominals, such as gerunds:

(6)  Wéma ɔ́   wìwlán yì tàn.
     book DEF write   go time
     "Writing the book took time." (ibid. 196)

In Saramaccan, such concepts are encoded with a bare verb:

(7)  Sikiífi dí  búku bi   taánga.
     write   DEF book PAST hard
     "Writing the book was hard."

Fongbe also distinguishes between the passive and the resultative through choice of copula:

(8)  Àvɔ̀     ɔ́    nyí  wìwólɔ́n.
     loincloth DEF be   crumple
     "The loincloth has been crumpled."

(9)  Àvɔ̀     ɔ́    ɖɔ̀  wìwólɔ́n.
     loincloth DEF be.at crumpled
     "The loincloth is crumpled." (ibid. 205)

In Saramaccan the passive reading is conveyed with a bare verb:

(10) Dí   dɔ́ɔ  jabí.
     DEF door open
     "The door has been opened."

(11) Dí   dɔ́ɔ  dé   jabíjabí.
     DEF door be.at open.open
     "The door is open(ed)."

Moreover, on the phonological level, Fongbe reduplication (in many dialects) entails that the vowel in the copy be [i]: *gbì-gbá* "constructed" *tí-té* "swollen"; furthermore, the tone on the copied syllable is low before voiced consonants and high before voiceless (ibid. 200). In contrast, all productive reduplication in Saramaccan is total, there are no vowel changes, and there are no tonal alterations specific to reduplication (those that occur fall out of sandhi rules general to the language's phonology). Phonologically and tonologically, Saramaccan reduplication is less complex than Fongbe's.

The preceding demonstration makes it clear that Fongbe recruits reduplication for much more overspecification and in more complexification than Saramaccan. Saramaccan itself shows that a natural language need not have overt labeling of gerunds, have overt markers of both passive and resultative, or submit reduplication to phonological rules. Fongbe, however, does, and in this is more complex—by my metric—than Saramaccan.

Saramaccan also restricts the reduplication in terms of syntactic scope more than Fongbe does. In Fongbe, attributively, only a small class of true adjectives may be used in nonreduplicated form, such as the following:

(12) súnu ɖàgbé ɔ̀
     man good  DEF
     "the good man" (ibid. 350)

But the vast majority of items must be reduplicated in this position as a syntactic rule, even when the semantics are not resultative; note, for example, *wì* "black":

(13)   (a)   sáki ɔ́    wì
             bag DEF black
             "The bag is black."

       (b)   sáki wìwì         ɔ́
             bag black.black DEF
             "The black bag." (ibid. 358–59)


Saramaccan has no syntactic requirement that attributive items be reduplicated. Instead, it links the reduplication to a semantic distinction, the counterexpectational (Kramer 2002). *Dí jabíjabí dɔ́ɔ* "the open door" is more precisely translated as "the ajar door," referring to a door open against expectation. Otherwise, one would say *dí jabí dɔ́ɔ*. Note the difference in my translations for (3) and (5): the Saramaccan phrase means, properly, "the basket that is sitting open for some reason," or "the basket that is open as opposed to that closed one over there"; thus I gloss it as "the open basket," as against the Fongbe equivalent, which refers simply to a basket which has "been opened," the speaker being neutral as to how expected this was. Similarly, *dí baáka-baáka sáku* in Saramaccan would mean either "the blackened bag" (as by fire) or "that bag that is, against what you would expect, black." "The black bag" is simply *dí baáka sáku*.

This could be taken as Saramaccan equaling Fongbe here in complexity in the attributive usage, matching Fongbe's syntactic "wrinkle" with a semantic one. But the larger picture reveals Fongbe as the more complex language—by my metric—here.

Saramaccan links property item reduplication to a single semantics grammar-wide: it has the counterexpectational connotation when used predicatively also. *Dí bóto dé láilái* properly means "the boat is loaded up"—in a context where one would be moved to remark upon this as a new development whereas a neutral observation that a boat was loaded would evoke *Dí bóto lái*. But Fongbe links reduplication to the counterexpectational semantics as well, but only in the predicate construction:

(14)   Awu ɔ    ɖo   xu-xu.
       cloth DET COP dry-dry
       "The piece of clothing is dry" (as unexpected given its having lay under a leaky roof while it was raining) (Migge 2003: 63)


while *Wɔ́ ɔ́ bɔ̀* means "The dough is soft" rather than "The dough is softened" (Lefebvre and Brousseau 2002: 354). Note that the attributive use of the contruction in (13b) has no counterexpectational semantics. Thus while in Saramaccan the reduplication always has counterexpectational semantics, in Fongbe it only does so in a particular syntactic context; in the meantime, Fongbe uses the construction in more syntactic contexts than Saramaccan does.

Thus compared to Saramaccan, Fongbe uses the reduplication in a wider range of the grammar, is less consistent in its linking of the construction to semantics, and submits it to more complex phonology and tonology. This usage of reduplication itself demonstrates that in creoles, overt manifestations of relatively "quirky" distinctions that many languages leave unexpressed are hardly unknown, and that my thesis is not that creoles are anything approaching "the simplest possible languages," a misinterpretation of my reasoning that has distracted a number of writers. However, the fact remains that, overall, the Fongbe use of reduplication surpasses Saramaccan in complexity, according to my metric.

## 4.2. Serial verbs

*Pace* former arguments that resemblances between Saramaccan serial verbs and those in its substrate languages are accidental (e.g., Bickerton 1981: 118–32, Byrne 1987), scholarship since would appear to have rendered the source of Saramaccan serialization in Fongbe indisputable. As I have argued elsewhere, serialization varies typologically in its syntactic manifestation and in which verbs it entails, and on this score, Saramaccan parallels Fongbe and its close relatives too closely to be accidental (McWhorter 1997a: 30–35). Migge's (1998) related argument for Saramaccan's sister creole Ndjuka reinforces the point with its closer attention to specific syntactic behaviors.

Notwithstanding the differences between Saramaccan and Fongbe in how serialization manifests itself. The following two behaviors bolster my thesis that creole languages are identifiable as young languages and are less elaborated—by my metric—than older ones.

### 4.2.1. Compositionality over lexicalization

For one, serialization is much more fundamental to Fongbe lexical semantics than to that of Saramaccan. Unitary concepts are expressed with verb pairs in Fongbe to an extent similar to that in many Southeast Asian languages.

Here, the significance of noncompositionality to assessing a grammar's age comes into play. In many such Fongbe cases, the contribution of the two verbs to the meaning is relatively compositional, but in others, the unitary meaning is a rather abstract reflection of the two lexical items. This is, of course, a clinal phenomenon, and I do not claim that all lexical denotations are purely literal in creoles; there exists no natural language in which this is true. In chapter 1 I specify that creoles, like all natural languages, include *institutionalizations* as opposed to outright opaque lexicalizations (Matthews 1974: 193–94), given the centrality of metaphorical and metonymical inference to human cognition. Thus Saramaccan's *báka-ma* (after/behind-man) means both "a man who is your friend" ("behind" one) and "afterbirth" ("the 'guy' that comes afterward"). However, the compositionality of these institutionalizations is accessible, perhaps upon explanation, to the modern speaker. Lexicalizations are the cases where the compositionality is only accessible to those equipped with earlier documentation of the language or with the tools of academic historical semantic inference (such as English *understand* or Russian's *najti*).

Crucially, of the Fongbe serial verb pairs, Saramaccan has inherited only the compositional and institutionalized ones. Those that fall on the more opaque, lexicalized end of the cline are foreign to the language. Thus where Fongbe has *xò àsí* (hit hand) "clap," Saramaccan has *náki máũ* ("hit hand"). But alongside cases like this are the numerous ones Lefebvre and Brousseau (2002: 430–31) list such as:

| | | |
|---|---|---|
| *tśn wá* | exit come | "to appear" |
| *ḍè xlé* | remove show | "to demonstrate" |
| *bló dó* | do have | "to repair" |
| *té kpśn* | spread-out look | "to try" |

Pairs like this are alien to Saramaccan, which instead uses single verbs inherited from English or Portuguese to express these concepts. There are even intermediate cases: Fongbe for "to spend" is *ḍù àkwέ* "eat money" (ibid. 547). In Saramaccan, this means specifically "to spend *too much* money" that is, an institutionalized, but less arbitrarily abstract, interpretation of the concatenation "eat money" than merely *spend*.

The Saramaccan lexicon, then, does not include cases like *dú ábi* "do have" in the meaning "to repair," and my informants have never come up with serial verb pairs so compositionally opaque in their renditions of sentences given to them to translate or in running speech. That Saramaccan only incorporated a subset of Fongbe serial concatenations was not due to mere rolls of the dice: the choices that Saramaccan's creators made were determined by compositionality. In this sense, they began a language anew, starting (relatively) clean.

### 4.2.2. Lexical over grammatical

Saramaccan also reveals its youth in its serial use of *téi* "to take" in contrast with Fongbe's use of its equivalent, *sś*. In Fongbe, this item is first used in constructions where its semantics are particularly concrete, such as instrumental ones:

(15)   Kȝkú sś    àtín  xȍ  Àsíbá.
       Koku take stick hit Asiba
       "Koku hit Asiba with a stick." (Lefebvre and Brousseau 2002: 415)

However, its other uses fall upon a cline from the concrete to the abstract, instantiating the process of serial verb grammaticalization analyzed by Givón (1975), Lord (1976), and others. *Sś* is used in constructions involving objects in which the essence of "taking" is obviously a component of the event, but which a speaker of a nonserializing language would only mark with *take* if desiring to call attention to the taking. The result is that in many constructions, *sś* straddles the line between lexical item and grammatical marker. Example (16) involves "taking" in a literal sense:

(16)   Kȝkú sś    àsśn ḍś távȍ jí.
       Koku take crab put table on
       "Koku put crab on the table." (Lefebvre and Brousseau 2002: 410)

In (17), however, specifying the "take" component of the action would be less intuitive to speakers of nonserializing languages, because the "taking" of the watch was presumably a less-salient component of the event than its yielding by the seller after monetary exchange:

(17) Kòkú sɔ́  gàn  ɔ́   xɔ́.
Koku take watch DEF buy
"Koku bought the watch." (Lefebvre and Brousseau 2002: 411, from Da Cruz 1994: 49)

Then in (18), the "taking" is even less obvious as a necessary aspect of the event to specify, such that *sɔ́* appears to function essentially as an object marker (in some West African serializing languages the *take* verb has become just this, Yatye being an example [Stahlke 1970]):

(18) Kòkú sɔ́  nyɔ́nû ɔ́   dà.
Koku take woman DEF marry
"Koku married the woman." (Lefebvre and Brousseau 2002: 413, from Da Cruz 1994: 50)

This is precisely the type of stepwise grammaticalization that Lord (1976) describes regarding the evolution of verbs "to say" becoming complementizers in Kwa languages.

Meanwhile, with stative verbs, *sɔ́* functions as a causative marker of intransitive verbs:

(19) Kòkú sɔ́   xɔ́ntɔ̀n tɔ̀n  hwè.
Koku take friend  GEN be-small
"Koku humiliated his friend." (Lefebvre and Brousseau 2002: 412, from Da Cruz 1994: 47)

(20) Kòkú sɔ́  gbè  yì jǐ.
Koku take voice go up
"Koku raised his voice." (Da Cruz 1994: 46)

An analysis stipulating that creoles are chary of overtly marking that which is not necessary to mark would predict that Saramaccan would parallel Fongbe until roughly (16)—and this would be correct. Saramaccan uses *téi* in instrumental constructions:

(21) Kobí téi  dí   matjáu kóti dí   bɛ́ɛ.
Kobi take DEF axe    cut  DEF bread
"Kobi cut the bread with an axe."

Yet even here, my elicitations confirm Veenstra's (1996) observation that Byrne's (1987) characterization of the serial use of *téi* as Saramaccan's principal instrumental construction was mistaken. Consultants most readily give translations of instrumentals with the preposition *ku* "with," and the *téi* serials are only grammatical in cases where the taking is an immediately salient component of the event. Meanwhile, in Saramaccan *téi* is not used in serial constructions where its contribution is essentially object marking, nor is *téi* used to causativize intransitive verbs. Instead, while Saramaccan can use *mbéi* "to make" as a causativizer, just as often bare verbs can connote both causative and stative meanings:

(22)  Mi lánga dí   bóto.
      I  long DEF boat
      "I made the boat longer."

In sum, Saramaccan reproduces Fongbe serialization up to the point where it entails overt marking of abstract grammatical relations or valence, in which case it leaves the distinction to context. It also diverges from Fongbe where the semantics of latter's verb concatenations depart from institutionalized compositionality, in which case it appeals to lexifier items with immediately processible meanings. In both cases, Saramaccan reveals itself as a younger grammar than Fongbe.

4.3. Tone Sandhi

Saramaccan tone sandhi is blocked between adjectives, between adverbs, between verbs and nominal objects, between prepositions and nouns, and between verbs and adverbs (Rountree 1972). The blockage between verb and nominal object and between preposition and prepositional object is illustrated next, as well as the phenomenon where sandhi "jumps" across an object between two verbs in shared object serials (underlinings indicate where sandhi has occurred; # indicates blockage):

(23)  /mi wási koósu butá a  dí  sónu/ → [mi wásí # koósu bútá # a dí sónu]
      I    wash clothes put in the sun
      'I washed my clothes and put them in the sun.' (Rountree 1972: 325)

This is clearly one of Saramaccan's more elaborated features, so typical a "Field Methods" construction that no fewer than three linguists who as graduate students learned of it from me have written on it (Ham 1999, Good 2003, Kramer 2002). However, it is an inheritance from Fongbe, and as so often, the Saramaccan system is the simpler one.

Ham (1999) parses the Saramaccan system as, essentially, tone sandhi breaking at left edge boundaries of maximal projections. This is also broadly true of Fongbe, where when spreading high tone reaches the end of a tonal domain, it creates an HL tone on the last syllable (Lefebvre and Brousseau 2002: 22):

(24)  /é sà  àsɔ́n wè/ → [é sâ # àsɔ́n wê]
      he sell crab two

But the Fongbe system attends to more than left edges. For example, it must attend to phonology, in that sandhi does not break before monosyllabic objects (ibid. 23):

(25)  /à  só   tè/ → [à só tê]
      you mash yam

(In Saramaccan, the usual sandhi break between verb and object is suspended when the object is a pronoun, but this is compatible with the left-edge account, as these pronouns are cliticized onto the verb [Ham 1999: 79–80].)

Moreover, Fongbe sandhi is sensitive to constituent class as, within NP, sandhi is blocked between possessum and possessor (Wiesemann 1991: 77):

(26)  /ànyú àsɔ́n tɔ̀n/ → [ànyû # àsɔ́n tɔ́n]
      skin   crab GEN

In his comparison of Saramaccan's tone sandhi to that in Ewe, Ham (1999) reaches a similar conclusion that Saramaccan's rendition is the distinctly simpler one.[3]

## 5. Saramaccan and Fongbe: Creole equals or surpasses substrate in complexity

Yet this tendency toward simplification of inherited features, while a very strong tendency, is not universal. A scientifically responsible approach to this issue requires that exceptions to the trend be presented in full as well.

### 5.1. Temporal subordinators

Saramaccan has developed a distinction in markers of temporal subordination sensitive to both tense and aspect. In the present and future, the subordinate clause is marked with *te* and the matrix with *nɔ́ɔ:*

(27)  Te    mujɛ́ɛ sí Kobí, nɔ́ɔ de  tá   kulé.
      COMP woman see Kobi then they HAB run
      "When women see Kobi, they run."

(28)  Te    mi sí Kobí, nɔ́ɔ mi o   kulé.
      COMP I  see Kobi then I  FUT run
      "When I see Kobi, I will run."

However, in the past, the subordinate clause is usually marked with *dí* and the matrix with the sequential marker *hɛ̃́:*

(29)  Dí (*te) a bi   tá   duúmi, hɛ̃́ (*nɔ́ɔ) mi gó kumútu dé.
      COMP he PAST PROG sleep then       I  go leave there
      "When he was sleeping, I left."

(30)  Dí    mi bi   jabí dí  dɔ́ɔ, hɛ̃́ mi sí dí  goő   mũjá̋.
      COMP I  PAST open DEF door then I  see DEF ground wet
      "When I opened the door, I saw the ground wet."

But in the past, there is an additional aspect distinction: if the matrix verb expresses an unbounded event, then the sequential marker is *nɔ́ɔ:*

(31)  Dí   mi bi   kó   lúku de,  nɔ́ɔ (*hɛ̃́) de  bi   duúmi kaa.
      COMP I   PAST come look them then       they PAST sleep  already
      "When I came to see them, they were asleep."

(32)  Dí    mi kabá u  njã́ a    dí   sónúati njãnjã́, nɔ́ɔ hángi bi    kísi  mi éti.
      COMP I   finish for eat LOC DEF noon    food   then hunger PAST catch me still
      "After I finished eating lunch, I was still hungry."

Here, Saramaccan is overspecified (by my metric) compared to, for example, English, which has no such distinction in temporal subordination marking based on tense or aspect. Significantly, Saramaccan also surpasses Fongbe in complexity here. *Dí* is also a relativizer in Saramaccan (*dí wómi dí sábi* "the man **who** knows"), and, like Saramaccan, Fongbe marks the subordinate clause with its relativizer (termed a nominal operator in Lefebvre 1998 and thus below glossed NOM) in temporal constructions:

(33)  **ɖé-è**     ùn wá   ɔ́,   à   ɖò   xwégbé ă.
      NOM-3SG I   come DEF you be.at home    NEG
      "When I came, you were not at home." (*Éléments de recherche* 1983: XI 2)

In non-past temporal constructions, the subordinate marker is *nú:*[4]

(34)  **Nú**  jì  já  ɔ́,  jojɔn nɔ  gbé.
      when rain fall DEF cold  HAB exaggerate
      "When it rains, it's cold." (ibid. XII 1)

However, as is visible in (33) and (34), Fongbe lacks the sequential marking of the matrix clause that Saramaccan has. The closest possible equivalent is an item meaning "hence" that occurs in conditional rather than temporal clauses, with the phonetic similarity with *hɛ̃́* supporting a possible connection:

(35)  Nú   à   mà  wá   sɔ̀     ă   **hùn**, mí ná  wà àzɔ́ ă.
      COMP 2SG NEG come tomorrow NEG hence 1PL FUT do work NEG
      "If you don't come tomorrow, we will not work." (Lefebvre and Brousseau 2002:
      178)

Yet there is no feature of Saramaccan's phonology that regularly renders [ũ] in a source language as [ɛ̃] (nor [u] as [ɛ]); *hùn* occurs at the right edge of the subordinate clause rather than the left edge of the matrix; it also occurs in the non-past where *hɛ̃́* does not; and, of course, despite the semantic overlap between the conditional and the temporal, ideally we would seek a marker that occurred in temporal clauses as well. In any case, even this item offers no model for the sensitivity to boundedness in the matrix verb that *hɛ̃́* and *nɔ́ɔ* mark in Saramaccan.[5]

   Here, then, is an example of an elaboration in Saramaccan that took its substrate model as a springboard but "took the ball and ran with it."

## 5.2. Change-of-location marking

Saramaccan uses *túwε* "to throw" and *butá* "put" in shared-object serial concatenations to mark the end of a trajectory denoted by change-of-location verbs (generally those conveying abrupt, forceful, or disruptive processes):

(36)  I    tɔ́tɔ  mi túwε  a     wáta.
      you push me throw LOC water
      "You pushed me into the water."

(37)  Kobí tɔ́tɔ  dí    wómi túwε.
      Kobi push DEF man  throw
      "Kobi pushed the man and he fell."

(38)  Vínde dí   bíífi túwε.
      throw DEF letter throw
      "Throw the letter in [e.g., the trashcan]."

(39)  A kándi dí    amána    fátu túwε  a    dí   bɔ̃ɔ́.
      he pour  DEF "Amana" fat  throw LOC DEF flour
      "He poured the syrup on the pancakes."

(40)  A sáka híi soní butá.
      he drop all thing put
      "He dropped everything [literally]."

The only possible English model here is the distinction between *You pushed me in the water* and *You pushed me into the water,* where the first sentence is ambiguous between the entire event happening in the water and a person being pushed into it, while the second sentence only allows the latter interpretation. However, Saramaccan has a mere three prepositions (the locative *a,* comitative and instrumental *ku,* possessive and general associative *fu*), all with behavior vastly diverging from their lexical sources. This suggests that Saramaccan's creators were unlikely to have incorporated a prepositionally encoded nuance like the *in/into* distinction, especially given its extreme variability in the spoken register. Nor is such a development of a verb "to throw" into a change-of-location marker a cross-linguistically common pathway of grammaticalization, as the development of, for example, *go* into a directional marker is.

Unsurprisingly, Fongbe is the source. Fongbe differs from Saramaccan in often using the corresponding verbs in three-verb predicates. But the semantic idiosyncrasy of the usage of both of these particular verbs in this function, as well as the restriction to change-of-location constructions, confirms a causal link:

(41)  Kɔkú sɔ́  sìn   ɔ́   kɔ́n  **nyì**   àyí.
      Koku take water DEF pour throw ground
      "Koku spilled water on the floor."

(42) Kɔkú sɔ́ mὲ  ɔ́  zín  ɖɔ́ àyí.
 Koku take person DEF push put ground
 "Koku made the person fall." (Da Cruz 1994: 51)

The import of this feature to this esssay is that there would appear to be no differ-ence between Saramaccan and Fongbe in its *entrenchment,* to use the terminology of Langacker (1987: 59). Both languages have an overt marker of change-of-loca-tion, which qualifies as an overspecification compared to English and a great many other languages.

## 6. Saramaccan complexity developing internally

As presented thus far, my argument falls into a mistake common in creole genesis accounts—a working assumption that all features in a creole must be derivable from source language models—with a corollary tendency to trace all newly emerging fea-tures to "decreolization" toward a target. As I have argued in various articles, the problem here is the proposition that creole grammars do not undergo the natural in-ternal changes that all languages do, or that, for some reason, a few centuries is not long enough for such changes to have begun in any substantial way. Along these lines, various features in Saramaccan are internal developments in which overt mark-ings of underlying distinctions that context conveys just as well take the grammar ever further from a hypothetical pole of maximal simplicity.

These particular developments are not traceable to Fongbe, and their presenta-tion will illustrate a phenomenon I have previously mentioned only in passing: namely, like all natural languages, creoles "hit the ground running" after their emergence in a particular contact situation. A useful analogy is the reemergence of infinitives in the Balkan variety of Tosk Albanian after the famous contact situation that elimi-nated infinitives in the Balkan Sprachbund (cf. Joseph 1983: 85–100, 211–12). Though born in contact situations, creoles' subsequent development is no more en-tirely determined by the "ecology" of these situations than that of any other language. Moreover, there is no principled reason to suppose that internal developments play a role any less robust in creoles' development than that more readily assumed for older languages.

However, there is an important "rider" in these cases: in all but one of them, the feature is variable rather than tightly conventionalized. With all due cognizance of the fact that variability expresses itself in various shades throughout any grammar, I must emphasize that I refer here not to marginal exceptions or fossilizations but to variation of the pronounced degree that the historical linguist associates with a change in progress. The general impression in compiling a grammar of Saramaccan is that the quotient of rules that are robust yet amply violable are somewhat more prevalent than in older languages. Quite often, work with informants on a given construction yields less ironclad declarations of ungrammaticality than strong tendencies, with one finding (in the attempt to filter out inevitable discrepancies between isolated elicitations and spontaneous practice) that transcriptions of running speech and texts written by native speakers reflect the same optionality.[6] I analyze this as evidence that Saramaccan is a new grammar, such that a great many features have yet to harden into complete grammaticalization.


## 6.1. Inalienable possessive marking

There is a strong tendency in Saramaccan to distinguish inalienable possession from alienable: upon elicitation, the former is almost always expressed with preposed pronouns, while the latter is almost always expressed with a PP with (f)u:

(43)  mí hédi
      my head
      "my head"


(44)  Dí   wági u  mi boóko.
      DEF car  of me broken
      "My car is broken."


Fongbe distinguishes alienability in possession as well, but quite differently from Saramaccan. It is alienably possessed items that take a preposed pronoun, but with what Lefebvre terms an objective marker; at the same time, a construction with the pronoun postposed and followed (rather than preceded) by a genitive marker is also grammatical with no difference in meaning:

(45)  nyὲ sín   àsɔ́n / àsɔ́n nyὲ tɔ̀n
      me OBJ crab crab   me GEN "my crab" (Lefebvre 1998: 101–10)


Meanwhile, with inalienable possession, the distinction between the two markers distinguishes emphasis on the possessum from that on the possessor:

(46)  Àwà nyὲ tɔ̀n,  wé wὲn.
      arm me GEN this break
      "It's my arm (e.g. not my leg) that is broken."


(47)  Nyὲ sín   àwà, wé wὲn.
      me OBJ arm  this break
      "It's my arm (e.g., not someone else's) that is broken." (Lefebvre and Brousseau 2002: 71)


Obviously, this system has nothing significant in common with Saramaccan's.

However, it is also important to note that in Saramaccan, replacement of one form of marking with another is neither ungrammatical nor especially infelicitous with either type of possession: for example, informants readily accept Mí wági boóko "My car is broken." They also frequently give such examples in sentences elicited for other purposes:

(48)  A náki dí    tatá   u     mi.
      he hit   DEF father POSS me
      "He hit my father."

(49)  Mi ké   gó a      mí njúnjũ wósu.
      I    want go LOC my new    house
      "I want to go to my new house."

The distinction is also canceled out in the plural when overtly marked with a determiner, in which case inalienably possessed items as well as alienably possessed ones
take the PP rather than the preposed pronoun:

(50)  Mi ké   u    déé     mií   u     mi músu dé  límbolímbo.
      I    want that DEF.PL child POSS me must COP clean
      "I want my children to be clean."

Thus this construction gives indication of being an emergent distinction, contrasting
with the well-known tightly grammaticalized alienability distinctions in hundreds of
languages worldwide, where switched marking strategies are unhesitatingly rejected
by speakers as ungrammatical.

6.2.  Identification/class distinction in the copula

Much has been written about the parallels between many creoles and West African
languages in their separate copulas for the equative (*I am your father*) and the locative (*I am in the tree*). However, unlike even its sister creoles Sranan and Ndjuka,
Saramaccan overtly marks a finer semantic subdivision of the equative domain.
     For identificational equation, *da* is the only grammatical copula:

(51)  Mi da (*dé) Gádu.
      I   COP    God
      "I am God."

But where the equation is one denoting class membership, then the otherwise locative copula *dé* is grammatical:

(52)  Mi dé   wá kabitiéni.
      I   COP a   captain
      "I am a captain."

(53)  Alísi dé   wá soní dí    de   tá     séi.
      rice  COP a   thing REL they PROG sell
      "Rice is one thing that they are selling."

Fongbe, however, merely makes a cross-linguistically conventional two-way distinction between equative and locative in its copulas:

(54)  Ùn  nyí  Àfíáví.
      1SG be  Afiavi
      "I am Afiavi." (Lefebvre and Brousseau 2002: 144)

(55)  Wémâ ɔ́    ɖɔ́  távò  jí.
      book  DEF be.at table on
      "The book is on the table." (ibid. 147)

Many have argued that the equative/locative split in creoles created by Africans is a substrate inheritance and, as such, would classify this case as one befitting section 4. However, I have argued that the resemblance to West African languages in this case is accidental, on the basis of syntactic, historical, and typological arguments (McWhorter 1995b, 1997a). The evidence suggests that, in fact, Saramaccan (or, more properly, the single ancestor to all of the Atlantic English-based creoles that I have argued for in McWhorter 1995b, 2000a) began with no expressed copula, with the equative and locative ones present today having developed internally. For this reason, I view Saramaccan's mapping of two copulas to three semantic distinctions as unrelated to Fongbe. However, it also bypasses Fongbe in overspecification.

Yet this too is a highly variable feature. The following are also grammatical:

(56)  Mi da   wɛ́ kabiténi.
      I  COP a  captain
      "I am a captain."

(57)  Alísi da   wɛ́ soní dí    de  tá   séi.
      rice COP a  thing REL they PROG sell
      "Rice is one thing that they are selling."

Speakers vary according to which copula they give upon elicitation in class predications (and texts of transcribed speech are also variable here). Speakers even very occasionally accept (but in my data do not produce spontaneously) *dé* in identificational contexts:

(58)  Alísi dé  dí   soní dí    de  tá   séi.
      rice  COP DEF thing REL they PROG sell
      "Rice is the thing that they are selling."

It is impossible to tell whether there is a drift toward *da* occupying the class domain exclusively or *dé* becoming obligatory there (historical documentation, in which there are cases of identificational *dé*, suggest a gradual encroachment of *da* into an ever-broader domain). But at the current point, Saramaccan has developed an overt marking—albeit highly variable—of a semantic distinction within the copular domain that none of its source languages, or even its sisters, mark.

## 6.3. Morphophonemics on the march

Most morphophonemic rules in Saramaccan are relatively transparent phonetically, with their origin in contractions still easy to glean. This is another sign of the grammar's youth. Pidgins are generally spoken relatively slowly and have few or no morphophonemic processes (Sankoff and Laberge 1980: 198–99, Mühlhäusler 1997, Heine 1973: 172). Then, after a language has existed for only a few centuries, segments in morphological contexts have yet to be ravaged by phonetic assimilation and drift beyond perceptible relationship to their original manifestations by anyone but the historical linguist, of an extent typified by consonant mutations, new gender classes, et cetera.

Thus, a typical morphophonemic process in Saramaccan is where the fusion of third-person oblique pronominal clitic $\tilde{\varepsilon}$ with preceding verbs that end in [á] or [ɛ], or the preposition *fu,* leads the preceding vowel to assimilate to it: *paká* + $\tilde{\varepsilon}$ "pay him" > *pakɛ́ɛ́,* *túwɛ* + $\tilde{\varepsilon}$ "throw it" > *túwɛ̃ɛ̃, fu* + $\tilde{\varepsilon}$ > *fɛ̃ɛ̃.*

However, one related case where the connection between underlying and surface forms has become more opaque is where the locative marker *a* combines with $\tilde{\varepsilon}$ to yield *nɛ̃ɛ̃.* The relationship between *a* and *nɛ̃ɛ̃* in the sentences below is hardly phonetically transparent:

(59)  A  sindó **a**    dí   líba fɛ̃ɛ̃.
      he sit    LOC DEF top POSS.it
      "He sat on top of it."

(60)  Mi á    wá baási   mi nɛ̃́   sikiífi **nɛ̃́ɛ̃́**.
      I   have a   balloon my name write on.it
      "I have a balloon with my name written on it."

This contrast is the result of the fact that *a* is derived from an earlier *na* (still current in Sranan), as is clear in historical documents of Saramaccan:
      1778:

(61)  dem no    mussu komotto na    Jerusalem
      they NEG must   leave    LOC Jerusalem
      "They must not leave Jerusalem." (Schuchardt 1914: 2)

The initial consonant has since worn away from the item in isolation, but it persists in the portmanteau morpheme. The result is a morphophonemic rule stipulating an [n] in combination with a particular pronominal form.

However, the rule has yet to become completely opaque. The *na* form is still used with deictic adverbs—*na akí* "on here," *naãndé* "there, on there," *na alá* "over there, (on something) over there"—and some interrogative markers, such as *na-ú-tɛ̃* 'at which time' "when." Speakers also use *na* variably on its own in its isolated usage:

(62)  I   sa njã́ na  dí júu i   ké.
      you can eat LOC the hour you want
      "You can eat at whatever time you want."

I analyze this as a morphophonemic rule in the process of drifting into the depth of the sort that we see, for example, in Finnish consonant gradations.

## 6.4.    Negation

Saramaccan has two negator allomorphs, one used between subject and predicate:

(63)  Dí  wómi **á**   wáka.
      DEF man  NEG walk
      "The man doesn't walk."

and the other used elsewhere, as in imperatives and in propositional negation:

(64)  **Ná**   wáka!
      NEG walk
      "Don't walk!"

(65)  **Ná**   mi dú ẽ.
      NEG I   do it
      "It wasn't me who did it."

In chapter 7 I demonstrate that this is due to a diachronic development from an original situation where *ná* was the negator in both contexts:
      Reconstructed:

(66)  Dí   wómi ná   wáka.
      DEF man   NEG walk
      "The man doesn't walk."

   Documentary evidence and the principles of internal reconstruction strongly suggest that the modern predicate negator *á* developed from the coalescence of third-person singular pronoun *a* (with low tone) and the following *ná* in a topic-comment configuration. The phonetic coalescence would have first been interpreted as a portmanteau morpheme *ã́* "he-NEG," but eventually the topic-comment configuration was reinterpreted as a subject-predicate one, with the erstwhile topic recast as the subject and *ã́*, eventually denasalizing as heavily grammatical morphemes tend to in Saramaccan, edged aside into the VP and becoming a negator only:

| Stage One | Stage Two | Stage Three |
|---|---|---|
| Dí wómi, a ná wáka. | Dí wómi, ã́ wáka. | Dí wómi á wáka. |
| "The man, he doesn't" | "The man, he doesn't | "The man doesn't walk." |
| walk." | walk." | |

Because this process occurred as the result of the merger of a resumptive pronoun and the following negator, the original *ná* form persisted in positions where there was no preceding pronoun: hence *ná* remains in use in imperatives and in propositional negation, as in (64) and (65).

Here, then, Saramaccan has developed an overt marking of a syntactic negation distinction that is absent in, for example, Atlantic English-based creoles where a cognate to *ná* is still used whether a subject precedes or not (Jamaican *Im na siŋ* "She doesn't sing," *Na siŋ!* "Don't sing!" Hancock 1987: 299).

Fongbe offers no model here. As it happens, it too has a separate propositional negator; the neutral marker is *mà* while the propositional one is *a&*:

(67)  Kɔkú **mà**  wá.
      Koku NEG arrive
      "Koku has not arrived." (Lefebvre and Brousseau 2002: 120)

(68)  Kɔkú xɔ  àsɔn lέ  **ă**.
      Koku buy crab PL NEG
      "It is not the case that Koku bought the crabs." (ibid. 128)

But besides that (1) the Saramaccan distinction gives such strong indication of being an internal development and (2) the syntactic occurrence of Fongbe's propositional negator is so starkly unlike Saramaccan's, the division of labor between the items differs in Fongbe, where the neutral marker is also used in the imperative (INS = insistence marker):

(69)  **Mà**  ɖù ó!
      NEG eat INS
      "Don't eat!" (ibid. 120)

Rather, Saramaccan simply developed this overspecification by itself.

Moreover, in this case Saramaccan only has marginal exceptions, one being the negation of the shortened form *á* of *ábi* "to have," *áá* ("not have"), where *ná á* is grammatical as well (likely because in rapid speech *áá* threatens ambiguity with the *á* negator alone):

(70)  Dí  dágu u     mi áá /      ná  á   mɔ́ni.
      DEF dog  POSS me NEG.have NEG have money
      "My dog doesn't have money."

Wrinkles like this, however, merely exemplify that "all grammars leak"; overall, the negator allomorphy is thoroughly entrenched.

## 7. The bigger picture

### 7.1. Saramaccan and Fongbe: bird's eye view

I hope to have illustrated convincingly two things:

1. I do not believe that Saramaccan is a "simple" language.
2. Nevertheless, overall, Saramaccan's grammar is less complex than Fongbe's in the overspecificational sense I stipulated at the outset.

Importantly, my demonstrations in the preceding discussion constitute but a subset of the relevant data. Here are briefer descriptions of further contrasts (Fongbe data from Lefebvre and Brousseau 2002):

1. Fongbe has two phonological tones and three phonetic (including two contour tones); Saramaccan has two tones (with the low tone usually subject to sandhi but sometimes occurring in a lexically specified unchangeable rendition).
2. Fongbe has two overt case markers; Saramaccan covers the functions of both with one marker.
3. Fongbe has a logophoric pronoun; Saramaccan does not.
4. In Fongbe, first- and second-person singular pronominal clitics are not phonetically identifiable with the full forms and then also make a case distinction in the singular, yielding three-way contrasts such as *nyè* 1SG (full), *ùn* (nominative clitic), *mì* (oblique clitic); third-person singular pronoun clitics also make a case distinction. In Saramaccan, all pronominal clitics correspond phonetically with full forms except subject clitic *a* with third-person singular full form *hẽ*; also, there are case distinctions in two full pronouns.
5. Fongbe has a pragmatic negator *kún* marking especially insistent denial; Saramaccan has no equivalent item.
6. Fongbe has a complementizer *bó* used in purposive sentences where the clauses share a subject (e.g., *I will go in order to work*); Saramaccan has no equivalent item.
7. Fongbe has six derivational suffixes and two or three derivational prefixes; Saramaccan has one productive derivational suffix and one preposed derivational item (to give Saramaccan the most possible due, *ná* in compounds like *ná-buwá-fóu* 'NEG fly bird' "flightless bird").[7]
8. Fongbe has over twice as many spatial-marking postpositions than Saramaccan has of cognate postposed nominals, encoding finer distinctions than Saramaccan's (such as distinguishing "on top of" from "at the top of").

Readers might reasonably suspect that I have chosen features where Fongbe happens to come out more complex. In response I can only state that I have proceeded with as little theoretical bias as possible, which I hope to have demonstrated by highlighting the cases I have found where Saramaccan does surpass Fongbe in complexity.

But these cases are a compact set, and I am unaware of an eight-point list of Saramaccan features beyond them that are more complex than their Fongbe models or equivalents.

## 7.2. Saramaccan and the world's languages

It is also relevant that Saramaccan reveals itself as a young grammar not only in comparison with its substrate model Fongbe—which in itself leaves the possibility that the differential is merely a matter of happenstance in the cross-linguistic sense—but in comparison to grammars worldwide.

My claim that creoles' "overspecification quotient" is less than older ones predicts that grammars with constructions whose complexity rates as extreme within the context of the world's languages as a whole reveal themselves as ancient. To wit, a language with extensive inflectional paradigms, split ergativity, consonant mutations, and the like can only have developed these features over vast periods of time, as such features only emerge as the result of gradual recasting of original materials.

Therefore, my case would be weakened if it could be shown that in the constructions where Saramaccan surpasses or equals Fongbe in complexity, these constructions have drifted into a superlative degree of complexity in the cross-linguistic sense. This would indicate that constructions of this nature do not require millennia to develop: in short, that degree of overspecification does *not* correlate with age.

It is therefore germane that, in fact, Saramaccan reveals no such features that are overspecified to a cross-linguistically superlative degree. Even where it surpasses Fongbe in complexity, its manifestation of the construction is *much less* overspecified than is possible in natural language grammars.

### 7.2.1. Temporal subordination markers

For example, Saramaccan's tense- and aspect-sensitive temporal complementizers and sequential markers are certainly one of the "frills" in its grammar. However, many languages' equivalent items vary more baroquely according to semantic distinctions. Take the Papuan language Barai, which has distinct temporal complementizers for past, future, and "delayed past" (where the event of the matrix clause takes place considerably after the event of the subordinate) (ALT = alternative mood; DPS = delayed past sequencer; FS = future sequencer; INT = intentive aspect; PS = past sequencer; SW = switch reference):

(71)  ro    igia keke-**mo**, na-si    ku-a-e
     COMP here arrive-PS 1S-ALT say-3S-PAST
     "But when he arrived here, I talked to him next." (Olson 1973: 49)

(72)  bu   ije  furi-ga-**kuva**,  na vua-kiro-ke
     3PL this finish-SW-FS, 1S come-INT-FUT
     "When they are finished with this, I intend to come." (ibid. 53)

(73)  ivia   muge no gamia va-**eva**, suake    una     rua-e
     today night 1PL there  go-DPS  morning go.back come-PAST
     "Last night we went (over) there and then this morning we came back." (ibid. 56)

### 7.2.2. Change-of-location markers

Saramaccan's markers of the telicity of change-of-location events can be treated under Talmy's (1985) typological analysis of event structure as *path satellites*. Talmy (102–3) identifies satellites as "certain immediate constituents of a verb root other than inflections, auxiliaries, or nominal arguments," such as *over* in *start over* or *entzwei* in German's *Der Tisch brach entzwei* "The table broke in two." The satellites in English that connote path include *in*, as in *I went in*, and *off*, as in *I got off*. But path satellites are hardly limited to Germanic or even Europe; Mandarin Chinese has a whole paradigm, including *guò* "past":

(74)   Píng-zi piāo guò shí-tóu páng-biān.
       bottle   float  past  rock     side
       "The bottle floated past the rock." (ibid. 107)

For my thesis, it is important that Saramaccan's path satellites, in marking a subset of change-of-location verbs, are but a beginning in terms of how far overspecification of path can drift in the typological sense. The Hokan Native American language Atsugewi has a vast array of affixes specifying the precise nature of pathways (ibid. 108):

| | |
|---|---|
| *-ic't* | "into a liquid" |
| *-cis* | "into a fire" |
| *-isp-u·* | "into an aggregate" |
| *-wam* | "down into a gravitic container" |
| *-wamm* | "into an areal enclosure" |
| *-ipsn$^u$* | "(horizontally) into a volume enclosure" |
| *-tip-u·* | "down into a (large) volume enclosure in the ground" |
| *-ikn* | "over the rim into a volume enclosure" |
| *-ikc* | "into a passageway so as to cause blockage" |
| *-ik's$^u$* | "into a corner" |
| *-mik·* | "into the face" |
| *-mic'* | "down into (or onto) the ground" |
| *-cis$^u$* | "down into (or onto) an object above the ground" |
| *-ik's* | "horizontally into (or onto) an object above the ground" |

There are two important observations here. First, it must be clear that these affixes are not simply incorporated nominals, such that there would be no grounds for considering them more "elaborated" than expressing the nominals as separate arguments. Rather, the affixes are used redundantly along with free word arguments; here is a sentence:

(75)   w'-o-        q$^h$put-   **íc't**        -a         c$^ə$   ni?$^ə$ qáp$^h$ c$^ə$   c'um· é·y-i
       it- by.falling-dirt.move-into.liquid-FACTUAL NOM soot       NOM creek-to
       "The soot flowed into the creek." (Talmy 1972: 69)

Technically, this sentence would be readily comprehensible if the path marker expressed only direction without specifying the nature of the goal, since there is the argument *creek* denoting that goal in all of its liquidity. The semantic particularity of Atsugewi's path markers, then, is an overspecification in terms of what is necessary to human communication.

Second, the potential objection that it is inappropriate to compare creoles with heavily inflected languages weakens when we consider that analytic languages often contain the very constructions traditionally associated with inflectional ones. World-wide, ergativity, evidential marking, grammatical gender marking, and a great many other features are regularly expressed by free morphemes rather than bound. There-fore, our question is why, if there are no grounds for supposing creoles to be less overspecified than older languages, there are no creoles that contain the above-mentioned three features in *either free or bound form.*

The import of the Atsugewi sentence to this chapter, then, is not that its highly inflected nature qualifies in itself as "complexity" but, rather, in what concepts many of the affixes specify. Crucial here is my demonstration in chapter 2 that even older languages with little or no inflectional morphology according to any metric can be shown to display more overspecification of this kind than any creole. The Sino-Tibetan language Lahu, for example, is devoid of inflection but has unbound numeral classifiers, an accusative case marking particle, a vast array of highly conventional-ized pragmatic particles analogous to the modal particles in many Germanic lan-guages, and other features of a sort that all or the vast majority of creoles leave to context. In Maori, lacking inflection, the syntax of interrogative constructions never-theless differs according to *wh*-word; possessive marking is split between two par-ticles whose choice is determined not by a conventional and universally transparent alienability distinction but by semantic classes that are subtly distinguished by de-gree of personal control over the possessum, for example, with these features again unknown in any creole language known to this author.

No theory of synchronic linguistic structure offers any principled reason why a creole with a paradigm of free morphemes specifying path, as the Atsugewi markers do, could not exist, nor one with a complex of free noun class morphemes like those so famous from Dyirbal. My theory, however, provides that principled explanation, in highlighting that extensive adult acquisition creates a particular kind of grammar, which it would be logically impossible for any older grammar to embody.

## 7.2.3. Copulas

In its overt marking of the identity/class distinction, Saramaccan is relatively over-specified as grammars go, surpassing, for example, English and many other Euro-pean languages. But again, this degree of subdivision is distinctly moderate from a cross-linguistic perspective. For example, the Cariban language Panare has zero copula in the first and second persons but overt ones in the third person, and these distinguish between the inanimate and the animate, and then these latter between the proximal and the distal:

(76)  maestro ø yu/amën
      teacher   1SG/2SG
      "I/you am/are a teacher." (ø = zero copula)

(77)    maestro këj              e'ñapa
        teacher COP.ANIM:PROX Panare
        "The Panare (here) is a teacher."

(78)    maestro nëj              e'ñapa
        teacher COP.ANIM:DIST Panare
        "The Panare (there) is a teacher."

(79)    e'chipen mën          manko
        fruit    COP.INAN mango (Gildea 1993: 54–55)
        "Mango is a fruit."

Nor is extreme overspecification in the copular domain restricted to inflectional languages. Yoruba has separate copulas for permanence and temporariness in the equative, and then copulas restricted to the locative, the attributive, the imperative, the pejorative, and the summary (Rowlands 1969), the latter illustrated below:

(80)    Ó di   èèmérin   tí   mo ti   wá.
        it COP four-times that I   PAST come
        "It is now four times that I have come." (ibid. 156)

## 8. The Relexification Hypothesis

At this point, we are in a position to evaluate Lefebvre (1998), who has argued that her proposed Relexificationist Hypothesis explains the difference between creoles and their lexifiers better than my own (Lefebvre 2001). She argues that Haitian Creole arose through the replacement of Fongbe lexical and grammatical items with French phonetic strings.

This is a welcome attempt to cast creolist transfer arguments in a precise, falsifiable, and theoretically informed fashion. However, Lefebvre's fundamental assumptions instantiate a general frame of reference among some creolists which will be useful to address, as it has created considerable misunderstandings between scholars and touches on the very importance of creole studies to the larger field of linguistics. As such, in this section I show that my findings raise serious questions as to the ultimate validity of the relexificationist model as Lefebvre presents it.

To make my case, I begin with a list of Fongbe-Haitian comparisons analogous to the Fongbe-Saramaccan one in 7.1:

1.  Fongbe has two phonological tones and three phonetic (including two contour tones); Haitian is not a tonal language.
2.  Fongbe has two overt case markers; Haitian has equivalents of neither.
3.  Fongbe has a logophoric pronoun; Haitian does not.
4.  Fongbe has syntactic clitic pronominal forms alongside the full forms, some not phonetically identifiable with the full forms and making a case distinction in the singular. Like Saramaccan, Haitian has phonological clitics alongside full forms, but all are phonologically identifi-

able with them, and Haitian has *no* pronominal case distinction (Lefebvre 1998: 148–55).

5. Fongbe has two pragmatic negators marking especially insistent denial: *kùn* (Lefebvre and Brousseau 2002: 122–23) and *ó* (Lefebvre 1998: 215–16); Haitian has one (ibid.).

6. Fongbe has a complementizer *bó* used in purposive sentences where the clauses share a subject; Haitian has no equivalent item.

These observations alone do not constitute a refutation of Lefebvre's hypothesis: she fully acknowledges that Haitian has not incorporated the totality of Fongbe grammar. However, her explanations for the exceptions fall into five main types, and all of them either fail to account for the facts outside of Haitian—fatal for a model proposed as applying to creole genesis in general—or are speculative to the point of unfalsifiability. I will treat them sequentially.

## 8.1. Absence of lexifier parallels does not block transfer

Lefebvre stipulates that transfer was blocked when French provided no item readily identifiable with a Fongbe one that could provide a source for relexification. This would explain, then, why Haitian has no postposed negator clitic, as in:

(81)  Kɔkú xɔ  àsɔ́n lé  ǎ.
       Koku buy crab PL NEG
       "It is not the case that Koku bought the crabs." (Lefebvre and Brousseau 2002: 128)

*Pas* was already recruited as the general negator, presumably leaving no French item available that parallels the Fongbe *ǎ* in behavior (ibid. 216).

But quite often in creoles, where the lexifier offered no equivalent to an item, creators simply borrowed the item from the substrate wholesale along with its phonetic form. This was hardly confined to notorious cases such as Berbice Dutch's ample borrowings of Eastern Ijo morphology and functional items.

For example, English offers no ready model for Fongbe's contrastive focus marker, but, despite this, Saramaccan just borrowed the Fongbe item complete with even specifics of its behavior, such as conditioned omission of the copula:

Fongbe:

(82)  Masè vì   lé  **wè** wá.
       Massé child PL FOC arrive
       "It is the people of Massé who have arrived." (Hounkpatin 1985: 218, from Lefebvre and Brousseau 2002: 134)

Saramaccan:

(83)  Mí **we** tá  fá  ku  ju.
       I   FOC PROG talk with you
       "It is me talking to you."

Fongbe:

(84)  Àtín **wè**.
      tree FOC
      "It's a *tree*." (ibid. 186)

Saramaccan:

(85)  Páu **wɛ**.
      tree FOC
      "It's a *tree*."

Similarly, Guinea-Bissau Portuguese Creole borrowed a Manjaku suffix to en-code the causative, Philippines Spanish Creole varieties borrow a substrate valence prefix *man-* to mark verbhood on non-Spanish etyma, and so on. For every case where Lefebvre supposes that the absence of a French source was why Haitian Creole lacks a Fongbe construction, cross-creole data raises the question as to why Haitian did not simply borrow the Fongbe form. For example, Lefebvre (1998: 148) claims that Fongbe's logophoric pronoun *émì* was not relexified because it has no independent meaning and requires context for interpretation. But the same could be said of Fongbe's *wè*: why couldn't *émì* be simply borrowed itself if French offered no model?

Then there are cases where French *did* offer obvious sources for transfer of a Fongbe source, and yet the feature was *not* incorporated into Haitian. Lefebvre does not address the change-of-location marking in Fongbe, but French obviously offers sources for the relexification of the lexical items *throw* and *put*. Yet Haitian has no usage of *jeter* or *mettre* along the lines of Saramaccan's *túwɛ* and *butá*. If a lexifier source was so readily available, why did Haitian's creators ignore them?

8.2. "What you see is not always what you get"

Lefebvre (1998: 203–5, 2001: 201–2) also proposes that a major reason that creoles appear "simpler" than older languages is that they incorporate source language features in null form. The two examples she gives are the presumed null expression of case markers in possessive constructions and the null expression of Fongbe's nominal op-erator (glossed as OP) in relative or factive clauses. She justifies the latter on the basis that, just as Fongbe's item reveals its nominal nature in being unable to co-index PPs:

(86)  *Távò jí **ɖěè** Bàyí súsú 5     víví    nú mi.
      table on OP Bayi wipe DET please for me
      "It made me happy that Bayi wiped the table." (Lefebvre 1998: 203–4)

Haitian's PPs cannot pied-pipe, because a presumed null nominal operator parallels the Fongbe item:

(87)  *Fiy ak **li**₁ u    sòti    *t*₁ a
      girl with her you go-out DEF
      "The girl you went out with"

This positing of null forms is deft, but we wonder whether analysts of Haitian grammar unconcerned with its roots in Fongbe would be likely to have proposed these forms. The question looms as to whether a significant body of researchers on the creole would concur that there is substantial grammar-internal justification for these assorted "un-spelled-out" items.

But even if they would, a great many more examples would be required before we could conclude that my argumentation has been formally refuted by the idea that in creoles, as Lefebvre titles her response to the article that chapter 2 is derived from, "What you see is not always what you get." Our question must be whether Lefebvre could present principled, theory-driven evidence that in Haitian Creole, reduplication, tense-sensitive subordination markers, a distinction between inalienable and alienable possession, markers of change-of-location, propositional negation, contrastive focus, and a same-subject complementizer were simply "unlabeled." (Obviously such an endeavor would be especially difficult regarding tones and their sandhi processes.)

While my hypothesis is constructed to be falsifiable, it does not turn on a simple binary opposition between "simple" and "not simple." Because creoles are not, after all, maximally simple, as a constructive address of its data set my hypothesis is necessarily founded on degree. As such, to refute it on the basis of hypothesized null representations would require not just one or two examples but an address of, at least, most of the cases I have adduced. By my understanding of modern syntactic theory, such an attempt would almost certainly result in a distinctly ad hoc exercise. This is especially so given that we seek a cross-creole validity: for example, if Haitians mark Fongbe's two case markers with null forms, then what explains that Saramaccan marks both of them overtly, except with one form (*fu*)?

And even if it could be shown that creole languages expressed an unusual weight of syntactic and semantic distinctions in null form, then this would qualify as support for my basic thesis that creole grammars are synchronically identifiable—unless an older language were presented in which syntactic analysis could *rigorously demonstrate* an *equivalent* weight of demonstrably underlying but phonetically unlabeled items.

## 8.3. Lexifier differences and creole differences

Lefebvre (2001: 203) acknowledges that Fongbe did not "translate" into creoles in the same way in all instances. She proposes that discrepancies such as those between Saramaccans' and Haitians' "relexifications" of the same language will result from differing properties between lexifiers, based on two demonstrations referring to the definite determiner and reflexive *self*. But the question is, again, whether this kind of explanation has *general* application, especially given that her arguments here do not take into account that creoles often reproduce substrate features via radical reinterpretation and resyntacticization of lexifier items, regardless of lexifier syntactic structure.

I am skeptical that there are available feature-based or syntax-internal accounts to explain why a Fongbe contrastive focus marker is more inherently compatible with English grammar than French; why postposed spatial nominals or change-of-location-marking serial constructions are more predictive of a contact encounter with English rather than French; or why English temporal subordination led Fongbe speakers to create a tense/aspect-sensitive extension of their native version of this area while French temporal subordination prevented them from retaining anything but a hint of their native system (to such a minor degree that this area of grammar is not even covered in Lefebvre 1998), and so on.

Short of more extended justification—which would be vital to a refutation of a thesis based on degree rather than binary alternations—we cannot consider this explanation to have been constructively argued to date.

## 8.4. Dialect leveling

With other Fongbe-Haitian discrepancies, Lefebvre guesses that a Fongbe relexification competed with one based on another Gbe variety with a different structure, with the latter winning. An example is Haitian's lack of a distinct habitual marker, which parallels Ewe rather than Fongbe (Lefebvre 1998: 139). However, the hypothesis runs into unfalsifiability here, as there is no metric given (or, likely, possible) for determining when or why Ewe would have "won out" in this way.

It would be one thing if Lefebvre were addressing the *presence* of cross-linguistically idiosyncratic features. But since, for example, so many older languages (and creoles) lack distinct habitual markers, Ewe's lack of one does not qualify as a trait so idiosyncratic as to virtually force a transfer account (as does its homonymy mentioned in note 5 between the third-person singular pronoun and the word for *then* and the same trait in Saramaccan). One cannot help but sense this as a band-aid approach to recalcitrant data, and this explanation must be judged as a particularly weak link in Lefebvre's argumentation.

## 8.5. Speculations

In other instances Lefebvre must venture unsupported guesses, such as that Haitian lacks Fongbe's syntactic clitic forms because either perhaps Fongbe did not have syntactic clitics in the seventeenth century (Lefebvre 1998: 155), or that Haitian's creators "could not deduce the availability of syntactic clitics" (157). But this only leads to the question as to why Fongbe speakers in Surinam created creoles with clitic paradigms that are more similar to their native language's, including phonetically distinct forms and case distinctions. In Palenquero Spanish Creole, the creators simply borrowed many of Kikongo's subject-marking verb inflections as clitics, as Schwegler (1998: 258–60) demonstrates. By the tests adduced for Haitian clitics in, for example, Déprez (1992), these Palenquero clitics are syntactic rather than phonological. Thus a relexification theory cannot be built on an assumption that imperceptibility of the lexifier's syntactic pronominal clitics must result in a creole without them: Lefebvre's theory cannot account for why Palenquero's creators resorted to native items instead.

Later, Lefebvre attributes Haitian's absence of Fongbe's *say*-derived complementizer to an original relexification of this feature having been "abandoned," but with neither reference to historical documentation nor a systematic explanation as to why this would have occurred when it did not in so very many creoles based on other lexifiers (186–87).

## 8.6. The dangers of "syntactocentrism"

Much of the difference in approach between myself and Lefebvre (as well as DeGraff) stems from a basic philosophical contrast. Both of these scholars' approach to creole genesis is "syntactocentric," in the terminology of Jackendoff (2002). Both parse creole genesis as an essentially syntactic process of a "structure-preserving" nature, as it were—mere "shufflings of the deck" that leave an original syntax qualitatively unchanged. For DeGraff, this means that creoles' differences from their lexifiers result from the same predictable changes that occur when any language loses its inflections over time, modified beyond this by the shaving away of constructions encountered relatively rarely by the acquirer. For Lefebvre, creole genesis merely replaces the phonetic forms of a morphology and syntax that is otherwise transmitted essentially intact.

These authors' attempts to integrate creole studies and modern syntactic theory are welcome. However, their perspective is also informed by an assumption that syntax will be "the main course" in a theory of language, with other modules of grammar incidental (e.g., the assumption in Chomskyan syntax that the generation of grammar begins with the lexicon encountering syntax and with semantics and phonology "plugged in" afterward). Jackendoff cogently argues that this kind of "syntactocentrism," a legacy of the Chomskyan revolution, is extremely problematic as a method of addressing the full range of what natural language actually is. In that vein, the problem with syntactocentrism in creole genesis theory is that the difference between creoles and their source languages extends far beyond syntactic structures.

### 8.6.1. Core versus periphery

Much of this issue hinges on the "core/periphery" distinction, addressed in Chomskyan theory more in the 1960s and 1970s than it is today, such that my thesis would perhaps have been more intuitively coherent to syntacticians working then.

The theoretical syntactician explores Universal Grammar: what all natural languages have in common. Under this framework, grammatical constructions are of interest to the extent that they overtly instantiate the particular syntactic and semantic distinctions considered central to Universal Grammar: wh-movement, anaphors, unergative versus unaccusative, and so on.

But natural language consists of a great deal beyond Universal Grammar; any grammar contains a considerable weight of features that are compatible with Universal Grammar but incidental to it. Appropriately, this realm—which includes features we have seen above, like logophoricity, emphatic negation, same-subject purposive complementizers, noncompositionality, et cetera—is usually of little interest to the syntactician. Such things can appear mere "peripheral" variations, compatible with Universal Grammar but of little or no import to its investigation. As such, the presence of such features in one grammar as opposed to their absence in another naturally appears inconsequential.

"Peripheral" to Universal Grammar though it is, this realm happens to contain much of what distinguishes old from new grammars. These are the facts that our data set presents us with, regardless of what subset of that data has happened to attract the most interest over the past few decades from grammarians working in a tradition notoriously unconcerned with developmental and evolutionary issues. Hence it follows naturally that a theory attempting to account for the difference between creoles and older languages will dwell considerably in the areas most generative grammarians would consider "peripheral" and will be couched in terms more familiar to the typologist than the generative linguist.

This creates, however, a possibility of miscommunication across lines of theoretical tradition. As a theoretical syntactician whose work focuses on synchronic analysis of two grammars (French and Haitian Creole) within the Principles and Parameters tradition, DeGraff (2001: 267), for instance, understandably sees my formulation of complexity as "coarse." While I can hardly claim that it is anywhere near perfect, DeGraff's charge exemplifies a sense in some of the responses to my theory in the *Linguistic Typology* issue devoted to it and beyond that a formulation of creole genesis is formally incomplete unless it is couched in the terms of the generative frameworks of the moment.

I must make clear, then, that although my hypothesis will be refined in the future, this will not be in the direction of casting my ideas according to the tenets of Distributed Morphology, Minimalist Checking Theory, Optimality Theory, et cetera (although see Bresnan 2000 for the latter as applied to pidginization). This is neither because I consider these theories invalid nor that I lack familiarity with them (viz. chapter 12), but because in terms of the phenomena that my hypothesis addresses, these frameworks are, quite literally, too "coarse" to capture the generalizations I consider vital.

### 8.6.2. Object lessons

This point is so important, and has caused such a great deal of misunderstanding, that I will illustrate it with several examples.

*Propositional negation.* An example: Lefebvre (1998: 216) must suppose that Haitian failed to "relexify" Fongbe's propositional negator *ǎ* because French offered no model. But besides that, again, absence of such models did not prevent Saramaccan from calquing various Fongbe features, Lefebvre even argues that Haitian *does* maintain the syntactic configuration that would allow a slot for *ǎ* (214–16). Syntax alone, then, cannot explain this omission. Cases like this require a different explanation, and that is what I attempt to provide in stressing the role of simplification in creole genesis above and beyond syntactic configurations.

*"Serialization."* Lefebvre's model draws parallels between Fongbe and Haitian serial constructions and their behavior. But addressing the transfer of the general feature of "serialization" and its associated binary parameters alone (355–74) misses a larger point: that serialization is less central to Haitian grammar than Fongbe's.

For one, Haitian does not incorporate the noncompositional serial combinations outlined in section 4.2 any more than Saramaccan does (Lefebvre 1998: 278–86), even though the lexical items themselves were obviously available in French. That is, Lefebvre's model cannot explain why Haitian Creole does not have, say, *fè gen* (< *faire avoir*) for "repair," nor does she address this issue.

A model stipulating that pidginized varieties strip away source languages' non-compositionality and that this only reemerges over millennia explains much of Haitian's (and Saramaccan's) selective transfer of "serialization" from Fongbe. A framework designed to address the simple existence of "serialization" writ large yields fruitful analyses for generative syntacticians, but it cannot, in the formal sense, address or shed light on these cross-creole comparative discrepancies.

*Reduplication.* Lefebvre claims that Haitian lacks Fongbe's grammatical uses of reduplication because its grammar requires morphological heads in derived constructions to be the rightmost constituent. She claims that this explains why, although Fongbe has a diminutive suffix (*-vi*), Haitian instead has a preposed *ti-* derived from the adjective *petit,* allowing the root, as the head of the diminutive construction (by the definition of Di Sciullo and Williams 1987), to be rightmost. Along the same lines, then, since reduplication would entail a construction-initial head (the reduplicated prefix), it was presumably blocked from Haitian.

But then Saramaccan grammar could be argued to have the same constraint (although it does not have as many derivational affixes to demonstrate it). Like Haitian, Saramaccan has an agentive suffix—this being a morphological head—but also eschews Fongbe's diminutive suffix in favor of preposing the lexical item for *small, piki.* But then, it has the Fongbe-modeled reduplication anyway. Di Sciullo and Williams's and similar analyses cannot explain this.

*Postposed nominals.* Lefebvre (1998: 388) proposes that Haitian major-category lexical items follow French word order as a rule, with only minor-category items following Fongbe order, noting that Haitian's prepositions, a major category, precede the noun as in French, while its determiner *la,* a minor category, follows the noun as in Fongbe. Saramaccan exhibits this tendency to an extent: adjectives precede nouns despite following them in Fongbe, and nominal quantifiers precede the head despite following them in Fongbe.

But Saramaccan postposes a paradigm of nominals—a major category—to encode spatial concepts:

(88)  Dí  búku dé  a    táfa líba.
      DEF book COP LOC table top
      "The book is on the table."

This is calqued on Fongbe:

(89)  Wéma ɔ́   dɔ́   távò jí.
      book DEF be.at table top
      "The book is on the table." (Lefebvre and Brousseau 2002: 325)

But then, Saramaccan's definite nominal determiner precedes the noun English-style (*dí búku*) despite being a minor-category lexical entry under Lefebvre's analysis.

Lefebvre's hypothesis cannot explain why Saramaccan flouts the generalization she stipulates despite Fongbe's impact on Saramaccan's grammar even being *heavier* than that upon Haitian. Quite simply, the syntactic insight that distinguishes major from minor categories cannot help us here.

### 8.6.3. Why did Fongbe come out differently in Saramaccan than in Haitian?

There is a question remaining from my presentation. A thesis that creoles eschew the more complex aspects of their source languages leaves unaddressed just why Saramaccan nevertheless did incorporate so many Fongbe features that Haitian did not. The answer to this question reveals yet another instance where syntactocentric conceptions cannot explain our dataset.

Creolization, like complexification, is a clinal phenomenon. Haitian, like all of the French plantation creoles, is demonstrably closer to its lexifier than Saramaccan is to English. In French-based plantation creoles, there are contrasts such as the following with "radical creoles" like the Surinam and Gulf of Guinea Portuguese ones, in terms of incorporation of West African traits versus lexifier ones:

1. Little tendency toward CV phonotactics
2. No coarticulated or prenasalized stops
3. No phonological or morphosyntactic tone
4. Much less reduplication (Parkvall 2003)
5. Relatively little reanalysis of superstrate lexical items as grammatical (along the lines of the reanalysis of *there* as an imperfective marker in Sranan and Ndjuka)
6. Verb serialization is possible with fewer verbs and is less grammaticalized
7. Robust retention of lexifier derivational morphology
8. Reflections of French's inflectional distinction of infinitive and participle from finite verbs in a distinction between "short" and "long" verb forms

This instantiates a general observation among scholars (often with no commitment to the Prototype Hypothesis or my complexity metric) that there exists no French plantation creole as removed from French as there exist creoles removed from English or Portuguese (Muysken 1994, Alleyne 1998, Parkvall 1999). The contrasts that have led so many to this observation are neither random nor accidental. Haitian lacks features such as Fongbe's *wɛ̀* contrastive focus marker, the *throw-* and *put*-marked path satellites, a *say*-derived complementizer, morphosyntactic-marking reduplication, and postposed nominals instead of prepositions because these features depart so sharply from the Indo-European template: in other words, because they are so "un-French."

French-based plantation creoles' sociohistory neatly explains this hewing toward the lexifier. All of these languages emerged and jelled in colonies where French continued to be spoken diglossically with the creole. Certainly relatively few creole speakers had substantial command of French itself but "high" varieties in a diglossia regularly have profound impact on "low" ones even when bilingualism is limited to a small elite, as the Norman French impact on English demonstrates among myriad other cases. The Surinam creoles, the Melanesian English ones like Tok Pisin, and the Gulf of Guinea Portuguese ones have developed largely in isolation from their lexifiers. The context in which Saramaccan developed conditioned a much lesser impulse to eschew "un-English" features that Fongbe presented than did a colony where French ruled as the dominant language. There is no French creole that emerged among maroons, or under the rule of non-Francophones, or in a location such as a sparsely populated island, dense forest, or remote village where native French speakers were virtually nonexistent (although some, after jelling as natural languages, have lived on in contexts where English later replaced French and became an adstrate, such as Trinidadian or St. Lucian Creole French).

Here, then, we face another fundamentally clinal phenomenon that will not submit to the generative paradigm focusing on binary alternations. Just as my conception of complexity is necessarily relative, creoles depart from their lexifiers to a gradient degree. To the theoretical syntactician, creoles' varying degrees of distance from their lexifiers may appear a "squishy," perhaps "social" concept irrelevant to syntax-internal analysis. DeGraff (2001) gives this conception but an appendix's attention and just to the derivation point, while Lefebvre has never, to my knowledge, addressed it in her work.

But to acknowledge the reality of this gradience hardly exempts the analyst from theoretical rigor. For example, morphological theory predicts that a creole closer to its lexifier would retain its derivational rather than its inflectional morphology, since derivation is ascribed under most analyses to the lexicon, an aspect of the lexifier that creoles obviously retain a great deal of (cf. chapter 1). To wit, a gradience-informed creole genesis model predicts that along the cline of degree of pidginization, inflection will fall out before derivation, derivation being retained with the lexicon. And this prediction is borne out: there exists no creole retaining lexifier inflections without its derivational morphemes. This is one more demonstration that creoles are natural languages and that creole genesis is constrained by the same grammatical fundamentals that all natural languages are (it is a typological fundamental that languages with inflection but no derivation do not exist [Greenberg 1966a]).

Importantly, however, a creole genesis theory that neglects this gradience leaves the Saramaccan-Haitian discrepancies as loose screws. I believe that this would be inevitable of a theory couched in the frameworks of generative morphosyntax.

Thus, I believe that a theory based on degree of overspecification, while of little interest to the theoretical syntactician, has the advantage of explaining the path from lexifier to creole more specifically and falsifiably than could any framework focused on identifying a single, optimally generalized human grammar whose surface manifestations are distinguished by a small number of alternate parameter settings.

As such, I would hope that evaluators of my hypothesis, whatever their ultimate assessment, might avoid a background assumption that the "theoretical" approach to such a question will *necessarily* turn on phenomena such as Merge, head movement, LF, empty operators, DP, and so on, and that short of this, no substantial argument can logically have been made. These phenomena are eminently useful in the investigation of certain aspects of natural language. But modern syntactic theory simply *cannot* capture the entire picture that is of interest under my hypothesis.


8.7. Stacking the deck?

Once again, my argumentation could be invalidated if I were neglecting a collection of features whose Haitian manifestations are more complex than Fongbe's. However, just as with Saramaccan, I am unaware of a set of such features of any substantiality.

As it happens, DeGraff (2001: 284–85) has presented a list of general "complexities" in Haitian. Yet when we compare these features to Fongbe equivalents, we see the same obvious difference in overspecification that we have seen throughout this chapter (Fongbe data from Lefebvre and Brousseau 2002; Haitian from DeGraff 2001):

1. H: Nasalized and non-nasalized vowels occur in some contexts in free variation; there is regressive nasalization within stems and progressive nasalization across morpheme boundaries.

   F: Underlying nasal phonemes [ẽ] and [õ] are obligatorily lowered to their lax counterparts [ɛ̃] and [ɔ̃] on the surface (15–16); nasal vowels regressively either nasalize certain consonants (/w̃ãlã́/ > [w̃ãlã́] "to write") or condition segment-level changes in certain consonants (/bɔ̃/ → [mɔ̃́]) (27); regressive nasalization occurs in the particular contexts of reduplication and with the derivational suffix -ṽi (28).

2. H: "A set of personal pronouns with morphophonologically and syntactically conditioned clitic variants."[8]

   F: (See 7.1.)

3. H: The postnominal determiner has four morphophonologically conditioned allomorphs.

   F: The postnominal determiner has two morphophonologically conditioned allomorphs (37).

4. H: The prenominal determiner (presumably the indefinite) has four morphophonologically conditioned allomorphs.

   F: The indefinite determiner does not vary allomorphically (39–40).

5. H: "Demonstrative, definite, and plural-marking markers that are head-final in a language that's otherwise robustly head-initial."

   F: Fongbe also exhibits heterogenous headedness, although with fewer head-initial features than Haitian (cf. Lefebvre and Brousseau 2002: 5).

6. H: "Head-final definite articles alongside head-initial indefinite articles."

   F: This is not true of Fongbe given its leaning more toward the head-final pole than Haitian as mentioned above—but as such, DeGraff's listing it is merely a recapitulation of the above point.

7. H: Predicate clefting with copy left in situ, and predicate clefting with a nonverbal pro-predicate (ye, usually treated as a copula) left in situ.

   F: Fongbe has both strategies, the latter with wɛ̀ as the pro-predicate.

8. H: Certain bare nominals can either cleft with copy or leave ye; the former cases are neutral as to individual- or stage-level interpretation, while the latter forces an individual-level interpretation.

   F: Only stage-level (dynamic) predicates cleft with copy with neutral interpretation; clefted individual-level (stative) predicates are only grammatical as causal or factive protases, while temporal adverbial protases are only grammatical with stage-level predicates at all (509–11).

9.  H:  Predicate clefting with copy forms "various adjunct clauses."

    F:  (As described in (7) and (8) for Fongbe.)

10. H:  "Three strategies for the formation of causal clauses, each of which uses some distinct CP-related position—one of these strategies also uses the predicate clefting-cum-doubling pattern."

    F:  Fongbe has four causal constructions, each of which uses a completely distinct position in the syntax: (1) a predicate cleft strategy, (2) a strategy with a complementizer, (3) a strategy using a paratactic clause with the verb *zɔ́n* "to cause," and (4) a satellite with the meaning "cause" (*wútú*) (168–70).[9]

11. H:  "A resumptive pronoun that surfaces in the small-clause subject position of DP(-like) predicates."

        DeGraff refers here to the fact that *se,* often described as a copula, appears before determined constituents (*Malis se yon doktè / doktè a* "Malis is a doctor / the doctor") but not before APs, PPs, or NPs (**Malis se malad* "Malis is sick," **Malis se anba tab la* "Malis is under the table," *??Malis se abitan* "Malis is a peasant") (DeGraff 1993: 81).

        He analyzes this as due to a language-general trait where subjects are generated within small clauses and move to Spec of IP to get Case. For theoretical reasons internal to Government-Binding theory, when subjects move from AP, PP, and NP, the trace left behind is governed, but DPs involve an extra bar level, such that the trace left behind can only be governed if spelled out the result is *se* (ibid. 83–84).

    F:  In the strict sense, this Haitian feature, if simply "falling out of" Universal Grammar, does not qualify in any sense as "over-specified." However, for these purposes it is useful to note that in Fongbe the appearance of resumptive pronominals can be conditioned by type of maximal projection as well.

        In cleft constructions, a resumptive pronoun must be left behind from RelP and PP but not VP (332–36). To the extent that Lefebvre and Brousseau do not stipulate this as an epiphe-nomenon of Universal Grammar, it is an arbitrary rule which qualifies as an overspecification: a trait that does not follow from Universal Grammar but must simply be learned separately.

12. H:  "A [morphophonologically and syntactically conditioned] rule of apocope that applies to a subset of verbs with short and long variants."

    F:  DeGraff here refers to the only feature of Haitian Creole that might possibly submit to analysis as inflectional. In the same vein, many Fongbe nouns have a nonproductive prefix *à-* or *ò-*, apparently a vestige of earlier noun class marking, whose appearance is sensitive to syntax, obliged to be deleted in inalienable possessive constructions and compounds.

Like many analysts, DeGraff misinterprets my thesis as claiming that creoles are "simple." However, his list of "complex" features in Haitian does not refute my argumentation. Since I have made no claim that creoles do not contain complexities, we can be sure that such a list could be composed for any natural language. Rather, my claim is that creoles are *less* complex than older languages—and considerably so.

And in that vein, it is clear that Fongbe is more overspecified than Haitian Creole. Certainly there are a few instances where Haitian is the more complex: serendipity—or more precisely that Haitian is a natural language and has existed for three centuries—makes this unremarkable. But in the majority of cases, Fongbe at least equals and usually surpasses Haitian.

Point (1) above, for example, is one of many possible ones which would show that Fongbe has a deeper phonology than Haitian's, conditioning segmental changes in surface manifestations absent in Haitian. This is also true of Fongbe in comparison to Saramaccan: in the former, LH and H tones are in complementary distribution, with LH only occurring after voiced consonants and sonorants (Lefebvre and Brousseau 2002: 21); see also the voicing-conditioned tone rules described for reduplication in section 4.1. Crucially, phonologists describe the distance between one language's phonemic and phonetic levels as longer than in another's with little controversy, treating certain languages as having "more phonology" than others. It is only in syntax that, suddenly, distinctions in complexity become "controversial" and are often rejected as based on an illusory epistemology. I am not aware of a principled explanation in print as to the logical foundation of this contrast. It may be that phonologists go wrong somewhere in their sense that depth of phonology varies from language to language. However, it may just as well be that syntacticians' chariness of any equivalent gradation in the module they study is based less on empiricism than on tradition.[10]

Then on top of the set of features DeGraff presents, in our final assessment of the case we must consider the features listed earlier in this section, as well as those discussed throughout this chapter. Table 4.1 illustrates the nature of the contrast I refer to. In reference to the ever-present possibility that a table like this is misrepresentative, it must be noted that it includes the very features that DeGraff proposes as Haitian's *demonstration cases* of complexity.


## 8.8. Summation

Lefebvre's Relexificationist hypothesis as argued to date cannot explain differences between Fongbe and the creoles based on it. In earlier work (e.g., McWhorter 1997a), I argued pointedly for a substratist analysis of Saramaccan and, by extension, other creoles. Even then, however, I found that this framework could only take one so far in the explanatory sense, and that creole copulas, for instance, revealed that simplification played as central a role in creole genesis as transfer. My later work has been designed to address exactly the subset of creole grammars that does not yield gracefully to a substratist analysis.

Relexification operated, indeed, but within the context of a larger "filter." The plantation context led creole creators to build new languages from rudimentary pidgin-level competence. These new languages were based on a robust but *partial* relexification of their substrate languages. The main factor in determining which substrate features were transferred was a cline of necessity to communication that

TABLE 4.1. Overspecification and complexification in Fongbe and Haitian

| | Fongbe | Haitian |
|---|---|---|
| Grammatical reduplication | ■ | |
| Noncompositional serials | ■ | |
| Tone sandhi | ■ | |
| Tense-sensitive subordinators | ■ | |
| Change-of-location markers | ■ | |
| Inalienable possession | ■ | |
| Propositional negator | ■ | |
| Contrastive focus marker | ■ | |
| Tones | ■ | |
| Case markers | ■ | |
| Logophoric pronoun | ■ | |
| Distinct/case-marked clitics | ■ | |
| More emphatic negators | ■ | |
| Same-subject complementizer | ■ | |
| More context-specific nasalization | ■ | |
| Phonetically deeper nasal assimilation | ■ | |
| More determiner allomorphy | | ■ |
| Head ordering heterogeneity | | ■ |
| More clefting constructions | ■ | |
| More semantic correlates of clefting | ■ | |
| More causal constructions | ■ | |
| Arbitrary appearance of resumptives | ■ | ■ |
| Conditioned apocope of marginal affixes | ■ | ■ |

Note: A shaded box means that the language surpasses the other one in the indicated trait.

linguistic features fall upon. The density of useless redundancies and overspecifications typical of older grammars is strictly the product of millennia of gradual drift. The weight of such features is not sought out when humans build new languages, and the result reveals itself in tables such as the one here.

What demonstrates this is, to bring our argument full circle, (1) that the only grammars in the world with so little of this kind of "ornament" are new ones, and (2) that attempts to shoehorn this contrast into the broad-level binary alternations of theoretical syntax fail as coherent theory.

## 9. "The data aren't all in"

Arends (2001) claims that "not all creoles adduced by McWhorter as cases of grammatical simplicity have been described in sufficient detail to allow such a far-reaching claim." It is true that decades ago, theories about creole genesis were often proposed on the basis of preliminary grammatical studies. However, today creolists have access to four decades' worth of grammars and countless articles on dozens of creoles. Ideally we would like even more studies, and a great deal remains underexplored. But the claim that creole theorists have but random shards of data to work with is today anachronistic.

Besides, the tacit notion that theoretical hypotheses about creole genesis are hubristic until detailed grammars and dictionaries are available for all or even most creoles in existence presumes that scientific investigation must proceed with a full dataset. But this is not how any scientific endeavor proceeds.

Arends's position would also seem to imply that creoles are the world's only languages where complexity of the sort I address will remain obscure to all but the most sustained of investigations. But if this were true, it would only support my claim that creoles are synchronically distinct. The morphologized distinction of imperfective and perfective in verbs is apparent on the first encounter with a Slavic language. One immediately perceives the consonant mutations in a West Atlantic language like Fula. Even the few languages with neither inflection nor tone quickly reveal complexities of a similar order, such as Polynesian languages' division of possessive marking between the "o" and "a" classes. Creoles do not reveal overspecifications of this sort and degree upon initial investigation. This alone reveals a trait apparently unique to creole languages, speaking against claims that to taxonomically distinguish creoles from older languages is empirically unsupportable a priori.

I have argued in this essay that, in addition, even closer examination of creoles reveals starkly less overspecification than that in older languages. Given that creoles are the world's newest languages, I propose that the explanation we seek hinges on the age of creoles' grammars. Surely my analysis is subject to criticism and revision, but I present it with the scholarly aim of attempting to forge a path from the descriptive to the explanatory. Slavicists, Africanists, and Austronesianists rue the holes in the data sets available to them as regularly as creolists. Yet these holes do not lead experts on these groups to dismiss summary statements as to what unites the languages they study as a class as hasty or suspect.

## 10. Conclusion

My goal in this chapter has been to show that my hypothesis that creole languages are less complex in the sense of overspecification—than older grammars, and that they manifest other traits that reveal their youth (such as a marked paucity of noncompositional combinations of morphemes) is demonstrable via a sustained comparison of a single creole grammar with its substrate language.

I must reiterate that my claim is not that creoles are "simple" languages. However, I hope that this stipulation does not give the appearance of rendering my hypothesis unfalsifiable. My theory can be falsified by the identification of an older grammar that could be shown to parallel a creole in degree of overspecification. Because creoles have emerged and developed in a wide range of sociohistorical contexts, the appropriate comparandum will specifically be a creole that:

1. is not one of the few that was a compromise between closely related languages (e.g., Sango, Kituba), since this allows the retention of a

considerable degree of overspecifications shared by the language
group, given their familiarity to most or all of the creators;
2. emerged in relative isolation from its lexifier; and
3. has not lived since in an intimately diglossic relationship with that
lexifier, since the latter leads to semi-creole varieties that incorporate
a great deal of their lexifier's inherited overspecifications.

Importantly, this stipulation leaves a robust number of creole languages as appro-
priate sources of comparison. Relevant ones include Sranan, Saramaccan, Ndjuka, Tok
Pisin, Bislama, Solomon Islands Pijin, Torres Strait "Broken," the Aboriginal Creole
English varieties, São Tomense Creole Portuguese, Principense Creole Portuguese,
Annobonese Creole Portuguese, Angolar Creole Portuguese, Negerhollands Creole
Dutch, Haitian Creole, French Guianese Creole, Antillean French Creole, Mauritian
Creole French, Seychellois Creole French,[11] Baba Malay, and Riau Indonesian.[12]
In the years since I first argued from this perspective, there have been assorted
arguments to the effect that a given creole contains a "complex" feature or even a
few. These presentations are quite interesting and thoroughly welcome. But as addresses of my thesis, they qualify as merely tangential. What has not been presented
at this writing is an older language with no history of sharply interrupted transmission that either conforms to my Creole Prototype or parallels creoles like Saramaccan
in degree of overspecification. I suggest that this gap in argumentation indicates that
my hypothesis is an empirically valid address of its data set.
There is an assumption in creole studies, tacit but powerful, that creolists' guiding task is to show that creoles are "real languages"—synchronically indistinguishable from any other language and symbolic of the self-preservation of their creators.
This *primum mobile* reveals itself, for example, in the unlikelihood of the "the data
aren't all in" objection being leveled at a hypothetical argument that creoles were
*more* complex than older languages.
This advocational mission motivated the focus on the structuredness of creole
continua in the 1970s, and the furor over substrate influence (of which I was a part)
from the 1980s into the 1990s. However, this goal alone is, first, long accomplished.
No trained linguist in our moment supposes that creoles are not "real languages,"
and scholarly consensus among creolists and beyond now readily affirms that creole
grammars were substantially shaped by those native to their creators. Second, this
sociopolitical goal is a rather simplistic and limiting watch cry for an entire subfield.
The lingering of this obsolete impulse narrows the scope of creolist investigation,
and deprives linguists outside of the field of any reason to find creoles interesting.
When Celticists, Algonquianists, and Sino-Tibetanists convene, it is not to remind
one another that the languages that they study are systematic and complex.
If there is to be a creole studies field treated as a branch of linguistics as opposed
to anthropology, then one of the responsibilities of the creolist is to illuminate what is
cross-linguistically distinct about the grammars of these languages as a class. Otherwise, the reason for the institutionalization of "creole studies" as a subdiscipline of linguistics, with its own conferences, anthologies, and journals, is decidedly unclear. We
risk fashioning ourselves into a rather postmodern extended joke, in which dozens of
scholars are dedicatedly engaged in the assassination of their very subfield.

# The Founder Principle versus
# the Creole Prototype

*Squaring Theory with Data*

## 1. Introduction

Before the official establishment of creole studies, some prominent thinkers treated creole languages as genetic offshoots of their lexifiers, for example, Haitian Creole as a kind of French rather than as a separate language (Hjelmslev 1938, Hall 1958). However, concentrated research starting in the late 1960s suggested otherwise. Bickerton (1981, 1984) identified creoles as the product of catastrophic breakdowns of lexifier grammar. Meanwhile, Alleyne (1980), Boretzky (1983), Holm (1988), and others called attention to the extensive role that substrate languages played in the development of these creoles after the breakdown Bickerton referred to. By the 1980s, a consensus had emerged that creoles were challenges to the Stammbaum model of language change, being genetic descendants neither of their lexifiers nor of the languages spoken natively by their originators. This perspective finds its hallmark exposition in Thomason and Kaufman (1988).

Various Francophone creolists, however, led by Chaudenson (1979, 1992), have long maintained a superstratist perspective, analyzing plantation creoles as varieties of their lexifiers, in whose history pidginization and substrate transfer have played minimal roles (cf. also Fournier 1987, Hazaël-Massieux 1993, Fattier 1995). Working in relative isolation from other creolists, this school had little influence on general creolist thought until the 1990s. However, Mufwene (1986a, 1991, 1992, 1994a, 1994b, 1997a) has adapted the Francophone superstratist framework and brought it to the general attention of the linguistic community. In each of a series of papers, he has treated a given topic as a springboard for the gradual development of a model called the "Founder Principle," summarily outlined in Mufwene (1996a).

The superstratist framework proceeds on a series of three novel interpretations of creoles and their history. The first is Chaudenson's observation that for their first several decades, plantation colonies were generally dominated not by large plantations but small farms, where African slaves were often outnumbered by indentured whites. Chaudenson proposes that because they had free access to the colonizers' language, *early plantation slaves spoke not creoles, but close approximations of the lexifier,* non-native competence leading to only relatively slight reduction.[1]

As small farms were converted to large plantations, African slave gangs were gradually expanded. Chaudenson supposes that as this influx mounted, new slaves gradually came to be exposed less to whites' native variety of the lexifier than to slaves' approximations thereof, this becoming their primary model. Developing an approximation of this approximation, these new slaves, in turn, served as a model for subsequently imported slaves. Under this scenario, plantation creoles were the end result of a series of such "approximations of approximations."

Crucially, Chaudenson does not consider this series of approximations to have resulted in a variety appreciably removed, in any taxonomic sense, from the lexifier. In particular, he claims that there was no break in transmission of the lexifier, merely a gradual "transformation" thereof. This eliminates any pidgin stage, which in most models constitutes a critical genetic discontinuation between lexifier and creole. This motivates the second keystone of the superstratist model, that not only did early slaves speak relatively close approximations of the lexifier, but *even creoles are simply varieties of their lexifiers* (Chaudenson 1979, 1992; Mufwene 1996a: 124).

To support this claim, superstratists have rightly criticized the tendency to compare creoles with standard varieties of their lexifiers, calling attention to the models for creole constructions in now-obscure regional dialects spoken by the white colonists. Scholars in this vein are highly chary of appeals to substrate influence. Mufwene (1990, 1994d) is slightly less absolute than Chaudenson; but has been consistently skeptical of most substratist arguments. Indeed, the "founders" referred to by the Founder Principle are in essence the whites, with substratal influence largely restricted to cases of convergence with the lexifier (Mufwene 1996a: 114–22).[2]

Taken alone, the above-mentioned two positions would merely indicate a healthy difference in perspective among creolists. The model is doubtless a useful check on the excesses of various schools of creolist thought. For instance, the Haitian Creole future construction *m pu ale* "I will go" appears less radical a departure from French when we recall that regional Frenches include the construction *je suis pour aller.* Similarly, overt habitual marking in Gullah English Creole (*ee blant si i brera* "she sees her brother" [Hancock 1987: 288]) is less plausibly treated as a calque on West African habitual markers when we note sentences like *'e do b'long smawken' cigars* in the English of Cornwall (Hancock 1994: 104). However, the superstratist model proposes a radical reconception of the frame of reference within which creole studies have been conducted over the past forty years.

In a third key assertion, Mufwene claims that *nothing distinguishes creoles from other varieties that have undergone extensive language contact,* such as Romanian, Yiddish, or Persian:

> The histories of the colonies in which creoles developed suggest that no language-development processes were involved that were unique to these new vernaculars, just the same ones assumed in historical linguistics, except for the emphasis on language contact. (Mufwene 1996a: 107)

> There is really no particular reason why the developments of creoles should not be treated as consequences of normal linguistic interactions in specific ecological conditions of linguistic contacts. (ibid. 121)

Crucial is the seemingly natural conclusion to which Chaudenson (1992: 135) and, most explicitly, Mufwene take the previous three interpretations.

The fourth keystone of the superstratist model is the assertion that *creole is not an empirically valid classificational term*, since nothing distinguishes the creole from other languages:

> Creoles do not form a valid structural language type. (Mufwene 1994b: 71)

> The current inadequate usage of the terms "pidgin" and "creole" as *type* names should apparently be discontinued. (Mufwene 1997a: 57)

> Il n'y a pas de critère formel qui définisse les créoles à part des langues non-créoles. (Mufwene 1986a: 143)

Thus in treating creoles as varieties of their lexifiers, modern superstratists, unlike Hjelmslev and Hall, do not intend a broadening of our conception of the lexifiers in order to incorporate creoles. On the contrary, under their conception, our conception of the lexifiers remains constant, because creoles are considered simply contact-heavy vernaculars, not an empirically valid class.[3]

Mufwene finally takes the superstratist framework to a further conclusion: that since creole is presumably a vacuous term, *one language cannot be more or less "creole" than another* (1994b: 71, 1997a: 59–60).

Few creolists have adopted the superstratist framework as wholeheartedly as Chaudenson, his French followers, and Mufwene. However, the idea that creoles did not arise from pidgins is increasingly influential, appealed to even in genesis models diametrically opposed to the superstratist one. Lefebvre (1993: 256), for example, considers the purported lack of historical relationship between pidgins and creoles to support her relexificationist model. Most important, however, the idea that creoles differ from their lexifiers only in having undergone ordinary processes of inflectional loss lightly mediated by second-language acquisition provides support for the increasing prevalence of creolist syntacticians' hypotheses that the difference between a creole grammar and its lexifier's results largely from language-wide parametrical alternations that hinge on presence of inflectional morphemes (Veenstra 1996: 145–48, 193; DeGraff 1999a, 1999b; Déprez 1999). Thus the superstratist model has been adapted to support the assertion that the very concept of "creole language" is a reification.

Here I will demonstrate that while the superstratist model increasingly recruited to support that assertion has clear intuitive appeal, the data themselves do not bear it out. I have argued in chapter 1 that creole is a synchronically definable typological class. In this chapter I will build on that claim by showing that, contrary to superstratist claims, this class is demonstrably the result of the pidginization of lexifier sources and that linguistic plausibility and historical documentation speak against the foundations of the superstratist model.

## 2. Examining the foundational tenets of the superstratist framework

As noted in the introduction, the French superstratist model and the Founder Principle hinge upon a series of assumptions leading to the conclusion that *creole* is not a valid empirical class of language, extended to an additional stipulation. To review, the line of reasoning is as follows:

1. Early plantation slaves spoke not creoles, but close approximations of the lexifier.
2. Even creoles are simply varieties of their lexifiers.
3. Nothing distinguishes creoles from other varieties that have undergone extensive language contact.
4. *Creole* is not an empirically valid classificational term.
5. One language cannot be more or less "creole" than another.

In this section, I will show that the first three assumptions, while increasingly influential in creolist thought, in fact do not stand up to the actual evidence, and finally that the refutation of the fourth contention (chapter 1) leaves the fifth unsupportable as well.

## 3. "Early plantation slaves spoke not creoles, but close approximations of the lexifier"

This seemingly neutral claim is in fact a key component in the superstratist denial of creole as a valid class. Most writers see the difference between creoles and their lexifiers as evidence of a break in transmission of the latter. This hypothetical nonnative approximation is a keystone topic of address in the superstratist depiction of creoles as a gradual, unbroken series of "transformations" of a lexifier.

Indeed, since whites and blacks worked side-by-side in equal number in the early decades of most plantation colonies, it is a natural deduction that early slaves would have developed not creoles but relatively full varieties of the lexifier and that creoles would only have developed later as slave importations increased. Plausibility is not always truth, however, and historical documentation roundly contradicts this reconstruction.

### 3.1. Martinique

For example, Martinique was colonized by the French in 1635, and white indentured servants and blacks worked in relatively equal number on small farms there well into the 1670s (Munford 1991: 505). For example, in 1664, 529 out of 684 farms had fewer than six slaves, and there were often fewer slaves than white family members (Chaudenson 1992: 95). According to the superstratist models, we would expect that slaves in Martinique at this time would have spoken non-native but relatively fully transmitted varieties of French.

This prediction is not borne out. In 1990, a text was discovered of unequivocal French Creole from 1671 (Carden, Goodman, Posner, and Stewart 1990). Superstratist work has continued in mysterious neglect of this text, for which reason I will cite a selection in its entirety:

(1)  Moi miré bête    qui  tini  Zyeux, tini   barbe, tini   mains, tini  Zépaules
      I     see  animal REL  have eyes    have beard  have hands  have shoulders

      tout comme homme, tini  cheveux et   barbe gris, noir   et   puis blanc,
      all   like     man     have hair      and beard gray black and then white

      moi na pas miré bas   li    parce   li  té    dans diau, li  sembe pourtant poisson.
      I    NEG   look under him because he ANT in    water he seem   however fish

      Moi té    tini  peur bete   là     manger monde. Li regardé plusieurs fois,
      I     ANT have fear animal DET eat      person he look    many     time

      li  allé devant     savanne, puis li caché li   dans diau, puis
      he go  in-front-of meadow then he hide  him in     water then

      moi pas   voir li    davantage.
      I    NEG see  him more
      "1 saw an animal that had eyes, had a beard, had hands, had shoulders just like a man, had hair and a beard that were gray, black, and white. I didn't see the bottom part of it because it was in the water; however, it looked like a fish. I was afraid the animal ate people. It looked several times, it went in front of the meadow (part of the island), then it hid itself in the water, then I didn't see it anymore."[4]

The text contains several shibboleths of Caribbean French Creole, such as fossilized determiners (*Zyeux, diau*), postposed determiner *là:* (*bete là*), bare reflexive pronoun (*li caché li*), postposed pronoun as possessive (*bas li*), and conventionalization of *té* as anterior marker (*moi té tini peur*). Furthermore, a variety this variety stabilized surely existed long before the text was recorded, in the 1660s at the latest.

This document is thus counterevidence to the claim that creoles were not spoken by early plantation slaves. To be sure, it is quite plausible that because access to whites' speech was rich on such small farms, slaves acquired relatively fully transmitted varieties of the lexifier alongside the creole. Indeed, other speakers recorded in the 1671 Martinique text speak varieties closer to French. However, the text is unequivocal demonstration of a creole already in slaves' repertoire even on small farms.

## 3.2. Suriname

If there were only one such case, we might dismiss it as a fluke. However, such cases are common. While Sranan English Creole has been the lingua franca of Suriname for over three centuries now, the English in fact controlled the colony for a mere six-teen years, from 1651 to 1667, when the Dutch took over. More to the point, it was the Dutch who established a thriving sugar plantation system there. Under the English, Suriname was firmly ensconced in what Chaudenson has termed the *société d'habitation* stage: Africans were primarily distributed among small plantations of twenty people each on average (Voorhoeve 1964: 234–36), where indentured servants were as nu-merous as Africans and worked alongside them (Rens 1953: 58–61).

The superstratist models predict that slaves at this point would have spoken a non-native but viable approximation of English rather than a creole. Records of Sranan do not begin until over fifty years after its founding, when large plantations were well established. Yet it can nevertheless be firmly deduced that Sranan had already developed on these small farms by 1667. First, an English-based creole is unlikely to have developed under Dutch hegemony, and since the Dutch took over Suriname in 1667, this automatically places the birth of Sranan before this. The second piece of evidence is Maroon Spirit Language of Jamaica, spoken under possession by de-scendants of escaped slaves. As it happens, Maroon Spirit Language and Sranan are varieties of the same creole (Smith 1987a: 92). Below is a sentence in both varieties:

(2)  a.  Maroon Spirit Language:
         Cha  in  go na  da bigi pre,  kya  in  go na  indi.
         carry him  go LOC the big  place carry· him  go LOC inside
         "Take him to that big place, put him inside." (Bilby 1992: 9)

     b.  Sranan:
         Tja  en  go na  a  bigi presi, tja  en  go na  mi.
         carry him  go LOC the big  place carry him  go LOC inside

The correspondences extend to vast lists of idiosyncratic departures from vowel harmony (e.g., both have *naki* for *knock, dagu* for *dog*), a battery of identical idio-syncratic grammaticalizations, and close similarities between the languages' para-digms of innovated interrogative markers (for details, see Smith 1987a: 98 and McWhorter 1996b: 4–6, 2000a: 83–86).

The presence of early Sranan in Jamaica is crucial to dating the emergence of Sranan, because slaves were brought to Jamaica from Suriname in 1671 (Bilby 1983: 60). Given that Maroon Spirit Language had already stabilized the above-mentioned departures from vowel harmony, grammaticalized items, and paradigm of interroga-tives, it is sure to have existed in Suriname long before 1671. However, in order to give the variety enough time to have gelled to such an extent, we are forced to place the birth of Sranan well back into the 1660s at the very least. To both do this and place the birth of the language on plantations, we would have to place its birth after the Dutch arrival in 1667, since only they established plantations. But the MSL sys-tem certainly needed more than a mere four years to develop, and this thus places the birth of Sranan in the English period, in the early 1660s or before, on their small farms.

The third indication that Sranan existed even long before 1667 comes from the history of its sister creole, Saramaccan. These two creoles correspond so intimately on all levels that there can be no doubt as to their common origin. The following sentence combines several idiosyncratic correspondences between them which, along with many others, are discussed in more detail in McWhorter (1996a: 463–70) and (2000a: 102–5):

(3)    Sranan:        Odi    granman ben  sabi  taki    mi ben  njan en ([ñam ẽ) noo?
       Saramaccan: Undí  gaamá   bi    sábi  táa    mi bi   njá̃  ẽ[ñam ẽ]) nɔ́ɔ?
              which chief        ANT know COMP I    ANT eat  it            then
              "Which chief knew that I ate it, then?"

*Odi* and *undí* stem from an original "which-this," part of an interrogative paradigm unknown in the Caribbean outside of the Suriname creoles and, significantly, Maroon Spirit Language.[5] The use of *taki* (> *táa* in Saramaccan) as complementizer and the conventionalization of *now* as "then" are similarly unique to Suriname creoles. Most striking is the epenthetic [m], which appears only between a closed class of verbs with a final nasalized vowel and a following phonetically brief vowel-initial item. The specific conditioning of this [m] varies slightly among the three main Suriname creoles (Voorhoeve 1985, Kouwenberg 1987, Huttar and Huttar 1994: 591–92), but its appearance is unknown outside Suriname. The list of other similar correspondences is vast, including specific interactions between copulas, adjectives, and reduplication (Winford 1997a: 291–95), idiosyncratic uses of copular items and oblique pronouns, and a number of highly particular choices of etymon in various grammatical functions.

It is significant, then, that Saramaccan ultimately traces back to the 1660s. While fundamentally an English-based creole, Saramaccan has a heavy Portuguese component in its lexicon. This resulted from the partial relexification of an early form of Sranan by Portuguese, when Portuguese planters who emigrated to Suriname bought Sranan-speaking slaves from the English in the 1660s and 1670s (Goodman 1987: 375–82, Smith 1987a).[6] Once again, a particular sociohistorical window reveals a historical "footprint" from Sranan. By 1675, the English, making way for the Dutch, had withdrawn all but fifty aged slaves from Suriname (Arends 1995a: 238). This means that for Sranan to have been brought to the Portuguese plantations, as the vast correspondences between Sranan and Saramaccan require to have happened, it must have been between the Dutch takeover in 1667 and before 1675, by which time almost all English slaves were gone or bought. It thus follows that Sranan already existed by this time.

Thus all evidence points to Sranan having already emerged in the 1660s, on small farms amid heavy black-white contact. Once again, the superstratist prediction that early slaves spoke close approximations of their lexifiers fails.

3.3. Other examples

Examples continue.

1. *Louisiana French Creole* is explicitly documented in the mid-1700s, at which time even the few large farms in the region had only twenty slaves, most slaveholders having only one or two: in other words, a classic *société d'habitation* (Klingler 1992: 56–57, Speedy 1995: 102).

2. *Palenquero Spanish Creole*, from a reading of all evidence, developed among slaves living in extensive and intimate contact with Spaniards (Böttcher 1995: 38–40). For one, the creole has been widely argued to have been based on a Portuguese pidgin or creole which the original slaves brought with them from São Tomé (Schwegler 1993: 670–71; McWhorter 1995a: 229–31, 2000a: 17–20), eliminating the possibility that they developed Palenquero from the ground up within the colony itself. Second, its speakers are documented to have spoken Spanish alongside the creole from an early date (Bickerton and Escalante 1970: 255, Schwegler 1996a: 26–28).

3. *Pitcairn Creole English* developed on a tiny island among nine English speakers and nineteen Polynesians.

4. *Hawaiian Creole English* was created by children who not only were surrounded by an indigenized but full variety of English and were even being educated in English as they created it (Roberts 2000).

In short, the historical record clearly shows that despite the initial plausibility of the idea that creoles would not have yet existed before blacks outnumbered whites in European overseas colonies, they in fact did.

At this writing, this question is a significant conundrum in creole studies and has been addressed in various ways. Hancock (1969, 1987), Cassidy (1980), and McWhorter (1995b, 2000a: 41–98) have argued that a single English-based creole was transplanted throughout the Caribbean, rather than a new one emerging independently in each major colony; Parkvall (1995a) makes a similar argument for French Caribbean creoles. This would mean that slaves imported from a previously established colony would have spoken the creole variety that had developed there, even before demographic disproportion had set in in the new colony. Other evidence suggests that creoles existed in the pre-plantation phase even of colonies established so early that no plantation colonies existed yet to transplant a creole from (McWhorter 1996b, 2000a). For this reason and others, some analysts have argued that the English creoles of the Caribbean stem ultimately from a single English pidgin ancestor born on the West African coast (Hancock 1969, 1986; McWhorter 1996b, 2000a). Meanwhile, Klingler (1992: 56– 57) and Parkvall (1995a) suppose that creolists may have simply overestimated the degree of demographic disproportion necessary to produce a creole, proposing that creoles may well have simply emerged on small farms.

Which of these solutions proves the correct one remains to be seen. Whatever analysis one chooses, however, the fact remains that the keystone superstratist contention, that slaves on early plantations spoke not creoles but simply non-native but close approximations of their lexifiers, is contradicted by an overwhelming volume of evidence.

## 4. "Even creoles are simply varieties of their lexifiers"

This superstratist assertion is based on two claims. One is that creoles would appear less divergent from their lexifiers if more consistently compared to the regional varieties actually spoken by colonists rather than standard varieties. The second is that no pidginization occurred during the emergence of the creole and that the traditional conception of creoles as expansions of erstwhile pidgins is mistaken.

To the extent that Chaudenson acknowledges any divergence between regional lexifier varieties and creoles, he supposes that this was due (1) to the fact that the slaves were exposed to a koine of regional dialects rather than only one and (2) to relatively nondisruptive second-language "approximation." Mufwene (1996b) adds that the creole may have diverged further from the lexifier when lexifier features grammaticalized in ways they had not in the lexifier itself.

Of course, viewed broadly, whether one calls a creole a variety of its lexifier or a new language is a matter of perspective and is inherently unamenable to any absolute metric. However, it is difficult to avoid the conclusion that the superstratist depiction of creoles as mere "varieties of their lexifiers" requires a highly selective presentation of data. When the creole data are viewed more liberally, the superstratist claim takes on a different perspective.

## 4. 1. Language versus sentence

Generally favoring textual exposition over example, superstratist arguments typically refer to sentences such as the following:
    Mauritian Creole:

(4)  Zot  ti    pe    ale.
     they ANT PROG go
     "They were going."

Indeed, such a sentence has a clear source in regional French *eux autres étaient après aller,* especially when unmonitored pronunciation is considered.

However, when sampled less selectively, creoles are much less plausibly viewed as simply slightly "approximated" extensions of regional lexifier dialects, and, furthermore, creoles contain clear signs that their origin involved a break in the transmission of the lexifier that is, pidginization.

### 4.1.1. Sranan

For example, here is a representative piece of Sranan Creole English (Adamson and Smith 1995: 231):

(5)  Te   den   yonkuman fu wrokope yere na   tori dis,
     when the-PL young man for workplace hear LOC story this

     dan den e    lafu. Dati na    wan bigiman srefisrefi.
     then they PROG laugh that COP a    big-man self-self

     Basedi      srefi ben e    lafu tu  nanga ala den    tifi
     Master Eddy self ANT PROG laugh also with all the-PL tooth

di   blaka fu soso tabaka. Noo a ben  de   na   en yuru.
REL black for only tobacco now it ANT COP LOC his hour
"Whenever the boys at work heard this, they would burst out in laughter 'That's one hell of a guy.' Even Master Eddy would laugh too, baring all of his teeth which were black from pure tobacco. Now it was his turn."

Clearly there are features here derivable from regional English dialects, such as *den* from *them* as plural marker. Clearly there are "approximations" of English, such as the elimination of plural inflection, the prevalence of CVCV structure, the over-generalized plural *tifi* from *teeth.* One could easily make a superstratist case for Sranan via isolated sentences like *Den go waka* "they will walk."

However, other features are utterly foreign to even the most hardscrabble dialect of English, and it is extremely difficult to conceive of them even as "approximations" thereof. Copula *na* is an internal development derived from *that,* not any form of "to be" (Arends 1989; McWhorter 1995b: 299–305, 1997a: 93–103), and one would look in vain for any English dialect with such a usage. The use of *self* (*srefi*) as an emphatic marker is extended in Suriname creoles far beyond anything conceivable in English of any kind (Rountree and Glock 1977: 133–34).

Under the Founder Principle, these two developments are presumably explainable as independent grammaticalizations, as Mufwene (1996b) proposes. Other features, however, are outright transfers from West African languages, not simply independent grammaticalizations. The postposition of *dis* (< *this*) is a West African inheritance (Bruyn 1995a: 111–24). as is the use of *di* (< *disi* "this") as a relative marker (Bruyn 1995b). Such features are in no way treatable as continuations of English. They are inheritances from other languages, and in grammatically central functions. Indisputable substrate transfer of this kind is so prominent in the grammar of Sranan and other creoles that it has even been argued that creoles are outright relexifications of West African languages (e.g., the relevent works of Lefebvre). While most creolists have been skeptical that transfer has played a role quite this dominant in creole genesis, the very fact that such analyses have been proposed strongly questions the marginal, or at best convergent, impact that superstratists consider substrate languages to have had on plantation creoles.

Other features specifically suggest that English was pidginized, not simply transmitted. For example, the internal development of the copula *na* entails that Sranan emerged with no expressed copula. Elimination of the copula is a diagnostic feature of pidgins, whose source in interrupted transmission of a lexifier is uncontroversial.

These realities are unclear in superstratist arguments which, demonstrated via isolated sentences like Mauritian *zot ti pe ale,* risk misleading the uninitiated into supposing that such sentences are even reasonably representative of creole grammars as a whole. Certainly, nothing strictly rules out a scholar insisting that even in view of the data I have shown, Sranan is a "variety of English." Clearly, however, with the data presented, such an insistence takes on a certain light. When actually seen in the context of whole grammars of a representative range of creoles, the "approximation" mechanism is in fact only applicable via tenuous, ad hoc extension, and as Baker (1996) crucially observes, this leaves no distinction between "approximation" and pidginization as traditionally conceived.

The only sustained superstratist acknowledgement of Sranan is Mufwene (1996a: 94–96), who argues for Suriname as an unusual case, leaving the superstratist model generally intact. He proposes that because of the brevity of the English tenure in Suriname (1651–1667), slaves there had unusually little exposure to English and thus developed a variety unusually divergent from it. We must recall, however, that these slaves worked on small farms alongside whites and that the superstratist model stipulates that they would have developed non-native but relatively viable English. Mufwene would appear to imply that sixteen years was not long enough for the slaves to do so, but without a principled justification, it is unclear why.

### 4.1.2. Annobonese Creole Portuguese

In any case, there is other evidence that Sranan is not an unusual case. Other creoles just as tenuously treated as "varieties of their lexifiers" have arisen in more conventional circumstances, when speakers of the lexifier were available for over a century. Annobonese Creole Portuguese (Fa D'Ambu) is one of four closely related varieties of Gulf of Guinea Portuguese Creole (Holm 1989: 277). Here is a sample (Post 1995: 203):

(6)  Se     amu bila-oio tela-mu Ambu.  Amu na    xonse
     CONJ I    open-eye land-my Annobón I    NEG know

     pe-mu-syi        pali mu-f.    Se    amu sxa    ma
     father-my-DEM bear me-NEG CONJ I     PROG take

     mavida  ku   me-mu.    Amu na     suku
     suffering with mother-my I      NEG have

     nge-syi     zuda me-mu     pa
     person-DEM help  mother-my for

     da   ma  xa    pa amu bisyi-f.
     give take thing for I     wear-NEG
     "I was born in my homeland Annobón. I did not know who my father was and I suffered with my mother. I had nobody to help my mother to offer me something to wear."

Again, it is difficult to view this language as merely "a variety of Portuguese." The postposition of the pronoun to encode the possessive, the postposition of the demonstrative (*pe-mu-syi*), the serial verb construction *da ma* "give-take," and the postposed negator *-f* (< original *fa*) are unequivocal West African inheritances (Ferraz 1976), the latter even lacking a Portuguese etymological source. As with Sranan, far from being scattered or marginal, such transferred features are nothing less than central to the grammar.

Also as in Sranan, other features specifically indicate pidginization rather than simple transmission of Portuguese. A Portuguese dialect eschewing its subject pronouns in favor of dative-marked possessive adjectives is inconceivable (*amu* from *a meu* "to my"). In contrast, pidgins typically generalize a tonic pronominal, and in Portuguese plays of the fifteenth through nineteenth centuries, Africans speaking rudimentary pidgin Portuguese are even depicted as saying *a mi* (Naro 1978: 328–29). Similarly, progressive marker *sxa* is derived from a combination of *sa* from *são* "they are" and *xa* from *ficar* "to stay," neither lexical source used as a progressive marker in Portuguese. Both exemplify the tendency in pidgins to innovate aspect markers by remodeling lexical items in ways unknown in the lexifier (cf. Tok Pisin progressive marker *stap* from "stop"). Furthermore, both *sa* and *xa* (< *ka*) can appear alone in other Gulf of Guinea Portuguese creoles (Günther 1973); their combination into one marker is an internal innovation in Annobonese, rendering *sxa* even more alien to any lexifier source. In short, the superstratist analysis begs the question as to which Portuguese dialect included sentences like *a meu são ficar sufrir* "I used to suffer."

Thus Annobonese is no more "Portuguese" than Sranan is "English," and yet it was created under conditions in which Portuguese speakers were a dominant presence for generations. Annobón was settled with slaves from nearby São Tomé in 1503 (Holm 1989: 283), and the sisterhood of Annobonese and São Tomense therefore suggests that the latter existed by the first decades of the 1500s. The existence of São Tomense by this early date is further indicated by the fact that another of the Gulf of Guinea Portuguese creole speech communities, Principe, was also seeded from São Tomé in the early 1500s (ibid. 280–81). This date of emergence is significant because at this time blacks had yet to vastly outnumber whites either in the São Tomé population as a whole or on individual plantations. During the large stretch of time between the large-scale settlement of São Tomé in 1493 and the mid-1500s, its plantations typically harbored only fifteen or so slaves at a time (Brásio 1954: 33–45) and were few in number; there were only two sugar mills, for example, as late as the 1510s (Hodges and Newitt 1988: 19–20). In the meantime, crucially, interaction between whites and blacks on São Tomé was especially intimate: marriages between Portuguese settlers and Africans, as well as between Iberian Jewish refugees and Africans, were encouraged and predominant (Ferraz 1979: 15–16).[7]

The damage to Mufwene's attempt to explain Sranan as the result of unusually brief contact with English is clear. Furthermore, this situation continued for over a century, until the downfall of the colony in the early 1600s—and yet the result was a creole as divergent from its lexifier as São Tomense (as well as its transplanted sisters). Ferraz's surmise that these marriages were significant in the development of the creole is supported by the firm documentation of the emergence of Portuguese creoles from similar intermarriages in Asia.

Thus regarding the claim that creoles are simply varieties of their lexifiers, Annobonese and its sister dialects are just as dire as Sranan not only linguistically but also sociohistorically. Mufwene's strategy of setting aside Sranan as the result of unusually brief exposure to a lexifier is inapplicable in the Gulf of Guinea, where Portuguese speakers were available as planters and even husbands *in extenso*.

Again, examples continue, another being Tayo French Creole of Caledonia, quite clearly the result of the severe reduction of French followed by a reinterpretation thereof that was deeply influenced by substrate interference from Melanesian languages. It was created not by a brief encounter with French but through unions between Melanesian women who spoke non-native, but by no means pidginized, French, and Melanesian men, all living in a settlement with French-speaking missionaries (Corne 1995a). We are forced to conclude not only that many creoles do not lend themselves to treatment as simply varieties of their lexifiers but also that this was unrelated to whether their creators' exposure to Europeans was brief or prolonged.

### 4.2. The approximation mechanism

Even the fundamental conviction behind the "creoles as mere dialects" idea, that a creole could plausibly have developed gradually from a lexifier via a series of incremetal approximations, is questionable. Typical of superstratist arguments, Chaudenson's (1992: 156–67) demonstrations of how "approximation" would produce a creole are outlined less in citation and diagram than in text block, tending to spare linguistic demonstration in favor of extended sociohistorical extrapolation (Baker 1996: 117). When we get down to cases and attempt a sustained linguistic engagement with the "approximation" scenario, we find that it is in fact difficult to "generate" a creole without a break in transmission.

For example, Chaudenson (1992: 158–62) claims that the absence of inflection in creoles is traceable to regional dialects in which inflectional paradigms were much more eroded than in European standards. The point that vernacular French dialects have often radically reduced the number of inflections in the present *tense -er* verb paradigm, for example, is well-taken and demonstrates the tendency for such erosions to proceed more rapidly in colloquial varieties relatively unconstrained by prescriptive impulses (cf. Kroch 1978) (table 5.1).

However, the fact is that French creoles did not generalize [parl] but [parle]. This could be derived either from the second-person plural or the infinitive. In reference to the first alternative, Chaudenson (1992: 158–59) gives examples of some grammatically marginal vernacular overgeneralizations of the *first*-person plural inflection, but this is not germane to his thesis; presumably there are no examples of the overgeneralization of the second-person plural ending, which would be a highly unusual diachronic development given the tendency for the third-person singular to be the source of generalization (Watkins 1962, Hock 1991: 220–22). Indeed, what the regional French dialects offer is a source for overgeneralization of the third-person singular—but this is exactly what French creoles did *not* do. A search for a regional French that used only the infinitive would be similarly futile.

However, overgeneralization of the infinitive is a diagnostic of pidginization. Note, for example, that an unequivocally pidginized French, Tay Bôi of Vietnam,

TABLE 5.1. Comparison of *-er* verb present-tense paradigms

| English | Standard French | Colloquial French | Haitian Creole |
|---|---|---|---|
| I talk | je parle | je parle [parl] | m pale |
| you talk | tu parles | tu parles [parl] | ou pale |
| he talks | il parle | il parle [parl] | li pale |
| we talk | nous parlons | on parle [parl] | nu pale |
| you (pl.) talk | vous parlez | vous parlez [parle] | nu pale |
| they talk | ils parlent | ils parlent [parl] | zot pale |

overgeneralizes the infinitive, not the third-person singular (*Toi napas savoir monsieur aller où?* "You don't know where the man went?" [Schuchardt 1888, cited in Holm 1989: 360]). This suggests that there was indeed a break in the transmission of French in the birth of Haitian Creole. A similar case is zero copula in French creoles. Regional French speakers have never omitted the copula: *Je ø pêcheur* or *Moi* (regional [mwe]) *ø pêcheur* "I am a fisherman." By contract, zero copula is diagnostic of pidginization (Ferguson 1971, Ferguson and Debose 1977, Foley 1988: 165).

In addition to these problems, the approximation scenario is even less plausible when it is applied to those European languages that, even in regional varieties, are more richly inflected than French. To be sure, it is tempting (albeit, as we have seen, mistaken) to view French-based creoles as a mere step beyond reduced paradigms like those in table 5.1. However, "approximation" proponents have neglected the fact that there were no such leveled paradigms as sources for creoles lexified by more richly inflected varieties. An example is Palenquero Spanish Creole (table 5.2).

As we have seen, the "approximation" scenario, while preliminarily plausible, does not explain as much data as the conventional pidginization account. The fact that creoles as inflectionally stripped as the French ones have developed even from inflectionally rich languages would appear to deal the coup de grâce to "approximation" as a valid creole genesis model.

In sum, despite the vital role that regional constructions play in creole genesis, the fact remains that creoles also present a mass of data that are neither traceable to "evolved" regional dialects nor plausibly treated as the product of a series of "approximations." The claim that "creoles are varieties of their lexifiers" must be evaluated in view of the data in the preceding section.

## 5. "Nothing distinguishes creoles from other varieties which have undergone extensive language contact"

The cluster of three traits that defines the Creole Prototype directly belie the claim that creoles are indistinguishable from other speech varieties with heavy language contact in their histories, because our three traits do not cluster in these ordinary heavy-contact varieties. This is because the three traits are the legacy of former pidginization, and heavy-contact varieties like Romanian did not arise via pidginization and subse-

TABLE 5.2. Verbal paradigms in Spanish and Palenquero

| English | Colombian Spanish (Pacific Coast) | Palenquero |
|---------|-----------------------------------|------------|
| I speak | yo hablo | i ablá |
| you speak | tó hablas/vos hablas | bo ablá |
| he speaks | él habla | ele ablá |
| we speak | nosotros hablamos | suto-/-ma hende ablá |
| you (pl.) speak | ustedes hablan | utere ablá |
| they speak | ellos hablan | ané ablá |

Colombian Spanish based on Lipski 1994: 213–14; Palenquero data from Schwegler 1998.

quent reconstitution as creoles did. Romanian, for example, has a heavy Slavic lexical component and Balkan Sprachbund structural features which distinguish it from other Romance languages (e.g., the postposed determiner: *omul* "the man").[8] However, its rich inflection instantly distinguishes it from Haitian Creole or Tok Pisin, and, like all regular languages, its derivational affixation is often semantically irregular: the core meaning of the prefix *de-* is inversive, as in *degrada* "to degrade," but this meaning is obscured in words such as *deprinde* "to habituate" from *prinde* "to take" or *desemna* "to designate" from *semna* "to sign." The same could be said of Amharic or myriad other speech varieties that have undergone especially heavy language contact in their histories but not extensive rapid acquisition by adults.

## 6. "One language cannot be more or less creole than another"

Continua of lects ranging from English to creole have been studied for decades (DeCamp 1971, Bickerton 1975, Rickford 1987); similar creole continua have been identified elsewhere (Bhattachariya 1994, Staudacher-Valliamée 1994); Thomason and Kaufman (1988) elegantly and rigorously argue for contact-induced interference as a gradient process. Yet as a consequence of his claim that *creole* is not a valid classification, Mufwene (1994b: 71, 1997a: 42) has argued that there is an "absence of a structural yardstick for measuring linguistic creoleness" and that the classification of a language as more or less "creole" than another is inappropriate.

However, the Creole Prototype is precisely the structural yardstick Mufwene seeks, and the notion of creoleness as a matter of degree follows naturally from the identification of this prototype, since entities naturally conform to any prototype to gradient degrees.

Our prototype is a creole with no inflectional affixes, no use of tone to contrast monosyllables or encode syntax, and derivational affixes whose semantic contribution is consistently compositional. Along these lines, the most "creole" of creoles is typified by Sranan and its offshoot Ndjuka, which fulfill all three qualifications. Saramaccan, with its occasional contrastive uses of tone, and Fa D'Ambu, with its occasional use of the suffix *-du* to form participial adjectives (*xaba* "to finish," *xabadu* "finished" [Post 1995: 195–96]), depart slightly from the prototype. All of these creoles, however, have long been considered among the "deepest" creoles by most scholars. The uncertain light in which superstratist models like the Founder Principle place this characterization is eliminated under our framework.

Other creoles depart somewhat more from this prototype. For example, Nubi Creole Arabic has clearly drastically reduced the grammar of its lexifier, having eliminated all nonconcatenative morphology and developed new derivational morphology from compounds (Heine 1982: 29, 41–42). However, it encodes a few morphological and syntactic distinctions via tone, generating derverbal nouns (*kárabú* "to spoil," *karáb* "spoiling") and resultatives (*úo séregú kalamóyo* "he stole a goat," *kalamóyo dé seregú* "the goat was stolen") (ibid. 41–42).

Often, departures from the prototype result when source languages have been retained alongside the creole. For example, Guinea-Bissau Portuguese Creole has a causative marker /ntV/: *sibi* "to climb," *sibinti* "to make climb" (Kihm 1989: 372), which is inherited from a pattern in local languages like Manjaku (-*lenp* "to work," -*lenpandan* "to make work"). Palenquero, spoken in a code-switching relationship with Spanish for centuries, has not only two inflections *ma*- (plural and -*ba* (past marker) (albeit both weakly obligatory [Armin Schwegler, Jan. 1997 pers. comm.]), but also the Spanish gerundive marker -*ando* and adjectival participial marker -*ao* (albeit the latter weakly productive [Friedemann and Patiño 1983: 135–36]). A related phenomenon is when a single substrate language had a disproportionate impact on a creole at its origin. For example, Gbe speakers were so numerous in early colonial Suriname that Saramaccan retains some tone sandhi patterns that were directly inherited from Fongbe, including one that could be interpreted as a marker of a grammatical relation: tone sandhi is blocked between verb and object.

Slight differences in "creoleness" of this sort, however, are of minimal theoretical import. Nubi Creole Arabic, Guinea-Bissau Creole Portuguese, and Palenquero have clearly reduced, and then restructured, their lexifiers to the extreme degree that defines creole genesis as a distinct and interesting process. However, certain contact varieties have reduced their lexifiers so much less extremely than Ndjuka or Haitian Creole French that they stand out as intermediate cases, traditionally called *semi-creoles*. Afrikaans is a classic case, having reduced morphological paradigms to a degree unknown in regional Dutch dialects, but by no means eliminating them entirely like Sranan has eliminated English ones.

Mufwene (1997a: 59) has argued that the term *semi-creole* is vacuous, but this follows from the superstratist impression that creole is an invalid classification: "Should Afrikaans and African-American Vernacular English be called 'semi-creoles?' Again, in the absence of a structural linguistic definition, what do we learn from this label? Or, what do we need it for? What criteria justify this new category?"

The Creole Prototype, however, contains exactly the criteria in question. Afrkaans, for example, has significantly reduced the inflectional affix paradigms of Dutch, but it retains Dutch's derivational morphology in much of its evolved idiosyncrasy as well as a wealth of other elaborifications typical of Germanic (cf. Chapter 11). In contrast. Negerhollands Dutch Creole had no inflectional affixes, and what derivational morphology it had was semantically regular. For precisely this reason, we can confidently classify Afrikaans as a semi-creole, in contrast to the Dutch creole Negerhollands.

Along these same lines, we can resolve a long-standing ambiguity over the classification of Bantu-based contact languages like Kituba, Lingala, and Shaba Swahili. Nida and Fehderau (1970: 147–48, 152–53) classify Kituba as a pidgin and Lingala and Shaba Swahili as koines. Holm (1989: 552–55) considers none of them pidgins, treating all three as intermediate between dialect and pidgin. Meanwhile, Mufwene (1986a: 146–47; 1989) once approached the first two along the lines of Holm but considered Shaba Swahili to be indistinguishable from older languages. Of late, under the Founder Principle, he instead rejects any notion of gradient "creoleness" among these languages (Mufwene 1997a: 46–47), for instance proposing sources for the direct inheritance of Kituba features from Kimanianga Kikongo rather than treating them as pidginizations thereof (Mufwene 1994c). As the result of these conflicting analyses, the Bantu-based contact varieties hover at the edges of most creolist discussion;

meanwhile, linguists outside of creole studies are often perplexed that Lingala, in particular, is even treated as a "creole" at all.

With our Creole Prototype identified, we can resolve this conundrum. In all three
of these varieties, the affix paradigms of the lexifier are slightly reduced, as are tonal
distinctions where the lexifier had any (Swahili is not tonal). However, the grammars of all three bristle with allomorphic affix paradigms, and Kituba and Lingala
retain lexically and syntactically contrastive usage of tone (note Lingala's tonally
indicated subjunctive):

Kituba:

(7)  Mbóma ná   Kaniki kéle  ba-nduku . . . tüka ya bó   vand-áka b-ána.
     Mboma and Kaniki COP PL-friend since   of they be-PAST PL-child
     "Mboma and Kaniki have been friends since they were children." (Mufwene, pers.
     comm. to Holm 1989: 558)

Lingala:

(8)  Pételo a-yók-i       molungi. A-ke-i   na ebale mpó á-sokol-a     nzóto.
     Peter he-perceive-PF heat     he-go-PF to river for he-wash-SUBJ body
     "Peter felt hot. He went to the river to wash himself." (Mufwene, pers. comm. to Holm
     1989: 560) (PF = perfective, SUBJ = subjunctive)

Shaba Swahili:

(9)  Paka i-le     baati   mungu a-ri-ku-kubar-i-a           njo i-le    tuu.
     just  CL-DEM fortune God    he-PAST-you-grant-APP-FIN COP CL-DEM just
     "Only the good fortune God has granted you, only this." (De Rooij 1995: 183) (CL =
     nominal classifier prefix, APP = applicative)

The Creole Prototype allows us to readily classify these as semi-creoles, in comparison to Ndjuka or Haitian. Instructive is a direct comparison of Lingala with its
lexifier, rare in the literature, in a sample which few would consider unrepresenta-
tive (Mufwene 1994c has independently noted that the degree of pidginization in
Lingala is noticeably light):

(10)  a. Bobangi:
         Ngai, na-ko-ke o mboka no-tonga ndako.
         Me   I-FUT-go to village INF-build house (Dzokanga 1979: 6, cited in Samarin
         1990: 63)

      b. Lingala:
         Ngái, na-ko-kenda na   mbóka ko-tónga ndako.
         me   I-FUT-go     PREP village INF-build house (Mufwene, pers. comm.)
         "Me, I'm going to the village to build a house."

The obvious difference in degree of reduction between these languages and their
lexifiers compared to Ndjuka and Haitian and their lexifiers speaks against the claim

that sociohistory is the only thing substantially distinguishing the Bantu-based contact languages from plantation creoles, and that there exists no synchronic cline of "creoleness."[9] Indeed, the sociohistories differ crucially: plantation creoles were created by West Africans transported across the world to encounter languages entirely unrelated to their own; the Bantu-based semi-creoles were stabilized more or less where the Bantu lexifier was spoken, largely by people from nearby regions who spoke highly similar languages. What the data show is that these *sociohistorical* differences, because of the differences in closeness of relationship between the contact languages they led to, conditioned clear *synchronic* differences: specifically, a difference in the degree of reduction of the lexifier.

There are surely no distinct lines between the classes of creole, semi-creole, and older language. The inherently gradient nature of language restructuring is such that it would be quite futile—and ultimately of unclear utility—to propose any "metric of creoleness." This, however, no more invalidates the terms or their usefulness than the nondiscrete nature of growth invalidates the terms *puppy* and *dog*. Our intention is to suggest that the data do not support a collapsing of creole genesis under ordinary language contact, and that creoles indeed represent the end of a cline of lexifier reduction. It is inherent to a cline that intermediate cases will arise, and inevitable of human cognition to process these cases as such (cf. Thomason 1997a). A natural label for these cases will be semi-creole, a term that appropriately is applied to Réunionnais French, Afrikaans, Kituba, Lingala, and Shaba Swahili.[10] In practice, precisely where each linguist draws the terminological lines will differ according to frame of reference: this is unobjectionable and even beneficial. What this analysis puts into question is a taxonomic reconception that would eliminate the creole as a synchronic class altogether, and thereby obscure the gradient nature of the process that created them.

## 7. Conclusion

The status of creoles as resulting from a break in the transmission of a lexifier has long been intuited by thinkers such as Hymes (1971a), Kay and Sankoff (1974), Bickerton (1977), Mühlhäusler (1980), and Seuren and Wekker (1986). The superstratists have usefully challenged this assumption in seeking to better square creole genesis theory with the actual demographic trajectory of colonial plantations, in reexamining the definition of *creole* in view of other contact varieties, and in pushing theoretical implications to stimulating extremes. In the final analysis, however, the data ultimately dictate that we maintain the conception of creoles as a unique language type, born from the pidginization and subsequent reconstitution of a lexifier, within a context of rich transfer from substrate languages.

# PART II

# IS CREOLE CHANGE DIFFERENT
# FROM LANGUAGE CHANGE
# IN OLDER LANGUAGES?

When creole studies were initiated at the Mona conference in 1968, one of the main manifestos was to show the world that creoles are true languages, deserving of study and celebration. Four decades later, this goal, although more tacitly, persists as a guiding notion in the field even to the point that some decry the very implication that there is any difference between creolization and ordinary language contact.

Yet ironically, a major current in creolist work proceeds on the assumption that, diachronically, creoles are distinct; namely, that creole life cycles are somehow exempt from the processes established as central in older languages. Thus, most work on change over time in creoles is couched in a fashion that implies that creoles are not only the products of language contact but are forever constrained by contact factors in their evolution. The scholar of continuum creoles has looked almost exclusively to decreolization towards the lexifier language as the source of changes over time. In a separate tendency, when changes in a creole in documents or via reconstruction are noted, it is taken as imperative to seek models for the change in the creole's substrate languages.

Certainly contact plays a part in creole diachrony. Mauritian Creole French has developed optional marking of inherent reflexivity due to French influence over time, as in *Mo pu aloñz mwa ler mo fatige* "I shall lie down when I'm tired" (Corne 1988: 73). Keesing's (1988: 213–15) demonstration that Solomon Islands Pijin, long spoken alongside Oceanic languages, has modeled adverbs on substrate language equivalents of identical behavior is unassailable.

But then all of the world's languages exist in contact situations, and historical linguists are more aware by the year that contact has played a major role in all of their life cycles, to the point of obscuring family-tree relationships in a great many cases (cf. Dixon 1997). However, historical linguists receive the latter realization as an urgent and novel insight, elbowing for space with a long tradition of charting the internal changes these languages have simultaneously undergone.

In creole studies, the situation is reversed. It is too often relegated to the margins of creolist work that, just like older languages, creoles, as natural languages that have existed for centuries, have undergone internal transformations independently of contact. No one would deny the fact in itself, but the focus on decreolization and substrate models suggests that most writers on creole change consider the internal changes somehow subsidiary in import or perhaps less important to document.

The result is a philosophical contradiction. We are told that creoles are just languages like all the others, and yet that their transformation over time is determined by factors local to creoles' sociological circumstances. One gleans a sense that creoles' being products of subordination and racism plays some part in this essentialization. But these sad realities are, after all, a norm in societies worldwide.

The reason for this paradoxical perspective is another guiding principle, which creole studies inherits from the leftist tilt of the academic climate since the 1960s and its focus on multiculturalism. Scholars in the humanities and social sciences are taught to cherish the fact that languages reflect the cultures of their speakers, to an extent that would confuse many pre-1960s linguists transported to our time, many of whom would see us as rather curiously stressing a valid but obvious point. In our era, this emphasis is seen as valuable in defending non-Western peoples against dismissal as "primitives"—while also reminding Westerners of the comparative sterility, arrogance, and greed of their own culture. The fact that most creoles are spoken by dispossessed non-whites makes this impulse especially robust in creole studies. The theoretical syntactician expert on a little-known language is judged primarily on the quality of their argumentation. But in creole studies, whether or not a scholar has lived long-term among speakers of the creole they study and learned their "culture" is an ever-looming issue, unless the scholar is a native speaker.

This "culture cult" explains the disjunction between insisting that creoles are not a definable class of language and charting their diachrony under different paradigms than other historical linguists. An enterprise dedicated as much to defending creoles as describing and analyzing them discourages defining creoles as a taxonomic class, out of an imperative to recast Western culture as just one alternative way of being human out of many equal, with creolophone cultures being one. But then this same focus just as naturally encourages approaching creoles' processes of change as a demonstration of cultural survival this comprising their creators' retention of native language traits (the substratist school) and their graceful coping with imposed Western ones (the decreolization paradigm).

The culture cult is hardly an error in itself, tracing to the teachings of Franz Boas and often benefitting scholarly inquiry. But the idea that linguistic analysis is inherently incomplete without sustained engagement with issues of culture, identity, and social stratification, despite how readily linguists are trained to concur with it regardless of the nature of their own work, is underargued. Discussing the creolist work he and others had done in the 1970s, the late Chris Corne (1983: 181) memorably noted that "if the omission of 'social context' in such studies was a serious methodological error, someone should have pointed out by now mistakes in published analyses which could have been avoided had social factors been considered."

And in creole studies, the culture cult limits the field's scope and influence as much as it enhances it.

For example, the interest in decreolization and statistical models of variation in the 1970s stemmed not from a disembodied fascination with the variation itself but with a desire to show that the multilectal languages that appeared so chaotic to the untutored observer were actually the products of constrained structure. It was often stated at the time that this work revealed a vibrantly varilectal language competence, the speaker negotiating between the personal, the local, and the wider world in ongoing "acts of identity." It's no accident that Robert LePage and André Tabouret-Keller's 1985 book of that title is so often checked out from university libraries: its message speaks deeply not only to creolists but to social scientists across any campus.

But the problem is that the creole continuum school has developed a highly local tradition of demonstration and argumentation. A decreolization case or even a case against it, such as the growing body of work questioning Black English's roots in Gullah—is likely cast in a statistically based format, often in text dedicating more space to discussing tables and graphs than to linking the findings to issues beyond variationist work, and is usually presented in venues that most diachronic linguists are unlikely to frequent. This paradigm is hardly alone in having become perhaps a bit unsuitably inbred. Algonquianist tradition, for example, has accreted a notoriously particular jargon and perspective that can discourage other linguists from engaging its work. But the problem remains, and I am uncertain whether creolophones' multilectal competence has had much effect on historical linguistic thinking since the inauguration of this school over three decades ago at this writing.

Meanwhile, substratists in the 1980s often claimed that the goal of their inquiry was formulating models of language transfer. But what truly drove most of this work was a visceral indignation towards Derek Bickerton's claim that African languages played no significant part in creoles' development. That claim, after all, was readable as denying that oppressed slaves had "retained their cultural identity" in creating their new languages. Notably, the most detailed and closely argued genuine "model of language transfer" to date was created not by creolists but by Native American language specialists Sally Thomason and Terrence Kaufman (1988), in a work addressing languages worldwide rather than a subset of them spoken by a particular ethnic group. Meanwhile, most substratist work in creole studies has simply pointed to isolated correspondences between a given creole and its substrate languages.

Thus the impulse to look first to substrate languages in charting a change in a creole over time has been as much politically as empirically based. I address an example of this in chapter 6: the assumption that if copulas in Atlantic English-based creoles were innovations, then the innovation must have been spurred by the West African copulas native to the creoles' creators. But only under the sociopolitically determined restriction of one's view to West Africa the black motherland can this brand of analysis maintain an illusion of legitimacy. The West African copulas only resemble creole copulas in a superficial way, while grammars worldwide develop copulas internally without substrate models.

And the problem is that at the end of the day, tracing so many creole changes to possible substrate templates—especially where the resemblance is either too approximate or too general to yield more than a tentative case—often renders that change inherently less interesting than one that proceeded language-internally. The substratist enterprise in creole studies has been necessary, and I participated in it lustily in my early work. But after a certain point it borders on becoming a kind of matching exercise of questionable intellectual import. When one language simply copies something in another one, the process is less likely to have significant theoretical implications for linguistics as a whole than does a change that occurred independently, affected by the rules and tendencies typical in all natural language grammars. This is another local tradition, then, that keeps creoles from playing as much of a part in developments in historical linguistics than they could. Chapter 7 is another address of the issue, outlining a change in Saramaccan that is no more connected to superstrate or substrate factors than is the loss of atonic word-final vowels in Germanic languages.

Another way that the culture cult places a barrier between creole studies and general linguistics is the common wisdom that each creole emerged in the setting that it is spoken in today. In actuality, large subsets of creoles, such as the Atlantic English-based ones and all of the French-based plantation creoles, are idiosyncratically correspondent to an extent that the historical linguist would consider diagnostic of sisterhood to wit, direct descent from a common ancestor.

It is often assumed that the similarities between these groups of creoles are convergences due to similar substrate languages or universals of second-language acquisition. But in chapter 8 I argue that a significant body of correspondences between the Atlantic English-based creoles cannot be traced to these sources and are, rather, the kinds of happenstance development that reveal common origin in a single language. That is, an Ur-creole formed in one place and was then transplanted from one to the other as slaveholders founded new colonies with slaves from earlier ones.

I think historical linguists might be somewhat surprised at the extent to which this is considered a bold claim in creole studies, where tradition traces each creole to interactions between colonizers and slaves in its individual colony. But that tradition is predictable from how politics subtly shapes inquiry in the field. To treat creoles as reflections of local culture and sociohistory is felt as legitimizing the creole as a "real language," in integrating it within a socioculturally dynamic indigenous context. Then another side of the culture cult plays a part as well. Salikoko Mufwene's claim, for example, that Gullah was a local creation rather than an import from Barbados feeds into the claim that the term *creole* is a mere reification. To trace Gullah to simply local "contact" is to imply that nothing significant distinguished colonial South Carolina from, for instance, Asia Minor where a deeply Turkish-inflected Greek arose.

While these tendencies are understandable, they ultimately hinder creole studies from contributing more richly to comparative historical linguistic inquiry. Creolists have at their fingertips vast arrays of sister languages whose divergences could be as instructive to diachronic theory as those between Romance and Austronesian or Algonquian languages. Barbadian Creole English, Gullah, Sranan, Jamaican patois, Nigerian "Pidgin" English, and Guyanese Creole English are all sister languages descended from a single parent as ineluctably as Russian, Ukranian, Czech, Polish, Serbo-Croatian, and Bulgarian are. Certainly, specifics of their contexts have determined many of the creoles' differences but then comparative Slavicists would be surprised to hear that local sociohistorical circumstances were not crucial to the development of the Slavic family.

Despite this, common practice traces the close similarity of Haitian and Martiniquan Creole partially mutually intelligible to universals of non-native acquisition, general West African traits, vaguely defined concepts of "diffusion," or regional French models. Hence we lose a rich data set, and this helps creolist discussion remain balkanized off in a corner upstairs at the Linguistics Society of America conference.

In chapter 9, I show that there are also long-standing conundrums in creole studies that appear irresolvable under assumptions emphasizing creoles as products of local identity, but which evaporate under a conception of most creoles as imports from another location. Here, one of my suggestions is my hypothesis that most plantation creoles were born as pidgins on the West African coast (the Afrogenesis Hypothesis). However, this is the only engagement in this book with that hypothesis, an unavoidably sprawling affair that requires a book-length monograph to present effectively (McWhorter 2000a). The article version of chapter 8 was also originally fashioned to argue for both the sisterhood of the Atlantic English-based creoles and their parent language's origin on the West African coast. This latter argument was based on a preliminary version of the Afrogenesis concept I had formulated at the time, which I later revised considerably. Given the obsolescence of that version of the argument, I have recast the article to outline the sisterhood issue alone, as this is most important to the aims of this anthology.

The culture cult is behind one additional artificial taxonomic division that, paradoxically, essentializes creoles just as a certain set so robustly deplore. This is between creoles and "mixed" or "intertwined" languages like Media Lengua (Quechua morphology and syntax, Spanish lexicon). A conventional wisdom has set in over the years that intertwined languages are created by ethnically mixed people as expressions of a bicultural "identity." But the closer one views the languages and their histories, the "cultural" difference between intertwined languages and creoles becomes ever more unclear. For one, it is hard to argue that creole creators did not have a "bicultural" identity. It is well-documented that the first generation of slaves born on plantations separated themselves from and often scorned African-born slaves, cherishing the fact that they were locally-born, while certainly not considering themselves white, either. Meanwhile, intertwined language specialists often present as a diagnostic of the type that the languages' creators were fluent in both source languages, but the creators of many actually were not.

In chapter 10 I show that the difference between intertwined languages and creoles was simply a matter of how many languages were widely spoken in a contact situation. If there were only two, the result was a language like Media Lengua; if there were several, the result was a creole, retaining substrate features general among the subordinated, but not language-specific features like morphological markers.

This process, like all in language contact, operated according to degree. Many languages straddle the two categories, such as Philippines Creole Spanish, which retains a fair amount of grammatical items from closely related Central Philippines languages, but hardly to a degree comparable to the almost total retention of Quechua morphology in Media Lengua. Here again, I hope help to bring creole genesis accounts into the linguistic mainstream, which requires full acknowledgment that contact is a gradient phenomenon. There is no question that French influenced English lexically more than Japanese did, that it influenced English syntactically less than Balkan languages did Romanian, that the Arawak language Bora had a greater morphological effect on the related language Resígaro in lending it ample amounts of number and case markers and classifiers (Aikhenvald 2001: 185–88) than French did upon English in lending it some derivational affixes.

In the same way, then, we would expect that the types of mixture exemplified by Media Lengua and Sranan represent points on a cline rather than discrete categories, even though this is incompatible with the temptation, based more on fashion than empiricism, to reify intertwined languages as uniquely instructive expressions of bicultural identity.

The message of this section, in sum, is that certainly creoles are cultural creations, but no more or less so than Uzbek, Apache, or Burmese. Beyond this, they are human language grammars, subject to the same fascinating processes of contact-independent and culture-independent change as any others.

# Looking into the Void

## *Zero Copula in the Creole Mesolect*

## 1. Introduction

In their investigations of the copula in English-based creole continua of the Caribbean in the 1970s, various scholars documented that the copula in these creoles manifested itself in a wide range of forms according to (1) type of following complement
and (2) level of register within the continuum (Stewart 1969, Bickerton 1973, Fasold
1976, Holm 1984, Rickford 1979, Baugh 1980). Among various patterns replicated
in several studies of various creoles, it was shown that when preceding an NP, the
copula is manifested overtly in the basilect (as *do*, *na*, or *a*), as well as in the upper
mesolect and acrolect (as the standard English-modeled *iz* or *waz*), but as zero in the
lower mesolect. These studies have sparked fruitful debates on issues such as the
nature of polylectal competence, targeted language change, and the creole origins of
African-American Vernacular English (henceforth AAVE).

     However, amid these controversies, some pressing questions raised by the seem-
ingly innocent behavior of the copula followed by NP remained largely unaddressed.
A language-internal diachronic approach to this fragment of grammar reveals multiple insights into the relationship of these continua to the tenets of language acquisition and reduction; the relationship between AAVE, standard English, and Caribbean
creoles; and the West African contribution to the creoles in question.

## 2. Questions raised by the mesolectal zero copula

### 2.1. The continuum as creation

When the manifestation of the copula across the creole continuum was first systematically investigated starting in the late 1960s, the continuum was thought to have

stemmed from an original situation in which the basilect and the acrolect had existed in opposition, with registers in between only developing over time as the result of increased interethnic contact after the abolition of slavery.

During the reign of this paradigm Bickerton (1973), for example, schematized the copulas in Guyanese Creole English as a systematic progression that speakers followed in a movement from a basilect towards an acrolectal target. He hypothesized this progression as a gradual unlearning of the patterns of one's native register in favor of new rules of the register "above." Bickerton's study showed a typical patterning of the manifestation of the copula before NP (as in the English *He is the captain* or *He is a doctor*) in Anglophone creole continua.

Table 6.1 depicts the copula in the Guyanese Creole English mesolect; the isolects are ordered according to increasing closeness to an acrolectal system. We see a general trend in which throughout the mesolect, the occurrence of *da* yields to an alternation between zero and forms of the English *be*. Thus we can conceive of this creole's copula as manifesting itself according to the deliberately oversimplified, but heuristically useful, conception shown in table 6.2.

Bickerton analyzed zero copula as an intermediate stage between the shedding of the basilectal *da* and the acquisition of the acrolectal *iz/waz*.

But under the historical account of the continuum outlined above, these data posed certain questions.

First, zero copula is a trait typical of reduced language, including pidgins, foreigner talk, and child language (e.g., Ferguson 1971). As such, we would expect that along a continuum of development from basilect to acrolect, if zero copula were to appear in any single register it would be the basilect. This follows from the fact that the basilects developed with the least input from the target, which would be expected

TABLE 6.1. The copula in the Guyanese Creole English mesolect

| Isolect | Copula form |
| --- | --- |
| A | 1 |
| B | 1 |
| C | 1, 3 |
| D | 1, 3 |
| E | 2 |
| F | 2, 3 |
| G | 3 |
| H | 3 |
| I | 3 |
| J | 2, 3 |
| K | 2, 3 |
| L | 3 |
| M | 2, 3 |
| N | 3 |
| O | 2, 3 |

1 = *a* (<*da*); 2 = ø; 3 = *be* (all forms).

Adapted from Bickerton 1973: 652.

TABLE 6.2. The copula before NP
in Guyanese Creole English

| |
| --- |
| Acrolect: *iz/waz* |
| Mesolect: ø |
| Basilect:    *a* |

to have favored the radical grammatical reduction of which zero copula is a widely-documented symptom.

Second, we must ask why speakers, in moving from a basilectal to a mesolectal register, would eliminate an overt copula in favor of zero rather than either retaining the old one or adopting the acrolectal one. In other words, what would the motivation be for zero as an intermediate stage of acquisition? It would seem that if the speakers were invested in approximating a target such as English, which has categorically expressed copulas, it would be an anomalous step backward to adopt zero copula—especially when even their native register had an expressed one.

In particular, such a development would recapitulate no known cline of grammatical development. Children do not acquire, drop, and then reacquire copular morphemes. Furthermore, while the *emergence* of copulas in previously zero-copula languages is well-documented (Li and Thompson 1975, Luo 1991, Devitt 1990, Gildea 1993), the reverse development, the dropping of previously overt copulas, is rare as a regular grammatical change (Russian is one exception, but just that).

2.2. The continuum as adoption

In the 1980s a new conception of the continuum became established. Based on historical research and historical documentation, the general consensus (Chaudenson 1979; Alleyne 1971, 1980; Bickerton 1983: 9, 1996; Baker 1990; Singler 1993) now depicts the continuum as having existed since the founding of the colonies, representing the variant degrees of exposure that individual Africans had to English according to life circumstances (residence in town or country, size of plantation, occupation within the plantation hierarchy, etc.).

Even under this conception, however, the mesolectal zero copula is an anomaly. In positing slaves as acquiring mesolectal competence (or beyond) in the early period of colonization rather than generations later, the revised conception raises a question regarding the traditional substratist treatment of Caribbean copulas.

Specifically, if (as many scholars have proposed) the basilectal copulas such as *da* (*na, a*) are calqued on equivalents in the West African languages spoken by the original slaves in the English Caribbean (Holm 1984, Alleyne 1980: 165–66, Boretzky 1983: 161, Migge 1998), then why did only the forgers of the basilect do this calquing? What blocked this calquing among speakers acquiring a mesolectal register? Furthermore, if one counters that mesolectal speakers may have had less need or inclination to draw on African sources in fleshing out their language, then we are again faced with the question from the previous section: Why would the speakers with more access to the target model, the mesolectal ones, choose zero-copula rather than the basilectal ones?

As Rickford notes (1987: 35), the new historical account of the continuum entails that speakers *adopt* previously existent registers as they move toward a target rather than *create* them. Rickford goes on to point out that this conception need not be seen as ruling out that speakers may create as well as adopt in the process of decreolization. While this point is well-taken, we must note that in relation to the issue treated here, it returns us to the questions posed in section 2.1. In short, under either of the conceptions of the continuum that has guided its investigators, the mesolectal zero-copula is an anomaly that appears to contradict known principles of language contact and change.

## 3. The basilectal copula as innovation

A resolution requires addressing the issue of the source of the basilectal copula *da* (*na, a*).[1] As mentioned, the traditional account is that the basilectal copula is feature of substrate transfer. However, diachronic, synchronic, and comparative facts conspire to indicate that, in fact, the basilectal creole equative copula is an internal innovation, its resemblance to its West African equivalents being accidental (or, more precisely, due to strong typological tendencies).

The importance of this to the current argument is that if the creole equative copulas are internal innovations, then this entails that we reconstruct an original stage of the basilect in which the copula was unexpressed overtly, just as in the mesolect today.

### 3.1. The equative/locative division of labor

The substratist account of *da* (*na, a*) (henceforth referred to as DA, intended as a generic designation denoting all forms of the basilectal equative copula in the English-based Caribbean creoles) proceeds from an argument of wider scope that centers on the fact that in both English-based Caribbean creoles and many of their West African substrate languages, there is a division of labor between an equative and locative copula, such as in Saramaccan[2]:

| *SARAMACCAN* | *FONGBE* |
|---|---|

*Equative*:

(1)  Mi **da**  í    tatá.        (2)  Ùn  **nyí** Àfíáví.
    I   COP your father           1SG be  Afiavi
    "I am your father."          "I am Afiavi." (Lefebvre and Brousseau 2002: 144)

*Locative*:

(3)  Mi **dé**  a    páu déndu. (4)  Wémâ ɔ́  **ɖɔ́** távò jí.
    I   COP LOC tree inside        book  DEF be.at table on
    "I am in the tree."          "The book is on the table." (ibid. 147)

However, this argument becomes less powerful in a cross-linguistic perspective on the copula. The transfer argument for Caribbean creole copulas would be compelling if the equative/locative split were a relatively idiosyncratic trait cross-linguistically. However, despite its anomaly to the European eye, the equative/locative copula split is quite commonly encountered around the world, to the point of being a common-place.[3] Particularly typical is for languages to divide labor between an equative zero copula and a locative expressed one for example. Bengali *lokti ø kerani* "the man is a clerk," *lokti ekhane ache* (clerk here is) "the clerk is here". However, it is also common for both equative and locative copulas to be overt. For example, note table 6.3.

These data do not categorically rule out a causal relationship between the West African scenario and that in the creoles. But, clearly, the transfer argument would be stronger if the equative/locative configuration were an idiosyncratic, rather than common, configuration.

## 3.2. The equative copula in creoles of other lexical bases

The transfer account of creole copulas is further weakened by an investigation of the equative copula in creoles of other lexical bases. It may seem unwarranted to some readers to disassociate the creole copular configuration from their West African ana-logs, given the simple fact that the Africans, after all, had acquired such a configura-tion natively and thus could be expected to have passed it onto the creoles. In fact, however, in creole languages equative copulas are absent as often as present.

For example, if we are to maintain the hypothesis that DA was modeled on its West African equivalents, then we would expect that a similar transfer would have occurred in Haitian Creole French, which formed under similar sociological and demographic conditions to those that created the English-based creoles, with the simi-larities extending even to its substrate composition (visible in a comparison of LePage and De Camp 1960 on the English-based creoles with Singler 1993 on Haitian). Yet Haitian has no equative copula.

Many sources on Haitian misleadingly imply that Haitian has a regularly ex-pressed equative copula *se*. However, quantitative data from the spoken language does not bear this out, as Phillips (1982: 247–49) showed in her dissertation on the Haitian verb phrase: "In Haitian Creole, utterances with no overt, i.e. morphologi-cal, 'to be' are extremely common. . . . Emphatic and interrogative constructions from their verb-less declarative, informal models . . . provoke the use of one or the other formal 'to be.'"

TABLE 6.3. Languages other than West African with separate equative and locative copulas

|  | Equative | Locative | Source |
|---|---|---|---|
| Irish | *is* | *tá* | Stenson 1981 |
| Vietnamese | *là* | *o* | Thompson 1965 |
| Nama | *'a* | *hàa* | Hagman 1977 |
| Hawaiian | *he* | *aia* | Hawkins 1982, Linda Uyechi, pers. comm. |
| Mandarin | *shì* | *zài* | Hashimoto 1969 |
| CiBemba | *ni* | *lì* | Sadler 1964 |

(5)  Etazuni ø o peyi    sosialis.
     U.S.       a country socialist
     "The United States is a socialist country."

(6)  M ø pešr.
     I    fisherman
     "I was a fisherman." (ibid. 250)

DeGraff (1992) shows that the use of *se* is categorical only when the predicate is
marked with a determiner, as in the following contrast:

(7)  Bouki (??se) doktè.
     Bouki SE    doctor
     Bouki is a doctor.

(8)  Bouki se **yon** doktè.
     Bouki SE a   doctor
     Bouki is a doctor.

DeGraff comes to the conclusion that *se* is a demonstrative pronoun.
     Furthermore, this indeed represents the language's original state, as we can see
in the earliest documentation. In Dueoeurjoly (1802), sentences with zero copula are
the norm:

(9)  Mo ø entrepreneur.
     I    entrepreneur
     "I am an entrepreneur." (366)

(10) Mouché et   moué, nou ø z'habitans de . . .
     Monsieur and I    we    inhabitants of
     "Monsieur and I, we are inhabitants of . . ." (368)

The situation is similar in most of the Caribbean French-based creoles, and in the
Indian Ocean French creoles as well (*li ø en kuyoh* "He is an idiot" [Baker 1972:
139, cited in Holm 1984: 304]). Guinea-Bissau Creole Portuguese is another example:

(11) Kabra i     ø     amigu di kačur.
     goat   CLIT COP friend of dog
     "The goat is friend to the dog." (Kihm 1980b: 91)

Thus we see that the transfer of the equative copula was by no means an inevitable
process in the emergence of the Caribbean creoles in general, lending further impetus to search elsewhere for a systematic source of these items in the creoles.

## 3.3. Diachronic evidence

Diachronic analysis makes a particularly compelling case for DA as an innovation,
especially in light of the evidence previously presented.

### 3.3.1. DA as innovation: Typological evidence

*DA* is most plausibly derived not from a verb "to be" but from the English demonstrative *that*. There is no variety today which preserves an exact homophony between the demonstrative and the copula, and the earliest historical documents available (such as of Sranan) show a copula *da* already having evolved. However, we can reconstruct this etymology from a comparative perspective.

Belizean (Escure 1983) has the portmanteau morpheme *dada*, which serves as a demonstrative pronoun while also overtly representing tense. As such, it is likely to have arisen from the adjacency of a demonstrative *da* and a copula *da*:

Belizean Creole English:

(12)  **Dada** we  a de    tel yu.
      that-is what I PROG tell you
      That's what I'm telling you. (ibid. 193)

As an example of the phonological plausibility of the erosion of *dat(i)* into *da*, the Krio demonstrative is *dat* when the demonstrative is used as a pronoun, but *da* when it modifies a noun:

Krio:

(13)  a. **Dat** na  di tin.
         that COP the thing
         "That's the thing." (Fyle and Jones 1980: 66)

      b. Yu get  **da** tin   de?
         you have the thing there
         "Have you got that thing?" (ibid. 63)

What is significant about this derivation from a demonstrative is that in all of the West African languages significantly represented in the substrate of the creoles in question in their formative stages,[4] the equative copula is rendered with a verb "to be" and never a demonstrative. Note, for example, the Ewe *nye*, which takes TMA markers, as do all verbs in the language:

(14)  Ló       é-**nye**  tɔmelã.
      crocodile he-COP aquatic-animal
      The crocodile is an animal that lives in the water. (Westermann 1930: 91)

(15)  Etsɔ     **a-nye**    asigbe.
      tomorrow FUT-COP market-day
      Tomorrow will be market day. (Kozelka 1980: 55)

(16)  AνéΦòΦo   é-**nye-a**  dɔ.
      woodcutting it-is-HAB work
      Woodcutting is supposed to be hard work. (Westermann 1930: 91)

Thus if DA is a West African transfer, then we must ask why a demonstrative was chosen to denote what in the substrate was a verb.

The functional unlikelihood of the recruitment of a demonstrative pronoun in the copular function when originating a contact language is clear in the following list. Note the conceptual leap involved:

|        | *Subject* | *Copula*      | *Predicate*  |
|--------|-----------|---------------|--------------|
| Ewe    | *Kofi*    | *is*          | *the chief*  |
| Creole | *Kofi*    | ***that (??)***| *the chief* |

We might suppose that a chance homophony in one or more of the substrate languages between an equative copula and a distal demonstrative may have served as a model for the creole homophony, but no such homophony occurs in any plausible substrate language examined (see table 6.4).

Note in addition that there is no morpheme here which could even have served as a plausible direct borrowing for DA.

However, we find a cross-linguistically productive explanation for the homophony of an equative copula with a demonstrative pronoun in several studies that have appeared over the past fifteen years. Significantly, these reinforce the hypothesis that DA is an innovation, not a caique.

Specifically, demonstrative-copula homophony represents a diachronic phenomenon. Equative copulas often emerge in initially zero-copula languages through the semantic bleaching of the demonstrative used resumptively in topic-comment constructions (Li and Thompson 1975, Luo 1991, Devitt 1990, McWhorter 1994b, Gildea 1993). Thus in, for example, an earlier stage of Saramaccan, the demonstrative would have been used as a resumptive to a preceding topic, as in:

(a)   [dí Gaamá] [da]   ø   [Kófi] (Who the leader is is Kofi.)
      topic      subject COP predicate
      TOPIC COMMENT

Note that since the language begins as a zero-copula language, there is no overt copula.

Over time, a rebracketing of the sentence occurs: the topic comes to be perceived as a subject, and the resumptive demonstrative comes to be perceived as a copular item between the new subject and predicate:

TABLE 6.4. Equative copulas and demonstrative pronouns in West African languages

|            | *Equative cop.* | that (*pron.*) |
|------------|-----------------|----------------|
| Wolof:     | *la*            | *boobu*        |
| Mandinka:  | *mu*            | *wò*           |
| Akan:      | *yè*            | *nó*           |
| Gbe:       | *nye*           | *má*           |
| Igbo:      | *bù*            | *áhù*          |
| Yoruba:    | *şe/jẹ́*        | *èyí*          |
| Kikongo:   | *ni*            | *kiokio*       |

(b)  [dí Gaamá] [da]   [Kófi] (The leader is Kofi.)
     subject      COP  predicate

This reanalysis instantiates the tendency in grammaticalization for constructions conveying emphasis to lose their semantic potency through constant use (Lehmann 1985; Sweetser 1988; Heine, Claudi, and Hünnemeyer 1991).

   Li and Thompson (1975) show that this type of reanalysis is documented in several languages. For example, Archaic Chinese did not express a copula in equational sentences. Thus:

(17)  Wáng-Tai ø wù        zhě   yě.
      Wang-Tai   outstanding person DEC
      "Wang-Tai is an outstanding person." (ibid. 421)

Meanwhile, the demonstrative pronoun *shì* was used in topic-comment sentences, as in:

(18)  Qíong  yù  jiàn,       **shì** rén   zhǐ  sǔo  wù   yě.
      poverty and debasement this people GEN NOM disike DECL
      "Poverty and debasement, this is what people dislike." (ibid.)

By the 1st century A.D., however, *shì* can be seen used unequivocally as a copula:

(19)  Yu **shì** sǔo   jià   fū-rén zhǐ  fù    yě.
      I   be  NOM  marry woman GEN father DECL
      "1 am the married woman's father." (ibid. 426)

And today this copula occurs regularly in equational sentences:

(20)  Nèi-ge    rén  **shì** xuéshēng.
      that-CLAS man be  student
      "That man is a student." (ibid. 422)

Li and Thompson describe similar processes in Hebrew, Palestinian Arabic, and Wappo.
   Thus we see two things: (1) equative copulas, which are homophonous with demonstrative pronouns, have been shown to be diachronically derivable from those pronouns; and (2) indeed, this is the only semantically plausible way in which a demonstrative pronoun could enter the copular function. Therefore, the etymology of the Saramaccan copula *da* is a clue to its having not existed at the earliest stage of the language, for the simple reason that such a reanalysis requires time.

### 3.3.2. DA as innovation: Historical documentation

There is some empirical evidence of this process having occurred in early documents of the Suriname creoles. Arends (1989) shows sentences in the oldest Sranan documents which contain zero copula where an overt one is required today:

Sranan c. 1770:

(21)  Mi ø no   negeri      fo joe.
      I    NEG black-person for you
      "I am not your slave." (ibid. 160)
      (cf. modern *Mi ano negri fu ju; ano* = COP + NEG)

(22)  Mi blibi   joe ø wan bon  mattie fo dem.
      I    believe you  a    good friend for them
      I believe you're a good friend of theirs. (ibid. 160)
      (cf. modem *Mi bribi taki ju de wan bon mati fu den.*)

Arends indeed hypothesizes that Sranan copula *na* is derived historically from a distal demonstrative.

These attestations do not close the case, because the earliest Sranan documents are sketchy, and even in them, there are many sentences with overt copulas.[5] However, given the typological evidence given in the last section, it seems plausible to interpret the early Sranan data as the documentation of a change in progress which began with zero-copula.

### 3.3.3. DA as innovation: Subject pronoun
###         in equative constructions

Equative sentences in Saramaccan present a feature that makes it all the more likely that such sentences began as topic-comment constructions. The third-person subject pronoun in Saramaccan is *a*:

(23)  A téi   fáka kóti dí gwámba.
      he take knife cut the meat
      "He cut the meat with a knife."

However, in equative sentences, the form *hɛ̃*, an oblique form usually used for emphasis or in isolation (24), must occur in subject position, and never *a* (25):

(24)  **Hɛ̃** a  mbéi dí wósu.
      him he make the house
      "He's the one who made the house."

25)   **Hɛ̃** da   dí Gaamá. (**A da dí Gaamá.*)
      he  COP the chief
      "He is the chief."

Yet in equative sentences *hɛ̃* has neither oblique nor, as one might expect, emphatic meaning. The use of *hɛ̃* in this context is thoroughly grammaticalized: informants spontaneously give these sentences and reject equivalents with *a*.

This anomaly is explicable as the phonological fossilization of a construction that began as a topic-comment structure with zero copula. *Hě* would have been used as topic (just as it is today), and a sentence like *hě da di Gaamá*, then, began as:

(a)  [hě]  [da]    ø    [dí Gaamá] (Him, he's the chief.)
      topic subject COP predicate
      TOPIC COMMENT

and became:

(b)  [hě]    [da] [dí Gaamá] (He's the chief.)
      subject COP predicate

Importantly, this process requires an original zero copula; otherwise, there would not be a position for the erstwhile subject demonstrative *da* to move into. This account inherently requires no transfer of a West African equative copula. Thus the anomalous presence of *hě* in subject position in equative sentences provides further evidence that zero copula was the original rule. It would be difficult to explain the categorical presence of *hě* rather than *a* in such sentences in any other systematic way.[6]

Note that resumptive topic-comment constructions are highly productive in identificational sentences even in modern Saramaccan, showing that such constructions would have been central enough to the grammar to provide ready fodder for a reanalysis. Of course, it is impossible to show examples of *hě-da* resumptive constructions, since these have all long since been reanalyzed as subject-copula sentences. However, *hě-da* sentences are today "recycled," in a sense, in topic-comment constructions in which the comment was, in earlier Saramaccan, a topic-comment construction itself:

(26)  Alísi **hě** da   dí súti  njǎnjá u  Saamáka.
      Rice it  COP the sweet food for Saramaka
      Rice is the tastiest food in Saramaka. (Rountree and Glock 1976: 41)

(27)  Dí bɛ wáta dé   wɛ **hě** da   buúu.
      the red water there well it COP blood
      The red water is blood. (Rountree and Glock 1977: 186)[7]

### 3.3.4. Summary

Despite the superficial attractiveness of deriving DA from West African equative copulas, the conclusion that DA was an independent innovation is virtually inescapable.[8]

That equative copulas were not transferred is predictable from the nature of pidginization, which strongly discourages the transfer of items that make no semantic contribution. Lyons (1968: 322) notes that in many languages the copula is unnecessary. The function of the copula is, in Lyons's words, "to serve as the locus in a surface structure for the marking of tense, mood, and aspect," "generated . . . when there is no other element to carry these distinctions." In zero-copula languages, the copula is not used in unmarked contexts. Thus in Russian, "Mary is beautiful" is *Marija ø krasivaja*, a sentence in the unmarked present tense. However, in the past a copula is used: "Mary was beautiful" *Marija byla krasivaja.* In languages such as English, the copula has been generalized to use in all contexts. However, in all cases, its function is simply to carry tense, mood, and aspect; it has no meaning in itself, being instead a "semantically-empty 'dummy verb'" (ibid.).

## 4. Implications

The creole continuum has often been seen as representing an ontogeny on view, with the basilect as the original stage. What I have shown in the discussion here, however, indicates that in terms of equative copula constructions, even the most basilectal registers available to us today display the results of evolution from an original stage now long vanished. While today, basilects are marked by the overt copula DA, we see that at their inception, they had zero copula.

This, in turn, allows a new perspective on the mesolectal zero copula. Specifically, we can see that the copula scenario in, for example, Guyanese Creole English is actually a derived one, having begun as shown in table 6.5.

What is most significant here is that originally, zero copula reigned in *both the mesolect and the basilect.*

### 4.1.  Life-cycle issues

This new picture explains the anomaly of zero copula appearing oniy in a continuum variety closer to the standard.

First, to the extent that *creation* of varieties while moving toward the target is still considered a perhaps partially valid account, the advantage of this scenario is obvious: we no longer need posit an awkward, acquisitionally unmotivated stage of zero copula in between stages in which it is expressed overtly.

Second, in terms of the more widely accepted conception of the continuum as an original condition, the new scenario allows a more graceful incorporation into continuum theory of the association between zero copula and contact-induced reduction. As previously noted, it is difficult to reconcile the findings of Ferguson (1971), Corder (1978), and others with the copula in the creole continuum if basilectal DA is treated as original. Holm (1984), for example, points to a possible connection between creole zero copulas and Ferguson's identification of zero copula with simpli-

TABLE 6.5. Diachronic account of the copula before NP in Guyanese Creole English

|  | *Original* | *Modern* |
|---|---|---|
| Acrolect: | *iz/waz* | *iz/waz* |
| Mesolect: | ø | ø |
| Basilect: | ø | *da* |

fied speech registers (296), but then associates the tendency towards overt copula before NP to calquing on West African equative copulas (298). However, this analysis locates the application of a prototypical pidginization phenomenon to the mesolect, a level above the basilect in which we would expect such effects to be most visible.

Approaching the continuum as I suggest, however, an analysis such as Holm's can be seen as applying to both of the lower lects rather than just the middle one. Thus the effects of reduction associated with limited access to a target are applied to both of the registers more removed from the standard, which is obviously preferable to positing that these effects somehow "skipped" the basilect and applied only to the mesolect. In the meantime, the superficial similarities between DA and West African copulas reveals themselves to be deceptive, despite the validity of transfer accounts of many other parts of Caribbean creole grammars.

## 4.2. Substrate transfer

The new scenario also provides new guidelines for the documentation of the role of substrate transfer in creole continua. The analysis leaves much of the traditional transfer account in this area unchallenged. For example, Holm (1984: 298) attributes the high rate of copula absence before adjectives to the fact that in the predicate position, adjectival concepts are expressed with verbs in the basilect (this point is elaborated by Baugh 1980). Because this strategy, in turn, is typical of the West African languages in the Caribbean substrate (cf. Welmers 1973), transfer is indeed the likely source of this trait in the creoles.

However, my continuum scenario suggests that when charting the role of the substrate in the manifestation of the creole copula, the West African equivalents themselves (as opposed to issues regarding verbs and adjectives) will be of little use. This is preliminarily clear in that, contrary to the implications of some analyses, *the equative (and locative) copulas are categorically overt in all of the plausible substrate languages*; there is no model whatsoever in the languages for copular absence. I have shown that these facts are actually unsurprising, given that the West African copulas were not transferred to the creoles in the first place.

This left zero copula as the original rule in the basilect and mesolect, with the subsequent independent development of overt copulas in the basilect, obscures the original configuration and makes a connection with West African equivalents mistakenly attractive. West African copulas will not explain either DA, its acrolectal equivalents, or copular absence at any level of the continuum.[9]

## 4.3. Zero copula as deletion in AAVE?

This analysis also sheds light on whether zero copula in AAVE is due to a copula not being generated at all or to its being deleted before surface structure. Labov (1969) argued for the latter explanation, a deletion account, proposing a rule taking the standard English contraction of *to be* a step further into deletion. Crucial to the argument was that copular absence is grammatical in AAVE just where contraction is in the standard (AAVE *He ∅ a man* vs. standard *He's a man*), and ungrammatical just where contraction is in the standard (AAVE *He know where she ø*, given that in the standard, *\*I know where he's*).

Fasold (1976) provided a historical gloss to this analysis, noting that while deletion rates were quite similar in recorded narratives by aged slaves in the late 1930s, the contraction rates were much lower, suggesting that a deletion rule was operating independently of the contraction rule some 100 years before his writing. Based on these findings, Fasold allowed the validity of Labov's analysis to AAVE as spoken today, but he constructed a separate pathway of development for the copula during AAVE's hypothesized decreolization towards the English target.

However, this account entails deletion as well. Fasold proposed that in AAVE, an original *da* developed immediately into *is* (indeed, thereby avoiding the superficially awkward zero-copula intermediary stage), but that *is* then became optional rather than categorical, by analogy with an optional usage of *is* before the V-*ing* construction, which itself only later in the dine becomes categorical, as table 6.6 shows:

Note that in the mesolect, grammaticality of zero copula before NP only emerges as the result of analogy with the V-*ing* construction. At stage six, contraction enters as a new alternate, modeled on the standard; in stage seven, deletion is no longer syntactic and is derived, after Labov (1969), from deletion after contraction. Thus we see that Fasold's new conception depicts *is* as originally categorical in the mesolect (stage four), with its optionality resulting only from a later analogy with a separate optionality in the V-*ing* construction (stage five). The analysis would seem to have the advantage of avoiding an awkward transition from overt copula through zero copula to overt copula again. The question arises, however, as to what motivated the direction of the analogy. Why wouldn't the categorical overtness of the copula before NP have rendered the copula before V-*ing* categorical, rather than the V-*ing* construction passing on its optionality?

With the continuum reconstructed as above, we can account for zero copula without recourse to two rules, avoiding the lack of directional motivation noted above as well. Instead, the new scenario allows us to designate the zero copula in AAVE as a simple case of dialectal mixture, in which a mesolectal zero stemming

TABLE 6.6. Fasold's conception of the development of zero copula before NP in AAVE

| Stage | A. *They are fish.* | B. *They are fishing.* |
|---|---|---|
| 1. Pure basilect | *Dem da fish.* | *Dem da fish.* |
| 2. *da > V-in* in B | *Dem da fish.* | *Dem ø fishin.* |
| 3. *da > is* in A | *Dem is fish.* | *Dem ø fishin.* |
| 4. Optional *is* in B | *Dem is fish.* | *Dem (is) fishin.* |
| 5. Optional *is* in A | **Dem (is) fish.** | *Dem (is) fishin.* |
| 6. Contraction enters as alternate from standard | *Dem (is) fish. / Dem fish.* | *Dem (is) fishin. / Dem's fishin.* |
| 7. Deletion now entirely phonological | *Dem is fish. > Dem's fish. >* **Dem ø fish.** | *Dem is fishin. > Dem's fishin. > Dem ø fishin* |

Adapted from Fasold 1976: 79.

from contact-induced reduction alternates with an acrolectal overt copula, as a reflection of the continuum nature of African-American speech. The preferability of this conception is only clear when we are able to thus account for mesolectal zero as a typical Fergusonian trait of reduction. The tendency to account for it as a "deletion" would seem to have been motivated by the presence of overt copula in the basilect as well as the acrolect, which we have now seen is a derived configuration stemming from an original one in which both the basilect and the mesolect were zero-copula dialects.

# The Diachrony of Predicate
# Negation in Saramaccan Creole

*Synchronic and Typological Implications*

## 1. Introduction

In this chapter I examine the diachrony of predicate negation in Saramaccan Creole (henceforth SM). It is possible, through reference to historical documentation in conjunction with comparative and internal reconstruction, to chart the emergence of the synchronic predicate negator allomorphy in SM. The diachronic process in question differs significantly from the relatively straightforward one which the synchronic facts would lead one to expect, an aspect of the analysis that makes the study particularly valuable in the area of diachronic syntax. In addition, the results are of interest for the light they shed on typology and creole studies.

## 2. Predicate negation in modern Saramaccan

There has been only one relatively extended description of SM negation in the literature other than this one, in Byrne (1987: 169–70). The description is representative of what briefer accounts there have been elsewhere (Glock 1972: 55–56; Rountree 1992: 41–42).

There are two predicate negators in SM, *á* and *ná*. Byrne notes that the more frequently occurring negator, *á*, occurs between a subject and a VP. Examples:

(1)  Mi **á**   o   dá  i   dí  pindá.[1]
     I   NEG FUT give you the peanut
     "I am not going to give you the peanut."

(2)   Dí mujếề **á**   dế   a   wósu.[2]
      the woman NEG COP LOC house
      "The woman is not at home."

The negator *ná*, according to Byrne, "appears when there is no pleonastic pronoun or theta-marked external role (whether overt or not) preceding." This accounts
for various occurrences. For example, it is also used with negative imperatives:

(3)   **Ná**   wáka! (\*Á wáka!)
      NEG walk
      "Don't walk!"

*Ná* is also used with certain predicate adjectives that take no subject:

(4)   **Ná**   tuú.
      NEG true
      "That isn't true."

Byrne does not mention that *ná* is also used when the negator has scope over the
entire proposition as in (5), but this falls within his description in any case:

(5)   **Ná**   mi dú.
      NEG I   do
      "It wasn't my fault." (DeGroot 1981: 202)
      (i.e. "That I did it is not the case," in contrast to *Mi á dú* "I did not do it")

(6)   **Ná**   i   bi   tjá   dí soní akí gó alá,   o?
      NEG you ANT carry the thing here go there INT
      "Haven't you carried this away?" (ibid.)

Byrne designates *á* as a "derived" form. The implication is that *á* is a reflex of *ná*
generated after the subject, the initial consonant of *ná* having been eroded as the result
of the phonological effect of preceding NPs as the result of heavy usage. Byrne's
analysis implies that, diachronically, the initial consonant of *ná* would have simply
eroded after the subject across the grammar, resulting in the current complementary
distribution of allomorphs:

(7)   Kófi **ná** wáka. > Kófi **(n)á** wáka. > Kófi **á** wáka. "Kofi is not walking."

A closer examination reveals that the distribution is not quite this tidy, however.
      Byrne's treatment is primarily concerned with issues relating to finiteness of VP,
and as a result there are aspects of SM predicate negation which he does not discuss.
Specifically, Byrne states that "*ná* never follows a subject whether pleonastic or not"
(169). However, this is belied by two occurrences of heavy use. First, when equative
sentences with the copula *da* are negated, *ná* is used categorically, always preceded
by a subject in such cases:

(8)  Dí wómi **da**   dí  kabiténi.
     the man   COP the captain
     "The man is the captain."

(9)  Dí wómi **ná**   dí  kabiténi.
     the man  NEG the captain
     "The man is not the captain."

Second, when sentences of possession using PPs with *fu* "for" are negated, *ná* is also used, again preceded regularly by a subject (before *mi* in this usage, *fu* regularly occurs as allomorph *u*):

(10)  Dí pindá **ná**   u  mi.
      the peanut NEG for me
      "The peanut is not mine."

Thus we see that while Byrne proposes a division of labor between *á* and *ná* where *á* is generated after a subject and *ná* appears otherwise, the fact is that *ná* regularly appears after the subject in two grammatically central contexts: (1) identificational sentences and (2) possessive sentences with *fu* PPs. These sentences render invalid an account which proposes that *á* arose via the phonological erosion of *ná* by preceding subjects across the grammar, since if this had been the case, *á* would be grammatical in these sentence types as well.

These cases do not, in my opinion, license a reformulation of Byrne's account from a *synchronic* perspective, stipulating that *á* is generated after the subject. Instead, from the perspective of the synchronic mental representation of SM, these cases are best analyzed as exceptions within the grammar. While there is a temptation to seek some general feature of equative sentences which would condition *ná* rather than *á* in sentence (9), the fact is that in semantically similar sentences with the other copula in SM, *dé*, *ná* is ungrammatical and *á* appears:

(11)  Dí búku **á**    **dέ**  wá mbéti.
      the book NEG COP a  animal
      "The book is not an animal."

The likelihood that sentences like (9) are exceptions is reinforced by another anomalous behavior that they exhibit: *ná* suppletes da rather than preceding it, while the negator precedes other copulas as well as all other verbs:

(12)  a. Dí wómi **ná**    kabiténi.
         the man  NEG captain
         "The man is not the captain."

      b. Dí búku **á**    **dέ**  wá mbéti.
         the book NEG COP a  animal
         "The book is not an animal."

Similarly, possessive sentences such as (10) are also best analyzed as exceptions. First of all, the affirmative reflex of such sentences is anomalous in its configuration as well. Generally, in the affirmative the copula *dé* appears before nonverbal predicates consisting of a PP:

(13)   Dí wómi **dé**   a      páu déndu.
       the man   COP LOC tree inside
       "The man is in the tree."

Nonverbal predicates with *fu*-headed PPs, however, are unique in that no overt copula appears in them in SM:

(14)   Dí búku ø     u   mi.³
       the book COP for me
       "The book is mine."

(15)   Dí pindá ø     u   mí máma.
       the peanut COP for my mother
       "The peanut is my mother's."

Correspondingly, sentences like (10) are the only nonverbal PP predicates in the grammar which take *ná*, rather than *á dé*, when negated:

(16)   a. Dí pindá **ná**   u   mi.
          the peanut NEG for me
          "The peanut is not mine."

       b. Dí mujɛ̃ɛ́ **á**    **dé**   a      wósu. (*Dí mujɛ̃ɛ́ ná a wósu.)
          the woman NEG COP LOC house
          "The woman is not at home."

   Nevertheless, as it happens, these behaviors reveal that despite the apparent plausibility of a phonological account for the development of *á*, it is inescapable that *á* arose via a different pathway. This pathway, in turn, sheds light on various more general issues.

## 3. Diachronic development of the modern distribution of negators

### 3.1. The reanalysis pathway

We have seen that on first glance, it would appear that *á* arose from the erosion of the initial consonant of *ná*. However, taking into account synchronic phenomena, known diachronic tendencies, comparative data, and historical documentation, it is possible to establish that in actuality, *á* arose via a reanalysis resulting from the fusion of the third-person pronoun *a*, when used as a resumptive after a topic NP, with a following *ná*. Thus *á* arose in contexts such as (17):

(17)    Kófi, a  ná    wáka.
  Kofi  he NEG walk
  "Kofi, he's not walking."
  [Kófi] [a ná wáka]
  TOPIC COMMENT

The pronominal *a* fused with the following negator *ná* to produce *á*, at which point the new item was presumably interpreted for a time as a portmanteau morpheme, combining the functions of the pronominal and the negator:
  Reconstructed:

(18)    *Kófi, á*  *wáka.*
  Kofi he-NEG walk
  "Kofi, he's not walking."
  [Kófi] [*á wáka*]
  TOPIC COMMENT

The modern interpretation would have arisen through a reanalysis of the topic in such sentences as a subject, with a subsequent reinterpretation of *á* without a pronominal component, encoding solely negativity:

(19)    Kófi **á**    wáka.
  Kofi NEG walk
  "Kofi is not walking."

This reanalysis would have been spurred initially by the coalescence of pronominal *a* and negator *ná*, which was predictable given their common status as monosyllables with back vowels. This coalescence paved the way for the operation of the strong tendency observed cross-linguistically for topics to be reanalyzed as subjects (Li and Thompson 1976, Givón 1976, Shibatani 1991).

  In reference to the occurrences of the negators that Byrne treats, this revised conception accounts for the facts just as well: *á* occurs in the context in which it was produced as a result of the adjacency of pronominal *a* and negator *ná*, while in contexts in which no such adjacency has or does occur, the original *ná* remains. Thus:

 a. *Á* between subject and VP:
  *Kófi á wáka.* "Kofi is not walking."
  *Mi á o dá i dí pindá.* "I will not give you the peanut."

 b. *Ná* elsewhere:
  Impersonal predicate adjectives: *Ná tuú.* 'It isn't true.'
  Negative imperatives: *Ná wáka!* 'Don't walk.'
  Sentential negation: *Ná mi dú.* 'I didn't do it.'

However, my conception has the advantage of accounting as well for the anomalous occurrences of *á* that Byrne did not treat.

## 3.2. Evidence for the reanalysis

Here (sections 3.2.1 and 3.2.2), I present seven arguments supporting my revised diachronic derivation of *á* in view of the occurrences of negators that Byrne treats.

### 3.2.1. Ná *as the original allomorph*

There are four principal clues suggesting that *ná* was originally the only predicate negator in SM (a fact which Byrne's analysis does not contest).

3.2.1.1. COMPARATIVE ANALYSIS    Most of the Atlantic English-based creoles have only one predicate negator, with an *n*V shape, often *na*. If the negator does exhibit allomorphy, the allomorphs differ only in the quality of the vowel. This suggests that the situation in SM is a derived one, arising from a phonetic and syntactical reconditioning of *ná* in certain environments. Following are sentences from Jamaican and Guyanese Creole English, showing the use of the same predicate negator, both preceded by subjects and not:

Jamaican:

(20)  a. Im **na**  siŋ fí wi.
        he NEG sing for us
        "She doesn't sing for us."

      b. **Na**  siŋ!
        NEG sing
        "Don't sing!"

Guyanese:

(21)  a. I  **na**  a     siŋ fo awi.
        she NEG PROG sing for us
        "She doesn't sing for us." (Hancock 1987: 299)

      b. **Na**  siŋ!
        NEG sing
        "Don't sing!" (John Rickford, pers. comm.)

3.2.1.2. SYNCHRONIC DISTRIBUTION OF ALLOMORPHS    *Ná*, and not *á*, occurs in negative indefinite nominals, as in *ná wã soní* (not one thing) "nothing" and *ná wã sɛmbɛ* (not one person) "nobody":

(22)  Ná  wã soní tá-pasá.
      NEG one thing PROG-happen
      "Nothing is happening."

Given that *á* appears only in the domain of VP, while *ná* appears not only there but also with NP, it becomes more likely that *ná* was diachronically primary.

3.2.1.3. PROVERBS    Proverbs are often indicative of conservative registers of a language. It is significant, then, that in SM proverbs we find usages of *ná* after a subject in contexts in which *á* would be required today:

(23)  Fúkuma      **ná á'**  wójo.
      needy-person NEG have eye
      "The needy have no eyes." (Summer Institute of Linguistics 1982: 7)

3.2.1.4. HISTORICAL DOCUMENTATION    As it happens, the earliest documents we have in SM support the account I am proposing. These documents were transcribed by Moravian missionaries whose competence in SM appears to have been quite proficient, on the basis of the generally accurate representation of modern SM structure they present. Here we see no sign of *á*, and instead the CV negator occurs after the subject (24) as well as where *ná* appears today (25):

(24)  A takki da   dem: dem **no**   mussu komotto na   Jerusalem.[4]
      he talk  give them they NEG must   leave   LOC Jerusalem
      "He told them that they must not leave Jerusalem." (Wietz 1805: 1)

(25)  **No**  so   a de?
      NEG thus it be
      "Isn't that so?" (Randt 1781)

Note that the negator here is *no* rather than *ná*. Given the lack of evidence in the current grammar of *no* as the original negator, there is a temptation here to question the accuracy of the source. The transcription of pidgins and creoles in the eighteenth and nineteenth centuries is notoriously unreliable in many cases, due to ignorance of, or disrespect for, the languages by the transcribers. The possibility of faulty transcription is particularly likely in this case because the missionaries who transcribed SM in the late eighteenth and early nineteenth centuries had extensive previous experience in transcribing Sranan, a lexically and grammatically similar creole spoken on the coast of Suriname. Despite the good intentions of the Moravians, and the accuracy of their transcriptions in many aspects, these early SM documents contain the occasional indisputable Srananism that was highly unlikely to have been uttered by actual speakers of the language, such as *nanga* for "with" (SM uses *ku*).[5] As it happens, Sranan also has apparently always had *no* as a general negator (*Mi no sabi* "I don't know"). Confronted with no evidence for *no* in modern SM on the one hand, and these Srananizing tendencies on the other, it is tempting to suppose that the negator *no* in these early SM documents represents a mistranscription on the part of Moravians accustomed to hearing *no*, perhaps hearing *ná* as a variant thereof.

However, a comparative consideration leads to a reassessment of that judgement. Ndjuka is another Surinamese creole spoken by descendants of maroon slaves, which has taken shape in similarly isolated conditions until recently. The originators of Ndjuka fled from plantations where Sranan was spoken, and thus the language is quite similar to Sranan today and is partially intelligible with it; as a result, Ndjuka can rightly be viewed as an offshoot of Sranan. In the domain of negation, while Sranan uses *no*, Ndjuka uses *ná* as SM does (Huttar and Huttar 1994) for example, *U ná abi* "you don't have." It is clear in this case that *ná* represents an internal phonological evolution of Sranan *no*. This demonstrates the possibility that a similar development occurred in SM and that therefore, in the earliest stage of the language, the negator was *no*, as it must have been in Ndjuka.

I am inclined to believe that this was indeed the case. The material in question closely reflects the subtleties of spoken SM in many other areas, such as the transcription of certain marginal contexts in which the copula is omitted; the use of an emphatic discourse particle difficult to elicit today; and the use of topic-comment constructions with resumptive pronouns where a European transcriber would often be tempted to resort to simple subject-predicate sentences, and so on. On the phonological level, there is an attempt (albeit inconsistent) to reflect the opposition between open and closed middle vowels (*weki* [weki] "to wake" vs. *keh* [kɛ] "to want"). It is hard to imagine that the transcribers could have heard *ná* as often as they would have in the case of so high-frequency an item and nevertheless have insisted on transcribing *no*.

Thus the historical documents strongly suggest that at an earlier stage in SM history, *ná* was the only negator. In addition, the documents show that at its origins, this negator is likely to have had the form *no*.

### 3.2.2. *The fusion of pronominal* a *and negator* ná

I now present evidence that *á* is indeed derived from the fusion over time of third-person singular pronominal *a* and negator *ná*.

3.2.2.1. TOPIC-COMMENT CONSTRUCTIONS IN SM    I suggested in section 2 that *á* arose as a concomitant of the reanalysis of topic-comment sentences as subject-predicate sentences. This account does not depend on a hypothetical reconstruction of such a configuration, since topic-comment constructions are very common in the language today. Next I show two such sentences in which the third-person pronominal subject is coreferent with the topic, just the configuration which produced today's negator *á*:

(26)  Hélipe,  a  lúku dí  dédɛ dé  píí.
      monkey he look the dead be quiet
      "The monkey, he looked at the dead body laying there quiet."

(27)  Dí mujɛ̃ɛ̃,  a  paí dí mií  a    wã́ dáka.
      the woman she bear the child LOC one day
      "The woman, she bore the child one day."

We see, then, that the configuration I propose as the source for the current distribution of negators is still vital in SM.

3.2.2.2. FUSION OF *Á* WITH PRONOMINALS    Most subject pronominals regularly combine with the following negator in SM, according to morphophonemic processes, as in:

(28)  *má wáka* "I am not walking"[6]
      *já wáka* "You are not walking"
      *á wáka* "He/she/it is not walking"

Here, then, is an incontrovertible synchronic manifestation of the fusion of *a* with *ná*, yielding a form identical to the predicate negator:

(29)  a. **Á**        wáka.
         he-NEG walk
         "He is not walking."

      b. Kófi **á**    wáka.
         Kofi NEG walk
         "Kofi is not walking."

3.2.2.3. PHONOLOGICAL FACTS    Finally, the derivation of *ná* from pronominal *a* + negator *ná* is predictable from the high tone of *á*: the nasal consonant disappeared during the fusion, and the two vowels became one (presumably as the result of heavy usage), but the high tone of *ná* was left behind.

As discussed in note 1, in the Upper River dialect the form is *ã́* trather than *á*. The Upper River dialect is in some respects slightly more conservative than the Lower River dialect. Along these lines, it is possible that *ã́* represents an evolutionary stage intermediate between pronominal *a* + *ná* and *á*, in which [n] had been eroded but left behind a reflex of itself in the form of a nasal quality on the vowel. Thus this variant can be seen as further evidence that the source of *á* was *a* + *ná*: *a* (pron.) + *ná* > *ã́* > *á*.

Thus we see that there is a wealth of evidence from a variety of perspectives, which strongly suggests the validity of the account I have proposed. Next I demonstrate how the validity of this account is bolstered in explaining the seemingly idiosyncratic occurrences of *ná* I described in section 2.

## 3.3. Anomalous occurrences of *ná* in modern SM

### 3.3.1. Identificational predicates

As I showed in section 1, although the conventional description of *ná* stipulates that it never appears after a subject, it does so regularly in two contexts, one being in negated identificational sentences in which the copula *da* appears in the affirmative:

(30)  a. Dí wómi **da**   dí kabiténi.
         the man   COP the captain
         "The man is the captain."

      b. Dí wómi **ná**   dí kabiténi. (*Dí wómi a dí kabiténi.)
         the man   NEG the captain
         "The man is not the captain."

(31)  a. Hẽ **da**   dí kabiténi.
         he COP the captain
         "He is the captain."

b. Hɛ **ná**    dí  kabiténi. (\*hɛ̃ á dí kabiténi.)
   he  NEG the captain
   "He is not the captain."

If *á* were indeed generated after the subject across the grammar, then we would expect *á* to appear in these cases. The reasons that it does not lend further confirmation to my account of the emergence of *á*.

The reason for the strange occurrence of *ná* in these cases is revealed through a closer look at sentences like (31a) in which the subject is a third-person pronominal. As we have seen, the third-person singular subject pronominal in SM is generally *a*. *Hɛ̃*, in contrast, is an oblique form used in isolation or for emphasis:

(32)  **Hɛ́**, a  mbéi dí  wósu.
      him he make the house
      "He's the one who made the house."

Yet before identificational predicates, and only in this context, *hɛ̃* appears in subject position, and *a* is ungrammatical:

(33)  **Hɛ̃** da    dí  kabiténi. (\*A da dí kabiténi.)
      he  COP the captain
      "He is the captain."

Of course, this occurrence of *hɛ̃* can only have blocked the emergence of *á* if it was indeed in place before *á* began to arise. The documents confirm that this was the case: *hɛ̃* as subject in identificational sentences is well in place in late eighteenth-century documents, while, as we have seen in the previous section, the predicate negator is still *no* across the board:
      SM 1781:

(34)  **Hem** da    marka.
      it    COP miracle
      "It is a miracle." (Randt 1781)

SM 1805:

(35)  **Hem** da    wan krutuman.
      he    COP a   wise-man
      "He was a prudent man." (Wietz 1805: 56)

(36)  Dem **no**    mussu komotto na    Jerusalem.
      they NEG  must  come-out LOC Jerusalem
      "They must not leave Jerusalem." (ibid.: 1)

Upon analysis, it becomes clear that there was a causal relationship between this quirk in this sentence type and the fact that it is negated with *ná*. The negator *á* does not appear in identificational sentences because *á* arose through a phonological fusion which never occurred in them, for the simple reason that as the fusion was taking place elsewhere, in these sentences *ná* was preceded by the oblique *hɛ̃* rather than the subject *a*. Thus the emergence of *á* in this context was "blocked" by the fact that a separate reanalysis had left an oblique form in subject position in this particular sentence type.

It would appear that this occurrence of *ná* is indeed licensed by *hɛ̃* and is not a more structurally general aspect of these sentences. For example, we might be tempted to stipulate that predicate negation in SM is sensitive to the occurrence of copulas in general. However, predicates with the locative copula *dé* are negated with *á*, as are regular VPs:

(37)  Dí mujɛ̃́ɛ̃ **á**    **dé**  a    wósu. (\*Dí mujɛ̃́ɛ̃ ná a wósu.)
       the woman NEG COP LOC house
       "The woman is not at home."

There is another account that at first glance appears promising. We might be tempted to stipulate that *ná* is licensed by the equative relation in general rather than by *hɛ̃*. But then, in SM the identificational sentence type (A = B) is a subtype of a more general class of sentences, the equative, the other class of which is class sentences (A ⊂ B). While *da* is used in identificational sentences, *dé* is often used in class sentences (as in [10]):
Identificational (A = B):

(38)  Hɛ **da**   dí kabiténi.
       he COP the captain.
       "He is the captain."

       Class (A ⊂ B):

(39)  A **dé**   wɑ̃́ dágu (\*Hɛ̃ **dé** wɑ̃́ dágu.)
       it COP a  dog
       "It is a dog."[7]

However, as we have seen, *ná* only negates the identificational sentence; even in the equative, *dé* is negated like other verbs via the preposing of *á*:

(40)  Búku **á**    **dé**   wɑ̃́ mbéti. (\*Búku ná wɑ̃́ mbéti. / Búku ná dé wɑ̃́ mbéti.)
       book NEG COP a  animal
       "A book is not an animal."

Thus we see that the occurrence of *ná* in identificational sentences must be ascribed to the presence of *hɛ̃* in subject position, this having prevented the emergence of *á* in such sentences.

It is important to note that if *á* had arisen simply as the result of erosion affected by preceding subjects, then *á* would certainly have arisen in identificational sentences as well. Sentences such as *Hɛ̃ ná dí kabiténi* constitute synchronic clues to the invalidity of the erosion account of *á*. The next section presents another such clue.

### 3.3.2. Ná *in PPs with* fu *"for"*

The other context in which *ná* appears unexpectedly is before nonverbal predicates with *fu* "for," as shown in section 1:

(41)  Dí  pindá  **ná**  u  mi. (*Dí pindá á u mi.)
      the peanut NEG for me
      "The peanut is not mine."

As it happens, like the identificational sentences, this sentence type demonstrates another idiosyncratic behavior that reinforces an account of *á* emerging in topic-comment constructions.

What must first be explained is why *fu* sentences take *ná* rather than *á dé* NEG COP, as do all other nonverbal PP predicates. As we have seen, the copula *dé* appears before other nonverbal predicates consisting of a PP in the affirmative:

(42)  Dí  wómi  **dé**  a  páu déndu.
      the man   COP LOC tree inside
      "The man is in the tree."

Nonverbal predicates with *fu* PPs, however, are unique in that no overt copula appears in them in SM:

(43)  Dí  búku ∅  u  mi.
      the book COP for me
      "The book is mine."

(44)  Dí  pindá ∅  u  mí máma.
      the peanut COP for my mother
      "The peanut is my mother's."

This anomaly represents a fortuitous fossilization of a previous stage of SM grammar, largely recoverable only through inference today, in which there were no overt copulas in the grammar at all (cf. chapters 6 and 8). Thus while *dé* now appears before all other PPs, they are absent in *fu* sentences, most likely as the result of the heavy usage possessive constructions undergo in spoken language and the resistance to change that is often observable in items of particularly heavy usage (such as the plurals *men*, *women*, and *children* in English).

One argument for this account is that it is more systematic to explain such a zero-allomorph as a fossilization of a previously categorical rule than to propose that a previously overt copula disappeared in so narrow a context and not elsewhere. While fossilization is a widely observed phenomenon, there is no observed mechanism to account for the disappearance of an overt copula solely before *fu* PPs.

A result of this absence of the overt copula in *fu* sentences, and their general resistance to change in SM, is that they would have retained the original predicate negation strategy, the preposing of *ná*. This, however, does not explain the presence of *ná* in these sentences *today*, for this reason: All other occurrences of *ná* after the subject have been transformed into *á* through fusion with preceding pronominal *á* (except in identificational sentences for the reasons described above). Why has this not happened in *fu* sentences? To illustrate:

> If: *Kófi*, *a ná wáka*. > *Kófi á wáka*.
> Then why not: *Dí búku*, *a ná fu mi*. > *Dí búku á fu mi?*

We find the explanation in *fu* sentences in which the subject is a third-person singular pronominal. Negated nonverbal predicate PPs with *fu*, and only those with *fu*, license an empty subject in the third person:

(45)  a. **Ná**  u   mi.
       NEG for me
       "it is not mine."

    b. Á     **dé**  a    páu déndu. (*Ná dé a páu déndu.)
       he-NEG COP LOC tree inside
       "It is not in the tree."

This most likely falls out of a general trait of the negator *ná*, which appears to license empty subject sentence-initially provided the subject is inanimate, as in *ná tuú* "It isn't true." The import of this is that here is another case where in topic-comment constructions, the appearance of *á* would have been blocked by the fact that the configuration producing it did not occur in this context. Where in most topic-comment configurations with resumptive subject pronouns, *a* would appear, in these *fu* sentences, *a* was not overt, and as a result the fusion requisite to the emergence of *á* never happened:

(46)  a. [*Dí búku*] [*ø*]    [*ná*] [*ø u mi*]
       topic      subject NEG COP-predicate
       **TOPIC COMMENT**

    b. [*Di búku*] [*ná*] [*ø u mi*]
       subject   NEG COP-predicate

Thus we see that the validity of a diachronic account of *á*, which depends on topic-comment structures, is strongly reinforced by the elegance with which it is possible to explain the anomalous synchronic occurrences of *ná* with reference to those same structures.

## 4. Implications

### 4.1. Issues within creole studies

#### 4.1.1. Saramaccan as the creole base

The originators of SM were slaves who escaped from plantations on the coast of Suriname beginning in the mid-1660s and founded communities in the interior, which survive today. As a result of this geographical isolation, SM has been observed to retain a particularly rich concentration of features derived from transfer from the West African languages native to its originators; unlike most creoles, SM has had only light adstratal exposure to European languages since its inception. As a result, SM has traditionally been seen as one of the purest, most extreme instantiations extant of the effects of creolization.

However, the predicate negator allomorphy in SM suggests that, despite the basic appropriateness of the conception of SM as a highly conservative creole, specific conclusions resulting from these phenomena must be made with great caution. Through comparative and internal reconstruction, it is possible to ascertain that SM syntax has undergone significant diachronic change despite having existed for only three centuries. As a result, it displays features that must be seen as internal developments rather than original endowments. This is also the case in the area of the copula, which has been a feature of prime concern in continuum studies (e.g., Day 1973, Bickerton 1975). Thus we have seen that while a creole like Guyanese Creole English has a straightforward predicate negation rule, which stipulates the preposing of *na* to any predicate, SM has two predicate negator allomorphs rather than one, and their distribution is determined by a rule which has two grammatically central exceptions. In other words, SM predicate negation is actually aberrant in comparison to related creoles, and cannot serve as a basis for reconstruction of a Proto-Atlantic English creole.[8]

This casts in a new light claims that creoles' youth precludes their having undergone significant structural change over their lifespans apart from decreolization. Bickerton (1984: 179), for example, suggests that SM has undergone little or no syntactic change since its inception, the one change possible having been a conventionalization of word order. In the meantime, while other scholars have acknowledged the effects of change upon SM, their observations have been largely limited to the phonological changes that are readily apparent from a comparison of SM with its more phonologically conservative sister creoles Sranan and Ndjuka, as well as its lexifiers (e.g., Alleyne 1980).

### 4.1.2. SM as Universal Grammar in vitro

Related to this view is that of some creolists who have proposed that SM represents Universal Grammar on display, unobscured by the diachronic accretions that make the operations of UG so difficult to perceive in other languages (see Bickerton 1984: 178, Byrne 1987). This view is based on a supposition that the originators of SM escaped into the bush having had the opportunity to acquire only the rudiments of a contact language, forcing their offspring to generate a new language on the basis of an inherited "bioprogram" (Bickerton 1981, 1988), similar in basic precepts to Chomsky's UG. A primary benefit of such a view of SM, if viable, is that it would call for an enhanced cooperation between creolists and syntacticians in pursuit of the universals of language.

I have elsewhere shown that some significant, grammatically central configurations in SM are inescapably derived from transfer from older, historically "accreted" languages (McWhorter 1996a, 1997a), which puts into question a conception of SM as arising independently from an innate fundamental linguistic endowment. One might respond that creoles tend to incorporate source language features in fashions more reflective of unadorned UG. Be this as it may, the language-internal changes creoles undergo are less amenable to such an analysis.

For example, predicate negation in SM is hardly what one would expect of a fundamentally transparent, elementary structure. As we have seen, Byrne (1987) implies that the relationship between *á* and *ná* is that of a neatly conditioned allomorphic distribution between an *á* appearing after the subject and *ná* appearing elsewhere. Such an alternation is analyzable as a mere and shallow instance of morphophonology, as such a minor deviation from an idealized reflection of UG unadorned.

As I have shown, however, this phonological derivation of negator *á* is a red herring. The allomorphy was created through a more deeply transformational process entailing the reanalysis of topic-comment configurations as subject-predicate ones. This process left behind grammatically central exceptions—syntactic suppletions, as it were—which render the rules generating predicate negation in SM a distinct departure from a maximally simple reflection of basic principles of UG. Ironically, it is related creoles, seen as less conservative, which preserve the simpler negation strategy SM began with.

The data indicate, then, that we must address with caution the implications of even conservative creoles as reflections of UG. If creoles offer insights into this area, useful analyses will only come from comparison of several at a time, in order to evaluate which languages preserve the ontogenetically primary configurations.

## 4.3.  SM and typological classification

Li and Thompson (1976) have proposed a typological distinction between what they call subject-prominent languages and topic-prominent languages. The authors suggest that languages fall along a cline, one end of which is occupied by languages like the Tibeto-Burman Lisu, in which there are no subject-predicate structures at all, and the other by languages like English in which topic-comment sentences are less central to the grammar, are grammatically derivable from subject-predicate sentences, and, as often as not, operate on the level of discourse, via the preposing of an independent proposition to another (as in *You know Tom? Well, he fell off his bike yesterday*).

We have seen that topic-comment structures were vital to the emergence of the current predicate negation scenario in SM. That a reconfiguration of the grammar would proceed from a particular construction suggests that such constructions occupy a relatively central place in that grammar. This proves to be the case. While a subject-predicate analysis of the grammar is fundamentally valid, under Li and Thompson's conception SM is considerably more topic-prominent than English or Portuguese. Topic-comment constructions are used quite frequently, as in the sentence cited earlier:

(47)  Dí mujéé a   paí dí mií a    wá daka.
      the woman she bear the child LOC one day
      "The woman, she bore the child one day."

It becomes clear from collected narratives that in SM, topic-comments serve a discourse function, one of introducing a new referent or calling attention to that referent. For example, note the use of the topic-comment structure in this selection:

(48)  Tatá  péndɛmbéti  dédɛ . . . Kɔkɔ́ni tá-kó,
      father color-animal dead    rabbit  PROG-come

      djɔnkɔ́fútu tá-kó,       pakía   tá-kó,      píngo tá-kó,
      rodent     PROG-come peccary PROG-come pig   PROG-come

      hélipe  tá-kó,      dée    mbéti tá-kó      gbítíí,
      monkey PROG-come the-PL animal PROG-come IDEO

      dí  wósu fúu póóó! Ma te      wấ písi, ma, **hélipe, a lúku** dí dédɛ dé   pííí,
      the house full IDEO but when one time but monkey he see   the dead there quiet

      a   táa "Hế!"
      he say well
      "Papa jaguar is dead. Here comes rabbit. Here comes rodent. Here comes peccary, here comes pig, here comes monkey. The animals are coming in hordes. The house is packed up *full!* But suddenly the monkey, he sees the body laying there so quiet, and he says 'Well!'"

After a description of all of the animals who have come to the house, the use of the topic-comment structure here directs the focus onto a single animal, the monkey, and his subsequent exploits.

Li and Thompson (1976) propose that languages evolve continually from topic-prominence to subject-prominence and back again in a circular typological evolution. The mechanism of evolution from, specifically, subject-prominence to topic-prominence is not clearly defined, but the validity of the reverse process has been confirmed by various scholars (e.g., Givón 1976, Shibatani 1991). However, it must be said that evidence from synchronic SM suggests that, in fact, the degree of topic-prominence it exhibits is currently a relatively stable feature in the grammar.

For instance, topic-comment constructions are quite common in historical documents of SM:
SM 1781:

(49)  Di  mutjama **hem** da    marka.
      the rainbow it    COP miracle
      "The rainbow was a miracle."


SM 1805:

(50)  Petrus ku Johanes **dem** go nanga makandra na   grang kerki va Dju.
      Peter  and John      they go with each-other LOC big   church for Jews
      "Peter and John went together to the Temple." (Wietz 1805: 10)

(51)  Di Gado va dem tatta   va wi, **a**  meki hem minini Jesu  limbo.
      the God  for them father for us  he make his   child   Jesus clean
      "The God of our fathers has made his son Jesus clean." (ibid. 12)

Thus topic-comment structures have been common in SM throughout its history. What is important to note is that although in some instances, these sentences become subject-predicate sentences, creating new formatives in the process, the grammar-wide employment of the topic-comment configuration persists. This can have the effect that subject-predicate sentences that began as topic-comment sentences are "recycled" into new topic-comment structures themselves. For example, I have shown that sentences such as (52) began as topic-comment structures, the oblique form of the subject pronominal indicating its previous status as a topic:

(52)  Hɛ̃ da   dí  kabitɛ́ni.
      he  COP the captain
      "He is the captain."

Today, this very sentence type occurs in topic-comment constructions.[9]

(53)  Nɔ́ɔ dí  nɛ̃́,  hɛ̃́ da   sukúma.
      then the name it   COP foam
      "Now, the name was foam."

Thus despite the fact that certain topic-comment constructions in SM have been reanalyzed as subject-predicate structures, the grammar overall has retained its degree of topic prominence as a discourse strategy. There would appear to be no teleological conspiracy toward the elimination of topic-comment structures in the grammar. The evidence corresponds with the observation that spoken language is, in general, topic-prominent (cf. Givón's 1979 "pragmatic mode"), and Escure's (1997) argument that topic-prominence is inherent to creolization.

# Sisters under the Skin

*A Case for Genetic Relationship between
the Atlantic English-Based Creoles*

## 1. Introduction

This chapter is an argument for the classification of the Atlantic English-based creoles (henceforth AECs) as the direct descendants of a stabilized progenitor of West African origin.

I am by no means the first author to suggest this thesis. Its earliest attestation is Stewart (1971), followed by Alleyne (1971: 179–80), Carter (1987), and Smith (1987a). Hancock (1969, 1986, 1987) has been the most comprehensive advocate (also arguing that the parent pidgin was transported from the West African coast, an argument that I agree with, despite having attempted a revision of its particulars in McWhorter [2000a], to which I refer interested readers [that argument will not be presented in this chapter]).

However, despite the excellent research on the part of these scholars, this thesis has yet to gain unhesitating acceptance in the creolist community. It would seem to be the general consensus that some Atlantic creoles arose via the transplantation of registers from other islands and that sociohistorical contacts between locations have effected some diffusion of linguistic features. However, the canonical conception remains: that of remarkably similar creoles emerging independently in various Caribbean locations. English is said to have been "creolized in Jamaica," "transformed in Charleston," and so on.

A principal reason for the resistance to conceiving of the AECs as sister languages is that previous arguments, while highly indicative, did not center on the types of correspondences that are formally diagnostic of genetic affiliation namely, those that are flatly idiosyncratic and highly unlikely to be borrowings. The comparison of core lexical items, vital to establishing diachronic developments in older languages, is less powerful when it is applied to creoles with a lexical base and substrate in common, because we can assume that the interaction of a particular superstrate and substrate will have considerably similar results even in separate locations.

This obstacle is surmountable, and the establishment of the sisterhood of the AECs with no hedges along the lines of claiming less direct relationships due to "diffusion" and the like would be immensely beneficial to creole studies and to linguistics in general. Building on the vital scholarship of the authors mentioned above, and applying the tenets of diachronic linguistic inquiry to these languages, in this chapter I build a case for the common parentage of the AECs.

## 2. Methods and assumptions

In building such an argument, we must identify shared features that are impossible to attribute either to a common superstrate or to a common substrate, which have also been shown cross-linguistically to be resistant to borrowing, such that their widespread distribution is unlikely to be due to subsequent interdialectal diffusion. Only such features can be seen as unequivocal evidence for shared ancestry. Historical linguistics points us in three directions in such a pursuit:

1. *Idiosyncrasies in grammatical morphemes.* While many kinds of lexical items are easily borrowed, grammar is less easily borrowed outside of contexts of widespread bilingualism (Thomason and Kaufman 1988). As such, grammatical, as opposed to lexical, morphemes, are much more resistant to borrowing cross-linguistically. When shared uniformly by several languages, they thus strongly indicate common ancestry rather than borrowing.
2. *Idiosyncrasies in core lexical items.* Words denoting concepts that appear to be universally central linguistically are generally more resistant to replacement by borrowings than is more "marginal" vocabulary. Thus common idiosyncrasies in core vocabulary items, as opposed to broader similarities between them possibly attributable to superstrate or substrate influence, is best analyzed as evidence of common ancestry.
3. *Idiosyncrasies in grammatical behavior absent a superstrate or substrate model.* Such behaviors found uniformly in several languages, when there is a wealth of other evidence of relationship, strongly bolster the case for common ancestry.

All three of these domains are represented in the features I present in this chapter. It is predictable that the number of such features found among the AECs will be constrained, given that the creoles took shape under highly similar circumstances in both time and space. I present six such features, which I consider to be hidden but precious evidence of common ancestry, obscured by a preponderance of superstrate- and substrate-derived correspondences inherent to the sociolinguistic circumstances of creole origins.

# 3. Evidence for the descent of the English-based Atlantic creoles from a common ancestor

## 3.1. The equative copula *da/na/a*

Among AECs, the equative copula is realized variously as *da*, *na*, or *a*. I treat the latter two as derived from the first, which the evidence seems to warrant. For example, we can observe an evolution from *da* to *na* over time in Sranan (Arends 1989: 151); similarly, we find *da* in earlier documents of other varieties which now have *a* (e.g., Rickford 1980, Lalla and D'Costa 1990). Furthermore, this process instantiates a general phonological tendency for initial consonants to elide in monosyllabic grammatical morphemes undergoing heavy usage in such varieties (Rickford 1980). We also find *da* and *a* coexisting in some varieties (e.g., Escure 1983 on Belizean), while other varieties have preserved the original alveolar stop. Thus, over time:

> *da* Saramaccan, Belizean >
> *na* Krio, Sranan
> *a* Guyanese, Jamaican

In this chapter, for convenience, I refer to these allomorphs collectively as *DA*.

### 3.1.1. Superstrate derivation?

*DA* is uniformly distributed among Atlantic English-based creoles (see table 8.1) and is most plausibly derived from the demonstrative pronoun *that*. There appears to be no variety today which preserves an exact homophony between the demonstrative and the copula, and the earliest historical documents available show a copula *da* already present alongside a demonstrative *dati*. However, we can reconstruct this etymology from a comparative perspective. For example, in Belizean (Escure 1983: 193), we find the item *dada*, likely to have arisen from the adjacency of a demonstrative *da* and a copula *da*: **Dada** *we a de tel yu* "That's what I'm telling you." Also, Krio, in which the copula has become *na*, has *da* as the adjectival demonstrative: Tel **da** *man* "Tell that man" (Hancock 1987: 308).

However, while the homophony is obvious, learners would be highly unlikely to have directly chosen a demonstrative pronoun as an equative copula when forging a contact language. Note the conceptual leap involved:

|      | *Subject* | *Copula* | *Predicate* |
|------|-----------|----------|-------------|
| Ewe  | *Kofi*    | *is*     | *the chief* |
| SM   | *Kofi*    | **that??** | *the chief* |

### 3.1.2. Substrate derivation?

There is no substrate model for this homophony. In almost all of the West African substrate languages, the equative copula is rendered with a verb "to be," and in none of them is it rendered with a distal demonstrative. Ewe is typical:

TABLE 8.1. Equative copulas in AECs

|  | *He's my partner.* |
|---|---|
| Krio | *Na mi padna.* |
| Nigerian | *Na ma fren.* |
| Sranan | *Na mi mati.* |
| Saramaccan | *Hẽ da mí kɔmpé.* |
| Guyanese | *I a mi kompe.* |
| Antiguan | *Hi a mi paadna.* |
| Jamaican | *Im a mi paadna.* |
| Belizean | *Da mi paadna.* |
| Gullah | *Hi duh mi paadnuh.*[a] |

a. Adapted from Hancock (1987: 284).

(1)   Etsɔ    a-**nye**    asigbe.
tomorrow FUT-COP market day
"Tomorrow will be market day." (Kozelka 1980: 55)

Note the future marker, demonstrating the verbal status of the copula. Nor do the substrate languages display a homophony between these verbs and distal demonstrative pronouns, as in table (8.2). Moreover, as we can see from the table, there is no copula with the phonetic form [da] or anything similar, in the substrate which could possibly have served as a direct borrowing.

### 3.1.3.  Da *as an internal development*

As it happens, this demonstrative-copula homophony is a common phenomenon cross-linguistically and has been widely documented to indicate an evolutionary relationship. In other words, these studies indicate that *da* is an innovation in the creole system, not an original component. Equative copulas often emerge in initially zero-copula languages through the semantic bleaching of the demonstrative as used in topic-comment constructions (Li and Thompson 1975, Luo 1991, McWhorter 1994b, Devitt 1990, Gildea 1993). Li and Thompson (1975) document this type of reanalysis, for example, in Chinese. Archaic Chinese did not express a copula in equative sentences. Thus:

(2)   Wáng-Tái ø wù        zhě    yě.
Wang-Tai    outstanding person DEC
"Wang-Tai is an outstanding person." (Li and Thompson 1975: 421)

Meanwhile, the demonstrative pronoun *shì* was used in topic-comment sentences, as in:

(3)   Qíong  yù  jiàn,       **shì** rén    zhǐ  sǔo   wù    yě.
poverty and debasement this people GEN NOM disike DECL
"Poverty and debasement, this is what people dislike." (ibid.)

TABLE 8.2. Equative copulas and distal
demonstratives in the AEC substrate

|  | Equative copula | That pronoun |
|---|---|---|
| Wolof | la | boobu |
| Mandinka | mu | wò |
| Akan | yὲ | nó |
| Gbe | nye | má |
| Igbo | bù | áhừ |
| Yoruba | ṣe/jḗ | èyí |
| Kikongo | i | kiokio |

By the 1st century A.D., however, *shì* can be seen unequivocally as a copula:

(4)  Yú **shì** sǔo  jià   fū-rén zhǐ fù   yě.
     I   be  NOM marry woman GEN father DECL
     "I am the married woman's father." (ibid. 426)

And today this copula occurs regularly in equational sentences:

(5)  Nèi-ge    rén  **shì** xuéshēng.
     that-CLAS man  be  student
     "That man is a student." (ibid. 422)

While this comparative and typological evidence alone strongly supports the hypothesis that *DA* is a grammaticalized innovation, there are other arguments in support.

   For example, in early documents of Sranan some evidence appears to capture a stage at which the generalization of the copula *da* was not yet complete. Arends (1989) shows that in the oldest Sranan documents, although there are many sentences with overt *da*, the omission of the equative copula is grammatical at least in some contexts. For example:
   Sranan c. 1770:

(6)  Mi ø no   negeri      fo joe.
     I    NEG black-person for you
     "1 am not your slave." (Arends 1989: 160)

(7)  Mi blibi   joe ø wan bon mattie fo dem.
     I  believe you   a   good friend for them
     "I believe you're a good friend of theirs." (ibid.)

Many of the sentences Arends cites actually allow zero copula in the modern language as well; the sentences I provide are the only ones that contrast with their modern equivalents. But the sentences remain highly suggestive.

   Another feature typical of more basilectal varieties is that negation, tense, and aspect markers may appear after *DA* rather than before, as they do with main verbs:

Krio:

(8)  Moussa **nà-bìn**    màràbú.
     Moussa COP-ANT Muslim
     "Moussa was a Muslim." (Nylander 1983: 206)

Jamaican/Guyanese:

(9)  Jan **a**   **no**   di liida.
     John COP NEG the leader
     "John is not the leader." (Winford 1993: 167)

As Arends (1989: 30–31) and Winford (1993) have pointed out, this is accounted for under an analysis deriving *DA* from a demonstrative, as negation and TMA markers would naturally occur after the subject position. The current anomalous word order is a fossilization that reflects the earlier demonstrative syntactic function of today's copula:

(10)  Early Krio:
      [*Moussa*] [*dà*    *bìn*   *ø*    *Màràbú*]
      topic      subject ANT COP predicate
      TOPIC COMMENT
      Modern Krio:
      [*Moussa nà    bìn    Màràbú*]
      subject   COP ANT predicate

### 3.1.4. The implication of da *as an internal development*

The crucial aspect of the development of *DA* is that it would strain credulity to propose that just this process occurred, with such consistent results, in several separate locations.

While indeed it is a common process of language change for copulas to develop out of deictic elements in topic-comment constructions, there is a wide range of alternatives as to which specific pathway this development will follow in a given language, as is to be expected from the fact that, in general, the study of historical syntax yields tendencies, not predictive formulations. The AECs brought a distal demonstrative into the copula slot. However, as we have seen, in Chinese it was the proximal demonstrative that underwent the reanalysis. In Swahili, it was the existential presentative that was treated thus:

Early Modern Swahili Reconstructed:

(11)  a. *Vita, **ni**   taabu.
         war    it-is trouble
         "War, that's trouble."

Modern Swahili:

      b. Vita **ni**   taabu.
         war  COP trouble
         "War is trouble." (McWhorter 1994b)

In Panare, a Cariban Amerindian language, both the proximal and the distal demonstrative became copulas, and both copulas retain the proximal/distal distinction in their semantics:

(12)  a.  Maestro **këj**        e'ñapa.
          teacher  COP-PROX Panare
          "The Panare here is a teacher."

      b.  Maestro **nëj**        e'ñapa.
          teacher  COP-DIST Panare
          "The Panare there is a teacher." (Gildea 1993: 55)

In Hebrew, the third-person subject pronominals undergo such reanalysis:

(13)  David **hu**      ha-ganav.
      David he/COP the-thief
      "David is the thief." (Li and Thompson 1975: 429)

Moreover, as we see, it is quite possible for zero copula to persist *despite* the availability of a demonstrative or pronoun for reanalysis; the equative copula in Tok Pisin *Mi ∅ tisa* "I am a teacher" has been expressed with zero for well over a century, despite the availability of a pronoun for reanalysis. Finally, and crucially, we find divergent outcomes even within language groups. For example, Moroccan and Egyptian Arabic are developing demonstratives into copulas, but Kuwaiti, Lebanese, and Syrian Arabic are not (Brustad 2000: 157–58).

Given all of these alternative outcomes that cross-linguistic analysis presents, we would expect, if the AECs arose separately, for there to be a variety of the above strategies represented among them. Some creoles would indeed have a *DA* copula; others would have a *di* copula resulting from the reanalysis of proximal demonstrative *disi*; others would have an *i* or *a* copula from the third-person subject pronoun; others would certainly have no overt equative copula (note that none of the Melanesian English-based pidgins and creoles do). Instead, we find *DA* in every single AEC with anything approaching a basilectal or lower mesolectal register. This distribution argues strongly for the reconstruction of a common ancestor.

Specifically, the historical documentation and the comparative data suggest that the reanalysis of the demonstrative into a copula *da* had already progressed in West Africa before its transplantation to the New World, which had the result that the *da* equative copula occurs throughout the Anglophone Caribbean.

## 3.2. The locative copula *de*

In all of the Atlantic English-based creoles save the most acrolectal, the locative copula is the item *de*. In table 8.3, we see the presence of this item in a representative sample of nine Atlantic English-based creoles, representing the African varieties Krio and Nigerian; the Surinamese varieties Sranan and Saramaccan; the Eastern Caribbean varieties Guyanese and Antiguan; the Western Caribbean varieties Jamaican and

TABLE 8.3. Locative copulas in AECs

|  | Where is he? |
|---|---|
| Krio | *Na usai i de?* |
| Nigerian | *I de husai?* |
| Sranan | *Na usai a de?* |
| Saramaccan | *Naáse a dé?* |
| Guyanese | *Wisaid am de?* |
| Antiguan | *We i de?* |
| Jamaican | *We im de?* |
| Belizean | *We i de?* |
| Gullah | *Wisai i de?*[a] |

a. Adapted from Hancock (1987: 284).

Belizean; and a North American variety, Gullah. This presentation, and corresponding ones throughout this section, would be virtually impossible without the invaluable research of Hancock (1987).

The widespread distribution of *de* on the West African coast and across the Caribbean constitutes in itself one of the most powerful arguments for the common ancestry of these languages, for the simple reason that it, as we will see, is all but impossible that the incorporation *of de* into a pidgin English grammar occurred in more than one place. We must arrive at this conclusion no matter which account of its derivation we subscribe to.

### 3.2.1. Superstrate derivation?

The source of *de* is not an English verb "to be," but the adverb *there*, and crucially, a deictic adverb is a highly unusual source for a copular morpheme. In a survey of twenty-five languages from a wide sample of families (NSF project BNS-8913104, which I participated in),[1] there were no copulas derivable from adverbs, and no such examples have been documented in other studies of copula derivation (e.g., Devitt (1990). Indeed, while recategorialization of superstrate morphemes is a well-documented concomitant of pidginization (Miskito Coast Creole English *He advantage her* "He took advantage of her," *He catch crazy* "He became psychotic" [Holm 1988: 103]), the extension of an adverb into a verbal domain of limited lexical content such as a locative copula is quite unusual. The fact that the adverb *de* "there" exists alongside the homophonous copula in the creoles makes it even more of an intuitive stretch to view the copula as simply a reconceptualization of the adverb. It seems unlikely that learners of English would acquire the adverbial meaning of *there* and extend it to a copular function, especially given the typological anomalousness of such an extension:

|  | Subject | Copula | Predicate |
|---|---|---|---|
| Gbe | *Kofi* | *is* | *in the tree* |
| Creole | *Kofi* | ***there??*** | *in the tree* |

The one systematic cause for such an extension would be if the substrate provided a model homophony. However, this is belied by an examination of substrate languages, in none of which the distal deictic adverb and the locative copula are homophonous (see table 8.4).[2] Thus even if it happened that an adverb was reconceptualized as a locative copula at some point, what is important is that it is unlikely to have happened in West Africa, Suriname, Guyana, Antigua, Jamaica, Belize, and South Carolina separately.[3]

### 3.2.2. Substrate derivation?

Another hypothesis has been proposed as to how copula *de* came about. Alleyne (1980: 163–64) has suggested that *de* is a compromise between a copula *de* from the Twi dialect of Akan and the adverb *there* in English.

The first problem with this hypothesis is that Twi's *de* (which in the modern language is now *ne*) is actually a specialized identificational equative copula, used to indicate complete identity between two entities; the locative copula is *wo*:

(14)  mé nùá    **ne**    Kòfí
      my brother COP Kofí
      "My brother is Kofí." (Alleyne 1980: 110)

(15)  ɔwɔ    dáŋ    mù.
      he-COP house inside
      "He is in the house." (ibid. 118)

Alleyne's hypothesis requires, then, that this Twi identificational copula was recast as a locative copula, presumably under the influence of the semantics of English *there*. Meanwhile, in the minds of non-Twi speakers, the incorporation of *de* into the new grammar as a copula would entail the reconceptualization of the syntactic behavior of an English adverb as that of a copula *without* the model of the Twi copula as a motivation. Obviously, then, the origin of copula *de* in the Twi *de* would have been an idiosyncratic type of reconceptualization—and thus unlikely to have occurred, as the polygenetic hypothesis requires, in several separate places at once.

TABLE 8.4. Locative copulas in AEC substrate languages

|           | Locative copula | There      |
|-----------|-----------------|------------|
| Wolof     | nekk            | fa         |
| Mandinka  | be              | jèe        |
| Akan      | wɔ              | ɛ-hɔ       |
| Gbe       | le              | afíma      |
| Igbo      | dị              | n'ébe ahụ  |
| Yoruba    | wà              | níbɛ̀       |
| Kikongo   | -ina            | kuna       |

Furthermore, as Mufwene (1986b: 172–75) points out, we must ask why those originating these languages would have chosen a Twi morpheme out of the range of choices represented. To bolster Mufwene's observation, recall the range of choices in table 8.4.

Alleyne (1971: 176; 1993) has elsewhere noted the social and cultural dominance of the Akan which could be invoked as a spur for the choice of borrowing from Akan rather than from other languages represented. However, this dominance notwithstanding, how likely is it to have led to the *specific* recruitment of a locative copula, rather than any number of other items, in several separate locations?

A final argument against the substrate-borrowing argument is that there is a very strong tendency for pidgins and creoles to recruit a superstrate positional verb as a locative copula, even when eschewing an expressed equative copula. Locative copulas thus fall outside of the range of items which are typically enocoded with substrate borrowings. To account for *de* as a substrate borrowing requires that all the AECs, with no exceptions, went against that tendency:

Guinea-Bissau Creole Portuguese:

(16)   Tuga      i   **sta**   ba    li.
       Portuguese CL COP ANT here
       "The Portuguese were here." (Kihm 1980b: 91)

Tok Pisin:

(17)   Bikpela fiva  i    stap  long yu.
       big     fever PM COP LOC you
       "A great fever is among you." (Sebba 1997: 22)

Naga Pidgin:

(18)   Moy yate ǝse
       I    here COP
       "I am here." (Sreedhar 1985: 107)

In short, it is impossible that in West Africa, Suriname, Guyana, Antigua, Jamaica, Belize, and South Carolina, separately, slaves (1) in each place bypassed the superstrate locative copula completely, counter to a strong opposite tendency in pidginization in general, and then *in each place* either (2) borrowed one from the same single language represented in the learning community, despite the general objective being to forge a language of interethnic communication, or (3) effected a quirky reconceptualization of an English adverb into a copular morpheme independently of any motivation from the substrate or diachronic tendency. Obviously, given the confluence of fortuitous circumstances which even one occurrence of such a borrowing would require, if it did happen, it indeed happened only once. Given the distribution of *de* today, it is most plausible that this would have happened in West Africa.

### 3.2.3. De *as an internal development*

I have shown that the immediate recruitment of an adverb as a locative copula would be highly unlikely on the grounds of syntax, semantics, and cross-linguistic tendency. However, the synchronic homophony is nevertheless a fact. What we can ascribe this homophony to is change over time specifically, grammaticalization. Grammaticalization entails the passing of lexical items into grammatical functions over time via semantic bleaching and generalization of syntactic occurrence, often leaving homophonous coexisting lexical and grammatical reflexes of the same item.[4]

Here, then, is a systematic and well-documented process to account for the synchronic distribution of *de*. While empirical documentation of this process in the AECs is most likely permanently unavailable to us, it is possible to infer how the grammaticalization of adverbial *de* proceeded through analysis of, for example, Saramaccan.

At the outset, however, we must bypass the garden path of attributing *de* to the reanalysis of the progressive aspect marker *de* coexistent with the adverb and the copula in many of the creoles in question, as in Krio *I de wok* "He is working." While the development of a lexical item—adverb *de* "there"—into a grammatical item such as the progressive marker is to be expected, according to the tenets of grammaticalization, the reverse development would contradict the strong tendency toward lexical-to-grammatical directionality, which is characteristic of the process.

Thus we proceed to a more likely derivation. In Saramaccan, the adverb *de* is often optionally inserted into sentences in order to lend pragmatic emphasis; note:

(19)  Nóiti fa     mi **dé**   a     Winikíi **dé**,  nóiti  mi jéi   táa ...
      never since I   COP LOC Winikii there never  I    hear talk
      "Never since I've been there at Winikii have I heard that . . ." (Glock 1986: 51)

(20)  Dí Gaamá dí    Kófi gó lúku **dé**   **dé**  ku    suwáki **dé**.
      the chief   REL Kofi go see   there COP with sickness there
      "The chief who Kofi went to look at is sick." (Byrne 1990: 673)

It is this expressive usage of the adverbial *de* that most plausibly sparked a grammaticalization. Presumably, in the initial stage, there was no expression of the locative copula just as there was none of the equative. For now, remaining agnostic as to whether this was in a parent language, we will use a hypothetical Proto-Saramaccan as a demonstration case:

(21)  Dí wómi ø     a     wósu.
      the man   COP LOC house
      "The man is at home."

However, it would have been a common expressive strategy to insert a deictic *de* between subject and predicate, similar to today's usage:

(22)  Dí wómi **dé**    a    wósu.
      the man   there LOC house
      "The man (there) is at home."

Colloquial English offers a possible model for this usage, in utterances such as *She gets cranky when she's there at Tony's.*

When the "expressive" *de* occurred in this position, it was ripe for a gradual reanalysis as a copula, especially given its phonetic similarity to the other copula morpheme *da* that was emerging at the same time. As a result, *de* came to be interpreted, in this usage, as a copular rather than an adverbial item:

(23)  Dí wómi **dé**    a    wósu.
      the man   COP LOC house
      "The man is at home."

This account describes a process which, while systematically plausible, hardly instantiates a strong tendency that is likely to be replicated in nine separate creoles. We are still faced with the typological anomaly of the homophony and diachronic relationship of adverb and copula cross-linguistically. In the literature on the diachronic origins of copular morphemes cross-linguistically (Li and Thompson 1975, Arends 1989, Devitt 1990, Luo 1991, Gildea 1993), it has become clear that there is a strong tendency for locative copulas to be derived from both positional verbs and the verbs "to be." Given this fact, we again see the use of an adverb as a copula as an aberration which, when encountered in so wide and uniform a distribution, is most realistically designated an inherited trait, in line with the basic tenets of comparative reconstruction.

One might propose that there is something inherent to English which hindered the perception of its copulas by learners. While we might suppose that the frequent contraction of the copula in English may have had just such an effect, comparative analysis reveals that this was not the case. Specifically, the French reflexes of the copula are not contracted and are generally perceptible even in rapid speech: *suis, es, est, sommes, êtes, sont.* Yet, the French plantation creoles have not incorporated them sentence-medially: Haitian Creole *mwe ∅ nã bulõžeri* "I am in the bakery." This indicates that perceptibility is not the crucial factor in the realization of the copula in creoles. Moreover, even if contraction had led learners to bypass superstrate copulas in selecting a creole copula, we would again face the question, why is an adverb, which we encounter nowhere else in the world used this way, rather than the positional verbs which we encounter in almost all other pidgins and creoles as locative copulas, and *in so many separate places*?

### 3.2.4. Conclusion

I prefer to derive *de* via a grammaticalization process. However, the acceptance of that specific argument is less important than my main aim, which is to demonstrate that *de* can only be an inherited trait and argues strongly for a single parent to the AECs. We must ask: whichever account of the origin of copula *de* one prefers, how plausible is it that the process occurred in West Africa, Suriname, Guyana, Antigua,

Jamaica, Belize, and South Carolina separately? On the basis of *de* alone, over a century of historical linguistics virtually forces the reconstruction of a West African proto-pidgin ancestor.

### 3.3. Modal *fi/ fo/ fu*

There is a homophony in AECs between a benefactive, possessive, or directional preposition; a complementizer; and a modal verb (Washabaugh 1975, Koopman and Lefebvre 1981, Bickerton 1981, Boretsky 1983, Winford 1985). Note, for example, Providencia Creole English (Washabaugh 1975):

(24)   a. Preposition:
           Wan a  di  granson **fi**  di  daata . . .
           one  of the grandson  for  the daughter
           "One of the grandsons of the daughter . . ." (116)

       b. Complementizer:
         ˙Ai mek **fi**   stan op.
           I   make for stand up
           "I tried to stand up." (ibid.)

       c. Modal:
           Dem **fi**      put im  ina i    yaad . . .˙
           they should put him in  the yard
           "They should put him into the yard . . ." (129)

The prepositional usage is relatively transparently derived from the superstrate usage; the complementizer usage is traceable to British dialects (Orton, Sanderson, and Widdowson 1978, cited in Hoim 1988: 168). Less obviously derived is the modal usage, which we will be concerned with in this section.

### 3.3.1. *Distribution*

This modal usage appears in all of the more basilectal AECs, although it gives way to superstrate constructions such as *must* and *have to* in all but the varieties with the most conservative basilects adapted from Hancock (1987: 295–96) unless otherwise noted (table 8.5).

### 3.3.2. *Substrate borrowing?*

Edwards (1974) suggested that the Caribbean *fi* was a borrowing from the Twi verb *fi* "to come from." This derivation was widely quoted, but upon examination it would seem unlikely.

   First, Byrne's (1984) elegant demonstration that *fi* is actually derived from an earlier *fu* makes Twi *fi* a less likely source. As Byrne states (106), Edwards's hypothesis was spurred in part by the unlikelihood of the phonological evolution of the mid back vowel in English "for" into the high front vowel in *fi*. *Fu* as the original form eliminates this problem.

TABLE 8.5. Modal *fi/fo/fu* in AECs

|  | *You have got to do it.* |
|---|---|
| Krio: | *Una fo du am.* |
| Nigerian: | *Una fo du am.* |
| Sranan: | *Mi ben fu suku mi futbal-susu* "I had to look for my football shoes"[a] |
| Guyanese: | *Mi fi go tumara.* "I ought to go tomorrow."[b] |
| Jamaican: | *Unu fi dwiit.* |
| Gullah: | *Hunnuh fuh du um.* |

a. Sordam and Eersel (1985: 59). Saramaccan, despite being perhaps the quintessence of the basilectal among the AECs, lacks this feature. Neither Tonjes Veenstra, Marvin Kramer, nor I, all working with multiple informants over many years, have been able to reproduce Byrne's elicitation (e.g., 1984: 101) of the construction: informants categorically reject it, and it does not occur in texts. Apparently the trait has fortuitously disappeared in this language, but this does not speak against the reconstruction of a parent to the AECs since Saramaccan idiosyncratically parallels the others in all other cases.

b. Bickerton (1981: 109).

Second, we are again faced with the question as to why speakers across the Caribbean would choose an item from Twi in particular with such consistency, and again, this is particularly significant with reference to the West African creoles spoken far westward of the Akan-speaking area.

Third, the semantics of Twi *fi* make it even more difficult to posit it as a source of the modal verb in the modern creoles. In Twi, *fi* means "to come from," used as in:

(25)  ɔsafohéne yi  **fi**      Akyém.
      captain    this come-from Akyem
      "This captain comes from Akyem." (Byrne 1984: 120)

(26)  onípa yi  a-bé-**fi**        mè mú.
      man   this PERF-INGR-come me unawares
      "This man has come to me unawares." (ibid.)

There is no documented, or intuitive, relationship between the obligative semantics of the modal usage of *fu* and this verb. Winford (1985: 621) notes that there are "almost identical" reflexes of this verb in other West African languages, which is indeed the case. However, none of them resemble *fi* phonetically, which would presumably be the motivation for its recruitment (table 8.6).

TABLE 8.6. Verbs "to come from" in West African languages

| Wolof | *woo* |
|---|---|
| Mandinka | *bo* |
| Gbe | *tsó* |
| Igbo | *ísí* |
| Yoruba[a] | *ti* |

a. From Rowlands (1969: 142).

Finally, even if by chance Twi *fi* was the source, why would this particular verb be recruited consistently, in several separate locations, when its semantics have no specifically West African significance?

Thus *fu* as a substrate borrowing seems highly tenuous. Furthermore, no other substrate verb with the phonetic form *f*V has a meaning relatable to any of the functions of *fu* (table 8.7).[5]

Finally, not only do none of these languages have an item resembling *fu* phonetically in obligative constructions, but also there is no homophony between the benefactive, complementizer, and obligative constructions in any of them:

(27) Wolof:

    a. **War**   naa ko defari.
       should I   it  take-care-of
       "I should take care of it." (WEC International 1992: 174)

    b. **Pur** xale    yi
       for  children the
       "For the children" (Njie 1982: 239)

    c. Man damma géna ag   moom **ndax**  ma gis ko.
       I   I       leave with him  so-that I   see him
       "I'm leaving with him to see him." (ibid. 248)

(28) Mandinka:

    a. Í  **si**     n  kòntong.
       you should me greet
       "You should greet me." (206)

    b. A sàng n  **ye**.
       it buy  me for
       "Buy it for me." (36)

    c. Ali bambang, **fo**   bànku jiyo si     sìi.
       you hurry    so-that clay  water should suffice
       "Hurry so that there will be enough water for the clay." (50)

TABLE 8.7. Meanings of *f* + V verbs in AEC substrate languages

| | *fi* | *fo* | *fu* |
|---|---|---|---|
| Wolof | here | to play | where |
| Mandinka[a] | *fii*: to plant | *fó*: until; *fóo*: to say, to miss | *fúu*: to be stupid; *fùu*: to lend |
| Gbe | to steal, to bleed | to strike, to shake | to be white, to project, to be dry |
| Igbo | | *ífó*: to uproot; *ífò*: to narrate | *ífù*: to get lost; *ífú*: to roll up, to hurt |
| Yoruba[b] | *fi*: to *swing*, *fí*: to dry, to put | *fó*: to float, *fò*: to fly | |

a. From Gamble (1987b).

b. From Wakeman (1979).

(29)  Akan:
  a. E-**twa me**      sɛ  me-kɔ.
     it-pass give-me say I-go
     "I must go." (Christaller 1933: 546–47)

  b. Me-yɛ iyi **ma** wo.
     I-do  this give you
     "I do this for you." (Balmer and Grant 1929: 121)

  c. O-ba-a        **ma** o-a-boa       me.
     he-come-PRET give he-PERF-help me
     "He came in order to help me." (ibid. 169)

(30)  Gbe:
  a. E-**dzè ná**   wò bé n-à-vá.
     it-fall give you say OBL-FUT-come
     "You have to come." (Rongier 1988: 156)

  b. É-wò-e **ná**-m.
     he-do-it give-me
     "He did it for me." (Westermann 1928: 129)

  c. Tsó-è ná-m'    **né**  m-á-ù.
     take-it give-me that I–FUT-eat
     "Give it to me so that I can eat it." (ibid. 174)

(31)  Igbo:
  a. **Kà**      ọ́  gaa.
     HORT he go
     "He should go." (345)

  b. Sìé-**re**    há    nri
     cook-for them food
     "Cook food for them." (244–45)

  c. Ọ́ byà-ra     **ka**     ó  wèé   rie nrí.
     he come-PAST HORT he CONS eat food
     "He came in order to eat." (307)

(32)  Yoruba:
  a. Bàbá **gbọ́dọ̀** lọ.
     father must   go
     "Father must go." (110)

  b. Ó pè   Òjó **fún** un.
     he call Ojo for  him
     "He called Ojo for him." (74)

  b. Bádé jí     Àjàyi **kí**    o jẹun.
     Bade awake Ajayi COMP he eat
     "Bade woke up Ajayi to eat." (110)

(33)  Kikongo:

    a. Mbatu tu-**xinga** kwenda.

       soon  we-must go

       "We must go presently." (Bentley 1887: 142)

    b. N-sumb-**ila**        emfumi embiji.

       I-buy-OBJECTIVE chef    meat

       "I buy meat for the chief." (28)

    c. . . . **kimana** ke    ba-mona nzala.

       so-that      NEG they-see hunger

       ". . . so that they are not hungry." (82)

Only in the case of Akan do we see the same item in all three constructions. But if the homophony were modeled on Twi, then given how regularly serial uses of *give*-verbs were transferred from West African languages into plantation creoles—including in highly grammaticalized functions—we would expect that the AECs would instead have recruited a *give*-verb in the three usages. And again, a derivation from Twi alone in several locations in the Caribbean is difficult to support in general, and if valid, would only take us back to a monogenetic explanation given its anomaly.

Elsewhere, we see scattered examples of semantically typical bifunctional polysemy, but none distributed with the uniformity which is necessary to logically rigorous substrate attribution compared to the standard espoused in Singler (1988). In short, then, we see that the obligative usage of *fu* has no likely model in the substrate, neither in the form of a source for a direct borrowing nor in the form of a parallel homophony with a preposition and complementizer.

### 3.3.4. Superstrate derivation

Washabaugh (1975: 130) suggested that *fu* in its modal usage was not a verb, but a reflex of the preposition which occurs after an underlying, but unexpressed, verb of obligation: *Im fi kom op ya.* "He should come up here."

The intuition that modal *fu* is indeed a reflex of the preposition, regardless of the presence of an unexpressed verb, is supported by other facts. First, while verbs evolve into prepositions frequently in language change (Lord 1976, Lightfoot 1979: 214), the evolution of prepositions into verbs is vanishingly rare, and as such would be unlikely to have occurred with such consistent results in so many places in Africa and the Caribbean. Thus crucially, if the three reflexes of *fu* represented a diachronic progression, then modal *fu*, as a verb, would have to have come first—which we have seen would pose a problem in that there is neither a superstrate nor substrate source for such a modal verb. Using the classification of the modal as an extension of the prepositional function surmounts this problem.

Second, in Saramaccan, one of the most basilectal of the creoles in question, the obligative construction is not the only one in which *fu* can appear after an empty VP. Specifically, in Saramaccan, when used in possessive constructions, *fu* regularly appears without a preceding copula, as in:

(34)    Dí búku ø fu mi. *Di búku dá u mi.
        the book for me
        "The book is mine."

In chapter 7 I show that this situation is a fossilization of an earlier stage in the grammar
in which the copula was unexpressed across the board. We can easily propose that modal
*fu* is a further instantiation of this fossilization that is, "I am for leaving" for *I should
leave* and if this is correct, it is important that this analysis casts modal *fu* as prepositional following an empty copula slot, rather than Washabaugh's unexpressed full verb.

    Under this prepositional analysis, Louden (1993) has noted that in earlier En-
glish dialects, there was a *to be for* construction which denoted futurity and, by extension, intention, as in *I'm for doing it* "I am going to do it," and *Are you for going?*
"Do you intend to go?" (Patterson 1880: 39). This derivation is promising, in that
the semantic relationship between futurity and intention on the one hand and obligation on the other is not implausibly distant.

    But that derivation still brings us back to requiring a common ancestor. First, if
we derive the modal *fu* which appears across the Caribbean and beyond from this
dialectal English future construction, it is curious that the exact same obligative, rather
than future, semantics emerged in all of these locations. As in the case of *DA*, we
would expect an array of outcomes in the various creoles: some would preserve the
future meaning; in some, the *fu* construction would have entered into competition
with alternate future constructions *go* and *sa* and then dropped out; in some, the choice
of *go* or *sa* would have prevented the incorporation of the *fu* future at all; in some,
the future construction would indeed evolve into an obligative. Hardly would we
expect, however, that so many creoles would separately incorporate or develop the
dialectal *for*-future into the selfsame obligative construction. Semantic change is
almost never this regular, even across related languages. It is more plausible that the
reinterpretation of the *for*-future happened once and was then dispersed.

    Second, we must return to the absence of copula in the modal construction. In
the pertinent register of all of these creoles, the expression of the copula is required
across the grammar, as we have seen in sections 3.1. and 3.2. The unexpressed copula
before *fu* can only be classed as a grammatical anomaly. I suggested that this anomaly
stems from the fossilization of a previous zero-copula state, but we must ask: Why
would *fu*, in particular. not only exhibit anomalously conservative behavior, but the
exact same anomalously conservative behavior, in so many separate locations? As I
noted, such a fossilization is explainable, but hardly predictable. As a rule in all of
these creoles, PPs do *not* license empty copula. There is nothing inherent to the semantics or syntactic behavior of *fu* that would *predict* its licensing empty copula in
*one* creole grammar, much less several across the Caribbean. If these languages arose
separately, then we might expect fossilization effects in *fu* constructions in one, or
perhaps two, of them—but hardly uniformly in all.

## 3.3.5. Conclusion

Just as with locative copula *de*, whatever derivation we propose for modal *fu*, how
likely is the process we choose to have occurred separately in Gambia, Nigeria,

Suriname, Guyana, Providencia, Jamaica, and South Carolina? A sentence like *Im fi kom op ya* "He should come up here," when grammatical in such a wide array of languages with such suggestive sociohistorical links, calls strongly for the reconstruction of a common ancestor.

### 3.4. Second-person plural pronoun *unu*

The second-person plural pronoun in many AECs takes a form that is impossible to derive from English in most of the more basilectal English-based creoles (table 8.8).

The reason for the substitution of an indigenous etymon for plural *you* is relatively transparent: West African speakers were accustomed to a morphologically encoded number distinction in the second person and thus substituted a native item for plural *you* rather than incorporating the ambiguity that English offered. What is fascinating is the uniform distribution of a single phonetic form.

We might expect that such a distribution would be traceable to a cognate present in a range of the substrate languages. However, as it happens, *unu* is neatly traceable to exactly one of these languages, Igbo (table 8.9).

As we see, the Igbo item is phonetically (or virtually) identical to the form found across the Caribbean and beyond. The importance of this is that Igbo contributed its pronoun to such a wide range of creoles of supposedly independent emergence. While Igbo was a relatively well-represented language in the substrate of most of the creoles in question, its presence was nowhere so overwhelming as to account for the occurrence of *unu* in so many separate locations. Culturally, for example, Twi, Ewe, and Kikongo cultures are much more strongly represented in the areas where the creoles in question are spoken than is Igbo (Alleyne 1971, 1993; Smith 1987a). Moreover, the English came to disprefer Igbo slaves, given their tendency to commit suicide in response to the harshness of plantation life (LePage and De-Camp 1960).

Furthermore, an account proposing that *unu* originated in one register and then somehow was diffused to the other dialects is implausible as well, in that core vocabulary items such as personal pronouns are traditionally relatively resistant to replacement and change in situations of language contact and language change.

While there is no explanation as to why plantation communities across the Caribbean and colonies in West Africa would have all unanimously chosen an Igbo item as a second-person plural pronoun, the recruitment of this form in a single-parent

TABLE 8.8. Second-person plural
pronouns in AECs

| | |
|---|---|
| Krio | *una* |
| Nigerian | *una* |
| Sranan | *unu* |
| Saramaccan | *ū* |
| Providencia | *unu* |
| Jamaican | *unu* |
| Belizean | *unu* |
| Gullah | *hunnuh*[a] |

a. Adapted from Hancock (1987: 295).

TABLE 8.9. Second-person plural pronouns
in AEC substrate languages

|          | Subject | Independent |
|----------|---------|-------------|
| Wolof    | *ngeen* | *yéen*      |
| Mandinka | *ali*   | *altolu*    |
| Akan     | *mo*    | *mo*        |
| Gbe      | *mìe*   | *mìawo*     |
| Igbo     | ***únù*** | ***únù***  |
| Yoruba   | *ę*     | *ènyin*     |
| Kikongo  | *nu*    | *yeno*      |

language and its subsequent distribution across the AECs would elegantly account for the current distribution.

### 3.5. Anterior marker *bin*

The anterior marker *bin* occurs in all Atlantic English-based creoles with a basilectal register (table 8.10). The Jamaican form is derived via a rule that deletes the initial /b/ in items of heavy usage (Rickford 1980); the Antiguan forms and the Belizean forms arise from assimilatory nasalization of the initial consonant.

While there has been much debate about the behavior of the anterior markers in creoles and its implications for the bioprogram, the area with which I will be concerned in this subsection is a seemingly mundane, but ultimately revelatory one—the etymology of *bin*. Put simply, we must ask why the anterior marker is encoded with *bin* in every single one of these creoles.

### 3.5.1. Substrate model?

While we might suppose that the substrate languages would provide a model for the recruitment of a form of the verb "to be" in the anterior usage, a survey of the substrate reveals that these languages use a wide variety of strategies to encode various forms of the past tense. Importantly, the verb "to be" figures in none of them.

TABLE 8.10. *Bin* in the AECs

|            | *Three of his friends were there.* |
|------------|-------------------------------------|
| Krio       | *Tri ipadi **bin** de de.*          |
| Nigerian   | *Tri fo hi fre **bin** de de.*      |
| Sranan     | *Dri fu e mati **ben** de de.*      |
| Saramaccan | *Dií máti fɛ̃ɛ̃ **bi** dé alá.*       |
| Guyanese   | *Tri a i mati **bin** de de.*       |
| Antiguan   | *Tri hi fren **min** de de.*        |
| Jamaican   | *Tri a fi-im fren **en** de de.*    |
| Belizean   | *Tri a fi-i fren **mi** di de.*     |
| Gullah     | *Tri uh hi fren **bin** de de.*[a]  |

a. Adapted from Hancock (1987: 282).

Wolof and Mandinka use postposed inflectional markers, which appear unrelated to verbs "to be":

Wolof terminative aspect:

(35)  Bey    **na**    dugub.
cultivate TERM millet
"He cultivated millet." (25) (Verbs "to be": *Ia, nékk*)

Mandinka past:

(36)  Dindingo bòri-**ta**.
child      run off-PAST
"The child ran off." (17) (Verbs "to be": *mu, be*)

In Kwa and Nigerian languages, the category closest to the creole anterior is what most grammarians term the perfective. In Akan, this is encoded with the infix *-á-*, as in *o-á-bà* he-PREF-come "He has come" (Balmer and Grant 1929: 106–7). This infix seems unrelated to the copula forms, *yè* and *wɔ*. Ewe appears to have lost its cognate to this infix. Westermann cites it only in the Anlo dialect, and subsequent grammars do not mention it at all; the modern language extends the FINISH serial verb construction as in:

(37)  Me-wo do    vo.
I-do    work finish
"I have finished working." (Fiagã 1976: 38)

Igbo has a postposed inflectional marker *-le O rie-le jí* "He has eaten yams" Emenanjo (1978: 80); its verbs "to be" are *bù* and *di*. Yoruba has the marker *ti*, derived from a verb "to come from": *Mo ti jeun* "I have eaten"; copulas are *jɛ́, şe,* and *wà*.

Kikongo has a postposed perfective inflection whose morphological form varies according to phonological constraints: *ntond-ele* "I loved," *ngij-idi* "I came." The copulas are *i* and *-ina* (Fiagã 1976: 33).

Thus we search in vain for a substrate tendency to encode anteriority with any reflex of a verb "to be." In addition, we see that the substrate presents a wide range of strategies for expressing pastness, in contrast to the usual similarities they display in most basic grammatical behaviors.

### 3.5.2. Superstrate model?

Could it be English, then, that forces the absolute uniformity in the distribution of *bin* today? Indeed, the Pacific English-based contact languages all have *bin* as a past marker. However, Keesing (1988) and others have shown that these registers are descended from a common ancestor, such that we can see this as one instance of the incorporation of *bin* rather than several. Indeed, *been* is an obvious candidate for past marking in an English-based contact language. However, elsewhere in the world, we find demonstrations that *been* is hardly the only potential past marker that presents itself to learners of English in contexts of filtered acquisition.

Some less basilectal English-based creoles use *did*, as in Barbadian *Hi di boi mi* "It bit me" (Le Page and Tabouret-Keller 1985: 93). Native Americans are documented to have used both *have* and *was*, rather than *been*, in the restructured registers of English which they acquired in the nineteenth century, as in *I* **have** *work, Columbus* **was** *discovered America, and I* **was** *feel* (Schuchardt 1980: 36). Because there is a range of choices available for the recruitment of an anterior marker, how likely is it that speakers in over a dozen localities would have independently chosen the exact same item in this function?

This would be explainable if the substrate provided a template; indeed, the fact that most of these creoles encode the progressive with the locative copula, and the irrealis with the verb "to go," is most probably a result of the fact that the substrate languages are relatively uniform in encoding these aspects similarly (see, e.g., Boretsky 1983). However, this is not the case with the anterior tense: (1) none of these languages encodes the past with a form of the verb "to be"; (2) no other strategy prevails; and (3) because most of the substrate languages encode pastness inflectionally, their contribution to the creole structure was inherently limited by the fact that inflection is rare in creoles.

Thus it is likely that the choice of an etymon in the creoles proceeded largely independently of the substrate strategies. If the creoles emerged separately, then we would expect at least a few creoles with *have, was, did,* or other superstrate items as past markers. The absolute uniformity of the distribution of *bin* across the creoles in question, then, is most plausibly ascribed to the creoles having descended from a parent creole which happened to have selected *been* as its anterior marker.

### 3.6. *Self* as an adverbial

A final trait common to too many AECs to be a matter of chance is documented by Hancock (1987: 320): the semantic extension of the word *self* to the adverbial meaning of *even* (table 8.11).

TABLE 8.11. *Self* as adverbial in AECs

|  | He even had another horse. |
| --- | --- |
| Krio | *I bib get oda os* **sef.** |
| Nigerian | *I bin get wan oda hos* **sef.** |
| Sranan | *A ben abi wan tra asi* **seefi.** |
| Saramaccan | *A bi ábi wǎ óto hási* **seéi.** |
| Guyanese | *I gat wan neks haars* **self.** |
| Antiguan | *I gat wan neks haas* **self.** |
| Jamaican | *Im ha wan neks haas* **self.** |
| Belizean | *Im av a neks aas* **self.** |
| Gullah | *I haa noduh hoos* **sef.**[a] |

a. Adapted from Hancock (1987: 320).

As in the cases discussed here, we are confronted with a remarkably uniform distribution of a construction with no apparent substrate or superstrate model, which must thus be an independent development. And again, for such an independent development to proceed so uniformly in so many languages would be an unprecedented phenomenon unless they had a common ancestor.

A survey of the substrate reveals no hint of a source for the extension of the word for *self* to the adverbial meaning of *even*. This adverbial usage is fundamentally one of pragmatic subjectively-based intensification, and thus can be presumed to have been derived from the intensificational usage of *self* as in *I myself am the father*, as opposed to the reflexive usage *I washed myself*. Thus I will present citations of the word for self in the intensificational usage.

Note that the item used to intensify pronouns is not used adverbially in any of these languages:

Wolof:

(38)   a. Moom    moo dem.
    · he:EMPH he-be leave
    "It is he who left." (Njie 1982: 107)

   b. Lépp la    mën, woy **sax**.
    all    DEF can   sing even
    "He knows everything, even singing." (189)

Mandinka:

(39)   a. **Nne** "I myself" (Spears 1973: 36)

   b. **Hani** suutoo a  be yaayi    la.
    even night   he be wander PROG
    "Even at night he is wandering around." (41)

Akan:

(40)   a. **Méara** m-a-fà.
    I-same I-PERF-take
    "I myself have taken it." (42)

   b. **Mpo** m-a-di          awu    a . . .
    even I-PERF-commit murder EMPH
    "Even if I had committed a murder . . ." (Christaller 1933: 397)

Ewe: .

(41)   a. Nye **ŋútɔ** me-wo-e.
    I    self I-do-it
    "I myself did it." (262)

   b. Éya **gõ**   hã  mé-va    o.
    he   even also NEG-come NEG
    "Not even he came." (116)

Igbo:

(42) a. Ọ́ bụ̀ **ọŋwé** m̀ mè-re   ya.
       it be self   I  do-IND it
       "I myself did it." (340)

   b. **M'ọ̀bụ́lá dí** nwatàkị́rị̀   ŋwère íke imé ya.
       even           small-child can       do it
       "Even a child can do it." (235)

Yoruba:

(43) a. Èmi **tìkálára** mi lọ síbẹ̀.
       I     self    I  go there
       "I myself went there." (67)

   b. Èmi **tilẹ̀**   mọ̀.
       I   even know
       "Even I knew it." (Abraham 1958: 643)

Kikongo:

(44) a. Mònò **kibêni**. "I myself." (Swartenbroeckx 1973: 135)

   b. Gâna **kána** fióti.
       give  even a-little
       "Give even a little." (117)

Thus we see that the extension of *self* to the adverbial meaning of English *even* has no model in any possible substrate language.

In the meantime, no source I have consulted on English of the seventeenth century, when most of the creoles in question formed, indicate that *self* was used in this semantic domain at the time, as would intuitively seem to be the case to native speakers.

As it happens, there is indeed a source language model for this usage: the Irish English that would have been spoken by indentured servants working alongside slaves in the early English Caribbean. In Irish Gaelic there is a homophony between *self* and *even* in the word *féin*, such that sentences such as *If I got it itself it would be of no use* for *Even if I got it it would be of no use*, or *If I had that much itself* for *Even if I had that much*, are recorded from Irish English speakers (Joyce 1910: 37, cited in Allsopp 1996).

But the question is how likely it would have been that slaves would have picked up this usage across the Caribbean. There would have been a number of Hiberno-Anglicisms available to adopt, and since no creole adopted all or even most of them, we must wonder why all of them would have adopted any particular one. It is much more graceful to assume that the construction was adopted by one creole and subsequently passed down to descendants of it.

Moreover, the Irish, although well represented among Caribbean bondservants, were not the majority. Whites from England dominated in Barbados (Niles 1980: 22–54) and in St. Kitts and the Leewards (Dunn 1972: 134), and Jamaica was relatively poor in bondservants at all (ibid. 157; all cited in Rickford (1986: 253–54). This would make it even less likely that slaves would have adopted one particular Gaelic-modeled construction across the Caribbean so consistently.

The uniformity of the distribution of this *self/even* homophony, then, is a classic case of a trait that suggests a common ancestor. When Hancock solicits a translation of the sentence *He even had another horse* from three dozen creolist scholars, and their independent answers are as uniform as we have seen above, sisterhood becomes a compelling analysis.

## 3.6. Summary

I have presented six features distributed uniformly in the AECs that are so vanishingly unlikely to have emerged in so many separate locations that they are strongly indicative of a common ancestor diffused throughout the Caribbean and subsequently to the West African coast to become Krio, Nigerian Pidgin English, and other varieties of that area. Unlike serial verbs, common phonetic shapes in core vocabulary, absence of gender marking, or the like, these six features can *only* be derived from a shared ancestor.

## 4. Conclusion

According to the established tenets of diachronic analysis, the AECs are sister languages. This argument compliments and reinforces the lexical correspondences previously brought to light by Hancock (1969, 1987) and Smith (1987a).[6]

Furthermore, the nature of the correspondences in question is such that we must conclude that the parent language was by no means a rudimentary pidgin but, on the contrary, was already relatively elaborated. What suggests this is that many of the diagnostic shared traits that would be present in the parent language are the result of evolution over time, such as the copulas *DA* and *de,* as well as *self* as *even.* A similar case can be made for *bin,* in that early pidgins often eschew VP-internal past marking. Thus this contact language was already elaborated enough to contain grammaticalized items, exhibiting a structural expansion analogous to that of Tok Pisin before creolization, as opposed to the rudimentary structure documented in pidgins of limited social function such as Russenorsk or Chinese Pidgin English.

In other words, it would seem that this parent had passed far beyond the stage of a jargon, and thus contributed to the Caribbean scenarios far more integrally than simply providing some isolated lexical items and expressions. Instead, this contact language seems indeed to have been the direct parent to the creoles in question, having consisted of a full grammar. Of course, as Hancock (1987, 1993) has proposed, this variety would have composed one of several ingredients in each context which contributed to the particular creoles that emerged, other ingredients being particular

British dialects, specific substrate compositions, timings in arrivals of slaves and whites, interdialectal contact, and so on. However, the nature of the idiosyncratic correspondences I have demonstrated indicate that we can see the parent language as having been a central and robust constant in the varying mixes across the Caribbean and down the West African coast.

My hope is to have made one thing clear: the principles of historical linguistics reveal that it is virtually impossible that the AECs were *not* descended directly from a stabilized common ancestor.

# Creole Transplantation

*A Source of Solutions to Resistant Anomalies*

## 1. Introduction

One of the most important aspects of creole studies is reconstructing how and why these languages developed. The dominant reconstruction has become what I will call the *limited access conception.* According to this, creole languages emerged when learners of a language, most often plantation slaves, received only fragmentary input from that language as the result of social or psychological distance. In need of a full language nevertheless, they created one from this material via transfer from substrate languages and the operations of universals of various kinds, be this through an innate bioprogram or more cognitively general universals of second-language acquisition.

To be sure, there is a wide range of creole genesis theories, and limited access to a target is by no means the sum total of any of them. However, whether concentrating on the expression of a bioprogram in response to dilution of target input (Bickerton 1981, 1984), relexification of substrate languages (Lefebvre 1998 or, less schematically, Alleyne 1980, Boretzky 1983), "creative" forging of a new interethnic communication vehicle (Baker 1 995a), or the development of "approximations of approximations" of the lexifier as slave populations gradually increased (Chaudenson 1992), all creole genesis theories incorporate the basic limited access conception as a key component. Very few working creolists could claim to consider disproportion of black to white unimportant to the emergence of plantation creoles. Examples:

> In the plantation situation, the preparatory phase of sugar colonization gave way
> . . . to the exploitative phase . . . requiring a rapid increase in the numbers of unskilled

manual laborers; . . . dilution of the original model must have resulted. . . . In fact, what took place . . . was second language learning with inadequate input. (Bickerton 1988: 271–72)

In the New World, on sugar plantations, production was organized on the basis of a kind of occupational stratification according to which field slaves were most numerous and were furthest removed from contact with Europeans. Social intercourse of the field slaves was almost exclusively confined within the group; and so, among them, linguistic forms showing a high degree of divergence . . . were able to crystallize and achieve the appearance of stability. (Alleyne 1971: 180)

The greater the proportion of people of color in a Caribbean colony during the period of genesis, the more "radical" the creole that emerged, with "radicalness" being measured as distance from the lexifier language. . . . [This assumption], linking the proportion of people of color in the population to degree of radicalness, is apparently uncontroversial. (Singler 1995: 219–20)

If it is accepted that Mauritian Creole emerged and jelled in that formative period (roughly fifty years or three generations long) of the eighteenth century and in demographic conditions which by definition rendered access to French next to impossible for most people . . . (Corne 1995b: 12)

While lack of ready access to a dominant language; or indeed lack of social compunction to acquire it fully, certainly has been a factor in the birth of creoles, the concentration on this aspect has entailed the neglect of an equally important factor in explaining why we find creoles where we do today.

Specifically, quite often, it can be shown that a creole is spoken in a given place not because it emerged there, but because a pidgin or creole had already existed in that location and served either as a template or as a direct ancestor for the new creole that developed. (Chaudenson [1981, 2000] has long noted this fact, but given that his work is written in French, this subsidiary observation in his work has had no significant impact on Anglophone creolist work.)[1]

In comparison to limited access-based scenarios, the development of a creole as a mere continuation of one imported from elsewhere seems at first rather mundane, which partly explains the general marginalization of this phenomenon even in studies of cases where its importance is clear. For example, no one comparing Haitian and Antillean French Creoles could deny that Haitian has obvious direct historical links to Antillean, to the extent that Haitians and Antilleans can manage conversation. Yet while this is occasionally acknowledged briefly (e.g., Baker 1987: 73, Singler 1995: 203–4), accounts of the genesis of Haitian largely imply that the language emerged in situ (e.g., Lefebvre 1998), with the implication that the influence of preexisting creoles was at best adstratal.

It is not difficult to see the reasons for this: the Language Bioprogram Hypothesis suggests that creoles will lend especial insight into Universal Grammar; relexificationist/substratist conceptions depict creoles as fascinating strategies of cultural hybridization and survival; the "creativist" analysis uses science and history to help rid creoles of the Sisyphean taint; et cetera. There is more apparent fascination in processes like these than in simply tracing the birth of a creole to the fact that seasoned immigrants were already speaking one. In short, the limited access model simply seems more *interesting*.

Yet the emergence of certain creoles as continuations of preexisting ones, while seemingly a rather inert affair, in fact sheds vital insights upon a number of problems long unsolved in creole studies. This chapter shows the benefits that more explicit acknowledgment and study of these historical links can yield to the discipline.

## 2. Hawaiian Creole English: *Sine pidgin non?*

Bickerton (1981) argued that Hawaiian Creole English (henceforth HCE) developed when children of parents speaking various languages were exposed to a mixture of structurally minimal and irregular English interlanguages spoken by the adults around them, and thereby were forced to transform this farrago into a full language via an innate language bioprogram.

The validity of Bickerton's extension of this scenario to other plantation colonies has, of course, been hotly disputed. Of interest to us for the purposes of this essay is that Bickerton's application of this limited access-based scenario to HCE has been refuted by recent work (Roberts 2000). Roberts's work by no means invalidates Bickerton's conception completely. For example, Goodman (1985), Holm (1986), and even myself (McWhorter 1994a) have argued that it was adults from the mid-1800s on, rather than children at the turn of the century, who created HCE. This conclusion was warranted by the evidence Bickerton brought to bear viewed against the other evidence available at the time. However, through assiduous examination of a lode of historical documents, Roberts has conclusively shown that, while many adult immigrants in Hawaii did speak a range of pidgin Englishes, children were indeed central in creating the stabilized language we today recognize as HCE, including the development and/or conventionalization of the tense, mood, and aspect markers.

However, it is equally important to note that these children created this creole in a context in which they were nothing less than bathed daily in rich input from full varieties of English, which would hardly have necessitated resort to a bioprogram. For example, a newspaper editorial of 1887 includes the following description of a fuller English spoken by adults:

> The colloquial English of Hawaii *nei* is even now sufficiently *sui generis* to be noticeable to strangers. It is not a dialect, but a new language with English as its basic element, wrought upon by the subtle forces of other languages, not so much in the matter of a changed vocabulary as a changed diction. (Reinecke, Tsuzaki, DeCamp, Hancock, and Wood 1975: 595, 609, cited in Goodman 1985: 111–12)

Goodman, Holm, and I have all argued that this suggests that HCE already existed by the 1880s, long before Bickerton reconstructed the creole as having been born. However, Roberts (2000) has convincingly shown that the author was in fact referring to a full indigenized Hawaiian English.

Crucially, however, earlier in the editorial the author makes specific reference to a "pigeon" English spoken by children. This is important in showing that HCE, or its precursor, was indeed already being spoken in the 1880s, even if the excerpted passage above itself is not referring to it. In other words, children created HCE in the very context in which this "colloquial English" was coin of the realm. With input of this richness, children would not have needed to create a language from the ground up.

Furthermore—a fact markedly deemphasized in Bickerton's writings—the children who created HCE attended schools where they were taught in English. Alone, this fact eliminates any reason for supposing that their English input was limited to any jargon or pidgin.

Thus we see that second-generation immigrant schoolchildren created HCE not as a solution to inadequate English input but as the linguistic expression of a new, young, Hawaiian identity.

Many have been uncomfortable with Bickerton's attempts to parse creole genesis as a mere matter of demographic ratios, an approach most explicitly espoused by Bickerton via his "pidginization index" (1984: 176–78). For those committed to a more sociologically rooted approach to the subject, it might be tempting here to suppose that expression of identity was the dominant factor in the birth of HCE. However, in broader view, this would raise a difficult question: if group identity was why multiethnic schoolchildren in Hawaii developed a creole despite being surrounded by full English, then why has this not happened throughout the world in multiethnic nations where a single official language is the medium of instruction in schools?

For example, if HCE arose simply as a vehicle of identity, then why have multiethnic schoolchildren in urban schools in countries like Congo or Tanzania not spontaneously developed creolized varieties of the language of teaching? As long as we find it unremarkable that no French creole has developed in Kinshasa or that no English creole has developed in Dar es Salaam (or even in schoolyards in American cities like Oakland, where children often speak as many as a dozen foreign languages natively), we must assume that something more was at work in the emergence of HCE.

In this light, a factor that distinguishes turn-of-the-century Hawaii from Tanzania is that in Hawaii there was, in addition to the varieties of full English, the range of pidgin Englishes spoken by immigrant adults, as demonstrated by Roberts (1998). While hardly discounting the concomitant presence of pidgin Hawaiian at the time (Bickerton and Wilson 1987, Roberts 1995), pidgin Hawaiian was strongest on plantations; in towns and cities, pidgin English was a vigorous presence by the 1880s, and it is here that schoolchildren developed HCE.

It is impossible that these children created HCE because of input deprivation when they spent five days a week being instructed in English. Nevertheless, it is plausible that for children surrounded by parents and other adults using pidgin English, to use as a vehicle of identity an English with reduced morphology, simple syntax, and fluid lexical categorial boundaries was a natural choice. Where no such pidgin varieties of the school language are "in the air," even schoolchildren speaking a wide variety of home languages simply learn the full school language, with slang lexical items and expressions serving as the markers of in-group identity, rather than a vast reduction and reconstitution of the language's structure per se.

There is a "control case" available to support this analysis of creole in Hawaii, in the form of the development of Singapore English ("Singlish"). Like HCE, Singapore English was created in English-language schools by children speaking a range of first languages (Chinese dialects, Hindi, Bengali, Tamil, and Malay), and expresses a local identity much as HCE today does, with even fluent speakers of English retaining Singapore English as a casual alternative (Platt 1975).

Yet Singapore English would not be considered a creole under any analysis. English inflections are somewhat reduced, but vigorous: bare third-person singular verbs are found, but quite variably even in basilectal speakers, and zero past marking occurs largely in a systematic opposition to marked pasts to encode subtle semantic and discourse distinctions. Zero copula occurs variably, but there are no distinct equative and locative copulas, no complex of preposed tense and aspect markers, no restructuring of the NP determination apparatus, and, in general, none of the sharp departures from English syntax that distinguish Jamaican patois, Sranan, or Tok Pisin. (Ho and Platt 1993). Here is a typical sample:

> Then sekali (Malay 'suddenly') the teacher come in. We all chabot (Malay 'run away') off ah. Then when de Sir (teacher) want to sit down den she shout you know. She shout you know. Den de Sir tot (thought) what happen [y']know. Den he se, "Got kum—dose pin ah, kum (thumb) tacks ah.' So den de Sir as(k) who lah (expressive particle). (ibid. 135)

Clearly, while this variety could be classified as a "creoloid" or semi-creole (Platt 1975), in general it registers more as a "kind of English" than as a completely different language.

An important difference between the genesis contexts of HCE and Singapore English is that pidgin English was a much more marginal presence during the development of Singapore English in the 1940s. Rather than being the increasingly prevalent interethnic lingua franca that it was in late-nineteenth-century Hawaii, pidgin English in mid-twentieth-century Singapore was spoken only by some older immigrants when communicating on a utilitarian basis with whites. The interethnic lingua franca was Bazaar Malay (Platt 1975: 364). As a result, pidginized English was a much less integral part of the linguistic context the creators of Singapore English lived in.

We must now recall that in most countries where there is no preexisting pidgin English model at all, multiethnic schoolchildren's in-group language is not even as reduced as Singapore English. In this light, in seeking to attribute the different outcomes in Hawaii and Singapore's schools to a systematic factor, we can hypothesize that the lesser influence of Singapore's pidgin English resulted in an in-group language that was less reduced in comparison to English than HCE. In other words, it may be that Hawaii, Singapore, and Tanzania represent a cline of contexts in which the prevalence, marginality, and absence, respectively, of a preexistent pidgin English have determined the extent of reduction and restructuring in the in-group speech developed by its multiethnic urban student bodies.

Certainly, in attributing the birth of HCE to the presence of a pidgin spoken by adults, I am in no sense attempting to rescue or recast my earlier claim that HCE was developed by adults. On the contrary, Roberts's work has convinced me, in a way that Bickerton's nimble but insufficiently supported guess did not, that the grammar of what we know as HCE was essentially a child creation, and I find this fascinating. Part of what fascinates me is that these children created this language despite having full access to English, contra Bickerton's reconstruction. Given that children of various ethnicities do not create creoles in schoolyards every day, and the availability of useful sources of comparison like Singapore, I am suggesting that the adults' pidgin varieties served less as a direct ancestor to HCE than as the spur for a degree of paradigmatic and structural reduction that would not otherwise have been the case.

Specifically, Hawaii shows us that a creole can develop as an in-group code even amid rich, directed input from its lexifier—but only when a pidginized variety of the lexifier is already spoken by some segment of the society to serve as a model and inspiration. Hawaiian Creole English, under this analysis, did not simply spring into existence on its own: the preexistent pidgin was a necessary condition for its birth.


## 3. The French continuum anomaly

### 3.1. The problem

One of the strangest, most persistent problems in creole studies is that French plantation creoles do not exhibit a continuum of lects shading gradually into the local standard, as English Caribbean creoles do. To be sure, some varieties of a given French creole do lean toward the standard, such as varieties of Haitian which incorporate front rounded vowels. However, the fact remains that in Haitian and the various Antillean varieties, Guianese, and Seychellois, there is a distinct break between creole and French, such that there is no band of lects classifiable neither as standard or creole as, for example, in Jamaica and Guyana.

It is difficult to see how creole genesis theory, as currently configured, could ever provide an answer to this contrast. We must note that even an answer based on exquisitely detailed sociohistorical research on a single colony, read to suggest that the local conditions would have kept a standard and creole separate, would be inadequate because of the nature of our data set. That is: continua are oddly absent in colonies formerly run by *one particular power*, and thus our explanation must apply "productively," so to speak, across the French Caribbean, as well as in the Indian Ocean.

Any sense that the French may have maintained more social distance between themselves and their slaves than the English appears belied by the ample documentation of mulatto classes of slaves in French Caribbean colonies. One must also ask how likely it would be that any such cultural tendency, even if nominally enshrined in *codes noirs*, would be upheld so consistently by every plantation supervisor in each of so many separate colonies. Clearly, something broader and more decisive was at work.

That this problem has remained a puzzle for thirty years suggests that it will be useful to consider a complete change of lens in addressing it. For example, we might surmise that the French situation, where plantation societies led to two distinct varieties, standard and creole, was not exceptional, but a norm. This would eliminate the

French situation as a "problem" and render it simply predictable, leaving us with the English continua as an anomaly to "explain." The advantage is that, upon examination, there is promise in this approach.

## 3.2. The history of the English creole continua

To see why, we must first briefly refer to my argument in chapter 8 that all of the Atlantic English-based creoles (AECs) trace to a single ancestor distributed across and beyond the Caribbean. This argument is based on six features shared by most or all of these creoles, which are distinctive in being too idiosyncratic to have emerged in several separate locations and can only have emerged in a single grammar. The equative copula *da* (with its cognates *na*, *a*, and *duh*), the locative copula *de*, and the modal use of *fu* (or cognates *fi* or *fu*) to mean "should"[2] are all idiosyncratic grammaticalizations representing particular choices out of many possible, with it thus being impossible that the "roll of the dice" would have come out so similarly in several separate colonies. The second-person plural pronoun *unu*, the past marker *bin*, and the use of *self* as "even" are, respectively, a borrowing, an etymological recruitment, and an adstrate calque, and, again, are all particular choices out of many possible and thus also indicate a single ancestor. For example, would every AEC use an African word for a *second-person plural* pronoun specifically, and all from the *same particular language*, Igbo?

The influence of the polygenetic frame of reference is so powerful in the field that it is tempting to suppose that the creoles emerged independently, but that these features "diffused" from one creole to another. Yet while diffusion can certainly explain some AEC commonalities, it is inapplicable to these six features. First, they are core grammatical items and thus relatively unlikely to be borrowed into a grammar; second, it would strain credulity to suppose that no fewer than six items, all already unlikely to diffuse, would end up distributed so uniformly across several creoles. Basic historical linguistics, bolstered by the rich sociohistorical relationships between the various colonies, makes the reconstruction of a single ancestor obviously the most economical choice.

To wit, the ancestor of the AECs is most likely to have been distributed from Barbados, one of the earliest colonies settled by the English and the source of the colonization of many subsequent locations, such as Suriname, Jamaica, South Carolina, and Guyana (Cassidy 1983).[3] Settlers of new colonies often either brought slaves with them or later bought slaves from Barbados, thereby transplanting the ancestral pidgin or creole from one colony to another (Baker 1999).

Today, even the Barbadian speech furthest from standard English is essentially mesolectal compared to the basilects of Jamaica or Guyana. However, even Bajan has four of the six ancestral AEC features (*de*, *unu*, *self*, and *bin* [the latter recorded in Rickford 1992]), with the absence of the particularly basilectal *da* and modal *fu* unremarkable. Moreover, sociological and historical evidence suggests that a more basilectal variety was once spoken in Barbados (Rickford and Handler 1994). Indeed, it is virtually impossible that this was not the case: the six features that AEC as a whole share must trace to a single source, and history demonstrates that this source must have been Barbados. Thus comparative reconstruction takes its place alongside the sociological and historical indications to make the former existence of a Barbadian basilect almost certain.

Where this applies to the continuum issue is that while chapter 8 addresses basilectal AEC features, there is no a priori reason to assume that only the basilect was transplanted from one colony to another and, in fact, all reason to suppose that the basilect was transplanted along with the mesolect (cf. Bickerton 1996: 324 for a similar observation). What suggests this is that the AEC mesolects, too, show signs of being traceable to *one* instance of restructuring rather than separate ones in each colony.

First thought to have developed after emancipation as blacks had richer encounters with the standard, today the mesolect is thought by most creolists to have been in place at the outset of a colony's history, developed by those slaves whose positions gave them more access to the standard than field hands (Baker 1990, Bickerton 1996). Whether we conceive of the continuum as having developed early or late, however, the implication of most authors is that this development would have been in a given colony itself. If this were true, however, we would not expect AEC mesolects to share certain features.

Most strikingly, for instance, AEC mesolects have zero copula in equative and locative sentences, in contrast to AEC basilects, which have overt copulas in such sentences. For example, see table 9.1 for Guyanese.

The facts are similar in Jamaican (LePage and De Camp 1960, Holm 1984), Gullah (Geraty 1990), Bajan (Rickford 1992), and other AECs. Under the old "bottom up" conception of continuum development, this was attributed to mesolectal speakers having "unlearned" their basilectal copulas but not yet acquired the acrolectal ones (Bickerton 1975). While ingenious, this notion was already problematic (chapter 6), but under the current "top down" conception it becomes utterly untenable: Why would those speakers with more contact with the standard have zero copula, a hallmark of pidginization, while those with the least contact, likely to pidginize the lexifier to the greatest extent, have overt ones? Moreover, exactly what would explain mesolectal speakers not retaining the acrolectal copula, if their access to the target was relatively free?

Finally and most important, whatever answers one could provide to those two questions, what is the likelihood that things would come out in these particular ways as a *regular* occurrence, happening in Barbados, Jamaica, South Carolina, Guyana, Trinidad, Antigua, and so on? Thus of course, "things happen" in language change and language contact; flukes are part of the territory, Grimm's Law being a prime example. Certainly it is not unheard of for a mesolectal, or semi-creole, variety to

TABLE 9.1. The copula along the Guyanese creole continuum

|  | *Equative* | *Locative* |
| --- | --- | --- |
| Acrolect | *iz* | *iz* |
| Mesolect | ∅ | ∅ |
| Basilect | *a* | *de* |

Adapted from Bickerton (1973)

have zero copula. Crucially, however, semi-creoles retain copulas as often as they drop them: Popular Brazilian Portuguese retains the copula, Singapore English can drop it; Afrikaans retains the copula, Réunionnais can drop it (Cellier 1985: 73), et cetera. In other words, zero copula in a mesolectal variety is not something we would reasonably expect to have occurred in *all* AEC mesolects; what we would expect is for it to occur in some but not all. Thus its actual distribution suggests that mesolectal AEC developed *once* and was subsequently distributed.

Another feature of mesolectal AEC suggesting this is the use of *did* as a past or anterior marker, in Guyanese, Jamaican, and Trinidadian (Winford 1993: 64–66) and other AECs. As Bickerton (1996: 315–16) notes, it is unlikely that this feature is simply a reflection of the pleonastic use of *do* in simple declarative sentences in earlier English, because this feature was passing out of general usage in most English dialects as early as the 1500s. This is especially important in reference to Guyana, where the English did not establish plantations until as late as the mid-1700s. While the feature held on somewhat longer in Irish and West Country English dialects, such speakers were hardly distributed so uniformly and predominantly across the English Caribbean that we would expect this particular feature to be incorporated by so many separate creoles. Once again, if these mesolects had developed independently, we would expect more variation between them: one or two would have *did*, while another might have overgeneralized *was* (as one variety of Liberian Pidgin English does [Singler 1981]) or *had* (as African-American Vernacular English now does in narratives [Rickford and Théberge 1996]). Much more likely, then, is that this feature was incorporated once in one place, most likely from regional British dialect influence in the 1600s, and subsequently spread elsewhere.

Thus basic principles of reconstruction lead us to the conclusion that not only the AEC basilect traces to a single ancestor but the AEC mesolectal band does as well. The argument is not that this basilect and mesolect remained pristine during these transplantations. The basic template was obviously altered in each location it reached, according to the nature of the English dialects spoken, the substrate lanuage mixture, degree of contact between slaves and whites, and so on, the result being the differing creoles extant today. Yet while obviously distinct enough to be considered separate languages, all of these creoles share a particular core of features whose nature clearly reveals a direct historical relationship between all of them, rendering it implausible that, for example, Gullah formed independently in Charleston with mere marginal "influence" from Bajan.

## 3.3. Brief excursus: The reality of transplantation

Some creolists may find themselves resisting this argumentation on the basis of a conviction that even if slaves from a former colony imported something identifiable as a grammar, it would have been impossible for this grammar to survive transmission to massive numbers of new adult slaves (e.g., Bickerton 1998: 85–86). This is an understandable intuition, but is, quite simply, refuted by the comparative linguistic data: the AECs are too closely similar in idiosyncratic ways for each imported variety to have been "pulverized" by waves of new imports. If these languages had developed in any sense independently, even with correspondences in superstrates, substrates, and universal tendencies, we would expect much more variation than we in fact find. This is because of the vital role that chance plays in language contact, expressing itself even within the broad constraints that source languages and universals impose.

For example, it is uncontroversial that Tok Pisin English Creole is the result of an encounter with English that was completely separate from the one that created AEC. Here we contrast equivalent sentences in Tok Pisin and Sranan:

(1)   a. Tok Pisin:
           Em mipela i     bin   kirap-im       dispela wok.
           it   we     PRED ANT start-TRANS this     work
           "It is us who started this work." (Mühlhäusler 1985: 352)

      b. Sranan:
           Na  wi di    ben  bigin a   wroko disi.
           it-is we REL ANT start the work  this
           "It is us who started this work."

(2)   a. Tok Pisin:
           Mi stap  long haus.
           he COP LOC house
           "I am in the house."

      b. Sranan:
           Mi de    na   ini    a    oso.
           he COP LOC inside the house
           "I am in the house."

Some creolists might suppose that the differences between these two creoles are attributable to differences in the superstrate, substrate, or timing of demographic developments. This is definitely valid to an extent—but leaves a crucial realm of the evidence unaccounted for.

For example, substratal influence is clearly one factor in the differences between the two creoles. The predicate marker and transitive marker in the Tok Pisin example (1a) are undisputed calques on Melanesian languages (Keesing 1988: 119–27, 143–70), and the -pela marker is also possibly traceable to substrate behaviors (ibid. 113, 137–39). Meanwhile, the choice of di (> disi "this") as a relativizer in Sranan is firmly traceable to West African patterns (Bruyn 1995b).

However, other things are more fortuitous. It is a universal tendency for positional verbs to serve as locative copulas, whether cross-linguistically or in pidgins and creoles. However, while Tok Pisin observes this universal, Sranan happens not to have, opting instead for an adverb there. It would be difficult to ascribe this to any parseable factor; for example, it cannot be traced to the substrate, since Sranan's West African substrate languages use verbs, not adverbs, as locative copulas. The AEC choice of de was a matter of chance (see chapter 8).

Similarly, there is a universal tendency in pidginization to use one or two items alone as prepositions. However, this universal allows a wide variety of etymological choices. What factor could "explain" the choice of *long* (< *along*) in Tok Pisin as opposed to *na* (either from Portuguese "in + DEF" or the Igbo general preposition) in Sranan? Tok Pisin radically reinterpreted a preposition from English; Sranan chose a foreign item—one would search in vain for a "reason" for the difference in outcomes.

Because chance alone ensures such distinct outcomes in separate instances of pidginization even apart from differences in source languages, it is clear that the AECs must indeed be the result of the transplantation of a single system to various places, in each colony adapted, to be sure, but by no means rebuilt from the ground up. If they had developed in any sense separately, then the AECs would be much more different on all levels than they are.

## 3.4. Solution: The French colonies as default

To return to the French colony issue: at this point, many readers will naturally suppose that whether or not the English continuum had been transplanted from colony to colony, continua would have developed independently in each place anyway. Crucially, however, the French colonies may be telling us that, in fact, this is not what would have happened. To wit: the genetic relationship between the English creole continua on the one hand and the odd absence of French creole continua on the other can be subsumed under a coherent analysis if we propose the following.

One interpretation of the current distribution of creole continua in the Caribbean is that the typical sociolinguistic result of plantation slavery was a creole distinct from the standard, with no unbroken continuum of lects in between; this result would be represented by the French colonies. Barbados, however, can be seen to have been uniquely suited to the development of such a continuum, and when the creole that developed there was transplanted to other colonies, the continuum of lects was transported along with it. This continuum thus took its place in colonies where, if AEC had not been imported and a creole had formed locally, the default situation—a creole distinct from the standard with no continuum, as in the French colonies—would have obtained. (I owe this hypothesis to my always stimulating exchanges with Mikael Parkvall.)

In evaluating this hypothesis, the first thing we must ask is whether there indeed was anything about colonial Barbados which would have made the development of a continuum particularly likely where it was not elsewhere. Presumably, what we seek is evidence of contact between white and black that was significantly richer than it was in other English colonies. In fact, as those familiar with English Caribbean history will immediately note, Barbados is just such a place. It is hardly accidental that today Bajans are the most notoriously acrolectal English Caribbeans, with mesolectal registers available but hardly as readily elicited as in Guyana, Jamaica, or even the Sea Islands, and now spoken regularly only by isolated, elderly people. As in other plantation societies, blacks vastly outnumbered whites in Barbados by the mid-1600s; however, the proportion of whites nevertheless remained higher than in other English Caribbean colonies (Handler 1974: 10), partly because indentured servitude was particularly prevalent. In general, as Roy (1986: 143) notes, the small size, flat topography, and early construction of roads ensured a richer contact between black and white than was possible in, for example, much of mountainous Jamaica.

Thus the absence of French creole continua, when viewed against the origin of the English continuum in Barbados, may suggest that plantation conditions alone were not sufficient to the development of a continuum, and that typical plantation societal conditions, such as, for example, those in Martinique, kept a standard and a creole distinct in the minds of speakers. Instead, it would appear that *particularly* rich contact between black and white was necessary. In support of this, it is significant that we also find a creole continuum, less assiduously documented than the English Caribbean ones but obviously similar, in Cape Verde (Bartens 1999), where plantations were always small because of poor soil and thus black-white contact was always relatively intimate, but not in São Tomé, where in its initial colonial period, large plantations were worked by Africans in relative isolation from whites. Similarly, the one New World French creole that has developed a mesolect is Louisiana French Creole, whose speakers have existed in a uniquely intimate relationship with similarly poor, isolated Cajun French speakers for centuries. Another useful example is that there has never existed a continuum between Spanish and Palenquero, despite its speakers having apparently always been bilingual in Spanish (Schwegler 2000). The social demarcation between Palenquero speakers and outsiders has prevented any such continuum from emerging.

In sum, then, if we shift our focus from polygenetic conceptions to the seemingly mundane fact that most creoles are descendants of preexisting ones, then one advantage is that we have a possible solution to a uniquely intractable anomaly, which has otherwise remained unsolved for decades.

## 4. The Spanish creoles

If we are positioned to focus as much on preexisting pidgin or creole models as on demographics, then we are also prepared to constructively address another truly baffling problem in creole studies, the scarcity of Spanish-based creoles.

The problem here is much more serious than most authors acknowledge. It is relatively well- known that the Spanish established plantation societies worked by Africans in Cuba, Puerto Rico, and the Dominican Republic. However, Chaudenson (1992: 124–28) and I (McWhorter 1995a: 223–26) have shown that the absence of creoles in these locations can be attributed to timing of demographic developments namely, slaves were used in small numbers for long periods during which they were able to learn relatively full Spanish; when massive importation of slaves finally began, these older slaves could pass their competence on to these new ones (for the introduction of this model, see Baker and Corne 1982).

What is virtually unacknowledged in the field, however, is that the Spanish also established thriving plantation colonies worked by Africans in their mainland colonies, such as modern-day Colombia (particularly the Pacific lowlands), the Chota Valley of Ecuador, Mexico, Peru, and Venezuela. Most important, in these places Africans were imported in large numbers at the outset, with no *société d'habitation* phase at all. Furthermore, the Iberian racial tolerance and restraining influence of Catholicism often cited as having impeded the development of Spanish creoles was nowhere in evidence in these settings, where large-scale agriculture or mining engendered the same dehumanization of African laborers as obtained in better-known colonies like Suriname and Haiti. I discuss this issue in detail in McWhorter (2000a).

Why no creoles appeared in these colonies is an issue I address in the following section. However, the first question to be resolved is why Spanish creoles did appear in Curaçao (Papiamentu) and El Palenque de San Basilio (Palenquero). In light of the past two sections, what is most interesting here is that Papiamentu and Palenquero share a certain factor: specifically, there is concrete evidence that a pre-existing pidgin or creole was highly influential in the genesis contexts of both.

Until recently, older people in Curaçao controlled a secret variety they called Guene (< Guinea, i.e., the Guinea Coast of Africa), which they considered to be the language spoken by their ancestors. Significantly, "Guiné" is still what some native speakers of Guinea-Bissau Creole Portuguese call their language (Birmingham 1976: 19), and in general Guene had features tracing it to Portuguese-based contact languages of West Africa, most strikingly the third-person pronoun *ine*, a substrate borrowing also found in the Gulf of Guinea Portuguese creoles. If Papiamentu had emerged as a Spanish-based contact language, then we would expect any preserved "slave" language to be Spanish-based, like the *bozal* Spanish similarly preserved as a ritual language among Afro-Cubans (Cabrera 1954).

The relationship between a Portuguese creole and Papiamentu is further bolstered by well-documented clues in the language itself, linking it to Portuguese creoles still spoken on the West African coast. For one, there are a healthy number of lexical items in Papiamentu that are derivable only from Portuguese rather than Spanish (most assiduously and rigorously identified by Grant 1996b). In addition, on the grammatical level, the plural morpheme *nan* is also found in the Portuguese creole of Annobón (Birmingham 1976: 22). Similarly, the parallel between the Cape Verdean Portuguese *el taba ta kanta* "he was singing" and Papiamentu *e tabata kanta* is striking (ibid. 20), since this usage is impossible to derive from any Iberian construction and is only one of many possible reconceptualizations of the lexifier material. Quint (1998) has documented an impressive range of parallels between Papiamentu and Cape Verdean Portuguese Creole which render the case for a direct relationship even stronger.

Meanwhile, in the case of Palenquero, in reference to his long-term residence in Cartagena, near where Palenquero is spoken, the father Sandoval noted in 1627 that there were many slaves who had lived in São Tomé who used a "highly corrupt and backwards" version of Portuguese "which they call the language of São Tomé" (*un género de lenguaje muy corrupto y revesado de la Portuguesa que ilaman lengua de S. Thome*) (cited in Schwegler 1998: 229). This passage suggests that many of the originators of Palenquero already spoke a form of what is today São Tomense Creole Portuguese.

The connection between São Tomense and Palenquero is supported by linguistic evidence. The third-person plural subject pronoun is *iné* in São Tomense, while it is reflexes of standard *êles* in other Portuguese-based creoles (*élis* in Guinea-Bissau Creole, for example [Kihm 1980b: 44]). Palenquero has *ané*, rather than a reflex of Spanish *ellos*).[4] Palenquero also has a postposed anterior marker *-ba* (*ele kelé ba* "he wanted"), which is also found in the Upper Guinea Portuguese creoles. The most likely source for this *-ba* is *acabar* "to finish," found as *kabá* in other Caribbean creoles such as Sranan and Saramaccan. The particular elision to simply *ba* in both

Palenquero and the Upper Guinea Portuguese creoles suggests yet another link between Palenquero and West African coastal Portuguese pidgins (although São Tomense lacks this particular feature).

The Guene connection in Curaçao and the São Tomé connection in Cartagena are striking, in that it is *precisely* where we have these two historical indications of a contact language already in the air that Spanish creoles exist today. If, in addition to the historical clues from Curaçao and northwestern Colombia, we had documentation of Cape Verdean-speaking slaves in Venezuela and mentions of slaves from São Tomé in Mexico, and yet creoles were spoken only in Curaçao and northeastern Colombia, then there would be no reason to view these preexisting contact languages as significant in the linguistic outcomes in various locations. However, what we have is historical citations of preexisting creoles in Curaçao and northwestern Colombia, and creoles spoken today in Curaçao and northwestern Colombia. What clinches the case is that both creoles have clear signs of Portuguese creole influence: if they had arisen simply via slaves' limited access to Spanish, we would expect much less, if any, of this kind of influence.

It would be unrealistic to analyze Papiamentu as a relexification of Cape Verdean itself, or Palenquero as a relexification of São Tomense. Nevertheless, the existence of Spanish creoles in just the places where Portuguese creoles are documented to have been imported by early slave populations suggests some causal link. In view of the role that we have seen that preexisting contact languages can play in Hawaii, these facts suggest that the presence of forms of West African Creole Portuguese in Curaçao and Cartagena were crucial to the emergence of creoles in these two locations. It is plausible that the very prevalence of a reduced contact language, especially one based on Portuguese—even more closely akin to Spanish in the 1500s and 1600s than it is today—made the adoption and stabilization of a reduced version of Spanish as an interethnic communication vehicle seem natural. Just as pidgin English seems to have served as a model modus operandi for young Hawaiians, if not as a direct template, the preexisting Portuguese creoles in Curaçao and Cartagena, while not serving as direct sources of relexification for the new creoles, obviously played an adstratal function. They left not only lexical items, but had a grammatical impact, their analytic typology serving as a model for the new language developing. Most important is to recall that *where such creoles are not documented to have existed in the genesis context, no creole emerged.*

Under limited access-based theory, the fact that a creole emerged in Curaçao but not in Venezuela is an eternal problem, which demographic tallies would be extremely unlikely to shed useful light upon (e.g., blacks and whites had rich contact in Curaçao, and yet there is a creole; in contrast, there was little contact on Venezuela plantations, and yet there is no creole). On the other hand, we see that once again, calling attention to preexisting contact languages allows a potential solution.

## 5. The afrogenesis hypothesis

However, we are now left with the question as to *why* no creole formed in Venezuela and similar Spanish colonies. Along those lines, let us review these two statements from leading creolist thinkers, first quoted early in this chapter:

In the New World, on sugar plantations, production was organized on the basis of a kind of occupational stratification according to which field slaves were most numerous and were furthest removed from contact with Europeans. Social intercourse of the field slaves was almost exclusively confined within the group; and so, among them, linguistic forms showing a high degree of divergence . . . were able to crystallize and achieve the appearance of stability. (Alleyne 1971: 180)

In the plantation situation, the preparatory phase of sugar colonization gave way . . . to the exploitative phase . . . requiring a rapid increase in the numbers of unskilled manual laborers; . . . dilution of the original model must have resulted . . . In fact, what took place . . . was second language learning with inadequate input. (Bickerton 1988: 271–72)

These statements are nothing less than canon in creole studies, and yet they touch upon what is in fact the most pressing discrepancy in the field.

Namely, on sugar plantations in Venezuela, the "social intercourse of field slaves was almost exclusively confined within the group," as Alleyne puts it with Jamaica in mind; and yet "linguistic forms showing a high degree of divergence" are nowhere in evidence: black Venezuelans simply speak Spanish even when living in Afro-Venezuelan communities (Megenney 1985). Similarly, when in seventeenth-century Ecuador there was "rapid increase in the numbers of unskilled manual laborers," as Bickerton puts it with Guyana in mind, there was no appreciable "dilution of the original model" in terms of slaves' acquisition of Spanish. The descendants of slaves brought to work in sugar plantations in Ecuador's Chota Valley today speak a Spanish that only minimally varies from the local standard, despite having always lived a "life apart" from other Ecuadorans (Lipski 1986).

Thus our crucial discrepancy is that vast disproportion of black to white, so confidently adduced as key to the development of creole languages, had no such effect throughout mainland Spanish American colonies. We have seen an explanation for why Spanish creoles *did* appear in two places; however, the question remains as to why they did *not* appear in the Chocó Valley of Colombia; in the Chota Valley of Ecuador; or in Mexico, Peru, or Venezuela—all places where huge numbers of African slaves were imported to work under conditions in all ways akin to those obtaining under other colonial powers. None of the strategies used to explain the absence of creoles in other locations works for these cases.

The enormity of this problem will become clear with one brief "case study." In the late 1600s, the Spanish began importing massive numbers of West Africans speaking a wide variety of languages into the Pacific lowlands of northwestern Colombia to work their gold mines. Today, the descendants of the Chocó slaves live in the same lowlands, leading a subsistence existence via small-scale mining. Whites are a negligible presence, and interethnic relations are distant (Rout 1976: 243–49). Yet the Spanish of black Chocoanos is essentially a typical Latin American dialect of Spanish, easily comprehensible to speakers of standard Spanish varieties:

(3)   Esa gente  som  muy amoroso. Dijen    que . . . dijeron        que
      that people COP very nice      they-say that     they-say-PRET that

volbían          sí   . . . cuando le     de        su   gana a ello vobe.
they-return-IMP yes when        to-them give-SUBJ their desire to them return

"Those people are really nice. They say that . . . they said that they would come back
. . . when they felt like it." (Schwegler 1991: 99)

(PRET = preterite, IMP = imperfect, SUBJ = subjunctive)

The reason for this is not that blacks did not outnumber whites significantly. There
were no fewer than 5,828 black slaves in the Chocó by 1778, while there were only
about 175 whites—a mere 3% of the total population (West 1957: 100, 108).

The reason is not that slaves and whites had an unusual degree of contact. Slaves
were organized into large teams, or *cuadrillas*, each formally supervised by a white
overseer but actually directed by a black *capitanejo* (ibid. 131–32). *Cuadrillas* typically
consisted of two hundred blacks or more, with ones as large as 567 reported (115–16).

The reason is not that there was a long *société d'habitation* phase, where Africans and whites existed in equal numbers such that Africans could acquire relatively
full Spanish and pass it on to later arrivals. The nature of mining is such that relatively large numbers of slaves were needed from the outset. One of the earliest
*cuadrillas* was established with forty slaves and was increased to sixty-five later that
year (Restrepo 1886: 77–78), and sharp disproportion of black to white increased by
leaps and bounds: there were 600 slaves in the Chocó in 1704; 2,000 in 1724; and
7,088 by 1782 (Sharp 1976: 21–22).

Finally, the reason was not that the Spanish were gentler masters. There was a
slave code enacted in Colombia in 1789 to protect slaves from abuse, but besides the
fact that its very institution suggests the brutality that had obtained over the century
of mining beforehand, it was barely enforced (Sharp 1976: 128). Catholic clerics were
in short supply and were often slaveowners themselves (ibid. 130–31). Flogging was
a regular punishment for any perceived offenses (139–40), and the most unequivocal evidence of the misery of the slaves' lot is the simple fact that escapes and re-
volts were common (140).

The facts are similar in all of the mainland Spanish colonies I have mentioned
(see McWhorter 2000a for details). The Spanish American mainland stands as a stark
contradiction to the very fundamentals of creole genesis theory, which all, despite
their variety, stipulate that disproportion of black to white led to vast reduction and
restructuring of a dominant language.

A general distrust of mechanistic approaches to creole genesis reigns among
creolists, sociolinguists, and anthropologists. In this light, a natural response to these
observations might be to take them as evidence that creolization will not reduce to
ratios and formulas, and to suppose that our solution will come from thorough study
of the social history of each of these anomalous colonies.

However, acknowledging the usefulness of such studies in themselves, our problem runs deeper than this approach could reach. An attempt to account for why a
creole would not have formed in *one* of these colonies, no matter how assiduous in
itself, would fail to address the heart of this problem, which is that creoles failed so
consistently to appear *under the Spanish*. If idiosyncratic combinations of intra-

colonial factors were the culprit here, then we would expect mysteriously absent creoles not in all mainland Spanish colonies, but in maybe two, and also in, say, Guadeloupe and Antigua as well. Thus we seek not to speculate on the operations of the local factors that happened to obtain in *one* given place, but a systematic factor that could determine the linguistic outcomes in *several* separate places having a common feature—in this case, proprietorship by one particular power.

In this light, then, it is also highly implausible that creoles were once spoken in all of these former Spanish colonies but have since disappeared, *pace* Granda (1978) and Schwegler (1993, 1996b). One might propose an account as to why a creole might have disappeared in *one* of these places, but, properly speaking, the only valid address is one that explains why this would happen so anonymously and frequently only under the Spanish. Moreover, claims that prescriptivism is strong in Spanish culture must account for the fact that French creoles survive despite equally strong prescriptivist impulses in French culture.

One identifiable factor truly sets the Spanish apart from other powers. The Spanish were the only slaving power not to establish trade settlements on the West African coast, because of the Treaty of Tordesillas, under which the West African coast fell on the Portuguese side of a line dividing exploration rights between the two Iberian powers. Seemingly irrelevant to sociolinguistic outcomes across the Atlantic Ocean, this absence of trade forts becomes more interesting in that some creolists have surmised that English West African trade settlements were the birthplace of the pidgin which, transported across the ocean, became the AECs, while others have surmised a similar origin for French plantation creoles.[5]

To outline the argumentation for these reconstructions would take us too far from the concern of this chapter, but following and suggesting revisions to Hancock (1969, 1986), I have presented a case for the birth of AEC on the Ghanaian coast in McWhorter (2000a). Meanwhile, Parkvall (1995a) has been the most recent adherent of this kind of scenario for the French creoles. For our purposes, it will suffice to observe that a great many aspects of English and French creoles' linguistic structure and history point in the direction of a West African pidgin origin.

Oddly enough, these trade fort scenarios relate to our Spanish anomaly. If the AECs show signs of tracing to a West African trade fort pidgin, and the French creoles do as well, while the one power that had no such trade forts also left behind very few creoles, then one interpretation of the facts is that *the trade forts were pivotal, rather than incidental, to the birth of the New World creoles.* In other words, it may well be that New World creoles were born in West African trade forts and only imported to, rather than emerging on, plantations. If so, then the reason the Spanish left behind so few creoles would be because they had no trade forts where an ancestral pidgin could form and be spread throughout its New World colonies. Supporting this would be the very fact that the two Spanish plantation creoles that do exist both apparently trace their origin to contact languages imported from the West African coast, in these cases Portuguese pidgin or creole. It is unlikely to be accidental, as we have noticed, that we have Spanish creoles precisely where history or anthropology reveals these imported Portuguese contact languages to have been spoken by early slaves, but none where we do not.

McWhorter (2000a) is a full-length presentation of the evidence for the Afrogenesis Hypothesis. If it is valid, it suggests another change of lens, along the lines of the one I suggested regarding the conditions for creole continua to emerge. Once again, we can account for the facts if we transform what we now take as a problem into the default situation, and recast what we now think of as ordinary as the "exceptional" case. Namely, the mainland Spanish colonies appear to be telling us that ordinarily, slaves were capable of learning a relatively full version of the whites' language on a plantation *even when outnumbering them vastly.*

As counterintuitive as this seems to anyone familiar with the limited access paradigm that creole studies has settled upon, in fact this is precisely what we see again and again in the mainland Spanish colonies. It is obvious that most adults are not capable of full acquisition of second languages, and the sociological conditions on plantations and in mines would have exerted even more of a downward pull on the competence of all but a few slaves. Most likely, it was children who had richer opportunities for acquisition than we might think. Hence technically speaking, plantation conditions may well have limited *adults'* access to Spanish, working in tandem with the lesser language-learning abilities of most people after their early teens. However, what we see is that such conditions did not limit access to such an extent that the only Spanish that slave *children* heard was the pidginized varieties spoken by their parents. Hopefully, future research will elucidate how these children acquired full Spanish. Most important for us to realize, however, is that there is a question only as to *how* the slaves did this; as we have seen, there simply is no question as to *whether* they did it—the Spanish-speaking isolated Afro-Hispanics in Mexico and South America admit no other interpretation.[6]

Why, then, if slaves could learn the lexifier, did slaves under the English and French develop creoles? Here is where we come back to the topic of this essay: I have hypothesized that castle slaves working in the Cormantin trade fort in Ghana, and speaking a pidginized English, would have been transported most likely to Barbados, serving as models for the sale slaves who arrived alongside or after them.[7] Just as in Hawaii, children, although going to school in English, developed a creole because a pidgin English was available as a model, and plantation slaves, though quite capable of acquiring the lexifier itself—as the mainland Spanish colonies prove—could have developed a creole variety because an English pidgin variety was available as a model. Just as Hawaiian kids thought of themselves as developing a "kind of English," plantation slaves would have thought of themselves as developing a "kind of English," not constrained by the taxonomic boundaries around our modern conception of "English" (note that today, Jamaican patois speakers are much less likely than creolists to consider their in-group speech a "different language" than English).

Some might object that pidgin-speaking castle slaves cannot have been numerous enough to have had such an effect on colony-wide speech habits. Yet small numbers of people, with sufficient prestige, can have impact far beyond what their numbers would lead us to expect. At the turn of the 1900s in Papua New Guinea, the British stationed a squadron of just over 400 Papuan constables in inland villages who spoke the pidginized form of Motu called Hiri Motu, with at most just two constables per village (Dutton 1985: 72). Yet because of the prestige of these mere 400 constables, 150,000 people spoke Hiri Motu in 1971 and more do now (ibid. 3).

The idea that creoles formed on plantations as the European language receded from most slaves' everyday contact has great intuitive appeal and is, in fact, an almost inevitable interpretation based on the fact that, say, Jamaican patois, Gullah, Haitian Creole, Sranan, Cape Verdean, and Louisiana French Creole are all spoken by descendants of slaves in former plantation colonies. However, this genesis scenario, thoroughly reasonable in itself, was developed in neglect of mainland Spanish America, former plantation colonies where no creoles are spoken. It is natural to suppose that explanations for this discrepancy will turn up which leave the limited access idea intact, but as I have shown, if such an explanation is found, it is vastly unlikely to involve the tools and approaches currently at creolists' disposal.

The Afrogenesis Hypothesis is motivated not by a mere predilection for monogenetic scenarios, or a natural bent toward revisiting past approaches rather than participating in current ones. It is motivated purely by a desire to resolve the fascinating problem of the absence of Spanish creoles in almost all of mainland Spanish America, in a falsifiable rather than an ad hoc fashion. The facts suggest that this is one more problem whose solution may center on the importance of preexisting contact languages in determining the language choice of multiethnic groups seeking a lingua franca.

## 6. The Portuguese creoles

A final area which an acknowledgment of the role of preexisting pidgins might shed light on is the Portuguese creoles of Africa. Cape Verdean and the Gulf of Guinea dialect complex are generally thought of as "plantation creoles" because they are spoken in former plantation colonies. However, recall that canonical plantation conditions failed to produce creoles in all Spanish colonies except in two cases where a preexisting pidgin/creole is known to have been widely spoken in the early colony. In this light, it may be significant that Portuguese pidgin is known to have been an integral part of the genesis contexts of Cape Verdean and the Gulf of Guinea creoles.

The prevalence of a Portuguese pidgin at the site of present-day Guinea-Bissau and its environs is uncontroversial (e.g., Boxer 1963: 9–12). It is presently unknown whether Portuguese pidgin was incidental or crucial in the birth of the Guinea-Bissau creole. If it was crucial, then by implication, we must trace the genesis of Cape Verdean ultimately to this pidgin, since Cape Verdean and the Guinea-Bissau creole are variants of the same language and thus must have a common source.

On the other hand, some consider Cape Verdean to have been born first and later transported to present-day Guinea-Bissau (e.g., Quint 1998). However, Cape Verde was supplied with slaves from Guinea-Bissau, and the two regions were in fact administrated as a single colony until 1879. As such, it is likely that Portuguese pidgin had a role in the sociolinguistic context of slaves in Cape Verde. This is especially the case given that plantations were generally small on Cape Verde due to poor soil, and its main role was to supply passing ships with food. Much interaction between the slaves and passing sailors would likely have been conducted in Portuguese pidgin.

Portuguese pidgin was also used in the slave trade conducted at São Tomé (although it is unlikely that this was the same pidgin used further north; Upper Guinea and Gulf of Guinea Portuguese creoles do not appear to trace to a single ancestor [Ferraz 1987]). Once again, it is possible that this trade pidgin had no effect on the contact languages developing on the sugar plantations. However, it is also possible that there was indeed influence, and this is suggested by correspondences between Portuguese pidgin recorded from the nearby Slave Coast and modern São Tomense, such as the idiosyncratic etymological source of copula *sa*, a combination of *ser* and *estar* (I thank Mikael Parkvall for this observation).

In both of these cases, my suggestion is not that the creole was necessarily a direct development of the pidgins. The available citations of Portuguese pidgin almost never correspond in any meaningful way to the modern creoles in the way that, for example, pidgin varieties of Tok Pisin were clearly the direct precursors to the modern creole. I suggest, rather, that the presence of reduced Portuguese "in the air" in Cape Verde and São Tomé were important in leading slaves to develop a creolized version of Portuguese as their lingua franca.

Of course, this speculation would be of questionable value if there were no explicit "necessité," as Chaudenson (1992: 44) puts it, for the hypothesis. Once again, I suggest this as a way of grappling with the anomaly of mainland Spanish colonies. Specifically, we find slaves having learned the full lexifier only in the contexts where (1) there is no documentation of early slave arrivals speaking a pidginized version of the superstrate (or a close relative), as there is in Curaçao or Cartagena, and (2) linguistic and sociohistorical reconstruction do not suggest the existence of such pidgin ancestors, as they do in English, French, and Portuguese colonies.

## 7. Implications

I do not mean to imply that restricted contact with a dominant language plays no part at all in creole genesis but, rather, that this aspect has come to play a more important part in our creole genesis scenarios than the distribution and histories of today's creoles actually indicate.

If the limited access conception had truly been as central to the birth of these languages as the literature suggests, then we would find that (a) every creole, or at least most creoles, had developed in situations in which access to the lexifier had been restricted, and (b) in every situation, or at least almost every situation, in which current theory presumes that access to a dominant language would be limited, such as plantations and mines worked by massive African crews, the language had been creolized.

This, however, is not what we find. Instead, on one hand, we find many situations where people developed creoles even with rich access to the lexifier language, such as Hawaii; as well as Curaçao, where Papiamentu developed, despite most slaves working in small groups in close proximity to whites; and Suriname, where Sranan developed among slaves working on small farms alongside equal numbers of English-speaking whites. On the other hand, we have many situations where people learned the dominant language fully in situations where current theory tells us that they could not have, such as slaves under the Spanish in Mexico and most South American colonies.

The actual distribution of pidgins and creoles around the world suggests, then, that the drastic reduction and reconstitution associated with these languages occurred most often where learners had neither need nor inclination to fully acquire the dominant language. This seems an unremarkable statement, but in fact it is not: contrary to appearances, plantation colonies in themselves apparently were *not* situations where learners "had neither need nor inclination to fully acquire the dominant language," at least not past the first generation. This is what the Spanish colonies, where today's isolated Afro-Hispanics speak no creoles, show us.

Rather, lack of need or inclination to acquire a superstrate fully manifested itself most clearly in the case of pidgins like Melanesian Pidgin English, which began as a work and trade vehicle between Australian Aboriginals and Englishmen (Baker 1993) and developed as a lingua franca between multiethnic labor crews in the South Pacific working under temporary contract (Keesing 1988), who thus had no inclination to acquire English as their new principal tongue. This pidgin has creolized in various locations where it has had a similar role, where native languages thrive and English itself has been the primary language only for a small elite until recently (Papua New Guinea, Vanuatu, the Solomon Islands, Torres Strait). The pidginized Zulu Fanakalo arose similarly (Mesthrie 1989).

Plantation slaves under the Spanish did not creolize Spanish so often that it begs explanation, and one way of doing this coherently is to read the independent evidence of West African pidgin ancestors for AEC and French creoles in the new way I have outlined. Namely, the introduction of these pidgins into English and French plantation colonies appears to have given the *illusion* that plantations themselves pidginized and creolized a dominant language. What in fact may have occurred is that the introduction of these West African pidgins—which had developed among castle slaves under conditions akin to the birth of Melanesian Pidgin English—into these colonies at their foundation provided models that made them, rather than the superstrate language, the basis for an interethnic lingua franca. Thus just as immigrants' children in Hawaii created HCE not because they had limited access to English but because they were surrounded by intimates whose English was at pidgin level, slaves in English and French colonies may have developed creoles not because learning English or French would have been impossible but because they were offered a pidginized version of the superstrate as a model.

The Spanish colonies suggest that these slaves could well have learned actual English or French if such pidgins had not been introduced, and that under *ordinary* circumstances, in a context where slaves were forced to use a European language not as a mere temporary work jargon but as a primary language, the result was not pidginization and creolization but relatively full acquisition. The introduction of West African pidgins was, in this sense, an *extraordinary* circumstance and one more demonstration of the central thesis of this essay—that preexisting contact languages played a crucial role in the establishment of creoles around the world.

It is natural to question why slaves would "settle for" or "stop at" the creole if they were capable of acquiring the superstrate. Here is where Hawaii is again useful: as a demonstration not of the limited access model, which we have seen is inapplicable to it, but as a demonstration of the powerful influence that a pidgin register can have on in-group vernaculars *even when the superstrate language is readily available*. This question also shows us the subtle effects of prescriptivist thinking, even on linguists. Despite the well-known *overt* denigration of creoles by their speakers, on the *covert* level, creole speakers perceive their languages not as steps on the way to a standard but as vehicles of group identity in their own right. Today, just as Jamaican patois speakers are often perplexed or even taken aback to be told that they are not speaking "English," Huber (2000: 283) documents a similar tendency among speakers of early Sierra Leone Krio. This would have been magnified among slaves, for whom the evaluative norms of larger society would have played a distinctly more marginal role than among today's postcolonial creolophones.

Ascribing a central role to the limited access scenario in creole genesis leaves open a number of questions that are unlikely to be resolved within its framework: why Hawaiian children developed a creole; why there are English creole continua so consistently but almost never French ones; why the English creole mesolects are so similar to one another; why Spanish creoles almost never appeared on Spanish plantations; why the Spanish creoles that do exist emerged where they did. Allowing the seemingly mundane evidence of preexisting contact languages a greater role in our reconstructions presents a way of transforming these problems into predictions, which is, of course, the principal goal of scientific inquiry.

# Creoles, Intertwined Languages, and "Bicultural Identity"

## 1. Introduction

As creolists have widened their purview beyond trade pidgins and plantation creoles, it has become increasingly apparent that certain contact languages strain the boundaries of categories established on the basis of languages like Chinese Pidgin English and Haitian Creole French. "Intertwined" languages such as Media Lengua have been especially interesting in this vein. In this chapter I argue that a common analysis of these languages as products of a cultural configuration distinct from those that produced creoles does not account for the data when we pull the lens back from the relatively few languages usually addressed on the subject.

## 2. The "challenge" to creole studies

In "mixed" languages, more usefully designated "intertwined languages" by Bakker and Muysken (1995),[1] inflectional morphology and grammar from one language is used with lexicon from another. Some examples:

(1) Media Lengua: Spanish and **Quechua**
    a. Media Lengua:
        Unu fabur-**ta**    pidi-**nga-bu**    bini-**xu-ni**.
        a    favor-ACC ask-NOM-BEN come-PROG-I
        "I come to ask a favor."

    b. Spanish:
       Vengo para pedir un favor.
       come-I for ask  a  favor

    c. Quechua:
       Shuk fabur-da  maña-nga-bu  shamu-xu-ni.
       one  favor-ACC ask-NOM-BEN come-PROG-I (Bakker and Muysken 1995: 43)

(2)   Michif: French and Cree
    a. Michif:
       **Kî-nipi-yi-w-a**    son frère  **aspin kâ**-la-petite-fille-i**wi-t**.
       PAST-die-OBV-he her brother since COMP-the-little-girl-be-3S
       "Her brother died when she was a young girl." (ibid. 45)

    b. French:
       Son frère   est mort quand elle était une petite fille.
       her brother is  died when she was a  little  girl

    c. Cree:
       Kî-nipi-yi-wa     o-stês-a         aspin kâ-oskinîkî-wi-t.
       PAST-die-OBV-he her-brother-OBV since COMP-young woman-be-3S (Richard
       Rhodes, pers. comm.)

(3)   Angloromani: Romani and **English**
    a. Angloromani:
       **The** Beng wel'**d and** pen'**d**: Av  **with** man-di.
       the  Devil came and said  come with me-DAT
       "The Devil came and said 'Come with me.'"

    b. Romani:
       O  Beng vi-as.     Yov pen-das:  Av   man-tsa.
       the Devil come-PAST he  say-PAST come me-with (ibid. 41)

In such cases, the precise contributions of the source languages are especially clear. This contrasts with creoles, where teasing out instances of transfer is often more difficult. When there are multiple substrate languages (the usual case), language-specific features such as inflections are rarely transferred, and native lexical items are most often incorporated in the "cultural" margins of the vocabulary. Meanwhile, creoles tend to incorporate substrate features in less complexified renditions (cf. chapter 3), which makes rare the precise correspondences with source-language models typical in Quechua and Michif.

    The result is that intertwined languages appear fundamentally "different" from creoles. But surfaces can deceive: in fact, creoles and intertwined languages are simply variations on a general theme, their differences determined by clinical aspects of language contact.

## 3. Grounds for intertwined languages as a "class": Bilingualism

The conventional wisdom is that intertwined languages are a response to unusual circumstances, distinct from those that produced creoles. One can distill from leading writings on these languages (Muysken 1981, Bickerton 1988, Bakker and Mous 1994, Bakker and Muysken 1995) two basic criteria thought necessary for such languages to emerge:

1. The creators must be proficient in the lexifier.[2]
2. The languages are used as in-group codes, reflecting a pointedly intermediate bicultural identity.

However, neither of these criteria motivates the establishment of a new class of contact language. On the contrary, on the basis of these criteria there is little to distinguish intertwined languages from the creoles that they are supposedly so ontogenetically distinct from.

### 3.1. Creators of intertwined languages are not always proficient in the lexifier

The bilingualism criterion is not an empirical observation based on a wide sample of intertwined languages. Rather, it is a hypothesis, extrapolated largely on Media Lengua and Michif, which happen to be among the most-cited and best-documented cases. Indeed, the sources on these two intertwined languages leave little reason to doubt that their creators spoke the lexifiers (Muysken 1981 on Media Lengua, Bakker 1997 on Michif). However, from cases like these, writers have extrapolated proficiency in the lexifier as a defining trait of intertwined languages, with creole creators thought to have labored under contrasting conditions—namely, impeded access to the lexifier.

There is certainly nothing remiss in attempting to impose order on data by approaching it via a model. However, in this case, a broader look at the evidence does not support the model. Specifically, a number of intertwined languages have emerged when speakers were not proficient in the lexifier.

For example, Angloromani, lexified by Romani, has been argued to have emerged when command of Romani had eroded among Gypsies in England (Boretsky and Igla 1994: 62–65), with English thus fully controlled. In strong support of this analysis, they note that Romani would have served as the Gypsies' in-group language if they had still controlled it.

Another case is Ma'a of Tanzania, which superimposes a Southern Cushitic lexicon on a Bantu structure, complete with Bantu inflections. Thomason and Kaufman (1988: 223–28) conclude that Ma'a was born of a language shift from Southern Cushitic to Bantu, the Ma'a retaining the Cushitic lexicon because of a marked cultural pride. Language shift inherently entails loss of bilingual competence. Thus Ma'a would have been born at a point where the Cushitic language was no longer productively controlled except for the lexicon.

## Ma'a: Southern Cushitic and **Mbugu Pare**

(4)    Kwá kubá   te-vé-**dúmú**-ye           va-**bó'i**           ká    **nyamálo** . . .
       with reason NEG-CL-want-APP/PF CL/SUBJ-make DEM work
       "Because they didn't want to do this work . . ." (Mous 1994: 176)
       (APP = applicative; PF = perfective; SUBJ = subjunctive)

Chinese Indonesian, less well-known, mixes Indonesian lexicon with Javanese inflections:

(5)    Chinese Indonesian: Indonesian and **Javanese**
       O, **ne?** **di**-dateng-**no**      pigi rumah **s**-ribu?
       oh if   PASS-come-BEN go house a-thousand
       "Oh, if he's called to the house, a thousand?" (Dreyfuss and Oka 1979: 264)

Dreyfuss and Oka (1979) argue that the creators of this language were most likely Javanese wives who partially acquired Bazaar Malay from the Chinese traders they married, who spoke this language. It is implausible that these women both spoke Bazaar Malay and created an intertwined Javanese-Malay. In such a case, presumably the intertwined language would have served as a marker of intermediate cultural identity—but there would be no reason for these women to develop such an identity. As Javanese women living in their native land, they would have retained Javanese as their in-group language. Their mixture of Javanese and Malay, then, would have resulted simply from the typical phenomenon under which adults tend to learn new languages only partially—that is, these women did not speak actual Malay/Indonesian.

The historical record is scanty. however, which has left the field open for other analyses. Bakker (pers. comm.), for example, supposes that it was not the Javanese mothers, but their hybrid children, who created Chinese Indonesian, presumably speaking Indonesian (a derivant of Malay) and Javanese alongside a special intertwined language marking their bicultural identity. However, short of positive evidence to the contrary, this account raises difficult questions as well. Today, only educated Chinese Indonesians speak Indonesian (Dreyfuss and Oka 1979: 253). Dreyfuss and Oka note that, in interactions with others, Chinese Indonesians are usually known for speaking a variety of Indonesian perceived as incomplete and incorrect. Whether or not this variety is identical with Chinese Indonesian itself, it is clear that Chinese Indonesians' command of Indonesian is partial. Crucially: if this is the case today, then it is unlikely that at an earlier point, all Chinese Indonesians spoke Malay/Indonesian—what would have motivated them to stop transmitting a prime lingua franca of the society? Without an explanation for this, it is most plausible that most Chinese Indonesians have never been fluent in Malay/Indonesian. In other words, Chinese Indonesian does not appear to have been born among people who spoke the lexifier language.

To propose otherwise raises the question as to why bilinguals do not form intertwined languages regularly, for example, Hispanic Americans. Any scenario one can conceive for the birth of Chinese Indonesian virtually requires that the creators did not speak Malay/Indonesian fully.

This is particularly likely given other intertwined languages in Java whose originators were even more clearly only partially competent in the lexifier. Van Rheeden (1994: 234–36) is quite explicit that the creators of Petjo, a Dutch-Malay hybrid, had only perfunctory competence in Dutch. De Gruiter (1994) makes the same point about the birth of Javindo, a Dutch-Javanese hybrid, and even traces its emergence specifically to Javanese-speaking mothers (151–53):

Petjo: Dutch and **Malay**

(6)   Kleren **njang di**–wassen  door die frouw . . .
      clothes REL   PASS-wash by   that woman
      "The clothes washed by that woman . . . " (Van Rheeden 1994: 226)

Javindo: Dutch and **Javanese**

(7)   **Lho**, als jij  snapnul,      . . . **taq** maken-**ké**.
      oh   if  you understand.not I-PASS do–CAUS
      "Oh, if you don't understand, I'll do them for you." (De Gruiter 1994: 156)

Examples continue: Island Carib mixes Carib lexicon with Iñeri grammatical items, and traces back to Iñeri-speaking women's incomplete acquisition of Carib (Hoff 1994):

Island Carib: Carib and **Iñeri**

(8)   Nemboui-**a-tina t**-ibonam.
      Come–PERF-1  her-towards
      "I have come to her." (ibid. 162)

In most of these cases, the sociohistory must be largely reconstructed. However, where the creation of intertwined languages can be synchronically observed, the proficiency-in-the-lexifier requirement is weakened even further. For example, Javanese with faulty command of Indonesian spontaneously created a Chinese Indonesian-like variety today (Dreyfuss and Oka 1979: 254). Regarding Ma'a, to be sure, nothing formally disproves that the Ma'a at some point spoke the Cushitic language fully at the same time that the intertwined language had already arisen. However, intertwined languages are concretely recorded to have developed where the lexifier was definitely not retained, such as Asia Minor Greek, a highly Turkicized Greek. The Cappadocian dialect of Asia Minor Greek can affix Turkish inflection to Greek roots, as in *kétunst-iniz* "you came," and Turkish influence on the syntax is also extensive (Thomason and Kaufman 1988: 219–22).

In sum, proficiency in the lexifier is not a requirement for the development of intertwined languages. This is hardly to say that the creators of intertwined languages are *never* proficient in the lexifier—clearly, they often are. However, proficiency is not a necessary condition and is therefore not a defining aspect of the creation of intertwined languages.

To found proficiency in the lexifier as a "principle" of intertwined language genesis on the basis of some examples that happened to come to attention the earliest is analogous to a Martian asserting "all animals have hair" based on having first encountered dogs and cats. Now that we have encountered other examples, the proficiency-in-the-lexifier "principle" requires revision, just as the Martian would revise their "principle" after encountering sparrows and salamanders. But this means that *intertwined languages cannot be said to differ from creoles on the basis of proficiency in the lexifier.*

### 3.2. Creoles did not result from "interrupted transmission"

To be sure, Bakker and Muysken (1995: 51) allow that "fluent knowledge of the language that provides the lexicon is not necessary, but it has to be spoken to a reasonable degree," a statement probably uncontroversial to writers on these languages. However, this assertion nevertheless maintains the conception of intertwined languages as crucially distinct from creoles. To Bakker and Muysken, there presumably remains a gulf between this "reasonable" competence and the "interrupted transmission" of the lexifier that creole creators are often thought to have labored under. However, Bakker and Muysken's point in fact brings intertwined languages even closer to creoles than might appear, especially in light of recent developments in creole theory.

The "interrupted transmission" model entails slaves sharply removed from the lexifier, especially by the time they significantly outnumbered whites. It has been most articulately promulgated by Bickerton (1984) and Baker and Corne (1982) and espoused by Thomason and Kaufman (1988: 147–66). However, a closer look at contemporary accounts suggests that plantation slaves were generally at least partially competent in the lexifiers. For example, Du Tertre (1667: 510, cited in Wylie 1995: 88) noted that slave children born in the French Caribbean spoke French alongside their parents' pidgin. Thus the creators and/or stabilizers of French Caribbean creole may well have had a diglossic competence operating between French and the emergent creole. Most important, they had competence in the lexifier.[3] Meanwhile, accounts of English plantations such as Lalla and D'Costa (1990: 79–92) on Jamaica depict a range of competences in standard English coexisting quite early on, again suggesting that the creators of plantation creoles were at least partially bilingual in the lexifier, even when blacks greatly outnumbered whites. Similarly, historical documentation of Negerhollands shows that slaves had a range of competences and that Dutch itself surely was not opaque to a number of them (Stein 1995).

Thus, fluency in the lexifier is not a requirement for the emergence of intertwined languages; meanwhile, creoles emerged in contexts of at least partial fluency in the lexifier. In other words, partial fluency in the lexifier can create both intertwined languages and creoles. The criterion of fluency in the lexifier fails as a distinguishing trait of intertwined language genesis.

## 4. Grounds for intertwined languages as a "class": Culturally intermediate identity

Thus we must attempt to stake the intertwined language "class" solely on the basis of their function as expressions of uniquely culturally intermediate identity. Bakker and Muysken (1995: 51) distinguish intertwined language speech communities on the basis of the fact that "members of the group do not identify themselves as belonging to either of the group whose languages they speak."

Here, however, it is again difficult to see how this criterion excludes creoles. Bakker and Muysken's statement, after all, could just as well apply to early plantation slaves, whose culturally intermediate identity has been the foundation of innumerable anthropological, sociological, and linguistic studies. The Caribbean identity, for example, is neither African nor European and is defined by the dynamic synergy between the two poles (cf. Alleyne 1994: 10). For example, "Me Bajan!" was the watchcry of Barbadian slaves described by Pinckard (1806: 133); they considered themselves neither "English" nor by any means "African." Recently arrived Africans were looked down upon by locally-born blacks in the Caribbean (e.g., Patterson 1967: 146). Note the dismissive attitude of a former American slave describing his grandmother's African competence: "My granny could never speak good like I can . . . I can't talk no African" (Wood 1974: 168). Clearly Caribbean blacks often retained a degree of African identity, but this was generally covert, expressed in the form of private ritual ceremonies and practices, and only one component of an identity appropriately described as culturally intermediate.[4] Again, then, what has been proposed as a distinguishing trait of intertwined languages in fact applies equally well to creoles.

## 5. A new typology

Yet clearly, we must account for why intertwined languages mix grammars on so intimate a level while creoles do not. We have seen that this difference is not due to degree of bilingualism or bicultural identity. I claim that the difference is something much simpler: the number of native languages in the contact situation. To wit, *in contexts generating a pointedly bicultural identity, when there is only one native language, an intertwined language results; when there is more than one, a creole results.*

Since language encodes identity, language mixture is a natural response to bicultural identity. Where there are two or more native languages, then the need for communication bars mixing of arbitrary components of grammar which differ from language to language, such as inflection. Thus in creoles, substrate influence is largely restricted to syntax and semantics. For example, serial verbs are present in the Kwa languages and those spoken eastward in the lower half of Nigeria, such as Yoruba and Igbo. A significant number of slaves from these areas were brought to English Caribbean plantations. Where bicultural identity led to language mixture on these plantations, substrate transfer from any one language would have impeded communication, and thus there are no Twi, Fon, Yoruba, or Igbo inflections in Atlantic English-based creoles. What was transferred into these languages was broader, less idiosyncratic features common to all or many of them, such as certain lexical semantic subdivisions (e.g. Huttar 1975), serial verb constructions, and other syntactic constructions.

In contrast, where there is only one native language, then inflections from that language, if transferred into the new culturally intermediate language, do not impede communication. The result is a language like Media Lengua, whose Quechua inflections are readily comprehensible to native Quechua speakers, but would have rendered it opaque if it had emerged for use among more than one Amerindian group.

To be sure, the formula I am proposing refers to the emergence of stabilized new languages linked firmly to a new culturally intermediate identity. The formula must not be taken to imply that any encounter between two languages will lead to intertwining of the Media Lengua type, as this is clearly not the case. Tây Bôi Pidgin French, for example, is in no sense an intertwining of French and Vietnamese: Vietnamese influence is largely restricted to general levels such as phonology and syntax. We would not expect Vietnamese inflections, since Tây Bôi speakers remained Vietnamese in their identity, with the contact language serving simply as a communication medium between the French and those in their employ.

## 6. Testing the typology

This formulation will strike many as oversimplified. A possible objection is that the analysis fails to take into account the differences between the colonial plantation context and the various contexts that have given rise to intertwined languages. However, those taking this position must specify exactly *what* about plantation conditions was crucially different. Sections 3 and 4 in this chapter were devoted to explicitly show that the two purportedly defining conditions for intertwined language in fact reigned on plantations as well.

To test whether my hypothesis neglects something about plantation conditions, we need a situation in which plantation conditions were conventional, with the sole difference being that there was only one substrate language instead of several. As it happens, we have such a situation at our disposal, Berbice Dutch Creole, only brought to light in the late 1970s.

When the Dutch founded the Berbice colony in Guyana, they apparently brought all of their first slaves from the Calabar River area. These slaves are likely to have all spoken one language, Eastern Ijo (Smith, Robertson, and Williamson 1987: 65–68); the massive component of lexicon and even grammatical items from exactly this language would seem to allow no other interpretation. The Berbice plantations were developed along typical colonial lines, starting small in the 1600s and expanding in the 1700s (ibid. 64). My hypothesis would predict that in Berbice, an intertwined language would have emerged. This is exactly what happened:

(9)   Berbice Dutch: Dutch and **Eastern Ijo**
      **Eni** kanti   lefu santu **mingi anga ka**
      they cannot live salt   water side   NEG
      "They cannot live next to salt water." (Silvia Kouwenberg, pers. comm.)

This language has a range of Eastern Ijo inflectional recruitments, such as a plural marker -*ap* (*frendi-ap* "friends"). Because of its plantation origins among Africans, the language has been treated as a "creole" in the literature. However, as the above example shows, nothing taxonomically distinguishes it from the languages traditionally treated as "intertwined."

To be sure, Berbice Dutch has only retained a subset of the Eastern Ijo morphology; furthermore, while Eastern Ijo (and, less pronouncedly, Dutch) is SOV, Berbice Dutch is not. However, over time in the Berbice colony, the number of Eastern Ijos declined at the expense of slaves of other extractions (Smith, Robertson, and Williamson 1987: 69). Most likely, an originally more complete relexification of Eastern Ijo was gradually pidginized (but only to a degree) by these new imports, eroding the specific Eastern Ijo component to an extent. However, it is obvious that the intertwining process was at work. It surely is no accident that the only known single-substrate plantation setting in the Caribbean yielded an unusual language like Berbice Dutch.

We could further confirm that my analysis is not neglecting some aspect of plantation conditions via a corresponding test. We need a context with multiple substrate languages, but with the plantation variable altered. Again, a recent discovery allows us to do just this. Tayo Creole French of New Caledonia is spoken by descendants of marriages between Melanesian women raised at a French-language boarding school (some actually Euro-Melanesian) and Melanesian men. The predominant Melanesian languages represented were Cèmuhî and Drubéa, related but mutually unintelligible (Corne 1995a). The French presence has had a significant influence on local identity. The consensus emerging about intertwined languages would predict that two intertwined languages would have developed among the children of these marriages, one French-Cèmuhî and another French-Drubéa. In fact, however, what developed was simply a French-based creole, with structural transfer on the semantic and syntactic levels largely reflecting the typological features common to Cèmuhî and Drubéa, including pronominal classes, relativization strategies, and imperative configuration (ibid.). Tayo emerged not in a plantation setting but in a single settlement amid marriages in which one partner was fluent in French. Thus we cannot ascribe the creole outcome to "interrupted transmission" or "distance from a target." The creole arose because there was more than one substrate language. If there had been only one, we can assume that an intertwined language would be spoken at St. Louis.

This analysis is further supported in that even intermediate cases are predictable. What would happen in a setting conditioning culturally intermediate identity, if there were multiple substrate languages, but the languages were closely related enough to share some inflections and closed-class lexical items (unlike the Kwa languages of Africa or Cèmuhî and Drubéa in New Caledonia)? My analysis would predict a moderate degree of intertwining, but less than that in Media Lengua and others. This is precisely what we encounter in the Zamboangueño dialect of Philippine Creole Spanish. History suggests that the substrate languages here were very closely related Central Philippines languages as Tagalog and Hiligaynon Bisayan (Whinnom 1956: 14, Frake 1971: 224–30). The result was moderate transfer of closed-class lexical items and affixes. Conventionally treated as a "creole," Zamboangueño is, in fact, quite reminiscent of intertwined languages, differing from them only in the degree of intertwining:

(10)    Zamboangueño Philippine Creole Spanish: Spanish and **Central Philippine**:
         **Hindi? kitá** ay-**man**-enkwentro el   **mana** muher.
         NEG   we FUT-V-meet         the PL    woman
         "We will not meet the women." (M. Ong, John Wolff, pers. comm.) (V = verbalizer)

## 7. Exceptions?

There are two main cases that are superficially problematic for this hypothesis. There have indeed been some instances where only two languages met and the result was a creole rather than an intertwined language. Pitcairnese stemmed from an encounter between Tahitians and English speakers. The Asian Portuguese creoles (the ones of India, Sri Lanka, Malaysia [Papia Kristang]), Indonesia, and Macao usually resulted from encounters dominated by interaction between Portuguese and a single language (Marathi for Korlai Creole Portuguese of India, for example).

### 7.1. Transplantation

However, aspects of both cases are relevant to assessing whether they constitute true exceptions.

For example, some argue that Pitcairnese, for example, is less a creole than a highly divergent dialect of English itself (e.g., Mühlhäusler 1998). From a cross-creole perspective, Pitcairnese does not give an especially "creole" appearance, especially when one looks past the exotifying effect of the phonetic transcription many of its signature academic sources are transcribed in. Pitcairnese seems less "un-English" in the light of the regional dialects of Great Britain most divergent from the standard, less immediate to most today as so many are extinct, moribund, or "diluted" toward the standard, to the point that their uniqueness is now mostly a matter of phonology and local lexical items. Also germane is that one of the uniquely small number of Anglophones (nine) at Pitcairnese's genesis was a West Indian.

Meanwhile, scholars of the Indo-Portuguese creoles generally assume that a widely used Portuguese pidgin was a significant component of the lexifier that these creoles' creators were exposed to. Dalgado (1906: 143) notes that priests were encouraged to preach in *linguagem facil e simples* (easy and simple language), and Whinnom (1956: 9) cited missionary St. Francis Xavier as attesting to having done so in the sixteenth century, as well having ordered other priests to do the same. In addition, idiosyncratic structural similarities between the Portuguese creoles of Asia are such that it is generally assumed that the varieties impacted one another's development through contact of various kinds (e.g. Dalgado 1900, Holm 1989: 291, Clements 1996: 13). This suggests that the Asian Portuguese creoles may have been cases of the sort I discussed in chapter 9, where imported models decisively affected linguistic outcomes that would have been different otherwise.

### 7.2. Religious instruction

Thus it may be that these cases do not constitute exceptions at all. But there is another sociohistorical factor that Pitcairn and Portuguese Asia share that would plausibly have been vital in determining the type of contact languages that arose. In both cases, the creoles emerged within a context of intimate and sustained religious instruction. On Pitcairn, John Adams, who was the only native Anglophone who survived the first ten years of settlement and became a respected elder on the island, carefully indoctrinated the Tahitians in Christianity. The community was "in effect, regulated by the Church of England Book of Common Prayer," with later visitors noting frequent prayer and saying of grace (Ross and Moverley 1964: 60–61). Portuguese priests played a central role in imparting Portuguese in the Indo-Portuguese contexts (cf. Clements 1996: 13–14), and speakers of all of the Asian Portugueses have constituted distinct castes of Christianized locals familiar with Portuguese or restructured versions of it (Papia Kristang means "language of the Christians," for example).

It may have been that when the lexifier was the vehicle of spiritually urgent scripture whose preaching transformed the lives of its learners, a prescriptivist impulse led them to seek a fuller rendition of that language rather than simply mixing it into their own via constant code-switching and creating an intertwined language. To the untutored learner, an intertwined language is a matter of "mixing up the two languages," while a creole more approximates actually "speaking" the new language—keeping in mind that creolophones, especially mesolectal ones, often do not spontaneously draw the taxonomic line between their speech and the lexifier itself that linguists do.

The timeline of Sri Lankan Creole Portuguese supports this surmise. Today it is virtually an intertwined language of Portuguese lexical items with syntax and grammatical functions from Tamil and Sinhala (cf. chapter 1, ex. 2), whose basic grammars have become akin due to Indo-Aryan/Dravidian Sprachbund effects. But evidence suggests that this is a latterly development since English's takeover as a "high" language, with a variety much closer to Portuguese (i.e., more typically "creole") having reigned while Portuguese language, culture, and religion thrived in earlier speakers' communities (during which missionaries even published books in the creole) (Smith 1984).

Surely religious instruction occurred in other creolophone contexts, such as under the French (e.g., Wylie 1995) and Spanish (e.g., Castellanos and Castellanos 1992). But the historical record of these practices gives all indication of rather perfunctory exercises, in comparison to the intense and immediate face-to-face tutelage typical in the Pitcairn and Asian Portuguese contexts.

If the religious factor was decisive, then here, obviously, is a case where culture indeed mattered, rather than linguistic factors alone. This is a useful point in showing that my attempt to point out where intellectual fashions of the moment may discourage empiricism hardly requires that culture plays *no* role in shaping how people speak. However, the fact remains that treating the difference between creoles and intertwined languages as a linguistic rather than cultural result accounts for a vast preponderance of our data set—that is, all creoles and all documented intertwined languages taken together.


## 8. Taxonomy

I suggest, then, a revision of the emerging consensus on intertwined languages. That consensus can be roughly stated as:

> Creoles result from interrupted transmission while intertwined languages are created as markers of in-group identity by bicultural people proficient in the lexifier language.

The data indicate that instead:

> In contexts conditioning a culturally intermediate identity, of which plantations are
> one of several, an intertwined language results when there is one substrate language,
> and a creole when there are two or more.

The former consensus is ultimately based on a model extrapolated from plantation creoles, Media Lengua, and Michif. My revision is a response to the wider range
of data available today. Its implication is that intertwined languages be seen as one
manifestation of a general process of language mixture. This process has usually
resulted in creoles, but only because historical realities have brought multiple substrate languages to most contexts in which the process took place. In other words,
intertwined languages retain substrate morphology not because of sociological circumstances unique to them, but simply because when there is only one substrate language, it is feasible for such morphology to be retained by substrate populations.
Terminologically, then, intertwined languages *are* creoles. This is not to suggest that
the term *intertwined language* be discarded. What I suggest be discarded is the idea
that intertwined languages are a discrete phenomenon, taxonomically and ontogenetically distinct from creole languages.

## 9. Further implications

The subsumption of intertwined languages into the creole category may allow sociohistorical deductions in cases where documentation is unlikely to provide more than
general outlines. French Guiana is one example.

On the basis of the predominance of speakers of the Gbe dialects Fon and Gun
in early French Guiana, Jennings (1995b: 32–35) concludes that the first contact language in this colony was specifically a Fon-French pidgin, rather than a pidgin with
a more general West African substrate. Evinced from the demographic evidence, this
is eminently plausible, but from the comparative perspective, a question arises.

We must ask: If an early predominance of Eastern Ijo in Berbice led to an intertwined Dutch-Eastern Ijo, then why did the early Gbe predominance in French Guiana
not establish a lasting intertwined French-Gbe? My analysis predicts that if one substrate language (or two closely related dialects like Fon and Gun) encounter a lexifier,
the result will be an intertwined language. This is what happened in Berbice. However, while displaying the broad syntactic and semantic West African influence that
all Caribbean creoles do, modern Guianese has no West African inflections and is in
no sense an intertwined language.

There are many ways of approaching this discrepancy. Many will prefer to suppose that sociohistorical differences between Berbice and Cayenne, lost to history,
conditioned the different outcomes. However, with my formulation we can approach
Jennings's data in a different way. Specifically, we can treat the lack of Gbe remnants in Guianese as a departure from the result we would expect, and search for an
explanation for this departure.

If we assume that an encounter between Gbe and French would have led to an intertwined French-Gbe, then one scenario that would have deflected this result is if slaves in French Guiana did not create the contact language in situ. If the slaves were exposed to a pidgin imported from elsewhere, which itself did not have a strong Gbe imprint, then they would have acquired patterns from this pidgin. This would have prevented Gbe from having the direct impact in French Guiana that Eastern Ijo, unintermediated, had in Berbice. An analogy is Tok Pisin in Papua New Guinea, where the influence of local languages like Kuanua (Tolai) is shallow in comparison to its Eastern Oceanic foundation, incorporated elsewhere in the South Pacific long before Melanesian Pidgin English was brought to New Guinea (Keesing 1988).

In identifying the origins of an imported French pidgin, we note that Guianese not only has no idiosyncratically Gbe cast, but in the meantime corresponds quite idiosyncratically on all levels with Caribbean and Indian Ocean French creoles (cf., e.g., Goodman 1964). These comparative facts have led Hull (1979), Parkvall (1995a, 1995b), and me (McWhorter 2000a) to reconstruct a West African pidgin French as having played a major part in the genesis of the French plantation creoles, most likely emerging on the Senegambian coast. The discrepancy between Guianese structure and French Guiana's sociohistory, then, supports the Afrogeneticist hypothesis of French creole origins. The typology I have proposed allows a solution to a conundrum which sociohistorical evidence probably cannot.

## 10. Conclusion

While there is no harm in retaining the term *intertwined language*, the languages ought be seen not as a "challenge" to creole theory but simply as one manifestation of creole genesis itself.[5]

# PART III

# THE GRAY ZONE

*THE CLINE OF PIDGINIZATION*
*OR THE INFLECTIONAL PARAMETER?*

It can be easy to miss guiding impulses in a body of work that one engages for reasons that do not include all of those for which it was created.

Medieval paintings concentrate on religious themes. The modern viewer may cherish the paintings for their formal excellence and their awesome beauty, while assuming that the Madonnas and illustrations of biblical stories are just "what people painted then," in contrast to the more quotidian, intimate themes that enchant us with their more immediate accessibility in later painters like Vermeer and his Dutch contemporaries.

But that biblical strain was not mere fashion. The religious focus in these paintings stemmed from a fundamental difference in world-view between us and the medievals, for most of whom fervent religious belief was part of the warp and woof of existence, determining royal decisions and even motivating wars. In other words, medieval painters really meant what they were communicating, or at least were constrained by the societally determined demands of their patrons. In the strict sense, we can only fully engage their work by attempting to put ourselves in the head of a medieval European human being, whose relationship to religion was usually much less abstract, private, and ambivalent than it is for most academics today.

In my career as a creolist, for years I read and enjoyed the papers of several colleagues for its implications for my own work, for the sheer grace of their lines of argumentation, and out of a desire to be familiar with as wide a range of creolist thought as possible. But after a while, I started to realize that with certain of these works, my personal interests and assumptions were distorting my interpretation of their core intent.

Salikoko Mufwene has written a great many papers (e.g., 1994b, 1994c, 1996b, 1997a) situating particular topics within reiterations of the fact that creoles were products of the contact situations that they arose in, their makeups determined by the features of the languages spoken by the people in the colony. That point struck me as, in itself, unexceptionable, and I read the papers for their insights on the particular topic situated into the point.

I read Michel DeGraff's papers (e.g., 1992, 1993, 1994, 1997) as interesting arguments situating various constructions in Haitian Creole into the framework of Chomskyan syntactic theory. But I misread as "garnish" his sidebar and final-paragraph notices that these arguments showed that the differences between Haitian and French were largely due to syntactic parameter settings determined by inflectional loss. Claire Lefebvre's (1993, 1998, 2001) increasingly comprehensive relexificationist model of creole genesis struck me as reinforcing, albeit more extremely than I would personally concur with, the kinds of arguments I had made in my own early substratist work.

What I was missing because of my personal "glasses" was that all of these scholars had been arguing for years that, essentially, there is no such thing as a creole.

Mufwene, for example, was not simply restating his Founder Principle in so many of his papers as a professional courtesy. His very intent was to propose that the vast array of issues he has treated (decreolization in Gullah, the emergence of Kituba, the substrate hypothesis, grammaticalization, etc.) all lend themselves to showing that *creole* is a vacuous term applied to languages that emerged amidst "contact" just like so many others not called creoles. DeGraff's choice of features to discuss was not random. He was especially interested in features whose behavior was especially suited to outline his view that creole genesis was largely a matter of the same parametrical alternations that determined the differences between Old and Modern English. Lefebvre (1998) has published a book-length compendium of arguments for relexification in Haitian not for the mere sake of dutiful thoroughness; her larger aim is to show that creole genesis essentially replicates a substrate language grammar, with "dropouts" in transmission determined by predictable aspects of Universal Grammar, unconnected with any independent tendency toward reduction of French structure.

In response to my arguments that, indeed, there is such a thing as a creole, these scholars and others have been more explicit in their intent. In Part I of this volume I addressed Mufwene's and Lefebvre's frameworks. But a question that arises repeatedly within our differences in approach is whether the difference between creoles and their source languages can be traced largely to inflectional loss flipping a syntactic switch. Chapter 3 addressed this in relation to creoles and their source languages, where I showed that inflectional loss alone vastly undershoots the nature of the difference between creoles and their source languages.

However, the application of the "syntactocentric" paradigm to creole studies merits attention from a broader perspective, especially given the unspoken sense woven into the culture of modern linguistics that arguments couched in the Chomskyan paradigm, such as DeGraff's and Lefebvre's, carry a certain authority. When American opera aficionados resist English-language versions of tragic operas more than comedic ones, they evince a common human tendency to associate substance with incomprehensibility. In the same way, it can be tempting to assume that the dense jargon of theoretical syntax inherently signals a higher level of argumentation.

Thus in Part III I show that my arguments about inflection such as those in chapter 3 neither are an attempt to reify creoles nor are composed in neglect of general linguistic thinking about inflection. In chapter 11 I argue that theoretical syntacticians studying the history of English itself have been mistaken in assuming that the difference between English and its Germanic sisters is merely a matter of inflectional loss and its syntactic correlates. Inflection was but one of a great many losses of the Proto-Germanic inheritance in English which, taken together, rendered it the least semantically overspecified and structurally elaborated sister in its family. English teaches a lesson that extensive adult acquisition of a language can "semi-semi-pidginize" it, passing to future generations what can be termed a conventionalized second-language rendition. That is: creoles represent an extreme of a clinal phenomenon of reduction that operates upon languages worldwide, including geopolitcally dominant ones that are vehicles of massive literatures.

In chapter 12 I pull back the camera from creoles even more, arguing that the very postulate that Universal Grammar even includes parameter settings contingent on inflectional morphology is impossible to support under a conception of human language as a product of natural selection.

Chapter 13 uses as a springboard this argument that heavy non-native acquisition can give a "close shave" to a grammar which nevertheless remains a natural language. Many have argued that the difference between standard English and Black English is due to an influence of African languages on the latter. But Black English displays none of the indisputable West African inheritances that so many creoles do, such as multiple copulas, serial verbs, and CVCV phonotactics. Rather, Black English only parallels West African languages in features that represent *losses* of standard English features (e.g., zero copulas, noninversion in questions) or *overgeneralization* of them (e.g., spread of negative concord).

This is not an accident: Black English is the product of adults acquiring English in robust but slightly abbreviated form, just as I believe standard English to be the product of Scandinavian invaders acquiring Old English in the same way. That the losses in Black English so often recall West African languages is a mere epiphenomenon of these latter languages' analyticity, given that second-language acquisition inherently entails the elision of the target language's features, drawing it closer to the analytic pole. It is natural to assume that there must be room for reconstructing that Africans directly modeled their rendition of English on the analyticity of their native languages. But cases like Palenquero Creole Spanish reveal simple non-native acquisition as the determining factor. Its creators spoke the heavily agglutinative Kikongo, and yet Palenquero retains only a few inflections—vastly fewer than those in Black English—and usually optional in usage.

That is: transfer is a crucial aspect of language contact, but second-language acquisition has decisive *subtractive* effects, regardless of the typology of the learners' native languages. It is not accidental that even the creolized version of Chinook Jargon, developed among speakers of fearsomely inflected languages, was thoroughly isolating in structure. My argument here and in chapter 11 calls attention to the role that reduction often plays in language contact, often missed in favor of the role of transfer.

The traditions of our moment have a way of shunting attention to the latter, because of its usefulness to the paradigm treating creoles as evidence of cultural retention and the incompatiblility of the reduction concept with the imperative to signal creoles as "real languages." But in this, a parallel beckons with scientists of yore, living in societies permeated with the unquestioned religious devotion I mentioned earlier.

Constrained by the Bible's teaching that the world had been created a few thousand years ago with all of its animals, scientists presented with fossils of creatures no one had encountered assumed that they were the remains of living oddities not yet discovered by Europeans, such as giants or dragons. An awareness that these enormous bones might represent an earlier circumstance hovered at the margins of respectable thought, but then only amidst studied constructs such as that God had ordered a series of floods within those few thousand years, after each of which he created many new animals. Because of its contradiction to strict interpretation of the Bible, the idea that evolution had produced an ever-morphing procession of creatures over millions of years was as yet alien and even emotionally discomfitting, and therefore unavailable to even the most brilliant minds.

In the same way, in creole studies and beyond, the role of reduction in language contact hovers at the margins; but is rarely processed as a central factor. The creolist literature is fairly strewn with acknowledgments that a given creole has inherited a given feature in less complex form than in its substrate language or languages, occasioning no opposition. For example, of the eleven papers in Siegel's (2000) anthology on creoles of Australia and Oceania, no fewer than six make such points. Only a statement that this kind of reduction is diagnostic of creoles as a class attracts questioning and dismissal.

But I suggest that a truly empirical engagement with the data requires that we take the myriad papers making such arguments for so very many creoles as indicative of a larger phenomenon, given that the heart of scientific inquiry is to generalize from the particular.

From our perspective, the sequence of eons-long transformation that fossils show is obvious, and we can barely help wondering why top thinkers just a century-and-a-half removed from us could not perceive this immediately. But we need not wonder: they were constrained by a reigning paradigm couched in religion, based on the type of conviction that occupies the heart as much as the head. Today's equivalent in creole studies viscerally distrusts the notion of reduction for similar reasons: sociopolitical sentiments local to the Western world over just the past four decades.

I present six statements that I presume all linguists would consider to be fact:

1. Some 6,000 languages jostle for space on a small planet where human groups have always migrated, encountered one another, and found it necessary to acquire one another's languages.
2. This has been especially common since technological developments combined with economic imperatives in the middle of the last millennium to lead speakers of a certain few languages to impose them on speakers of others worldwide.

3. Human migration typically spurs language shift, where adults gradually give up their native languages for a new one.
4. All languages are replete with features unnecessary to even nuanced human communication, including many that are especially challenging to non-native acquirers.
5. Adults typically acquire languages in abbreviated fashion, and more so in untutored situations.
6. In many cases, a large enough proportion of adults acquires a language non-natively that their rendition becomes the main model for new generations of speakers. (I assume that regardless of philosophical inclinations, any creolist will see creoles themselves as demonstration cases here.)

And I now suggest that these six facts logically imply the following one:

A crucial factor in language change is adults *abbreviating* the machinery of a language, along a gradient of degree according to typological distance between native language(s) and acquired language, demographic proportion of learners to native speakers, and the extent to which the native version of the acquired language remains available in the genesis context over time.

The chapters in Part III address the intermediate point along that gradient.

# What Happened to English?

## 1. Introduction

Since linguistic investigations as early as Paul (1880), it has been well known that simplification and complexification have complementary roles in the evolution of grammars. I argue in this chapter that in the emergence of Modern English, simplification dominated complexification to a greater extent than in any other Germanic language. Specifically, I claim that at a certain point in English's history, simplification dominated in a fashion suggesting a sociohistorical factor hindering the full transmission of the grammar across generations.

This chapter does not revive the hypothesis of Bailey and Maroldt (1977) (followed by Domingue 1977 and Poussa 1982) that Middle English was a creole that developed when Norman French invaders learned English imperfectly and expanded their reduced English into a full language. This hypothesis was motivated partly by the heavy admixture from other languages in English's lexicon and derivational apparatus. But lexical mixture itself does not equate with creolization. Languages can borrow massive amounts of lexicon and even morphology without evidencing any traits that would suggest the label *creole* to any linguist, such as many languages of Australia (Heath 1981) and "mixed" or "intertwined" languages like Michif (Bakker 1997) and Media Lengua (Muysken 1997).

Bailey and Maroldt and their followers also based their argument on English's notorious paucity of inflection in comparison to other Germanic languages. However, Thomason and Kaufman (1988: 263–342) refute this thesis. The inflectional loss had proceeded considerably before the Norman Invasion, and even in dialects not in contact with French. In addition, today's Mainland Scandinavian languages, unaffected by any contact as heavy as that caused by the Norman invasion in England, are little more inflected than English. Moreover, during the Norman rule, French speakers were but a numerically small elite, whose rendition of English can hardly have influenced a vast majority of monolingual English speakers. These and other arguments are taken as conclusive in this chapter.

Thomason and Kaufman's argument, however, entails that English's heavy inflectional loss was due simply to its being less "conservative" than its sisters, implying that no external factor distinguished English's development. Meanwhile, to the extent that English manifests other features we might treat as less marked than their equivalents in its sister languages, the generative historical linguistics tradition tends to ascribe these to "chain-style" effects of inflectional loss that modern syntactic theory would predict. Examples include the rich literature on the loss of OV and V2 word order, and other features such as obligatory postposing of particles to the verb (e.g., Platzack 1986; van Kemenade and Vincent 1997; Fischer, van Kemenade, Koopman, and van der Wurff 2000). The common consensus among specialists on the history of English is that features suggesting a break in transmission or unusual simplification in the English timeline are merely trompe l'oeil's having in fact emerged by ordinary processes of change.

However, the focus on certain abstract syntactic features that the generative enterprise conditions has perhaps narrowed our purview, thereby causing us to neglect other aspects of grammar that suggest a larger story. I propose that loss of inflection is but the tip of the iceberg in terms of Germanic features that English has shed, complemented by many other losses unconnected with analyticity. Overall, a comparison with its sisters reveals English to be significantly less *overspecified* semantically and less *complexified* syntactically. Some scholars, such as Lass (1987: 317–32), recognize that English departs considerably from the Germanic template, but leave aside the question as to why, with the implication that the issue was a matter of chance. I argue that a contact-based, external explanation provides a principled account for the relevant facts.

## 2. The nature of overspecification and complexification

### 2.1. Overspecification

Any given language gives overt manifestation to particular underlying semantic or syntactic distinctions that are left unmarked in many other languages. The fact that many or most languages operate without marking the distinctions in question entails that to mark the feature at all is ornamental, rather than necessary, to human language. As such, in a given area, one language can be considered *overspecified* in comparison to another.

For example, the Northern Californian American Indian language Karok has grammaticalized different verbal suffixes for various containment mediums: *pa:θ-kúrih* "throw into fire," *pa:θ-kúrih* "throw into water," *pa:θ-rúprih* "throw in through a solid" (Bright 1957: 98, 102). (These morphemes are not perceivable reflexes of the words for *fire*, *water*, or *solid*, respectively.) Most of the world's grammars do not happen to have grammaticalized such fine-grained overt expressions of containment mediums, and it would be impossible to argue that Universal Grammar specifies such. On the contrary, as useful as these suffixes are in Karok grammar, their emergence was due to a chance elaboration within a particular semantic area, not communicative necessity. Thus: in the area of marking of containment mediums, Karok is *overspecified* in comparison to English, just as in its grammaticalized marking of definiteness and indefiniteness of NPs, English is overspecified in comparison to Karok. A similar argument could be made for other languages in regard to grammaticalized evidential markers or the regular overt distinction of alienable from inalienable possession.

Along these lines, my comparison of English with its sisters suggests that, overall, English manifests less of this kind of overspecification than its sisters. Hawkins (1985: 6) makes a similar observation regarding English and German: "Where the surface structures (morphology and syntax) of English and German contrast . . . English surface structures exhibit less correspondence with their semantic representations than do those of German," and later (28) "German speakers are forced to make certain semantic distinctions which can regularly be left unspecified in English."

Throughout this chapter, my delineations of *overspecification* refer to my characterization above, as usefully elucidated by Hawkins's conception.

## 2.2. Complexification

Complexity in syntax is certainly a difficult concept, with only fitful agreement among linguists working in various paradigms. For the purposes of this thesis, however, I stipulate that, within a given area of grammar, a language's syntax is more complex than another's when it requires the operation of more rules. Thus a grammar involving two kinds of alignment rather than one (i.e., ergative/absolutive and nominative/accusative) can be considered more complex than a strictly nominative/accusative one (cf. the approach of Henry 1995, Henry and Tangney 1999). Similarly, a language with a V2 rule, requiring under many analyses that the verb move to C for its surface expression (Den Besten 1983; Fischer, van Kemenade, Koopman, and der Wurff 2000: 110–14) can be considered more complex in this regard than a language with no such requirement of the verb. This conception is admittedly preliminary, but I feel that it will serve adequately to frame, elucidate, and support the particular thesis I wish to present.

Importantly, this conception of complexity addresses grammars solely as systems viewed from the outside, as products of millennia of drift and its attendant elaborations upon the rootstuff of the human linguistic capacity. Complexity under this metric is not indexed with relative difficulty of production or processing; this metric takes as a given that all languages are acquired with ease by native learners. Our assumption is that human cognition is capable of effortlessly processing great degrees of overspecification and complexification in language (cf. Trudgill 1999). While there is no reason to suppose that differentials in ease of production or processing do not exist, these issues are ultimately of little import to the thesis explored here, a diachronic and comparative one.

## 2.3. Epistemological caveat

Importantly, my argument is not that English is in any sense *radically* underspecified or simplified in a cross-linguistic sense. Its *do*-support, subtle subdivision of the semantic space of the future between four constructions (*I leave tomorrow, I'm going to leave tomorrow, I'm leaving tomorrow, I will leave tomorrow*). the subtle interplay of definiteness and referentiality underlying the use of its definite and indefinite articles, and other features are fatal to any argument that English is somehow a "simple" language.

Thus my argument proceeds in full acknowledgment of such features, but is predicated upon a *relative* argument: that overall, English is *less* overspecified and *less* complexified than its sisters are, to an extent suggesting something other than unbroken internal development.

My intention can be illustrated with an informal but heuristically useful observation. For both English speakers learning another Germanic language and speakers of other Germanic languages learning English, much of the acquisition task entails learning alternate, but in no sense more complex, strategies for expressing concepts. An example would be the arbitrary differences in semantic space that prepositions cover: *pale with fear* versus German *blass vor Furcht*, et cetera. However, it is my impression that for the English speaker, most of the acquisition task beyond this entails learning to attend to things English does not mark overtly, while for the speaker of another Germanic language, most of the task entails learning *not* to attend to features that their native language does mark overtly.

The centrality of inflection to modern syntactic theory leads to an impression that this contrast is largely a matter of English's relatively sparse declensional and conjugational paradigms. This, however, is in broad view an artifact of the interests that happen to dominate linguistic inquiry in our times: the contrast to which I refer encompasses a great deal beyond inflection.

## 3. Examples

### 3.1. Inherent reflexivity marking

Germanic languages overtly mark what is often called "inherent reflexivity." These differ from literal reflexives in that while these refer to an event involving two participants of which both happen, contrary to general expectation, to be the same entity (*He shot himself*), inherent reflexives entail a perception of one participant, performing upon itself an action whose reflexivity is the expected case rather than an anomaly (*He bathed*) (Haiman 1983, Kemmer 1993).

Inherent reflexives are the product of the grammaticalization and bleaching of the reflexive element in conjunction with verbs connoting inherently reflexive actions, such that in many languages, inherent reflexivity is marked in motion verbs (German *sich beeilen* "to hurry"), psych-verbs (*sich erinnern* "to remember"), and verbs of social behavior (*sich benehmen* "to behave"); this is a cross-linguistic developmental tendency (cf. Kemmer 1993, Peitsara 1997).

Inherent reflexivity marking is common in all of the Germanic languages but English and was also present in early Germanic languages such as Gothic (*ni idreigo mik* "I do not repent" [Dal 1966: 155]) and Old Norse (where it was already grammaticalized to the point of morphologization; cf. 5.3), suggesting that i was a Proto-Germanic feature. In table 11.1 and similar tables, for reasons of space, "Mainland Scandinavian" is represented by Swedish, the feature having also been identified in Danish and Norwegian.[1]

Note that pronominal form restricted to reflexive use (e.g., a cognate of German *sich*) is not necessary to inherent reflexive marking. The absence of a reflex of *sich* is not local to English but was already the case in Ingvaeonic, such that Frisian also lacks a *sich* reflex; Afrikaans does as well. In all Germanic languages, inherent reflexivity is marked in the first and second persons with the corresponding accusative or oblique pronoun (*ich rasiere mich, du rasierst dich* "I shave, you shave"), and in the third person, those without a *sich* reflex mark reflexivity with an accusative or oblique third-person pronoun; for example, Frisian *hy skeart him* "he shaves."

In Old English, inherent reflexivity was marked with either the dative or the accusative pronoun in all persons:

TABLE 11.1. Inherent reflexives in Germanic

| Language | Examples | Source |
|----------|----------|--------|
| German | *sich rasieren* "to shave" | |
| | *sich beeilen* "to hurry" | |
| | *sich erinnern* "to remember" | |
| Dutch | *zich scheren* "to shave" | Donaldson 1997: 203–4 |
| | *zich bewegen* "to move" | |
| | *zich herinneren* "to remember" | |
| Frisian | *hy skeart him* "he shaves" | Tiersma 1985: 66, 147 |
| | *ik skarnje my* "I am embarrassed" | |
| | *ik stel myfoar* "I imagine" | |
| Afrikaans | *hy bevind horn* "he is situated (at)" | Ponelis 1993: 288–91 |
| | *hy roer horn* "he gets going" | |
| | *hy herinner horn* "he remembers" | |
| Scandinavian | *raka sig* "to shave" | Holmes and Hinchliffe 1997: 105–6 |
| | *röra sig* "to move" | |
| | *känna sig* "to feel" | |
| Icelandic | *koma* "to come" / *komast* "to get to, reach" | Kress 1982: 105, 143 |
| | *snúa sér* "to turn around" | |
| | *kammast sín* "to be ashamed" | |
| Faroese | *raka sær* "to shave" | Lockwood 1955: 117–18 |
| | *snúgva sær* "to turn" | |
| | *ætla sær* "to intend" | |
| Yiddish | *bukn zikh* "to bow" | Lockwood 1955: 89–90 |
| | *shlaykhn zikh* "to sneak" | |
| | *shemen zikh* "to be ashamed" | |

(1)  þa **beseah**    he **hine**    to anum    his manna        and cwæð . . .
     then look.PAST he him.DAT to one.DAT his man-PL.GEN and say.PAST
     "Then he looked at one of his men and said . . ." (Visser 1963: 146)[2]

(2)  **Reste**    ðæt folc    **hit**    on ðam    seofoþan dæge.
     rest.PAST the people it.ACC on the.DAT seventh  day
     "The people rested on the seventh day." (ibid. 147)

Even at this early date its use was optional (ø where the reflexive pronoun would occur):

(3)  se sylfa Drihten wolde    ø of heofenum    on eorðan    beseon
     he self  Lord    want.PAST from heaven.DAT on earth.ACC see.INF
     "The Lord himself wanted to look upon the earth from heaven." (ibid. 146)

Throughout the Middle English period, however, inherent reflexivity was marked increasingly less (Mustanoja 1960: 431) and was likely preferred as a metrical device (Fischer 1992: 239). As early as Old English, texts suggest only vague semantic distinction between a given verb's usage with and without the reflexive pronoun (Mitchell 1985: 114, Visser 1963: 322, Rissanen 1999: 256).

By the Early Modern English period, Peitsara (1997: 303) finds inherent reflexive marking in only a third of potential cases from 1500 to 1570, and in less than a sixth from 1570 to 1640. By the latter period, Peitsara finds the marking in only a limited number of verbs, including ones of motion, posture, self-care, and equipment; of psych-verbs only *fear* retains it (optionally), and among social ones, *commend*. Eventually, inherent reflexive marking with simple pronouns is eliminated completely, except in scattered frozen archaisms (*Now I lay me down to sleep*).

As inherent reflexive marking declines in Middle English, *self*, which begins in Old English expressing emphatic reflexivity (among other uses: cf. Mitchell 1985: 115, Faltz 1985: 18–19, 35), increases in frequency; by the fifteenth century its use had bleached semantically into compatibility with verbs that previously took just a simple pronoun (Peitsara 1997: 320–23). Thus where Wycliffe in the fourteenth century has *Adam and his wijf hidden **hem** fro the face of the Lord God* (Old Testament, Genesis 3:8), Tyndale in the sixteenth has *And Adam hyd **hymselfe** and his wyfe also from the face of the LORde God* (Five Books of Moses, Genesis 3:8). However, instead of extending to the full range of verbs that the bare-pronoun reflexive strategy once covered, *self*-pronouns settle into the modern pattern, largely marking only literal reflexivity. Today, reflexivity is usually marked where operation upon the self is emphasized for clarity (*bathe oneself*) or stylistic purpose (*they hid themselves*). With some verbs, the reflexive usage has conventionalized into a particular meaning (*to behave* versus *to behave oneself*), while in only a limited number of verbs is the marking obligatory (*pride oneself, perjure oneself*).

The result of this process was that, as Peitsara (1997: 337) neatly puts it, English became unique among Germanic languages in "an individual tendency to treat overt reflexivity as redundant, unless marked for practical or stylistic reasons." This cannot be attributed simply to the fact that inherent reflexivity marking was already optional in Old English, given that such an account begs the question as to why English did not instead choose to conventionalize the initially optional usage rather than eliminate it. For example, the feature was also at first variable in German (Curme 1952: 155–56), but was eventually obligatorified; Curme (331) notes, "German is usually tenacious of reflexive form even after its meaning has changed."

Obviously, this was also the case in the other Germanic languages. In Mainland Scandinavian, the grammaticalization went so far that the reflexive pronoun has eroded into a mere suffix on many verbs, creating deponents such as *minna-s* "to remember"; Icelandic and Faroese's *-st* suffix is similar (and is also found in Nynorsk and other western Norwegian dialects; Peter Trudgill, February 2002 pers. comm.). Cornips and Corrigan (2002) document the development of reflexive *zich* into a middle marker over the past hundred years in the Limburg dialect of Dutch (*Dit bed slaapt zich goed* "This beds sleeps well"). The English situation must also be seen within the context of a similar generalization of inherent reflexive marking across Europe as a whole. Haspelmath (1998: 276), for example, describes the development of anticausative marking with the reflexive pronoun as a pan-European Sprachbund feature. Our question, then, is why English took so anomalous a path as to eliminate the feature after having partially conventionalized it.

Along those lines, the grammaticalization of inherent reflexives is obviously connected to the marking not only of shades of reflexivity, but to distinctions of valence (transitivity) and mood (passive and middle voice). These distinctions are commonly related cross-linguistically (e.g., Lyons 1968: 373–75), and the Scandinavian -*s*-marked verbs, for example, also encode passivity (*bakas* "to be baked"). In this light, the disappearance in English of inherent reflexive marking can be seen as one symptom of the general drift toward "transitivization" that Visser (1963: 127–35) describes, where the overt distinction between transitive and intransitive use of verbs erodes. Under this analysis, the eclipse of inherent reflexive marking was part of a general process that also included the disappearance of the *ge-* prefix that once distinguished transitive verbs (*ærnan* "to run," *geærnan* "to reach, attain by running").

While we might be tempted to suppose, as Visser's treatment implies, that this "transitivization" drift was the fortuitous result of various independent processes that just happened upon a single result, the question we must ask is why similar processes did not converge upon the same result elsewhere in Germanic. Scandinavian also lost its *ge-* prefix, and the coalescence of vowels that once marked causative distinctions (Old English *sincan* versus *sencan*) is hardly unique to English. Yet if there is a tendency for a grammar to fill in "open spaces" in syntax as well as phonetic inventories as Visser surmises (1963: 135), then we might ask why English did not, as its sisters did, seek to compensate for the ravages of phonetic erosion by obligatorifying its usage of reflexives to retain overt signaling of transitivity and passiveness. Put another way, why did English not submit these pronouns to "exaptational" usage, in Lass's (1990) conception borrowed from evolutionary biology, recruiting reflexive pronouns as valence and mood markers as dozens of other languages were concurrently doing across Europe?

Instead, English became a grammar markedly less *overspecified* than its sisters in this area, leaving inherent reflexivity, transitivity, and causativity to context to an extent unique in its subfamily, and unusual in the Indo-European family as a whole.

## 3.2. External possessor constructions

When a possessed object falls into a semantic class roughly definable as inalienable, Germanic languages typically encode the possessor as an argument distinct from the possessed NP itself, as in German's *Die Mutter wäscht dem Kind die Haare* "the mother washes the child's hair." While this construction is sometimes termed the "sympathetic dative," I follow Vergnaud and Zubizarreta (1992) and König and Haspelmath (1997) in referring to this as the *external possessor construction*, as the term captures the larger generalization that the "external" constituent can be marked with cases other than the dative. External possessive generally refers to animate possessors, and applies to body parts, relatives, clothing, habitations, and sometimes even emotional conditions: the motivating factor is membership in the "personal sphere" (König and Haspelmath 1997: 530–33).

This feature is found in all of the Germanic languages but English except Afrikaans; in Mainland Scandinavian and Icelandic the marking is locative rather than dative, while Yiddish has the dative for pronouns and the benefactive for nouns. Because Proto-Germanic surveys are notoriously sparse in their coverage of syntax, I have no data on this construction in Gothic or Old Saxon, and a mere hint in Old Norse, in the form of *skera tungu ór höfdi manni* "cut the tongue out of man's head" in Cleasby and Vigfusson's (1957) Old Icelandic dictionary, where the dative marking in *manni* suggests the presence of the construction. However, its uniform presence in Germanic indicates that it is an original Germanic trait (although König and Haspelmath 1997 and Haspelmath 1999 treat it as an areal feature, such that contact may have played a role in its distribution within Germanic as well).

German:

(4)  Die Mutter wäscht    dem      Kind die      Haare.
     the mother wash.3S the-DAT child the-PL hair.PL
     "The mother washes the child's hair."

Dutch:

(5)  Men heeft    hem      zijn arm gebroken.
     IMP have.3S 3S-OBJ his  arm break-PART
     "They broke his arm" (Konig and Haspelmath 1997: 554)[3]

Frisian:

(6)  Ik stompte    my      de holle.
     I  bump.PAST me.DAT the head
     "I bumped my head." (Jarich Hoekstra, July 2001 pers. comm.)

Scandinavian:

(7)  Någon  bröt      armen    på    honom.
     someone break.PAST arm.DEF PREP 3S.OBJ
     "Someone broke his arm." (König and Haspelmath 1997: 559)

Icelandic:

(8) Han nuddaði á henni fætur-na.
he massage.PAST on her.DAT leg.PL-DEF:ACC
"He massaged her legs." (ibid.)

Faroese:

(9) Eg hoyrdi røddina á honum.
I hear.PAST voice on 3S.DAT
"I heard his voice." (Lockwood 1955: 105)

Yiddish:

(10) (a) Di mame hot em gevasht di hor.
the mother have.3S 3S.DAT wash.PART the hair
"The mother washed his hair."

(b) Di mame hot gevasht di hor farn kind.
the mother have.3S wash.PART the hair for.the child
"The mother washed the child's hair." (Jim Matisoff, pers. comm.)

Old English had external possessor marking, as in:

(11) þa cnitton hi rapas . . . hire to handum and fotum
then tie.PAST they rope-PL her.DAT to hand.DAT.PL and foot.DAT.PL
"then they tied ropes . . . to her hands and feet" (Mitchell 1985: 125)

However, the construction, already optional in Old English (Mitchell 1985: 126), decreases in frequency throughout the Old English period (ibid. 126–27, Ahlgren 1946). Visser (1963: 633) notes it as "common" but not obligatory in Middle English, but almost completely obsolete by the Modern English period. Modern English retains but sparse remnants of the earlier construction, as in *She looked him in the eyes* (König and Haspelmath 1997: 554, 560).

Ahlgren (1946: 201–2) suggests that English may have lost the external possessor construction due to the collapse of the dative and the accusative in English case-marking. This early explanation has its echo in the emphasis in modern treatments on tracing historical developments in English to loss of overt case distinctions. But this surely cannot serve as an explanation for the loss of external possessor marking when Dutch and Scandinavian have experienced the same collapse of dative and accusative in pronouns and yet retain the feature. It is also germane that even a language that does retain the dative/accusative contrast robustly, Icelandic, has nevertheless shed dative-marked external possessives for marking them with the locative. Obviously collapse of case marking was not a causal factor in English (cf. Haspelmath 1999: 125). Nor can Ahlgren's suggestion (210–16) that Latin was a deciding factor stand, when French and other Romance languages retain dative external possessor marking (*il m'a frappé la main* "he hit my hand"), despite Latin playing as influential a role as a language of scholarship in their lifespans as it did in that of English.

Thus the question that arises is why it is ungrammatical in English to say "They broke him his arm," when Dutch has *Men heeft hem zijn arm gebroken*, or why English does not have "Someone broke the arm on him" as the Scandinavian languages do. Proposing a pathway of semantic evolution of prepositions on which external possessives fall at a highly evolved point, Haspelmath (1999: 130–31) suggests that English does not use the preposition *to* in the function because it has yet to abstractualize to this extent. This is well-taken in explaining why *They broke the leg to him* is ungrammatical, but it does not account for why English does not instead encode external possession with oblique pronouns *without* a preposition, as Dutch does, or with locative prepositions, as in Scandinavian. Under any internally-based account, it is indeed "difficult to find a proper explanation," as Visser (1963: 633) puts it, of the absence of external possessor constructions in English; like so many, Visser is left to simply describe the change.

König and Haspelmath (1997: 583) note that the general tendency throughout Europe is for dative external possessives to recede, with only Baltic, Slavic, and Albanian preserving them as robustly as in early documents. Yet our question regarding English must be why it has lost the feature so quickly and thoroughly. Today, in Europe Welsh and Breton are the only other languages that lack the construction (and Turkish if we count it as a European language), with even Finnish and Hungarian having picked up reflections of it, presumably through Sprachbund effects (ibid. 587–88).

Indeed, the loss of this construction in English must be viewed against concurrent cross-linguistic tendencies that are the very source of constructions such as these. Despite the broad trend over millennia to dilute external possessives, for instance, Romanian has extended the semantic boundaries of the "personal sphere" somewhat:

(12)  Ne-am              lăsat        bagajele     în autocar.
      1PL.DAT-have.1PL leave-PART baggage.PL in coach.
      "We left our baggage in the coach." (Deletant and Alexandrescu 1992: 108)

Also germane here is what Icelandic linguists term "dative sickness," whereby over time, the marking of experiencers as dative rather than accusative is increasing rather than decreasing, as in:

(13)  (a)  **Mig**      brestur kjark.
           1S.ACC lack.3S  courage.ACC

      (b)  **Mér**      brestur kjarkur.
           1S.DAT lack.3S  courage.NOM
           "I lack courage." (Smith 1992: 291)

Smith identifies dative sickness as symptomatic of a general diachronic tendency for case marking to decrease in what he terms "abstractness"; under his definition, abstractness decreases as the linking of grammatical relations (general) to semantic roles (specific) becomes more explicit.

Thus the pan-European tendency to dilute dative possessor marking coexists with a countervailing possibility that a grammar may also drift into increasing the overt marking of particular semantic roles applicable to a given general grammatical relation. English shunned the pathway that Romanian and Icelandic have taken, and did it so decisively that external possessor marking vanished completely.

Finally, it is relevant that the only other Germanic language that lacks external possessive constructions is Afrikaans, whose structure (it is now agreed) was decisively influenced by extensive acquisition of Dutch as a second language by people of various ethnicities. This is one piece of evidence that the situation in English is not simply a matter of internally-driven "business as usual."

English, then, is unique among its European sisters in having chosen not to mark an inalienable, "personal" shade of experiencerhood. While just beyond the British Isles, both northward and eastward, other Germanic languages developed and retained a degree of inalienable possessive marking, English makes no grammaticalized differentiation between *He grabbed my hand* and *He grabbed my folder*, and this, like English's lack of inherent reflexives, is quite unusual even among European languages as a whole.

## 3.3. Grammatical gender marking on the article

The mechanics of the loss of grammatical gender in English have been well covered, recent examples including Thomason and Kaufman (1988) and Lass (1992: 103–16). By the end of the twelfth century, grammatical gender was already all but lost in northern dialects; two centuries later, it had all but disappeared even in the south (cf. Strang 1970: 265).

However, in the emphasis on the phonological predictability of these changes, it has been less acknowledged that this change left English *the only European Germanic language with no grammatical gender marking*, despite the obvious vigor of phonetic erosion and analogy in its sisters.

Certainly, as Thomason and Kaufman emphasize, English is hardly unique in having lost grammatical gender marking on nouns themselves; Mainland Scandinavian, Dutch, and Frisian have only remnants of segmental indication of gender on nouns. Even Old English had already moved considerably in this direction, the emergence of multiple homophonies via phonetic change having already rendered the nominal morphology "relatively inexpressive and ambiguous," as Lass (1992: 104) puts it and so many others have noted. The Germanic syllable-initial stress system is well-known for having encouraged the erosion of unaccented word-final segments, which left nominal morphology especially vulnerable.

But nominal inflections were only a subset of the grammatical gender marking apparatus. To quote Lass again, in Old English "the richest and most distinctive marking for nominal categories is on determiners, in the strong adjective declension, and in pronouns" (ibid. 106). Here, the determiners are particularly important; specifically, the articles. Concurrently with the erosion of the nominal inflections, an initial three-gender distinction in the demonstrative-/-article *se* (masc.), *seo* (fem.) and *þæt* (neut.) collapses into the gender neutral *the*.[4]

Scholars on the history of English typically subsume the inflectional erosion and the collapse of the article's gender distinctions under a general "shift" from a grammatical to a natural gender-marking system; these include Strang (1970: 265, 268) and Lass (1992), who describes this as a "cumulative weighting of 'decisions' in favour of natural gender." However, in a broader view, the "drift" characterization can serve only as a description rather than as an explanation, primarily because it begs the question as to why all of the other Germanic languages of Europe, despite the erosion of the nominal inflections, maintained a grammatical gender distinction in the articles.

Surely, Dutch, Frisian, Danish, and Swedish collapsed the original Germanic masculine and feminine into a common gender contrasting with a neuter. But they only went this far, and it is unclear why English could not have done the same. It would even seem to have been phonetically plausible for *se* and *seo* to collapse into, perhaps, *se*, with *þæt* remaining as a neuter marker. Strang (1970: 268) states that "gender, as a grammatical system, can hardly survive the transformation of the personal pronoun system," but since Dutch, Frisian, and Mainland Scandinavian underwent similar collapses in their pronouns, it is unclear that the disappearance of grammatical gender in English was so foreordained. (Note also that some nonstandard Mainland Scandinavian dialects retain all three genders [e.g., Haberland 1994: 324].) Similarly, Lass's observation on "cumulative weightings" is obviously correct in itself but reveals English speakers to have been unique among Europe's Germanic languages in this regard.

Is it possible that the phonetic shapes of Old Norse's articles led to the collapse of gender distinctions in Old English's cognate items as English speakers intermingled with Scandinavian settlers? It would seem that this explanation will serve us, but so well. The definite articles English speakers would have heard Old Norse speakers using were *þænn* (masc.), *þe* (fem.), and *þæt* (neut.) (Gordon 1927: 302). It is logical that English speakers in contact with Old Norse might have replaced the initial consonant of *se* and *seo* with [θ], the varieties being so typologically close that small adjustments like these could have gone a long way in easing communication. Yet contact *qua se* gives us no reason to assume that the immediate result would have been a single gender-neutral item *the*. When bilingualism between Western Danish and Low German was common in the thirteenth to fifteenth centuries, Danish lost much inflection (Haugen 1981) but retained a two-way gender distinction in its definite article (rather than reducing all forms to, for example, [də] on the phonetic model of what was common to the German definite articles). On the contrary, one plausible scenario is that English would have developed, for instance, a common gender item such as [θe] and preserved its neuter *þæt*. If such had occurred, there are no grounds for assuming that phonetic erosion would inevitably have eliminated the distinction in final consonant between the two forms. Faroese is a living demonstration, with its cognate configuration, masculine and feminine *tann* and neuter *tað*. After centuries of regular use, the two remain distinct, partly due to the inherent conservativity of heavily used items. Only in English was this tendency overridden in favor of eliminating grammatical gender entirely.

Two broader observations highlight that English's lack of grammatical gender is a more "interesting" fact than generally assumed. First, among Germanic languages, again English's only parallel is Afrikaans, a language whose history was heavy with second-language acquisition.

Second, it has seldom been remarked that in its lack of any kind of grammatical gender within the noun phrase, English is unique not only among European Germanic languages but among *all the Indo-European languages of Europe*. As we would predict from the tendency for erosion and analogy to erase word-final morphology, there are scattered instances recorded in Europe of the loss of grammatical gender in Indo-European, but only in a few nonstandard dialects of particular languages, not all of the languages' dialects. Examples include Western Danish (Haberland 1994), Ostrobothnian Swedish, Tamian Latvian (Mathews 1956), and Màndres Albanian (Hamp 1965). Crucially, in the last two cases, gender was lost not through internal change but because of language contact (with Livonian and Turkish, respectively), and this is significant for our argument that English was crucially affected by contact. To be sure, the two cases of internal loss are both Germanic. Yet the question remains: Why is English the only European language in which *all* dialects have lost grammatical gender, such that today English speakers are the only Europeans who encounter grammatical gender marking as a new concept when acquiring another European language?[5] Or, to view this from another angle, English is the only language in Europe where loss of grammatical gender occurred so quickly and completely as to be a fait accompli across all dialects by the time European languages were being standardized in the middle of the last millennium.

Thus English contrasts with its sisters in lacking a particular type of overspecification: the obligatory marking of noun phrases according to categories generally only marginally correspondent with any real-world distinctions. Some linguists are uncomfortable with the idea of grammatical gender marking as "useless," and indeed once present, it can be useful in reference tracking (e.g., Heath 1975, Foley and Van Valin 1984: 326). However, here it is only one type of grammatical gender marking upon pronouns that serves the purpose in question, rather than gender distinctions marked by articles.[6] Furthermore, Trudgill (1999) rather conclusively refutes the notion that the gender marking arose *in order to* serve such functions, it being rather clear that the markers can be "exapted" into this function along the nonteleological lines of Keller's (1994) "invisible hand" concept. As such I am inclined to classify grammatical gender as equivalent to, in Lass's deft phrasing, "linguistic male nipples" (1997: 13).

Yet even if one is inclined to disagree, the point stands. Whether English was the only Germanic language disinclined to preserve a useless feature, or the only one that shed the feature despite its being useful to communication, it has been unique in its "streamlining" orientation.

## 3.4. Derivational morphology

As is well known, English is unusual among Germanic languages in the volume of original Germanic derivational morphology that it has lost: the rich Proto-Germanic battery of affixes (cf. Voyles 1992: 270–79) has been reduced to scattered remnants. The typical account focuses on the frequent replacement of Germanic derivational affixes with French ones. But some analysts note that the loss appears to have predated significant contact with French (Strang 1970: 191, Dalton-Puffer 1995: 39); while French lexical items often only appear in texts after the Norman occupation,

Hiltunen (1983: 92) describes the derivational loss as virtually complete as soon as Middle English texts begin. This means that in the strict sense, Old English apparently simply let a great deal of its derivational apparatus go; the French replacements were a later consequence of geopolitical developments.

### 3.4.1. Verb prefixes

Of course, in the case of many of the Old English prefixed verbs, we cannot speak properly of loss, given that they were simply replaced by equivalent phrasal verbs, as Hiltunen (1983) describes: *toberstan > to break apart*, *inlædan > to bring in*, et cetera. However, this only happened where the prefix either coexisted with a free preposition (e.g., *in*) or was of semantics robust and discrete enough to be readily substituted by an equivalent free word: *down* for *niþer-*, *around* for *ymb-*, *up* and *out* for the intensificational uses of *for-*, as in *forbærnan > to burn up*.

This process would then fall under the rubric of the general loss of morphology in the inflectional realm, where, similarly, distinctions encoded by affixation are often replaced by ones encoded by free morphemes (e.g., prepositions) or word order. But all of the derivational losses cannot be subsumed under a simple substitution of the analytical for the synthetic, as certain prefixes were instead eliminated from the grammar without any substitution—namely, the prefixes with semantics leaning more toward the grammatical, abstract pole simply disappeared, leaving only fossilized remnants. Thus English lost its transitivizing *be-* (*seon* "to see," *beseon* "to look at") and *ge-*, alternatively described as transitivizing (Visser 1963: 127) or perfectivizing (Mitchell and Robinson 1986: 58), as in *ærnan* "to run," *geærnan* "to reach, attain by running" and *winnan* "to toil," *gewinnan* "to conquer."

Another question arises with another use of *for-*. Grammars typically describe its relatively compositional uses, such as the intensificational one. However, a survey of its uses across the Old English lexicon shows that its contribution had often bleached to the point that there was little or no perceptible difference of meaning between the bare verb and its conjunction with *for-*, as in *helan/forhelan* "to conceal" and *þolian/forþolian* "to lack, be deprived of." This is also the case in German, Dutch, Afrikaans, Yiddish, Mainland Scandinavian, and Frisian, where there are doublets of this type whose differentiation of usage is, at best, highly subtle and sometimes register-bound (German *sterben/versterben* "to die"). It is likely that this was a step toward the reanalysis of the *for-* cognate in these languages as simply a marker of verbhood, connoting transformation, and in this usage extended to nouns and adjectives as well as verbs: German *verlängern* "to make longer," Dutch *vernederlandsen* "to Dutchify," Afrikaans *verafrikaans* "to Afrikaansify," Swedish *förgifta* "to poison," and others. Even heavy contact has not hindered this development, as we see in Afrikaans as well as Pennsylvania German, threatened by English, where nevertheless the cognate prefix is used to create new verbs: [fərbɔtʃt] "all botched up" (Van Ness 1994: 433). Old English could, theoretically, have replaced the compositional uses of *for-* (such as the intensificational one) with phrasal verb particles, but otherwise retained *for-* as a verbalizer of this kind as many of its sisters did. Instead, while the intensificational uses were indeed replaced by phrasal verbs, in its other uses *for-* simply disappeared as a productive morpheme.

In short, English's loss of prefixes entailed a significant degree of loss of *overt specification*. As it happens, Icelandic and Faroese have also opted for phrasal verbs to the virtual exclusion of the Germanic verbal prefixes, including losing *be-*, *ge-*, and *for-* cognates. My thesis hardly rules out that a given Germanic language other than English might have also shed a given feature, due either to developments elsewhere in the grammar or to sheer chance. However, my thesis is indeed that to couch the developments in English as unremarkable results of a "trend toward analyticity" misses a larger point. In that light, we must first note how very much *inflectional* morphology Icelandic and Faroese nevertheless retain, as well as the various other overspecified features discussed thus far. Moreover, it is also relevant that even Afrikaans, despite its heavy inflectional loss, has retained the verbal prefixes *be-* (*beslis* "to decide"), *ont-* (*ontken* "to deny"), and *ver-* (*verpletter* "to smash"), and not in fossilized form, but with a certain degree of productivity, as demonstrated by neologisms such as *beplan* "to plan," *ontlont* "to defuse," and *verafrikaans* "to Afrikaansify" (Ponelis 1993: 556–57).

When the derivational prefixes were lost in two languages otherwise heavy with morphology, and meanwhile preserved in a language that otherwise underwent major reduction in morphology, the loss in English appears traceable to something other than random phonetic erosion; something more specific was at work.

### 3.4.2. Suffixes

The losses of various derivational *suffixes* in Old English is overall less indicative of any trend against overspecification. Old English documents capture the language at a stage where some suffixes are robustly productive while others are falling by the wayside, some obscured from perception by the transformations of the root they caused (most notably, *the*, as in *foul/filthe*, *young/you(ng)the*), others losing out in Darwinian competition with ones filling similar spaces (*-reden* and *-lac* versus *-ness*). In any language we see affixes at various points on the dine between glory and oblivion, and thus it is not necessarily the case that these losses in themselves suggest that Middle English was a "recessive" language, as Dalton-Puffer (1995) proposes.

However, one case here again points to a trend toward underspecification. English loses its infinitive marker *-(e)n* by the end of the 1400s (Lass 1992: 98). Other than English, only Afrikaans, Germanic's contact language par excellence, has lost all signs of this marker completely. But in itself, the loss in English entailed no loss of overspecification. Already in Old English, there was a semantic difference between bare infinitives and those occurring with *to*, the former's conjunction with the preceding verb connoting more transitive actions processed as one event (Callaway 1913, cited in Fischer 1997). When the infinitive marker wore off and all infinitives were then marked with *to*, this distinction was not lost: *-ing*-marked verbs came in to connote the more transitive relationship with infinitives now processed as less so (e.g., *I saw him doing it* versus *I wanted to do it*) (Mittwoch 1990, Fischer 1997: 126).

For the purposes of this argument, however, it is important to note that English lost not only the verb-marking reflex of this morpheme. but also those that served derivationally as word-building devices. In Old *English*, *-sian*, *-ettan*, and *-lœcan* served to make nouns and adjectives into verbs (*ricsian* "to reign," *licettan* "to pretend," *geanlæcan* "to unite"; Mitchell and Robinson 1986: 60]). These were flushed away: English did not take the route of, for example, letting -*(e)n* erode but retaining markers -*s*, -*ett*, and -*læc* as derivational equipment (e.g., retaining enough pairs like *clean-/-cleanse* for the suffix to be processible and even productive). To be sure, cognates of these suffixes are now defunct in English's sisters, but they all retained machinery elsewhere that overtly marks analogous derivational distinctions. Meanwhile, English instead chose the pathway toward its now notorious fondness for zero-denominal and zero-deadjectival derivation. In German, I *telephoniere*; in English I just *telephone*. The German cannot get away with "*ich telephon*," nor is the cognate equivalent possible for speakers of any Germanic language but English.

### 3.4.3. Description versus explanation

The causes traditionally adduced for this rather striking sloughing away of derivational apparatus within a few centuries leave more questions than answers. The idea that lack of stress rendered the morphemes uniquely vulnerable addresses a tendency rather than an inevitable death sentence. German and others, after all, retain, for example, past participle marker *ge-*, and even southwestern English dialects retained its cognates *y-* and *a-* (cf. Barnes 1886: 27–28 on Dorset) as participial markers until pressure from the standard rendered them extinct. This last questions Marchand's (1969: 130–31) suggestion that the vowel-initial prefixes in particular were uniquely vulnerable, as well as the idea that erosion is the sole reason that the almost three dozen Old English verbs transitivized by *ge-* that Visser (1963: 127) lists were shorn of their valence markers.

Authors also sometimes suppose that an affix was ripe for elimination because it had many meanings (Dalton-Puffer 1996: 179 on adjectival marker -*ly*), or because its contributions to many stems were no longer semantically predictable (Marchand 1969: 130–31 on *for-*). However, in any language, a given affix may remain in productive use in a core meaning while its contributions to myriad roots have drifted into noncompositionality. The noncompositional uses are not evidence of imminent demise of the affix but are merely indications that the affix has been in use for a long time. The German *ver-* is a useful example. One usage conveys the notion of "away": *jagen* "to hunt," *verjagen* "to chase away." There are extended meanings from this one, such as error ("away" from the right path), creating antonyms such as *lernen* "to learn" versus *verlernen* "to forget." Meanwhile, many uses of *ver-* are unattributable to any of these meanings and must be learned by rote, such as *nehmen* "to take," *vernehmen* "to perceive." Yet this is not taken to signal that *ver-* is on its way out of the grammar; on the contrary, it is used productively to create new verbs (*verschlagworten* "to file under a subject heading" [Ingo Plag, pers. comm.]), with the non- and semi-compositional results of its historical legacy simply dragged along by speakers. Thus the question is why English does not drag along noncompositional cases like *forbid* and *forgive* at the same time as creating words like "forenglish" to mean "to Englishify."

Finally, there are explanations such as Visser's (1963: 134) that a given affix disappeared because a great number of the words displaying it "dropped into disuse." The implication would seem to be that the massive incursion of French words eliminated so much of the original Germanic lexicon that in some cases too few uses of a given affix remained to be processible by speakers. Yet it is well known that French words often took their place alongside Germanic words to create synonyms, often occupying different registers.

Visser's list of now lost words where *be-* was affixed to roots still used in bare form in Modern English is worth citing in full: *bebark, bechirp, bedwell, beflow, befly, begaze, beglide, beglitter, bego, behoot, beleap, belie, bemew, berain, beride, berow, beshite, beshriek, besit, bescramble, bescratch, besparkle, beswink.* First, why could a healthy subset of words of this kind not have persisted alongside French equivalents, as *help* persisted alongside *aid*, for instance? Certainly we would expect some to vanish by the sheer dictates of serendipity, but so many that today the prefix occurs on too few words to be processible to any but highly literate modern speakers? Even if all of the words on Visser's list did for some reason "drop into disuse" by chance, why did speakers not come to apply the native affix to borrowed words, as they went on to apply borrowed affixes to native words (*speakable, bondage* [Dalton-Puffer 1996: 221], or today, *faxable*)? An alternate interpretation of the disappearance of the words is that it was the *affix* that speakers were rejecting, not the words themselves, especially when they so often retained the root itself (i.e., in reference to Visser's list, *bark, chirp, dwell, flow,* etc.).

Thus the loss of derivational morphology in English takes its place alongside the loss of inherent reflexive marking, external dative possessor marking, and grammatical gender marking in rendering the language less accreted with overspecification. In this case, English shed overt marking of transitivity with the jettisoning of *be-* and one use of *ge-*, and overt marking of noun- and adjectivehood with its shedding of derivational uses of reflexes of the infinitive marker *-(e)n* and the prefix *for-*.

## 3.5. Directional adverbs

Germanic languages typically distinguish forms of adverbs of place according to location, motion toward, and motion away from (Swedish *här* "here," *hit* "to here," and *härifrån* "from here" [Holmes and Hinchliffe 1997: 115–16]). This was a Proto-Germanic feature (cf. Voyles 1992: 242).

Old English originally toed the Germanic line here (e.g., *her, hider, heonan*), but the system was already fragile, with *her* often used for motion toward, *-an*-suffixed forms losing their sense of "from" and being used as mere locationals, and so on (Mitchell 1985: 476; Meroney 1945: 386, cited in Mitchell). This uncertainty and variability can even be taken as a suggestion that in the spoken language the distinctions were even more fitfully observed. In any case, even in its written form the system was already what Meroney (1945: 386) describes as "a stage of compromise between Germanic and Modern English," and by the latter stage, English had become the sole Germanic language not to attend regularly to this distinction. Because these forms were widely used in high literary English into the 1800s, it is difficult to place exactly when they passed out of spoken English. However, all would agree that they are no longer current today beyond frozen expressions like *hither* and *yon* (which to this writer's ear are restricted for modern generations to the ironic, at least in the United States).[7]

The loss of the "motion away from" forms did not in itself lead to a loss in encoded meaning, since the word *from* was recruited to serve the same purpose: *heonan* became *from here*, and so on. However, motion *toward* a destination is often contained within the semantics of a verb of motion, and in these cases, English, as so often elsewhere, took the route of leaving the nuance to context (see table 11.2).[8] Certainly as directionality itself goes, the overt distinction is not entirely foreign to English, as in *in the house* versus *into the house*. Moreover, even with the adverbs themselves, colloquial English speakers often make the distinction variably with *where*, as in *Where is she at?* versus A: *We're going now.* B: *Where to?* But this is hardly the case with most applicable adverbs, and the point remains that it is obligatory in the standard *not* to mark the distinction on any adverb: *hither, thither,* and *whither* are strictly archaic words foreign to even the highest registers of Modern English. Moreover, arguably, the *absence* of the distinction is grammatical to all English speakers: there is probably no Anglophone context on earth where asking *Where?* rather than *Where to?* would sound non-native or clumsy.

Other Germanic languages differ slightly in the degree to which the distinctions are obligatory (Tiersma's Frisian grammar has the use of *hjir* with the *come-* verb as grammatical, and Faroese even has an outright gap with *hvar*), to their scope of application within the grammar (German's conventionalization of the conjunction of *her-* and *hin-* with prepositions and verb particles being an extreme), and where particular usages fall in terms of register. But in all of the languages, the distinction is a robust aspect of their grammars (to my knowledge, even nonstandard varieties), usually applying to a wide range of adverbs.

We cannot simply classify this loss as a mere symptom of the erosion of morphology in Old English. For one, the "motion" forms in Old English differed in shape from the locational reflexes far beyond the affix itself. If morphological loss were the smoking gun here, then we might expect, for example, *hid* and *heon* to have resulted, still distinct from *her* (> *here*). In any case, too often Germanic languages have maintained this distinction *despite* vast morphological losses: Afrikaans is the most pointed demonstration, followed by Mainland Scandinavian and Dutch.

TABLE 11.2. Directional adverbs in Germanic

| Eng | OE | Ger | Du | Fr[a] | Yi | Sc[b] | Ic | Fa | Afr |
|---|---|---|---|---|---|---|---|---|---|
| here | her | hier | hier | hjir | hi | här | hér | her | hier |
| | hider | her(-) | hiernaartoe | hjirhinne | aher | hit | hingaþ | higar | heirnatoe |
| there | þær | dort | daar | dêr | dort | där | þar | har | daar |
| | þider | hin(-) | daarnaartoe | dêrhinne | ahin | dit | þangaþ | hagar | daarnatoe |
| where | hwær | wo | waar waar. | wêr | vu | var | hvar | hvar | waar |
| | hwider | wohin | .heen | wêrhinne | vuhin | vart | hvert | | waarheen |

Abbreviations: English, Old English, German, Dutch, Frisian, Yiddish, Scandinavian, Icelandic, Faroese, Afrikaans

a. Frisian data in this table from Peter Tiersma (July 2001 pers. comm.)

b. The Mainland Scandinavian varieties differ in the fashions and extents to which they indicate direction in their adverbs, but the distinction is overall very much alive in both Danish and Norwegian.

But English alone shed these forms, and Sapir (1921: 169–70) artfully parsed the grammar-wide developmental impetus that this demonstrated:

> As soon as the derivation runs danger of being felt as a mere nuancing of, a finicky play on, the primary concept it tends to be absorbed . . . [an] instance of the sacrifice of highly useful forms to this impatience of nuancing is the group *whence, whither, hence, hither, thence, thither.* They could not persist in live usage because they impinged too solidly upon the circles of meaning represented by the words *where, here* and *there.* That we add to *where* an important nuance of direction irritates rather than satisfies.

Crucially, in Germanic only English speakers felt such an "irritation." Alone, this anomaly in English could be seen as a mere fluke; in conjunction with the previous four cases adduced, a larger process reveals itself at work.

### 3.6. *Be* with past participles

A hallmark of Germanic (and Romance) is the use of the verb *to be* with a large subset of intransitive verbs in the perfect: German *er hat gegessen* "he has eaten," "he ate," *er ist gekommen* "he has arrived," "he arrived." Of course, the precise domain of intransitives to which *be* applies varies across the languages, but the basic distinction is retained even in Afrikaans (*Ze zijn vertrokken* "they have left" [Ponelis 1993: 444]) and Yiddish *Ikh bin geblibn* "I stayed" [Lockwood 1995: 83]). The virtually uniform distribution of this feature suggests Proto-Germanic inheritance; it is found as early as Old Norse (Brenner 1882: 129) and Old Saxon (Ramat 1998: 403). Accordingly, Old English marked this distinction with the verbs *beon* and *wesan*:

(14)  hu  sio lar    Lædengeðiodes    ær  ðissum afeallen    **wæs**
      how the learning Latin-language.GEN before this.DAT fall-away.PART was
      "How the learning of Latin was fallen away before this" (Mitchell and Robinson 1986: 111)

Yet as so often with typical Germanic constructions, already in Old English the usage was apparently in flux, with *habban* encroaching on the domain of *beon* and *wesan.* Mitchell (1985: 302–4) suggests that none of the attempts over the years to delineate a principled semantic distinction between the use of a verb with *habban'* as opposed to *beon* or *wesan* withstand scrutiny, and he questions whether the documentation even indicates a grammaticalized *be*-perfect, as opposed to a typical use of a *be*-verb with stative adjectivals.

By the 1500s, the use of *be* in the perfect had largely shrunk to the change-of-state class of intransitives such as *come, become, arrive, enter, run,* and *grow*:

(15)  And didst thou not, when she **was** gone downstairs, desire me to be no more so familiarity with such poor people? (Henry IV, 11.i.96) (cited in Traugott 1972)

(Cf. also Rissanen 1999: 213). In their variationist analysis based on texts as representative as possible of the spoken language, Rydén and Brorström (1987: 200) show that by the early 1800s, overall usage of *have* over *be* surpassed the 50 percent mark, with prescriptive grammarians granting tolerance of the *be*-perfect to an ever narrower class of verbs over the century (206–11). Today the usage has vanished except for in frozen form with *go* (i.e., if I may, *The construction is gone*).[9]

The pathway English followed is striking, given that the development of *be*-perfects was an innovation in Germanic and Romance rather than an inheritance from Proto-Indo-European, and in many languages the domain of *be* has spread rather than contracted over time compare the varying extents of its application across Western European languages in Sorace (2000). English instead reversed this pathway of overspecification of intransitivity, thus joining the elimination of inherent reflexive marking and the derivational prefixes *be-* and *ge-* and rendering English the Germanic language with the least overt marking of valence.

Obviously we cannot lay this change at the feet of inflectional loss, nor can it be subsumed under the rubric of the drift toward analyticity.

Typically, the disappearance of the *be*-perfect is attributed to the recruitment of *be* as a marker of the passive (Mustanoja 1960: 501, Traugott 1972: 145, Mitchell 1985: 299, Rissanen 1999: 213). There is even comparative support for this explanation, in the fact that Swedish, the only Germanic language other than English that lacks the *be*-perfect (*Vi **har** rest till Spanien förr* "We have gone to Spain before" [Holmes and Hinchliffe 1997: 100]), has also recruited its *be*-verb *vara* to mark the passive (cf. Rissanen 1999: 215).

But the causal relationship here is not absolute. Icelandic, too, forms its passives with its *be*-verb *vera* (*ég **var** barinn* "I was hit") and in the perfect uses *have* with both transitives and intransitives (*ég **hef** komið* "I have come") (Kress 1982: 148–49). Yet Icelandic also uses *vera* with intransitive verbs of motion and change-of-state to connote the resultative: *ég **er** kominn* "I am come, I am here," and the class of verbs used this way is large (ibid. 152–53). But the strategy is by no means the recessive, marginal archaism that it was, for example, by Early Modern English.

It also bears mentioning that Swedish is unique even in Mainland Scandinavian in lacking a *be*-perfect. Danish and Norwegian retain it: Danish *Barnet **er** kommen* "the child has come" (Thomas 1911: 33–34), Norwegian *Han **er** reist* "he has left" (Strandskogen and Strandskogen 1986: 21). This highlights the general tenacity of this feature in a language once it arises (although it happens to be receding in Norwegian). Yet note that English *parallels* the Swedish exception as always, if a Germanic language other than English happens to opt for context where family tradition calls for being explicit, English will have done the same (the Faroese lack of a *to*-marked *where* being another example).

## 3.7. Passive marking with *become*

Another Germanic tribal marker is the use of a verb "become" to form the passive (German *Die Tür wird geschlossen* "The door was closed"), this including Afrikaans with its *word* (*Die trui word gebêre* "The jersey is put away"). Uniform distribution again suggests a Proto-Germanic pedigree, with its presence as far back as Old Norse (Heusler 1950: 137) and Gothic (Streitberg 1906: 182–83) reinforcing the reconstruction. While Swedish indeed uses its *be*-verb *vara* in the passive, it does so in conjunction with its verb "to become" *bli*: *vara* conveys a "stative" passiveness in line with its semantics: *Himlen är täckt av moln* "The sky is covered in cloud," while *bli* conveys more perfective semantics: *Han **blev** påkörd av en bil* "He was run down by a car" (Holmes and Hinchliffe 1997: 109). Icelandic, too, retains its *verða* along with its use of *vera* "to be" in the passive, in a division of labor in which *verða* is the marked, but hardly marginal, member (Kress 1982: 150).

As frequently, Old English followed the Germanic pattern in already rather atrophied fashion. *Beon* and *wesan* were already easing out *weorþan* in the passive, and Mitchell (1985: 324–35) rather spiritedly refutes common claims that this was instead a regularized distinction between perfective semantics conveyed by *weorþan* and stative ones by *beon* and *wesan* (along the lines of Swedish's *vara* and *bli*). Mitchell argues that all of the forms were used with both readings, but Denison (1993: 418–19) and Kilpiö (1989) show that more properly, *weorþan* was restricted entirely to the actional while *beon* and *wesan* were grammatical in both this and the stative meanings. By Middle English, the *weorþan*-passive is not just recessive; it's nonexistent (Rissanen 1999: 325).

Modern English has innovated the marking of passive with *get* (*He got hit*) and *have* (*He had his hair cut*), but both are pragmatically constrained, encoding especial activeness on the part of the subject, with the *have*-passive essentially a causative. Overall, English remains the only Germanic language without a lexical item dedicated to expressing a pragmatically neutral manifestation of the passive. Only in Icelandic is it even grammatical to use the *be*-verb to say *He was kicked*, and even it has retained *verða* alongside. Meanwhile, properly speaking, Swedish has recruited *vara* into a *subdomain* of the passive, retaining *bli* to distinguish the "true" passive as opposed to its more stative manifestations. Once again, English opts for underspecification where its sisters insist on dotting the *i*'s and crossing the *t*'s.

## 3.8. Verb second

All Germanic languages but English have verb-second (V2) word order, including Afrikaans. This is generally agreed to be a Proto-Germanic feature (Hopper 1975: 82, Ramat 1998: 410–13).

The languages differ in their particular manifestations of the phenomenon, often classified as "asymmetric" when V2 occurs only in root clauses and "symmetric" when V2 occurs in both root and subordinate clauses Which type of V2 Old English manifested is disputed (van Kemenade 1987 versus Pintzuk 1991), but it is uncontested that it was a V2 language:

(16)   On twam    þingum    hæafde    God þæs      mannes    sawle gegodod.
       in two.DAT thing.DAT have.PAST God this.GEN man.GEN soul  endow.PART
       "God had endowed this man's soul with two things." (Fischer, van Kemenade, Koopman, and van der Wurff 2000: 107)

V2 in English begins a decline in the fifteenth century and is essentially dead by the seventeenth (Jacobsson 1951, Nevalainen 1997). The question obviously arises as to why.

One current consensus links the loss to the erosion of verbal inflectional morphology. A general assumption is that V2 results from verb movement, specifically to C (Den Besten 1983), and inflection-based accounts of V2 loss suppose that the erosion of verbal morphology led to the verb staying in place rather than moving upward in its clause (e.g., Fischer et al. 2000: 135–36). But overall, the explanations offered in this case lack explanatory power or falsifiability.

For example, an inflection-based account of the loss of V2 presumes that the very small difference in degree of verbal inflection between Mainland Scandinavian and English determined that the former would preserve V2 while the latter would lose it. Yet this difference consists only of the fact that Mainland Scandinavian marks the present in all persons and numbers with -r (Swedish *jag arbetar* "I work") while English inflects in the present only the third-person singular. This would appear to attribute a profound configurational transformation to a rather minor discrepancy, especially given that discourse studies show that the third-person singular is by far the most frequent in speech (e.g., Greenberg 1966b: 45), such that the inflected form in English constitutes a disproportional component of input to learners. Where is the cut-off point that determines how "weak" inflection must be before it conditions a change in movement rules?

This question is all the more pressing given that in reference to a related process, Roberts (1993), Rohrbacher (1999), and others have argued that loss of verbal inflection in both English and Mainland Scandinavian led to the loss of verb movement to I in subordinate clauses. A demonstration case is English, in which previously the verb moved ahead of the negator, adverbs, and other elements, as in *if I gave not this accompt to you* from 1557 (Görlach 1991: 223). But there appear to be no principled accounts to date which motivate the differing fates of V-to-I and V-to-C movement in English. Precisely why did inflectional loss preserve V2 in matrix clauses but eliminate V-to-I in subordinate clauses in Mainland Scandinavian, while eliminating *both* movement processes in English?

We might be tempted to suppose that, for some reason, the small difference in degree of inflection was indeed responsible for the very specific effect of preserving V2 but not V-to-I movement in Mainland Scandinavian. But then the latest evidence suggests that the decisive causal link is solely between "strong" inflection and verb movement; when inflection is "weak," then the verb may or may not move (Roberts 1999: 292). The Kronoby Swedish dialect preserves V-to-I despite the inflectional erosion (Platzack and Holmberg 1989). Meanwhile, Kroch and Taylor (1997) argue that when verbal inflection eroded in English dialects in the north (under Scandinavian influence), the result was not the loss of V2, but a mere change in its configuration, from symmetric (the authors assume Pintzuk's analysis) to asymmetric. Baptista (2000) shows that there is evidence of verb movement in Cape Verdean creole despite its having but a single verbal inflection. Rohrbacher (1999) notes that Faroese verbs do not move to I despite robust plural inflection on verbs. He thereby surmises that "strong" inflection entails overt marking of the first and second persons in at least one number of at least one tense. But this stipulation is rather ad hoc, contradicting the centrality of the third-person singular in discourse, and would seem to have been invalidated by dialects like Kronoby Swedish. It would appear that, simply, the correlation between inflection and verb movement is a rather loose one. While work on the relationship of overt morphology to verb movement continues to be refined (e.g., Bobalijk and Thráinsson 1998), it seems clear that the link is too weak in itself to offer a conclusive explanation for what happened in English in comparison to its sisters.

Lightfoot (1997: 268–69) argues that this kind of gap in explanatory power is not problematic for generative diachronic syntacticians. In his view, their enterprise is strictly to use language change to illuminate the effects of synchronic parameters, and under this constrained conception, the reasons for the changes are irrelevant: "Sometimes the concern with explanation is excessive . . . such things happen for various reasons which are often of no particular interest to grammarians." Thus Lightfoot prefers to simply chart changes like the loss of V2 in terms of input gradually depriving learners of "triggers" motivating the setting of the appropriate parameters.

However, the reason for the disappearance of the "trigger" for V2 is crucial to this particular thesis, and I suggest that the reason is less obscure, or "contingent," as Lightfoot (1997) has it, than it might seem. In becoming the only Germanic language without V2, English opted for what can be argued to be the less complex syntactic configuration. Despite its air of "linguocentricity" when argued by an Anglophone, there is a great deal of evidence that SVO is a universally unmarked order. Kayne (1994) is an articulate generative demonstration. Pidginization and creolization data also support SVO as a "universal" order. Creoles tend to be SVO regardless of the word order of their substrate languages, such as Berbice Dutch Creole, formed between speakers of Dutch and the SVO Niger-Congo language Ijo (Kouwenberg 1994).

Linking the disappearance of V2 to a decomplexifying imperative also sheds light on another analysis of English's unique treatment of this feature, Kiparsky (1995). Kiparsky proposes that the development of COMP in both subordinate and matrix clauses was an innovation in Proto-Germanic, Proto-Indo-European being presumably a more clausally paratactic grammar (cf. Hermann 1895). He reconstructs that while all other Germanic languages conventionalized COMP in matrix clauses, English was unique in first having COMP as only optional in Old English, and then eliminating it. He notes that Old English is unique in Germanic in allowing matrix clauses, such as the one below, where the verb does not raise, while equivalent sentences were unattested in other early Germanic languages like Old High German and Old Norse:

(17)  He þa   his here  on tu  todælde.
      he then his army in two divide.PAST
      "He then divided his army in two." (Orosius 116.16) (Kiparsky 1995: 143)

But Kiparsky's analysis begs the question, like so many accounts of the history of English, as to just *why* English was unique in this regard. Kiparsky is concerned with diachronic syntactic analysis within the Principles and Parameters framework, and thus presumably concurs with Lightfoot regarding the theoretical import of such questions. However, within a frame of reference where such questions are more urgent, we see that English, in failing to develop an obligatory COMP node in matrix clauses, would once again be opting for the less complex path than its sisters, eschewing V2 in the vein of most of the world's languages while its sisters drifted into a typologically unusual quirk.

Importantly, Kiparsky notes that the presence of COMP in matrix clauses in Old English is variable rather than absent. But as with inherent reflexives, we must ask why English did not conventionalize rather than eliminate the feature. Old Norse did: by the time it is documented in about 1100, it has already grammaticized COMP in matrix clauses; Old High German was similar. Meanwhile, only in Old English does the variability persist and then eventually yield to dissolution.

In sum, in eliminating V2, English eliminated a feature requiring the operation of a rule to move the verb to C, a feature whose supplementary character in general is illustrated by the typological rarity of the V2 feature beyond Germanic. Other Germanic languages held on to V2 despite inflectional erosion as rampant as that in English for example, Mainland Scandinavian and Afrikaans. Inflection-centered, syntax-internal accounts have yielded stimulating explanations that are proper for assorted *variations* on the manifestation of V2. But for the complete elimination of verb movement, the best they have provided to date are loose correlations. No amount of refinements of this framework has been able to explain why *only English shed V2 in affirmative sentences altogether*. I suggest, along with Danchev (1997), that only a larger, contact-based explanation can surpass this obstacle.

## 3.9. The disappearance of *thou*

By the 1700s, the originally plural *you* had replaced *thou* in standard English. Recent research on court documents from the northeast suggest that in spoken English, *you* was already the conventional second-person singular form as early as the late 1500s, with *thou* used only in particular marked contexts (Hope 1994). Hope suggests that the wider use of *thou* in literary sources such as Shakespeare may have been a conservatism that spoken English had moved beyond.

This development is typically discussed within the larger context of the use of second-person plural pronouns in formal address to single persons across Europe. But Strang's (1970: 139) comment that "such a use, once introduced, must snowball," while obviously apt, does not explain why the "snowballing" went so far in English as to leave it the only Germanic language that lost a distinct second-person singular pronoun altogether. The usual result of the well-known development of "T-V" forms was for the V form to encroach ever more on the realm of familiarity but all of the other Germanic languages nevertheless retain the familiar form. If anything, the modern development has been toward the reassertion of the T form within the democratizing ideological tendencies of the post-Enlightenment age. Yet during just this period, English relegated *thou* to the archaism of the religious register. As Strang notes (140), it might not have persisted even here if the King James Bible had not happened to reproduce to such an extent the usage of Tyndale, who wrote in the early 1500s when *thou* was still in current use.

Clearly, neither inflectional loss nor a drift toward analyticity was related to a change that did not transpire even in Afrikaans, in which inflectional loss and analyticity were both rife. Furthermore, even highly isolating languages rarely display an isomorphy between singular and plural pronouns in the second person. Even the inquisitive undergraduate is often given to ask, when exposed to the

T-V pronoun issue, why English went as far as to eliminate *thou* entirely while German retained its *du*, et cetera. Often the professor can only offer an articulate shrug.

But in fact, this development correlates with the eight we have seen so far in rendering English less overspecified than its sisters. Obviously the lack of a number distinction in the second person occasions no significant communicational difficulties. However, every single Germanic language but English has preserved this distinction, frill though it is, to the present day. To be sure, Dutch and Frisian have lost the *du*-cognate itself but have nevertheless "exapted" other material to maintain a T-V distinction. English stands as unique among its sisters in having eschewed the nuance altogether.

## 3.10. The disappearance of *man*

English began with the usual Germanic endowment of an indefinite pronoun *man*, grammaticalized enough to have eroded phonetically to *me* by Middle English:

(18)  Ac **me** ne    auh   to bien hersum  bute      of gode.
      but one NEG ought to be    obedient except  in good
      "But one should not be obedient except in good things." (Rissanen 1987: 520)

The pronoun appears to trace to Proto-Germanic. The only Germanic languages that lack a distinct indefinite pronoun are Icelandic and Faroese (Icelandic recruits *maður* "men" [Kress 1982: 13], while Faroese uses *man* but only as a Danicism, preferring to use *tú* "you" and *teir* "they" like English [Lockwood 1955: 125]). But *man* is present (although variably) in their ancestor Old Norse (Heusler 1950: 147), suggesting that its eclipse in two daughters was a subsequent develonment. Meanwhile. Afrikaans does not retain Dutch's *men*, but instead uses the colloquial Dutch *'n mens* (< "a person"), and the tendency is to shorten this to *mens*, creating what Ponelis (1993: 224) analyzes as a new pronoun.

As always, where a few of its sisters eliminated a feature English followed suit: English's *man* rapidly disappeared, essentially gone in the written language by the late fourteenth century. To the extent that it appears in regional speech after this, it is marginally, such as in the early 1900s in Cumberland as attested by Brilioth (1913: 111). The original form *man* had split off to connote "a human being":

(19)  þanne **man** forgiet that  he seien     sholde.
      when  one  forget  what he say.INF  should
      þanne beð   his tunge  alse hit cleued were.
      then  be.3S his tongue as   it  stuck  were
      "When a person forgets what he should say, his tongue is as if it were stuck." (Rissanen 1987: 520)

Yet this usage as well did not eventually survive, and Modern English recruits *you*, *they*, and *people* in the function once served by its birthright *man*.

Rissanen surmises that the disappearance of *me* was due to two factors. If I read him correctly, his proposition that *me* "was too weak for the subject position" leads us to ask why similarly weak forms survive across Germanic, such as the unemphatic forms in Dutch (*je* for *jij*, etc.).[10]

His other suggestion is that homonymy with the oblique *me*, especially with impersonal verbs (*me semeth*), was a factor. Yet Rissanen himself elsewhere (517) notes that "admittedly, homonymy and disambiguation offer only a shaky argument for the loss of forms," and this is especially à propos here. Crucially, it is likely that in the spoken language oblique *me* and indefinite *me* were not homophones: the former retained a long vowel, while the vowel in *me* was likely a weakened one such as schwa (Meier 1953: 179–82, cited in Rissanen 1987). Thus especially given that we are dealing with phonetically similar but hardly identical forms, the homonymy argument is weakened in view of, for example, *det* ([de:]) "it" and *de* "they" in Swedish, which like oblique and indefinite *me* in Middle English occur with the same verbal ending in the present (since Swedish has but one across person and number). While one might argue that the increasing prevalence of *dom* as "they" in Swedish responds to this homonymy, note that *dej* ([dɛj]) is now established in colloquial Swedish in the second-person singular, creating yet another near-hononymy with *det* even in the absence of conjugational allomorphs of verbal inflection to signal a distinction in meaning. Then beyond Germanic, there are, of course, cases like *lei* used both as "she" and as a term of polite address in Italian (both with the same third-person verbal ending), and the absence of a number distinction in third-person pronouns in spoken French (*il/ils, elle/elles*), despite there being no verb endings to distinguish them.

And meanwhile, obviously neither of these two explanations would apply to the more robust form *man* that persisted alongside its more deeply grammaticalized descendant *me*. One might decide that the disappearance of the distinct indefinite pronoun 'lust happened." Yet as Strang (1970: 267) puts it, "No satisfactory all-purpose substitute for it has ever been found," thus leaving the absence of a single indefinite pronoun to combine with the concurrent disappearance of *thou* in rendering the English pronominal array the most context-dependent of any Germanic language. Of course, in larger view, this is just one of the many developments we have seen that are all symptomatic of a clear trend toward underspecification, and it is far beyond the realm of inflectional loss.

## 4. Implications

That one language can be overspecified in a *particular area* compared to another one is clear to all analysts. However, linguists often claim that overall, languages "balance out" in terms of complexity of this kind (e.g., Edwards 1994: 90; Bickerton 1995: 67; O'Grady, Dobrovolsky, and Aronoff 1997: 6; Crystal 1987: 6–7). But this assumption has never been investigated in any wide-ranging fashion, and it is ultimately more an article of faith than an empirical observation. Those few examining the issue more closely have tended to venture that, more properly, all languages are complex to a considerable, but not equal, degree (Crowley 2000, Gil 2001).

In this light, it must be reiterated that while I do not claim that English is a "simple" language in the cross-linguistic sense, I do claim that English is significantly less complex overall—in the specific senses of overspecification and complexity presented in section 2—than its sisters. The contrast I refer to is illustrated by the comparative (table 11.3). Lass (1987: 318) finds related results in an analogous table (table 11.4). Lass (332) also makes a comparison of English with Afrikaans and Yiddish specifically, treating these three as uniquely impacted by contact (table 11.5). He again shows that English surpasses the other two in loss of Germanic features (German and Dutch are included for contrast).

In Lass's first table, English and Afrikaans come out even and are close to even in the second table. However, Lass focuses on inflectional features, which automatically brings English and Afrikaans to the fore since both have been shorn of so much inflectional morphology. My treatment, in expanding our perspective to features beyond inflection, demonstrates that Afrikaans is in fact much more conservative than English overall. Importantly, the relative innovativeness of English has consisted not only of the *transformation* of original materials, but of simply *shedding* much of it where none of its sisters have.

Indeed, it is difficult to conceive of any complex of *original Germanic features* that would yield a chart where any Germanic language but English proved to have lost all of the features while the other languages including English had retained all or most of them. Obviously, my table 11.3 can fairly elicit the objection that it is not representative of the Germanic inheritance, my having potentially "stacked the deck" by choosing features absent in English and neglecting the possibility that English may have retained just as many features that many or most Germanic languages have lost.

However, the results are, in fact, the same, even when we bring to bear a more representative array of the Germanic legacy. Table 11.6 provides a generous outlay

TABLE 11.3. Losses in English compared to other Germanic languages

| | Ger | Du | Yi | Fr | Sc | No | Da | Ic | Fa | Afr | OE | E |
|---|---|---|---|---|---|---|---|---|---|---|---|---|
| Inherent reflexives | ▓ | ▓ | ▓ | ▓ | ▓ | ▓ | ▓ | ▓ | ▓ | ▓ | ▓ | |
| External possessors | ▓ | ▓ | ▓ | ▓ | ▓ | ▓ | ▓ | ▓ | ▓ | | ▓ | |
| Gender beyond noun | ▓ | ▓ | ▓ | ▓ | ▓ | ▓ | ▓ | ▓ | ▓ | | ▓ | |
| Loss of prefixes | ▓ | ▓ | ▓ | ▓ | ▓ | ▓ | ▓ | ▓ | ▓ | ▓ | | |
| Directional adverbs | ▓ | ▓ | ▓ | ▓ | ▓ | ▓ | ▓ | ▓ | ▓ | ▓ | | |
| *be*-perfect | ▓ | ▓ | ▓ | ▓ | | ▓ | ▓ | ▓ | ▓ | ▓ | | |
| Passive *become* verb | ▓ | ▓ | ▓ | ▓ | ▓ | ▓ | ▓ | ▓ | ▓ | ▓ | | |
| V2 | ▓ | ▓ | ▓ | ▓ | ▓ | ▓ | ▓ | ▓ | ▓ | ▓ | | |
| Singular *you* | ▓ | ▓ | ▓ | ▓ | ▓ | ▓ | ▓ | ▓ | ▓ | ▓ | | |
| Indefinite pronoun | ▓ | ▓ | ▓ | ▓ | ▓ | ▓ | ▓ | | | ▓ | | |

Abbreviations: German, Dutch, Yiddish, Frisian, Scandinavian, Norwegian, Danish, Icelandic, Faroese, Afrikaans, Old English, English

Shading indicates retention; white space indcates loss.

TABLE 11.4. Losses in English (Lass 1987)

| | Eng | Fr | Du | Afr | Ger | Yi | Ic | Fa | No | Da | Sc |
|---|---|---|---|---|---|---|---|---|---|---|---|
| Grammatical gender | | ■ | ■ | | ■ | ■ | ■ | ■ | ■ | ■ | ■ |
| Rich case marking | | ■ | | | ■ | ■ | ■ | | | | |
| 3-person verb morph. | | ■ | ■ | | ■ | ■ | ■ | ■ | | | |
| Sing./pl. Verb morph. | | | ■ | | ■ | ■ | ■ | ■ | | | |
| Subjunctive | ■ | | | ■ | ■ | | ■ | | | | |
| Strong/weak verbs | ■ | ■ | ■ | ■ | ■ | ■ | ■ | ■ | ■ | ■ | ■ |
| Strong/weak adjectives | | ■ | ■ | ■ | ■ | ■ | ■ | ■ | ■ | ■ | ■ |
| V2 | | ■ | ■ | ■ | ■ | ■ | ■ | ■ | ■ | ■ | ■ |
| Long/short vowels | ■ | ■ | ■ | ■ | ■ | | ■ | ■ | ■ | ■ | ■ |
| Robust umlaut | ■ | | | | ■ | ■ | ■ | ■ | ■ | ■ | ■ |

Abbreviations: English, Frisian, Dutch, Afrikaans, German, Yiddish, Icelandic, Faroese, Norwegian, Danish, Scandinavian

Shading indicates retention; white space indicates loss.

of grammatical features that are traditionally treated as tracing to Proto-Germanic, for good measure assembled through reference to two sources, Voyles (1992: 227–79) and Ramat (1998). It is clear from this list, especially to Germanicists, that it would quite impossible to derive from it a table of features that English has retained *that all or most of its sisters has not*. More to the point, there is not a single feature on the list of this sort. Admittedly, I added a few features from table 11.3 not traditionally examined in studies of Proto-Germanic: inherent reflexives, external possessor marking, the *be*-perfect, and the *become* passive. However, I am unaware of any other features omitted in Proto-Germanic surveys that are retained in English but are rare

TABLE 11.5. Loss in the "contact heavy" Germanic languages (Lass 1987)

| | Eng | Afr | Yi | Ger | Du |
|---|---|---|---|---|---|
| Loss of past vs. perfect | | ■ | ■ | | |
| Loss of infinitive suffix | ■ | ■ | | | |
| Loss of sentence-brace[a] | ■ | | ■ | | |
| Loss of SOV | ■ | ■ | ■ | | |
| Loss of gender | ■ | ■ | | | |
| Loss of verb marking | ■ | | | | |

Abbreviations: English, Afrikaans, Yiddish, German, Dutch

Shading indicates loss; white space indicates retention.

a. This refers to the separation of auxiliary and main verb by objects, adverbials, and so on (*Ich habe den Brief gestern geschrieben* "I wrote the book yesterday").

TABLE 11.6. Reconstructed Proto-Germanic features

1. Nominal inflection classes specific to Germanic
2. Nominative, genitive, dative, accusative case marking in NP markers in both numbers on nominals and demonstratives, instrumental in singular

3. Strong/weak distinction in adjectives
4. Masculine, feminine, and neuter adjectival classes
5. Nominative. genitive, dative, and accusative inflections in singular and plural in masculine and feminine, locative and instrumental inflections in masculine singular
6. Simple singular/plural distinction in neuter
7. Comparative and superlative suffixes -ō, -az
8. Small class of suppletive comparative and superlative forms
9. Interrogative adjectives decline as strong

10. Pronominals in nominative, genitive, dative, and accusative in singular and plural
11. Dual paradigms
12. Reflexive *sīn
13. Inherent reflexive construction
14. External possessive constructions

15. One to four declineable
16. Four to ten undeclinable
17. Eleven and twelve remnants of duodecimal system (*ain-lif "one left over," *twa-lif)
18. Thirteen to nineteen composed of unit numeral + "ten"
19. 20, 30, 40, 50, 60 composed of unit numeral + *tigīzjuz "10-ness"
20. 70 to 90 composed of genitive plural of unit numeral + derivational *-t + *kn̥tom
21. 1000 derived from pie *tūs "large" + *kn̥tom reflex[a]

22. Strong/weak distinction in verbs
23. Verbal inflection classes specific to germanic (class vii forms past and participial form via reduplication)
24. Present and preterite paradigms in active and subjunctive (dual inflections for 1P and 2P except in preterite subjunctive)
25. Present passive indicative and subjunctive paradigms (same inflection allomorph for all numbers in plural in both of the above cases)
26. Infinitive
27. Participles for present, past and past passive
28. Use of be in intransitive auxiliary + participle constructions
29. Use of become for passive
30. Preterite-present verbs
31. Athematic verbs (be, do, go, stand)
32. will-marked "subjunctive"

33. Adverbial suffixes—ē, -ō, -ba
34. Adverbial comparative and superlative suffixes -ōz,-ōst
35. Suppletive well for good
36. Directional adverbs for "at x," "to x," "from x"

37. Prepositions doubling as preverbs
38. Conjunctions *endi / *undi "and," *auk "also," þauh "but," *iƀa / *uƀa "if"
39. OV word order
40. Large number of derivational prefixes and suffixes

a. Numeral reconsuctions after Voyles (1992: 245–46).

to nonexistent elsewhere in Germanic, and I have the distinct impression that few could identify many such features if any.

Certainly English has developed *individual* features of overspecification and complexity that its sisters have not. My thesis is that there was a significant disruption in the transmission of English at one point in its history, but this scenario requires that, after this, English would naturally drift into its own elaborations, as all languages do. Thus English is unique among Germanic languages in its *do*-support; in its conventionalization of the present participle with *be* as obligatory in marking imperfectivity in the present, thereby rendering the bare verb zero-marked for habituality; and in its distinction of shades of futurity with *will*, *going to*, and *be* + present participle.

Nor, however, have the other Germanic languages simply retained more of the Germanic legacy while otherwise developing no new features. On the contrary, just as we would expect, they developed overspecifications and complexities of their own after branching off from Proto-Germanic. The result was the many well-known Germanic features absent in English that cannot be treated as Proto-Germanic, such as the conventionalized modal particles in German, Dutch, Frisian, and Mainland Scandinavian; tone in Swedish; and lesser-known cases such as noun incorporation in Frisian.

Thus to wit: while English consists of a massively abbreviated Germanic legacy plus a few later developments, its sisters retain much more of the Germanic legacy *plus* later developments of their own. A claim that English must necessarily be equal in overspecification and complexity to its sisters is, in the strict sense, illogical. It would require either that (1) *not one* of the several other Germanic languages has drifted into as many new developments as English over the past several centuries, or that (2) English for some reason was uniquely innovative, as if once "burned" by extensive second-language acquisition, a grammar is somehow inherently driven to restore a particular degree of needless elaboration. Obviously, neither scenario has any theoretical motivation, leaving the conclusion that English is, indeed, the least overspecified language in the Germanic group.

## 5. Reassessing the Scandinavian impact

One response to the contrast in table 11.3 might be to suppose that English just shed these features by chance. Certain members of a given family have long been observed to be more innovative than others. There are often no apparent "reasons" for this, with linguists treating the difference in conservativity as parents might treat personality differences among their children: they just "are."

While authors such as Trudgill (1989, 1996) have noted that widespread acquisition as a second language often renders a language less phonetically and morphologically complex than its relatives, Crowley (2000) gives clear demonstration of a case where a complexity differential of this kind is unlikely to trace to contact effects. The Oceanic language Ura is less complex morphophonemically and inflectionally, and it marks fewer categories overtly with its inflections than its sister Sye, despite Ura having no documented history of use as a lingua franca. Many might prefer to treat English as the "Ura" of Germanic.

However, the relative prevalence of contact in English's history (while hardly presuming that its sisters developed in isolation) offers a compelling suggestion that English is instead closer to being the "Swahili" of Germanic. Swahili is unusual among Bantu languages in lacking tone, having shed a number of noun class categories and verbal inflections and having simplified its nonverbal predication system, this being due to its being used more as a second language than as a first over the past several centuries (McWhorter 1994b). While hardly a creole, Swahili gives clear evidence of a slight but decisive break in transmission in its timeline, and few Bantuists would classify it as "innovative" due strictly to internal factors.

We will reject two other possible explanations. It is unlikely that English's departure from the Germanic template was a function of its isolation on an island; generally, this kind of isolation is associated with relative conservatism, Icelandic and Faroese being the obviously pertinent cases here. Furthermore, it cannot be upheld that the standardization of English was the culprit. While one might propose that koineization between speakers of various dialects of English in the London area led to a streamlining of the language, this would leave the question as to why similar processes did not leave standard French (developed amid contact between dialects brought to the Île-de-France region) or Russian (developed amid contact between several dialects in Moscow), similarly simplified in comparison to their sisters. In any case, most of the features I have covered were defunct or near-defunct long before the 1400s.

## 5.1. Evaluating the alternatives

It would seem, then, that the task facing us is to choose between possible contact explanations. To investigate where a contact-induced break in transmission might have occurred in English, we are faced with a choice between four potential culprits.

### 5.5.1. Norman French

I accept the arguments of Thomason and Kaufman (1988) and others that the Norman occupation cannot have caused a significant break in the transmission of English. The invaders were too slight in number and too far removed from the general population to affect the structure of a language that, meanwhile, was spoken by millions of people. I would propose that they could not have had any significant influence on the language beyond the lexical (which would thus encompass derivational affixes).

### 5.5.2. Low Dutch

I also find it implausible that Low Dutch varieties,[11] imported from 1150 to about 1700 by Flemish immigrants and agents of the Hanseatic League (Viereck 1993, Thomason and Kaufman 1988: 321–25), had any significant influence on English grammar. There is nothing in accounts of the Hanseatic League like Pagel (1983) to suggest that Low German speakers were thick enough on the ground in any one place to influence general speech patterns; on the contrary, such sources indicate that the Hanseatic agents were generally housed in their own quarters of town. Moreover, if

Low Dutch speakers' non-native English had influenced the language, we would also expect that their lexical contribution would extend into the grammatical realm. Yet it did not to any significant or conclusive extent (Bense 1939), which would include the -*kin* derivational suffix noted by Thomason and Kaufman (1988: 325). These authors (323) also propose that Low Dutch lent several dialects of English an enclitic object form for *she* and *they*, /əs/, but Voss (1995) is rather compellingly skeptical of this account, as well as others concerning sound changes. Overall, despite Viereck's (1993) and Danchev's (1997: 101) useful call to consider that Low Dutch had greater influence on English than traditionally thought, I suspect that in the final analysis, we will find that this influence was no more significant than that of Dutch on English in the New Amsterdam colony in early America. Large numbers of settlers almost always affect the lexicon of the language they encounter, but their numbers alone do not entail transformation of the grammar.

### 5.5.3. Brythonic

Vennemann (2001) argues that interference from Insular Celtic was the culprit in rendering English so typologically distinct from its sisters and Indo-European in general. While he stresses the absence of external possessive constructions and the presence of *be*-marked imperfectives in Insular Celtic, his argument can be extended in view of the fact that Brythonic also lacks inherent reflexives, Indo-European's derivational prefixes, V2, the *be*-perfect, an indefinite pronoun, and a *become*-passive (Martin Haspelmath, pers. comm.).

This hypothesis is superficially tempting. However, the first problem is that we would expect that a structural impact so profound would be accompanied by a robust lexical one. Yet the Celtic contribution to the English lexicon beyond place names, two now defunct items incorporated on the continent before the Germanic settlement of England, and seven mostly defunct ones introduced by Christianizing missionaries from Ireland is so small that Kastovsky (1992: 318–19) requires barely half a page to list the fourteen, most now obsolete. To be sure, Thomason and Kaufman (1988: 116–18) note that lexical loans amid shift-based interference are often not as numerous as in cases of one language borrowing from another. However, the paucity of Celtic loans in English is so glaring that it becomes appropriate to question whether any interference in fact took place.

An equally grave problem is timing. Vennemann (2001: 356) supposes that Celtic was no longer spoken in the north of England after the late eighth century at the latest, whereas English begins its sharp departure from the Germanic template after the Norman Invasion, four centuries later. Vennemann argues (364) that this delay may have been due to a diglossic distinction between the written register and common speech, the latter only committed to paper after the "liberation" of English upon the lifting of the documentational "blackout" during the Norman occupation.

This is a deft argument, and it is most likely true that Old English documents trailed behind developments in the spoken varieties (as remained the case throughout the language's history and is still the case, to an extent, to this day). But it raises a question: If the Celtic influence was decisive enough to erase external possessive constructions and contribute a new progressive construction, then why precisely did the influence stop there? Vennemann concurs with Gensler (forthcoming) that Celtic itself owes its VSO word order, lack of external possessive constructions, and other departures from Indo-European patterns to Semitic influence, considering English's transformation due ultimately to Semitic interference passed on through Insular Celtic. However, why, then, did Celtic interference not render English VSO?

In general, we have vivid evidence as to what happens to English with the extensive and concretely documented interference from Celtic namely, Hiberno-English. Here we see closer and unmistakeable parallels to Celtic, such the *after* + V immediate past calque and interrogative constructions such as *Is it out of your mind you are?* On top of this is a vast quantity of Gaelic lexical borrowings. Certainly there are differences between Irish and British Celtic varieties, but this merely leads us to ask why English does not display clear parallels to, for example, Welsh as opposed to Gaelic. As presented to date, Vennemann's hypothesis begs the question as to why English in Great Britain is not as rife with unequivocally Celtic-derived constructions and loanwords as Hiberno-English is.

### 5.1.4. Process of elimination

This leaves us with the Scandinavian invaders, who arrived in England in the late ninth and early tenth centuries; roughly speaking, Danes settled in the northeast area that came to be called the Danelaw while Norwegians later settled in the northwest. The Scandinavians settled among the general population rather than ruling from afar as an elite as the Norman French did, often marrying Anglo-Saxon women. The massive lexical effect of this contact is hardly in dispute, eliminating one serious problem in the Low Dutch and Celtic cases. In terms of sheer number of words, the Normans of course had a vast effect as well. But they imposed their language mainly "from above," lending content words, generally hewing toward the formal realm. In contrast, the Scandinavian legacy included content words of even the homeliest nature (*neck, window, knife, skirt, happy*, etc.), and extended to grammatical words such as *they, their, them, though, both, same, against*, and others since lost. This alone indicates a highly intimate contact scenario.

Our question, then, is whether the Scandinavian influence on English went even deeper. I propose that there are indeed indications that the Scandinavian invasions were responsible for the very decrease in overspecification and complexity that I presented in section 3. In this, I will attempt an argument similar to that of Poussa (1982) but in more extended fashion. I will also complement O'Neil's (1978) observation that English is one of *various* Germanic languages whose development was affected by contact: first, in fashioning an argument within the context of language contact studies as they have progressed since he wrote; second, by exploring why the degree of reduction in English was greater than in any other Germanic language.

### 5.2. Support for Scandinavian influence: Timing

The first piece of evidence pointing specifically to the Scandinavian influence is evidence that many of these features persisted longest in regions where Scandinavians did not settle, or in those where place-names suggest that they were less robustly represented. Under this perspective, we might assume that these features would be represented even more vividly in these regions even today if a particular dialect that emerged in the Danelaw standard English had not gone on to dilute the regional dialects via sociological pressure to such a degree. To wit: if England had remained a preindustrial society where literacy was largely limited to elites, then we might hypothesize that English varieties outside of the Danelaw would remain "card-carrying" Germanic descendants.

The evidence here is solely a first plank in my argument. The vast majority of our substantial sources on regional grammars (as opposed to lexicons and phonologies) were written after standard English came to prevail. As such, in the technical sense, most of our views of nonstandard dialects of England treat varieties in decline, having long ago taken their place on a pole of variation between standard and nonstandard forms. However, even these sources give some support to my thesis:

1. *External possessor marking.* Upton, Parry, and Widdowson (1994: 488) record *wring the neck of him* rather analogous to the locative Scandinavian configuration of this strategy in Derbyshire and, pointedly, Cornwall, where there was no Scandinavian settlement at all. (It may also be relevant that they record *He's pulling that chap his leg* in Yorkshire, the western region of which was rather thinly settled by Scandinavians.)

2. *Grammatical gender.* Scandinavian settlement was concentrated in the northeast; Lass (1992: 113) notes that "loss of inflection [in the noun phrase] is earliest in the east and north, the south and west generally remaining more conservative." The loss of gender on the definite article began in the north and then was attested only variably in the southwest Midlands in the late 1200s (Lass 1992: 113); meanwhile, the old three-way distinction persisted in the south at this time (Strang 1970: 267), and traces of gender marking hung on in Kent as late as 1340 (ibid., Lass 1992: 113).

   Indicatively, of the regions where Upton et al. (1994: 486–87) record the use of *he/him* and/or *she/her* to refer to objects), sixteen out of twenty are outside of Scandinavian concentration (most south of the Danelaw).

   There is also evidence that remnants of the gender distinction persisted in especially grammaticalized form in the Viking-free southwest. In the early 1200s, there is occasional gender marking of inanimates there in documents (Strang 1970: 265), and this was still attested in the late nineteenth century in Barnes's description of Dorset dialect. Here, Barnes (1886: 17–18) describes precisely what we might expect to have evolved in English short of "intervention": a distinction between common and neuter genders, which he terms "personal" and "impersonal." The "personal" class includes "full shapen things, or things to which the Almighty or man has given a shape for an end" and includes people, living things, and tools: thus of a tree, one said *He's a-cut down* but for water, *It's a-dried up*. The distinction extended to demonstratives (*"theäse"* vs. *this, "thik"* vs. *that*).

In reference to inflection in general, Upton et al. (490) record the infinitive marker *-(e)n* in Derbyshire, Westmorland, and Lancashire, areas of thin Scandinavian settlement (with the exception of *putten*, which occurs in Yorkshire and Lincolnshire as well). They record infinitives ending in [i] only in Monmouthshire, Kent, Cornwall, Somerset, Devon, Lancashire, Derbyshire, Shropshire, and Staffordshire.[12]

In sum, was it merely an accident that the loss of grammatical gender did not begin in the south? The evidence in this paper (including that to come) suggests that it was not.

3. *Directional adverbs.* Upton et al. (92) find variations on *come hither* only in regions south of the Danelaw except Lincolnshire. They find *Where to is it?* or *Where is it to?* only in Monmouthshire, Somerset, Wiltshire, Cornwall, Devon, and Dorset (ibid. 502).

4. *V2.* In one report, V2 persists in Kentish documents while eroding elsewhere in English (Kroch and Taylor 1997: 312). These authors' analysis even offers more fine-grained evidence that the erosion of V2 was caused by Scandinavian. They argue (318–20) that the transition from "symmetric" (verb movement in both matrix and subordinate clauses) to asymmetric (verb movement only in the matrix clause) V2 was occasioned by the inflectional loss that Scandinavian settlers' incomplete acquisitior of English led to. Under the assumption that complete loss of V2 would only be possible with sharp diminution of inflection, the implication of Kroch and Taylor's analysis is that the transition to asymmetric V2 was an intermediate stage between the original configuration and today's. By extension, this implies that the disappearance of V2 was initiated by language contact in the Danelaw.

5. *Inherent reflexive marking.* Upton, Parry, and Widdowson (1994: 488) show *sit thee down* and variants persisting in nonstandard dialects throughout England. While they find *laid him down* and *laid her down* only in regions where Scandinavian settlement was relatively thin according to Wakelin (1972: 20)—Cheshire, Derbyshire, and Staffordshire—it is also documented in heavily Scandinavianized Cumberland (Brilioth 1913: 107) and West Yorkshire (Wright 1892: 120, Hedevind 1967: 242). However, it is perhaps notable that Upton et al. only find attestations with other verbs (ibid. 488–89) (*they play(en) them* [*they disport themselves*]) in Lancashire and Derbyshire. Possibly the usage conventionalized as an archaism with heavily used *sit* and *lie* throughout England (cf. Hedevind's description of the feature as used only with "certain verbs," giving the usual *sit* and *lie* as examples [242]), but persisted more robustly in areas with less Scandinavian influence.

## 5.3. Support for Scandinavian influence: Transfer

Modern dialectal remnants, however, are only one indication that Scandinavian contact profoundly affected the course of English's evolution. Transfer evidence provides further, and more striking, support for the hypothesis.

Thomason and Kaufman's (1988: 302–3) verdict on the evidence of transfer from Scandinavian in English is the following: "The Norse influence on English was pervasive, in the sense that its results are found in all parts of the language; but it was not deep, except in the lexicon. Norse influence could not have modified the basic typology of English because the two were highly similar in the first place." This conclusion is justified for their masterful argument on the basis of the features they treat as part of their "Norsification package." However, other evidence suggests that the Norse influence was indeed deep, and that Thomason and Kaufman's Norsification package, comprising mostly phonological and morphological traits, various grammatical items, and some lexical items, constitutes but a subset of the relevant evidence.

Following tradition, Thomason and Kaufman assume that Old English and Old Norse were too similar for structural transfer to be particularly relevant to analyzing their effect on one another in contact. Yet a closer look at Old Norse reveals grammatical differences that are crucial to this thesis. Specifically, no fewer than six of our ten losses in English have parallels in aspects of Old Norse hitherto overlooked, to my knowledge, in studies of the Danelaw situation:

1. *Inherent reflexives.* In Old Norse, the reflexive use of the first-person and third-person pronouns had eroded and affixed to the verb as a suffix, the latter used in all persons but the first singular: *bindomk* "I tie myself," *býsk* "you arm yourself," *staksk* "he stabbled himself" (Heusler 1950: 107). This extended to inherent reflexives: *þeir setiask niþr* "they sat down," *er hefnezk á honom* "you revenge yourselves upon him," *þetta felsk honom yel í skap* "that felt good to him, agreed with him" (ibid. 137–38). Use of free pronouns in the reflexive was not unknown but was largely restricted to dative forms (*hann brá sér* "he wandered"), but even here was variable (*hann brásk* was also grammatical) (ibid. 138).

   The variability of inherent reflexive marking by Middle English may have been the result of a tendency for Old Norse speakers to omit the inherent reflexive pronouns in speaking English. Use of the full pronoun was the marked case in their native language, and meanwhile English lacked any equivalent of their reflexive inflection. English specialists often note that morphology could be shed in the Danelaw because it was incidental to communication. Morphological marking of inherent reflexivity would have fallen under this rubric by definition.

   Thus because it was encoded morphologically, Old Norse speakers would have been comfortable refraining from marking the distinction when speaking English just as Modern English speakers are.

2. *External possessives*. Scandinavian is unique in Germanic in encoding external possession with the locative rather than the dative (cf. examples (7), (8), (9)). Faced with this disjunction between external possessor encoding in the two languages, Scandinavians may have taken the choice of eliminating the distinction altogether, given that it was not vital to the expression of the relevant concepts. This is a common process in the development of koines, for example, where often the koine eschews features that were present in most or all of the source varieties but expressed with different morphemes or strategies (see discussion in section 5.4).

3. *Derivational prefixes*. The absence of the core Germanic verbal prefixes in Icelandic ar Faroese traces back to Old Norse (Heusler 1950: 40). It could be that the rapid eclipse of these prefixes in English was due to the absence of cognates in Old Norse speakers' native language.

4. Be-*perfect*. In Old Norse, as in Modem Icelandic, the *be*-perfect largely connoted the resultative and the passive (Heusler 1950: 136). Its use as a true perfect was limited to a few intransitive verbs such as "to go": *ek em gengenn* "I have gone" (Brenner 1882: 129). This may have been the spur for the disappearance of the feature in English, including the possibility Mitchell (1985: 302–4) notes that what has been analyzed as a *be*-perfect in Old English may have actually been *only* a resultative construction.[13]

5. Become-*passive*. In Old Norse, the passive was usually expressed with *vera* "to be." *Werþa* "to become" was relatively restricted in meaning, encoding roughly the saliently active semantics of Modern English's *get*-passive:

(20)    þǽr    saker    skal    fyrst dǿma,
        the.PL issue.PL should first adjudge.INF
        er    fyrra surnar    **varþ**    eige urn dǿmt.
        that last    summer become not to judgment
        "First the complaints should be decided upon that didn't manage to get to judgment last summer." (Heusler 1950: 137; translation mine)[14]

This restricted usage may have been a cause of the otherwise mysterious absence of English's *weorþan* after Old English.

6. *Indefinite man*. Icelandic and Faroese lack a *man*-cognate, and already in Old Norse it was recessive (Heusler 1950: 147), generally replaced by impersonal verb constructions or third-person verbs without pronouns. This may possibly have set in motion a deemphasis on the use of Old English's *man*-cognate that eventually resulted in its disappearance early in Middle English.

English is traditionally considered closest to Dutch and Frisian. But in many aspects where Old Norse and its descendants depart from the Germanic pattern, they parallel English, although having overall retained a great deal more of their Germanic legacy. Only Old Norse and its modern descendants offer anything approaching six out of ten features that could be expected to result in elimination in a contact situation with English, a clustering which I did not even expect to find upon beginning this investigation. This finding especially in congruence with the dialectal evidence adduced in 5.2 suggests a specific effect from Scandinavian. In addition, it further weakens the potential import of the correspondences between English and Celtic, given that Old Norse offered just as many features which we could expect to occasion loss in English in a contact situation but *in addition* left behind a rich lexical legacy.

To wit, in reference to Thomason and Kaufman's statement that "Norse influence could not have modified the basic typology of English because the two were highly similar in the first place," the similarity dilutes somewhat on closer examination, to an extent that may well have had significant impact on the development of Modern English.

## 5.4. Support for Scandinavian influence: Reduction

Generally, discussion of the Scandinavian influence on English is largely restricted to transfer effects: sound changes and lexical borrowings. I have attempted to add possible structural transfers to the relevant discussion. As such, however, it might be objected that my attempt to expand our conception of the Scandinavian influence is hindered where Old English and Old Norse have parallel structures, under the assumption that English would likely have retained these features rather than shed them.

But as Thomason and Kaufman (1988: 129) note, when a population shifts to a new language and their rendition of the language ousts the original native one, then transfer effects often occur alongside evidence of incomplete acquisition that is, outright *reduction* rather than transfer. Importantly, these effects often occur even where the languages in question have parallel or cognate structures.

### 5.4.1. Traditionally accepted: Inflection and grammatical morphemes

Scholars of English's history traditionally recognize this in the area of inflection, where it is often reconstructed that when Old English and Old Norse speakers were confronted with equivalent but phonetically differing inflections, they simply shed them to ease communication (O'Neil 1978: 256–60 being an extended presentation). For our purposes we must refine the conception somewhat.

Most writers appear to suppose that this must have been a two-way affair, communication occurring as speakers of both languages shaved away their native inflections, leaving an analytic "common denominator" comprehensible to both. However, it is questionable that this would have allowed significant communication. Lass (1987: 52) and Kastovsky (1992: 328–9) suggest that claims that Old English and Old Norse were virtually mutually intelligible are exaggerated, and I would agree: this idea strikes me as reflecting the written medium, allowing us to "wrap our heads around" phonetic correspondences at leisure and concealing the obstacles to comprehension effected by accent, intonation, and morphophonemics. Analyzed side by side, Old English and Old Norse suggest no more mutual intelligibility than that between, for example, Serbo-Croatian and Bulgarian or Spanish and Italian.

Moreover, mere contact between closely related varieties hardly *entails* the dilution of infection. Contact alone, amid extensive *first*-language bilingualism, can lead to a language with a mixture of inflections from several languages, but no less inflected overall than its pre-contact form. *Pace* arguments like O'Neil's (1978: 256–60), this is even true when languages are closely related, despite initial impressions that the confusions created by cognate affixes would simply drive speakers to shed morphology altogether. One example is Rusyn, formed through contact between dialects of Ukrainian, Slovak, and Serbo-Croatian (Harasowska 1999).

Inflectional loss is symptomatic of a more specific phenomenon: non-native acquisition. Specifically, it is more likely that the inflectional loss resulted from Old Norse speakers' incomplete acquisition of English (cf. Danchev 1997: 90). Thomason and Kaufman's (1988: 119–20) stipulation that interference effects are likely to be stronger in cases of rapid shift over "one or two generations" is also relevant, given that these authors are of the opinion that Norse was no longer spoken in England after 1100 (ibid. 282), disappearing within one or two generations of the reintegration of the Danelaw into the English polity (284, 286).

The Norse grammatical morphemes that English incorporated make a further case for the non-native acquisition effect. A language generally only borrows grammatical, as opposed to lexical, items in contexts of bilingualism (among at least a subset of the population). The question here is whether the Norse were more likely to be bilingual thus developing an English bedecked with Norse grammatical items than the native English speakers were.

There would appear to be little question here. The Danes and Norwegians were newcomers, who were largely illiterate and thus did not impose their language in writing or in government and eventually gave it up. Obviously the impulse toward bilingualism would have been much stronger among the Vikings than among the English. In this light, items such as *they/them/their*, *both*, *same*, and others would stand as remnants of Scandinavian brought into the English spoken by, first, immigrants and then, just as plausibly, by succeeding generations bilingual in Old Norse and Old English. It is rarely if ever acknowledged that after the first generation, descendants of the Scandinavian invaders may well have begun to speak English as well as Norse even among themselves, as is typical of shifting speakers, with Norse and English perhaps taking their place in a kind of diglossia. As such, for Norse deescendants born in England, an English sprinkled with the occasional Norse grammatical item would have been not only comprehensible but even a marker of, if we may, "ethnic" kinship.

## 5.4.2. *Extending the paradigm*

These observations, then, suggest that English could easily have shed even features it *shared* with Old Norse, if its fate was determined by non-native speakers' proficient yet approximate rendition, as the timing and transfer evidence suggest. This in itself is hardly a venturesome proposal, the conception having long been considered unexceptionable as applied to morphology, perhaps because the difficulty of acquiring a foreign language's morphology is so familiar and readily perceptible. My suggestion is simply that we extend this mechanism beyond morphology, especially given that modern language contact studies offer no grounds for supposing that this would be scientifically inappropriate.

The relevant comparison, for example, is with koines, such as Siegel's (1987: 185–210) description of the koine Hindustani of Fiji, developed during contact between speakers of a range of divergent varieties of the Hindustani dialect complex. Certainly, to an extent, the koine has picked lexical and morphological features "cafeteria" style from assorted dialects rather than shed the features. However, on balance, the koine is not as elaborated as any of these dialects, instead being markedly simpler in the formal sense than any of these, *even when the dialects all display the feature in question.* This includes the elimination of the three-way formality distinction in second-person pronouns, a general tendency toward replacing synthetic with analytic forms, and a strong tendency to replace SOV order with SVO (ibid. 198–99). (This last is especially indicative regarding the loss of V2 in English.)

A less well- known example is the Riau dialect of Indonesian (Malay) described by David Gil (1994). While developed among speakers of languages closely related to Indonesian and to one another, Riau Indonesian has vastly simplified Indonesian's valence-marking morphological apparatus which are of much greater semantic and syntactic import than are mere gender or person/number markers—and other grammatical features with close cognates in the languages spoken by its creators, such as Minangkabau.

These cases demonstrate that even when languages in contact are closely related, reduction can play as significant a part in the outcome as exchange of materials *far beyond mere inflection.*[15] In processes of linguistic accommodation, speakers often contribute a less overspecified and complexified rendition of their language. The extreme manifestation here is Foreigner Talk; a less radical manifestation would be the tendency for creators of creoles to contribute a "streamlined" version of their native grammars to the new language, such as among Oceanic speakers (Keesing 1988; Siegel, Sandeman, and Corne 2000). Koine scenarios exhibit an analogous process, and there is no theoretical reason that this would not have been the case in the Danelaw.

### 5.4.3. Two mechanisms for fostering underspecification and simplification in English–Norse contact

5.4.3.1. TRIGGER WEAKENING    In many cases, already in Old English features were ripe for marginalization in a contact situation, because they occurred only variably. This is the case with inherent reflexives, external possessors, directional adverbs, the *be*-perfect, the *become* passive, V2, and indefinite *man*.

It is tempting to hypothesize that the optionality of these features in Old English was itself due to Scandinavian contact. But this is unlikely given that most Old English documentation from 900 A.D. onward is in the West Saxon dialect, outside of Scandinavian settlement. Crucially, however, this hardly means that these features were used in more tightly conventionalized fashion beyond West Saxon. On the contrary, this kind of variability is attributable to speech varieties that are primarily spoken, as was true of Old English: while it comes down to us in writing, Old English was spoken in a society where literacy was largely limited to an elite. The prevalence of "unfocused" conventions is familiar to any linguist working on an unwritten indigenous language, and is even characteristic of other early Germanic varieties like Gothic and Old Norse itself (in the latter of which inherent reflexives, *become* with the passive, and indefinite *man* were variable). As such, we can assume that the "softness" of the relevant rules was typical of English dialects in general, not just West Saxon.[16]

In any case, this would mean that such features were especially vulnerable to falling below the line of acquirability, via a process outlined by Lightfoot (1997, 1999) namely, the general tendency toward isomorphism and simplification in the generation of non-native varieties would have led Norse speakers to use these features even less in their rendition of English. This could have initiated a decline in frequency of occurrence over generations of the sort that Lightfoot analyzes as weakening and eliminating the sufficient "trigger," in his terms, for its transmission to new generations. Importantly, the weakening of many of these features would have been reinforced by being variable or marginal in Old Norse itself: inherent reflexives, the *be*-perfect, the *become*-passive, and the indefinite *man*.

A modern parallel would be a feature of the Irish Gaelic spoken by second-language learners in Ireland (Henry and Tangney 1999). Equative predications in Irish Gaelic mark the subject as accusative, place it clause-finally, and use a distinct *be*-verb (*Is dochtuir é* [be doctor him] "He is a doctor"). This, however, is an exceptional feature in a language in which "ergative" constructions are otherwise nonexistent English-dominant learners tend to replace this quirk with a construction using the more commonly encountered *be*-verb *tá*, which occurs sentence-initially as verbs typically do in this VSO language, and takes a nominative subject: *Tá sé dochtuir* [be he doctor].

Importantly, *Lightfoot's framework entails no stipulation that a given feature would vanish immediately*. Rather, once initiated, the weakening of a trigger proceeds gradually towards its total obliteration, each generation using a feature less often than the previous one and providing even less stimulus for the next one.[17] As such, my claim is not that contact in the Danelaw would have obliterated the features in table 11.3 immediately, a scenario obviously impossible to support given the documentary evidence.

Certainly the optimally "clean" version of my argument would demonstrate that all of these features evanesce from English before 1200 A.D. but the documentary evidence obviously does not support such a scenario. Our goal is to construct a scientifically responsible explanation to account for the *gradual* disappearance of the features in question, this being as imperative to explain as their more abrupt disappearance would be, given that they were retained in a dozen-odd sister languages. Lightfoot's framework provides a basis for proposing that Scandinavian contact "tripped off" a decline of these features, that only later culminated in complete disappearance.

### 5.4.3.2. GENERAL "TRIMMING" OF OVERSPECIFIED AND COMPLEX FEATURES

Other features may have been eliminated even when robust in both languages. To reiterate, this is the very conception that is common consensus regarding grammatical gender in the noun phrase. I suggest that it was also the case with the collapse of gender distinctions on the articles. A non-native speaker of English, confronted with three forms of the article corresponding to gender assignments that often conflicted between Old English and Old Norse, would plausibly have made do with a single gender-neutral marker rather than applying their native genders to their version of English. Koine data worldwide, such as Fiji Hindustani discussed above, indicate that when structures are cognate but distinct in closely related varieties, the speaker of one of them is as likely to eliminate their reflex of that feature as to preserve it even when doing the latter would not appreciably impede communication.

I also suggest that the gradual disappearance of V2 falls under the same rubric. An analogy is the weakness of SOV order in Fiji's Hindustani koine, created by people all of whom spoke languages where SOV was obligatory. Here, the issue was less structural discrepancies—minor in both the Danelaw and Fiji than the simple impulse toward simplification in non-native speech varieties.

### 5.4.4. Where art thou?

Of the ten features in table 11.3, only *thou* is incommensurate in its history with a thesis that conditions in the Danelaw in general were the key to English's detour from the Germanic template. *Thou* disappears only in the written standard (and even then rather late), but remains robust in nonstandard dialects even within the Danelaw region, regularly appearing in dialect surveys even of twentieth-century speech.

One might suppose that the demise of *thou* in one dialect was merely an accident, just happening to occur in the region that went on to produce the written standard. However, the uniqueness of the development compared with (all dialects of) all of English's sisters as well as with European languages in general remains striking. As a chance occurrence, the eclipse sits as an eternal loose screw, but a more elegant analysis subsumes it under the general trend in English's development toward underspecification. To suppose that the death of a distinct second-person singular pronoun was mere happenstance means that one would find it unremarkable to see the decline occur in a hypothetical English where the other features of (table 11.3 remained intact. In light of the fact that not a single one of the other Germanic languages has taken this route over millennia of existence, I propose that such a development would have been highly unlikely.

Just why this occurred only in the East Midlands dialect will most likely remain a mystery. Perhaps it lends support to Poussa's (1982) argument that this variety was a particularly koineized one serving as a lingua franca between speakers of still-divergent Middle English dialects. But our perspective on *thou* must be informed by its utter anomaly, implausibly linked to any cultural factor local to England and impossible to trace to the influence of Latin on English standardization, since Classical Latin evidenced no such trait. In being the only Germanic language refraining from distinguishing number in the second person absence of pronominal plural marking being a cross-linguistically rare trait that the typologist associates with a few languages in Indonesia and Papua New Guinea—standard English displays one of a great many underspecifications and simplifications which, in their sheer number, suggest an external explanation.

## 5.5. The nature of evidence

Obviously at this point we yearn for particulars of the sociolinguistic terrain in the Danelaw. However, this was a largely illiterate setting of primarily oral communication lost to the ages; the writing that has come down to us was, in broad view, a marginal activity aimed at a small elite. Even the numerical size of the Scandinavian presence remains controversial and most likely unknowable. Thomason and Kaufman (1988: 276, 361–63) cite Sawyer's (1971) arguments that there is no evidence that vast streams of peasant settlers followed in the wake of the invaders, as is often supposed.

However, I propose that the clustering of the changes in the Danelaw region where Scandinavian settlement was heaviest, combined with the correspondences between the losses in English and features absent or marked in Old Norse, implicate the Scandinavian invasions *despite* the lacunae in the sociohistorical record. Sawyer may be correct that this influence was due more to prestige than to brute numbers, and the questions here naturally evoke an interest in the precise mechanics of how a language is transformed by widespread second-language acquisition. But at the end of the day, a preliterate society 1200 years removed from us is unlikely to ever shed much light on this question.

To serve our interest in the on-the-ground sociolinguistic aspects of this kind of process, there are various living or amply recorded analogues to what I propose happened in the Danelaw (e.g., see LaCroix 1967 on vehicular Fula or Siegel 1987 on pidginized and koineized Hindustani). My aim has been to demonstrate that even if we will likely never know precisely *how* the transmission of English was temporarily diluted in northeastern England, there is evidence allowing us to know that this *did* happen.

Clearly, my hypothesis can be vastly strengthened by closer engagement with the document literature, computer corpus-based techniques being particularly germane. However, I propose that such engagement would be a worthwhile pursuit, as it offers a possible answer to a contrast that must otherwise stand as a pressing anomaly to wit, table 11.3.[18]

## 6. English versus Afrikaans

A perhaps surprising conclusion of this thesis is that English experienced a significantly greater disruption of transmission during its timeline than Afrikaans did, despite the now established analysis of Afrikaans as a "semi-creole." Viewed in comparison to its Germanic sisters through the lens of table 11.3, Afrikaans differs largely in its loss of inflections, with the mere addition of loss of the external possessive construction and indefinite *man*. Overall it remains very much a "well-behaved" Germanic language. The losses in English vastly surpass those in Afrikaans.

That the difference between English and Afrikaans indeed suggests a difference in *degree* of transmission disruption is suggested by evidence that inflectional loss is a "first layer" along the dine toward outright pidginization. Along the dine towards pidginization follow losses in other grammatical features characterizable as "ornamental" upon the language competence (cf. McWhorter 2001). For example, there are contact languages that lack most or all of the inflections of their source languages but largely retain the remainder of their source languages' grammatical machineries, but none that lack source language features such as derivational markers, inherent reflexive marking, evidential markers, or inalienable possessive marking while retaining source-language inflections.[19]

Nevertheless, English also displays internal developments departing from the Germanic template which, in their "elaborative" nature, discourage any analysis of the language as "creole" or even "semi-creole": *do*-support is one such development. However, if my thesis is valid, then the reason English contains features that distract modern observers from the degree of its overall anomalousness among the Germanic group is that it underwent a profound change from extensive non-native acquisition so much further in the past than was true in Afrikaans.

Afrikaans emerged from Dutch after just 300 years ago, while the Scandinavian encounter with English occurred over 1,000 years ago. After this, English had roughly five centuries to evolve before the invention of printing and the advent of widespread literacy; thus, English remained relatively unfettered by the effects of prescriptivism and standardization. Moreover, only in the late eighteenth century would prescriptivism become a truly decisive force on general tendencies in English speech. As a result, after being "shorn" of so much of its overspecifications and complexities (according to the metric outlined in section 2) English had as long as 700 years to "get back on its feet," returning to the tendency towards drift into elaborations that is typical of natural languages as they are spoken over time. Crucially, *all of the internal elaborifications of English adduced above occurred long after the nativization of the Norse-speaking invaders*. Afrikaans, meanwhile, has existed for only a few centuries, and in addition, within this time the language has been codified as a written language, its natural change thus retarded.

Thus the reader is asked to imagine that printing and widespread literacy had arisen in England in, for example, 1000 A.D., the language thus subjected to standardization and prescriptivist impulses shortly after the Scandinavian influence, with internal developments in the nonstandard dialects marginalized or stanched by the dominance of the standard, as is the case today. I suggest that this (standard) English (roughly early Middle), devoid of *do*-support, *going to* versus *will*, or *I am speaking* versus *I speak*, would be as readily analyzed by the modern linguist as a "semi-creole" as Afrikaans is today if this hypothetical standard English were compared with its continental sisters.

In reality, although Gutenberg and universal education arose much later, a comparative analysis reveals that even 700 years could not erase what appears to have been more far-reaching an interference in transmission in English's history than that of Afrikaans.

## 7. Conclusion

My aim in this chapter has been to show that the difference between English and its sister languages comprises a much larger array of features than merely loss of inflection or a "tendency toward analyticity," and that the larger awareness that English has moved toward a "different typology" than its relatives (e.g. Lass 1987: 17–32) is traceable to a causal factor rather than being a random "uninteresting" development.

As many readers may have noticed, my list of features is hardly complete. Radiating outward from the core of losses that leave English unique or close to it in Germanic, there are other losses that English shares with a few Germanic languages, their interest being that where a subset of Germanic languages have departed sharply from the original Germanic "typology," English never fails to be a member. Examples include subjunctive marking (lost or marginal in Mainland Scandinavian, Dutch, Frisian, and Afrikaans) and verb-final word order in subordinate clauses (lost in Mainland Scandinavian, Icelandic, Faroese, and Yiddish). English is also alone in Germanic in lacking a strong–weak distinction in adjectival inflection (even Afrikaans retains this based largely on syllable count), which I omitted from my presentation to detract from the traditional focus on inflectional loss.

I must reiterate that my claim is neither that English is a "creole" nor that elaborations have been alien to its life cycle. However, our full cognizance of *do*-support and other features must be seen in conjunction with the striking losses that English suffered in the centuries during and in the wake of the Scandinavian invasions, of a disproportionate volume leaving it much more underspecified or complex *overall* than even Afrikaans.

And the result is that English is the most context-dependent grammar in the Germanic family by strikingly wide margin. Of course, if there were only three or four Germanic languages, then serendipity might remain a plausible explanation of the discrepancy. But instead there are about a dozen Germanic languages, each of them subsuming a number of dialects. To assume that the nature of the changes in English was merely a matter of chance would seem to require that the slings and arrows of outrageous fortune had led at least one of the many other Germanic languages or even dialects—to shed, rather than transform, a comparable volume of the Germanic legacy.

Otherwise, the conclusion would seem almost unavoidable that the English timeline was decisive influenced by what Trudgill (2001) has termed, in apt and savory fashion, "the lousy language-learning abilities of the human adult."

# Inflectional Morphology and Universal Grammar

## Post Hoc *versus* Propter Hoc

## 1. Introduction

A tradition in the Principles and Parameters framework of theoretical syntax hypothesizes that Universal Grammar includes parameters that differ in terms of the presence or absence of inflectional morphology. More specifically, various researchers hypothesize that inflectional morphology, or its absence, constitutes one of the signals that infants are innately disposed to attend to in setting the parameters that determine the structure of the grammar they are acquiring. Baker (1996) is a particularly explicit and comprehensive argument of this kind, paralleled by the school arguing that inflectional affixation determines whether or not the verb moves to INFL (e.g., Roberts 1993, Bobalijk 1995, Bobalijk and Thráinnson 1998, Rohrbacher 1999, and others).

Analysts in this tradition have demonstrated robust typological correlations according to the presence or absence of inflectional morphology. As such, the innatist implications that they draw from the data appear logical on their face. However, theorists positing that language is the product of natural selection (e.g., Pinker and Bloom 1990; Bickerton 1990, 1995; Dunbar 1996) assume that a useful theory of Universal Grammar will be compatible with the tenets of modern evolutionary theory.

I will argue that any conception of Universal Grammar that includes parameters distinguished by the presence, or "robustness," of inflectional affixes is, despite its *descriptive* attributes, incommensurate with the tenets of genetic inheritance. This implies that the concept of "inflectional parameter" be rejected, and that the descriptive correlations support the claim that a great deal of, if not all, of our language ability is an accidental by-product of the natural selection of other neurological features, as argued by Deacon (1997), Kirby (1999), Lightfoot (2000), and others, as well as Noam Chomsky in passing in assorted writings.

In the discussion that follows, it must be clear that the object of analysis is inflectional affixation, not "Inflection" as an abstract component of syntactic generation.

## 2. Demonstration case: The Polysynthesis Parameter

For example, Baker (1996) proposes that Universal Grammar includes a Polysynthesis Parameter, under which a subset of the world's languages require that arguments can be theta-marked only (1) via incorporation into the verb, as in the noun incorporation typical of his prime demonstration case Mohawk, or central to this discussion (2) when co-indexed with an inflectional affix on the verb. Baker formalizes this conception as the Morphological Visibility Condition:

> A phrase X is visible for $\Theta$-role assignment from a head Y only if it is coindexed with a morpheme in the word containing Y via (i) an agreement relationship or (ii) a movement relationship (Baker 1996: 17, 496).

In Mohawk, this property is demonstrated by three sentences that Baker gives (21):

(1)  (a)  *Ra-núhwe'-s ne  owirá'a.
          he-like-HAB  NE baby
          "He likes babies."

     (b)  **Shako**-núhwe'-s     (ne owirá'a).
          he/**them**-like-HAB  NE baby
          "He likes them (babies)."

     (c)  Ra-**wir**-a-núhwe'-s.
          he-**baby**-ø-like-HAB
          "He likes babies."

In (b), the object *baby* is co-indexed with an inflectional affix on the verb (contained within the portmanteau morpheme *shako*); (c) takes the alternative route of incorporating the object (*as -wir-*); (a) shows that using neither strategy, while most immediately intuitive to an Indo-European speaker, is ungrammatical. Baker proposes that various syntactic features, such as absence of adpositional phrase arguments and infinitives, or sharper restrictions on the incorporation of verbs than nouns, follow from the Polysynthesis Parameter.

Crucial to this conception is the requirement that a language with the Polysynthesis Parameter set to "on" have verbal inflectional affixes. The very "agreement relationship" that he stipulates implies this, and all of the languages that he classes as demonstrating the parameter are highly inflected. Moreover, his hypothesized reconstruction of how a grammar comes to be set with the Polysynthesis Parameter diachronically is centered on the development of inflectional affixes via phonological erosion (Baker 1996: 503).

Indeed, neither Baker nor any linguist to my knowledge has revealed any analytic language with regular and grammatically central noun incorporation. Absent any documented polysynthetic languages in West Africa, Southeast Asia, or Polynesia, it appears safe to assume that inflectional affixation is inherent to languages classed as polysynthetic according to Baker's definition.

And following from this, we assume a logical entailment of Baker's hypothesis: that sensitivity to the presence of inflectional affixation is part of humans' innate endowment for language.

## 3. Inflectional affixation as diachronic accident

In squaring this analysis with evolutionary biology, however, a diachronic perspective is germane. The relevant facts, while seeming at first glance tangential to synchronic analysis, are crucial to situating our conception of Universal Grammar within a Darwinian framework.

### 3.1. How inflections develop

A fundamental tenet of historical linguistic theory is that inflectional affixes develop from what begin as free morphemes. The development in Vulgar Latin, for example, of forms of the verb *habēre* into future and conditional marking inflections in many Romance languages is well-known: *amare habeo* "I have to love," or "I will love" > Italian *amerò*. Givon's (1971: 413) well-known dictum that "today's morphology is yesterday's syntax" is an eloquent distillation of historical linguists' basic assumption that inflectional affixes are the product of the phonetic erosion and semantic grammaticalization of erstwhile free morphemes.

This ontogeny of the inflectional affix is further supported by the existence of intermediate forms: clitics. Phonetically less integrated with the root than affixes but subsumed within their intonational contour, intimately associated with certain constituent classes but less likely to select idiosyncratic subclasses of same than affixes (cf. Zwicky and Pullum 1983), clitics are a "snapshot" of the intermediate stage between free morpheme and affix, in the same way that fossils of *Archaeopteryx*, a toothed, tailed, yet feathered creature intermediate between reptile and bird, show that birds evolved from dinosaurs.

Certainly, free morphemes are not the sole source of inflectional affixes. Nichols (1992: 141–42) notes, for example, that nominal gender marking has also arisen via the reanalysis of happenstance phonetic correspondences between nouns. However, in all documented cases, inflectional affixation arises by the recasting of material that previously served in other functions.

Inflectional affixation, then, is the result of historical accident: aspects of human anatomy combine with cognitive tendencies to gradually erode free morphemes and bind them to roots, or to reconceptualize phonetic correspondences, via pattern recognition, as classificational markers.

## 3.2. Inflections: Entrenched but unnecessary

Some have argued that inflections, once they develop, are not "useless" but serve various purposes, such as lending a grammar reference-tracking strategies (Heath 1975, Foley and Van Valin 1984: 326). But the fact remains that a great many languages do without the very features these scholars describe (a language can thrive and even acquire world dominance without switch-reference marking, such as the one I am writing in), and even often do without inflectional affixes entirely.

All linguists are aware that many languages are analytic, but less often is it acknowledged that this alone puts into question the idea that inflectional affixation is fundamental to natural language in itself. Even in inflected grammars, inflections' functional contributions are quite often redundant, serving at best to reinforce relations made clear otherwise. Trudgill (1999) usefully notes that while in many grammars inflections distinguish gender in the first person Russian *ja znal* "I knew" (masc.), *ja znala* "I knew" (fem.) this cannot be taken as "functional" given that in oral usage, the original and still fundamental modality of language, this distinction is utterly redundant, the speaker's gender always being obvious.

This evidence suggests that while inflectional affixes are highly *entrenched*, in the sense of Langacker (1987: 59), they became so in the absence of any functional purpose. They are, in Lass's (1997: 13) terms, "linguistic male nipples."

## 3.3. Most aspects of a grammar are not "cultural"

Arguments of this kind make many linguists uncomfortable, in part because of the roots of modern linguistics in anthropology, which stresses language as a reflection of culture. No one could deny that grammars reflect culture to some extent: Japanese and Korean honorifics, for example. However, such connections are unpredictable from one grammar to another; quite a few languages spoken in sharply hierarchical societies lack grammaticalized honorific marking of the Japanese type, such as Indo-Aryan languages, which emerged in caste-based societies.

Thus work such as Wierzbicka's (e.g., 1992) on grammatical reflections of cultural differences between, for example, "Anglo-Saxons" and Slavs, or Perkins's (1980) demonstration that languages spoken by small, less-"developed" groups have particularly rich deictic strategies because shared context among intimates encourages this in a way that less contextualized usage by strangers does not, are well-taken. But these observations must be seen in context: they hardly imply that anything but a small subset of a given grammar will submit to analyses such as these. Any realistic perspective on natural-language grammars must acknowledge that the bulk of any grammar morphophonemics, extent of overt marking of semantic roles, word order, ergativity, extractability constraints, phonological derivations, and most of the things that one attends to in controlling a grammar—has arisen quite disconnected from the culture of its speakers.

Hill (1993: 451–52), for example, argues against the notion that polysynthetic structure is the product of small societies based on intimate relations, the volume of shared information presumably allowing the null anaphora, loose word order, absence of a distinct subordinate clause structure, and other "pragmatic mode" features (in Givon's [1979: 229] terminology). The Aztecs created a hierarchical civilization, and yet Nahuatl is polysynthetic; meanwhile, languages of Southern Australia are not polysynthetic, despite their speakers having been small bands of hunter-gatherers. Baker (1996: 510–11) presents various features of Mohawk society and pointedly observes: "Does it follow from any of these features of their traditional society that their syntactic constructions should be consistently head marking?" In general, it is impossible to propose a cultural aspect uniting Germans, people of India, Ethiopians, and the Japanese that would predict verb-final word order, or one uniting Celts, Polynesians, and inhabitants of the Philippines that would predict verb-initial.

Few if any linguists would contest any of these observations. And they highlight the simple fact that inflectional affixation is no more "cultural" than any number of other grammatical features, and more important, that it is on the contrary a random, accidental development in natural languages.

## 4. Inflection-based parameters: The collision with evolutionary theory

If we acknowledge that inflections are linguistic "male nipples" that do not reflect culture in any significant way, then we are in a position to realize that conceptions of Universal Grammar based on the presence of inflectional affixes run up against the tenets of evolutionary biology.

### 4.1. Inflectional affixes lend no survival advantage

Evolution, under the Darwinian conception that all biologists consider valid regardless of controversies over the details, is driven by the selection of features that lead individuals to propagate their genes to future generations, as the result of greater fitness for their particular environment. The first problem, then, for a theory proposing an innate capacity for producing and processing inflectional affixation is the sheer number of languages that lack inflections. Presumably, we might assume that if inflectional affixation itself conferred an advantage in survival, then all languages would by now long have become inflected. But obviously they have not; neither do human groups demonstrate a correlation between inflectional affixation and historical success: the Chinese languages are an obvious example, as are the Polynesian ones.

Nor would an argument that modern technology largely exempts today's humans from the exigencies of evolutionary biology stand. Even in less-developed societies today, we find polysyntheticity, fusional and agglutinative inflection, and outright analyticity distributed randomly across the globe.

### 4.2. Was universal grammar "set" after inflections had already arisen?

One way around this problem would be to surmise that Universal Grammar happened to be incorporated into the human genetic code only after the first language (or languages) had developed inflectional affixes via drift. But this scenario is again decisively incompatible with a survivalist imperative. If UG was set after inflections had already arisen, then we would presumably predict that when languages were born anew as creoles, they would be inflectional and that perhaps analytic languages arise when natural processes of erosion eliminate affixes.

But that prediction is not borne out. Many creoles have no inflections at all, such as the creoles of Surinam, like Sranan and Saramaccan, or those of the islands in the Gulf of Guinea, such as the Portuguese-based creoles Angolar and São Tomense. Others have one or two, such as Tok Pisin and its sisters in New Guinea and the South Pacific, or perhaps, depending on one's definition of inflection, many French creoles, whose verbs are often realized in short and long forms depending on context.

Some creoles have more inflectional affixes than this, but this is not a random phenomenon; such creoles result only from contexts in which the languages in contact happen to be closely related genetically, or in which the creole develops in close contact with an inflected older language. Specifically, creoles with a moderate degree of inflection all (1) were created by people mostly speaking the same language who retained some native inflections (e.g., Berbice Dutch), or (2) were born from contact between speakers of very closely related languages whose kinship allowed retention of many cognate affixes (e.g., Lingala), or (3) have long existed in intimate contact with inflected superstratal or adstratal languages (e.g., Sri Lanka Creole Portuguese) (cf. McWhorter 2001).

And the fact remains that whenever a creole has emerged outside of these conditions that is, where genetic and typological distance among the creators' languages disallowed convenient compromises, and the creole then went on to develop in a context where there was only enough contact with older languages to yield lexical borrowings—the result has been an analytic language.

Proposing that UG was set after inflections developed leads to another problem as well, in that it would seem to predict that all languages in general would be inflected. Yet they are not, and this is another direct contradiction to evolutionary theory. Biology does not record cases where a feature selected *because of its aid to survival* is then regularly arbitrarily suppressed in some individuals while expressed in others. All sparrows have wings, not just most of them; among populations of venomous snakes, we do not find that only 60% have venom while the remaining 40% mysteriously lack it. A possible exception would be sexual dimorphisms, in which the rendering of an individual as male or female entails the suppressing of certain of its genetically encoded traits. But sex differences are crucial to the survival of the species, whereas humans accrue no such benefit from the coexistence of analytic and inflected grammars.

4.3. The Polysynthesis Parameter and Population Genetics

One might object that my characterization of the parameter school's argument as claiming inflections as a survival advantage is a reductio ad absurdum. Indeed, more properly, their argument is that the parametrical alternations themselves were selected for; that is, the *choice between* affixation and analyticity, not affixation alone. But even this is a formulation difficult to square with the tenets of evolution currently assumed by biologists.

At first glance, the population-genetics model of evolution (e.g., Fisher 1930, Haldane 1932) would appear to provide a way to incorporate the distinction between analyticity and inflectionality, without appealing to survival advantage. It is now accepted that within a species population, random mutation creates innumerable variations upon genes that are passed down generations, but expressed only rarely if at all. Those variations that are disadvantageous to survival when they are expressed will naturally tend to leach out over time, but many, if not most, such genes are neutral as to survival advantage. However, if conditions arise that render that mutation advantageous to survival and propagation, then it will increase in the population.

A classic demonstration would be the peppered moth case in late nineteenth-century England, under which it was argued that at first, blackness in the moths was a harmless deviation from a white norm. But when factory soot blackened the tree trunks the moths lived near, the black variant became a norm as their color rendered them less visible to predators. (This particular case itself has actually been rejected as fraudulent [Majerus 1998], but I cite it for its heuristic usefulness in conveying a general phenomenon whose validity is accepted.)

We might imagine that the Polysynthesis Parameter began as a random mutation in some individuals. It would have arisen while or after the first language emerged, but was unexpressed until phonetic erosion and grammatical reanalysis created inflectional languages compatible with it. This would allow the parameter to emerge unconnected from any survival advantage and yet be innate.

This scenario strains credibility even in a general sense. Inflectional affixation is, after all, just one of myriad aspects of human language. A population genetics account requires that of all of the mutations that serendipity could have conditioned on our innate specification for language, one of them occasioned an especial facility for producing and processing languages where a subset of grammatical items and relations are expressed, usually redundantly, via brief sequences of segments phonetically appended to major category constituents. Stranger things have happened, but the notion does give one pause. More important, the parameter model entails that *all* humans presumably harbor the mutation in question, not just a subset of them: humans acquire any grammar that they are exposed to, regardless of its typology. Thus the analogy with evolutionary biology is incommensurate: speakers of polysynthetic languages are not the "black moths," odd ducks producing mysteriously inflection-rich versions of analytic languages they are exposed to as children. Rather, the acquisitional scenario that the parameter school proposes is one under which all humans have the potential to be white or black moths.

## 4.4. The Polysynthesis Parameter "along for the ride"?

To be sure, nature provides examples of traits that occur in two or more variations from one individual to another, with neither or none of the variables conferring survival advantage. Handedness and blood types are commonly discussed examples. These examples of what is termed *stable polymorphism* could be seen as providing an account for the Polysynthesis Parameter that is compatible with evolutionary theory.

But the fate of inflectionality in human populations over time does not square with even this innatist framework. Handedness and blood type are specified genetically for each individual and emerge regardless of environmental stimulus (except, of course, societal custom often encourages individuals to suppress left-handedness). On the other hand, all humans are equally capable of acquiring analytic or inflectional languages: the hypothesized parameter is unset at birth; and thus differs sharply from stable polymorphism.

Nor does inflection subsume gracefully under other categories of features inherited independently of selective advantage. Nature displays innumerable phenomena which, in all of their salience and wonder, are ultimately accidents rather than selected features. The hemoglobin molecule in our red blood cells, for example, was selected for because it is useful in carrying oxygen and carbon dioxide; however, the fact that it happens to be red was not selected for. Clearly its color was irrelevant to ensuring that its bearers sired more offspring, and in fact many creatures that have thrived on earth much longer than humans have blood of other colors (Lightfoot 2000: 237). Fin whales' lower jaws and baleen plates are black on one side and white on the other, and there is no conceivable competitive advantage that this confers: it is apparently simply a happenstance development of their biologies (Ellis 2001: 237). All of the several dozen other whale varieties do quite well with jaws and baleen of just one color. It is a fundamental observation in evolutionary biology that only a subset of a biological organism's traits are evolutionary adaptations.

But where the Polysynthesis Parameter is concerned, we are dealing not with a single species-wide trait, but a hypothesized innate disposition to manifest either of two variations upon a trait, depending on environment. A theory of inflection compatible with evolutionary biology requires that there be parallels in nature to this particular phenomenon.

### 4.5. The Polysynthesis Parameter as an environmentally conditioned phenotype

Nature does provide examples of biological "parameters" that are initially unset in the individual, tipped one way or the other by environmental stimuli. In the life cycle of many organisms, sex is determined by environmental triggers. The sex of crocodiles and some other reptiles is determined by temperature at the time of hatching (Madge 1985). If a larva of *Bonellia*, an echiuran marine worm, lands on a substrates it becomes a female, but if an adult female takes it up with her proboscis, it becomes a male (and spends its life in her uterus!). Could it be that phenomena like these are the biological parallel to linguistic parameters, innate either-ors set by what kind of language the individual happens to acquire?

In fact, the fit is extremely approximate from both the synchronic and the diachronic perspectives. In nature, environmental factors inherent to our planet (e.g., temperature, habitat) control a distinction between individuals (sex) that is vital to propagation. In language, we would have to propose that an environmental factor that didn't exist when the species arose and only emerged via devolutional processes (polysynthetic grammar) controls a distinction irrelevant to survival (analyticity vs. polysynthesis).

Obviously, tautology looms large here: crocodile gender is determined by temperature at hatching, but how humans process grammar is determined by, well, what kind of grammar they hear after hatching. More pointedly, there is a clear lack of fit here between both nature of dimorphism and nature of environment. The biological phenomena are variations upon the theme of ensuring survival, while the Polysynthesis Parameter is irrelevant to it. The only way we could save the parallel here would be to surmise that the Polysynthesis Parameter simply "happened" for no functional reason, but obviously a more constrained and falsifiable account would be preferable.

## 4.6. Parametrical alternations as a survival advantage

Baker (2001: 211–12) explores the idea that parametrical alternation itself may have conditioned in-group linguistic traits reinforcing group solidarity, thereby encouraging altruism that operated to the benefit of the species as a whole by enhancing the propagation of genes within all human groups. This idea would demonstrate what biologists today term *species selection*, in which traits are selected that benefit the survival of the species overall rather than individuals. Thus while longer necks in giraffes' ancestors made the survival of individuals more likely, an ability among a species' individuals to survive in a wider range of environments makes the survival of that species as a whole more likely. But Baker rejects this explanation for parameters as "overengineered" differences in accent and lexical choice mark group boundaries quite well.

Of course, technically, evolution often "overshoots" the bounds of necessity, male peacocks' tail feather displays being an example. But there is further evidence against parameters as a survival advantage: the geographical distribution of language typologies. Too often vast areas of the globe are covered by uniformly well-inflected languages (all of North America and Australia until Europeans came, or most of the Bantu-speaking region of Africa), or analytic ones (China, Polynesia, much of the upper western coast of Africa). Nor is there any reason to suppose that this is just a latter-day, "post-evolutionary" development. Obviously, even in the most undeveloped, isolated regions of the globe, either highly inflected languages or highly analytical ones are the norm across imposingly broad geographical areas.

## 4.7. Implications

In general, attempts to incorporate the Polysynthesis Parameter hypothesis into evolutionary theory are either logically hopeless or, at best, depend on "just so" stories to a degree that ultimately suggests that analyses beyond the Darwinian will be more useful.

Specifically, the nature of language in time and space is such that the most useful theories will have room built into them for contingency. Lightfoot (2000) refers to reading and writing as examples of contingencies which, unlike inflections, have even been central in the success of human populations that have developed them. Yet no one would argue that the capacity to engage in them is specifically encoded genetically. Myriad civilizations have thrived in which most citizens were illiterate. Reading, requiring constant focus on tiny symbols, is ultimately detrimental to our vision. And none would claim that the illiteracy of a great many of the world's peoples past and present renders them any less human than the literate. On the contrary, since writing only traces back about 6,000 years, illiteracy has been the natural state of our species. We naturally assume that our ability to read and write is a contingent development that "piggybacks" on innate traits developed to other ends.

Indeed, modern evolutionary theory assumes that a vast weight of an organism's traits are random epiphenomena rather than inheritances selected because of advantage to survival. And this means the following: given that such epiphenomena are rife in nature, under any Darwinian conception of human language, *it would be unexpected that language would lack such "accidental" features.* The only question is which features would fall into this class. In that class, all linguists would include, for example, phonetic shape of a language's words. But for all of its centrality to linguistic theory, inflectional affixation gives every indication of being another such feature:

1. It arises via historical accident.
2. It serves no function in a grammar that complex, nuanced communication requires.
3. It has no connection to human culture.
4. It confers advantage in neither survival nor sexual attractiveness.
5. It is incommensurate with evolutionary accounts for traits inherited independently of survival advantage, including stable polymorphic ones.

The evidence is compatible, then, with an analysis stipulating that the Universal Grammar that was selected for in human evolution and passed on to all future generations of *Homo sapiens* lacked inflectional affixation (cf. Comrie 1992 for a related argument). Eventually, a subset of the manifestations of Universal Grammar developed inflectional affixes via inexorable processes that are inherent to human anatomy and cognition. These grammars were processible by the massively plastic human brain, but had no effect on our genome.

In broader view, if inflectional affixation is irrelevant to Universal Grammar, then *this disallows the existence of an innate Polysynthesis Parameter*, or any other that requires that sensitivity to inflectional affixes is innate to the human species.


## 6. A potential counterargument: Sign languages and inflections

Modern sign languages have inflectional affixation despite having arisen only within the past 200 years, a life cycle as brief as that of creoles. Specifically, for example, in American Sign Language, the signs for some verbs are expressed simultaneously with physical deictic indications of person and number: *I give to you* expressed by moving the hand from the speaker's body outward toward the interlocutor's. Many might take this as implying that sign languages, being recently-born natural languages, indicate that inflectional affixation is indeed innately specified.

But to treat sign languages' pronominal inflections as innate predicts that when analytic pidgins were transformed into natural languages or creoles that in at least a subset of cases, their pronouns would be manifested as inflectional affixes. But in twelve years' research on pidgins and creoles, amid investigations that have required reference to the grammars of all of the several dozen creoles extant, I have not encountered any such case. When Melanesian Pidgin English evolved into creoles like Tok Pisin, its pronouns remained free morphemes; the case was similar in other documented cases of the pidgin-to-creole transition such as the emergence of Sango in the Central African Republic and Hawaiian Creole English from Hawaiian Pidgin English. This is unexplained under a claim that sign languages' verbal inflections indicate an innate property.

To be sure, the pidgin stage of most creoles was not recorded, meaning that in most cases we cannot track the development from pidgin to creole. But there does not even exist a creole with a paradigm of person/number affixes that is segmentally homologous with its free pronouns, which would be an obvious indication that erstwhile free pronouns had been affixed as those in sign languages are. The one possible exception would be the more standardized variety of Lingala, created by speakers of closely related Bantu languages (the Bobangi cluster) that have subject-marking inflections. The result was a language with a paradigm of subject inflections varying according to person and number. But the source languages here were so genetically close (essentially a dialect continuum) that the result was essentially what most linguists would class as a koine; indeed, Bantuists often treat Lingala as an ordinary Bantu language rather than as a "pidgin" or "creole."

Technically, there could theoretically be pidgins lost to history that contradict my claim that truly new languages are always analytic. We might surmise that some pidgins may have indeed arisen with ample affixation, only for these to be, for some reason, transformed into free pronouns in the creole that developed from the pidgin. But such a surmise would be atheoretical: for affixes to evolve into free morphemes would contradict a very strong tendency in grammaticalization in the other direction. The grammaticalization literature notes occasional exceptions (usefully gathered in Newmeyer 1998: 263–75), but mere exceptions they are. As Newmeyer notes (275–76), "a rough impression is that downgradings [i.e., free morphemes becoming inflectional affixes] have occurred at least ten times as often as upgradings [i.e., inflections becoming derivations, clitics, or free morphemes]." The exceptions do not motivate positing a regular development of affixes into free morphemes in the pidgin-to-creole life cycle—which is what hypothesizing inflected pidgins would require.

On the contrary, where the occasional source-language modeled inflection occurs in a documented pidgin, if a creole develops from the pidgin, the inflection does not drift into becoming a free morpheme, but always remains an inflection in the creole. An example is the transitive marker -im in both pidgin and creole varieties of Tok Pisin, which neither here nor in any of its sister creoles has drifted into becoming a clitic or free morpheme. Pidginized Assamese (Naga Pidgin) is an example of a contact language developing in intimate enough contact with its lexifier to lend it some of its inflections. But its creole varieties retain the same inflectional affixes rather than recasting them as free morphemes.

This sharp contrast between the spoken and manual modalities suggests that the inflections in sign languages stem from something inherent to that modality rather than innate to our species. And a ready solution is that the structural nature of human limbs and hands inherently encourages some verbs and their deictic reference to be indicated within the same physical motion. That is, inflectional affixation in sign language gives all indication of being an exaptation a recruitment in a new function of a trait selected for other reasons (Gould and Lewontin 1979)—just as I believe inflection in spoken language to be. Our physical makeup allows and even encourages this feature in sign language without there being any motivation for treating it as an innately specified feature of our language competence.

## 7. Another example: The rich agreement hypothesis

### 7.1. The rich agreement hypothesis: Stage one

In the 1980s, various researchers converged on a hypothesis that ample verbal inflectional affixation in a grammar leads the verb to move to INFL, while when verbal inflection is sparse or absent, the verb stays in situ. The relevant contrast is illustrated by the heavily inflected Icelandic versus Danish, whose inflectional affixes are invariant across person and number. In subordinate clauses (chosen because in main clauses, most Germanic languages exhibit a V2 phenomenon that obscures the process), verbs in Icelandic precede various elements that occur at the left edge of the VP, such as sentential negators, while Danish verbs occur to the right of these elements:

Icelandic:

(4)    . . . a hann **keypti    ekki** bókina.
      that   he    buy.PAST NEG book.DEF
      ". . . that he did not buy the book."

Danish:

(5)    . . . at han **ikke købte**      bogen.
      that   he   NEG buy.PAST book.DEF
      ". . . that he did not buy the book." (Platzack 1986: 209)

Various scholars (Travis 1984; Roberts 1985, 1993; Platzack 1986, 1988; Pollock 1989; Vikner, 1995; Rohrbacher 1999) have taken this as evidence that there exists a parameter distinguishing richly versus weakly inflected grammars. The hypothesis appeared strengthened by diachronic evidence, where in some grammars, after inflectional affixes wore away, the verb that once moved to INFL came to rest in situ, such as Platzack's (1988) demonstration in Swedish and Roberts's (1985) for English.

However, various exceptions came to light: grammars with weak agreement in which the verb nevertheless moves to INFL. The Kronoby, Finland, variety of Swedish was a particularly noted problem (Platzack and Holmberg 1989), another example being the Tromsø dialect of Norwegian, where inflection is as weak as in Danish and yet the verb moves to INFL (Vikner 1995):

(6)   Vi va' bare tre    støkka, før det   at    han Nilsen **kom ikkje**.
      we were only three pieces  because that he   Nilsen came NEG
      "We were only three because Nilsen didn't some." (Iversen 1918: 83, cited in Vikner 1995).

Conversely, Faroese, with somewhat less inflectional allomorphy than its close relative Icelandic but vastly more than Mainland Scandinavian varieties, was shown to
variably allow the verb to remain in situ (Barnes 1987).

Among responses to the new data were attempts to refine the definition of inflectional "richness" in ways that risked the ad hoc from a cognitively plausible perspective (e.g., Rohrbacher 1999) and concessions that an empirically responsible
reformulation of the "parameter" must stipulate only that rich inflection requires the
verb to move to INFL, while weak inflection may or may not do so (Platzack and
Holmberg 1989, Roberts 1999: 292).

But as Rohrbacher (1999: 147) acknowledges, this latter conception is problematic
for a constrained theory of acquisition: "If examples of V to I raising in the input are
sufficient to trigger the acquisition of V to I raising, it is unclear why the morphological
richness of person or any other agreement should play any role at all in this process."
Concurring, Bobalijk (2002) cites evidence given by Lardiere (2000) that, indeed, word
order alone is acquired by children before they master inflectional affixes.

More generally, this initial version of the Rich Agreement Hypothesis founders
on the same arguments as the Polysynthesis Parameter: both innate sensitivity to
inflectional affixation and an innate *option for* inflectional affixation are hopelessly
incompatible with an account of language origins couched in Darwinian theory.

## 7.2.  The Rich Agreement Hypothesis: Stage two

In response to the exceptions, Johnson (1990), followed by Bobalijk (1995) and
Bobalijk and Thráinsson (1998), sought a resolution in recruiting Pollock's (1989)
recasting of the IP into separate agreement and tense nodes.

The hypothesis is that languages vary in their configuration of the INFL realm:
in some, the IP simply manifests itself as an INFL node and a VP node (a), while in
others, the IP consists of multiple maximal projections (b):

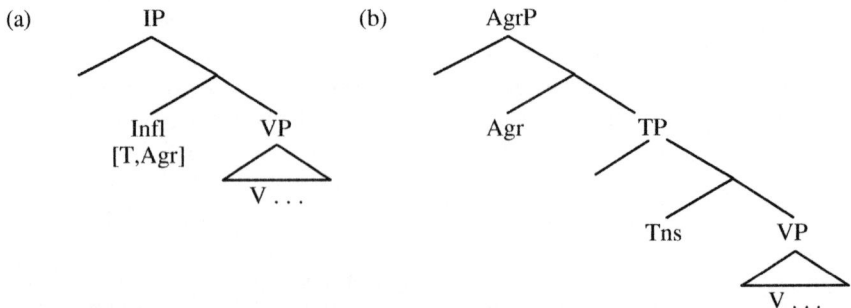

The proposal here is a "Split-IP Parameter," and its usefulness to retaining a version
of the Rich Agreement Hypothesis is that the driving force for verb movement is not
inflectional affixes per se but the split IP in the syntax. Crucially, this formulation

provides a principled reason for verbs to move even in grammars with weak inflection: split IP is a syntactic rather than a morphological feature, and thus a grammar
can presumably have a split IP even without rich inflectional affixation.

For adherents of this hypothesis, Kronoby Swedish and Tromsø Norwegian are
thus accounted for: despite the erosion of the affixes, the split IP remains, forcing
verb movement. Bobalijk (1995) and Bobalijk and Thráinnson (1998) present a principled account for such grammars within the Minimalist framework, under which
verbs in languages of the (b) type are forced to move to check their features, because
the multiplicity of projections deprives them of adjacency to the verb, in contrast to
the situation in languages of type (a). This revision could be taken as resituating the
relevant contrasts within an evolutionary framework, given that it removes affixation
as the spur for the parameter setting.

## 7.3. Old problems

Viewed more closely, as argued to date, even this new version reduces to maintaining inflectional affixation as an innate specification. The relevant linguists are themselves concerned mainly with synchronic issues, valuing the revision for its attribution
of the relevant contrasts to the syntactic rather than the morphological realm, and
the implications of this for the Distributed Morphology framework (Halle and Marantz
1993). However, our discussion addresses whether or not this scenario is plausible
as a product of evolution, and here, serious problems remain.

For example, Bobalijk (2002) stipulates that even in split-IP grammars where
the verb moves despite weak overt inflectional affixation, there remain zero inflectional morphemes in place of overt ones. This alone implies that the learner of a split-IP
grammar is still cued by inflectional affixes.

However, Bobalijk does not lay much emphasis on this presumption. As to the
question of what cues the acquirer to set their grammar as one with split IP, he and
Thráinsson note other features that split IP conditions. For example, they propose
that a split IP grammar, endowed with multiple specifier positions in contrast to simple
IP grammars, may recruit these nodes for pragmatic contrasts. A demonstration is
Icelandic, where subjects occurring to the left of an adverb connote old information,
while those occurring to the right of the adverb connote new information (Bobalijk
and Jonas 1996: 196):

(7)  (a)  Í gær      kláruðu {þessar mýs} sennilega *{þessar mýs} ostinn.
          yesterday finished these   mice probably these     mice cheese.DEF
          "These mice probably finished the chesse yesterday."

     (b)  Í gær      kláruðu {?margar mýs} sennilega *{margar mýs} ostinn.
          yesterday finished these   mice probably these     mice cheese.DEF
          "Many mice probably finished the cheese yesterday."

Certainly these authors have deftly demonstrated that verb movement need not depend strictly on affixation synchronically, their implication being that affixation is
merely one of many epiphenomena of a particular syntactic parameter. But the question is whether their hypothesis requires that the proposed Split-IP parameter was

incorporated as a genetic specification on the basis of overt inflectional affixation. In this light, it is crucial that all of the weakly inflected grammars with verb movement that these researchers present are well documented to have evolved over the past several centuries from languages with ample inflection. Specifically, the case for a Split-IP parameter has been to date based on Germanic languages, in various states of evolution from an inflection-heavy Proto-Germanic ancestor.

Demonstrations that some of the weakly inflected among these languages exhibit other evidence of a split IP, despite inflectional erosion such as the transitive expletive constructions grammatical in Icelandic but ungrammatical in Norwegian or English are well and good. But, strictly speaking, these phenomena can be taken as demonstrating that split IP arises first when inflectional affixation emerges, but that its configuration then spins off structural by-products that may, unremarkably, persist even after the inflections erode away. It may well be that the synchronic learner can infer a split IP from these constructions or simply from the fact that the verb moves in the grammar even when inflection is weak.

But in the evolutionary sense central to my argument, this conception entails that split IP first developed in natural-language grammars as a result of the emergence of inflectional affixes. What would belie such a conclusion is the existence of grammars (assumed to have been analytic for millennia) that distinguish new versus old information on the basis of orderings within a multiheaded IP, or other features derivable from split IP other than rich inflection. Only these would clinch a case that split IP is a parametrical setting independent of the development of affixes, but researchers arguing for the hypothesis have presented no such examples to date. All of the Germanic languages are disqualified by virtue of their recent and well-documented descent from a richly inflected ancestor.

In other words, the Split-IP hypothesis as currently argued on languages where rich inflection is either present or was present only recently—maintains, via logical implication, an assumption that inflectional affixation was a component of the Universal Grammar that was incorporated as an innate feature in our species. Specifically, the arguments give all indication of implying that *split IP arises when inflectional affixation emerges*, not as an independent feature.

Indeed, the very creation of the multiheaded INFL schema was driven not by observations such as Icelandic informational structure contrasts but by the functional division of labor in inflectional affixes between tense and concord. Icelandic's past-tense verbal paradigm is an example, where a segment ð- is treatable as connoting pastness, with further segments corresponding to person and number:

(8)   "hear," past tense
    *heyr-ð-i*       *heyr-ðu-m*
    *heyr-ð–ir*    *heyr-ðu-ð*
    *heyr-ð-i*       *heyr-ð-u*

In any case, even if we were to accept an argument that the Split-IP Parameter alone, unconnected from overt affixation, is a genetic inheritance, we would be brought before the eternal question: How could either a split IP or the option of having one have possibly conferred a survival advantage on the human species?

## 8. A thought experiment

In the end, we must acknowledge the risk inherent in native speakers of inflected languages proposing parameters of Universal Grammar based on the presence of inflectional affixation.

This is not to take a page from the traditional cavil that generative syntacticians found their theories on a mere few European languages. If this was true in the 1960s, it would be difficult to maintain this charge today in view of the typologically broad spectrum of languages that many theoretical syntacticians address, Baker's work on polysynthetic languages being an obvious example. However, in formulations of Universal Grammar that, despite incorporating "exotic" languages, hinge centrally on the presence or absence of features that are particularly salient in Indo-European languages, we must attend to the danger in what might be called the Mickey Mouse phenomenon.

### 8.1. Talking animals three feet tall

For decades in the twentieth century, Hollywood cartoon characters tended to be cast as jolly talking animals about three feet high. But this is hardly an inevitable choice in what to animate, as witnessed by the distinctly lesser role that such talking animals have played in foreign animated cartoons. Indeed, American cartoon characters tended to be human before the late 1920s. But when Walt Disney hit paydirt with a sunny talking mouse, all of the other studios followed suit in a quest for a piece of the monetary pie that Mickey had seized, and a tradition was set: enter Bugs Bunny, Woody Woodpecker, Droopy Dog, et cetera. It could be argued that American animation has been limited in scope by the imperatives of that tradition.

In the same way, a theory of Universal Grammar that includes sensitivity to inflectional affixation may be one that is more contingent on local traditions and biases than an empirically independent response to the cross-linguistic data set. The inflectional affixation that naturally appears so central to human language to a European is revealed by diachronic analysis to be less a sine qua non of language than a by-product of heavy use—a conspiracy of phonetic erosion, semantic bleaching, and syntactic reanalysis. Then this must be seen within the context of the plethora of uninflected natural languages worldwide, the strong tendency for new languages to lack inflections, and the impossibility that inflections (or the option to use them) could confer survival advantage. Hence the suggestion is strong that inflectional affixation is a contingent epiphenomenon in natural language grammars and as such, a poor candidate for innate specification in any sense.

### 8.2. Universal Grammar Nigeria style

A thought experiment makes this clearer. Imagine that modern theoretical syntax was founded not by Indo-European speakers in the United States, but by Southern Nigerians speaking Edoid languages like Edo (Bini), Urhobo, and Degema, in a hypothetical world where they were unfamiliar with any Indo-European languages. Under our scenario, let us imagine that the linguists in question were familiar only with Edoid languages and Mande languages spoken further up the West African coast.

In Edoid languages, various tenses and aspects are encoded solely by tone rather than affixes (Elugbe 1989: 299, Ben Elugbe, Jan. 2002 pers. comm.). Mande languages, in contrast, are notorious in Niger-Congo for making only moderate use of tone to distinguish lexical items or encode morphosyntactic contrasts, although tone plays a role phonologically and intonationally. As it happens, Edoid languages are SVO, while Mande languages are SOV.

Imagine that our Edoid-speaking linguists, steeped primarily in various Edoid languages beyond the ones they spoke natively, hypothesized that the word-order contrast between Edoid and Mande represented a parameter distinction, whose setting by the acquirer depended on tonally-marked tense and aspect marking. Under their analysis, the verb in Edoid languages had to move to the left of the object to "get tone." For them, Mande's SOV order was the result of verbs remaining in situ because there was no tense-marking tone to "get." Tone would naturally appear central to human language to them, since it is central to the grammars of the languages these linguists would be most familiar with. Meanwhile, inflectional affixation, absent in Edoid and sparse in Mande, would just as naturally seem "beside the point" in specifying what component of language is innate.

These Edoid speakers' scenario would seem even more plausible given that in Edoid, tone does not distinguish verbs themselves. Instead, they are only marked with tones that encode features such as tense and aspect. Thus a theory where verbs moved for a purely grammatical reason—to "get" the tone—would follow quite gracefully given their data set.

Now, let us suppose that these linguists then became aware of the many West African languages that have SVO order but, unlike Edoid, encode tense and aspect segmentally rather than with tones. One response they might have is to suppose that, because these languages do make ample use of tone to distinguish lexical items, acquirers are spurred to move the verb on the basis of a more general "high functional load tone" feature, with Edoid languages simply displaying a particularly robust overt manifestation of this parameter setting. We might even imagine that they provided a theory-internal mechanism requiring verb movement in such languages, founded perhaps on a notion of a TONE node that "contains" "abstract tone" even in grammars where tense and aspect are themselves encoded with clitics or affixes. Thus they might propose that a verb in, say, Yoruba can only "acquire" its lexically contrastive tone at "TONE," this requirement falling away only in languages like the Mande ones where tone's functional load is so sharply reduced.

For us linguists in the real world, such a theory appears almost laughably misguided. No theories of Universal Grammar treat tone as innately specified. We are aware of the tonogenesis literature demonstrating how tone emerges in grammars that initially lacked it, phonetic erosion leading to a reinterpretation of phonetic tonal distinctions as phonemic, or eliminating a grammatical segment and leaving behind its tone to carry its functional load. As such, we casually think of tone as merely one of many developments that a natural language may drift into over time, and we see its functional marginality in most European languages as reinforcing this assumption. Nor, in the evolutionary vein, would any of us see it as likely that tonality assured one more progeny. Similarly, the Indo-European-speaking linguist would never dream of proposing parameters based on alienable possession, switch reference marking, or other features that are largely absent in European languages that we classify as "frills" peripheral to Universal Grammar.

Things would quite naturally appear otherwise to the Nigerian linguist for whom lexically and morphosyntactically contrastive tone was central to all of the languages they encountered most, with those without it (such as the Mande ones) thus appearing "exceptional." My claim is that *diachronic linguistic theory reveals inflectional affixes as every bit as epiphenomenal to natural language as tone.* Like tone, they only arise as a result of the phonetic erosion that heavy usage conditions, and from a cross-linguistic perspective they are just one of many pathways of drift that a grammar may wend its way through.

To wit, for our hypothetical Nigerian linguists, a Universal Grammar comprising parameters hinging on inflectional affixation, rare to absent in the dozens of languages most familiar to them, would appear as parochial as their tonally-based parameters would seem to us.

## 9. So what's the "story"?

We are faced with the fact that, on the one hand, inflectional affixation conditions fascinating typological correlations, while, on the other, a conception of Universal Grammar that traces these to innate neurological configurations selected for in human populations is implausible. I have focused my argument on inflection-based parameter scenarios, but Baker is quite aware of this problem in relation to the very plausibility of parameters in general as products of natural selection.

In both Baker (1996) and Baker (2001), the rigorous and ingenious analysis of the synchronic correlations forming the body of his argument contrasts almost jarringly with final envoi chapters addressing the innateness question, where he can only offer highly speculative gestures constituting, essentially, a concessionaiy shrug of the shoulders. In Baker (2001: 228–30) he proposes that an evolutionary explanation for parameters may only emerge from modes of scientific thought far in the future, inconceivable to us at our current state of knowledge. And in Baker (1996) he even surmises, quite soberly, that the ultimate explanation may be divine inspiration.

Whatever the validity of these approaches, it must be acknowledged that the nature of this conundrum can be taken as suggesting that parameters and especially ones based on inflectional affixation are simply not innate.

However, resting here, my argument, whatever its validity, stands merely as what has been called a "nyah nyah" argument, and this is not my intention. Despite the implausibility of the specific innatist implications that Baker and the Rich Agreement Hypothesis school draw from their observations, the fact remains that they have revealed robust correlations that give indication of indeed being causally rather than accidentally linked. As such, I believe that it would be hasty to simply dismiss these arguments as just so much mumbo-jumbo rather, they beg for an alternate systematic account.

## 9.1. The Polysynthesis "Parameter"

For example, Baker's claim that obligatory agreement morphemes corresponding to arguments and noun incorporation represent a unified phenomenon is supported by the fact that the incorporated nouns in such languages are the only arguments that do not require a correspondent agreement morpheme (Baker 1996: 20). Moreover, his formulation of the Polysynthesis Parameter as the Morphological Visibility Condition (cited here in section 2) is further supported by otherwise anomalous traits that can be treated as falling out of a general requirement, that arguments either correspond with an inflection or are "swallowed" into the head via incorporation. Absence of adpositional phrases follows from the unavailability of agreement morphemes corresponding to such phrases, absence of infinitives from the fact that they have no marking of subject and would thus violate the requirement that subjects be inflectionally marked at all times, and so on.

### 9.1.1. Where do you draw the line?

Thus Baker's observations strongly suggest that these correlations reflect something real about mental representations of grammatical structure. The question is how plausible this grammatical reality is as an innate inheritance. Here, the problem is that the languages Baker classes as polysynthetic are actually a subset of those traditionally treated as such: Baker considers the Polysynthesis Parameter to apply only to those languages that *both* require arguments to correspond with agreement inflections and have robust noun incorporation. Yet as he acknowledges, there also exist many languages with only the agreement requirement but with no appreciable noun incorporation, such as Warlpiri, Navajo, and Choctaw, as analyzed by Jelinek (1984), as well as languages where the agreement and/or the incorporation is present but hardly required, such as Chichewa, Slave, and Papuan languages like Yimas.

That is, languages of Baker's "pure" polysynthetic typology can be taken as one end of a cline of polysyntheticity as traditionally conceived. That grammars occur along such a dine is a worthy observation in itself: it is significant that there are apparently no languages with noun incorporation without agreement marking, given that there would seem to be no a priori reason that such languages would not exist (i.e., why could not a few Polynesian, Sinitic, or Kwa languages not have robust noun incorporation?).

However, this clinal nature also throws yet another wrench into an innatist scenario: Baker's theory cannot explain *within the tenets of evolutionary biology*—just why the parameter was "set" at the end of the cline. Just what was it about the combination of obligatory agreement affixes and noun incorporation that would have increased the chances of propagation for those whose genomes rendered them as well predisposed to use this kind of grammar as an analytic one (this presumably being how a parameter, rather than a single option, would manifest itself)? Why would this mutation have only conferred this hypothetical advantage among speakers of languages like Mohawk rather than Warlpiri? And if we widen our lens to stable polymorphisms and the like, how scientifically valuable can we adjudge a theory that proposes that such a mutation "just happened" at some point in human evolution—

before grammars compatible with it yet existed—and encoding *precisely the grade of polysyntheticity* that Baker appeals to? Clearly there are problems with falsifiability and theoretical elegance here.

### 9.1.2. Cognitive versus autonomous

An alternate analysis beckons: that the cline represents a pathway of drift that languages may possibly take just as Edoid tonal tense/aspect marking does, and that both the implicational, "nested" nature of the cline and the syntactic features that seem to follow from particular degrees of polysyntheticity show that this drift is constrained by cognitive aspects of the human brain.

Other scholars have come to similar conclusions about parameters in general. Hawkins (1994) demonstrates that ordering of verb phrase constituents, proposed as parametrically based by Koopman (1984) and Travis (1989), submits gracefully to a cognitively-based parsing model. In line with my argument, Hawkins concurs (1997: 746) that the correlations in question are valid in a descriptive and even predictive sense, "But they are no longer part of UG itself." Similarly, Newmeyer's (1998: 364) conclusion, after comparing formalist and functionalist approaches to parametrical variation, is that "one can imagine the possibility of a theory in every respect like recent principles-and-parameters models, but in which the parameters are arrived at inductively by the child."

Nor does such an approach necessarily entail that language is not innate to some degree. Pinker and Bloom (1994: 183), in a follow-up to their seminal 1990 paper, write that parameters of variation "are not individual explicit gadgets in the human mind . . . instead, they should fall out of the interaction between the specific mechanisms that define the basic underlying organization of language ('Universal Grammar') and the learning mechanisms, some of them predating language, that can be sensitive to surface variation in the entities defined by those language specific mechanisms."

### 9.1.3. Exaptation and Universal Grammar

Once again, evolutionary theory has space beyond innateness for the emergence of just such a conception of grammar: exaptation, or the recruitment of pre-existing structures in new functions (Gould and Lewontin 1979). Many creatures have fashioned their hands into new structures enabling them to fly, but the extremities themselves were originally selected for the purposes of terrestrial locomotion and manipulation of objects. In the same way, as Lass (1997: 320–23), for example, argues, Finnish case-marking arose through the recruitment of assorted linguistic material which had served other purposes in earlier stages of its grammar.

The correlations that Baker identifies, then, can be seen as support for the exaptationist conception of linguistic evolution espoused by authors such as Deacon (1997) and Kirby (1999). A preliminary observation regarding polysynthesis is that it, like all language change, demonstrates a cognitive tendency toward entrenchment of habit, which natural languages manifest over time. Pointedly, there are myriad ways in which this happens in grammars that no linguist would treat as based on innate configurations.

Lass (1997: 318–19) notes, for example, that over time English came to require speakers to mark the present tense with the progressive marker rather than the bare verb: what begins as a marginal strategy in Old English becomes obligatory in Modern English. Yet the anomalousness of this construction within Germanic, as well as languages worldwide, makes it plain that there is no "progressively-marked present tense parameter."

Our question, then, is simply whether there is any more indication that polysyntheticity and its syntactic correlates require an innatist parametrical analysis. Along those lines, it would seem that traditional functionalist studies of grammaticalization processes serve well as an alternate account.

For example, languages in which resumptive pronouns, or the co-indexing of subject- or object-marking clitics or affixes with full NPs, are ungrammatical are unknown to me: *My mother, she eats a lot of vegetables; I never liked him, that guy;* the French election slogan *La France, nous, on l'aime.* This trait, rooted in the topic-comment configurational inclination typical of human grammars that drives so much of grammatical change (viz. Li 1976), is typical of oral language in particular (cf. Escure 1997). In any grammar, myriad features that are either optional or marked in terms of pragmatics or register are candidates for entrenchment as obligatory. Grammars differ in what choices they happen to make in this regard: some develop obligatory evidential marking, others develop verb-initial word order, and so on.

Baker's conception of polysynthesis could plausibly trace to grammars drifting into the entrenchment of the co-indexing of full NPs with pronominal elements. In languages with obligatory subject prefixes, residual phonetic likenesses between the prefixes and the full subject pronouns testify to this pathway of development (e.g., Swahili's second-person singular pronoun *wewe* and the corresponding prefix *u-*, and third-person plural *wao* and *wa-*). In some languages, this particular structural "genius" would become so very entrenched that constituents incommensurate with it would become infelicitous—just as the history of a verb-initial language includes a point at which verb-initial sentences, at first a pragmatic option amidst a subject-initial norm, became a new norm rendering subject-initial sentences ungrammatical. Hence, in a Bakerian polysynthetic language, *exeunt* adpositional phrases for which there exist no corresponding resumptive pronouns, and so on.

Germanic diachrony demonstrates that such grammatical correlations falling out from a particular feature need not be seen as suggestions of innateness. There are only two Germanic languages, English and Swedish, that recruited their *be*-verbs as passive markers (Rissanen 1999: 215). As it happens, these two languages are also unique in their family in not marking intransitive perfects with the *be*-verb (German *wir **sind** gereisen* "We traveled," but Swedish *vi **har** rest* with a form of its verb *have*). This is not an accidental correlation: few would contest an analysis here based on an ambiguity between the passive and perfect readings rendered by the same verb, resolved in favor of the former. That is, the habit of marking the passive with *be*, beginning through chance drift, eventually became so entrenched in these two grammars that it rendered *be*-perfects potentially opaque, with these thus eliminated. This was essentially an unremarkable cognitive process, and none would assume that it indicated a neurologically encoded parametrical choice for maintaining distinct forms for the intransitive perfect and the passive. Any such argument would founder when encountering Icelandic, in which the *be*-verb is used both to connote resultativity in the intransitive perfect with verbs of motion and change-of-state (*ég er kominn* "I am come," "I am here" [Kress 1982: 152–53]) as well as to connote a substantial resultative domain of the passive (*ég var barinn* "I was hit") (ibid. 148–49).

While the entrenchment of NP-pronominal co-indexing is readily intuitive, the analogous origin of the other defining feature of Baker's polysynthesis conception is perhaps less so to Indo-European speakers: the entrenchment of a "habit" of saying *He's house-building* for *He's building a house*. But we can see parallels in English to the beginning of such a process in items like *babysit*, and obviously the further entrenchment of such a feature is inherently no more remarkable than so many Indo-European languages' developing a verb *have* denoting possession—which has been argued to be a typologically unusual feature, encoded in most languages with case-marking or zero-marking (Lazard 1990: 246–47). Yet we would not accept a proposed "*have*-verb parameter."

Crucially, there would appear to be no principled motivation for specifying that polysyntheticity of any type be encoded as innate that would at the same time systematically rule out submitting English's progressive-marked present or *be*-marked passive to the same analysis. Moreover, that we are dealing with various stages of an acquired habit rather than a distinct "parameter setting" is supported by the very fact that natural languages evidence polysyntheticity along a cline of varying degrees along which there is no particular point that we have any principled reason to suppose would decisively enhance a species' propagation of its genes where previous points on the cline would not.

Such an account does leave open the question as to why languages apparently only drift into noun incorporation *after* having acquired the agreement morpheme "tic." But the fact remains that this developmental sequence does not submit any more gracefully to analysis as a selected feature than the parameter itself. And all indications are that a cognitively based address of this question is more immediately promising than one based on religion, or modes of thought too fundamentally unlike any presently known to even be productively addressed within our lifetimes.

## 9.2. The Rich Agreement Hypothesis

There are two possible alternate approaches to the Rich Agreement Hypothesis.

### 9.2.1. Another epiphenomenon of human cognition?

One approach would be to proceed according to the assumption, as seems unassailable regarding the Polysynthesis Parameter, that the relevant typological correlations are real. Supporting this would be the restriction of the Transitive Expletive Construction to languages with verb movement. Bobalijk and Thráinnson (1998: 56) argue that these constructions, where the logical subject occupies a lower position while the expletive fills a higher one, suggest a split IP, an example being Icelandic:

(9)  **það**   hefur einhver köttur étið   mýsnar.
     EXPL has   some   cat    eaten mice.the
     "A cat has eaten mice." (i.e., "There has a cat eaten mice.")

They predict that such constructions would only occur in languages with verb movement, and then demonstrate this with Norwegian and English where the Transitive Expletive Construction is absent:

(10)   *Det  har en katt ete    mysene.
       EXPL has a   cat  eaten mice.the
       "A cat has eaten mice."

Faroese lends encouraging support, in that speakers of dialects with verb movement accept Transitive Expletive Constructions while speakers of dialects where the verb does not move do not (Jonas 1996).

Data of this sort show that it would be inappropriate to reject the Rich Agreement Hypothesis as based solely on verb movement and various formulations of inflectional "richness." Arguments from adherents of this school are broader and more rigorous than this.

We might propose, then, that the emergence of inflectional affixation conditions a syntactic mental representation with a split IP without there being any innate specification or predisposition for this. Future research may reveal that even when affixes erode, such a syntax can persist in the mental representations of future generations on the basis of other "cues," such as manifestations of multiple specifier positions high in the tree. It is unclear that the current state of neurobiology or human cognition rules out such a hypothesis in any falsifiable way.

### 9.2.2. An artifact of a narrow data set?

Yet the fact remains that the Rich Agreement Hypothesis has to date only been argued on the basis of Germanic (one smallish subfamily only about a dozen languages strong) and Romance (a subfamily only about a dozen languages strong by conventional estimations), which are two conglomerations within just nine living subfamilies of just one smallish family (Indo-European is by no means fecund as language families go) out of dozens of language families worldwide. While, strictly speaking, a small subset of languages may well reveal language universals, surely this typologically narrow database qualifies as a potential weakness compared to the truly cross-linguistic focus of Baker's work.

This becomes especially urgent in view of another parameter argued for on the basis of a similarly narrow typological base, perhaps the "textbook case" for the parameter conception as a whole, the null-subject parameter. Rizzi (1982) and Safir (1985) together predicted five out of sixteen potential conglomerations of features in grammars, based on their conception of this parameter and its predicted effects on a syntactic configuration. Yet Gilligan (1987), checking a 100-language sample, found no fewer than nine such conglomerations that is, four configurations that Rizzi's and Safir's hypothesis ruled out.

Recently adduced evidence suggests that the Rich Agreement Hypothesis may be similarly threatened when the typological net is cast more widely, so that a second alternate analysis to the Rich Agreement Hypothesis may be to reject its cross-linguistic validity altogether.

Cape Verdean Creole Portuguese has but one inflectional affix, the past marker *-ba*. None of the metrics that Rich Agreement Hypothesis adherents have proposed would admit this one marker, invariant across person and number, as lending this grammar "rich" inflection. Yet Baptista (2000) shows that nevertheless in this language, the verb moves past adverbs and quantifiers left-adjoined to VP, *even when the past affix is not even phonologically realized*:

(11)  (a)  João xina   **ben** se  lison.
           John learned well his lesson.
           "John learned his lesson well." (Baptista 2000: 14)

      (b)  Konbidadu txiga    **tudu** na mismu tempu.
           guests        arrived all  in same  time
           "All the guests arrived at the same time." (ibid. 17)

Yet Baptista argues that Cape Verdean syntactic behavior gives no evidence of a split IP such as multiple specifier heads available to subjects.

The facts are even more problematic in Cape Verdean's close sister language, Guinea-Bissau Creole Portuguese. Here, the cognate of *-ba* is less an affix than a floating clitic, modifying not only verb phrases but even nominal predicates:

(12)  I un prosesu dificil   **ba**.
      it a  process difficult PAST
      "It was a difficult process." (Kihm 1994: 108, cited in Baptista 2000: 26)

But in this inflection-free language, the verb again moves leftward of floating adverbial quantifiers left-adjoined to VP:

(13)  Konbidadu **tudu** ciga   na mismu tenpu.
      guests        all  arrived at same  time
      "The guests arrived all at the same time." (ibid.)

Yet again, there are no residual indications of split IP in Guinea-Bissau Creole Portuguese either (unattested in the most complete grammar of the language [Kihm 1994] and confirmed as absent by Kihm himself [Mar. 2002, pers. comm.]).

Finally, there are dialects of Louisiana Creole French where verb stems alternate between short and long forms (Baptista 2000: 28). The short forms condition verb movement obligatorily with the negator *pa* and optionally with VP adverbs:

(14)  (a)  Mo mõzh **pa**   gratõ.
           I   eat  NEG cracklin'
           "I don't eat cracklin" (Neumann 1985: 321, cited by Rottet 1992: 277)

      (b)  Mo marsh (pa) **zhame** ni-pje   deor.
           I   walk  NEG never  barefoot outside
           "1 never walk barefoot outside." (Neumann 1985: 330, cited by Rottet 1992: 267)

But the long forms remain in place under both conditions:

(15)  (a) Na lõtõ      mo **pa**   mõzhe gratõ.
      in  long-time I   NEG eat    cracklin'
      "I haven't eaten cracklin' for a long time." (Neumann 1985: 321, cited by Rottet
      1992: 277)

      (b) Mo (pa)  **zhame** (te)   zhõgle õho   sa.                      ·
      I   NEG never  PAST think   about that
      "I never thought about that." (Neumann 1985: 330, cited by Rottet 1992: 267)

The variation here is difficult to square with an analysis positing a split IP categorically requiring verb movement: some finite verbs move and others do not. And it is
furthermore ominous that, to the extent that one might be moved to treat the final *e*
on the long forms as an inflection, it is precisely the verbs with this segmental ap-
pendage that *never* move.

   These data from three natural languages beyond the data set that the Rich Agreement Hypothesis school have addressed suggest that the correlations in question may
be restricted to a small subset of the world's languages, and that the explanation found
for them will fall outside of innateness.


## 10. Conclusion

Because inflectional affixation emerges as the result of contingent accident, is absent or marginal in languages that arise anew, and is impossible to square with the
tenets of evolutionary biology as currently configured, I submit that the syntactic
parameter whose setting depends on inflectional affixation is a logical impossibility.

   This implies that where typological correlations hinging on affixation are evident, they should be traced to factors beyond natural selection. In other words, this
argument supports positions such as Deacon's (1997), situating the language competence in general aspects of human cognition.

   In light of Baker's claim that parameters' evolutionary purpose will only become evident from forms of thought as yet unfamiliar, I surmise that the most promising infant paradigm for providing a principled explanation of the correlations in
question will be that charting the self-organizing principles of complex adaptive
systems (that is, Kauffman 1995) (cf. Kirby 1999).

# Strange Bedfellows

*Recovering the Origins of Black English*

## 1. Introduction

It always strikes me how difficult it is to answer a question I am often asked by students, professors, the media, and members of the general public: Where did Black English come from? The responsible scholar acquainted with the issues can only answer this question after a game swallow and a pause for gathering one's thoughts, because the origins of Black English have been hotly contested for thirty years now.

The two major schools of thought on the issue have been termed the Creolist and the Dialectologist Hypotheses. The former proposes that Gullah Creole was once spoken throughout, at least, the deep South instead of just on the Sea Islands and somewhat inland as it is today, and that today's Black English resulted from the decreolization of Gullah in most locations as the result of integration after the Civil War. After some early espousals most notably by Stewart (1967 and other works) and Fasold (1976 and other works) and a book-length treatment by Dillard (1972), the Creolist Hypothesis became an official institution with papers by Rickford (1977) and Holm (1984) pointing to features in Black English possibly traceable to African languages and/or a previous creole stage. Since then, various scholars such as Baugh (1980), Singler (1991), DeBose and Faraclas (1993), and Rickford (1997, 1998) have devoted significant attention to arguing further for this hypothesis, followed by "third-generation" contributors such as Hannah (1996) and Weldon (1996). This work has largely been couched in the quantificational frame of reference pioneered in the early 1970s for the analysis of highly variable grammars such as continuum creoles and Black English, and it bases arguments for historical relationship on the comparison of occurrence rates of variable grammatical features and their conditioning according to context.

The Dialectologist Hypothesis was originally associated with now deceased scholars who worked before the advent of two phenomena central to how most research on Black English origins has been conducted since the seminal Labov (1969): the variationist paradigm founded by Labov at the University of Pennsylvania, and the civil rights movement. Constrained neither by the rigorous attention to detail enforced by competing analyses of quantificational corpora nor by a guiding desire to delineate a unique African American heritage, scholars such as Krapp (1924), Kurath (1949), and McDavid and McDavid (1951) argued that Black English was traceable solely to archaic or regional white English sources, and that Africa had played no significant part in its birth.

In the early 1980s, however, a series of papers by Shana Poplack, in conjunction first with David Sankoff (1987) and later Sali Tagliamonte (1991), reignited the Dialectologist position. The "New Dialectologists" have made especial reference to sources of data that have been unexplored until the 1980s: the speech of communities of descendants from African-Americans who settled outside of the United States before Emancipation. Their general argument, inaugurated with Poplack and Sankoff's study of Samaná English (1987), is that contrary to the Creolist Hypothesis prediction that these varieties would be closer to creole than to modern Black English, they are, in fact, often no more or even less creole-like, suggesting that Black English itself has roots not in Gullah but in nonstandard English varieties. For better or for worse, amid the value that our post civil rights Zeitgeist places on diversity and cultural essentialism, the Dialectologist Hypothesis is somewhat Politically Incorrect. As such, the New Dialectologists have been especially attentive to statistical argumentation and fine-grained manipulation of the VARBRUL program, and have also been extremely prolific, with breadth of coverage thus complementing the quality of their argumentation in demonstrating that their position is empirically rather than ideologically based.

## 2. Epistemology of the volume

In this light, *The English History of African American English* is not simply one more collection of conference papers or articles united loosely by a general theme. This book is a manifesto, gathering between two covers several state-of-the-art analyses of various areas of Black English grammar, all arguing in favor of the New Dialectologist position pioneered by the editor. For maximum comparability, the papers all refer to one tripartite corpus, consisting of (1) the speech of blacks on the Samaná Peninsula, (2) the speech of blacks descended from American slaves relocated to Nova Scotia after the Revolutionary War and thereafter, and (3) the Works Progress Administration (henceforth WPA) recordings of aged ex-slaves made mostly in the 1930s.

In her introduction, Poplack makes three crucial observations. First, she notes (15):

> Work aimed at establishing the origins of AAVE has often invoked coincidental similarities with creoles and African languages, on the one hand, and differences from Standard English on the other. Inexplicably rare, with a few notable excep-

tions, are systematic comparisons with varieties approximating the older, regional and/or nonstandard forms of English to which the Africans were likely to have been first exposed.

I would have inserted a "possibly" before the word "coincidental" in this passage, but otherwise this is a crucial and sadly apt observation.

Most Creolist Hypothesis treatments, for all of their virtues, largely appear to assume that slaves in America were exposed to the kind of English I am writing in (Rickford 1986 is one of the few Creolist Hypothesis treatments that devotes attention as sustained to the British Isles as to the Caribbean and the Sea Islands.) Yet, in fact, nonstandard English varieties contain not just some but most of the features that today are associated with Black English, including habitual *be*, overgeneralization of third-person singular *-s*, omission of plural with certain types of lexical item, the *done* past, multiple negation, and a great many others. Yet nonstandard British English is less underacknowledged than outright ignored in a great deal of Creolist Hypothesis work, in contrast to concentration on Jamaican patois, Gullah, and African languages such as Yoruba, many of which were not actually significant elements in the ethnic mix of slaves brought to America.

This has constituted an unfortunate lapse in argumentation, because the basic outlines of the black experience in the United States require that nonstandard English dialects be nothing less than central in any address of the origins of Black English. To treat nonstandard English as a marginal issue is analogous to charting a history of ragtime that refers only to African-derived syncopation and "blue notes" while making only fleeting reference to the European harmonic system and American-born march format that are equally central to the architecture of the genre. This volume and the tradition it represents, then, is particularly welcome in addressing this problem by giving the English data their due weight.

Poplack's second observation addresses a notorious issue in the Black English origins debate. When New Dialectologist analyses have questioned Creolist Hypothesis conclusions, a frequent objection among advocates of the latter has been to question the representativeness of speech data collected under artificial conditions from black respondents from unfamiliar white interviewers, with accuracy of transcription another vital concern, particularly in reference to the WPA tapes. In fact, as much ink and verbal debate have been devoted to the representativeness of the WPA tapes and their transcriptions as to the linguistic data on the tapes itself (cf. Bailey, Maynor, and Cukor-Avila 1991). Here, however, Poplack observes that if possible interference factors significantly invalidated the representativeness of these three sources, then we would not expect the close correspondences between them in terms of rates of occurrence and grammatical conditioning of various features.

Finally, unusually for advocates of either position in the origins debate, Poplack takes the occasion to specify the epistemological motivation of the variationist focus of most work on Black English history. I will never forget a particularly outspoken graduate student colleague of mine in the 1980s who noted the anomaly in the tendency toward concentration on "counting copulas" in the study of Black English rather than on grammatical analysis. Certainly that designation is oversimplified; copulas are hardly the only variable to have received attention, and "counting" in this tradition is complemented by examination of surrounding grammatical conditioning.

Nevertheless, it is easy to forget that Black English is the only speech variety in the world where such a vast proportion of work devoted to it hinges on statistical analyses of the rates of occurrence of a few variable features—this frame of reference is largely alien to, for example, Indo-European or Algonquian studies, or dialectological studies of German or Chinese. One might suppose that this approach stems from historical accident in the vein of the QWERTY keyboard I am typing on, and this is not completely untrue. The graduate student aspiring to join the study of the history of Black English, instantly immersed in a culture where 90% of the best work is based on VARBRUL analysis, statistical tables, and Labov (1969) as a foundational point of departure, is highly unlikely not to follow in this tradition in her own work. But it would be difficult to deny that this has a somewhat limiting effect. It must give us pause that after over three decades of concentrated attention to the dialect, a great deal remains unexplored about Black English phonology, syntax, and semantics synchronically or diachronically: those features that do not happen to lend themselves to variationist analysis have attracted relatively little attention.

Poplack, however, provides a rare and useful stipulation: that the variationist approach is specifically necessary to untangling the history of Black English. She first notes that New Dialectologist studies' conclusions are based not simply on comparison of rates of occurrence of features, but on differences across varieties in their grammatical conditioning, as teased out by the VARBRUL program, the assumption being that parallels in such conditioning are evidence of historical relationship. She notes that this is particularly important to the study of Black English origins because so many of its features are attested in white nonstandard Englishes, creoles, and Black English (variable plural marking, zero-marked relative clauses, etc.). In her view, quantificational analysis constitutes the only way to choose which surface parallels stem from historical relationship rather than happenstance.

Following her introduction are six papers giving concentrated attention to particular variables' usage in black speech of Samaná, Nova Scotia, and/or on the WPA tapes, collectively designated "early African American English" or "early AAE" (as it will be here henceforth). Their general theme is that early AAE either diverged from creole patternings or displayed no significant likeness to them, rather than hewing closer to them as the Creolist Hypothesis would predict, and usually that instead, early AAE paralleled white nonstandard English varieties. The general implication intended is that modern Black English has its origins largely in nonstandard English itself and that features of the modern dialect that superficially parallel creoles, such as new negation concord strategies, are, in fact, independent innovations, since the English leaning of early AAE eliminates the possibility that Gullah or its ilk could have been their source.

This is a richly considered and highly welcome volume. I too have argued that Black English owes the bulk of its structure to nonstandard English dialects rarely heard or encountered on the page by most Americans (McWhorter 1998b). As such, I consider it a boon to Black English studies for a volume to now exist presenting such detailed and careful argumentation for a similar position. Yet the fact is that in the final analysis, I find it difficult to conclude that these six papers together make as conclusive a case against the Creolist Hypothesis as Poplack's introduction, or the claims of the authors themselves, would have it. This becomes clear with an evaluation of each of these papers in turn.

## 3. The papers

If the argument in each of these papers were as clean and persuasive as Sali Tagliamonte and Jennifer Smith's on the conditioning of *was* and *were* in early AAE as compared to white nonstandard English varieties, then this book alone would score a decisive victory for the Dialectologist position. The Creolist Hypothesis would propose that the overgeneralization of *was* in Black English is an inheritance from the creole copula, which is invariant according to person and number. Yet overgeneralization of *was* is equally characteristic of nonstandard English dialects, blunting the significance of the parallel between creoles and Black English.

Tagliamonte and Smith provide quantificational analysis of the occurrence of *was* in contexts disallowed in standard English (second-person singular, first-person plural, and third-person plural) in early AAE (Nova Scotia); in the English of Buckie in Scotland, chosen as representative of the Northern English varieties predominant in the South where early AAE would have formed; and in the English of white Nova Scotian villagers, used as a control to examine whether correlation between early AAE and the speech of Buckie would be meaningful or epiphenomenal of tendencies general in English. In an eloquent demonstration of Poplack's claim in the introduction that grammatical conditioning can reveal relationships obscured by surface similarities, the authors find that in both Nova Scotian early AAE and Buckie English, *was* is favored by second-person singular over plural pronouns; full plural NPs over *they* (single NPs are irrelevant in that *he*, *she*, and *it* take *was* in all varieties); and negative over affirmative contexts. Various possible objections are anticipated and refuted.

One might suppose that the conditioning of *was* in Buckie may have been innovated after northern British people had immigrated to the United States to serve as models for blacks, but the data show no gender differentiation, suggesting a long-established feature. One might also propose that the preference for *was* with second-person singular in Buckie arose from a hypothetical desire general among English speakers to disambiguate the singular from the plural in earlier stages of English when the use of *you* with singular as well as plural reference was newer, but, in fact, Southern varieties of English in Britain exhibited no such tendency in *was*, despite the inherent ambiguity. Finally, the white Nova Scotian English variety does not show the same effect for second-person singular, which is congruent with the fact that immigrants to this area came mostly from southern England where *was* was not used with second-person singular. A paper like this one usefully illuminates the intimate historical relationship between Black English and rural Britishers long departed from the American social fabric.

Gunnel Tottie and Dawn Harvie make a similar, if necessarily not as watertight, case for relativization strategies in early AAE. Under the Creolist Hypothesis, the omissibility of subject relative pronouns in Black English (*He got a gun sound like a bee*) and the use of *what* as a relative pronoun in early AAE are creole inheritances (there are cognates to the latter item in, for example, Gullah). Yet it is under-acknowledged in references to this feature that the same traits are also found in non-standard dialects in England. Tottie and Harvey indicate that relativization in early AAE is more plausibly treated as a development from nonstandard white varieties than from creoles. For one, early AAE includes not only *what* but *that*, a form alien to creoles but alternating with *what* in white varieties. Furthermore, apparently Nova Scotian early AAE prefers *that* while Samaná English prefers *what*. The reasons for this are currently a mystery and are most likely due to chance differences that *arose* over time, but certainly cannot be traced to any alternation inherent to Gullah or any other creole. Tottie and Harvey's argument does leave some questions, since we lack quantitative analysis of the expression of relativization morphemes in the pertinent creoles. An argument that the presence of *that* traces to slight decreolization from Gullah cannot be dismissed out of hand. However, this paper is useful in demon-strating that attempts to trace the history of Black English are incomplete without sustained reference to white vernaculars as well as black ones.

The remaining four papers, however, make much less compelling cases for early AAE as a koine of nonstandard white Englishes. James A. Walker proposes that the contraction and zero-realization of the copula in early AAE can be shown to be con-ditioned not by following grammatical environment, as stipulated in innumerable studies following in the framework of Labov (1969), but by phonological or prosodic features of preceding or following constituents, as analyzed within the framework of Nespor and Vogel (1986) and Selkirk (1986). Walker is correct that the quest to link the relative percentages of contracted or zero copulas in Black English before NP, locatives, adjectives, *gonna*, and V-*ing* to corresponding percentage gradients in creoles, the theme of most works addressing the seminal dialectologist argument of Labov (1969), has resulted in an almost overwhelmingly contradictory collage of findings, with data incongruent with Creolist predictions that are too often explained away via rather unconstrained argumentation.

Walker notes that studies such as Holm (1984), Singler (1991), and Rickford (1996), taking basilectal English creoles' overt equative and locative copulas *da* (and its allomorphs) and *de* as the model for Black English, cannot account systemati-cally for the high percentage of zero-copula before locatives in particular in Black English, given that the creoles (and the African languages their creators spoke) have an overt morpheme in that context. Meanwhile, there is a lack of consistency in the level of creole appealed to, which has wide-ranging implications for conclusions about historical relationship. Weldon (1996), taking the high incidence of overt copula before adjectives in mesolectal Gullah as the comparandum, argues that the same feature in the Black English data she analyzes supports the Creolist Hypothesis, whereas many other scholars argue for the same hypothesis on the basis of the low incidence of overt copula in basilectal creoles where "adjectives" often behave like stative verbs and thus take no copula. Finally, the Creolist work lacks systematic explanations for various differential rates of contraction and deletion between dif-ferent following contexts. As Walker notes, Rickford (1996) can only attribute the lesser rate of zero-copula before locatives as opposed to equatives in Jamaican patois in general to an unmotivated "persistence of creole copula de" (why exactly wouldn't the equative *a* copula "persist" as well?), while Winford's (1992) charting of Trinidadian Creole's decreolization patterns in the copula, intended as a reference point for corresponding work on Black English, provides little explanation of why, for example, zero-copulas in the mesolect become overt at higher rates for V-*ing* and *gonna* than before adjectives and locatives.

Walker tantalizingly suggests that phonological environment and prosody will provide explanations for the relevant facts where twenty-five years of previous work has not, but in the end, most of the old questions remain. Walker's quantitative results do show that proclitic personal pronouns and a preceding vowel or [r] favor contraction, while zero is favored elsewhere (although the effect is relatively slight in the case of the latter condition). This is a useful observation, but hardly one positioned to provide a general explanation of copula patternings between Black English and Caribbean creoles. As to rendering following grammatical environment irrelevant in favor of prosodic factors, it simply cannot be said that Walker has shown that, as he claims, "the analysis in this chapter has demonstrated that many of the purported grammatical effects are due to prosody" (67).

Walker's hypothesis is that contraction and zero-copula will be conditioned by following complex phonological phrases rather than simple ones, but in fact, the quantificational results do not support this meaningfully. Between the analysis of Nova Scotia English and Samaná English, in the results from testing the impact of prosody on the contraction and zero before the pertinent grammatical environments, there are twenty comparisons; i.e., contraction before a simple phonological phrase containing V-*ing*, zero-copula before a complex phonological phrase that is a locative, etc. (omitting from consideration the comparisons where there is no data for one context). Out of these twenty, in only eight cases is the impact of simple versus complex phonological phrases more than ten points; otherwise, either simple phonological phrases had a greater impact or the difference would appear to be too small to base broad historical claims upon. Pointedly, in the meantime, the general trend is that *gonna* and V-*ing* condition more contraction and zero than NPs and locatives, with adjectives, as so frequently observed in the Creolist literature, flipping maddeningly between more and less contraction and zero than locatives. It is unclear that the phonological and prosodic factors so carefully outlined by Walker have provided a compelling alternative to following grammatical environment as crucial factors here.

Walker appears to be aware that these results are not a decisive refutation of the Creolist approach to the data, and he provides some extremely apt directives for future research which fall outside of the phonological purview. These are as important to Creolists as to Dialectologists, and they provide a more rigorous definition of "copula," including an acknowledgement of the distinction between copula and auxiliary. If there is one element missing from all work on Black English and its history, it is a cross-linguistic, typological perspective, and in that light, it should be noted that it is hardly a universal configuration in the languages of the world for nonverbal predications (equative and locative) to be marked with the same item that marks progressives and futures. Many of the differences in rates of occurrence of zero-copula, or its rate of replacement in different contexts by overt morphemes, are likely to be attributable to grammatical differences between "true" copulas and auxiliaries, along with the particular configuration of these two categories in English grammar.

Early AAE marked the plural on nouns less than modern Black English does. This would appear to support the Creolist Hypothesis, according to which Black English has moved ever closer to standard over time but began as a creole, creoles being well-known in tending to mark the plural only in relatively constrained contexts. However, Shana Poplack, Sali Tagliamonte, and Ejike Eze attempt to build a case that quantitative analysis rules out a historical relationship between early AAE's less-frequent plural marking and the creole tendency, and instead suggests that the early AAE pattern was modeled on nonstandard English varieties. Yet in the end, their findings leave decreolization from a creole template not simply plausible but the most likely analysis as well.

This study makes the contribution, rigorous and useful in itself, of addressing quantitative analysis of data from Nigerian Pidgin English (NPE)—which, despite its name, is structurally a full language (i.e., creole) and is closely akin to sister creoles in the Caribbean—as a creole comparandum. The most important observation from this analysis is that plural marking is significantly favored by animacy in NPE, a trait they trace to the creole's substrate languages such as Igbo where there is a similar constraint. This, in turn, becomes a lynchpin of their argumentation, because early AAE exhibits no such animacy effect.

The implication the authors draw from this, however, is problematic. They treat this difference as indicating a general contrast between early AAE and "creole," but this is extremely hasty. For one, Nigerian Pidgin English is not the creole Black English is proposed to have arisen from (nor was Igbo a particularly dominant substrate language among slaves in the United States). Furthermore, it is undocumented that animacy plays a similar role in plural marking in Gullah or in any of the English creoles of the Caribbean that it stemmed from; neither are we told whether animacy plays this role in the marking of plural in African languages other than Igbo, such as Wolof, Mende, Twi, or Kikongo. The most responsible account of the given data is that Nigerian Pidgin English alone has borrowed this specific constraint from Igbo as the result of centuries of bilingualism; the application of these facts to the speech of blacks in Nova Scotia is unclear. Moreover, even if such an animacy constraint on plural marking were found in other African languages that slaves brought to the United States, we could not assume that the constraint was carried over into Gullah. Creoles spoken *long-term* alongside their substrate languages typically inherit particularly specific features from them (cf. Solomon Islands Pijin [Keesing 1988], Korlai Creole Portuguese [Clements 1992]), but substrate impact on creoles whose speakers lost the substrate languages early on is, while robust, generally less likely to include features as specific as animacy-marking constraints on plural marking (cf. chapter 3).

Thus it cannot be said that the absence of the animacy effect in early AAE constitutes a decisive distinction between these varieties and "creole," which leaves us with the other differences the authors note. These are that, unlike creoles, early AAE did not leave generics unmarked and that early AAE favored zero plural in a small class of lexical items and before following consonant, while creole plural marking is conditioned by deictic and semantic factors rather than lexical or phonological ones. If we could really say that animacy conditions plural marking in creoles in general, then this would discourage treating early AAE as a decreolization from Gullah. Divested of that block, though, there would appear to be no principled reason why these differences could not have arisen through the gradual movement of Gullah toward standard English—especially since, as the authors even observe, the lexical items that favor zero plural marking in early AAE are different from those that favor it in various nonstandard British dialects.

Darin M. Howe and Walker try to deflect the development of modern Black English negation patterns from a creole origin by proposing that much of today's patterning had yet to emerge in early AAE and only developed subsequently via internal innovation. That Black English has innovated some negation constructions is clear—and unremarkable of a living speech variety of any kind. Furthermore, these innovations cannot be attributed to African or "creole" patterns; rather, they are paralleled by developments in many nonstandard white varieties (Schneider 1989: 200), and to the extent that they are not, we must allow for the fact that as a living speech variety, Black English not only *may*, but most certainly *must*, develop features unique to it over time. However, Howe and Walker's claim that early AAE exhibited no significant differences from white nonstandard Englishes is only possible via rather frantically waving away an uncomfortable volume of data suggesting otherwise, which at least on the surface leaves some variant of the Creolist position plausible.

The basic problem that Howe and Walker face is that early AAE keeps popping up with tokens that parallel creole negator behavior in ways that they would not if early AAE were truly the koine of white nonstandard Englishes that this volume proposes. For example, *ain't* is tense-neutral in creoles, appearing in past as well as present. Interestingly, in early AAE but unlike modern Black English, there are examples of *ain't* used in the past. The authors' attempts to explain this away (118–19) are unsuccessful. They try to marginalize it by claiming that it is found only in the Nova Scotia data, but their own tables show tokens in Samaná and the WPA tapes as well. They claim that in Nova Scotia it is "essentially restricted to the present tense" and is thus not truly tense-neutral—but to designate sixty-nine tokens in the present and eleven in the past as "essentially present" is an ad hoc stretch. The fact that the item does not occur in this usage in a modern creole is irrelevant: the Creolist position would stipulate that the usage recruits a white nonstandard form for a creole usage. They dismiss the use of *ain't* for *don't* (*I ain't know nothing 'bout that*) as too "rare" to be admitted as evidence (121), but then just five pages before, in reference to another feature rare in some data but beneficial to their thesis, they argue that "small percentages of a feature do not indicate the underlying absence of that feature." Indeed, especially when we are dealing with limited corpora, there are no principled grounds for rejecting an uncommonly encountered token as "not a part of the speaker's grammar," a particularly important question given the Dialectologist claim that the early AAE speakers were taking their cue only from white nonstandard Englishes: where, then, did they acquire past-marking *ain't* even on the purported "margins" of their competence?

The authors suggest that negative concord with indefinites (*Nobody don't know about no club*), a creole-like feature, be classified as an innovation in modern Black English because its use shows "far more variability" in early AAE—but the crucial point would appear to be that the feature appears 89% percent of the time in the Nova Scotia data, 80% on the WPA tapes, and 66% in Samaná. The contrast between these rates and the 98% for modern Black English found by Labov, Cohen, Robins, and

Lewis (1968) is obviously not great enough to isolate the feature as a modern inner-city innovation: even if a hair less frequent, it was clearly a robust feature in early AAE. Negative concord with verbs in the same clause (*Nobody didn't go*) is found both in creoles and in early AAE, but the authors dismiss this as indicative of creole origins because (1) the feature is found in Southern White English, (2) the feature is found in Middle English, and (3) the feature is always variable rather than categorical in all varieties in which it is attested. But Black English could easily have lent the feature to Southern White English. The presence of the feature in a passage from *The Canterbury Tales* hardly suffices as demonstration that the feature was present in a representative number of nonstandard dialects four centuries later; and point 3 is simply not an argument at all: the entire Dialectologist school would appear to be based on the assumption that variable occurrence rates and conditions can be passed from one variety to another intact and may even be preserved over centuries of time.

The preceding cases alone cover most of the sentence types the authors treat, and suffice to show that this paper does not demonstrate that early AAE paralleled white nonstandard Englishes in its negation constructions.

Gerard Van Herk argues that noninversion of auxiliaries, often argued to be a creole inheritance in early AAE, is actually a continuation of a trait inherent to English throughout its history. It is true that the Creolist literature on this feature has not acknowledged, as this paper does, that noninversion is a vital feature in questions even in standard English (*It's near Billings Bridge?*), but the question is whether the *particular* types of noninversion in Black English and early AAE are traceable to white Englishes. The crucial cases are those identified by, for example, Debose (1996) in Samaná English, *Why I didn't see you?* (designated "causative" by Van Herk) and copula-final sentences like *From where you is?* and *Where you was?* Judging from Van Herk's presentation, these sentence types are found in early AAE (also documented in Nova Scotia), but the paper does not cite evidence of such sentences in any white varieties spoken by whites in contact with American blacks in the past or present, which we can take as indicating that there is no such evidence.

Instead, Van Herk makes a larger argument that noninversion of subjects and verbs as a general syntactic strategy has been on the increase in English as the result of the emergence of *do*-support (*How do you use it?*), but this argument would appear to miss the trees for the forest. The issue is why early AAE had not generalized *do*-support to the particular sentence types Debose presents, and moreover, these types are crucial in that they cannot be attributed to variable elision of *do* as Black English sentences like *How you do it?* can be. Van Herk's approach would appear to entail treating syntactic features as a whole rather than appealing to surface configurations, but here, this begs the question as to what conditioned the *extent and manner of application* of the syntactic process in question. The crucial sentence types—which are extremely difficult for any English speaker to imagine enunciated with a British or even vernacular American white accent—remain as evidence that white nonstandard English was not the only significant element in the birth of early AAE and, by extension, modern Black English.

Thus, taken together, the papers in *The English History of African American English* show that while English clearly played a large, and even dominant, role in the birth of Black English, there remain identifiable aspects of the dialect that are at least preliminarily parseable as support for some form of the Creolist Hypothesis. More specifically, this volume does not confirm the thesis that early AAE was for all intents and purposes a garden-variety English dialect, or that features in modern Black English that appear creole-like are all latter-day innovations whose resemblance to their creole equivalents is merely fortuitous. Salikoko Mufwene's claim in his epilogue to the volume that "nothing has been found so far which suggests that AAVE was more creole-like at the beginning of the nineteenth century" (247), for example, is not borne out by the sum of these papers.

In general, it is likely that a conclusive resolution of this issue will depend on the supplementary reference to broader but equally vital lines of attack. In the remainder of this essay I will suggest that these additional approaches indicate that the truth about the history of Black English lies between the Dialectologist and Creolist positions, albeit with a considerable leaning toward the former.

These alternate approaches are necessary because by themselves, the early AAE data are, from a wide-lens perspective, uncooperative with the expectations of advocates of either side. The Creolist collects data from the WPA tapes, as well as from the diaspora communities of Samaná, from Nova Scotia, and from Liberia awaiting a creole-like speech, only to find people most of whom sound more or less like my great-grandmother, an African American of little education who spent her life in Georgia—a deep Black English but in no significant sense a "creole" variety; my great-grandmother would have considered Gullah or "Geechee Talk" quite alien from her speech repertoire. In contrast, the Dialectologist searches the same sources for a kind of koine of white nonstandard Englishes, only to find people talking not unlike, well, my great-grandmother, whose speech patterns were clearly starkly distinguishable from any white English dialect, deep Southern vernacular included. Given this situation, does Black English have creole roots, and if so, what exactly was the nature of the relationship?

## 4. Supplementary approaches to the issue

### 4.1. Diaspora speech versus diaspora variables

It is useful to observe at the outset that contrary to the expectations of an extreme version of the Creolist Hypothesis, the speech of people descended from American slaves who left the United States before Emancipation was clearly not, in any meaningful sense, Gullah itself. The literature on this question focuses to such a degree on a small set of variable features and their quantificational analysis that the outside reader can possibly lose sight of the fact, as they peruse the plethora of tables and charts and discussions of chi-squares, that the varieties in question do not correspond to Gullah in the vast majority of respects. Of course, where one draws the line between creole and dialect is an inherently hazy and subjective affair. However, the existence of purple hardly eliminates the validity of the concepts of red and blue, and in that light, here are some sentences from Samaná English (from Poplack and Sankoff 1987):

(1)  She don't ax me what she gon' cook.

(2)   English ain't so easy to learn like Spanish is.

(3)   If anybody in the way, well, they'll mash him up.

The situation is similar with the descendants in Liberia of slaves transported there in 1822, at first mostly from Maryland, Virginia and North Carolina and then later from South Carolina and Georgia. Again, there is little in this speech (Liberian Settler English) that suggests that Gullah itself was transported to Liberia, as we see in these examples from Singler (1991):

(4)   1 done forgot it.

(5)   But still we so hard up.

(6)   The girl say she ain't want me.

Finally, Poplack and Tagliamonte (1991) analyzed the speech of blacks in Nova Scotia, descended from slaves and freedmen from various American colonies freed by the British after the Revolutionary War, other slaves freed after the War of 1812, and then other slaves fleeing until the Civil War. They find this speech, like the other diaspora dialects, closer to Black English than to West Indian creoles or Gullah (from Poplack and Tagliamonte 1991: 324, 327):

(7)   I never run from nothing else no more.

(8)   She know how my husband used to teat me.

(9)   When they speaks to me, say "Hello," I just lets it go, go on about my business.

In all of these cases, we must note the absence of features such as second-person plural pronoun *hunnuh*, habitual marker *blant*, postposed *dem* as plural marker, *wisseh* for "where," *duh* for "to be," gender-neutral pronoun *um*, and any number of other features that specifically distinguish Gullah, and the general likes of which distinguish creoles. Overall, only very occasionally do any of the sentences in these corpora give the impression in terms of lexical items, phonology, semantics, or syntax of departing significantly from what we would process as variants of Black English itself—allowing that Black English is no more uniform an entity than any other highly variable nonstandard dialect in a dynamic relationship with a dominant local standard. As such, it is difficult to view the diaspora varieties as indicating that Gullah itself was once spoken far beyond today's Gullah territory.

## 4.2. Identifying the pertinent lect to examine: The revision of the old continuum model

It is for this reason, then, that the Creolist work on the diaspora varieties focuses on what are considered to be *underlying* inheritances from creoles specifically, the rates of occurrence of certain features, especially the copula, and the weighting of their grammatical conditioning by surrounding elements. Along those lines, possible correspondences with creoles have indeed been found. Poplack and Sankoff (1987) examined Samaná English and concluded that "at least insofar as its copula usage is concerned it [Samaná] bore no more resemblance to English-based West Indian creoles than modern ABE [AAVE], and indeed less." However, Hannah (1996) has shown that Samaná English copular absence rates parallel West Indian creoles much more closely than Poplack and Sankoff's data suggests. Rickford (1998: 170–73) notes that copula deletion patterns in the Liberian data are again similar to those in West Indian creoles, and Singler (1989) suggests that Liberian Settler English shows signs of being more sensitive to aspect than tense as creoles tend to be.

Developments in creole studies over the past fifteen years suggest a clarification as to exactly what kind of creole ancestor is in question, and they provide a resolution of longstanding contradictions and ad hoc explanations in the Creolist literature. Much of the Creolist literature has been couched in the traditional creole continuum model, under which Black English and early AAE would have evolved from a basilectal creole variety with overt equative and locative copulas and a tense-aspect system expressed with preverbal particles, then proceeding to a mesolectal stage where these copulas were absent while the tense-aspect particles were replaced phonetically by lexifier items serving the same basilectal grammatical functions (as first analyzed in Guyanese Creole by Bickerton 1973, 1975), and finally moving into an acrolectal stage where lexifier forms of the copula were incorporated while tense-aspect forms took on their lexifier functions.

The apparent elegance of that model, and its indexical relationship with sociological currents of the Afro-American experience, were quite seductive: Bickerton (1975) remains, in itself, a uniquely satisfying read, for example. However, this continuum model would seem to have been conclusively refuted by evidence that English creole basilects and mesolects developed concurrently at the outset of colonization. The evidence for this is partly sociohistorical: most colonies were settled first with small numbers of slaves, who presumably would have had enough access to the lexifier language to acquire a second-language variety rather than create a basilectal creole (Baker 1990, Chaudenson 1992). This suggests that basilects developed after, rather than before, the mesolect, which, in turn, requires that the mesolect was not a latterly development stemming from increased access to the lexifier after Emancipation. As early as 1971, Mervyn Alleyne suggested that mesolects and basilects coexisted from the beginning of colonies' histories, and this is supported by historical evidence from Jamaica (Lalla and D'Costa 1990: 84–98) and other colonies.

The clinching evidence, however, is linguistic: there are discontinuities between English creole basilects and mesolects, which are hopelessly unexplainable under the old "decreolization" continuum model but are easily accounted for via the new "top-down" model. As Bickerton (1996: 314–15) notes, for example, it would have been impossible for Guyanese slaves to adopt *did* as a "calque" on basilectal *bin* after emancipation in the 1800s, given that *did* was no longer used in neutral affirmative contexts in most English dialects even by the 1700s. It makes more sense to reconstruct that slaves incorporated *did* into the mesolect in the late 1600s or early 1700s, when the feature was still available. Another problem is that third-person pronouns are gender-neutral but distinguished for case in the Guyanese basilect but case-neutral while distinguishing gender in the mesolect (Bickerton 1996: 324). This hardly makes sense under a model proposing that the mesolect reflected greater access to English, but it is accountable as a chance difference between lects that developed separately.

In chapter 6 I further noted that the traditional idea that after shedding the overt copulas of the basilect, creole speakers "passed through" a mesolectal stage of omitting equative and locative copulas altogether before incorporating the lexifier ones in the acrolect is extremely ad hoc. We would expect increased access to the standard to spur the incorporation of the lexifier copulas in the mesolect itself; there is no principled explanation as to why speakers would mysteriously "wait" until the acrolect to incorporate overt copulas, conventionalizing a distinctly non-native strategy but otherwise eagerly acquiring other lexifier features, many less salient than the copula. The zero-copula in the mesolect submits more gracefully to an analysis under which both the basilect and the mesolect arose without overt copulas, after which copulas arose in the basilect but happened not to in the mesolect (cf. chapters 6 and 7 for evidence that the basilectal copulas *da* and *de* were innovations rather than original features).

Surely, the basilect and the mesolect did not develop in complete isolation from one another—but these linguistic incompatibilities do not allow that we proceed from this to denying the overall validity of the new "top-down" model, or to doing so in essence by simply noting that unspecified aspects of the mesolect may well have been created after slaves' emancipation. Short of systematic alternate explanations of the observations in Bickerton (1996) and chapter 6 in this volume, I would suggest that future work of the Creolist school would be most empirically sound in working within the assumptions of the "top-down" model.

This is especially germane given that this new model eliminates the theoretical necessity, inherently entailed by the old one, of supposing that any creole precursor of Black English would have to have begun at a basilectal stage. This assumption naturally leads to attempts to find parallels or echoes in Black English of basilectal features such as overt equative and locative copulas (cf. some of the more adventurous interpretations of the WPA tapes in Sutcliffe 2001). Yet as noted previously, this necessitates reasoning around the tendency for zero-copula to appear as often before locatives as before adjectives in Black English, eternally awkward under a model assuming a basilectal template with locatives preceded by the overt *de* rather than a mesolectal one where zero-copula in the locative comes built in. The fact is that to the extent that Black English or its early AAE precursors resemble creoles, it is in what would be *mesolectal*— or more to the point, upper mesolectal—creole features: zero-copulas, variable absence of plural marking but almost never the more basilectal *dem* plural (notably present in the speech of WPA interviewee Wallace Quaterman, who was, pointedly, an acknowledged Gullah speaker), absence of inversion. This is in contrast to the basilectal features that diverge sharply from English itself such as serial verbs, multiple copula morphemes, and predominantly CV phonology. The top-down model allows the Creolist Hypothesis advocate to seek mesolectal rather than basilectal parallels, which would obviate the "static" that results when studies of Black English history take different creole lects as the relevant source, as noted above in the case of Weldon's (1996) mesolectal focus in contrast to Holm's (1984) basilectal one.

If this is accepted, then our task is to evaluate the plausibility of a *mesolectal* creole ancestor to Black English spoken beyond Gullah country—copulas *a* and *de* and all features more reminiscent of Sranan than Trinidadian become irrelevant to the inquiry. At this point, the question arises as to how deeply mesolectal this variety would have been, or: How "creole" was this ancestral variety? Was it the Gullah spoken today in the Sea Islands, a close relative, or a more acrolectal variety?

## 4.3. Historical evidence

It is here that the historical evidence becomes crucial, and I believe that it indicates that Gullah itself has always been spoken approximately where it is now: on the Sea Islands and small distances inland in South Carolina, Georgia, and Florida that is, "the Low Country." Meanwhile, elsewhere blacks spoke a variety that was not a creole under any taxonomic framework. The nature of language contact is such that there is no discrete line between "dialect of English" and "creole English," and thus there is no reason to rule out that varieties existed which fell on a continuum between Black English and Gullah, and, indeed, work such as Kautzsch and Schneider (2000) on documentary evidence from South Carolina and Sutcliffe (2001) on the WPA tapes strongly suggest that such varieties existed. I term these varieties "Black English-plus," which straddled the line between "dialect" and "creole" in the same way as Réunnionais French and Popular Brazilian Portuguese did.

### 4.3.1. Demographic evidence

As Schneider (1989) noted and Winford (1997b) covers in particular detail, plantations in America generally were relatively small, particularly beyond the rice-growing regions of the South Carolina coast and its environs. These conditions would presumably have conditioned slaves to acquire second-language varieties of English rather than creolize it as they did in colonies like Surinam and Haiti, where slaves typically worked in gangs as large as several hundred. This constitutes one historical argument in favor of a Dialectologist position.

Too often, however, data in this vein have been adduced with the implication that they constitute the bulk or even the totality of germane sociohistorical evidence in the case of Black English. The problem here is that the relationship between degree of language restructuring and demographic ratios is much less indexical than is often presumed in creole studies. As noted in McWhorter (2000a), on the one hand, in many Spanish American colonies, slaves were imported in massive numbers quite early in a colony's history, and yet nothing approaching a creole ever resulted. (Significantly, I refer not to Cuba, Puerto Rico, and the Dominican Republic, where the absence of a creole is potentially attributable to early periods when slaves were only imported in small numbers, but to the mainland Spanish colonies such as Mexico and present-day Colombia, Ecuador, Venezuela, and Peru, countries which are saliently absent in the development of creole genesis theory.) Meanwhile, on the other hand, Sranan and Martiniquan Creole can be firmly reconstructed to have existed in their respective colonies long before blacks significantly outnumbered whites, either in the colony as a whole or even on the typical individual plantation. Demographic ratios were but one of many factors central to determining depth of creolization, another being whether or not a pre-existing pidgin or creole was imported with slaves imported early in the colony's history (cf. chapter 9), and one other being degree of motivation to acquire the lexifier that the social context conditioned.

For this reason, size of plantations and headcounts of imported slaves in given decades can serve only as one "spoke in the wheel" of a decisive case regarding the origins of Black English. Another spoke is citations of the speech of early American blacks.

## 4.3.2. Citations

Especially in earlier arguments for the Creolist Hypothesis, great emphasis was placed on citations of black slaves speaking in what Dillard (1972) termed "pidgin" English. This pidgin English was seen as significant in being the presumed precursor to Gullah itself. However, in the strict sense, all citations of reduced Englishes in early America do not indicate that Gullah was once coin of the realm among blacks beyond the Sea Islands and the Low Country. Specifically, all of the reduced-English citations of blacks outside of today's Gullah-speaking territory in Stewart (1967) and Dillard (1972, 1992) fall into one of two categories. Neither category can be seen as a precursor to Gullah itself.

One is the unstable, utilitarian interlanguage of blacks born in Africa, who acquired English as a second language as adults. These citations are certainly in a reduced English, but none of them are recognizably correspondent with Gullah in any particular way. A typical example is from the play *The Fall of British Tyranny* of 1796, where an African-born slave named Cudjo says things such as "Eas, massa, you terra me, me shoot him down dead" (Dillard 1972: 90). This is non-native English, but not Gullah, where *I* is *ah*, there is no substitution of *r* for *l*, as in *terra* for *tell*, and paragoge as in *terra* is rare (the latter being readily explainable, however, as second-language transfer of West African languages' common CV phonotactics). Similarly, Frederick Douglass mentioned African-born slaves saying things like *Oo dem got any peachy?* for "Have you got any peaches?" on the Maryland plantation where he grew up. Again, this is interlanguage, but not Gullah, in which the mysterious *oo dem* is unknown. The same analysis applies to any number of citations from the 1700s and 1800s which depict blacks speaking varieties that are "broken" but show no traits specific to Gullah creole itself. The frequent paragoge in words such as *puttee* for *put* and *givee* for *give* in these examples is one of several examples of the mismatch in question. It should not surprise us that African-born slaves are not depicted speaking fluent, ordinary English; however, it is quite possible that their descendants acquired a full variety of English rather than transforming their parents' pidgin into Gullah.

Both Stewart and Dillard supposed that the descendants of these adults developed Gullah on the basis of this adult interlanguage; to wit, they supposed that this speech, as a pidgin, would have been a natural precursor to a creole that is, Gullah. In this vein, Dillard (1972: 81), for example, points out the prevalence of paragoge in Sranan Creole English of Suriname, with the implication that even American-born blacks' speech was once as far removed from English itself as these creoles are (indeed, Dillard was even known to surmise that black Americans once spoke

Saramaccan!). Dillard is particularly explicit in framing the interlanguage citations this way in Dillard (1993).

This idea would be quite unexceptionable except for the inconvenient fact that citations of blacks not designated as born in Africa—unless they were born in Gullah country—always appear to be early Black English instead of Gullah. Perhaps the earliest such citation is that of a Baltimore doctor's slave Dromo, who is quoted (most unfortunately, it must be said) as saying *Dis de way to York? You a damn black bitch* (Dillard 1992: 71). Dillard treats this citation as part of a broad conception of a black "pidgin English," but the copula deletion patterns are also reminiscent of Black English, and there is (1) nothing ruling out that this is what Dromo was speaking and, more important, (2) nothing specifically Gullah about the citation. Tabitha Tenney of Philadelphia's *Soon he want to know how old you be first* (ibid. 79) from 1829 and other citations are similar cases, which in themselves do not constitute a case for Gullah having been spoken in, for example, Baltimore or Philadelphia.

It is significant that whenever we find quotes of Gullah itself, the speaker is from Gullah territory, not Texas, Delaware, or Alabama. For example, here is the slave Jupiter in Edgar Allan Poe's *The Gold Bug* (1839), of Sullivan's Island:

> Somebody bin lef' him head up de tree, and de crows done gobble ebery bit of de meat off.

If blacks *outside* of Gullah territory spoke this way, we would certainly expect at least one citation indicating such. Even a contemporary observer supported the idea that Gullah was a local phenomenon spoken only more or less where it is now while a precursor to Black English was spoken everywhere else. Colonel Thomas Wentworth Higginson, in his *Army Life in a Black Regiment* (1870, cited in Dillard 1972: 105), casually notes:

> "Done" is a Virginia shibboleth, quite distinct from the "been" which replaces it in South Carolina. Yet one of their best choruses, without any fixed words, was "De bell done ringing," for which in proper South Carolina dialect, would have been substituted "De bell been a-ring."

Dillard, committed to Gullah having been spoken throughout the South and beyond, hastens to add that "there was a more complicated situation than Higginson's geographic statement indicates." To an extent, yes—Kautzsch and Schneider (2000) note that Gullah influence in South Carolina gradated as one moved inland, for example—but we must beware of the rhetorical strategy of recruiting unremarkable gray zones as a tool for denying decisively general tendencies. In that light, it is also possible that Higginson's statement was accurate in a general sense and reflected a basic difference between Black English and Gullah still prominent today.

### 4.3.3. Contemporary observations

Kay and Cary (1995: 49–50) and Rickford (1997) have treated observations of slave speech made by whites in the 1700s as evidence that the slaves spoke a creole variety. Three of these five observations refer explicitly to African-born rather than

American-born slaves, however, and their fragmentary command of English there-fore was to be expected. An example is Reverend James Marye, Jr., who observed in Virginia in 1754 that "there are great quantities of those Negroes imported here yearly from Africa, who have languages peculiar to themselves, who are here many years before they understand English."

The two other observations could refer either to African- or American-born slaves. Philip Reading in Delaware in 1748 had "difficulty of conversing with the majority of the Negroes" because they had a "language peculiar to themselves, a wild confused medley of Negro and corrupt English which makes them unintelligible except to those who conversed with them for many years." "Negro" here could refer to natively-spoken African languages, but to be maximally even-handed we must allow that Reading could also have been trying to say that the slaves had developed a new kind of natively-spoken speech with African influence—that is, Gullah. J. F. D. Smyth, visiting Virginia and North Carolina from England in the 1770s, described slaves' speech in those states as "a mixed dialect between the Guinea and the En-glish." Once again, Smyth could either have meant "Guinea" as a native language or as an influence on a new kind of English spoken by American-, rather than African-born slaves—again, perhaps, Gullah.

These two ambiguous observations must be seen in a certain perspective. Noth-ing in Reading and Smyth's observations by themselves explicitly rules out that they were referring to a creole variety to a form of Gullah. However, it is equally possible that their impressions arose from a lack of familiarity with forms of Black English, especially creole-leaning ones such as Sutcliffe has shown us existed. Many whites who have little contact with black speech, especially foreigners like Smyth, find Black English difficult to quite comprehend at first because of phonological features alone, this being especially the case with Southern Black English. I personally once ob-served an Anglophone Canadian finding the inner-city Black English spoken by cash-iers at a fast food restaurant utterly incomprehensible. I can also attest that in my childhood, it often took me about a week, as a Philadelphian, to get past needing to ask my grandparents, relatives, and their friends for frequent repetitions, given the largely phonological differences between their deep Southern Black English and the derivants of "inner-city AAVE" that I was familiar with hearing my relatives and playmates use. Similarly, a Hochdeutsch speaker who finds a nonstandard German dialect virtually opaque at first often finds that comprehension comes via wrapping one's ear around a few phonological differences and that the dialect itself hardly diverges from Hochdeutsch to an extent analogous to the distance between, for ex-ample, mesolectal Jamaican patois and standard English. Something similar may well have been the case with these two observers of Black English—especially in light of the aforegoing evidence and that adduced below rendering the previous existence of a true creole beyond Gullah territory difficult to support.

Which interpretation of these quotes might be the correct one, then—were these observers hearing a "creole English," or were they largely thrown by an unfamiliar accent? There is something favoring the latter interpretation: the sheer scarcity and vagueness of such remarks. In colonies where creole languages were indubitably spoken, there were dictionaries and grammars compiled of "the slaves' language," this being quite explicitly processed as different enough from its lexifier to necessitate such work for the purposes of religious conversion or even simple work supervision. This is the case in Mauritius, Haiti, St. Thomas, Suriname, and other colonies. Furthermore, in historical documentation on these colonies, references to the slaves having their own language are generally frequent and casual, the existence of this slave language being an unexceptionable part of the mise-en-scène. One could not study colonial Jamaica, for example, without noticing that slaves spoke patois; even a historian of Haiti with no interest whatsoever in language could not miss that slaves in Haiti spoke creole; and so on.

But this is not true of the American South. There are no grammars of slave language written in Mississippi, no dictionaries of slave "lingo" from Delaware, and in the mountains of archival material, memoirs, and literary depictions of slavery in the United States, we do not find the slaves referred to as having their own kind of "talk" that the white person must essentially learn as a new language. Instead, what we have is a mere two highly ambiguous observations that slaves could be tricky for whites to understand, which must be seen in the context of the fact that Danes are tricky for Swedes to understand despite the languages' revealing themselves as dialects of the same tongue on the page.

There is further indication in literary depictions that Gullah itself was not the coin of the realm among American blacks. For example, Scott Joplin set his opera *Treemonisha* in Texarkana, Texas, in 1884. This was a region where many former slaves lived at the time, many drawn from other parts of the South, and Joplin's having grown up in this and similar areas would have lent him solid acquaintance with the folk speech of blacks just a couple of decades after Emancipation. Moreover, the characters in *Treemonisha* are poor, isolated, uneducated sharecroppers. If Gullah, or something similar, had ever been spoken in East Texas, then Scott Joplin would most likely have given some indication of this in *Treemonisha*. Of course, he would not have written it in full-blown Gullah, but it is possible to convey the flavor of Gullah in literature without unduly straining the comprehension of the mainstream reader or listener.

Edgar Allan Poe's transcription of Jupiter's speech is an example. Another is the language of Dorothy and DuBose Heyward's play *Porgy* in 1927. This play, source of the better-known opera *Porgy and Bess*, depicted poor blacks living in an isolated quarter of Charleston, and the Heywards couched the script in a speech variety somewhere between Black English and Gullah, in order to convey the flavor of Gullah while maintaining comprehension for white audiences:

*From* Porgy:

No man ever take my 'ooman from me. It goin' to be good joke on Crown ef he lose um to one wid no leg an' no gizzard.

*Gullah translation (Geraty 1990)*:

No man ebbuh tek 'ooman 'way f'um Crown. 'E gwi be big joke on 'um ef e' loss 'e 'ooman tuh uh man wuh ent hab no laig needuh gizzut.

The Heywards managed to convey a Gullah "feel" with words like *'ooman, ef,* and the gender-neutral pronoun *um*. There is nothing of this kind in Joplin's *Treemonisha* libretto, however, whose speech runs along the lines of the following:

Who is that woman they am bringin' with 'em?
I's the king of Goofer dust land / Strange things appear when I says "Hee hoo"!

In the same vein, if Gullah had been spoken on Maryland plantations, we might expect Frederick Douglass to have mentioned it at least once in one of his three extremely detailed and prolix autobiographies. Instead, however, he mentions only the speech of African-born slaves. This would seem to have been a natural point for him to proceed to discuss the local Gullah or "Geechee Talk" or "patois" or "slave talk," and his not doing so suggests that native-born blacks spoke something we would process as Black English rather than Gullah.

Of course, to assess the Creolist Hypothesis solely on the basis of broadly conceived negative evidence in this vein would be insufficient. Rickford's (1992) discovery of a mesolectal level of Bajan creole demonstrates that lack of documentation can conceal hitherto unknown realities. The verdict on the Creolist Hypothesis, then, must be richly informed by concentrated analysis of positive evidence as well, including that referred to by Creolist Hypothesis advocates. Still, the negative evidence in the Black English case, such as *Treemonisha* or what observers *didn't* say, despite being perhaps reminiscent of trying to slice a tomato with a machete, must be given its weight as well.

There are two reasons for this. First, because the development of creoles is a worldwide phenomenon rather than one local to the United States, any conclusions we make about the American situation must be assessed in view of the ready documentation of creoles in other colonies. Second, while a verdict based *solely* on what certain authors did *not* mention would clearly be of little worth, there is conversely perhaps a risk of "missing the forest for the trees" if we neglect broader indications in favor of focusing our evaluation on issues as interesting, but ultimately local, as copular deletion rates.

### 4.3.4. The "African Pidgin English" citations versus Gullah

Finally, Dillard (1993) objects that the attestation of slaves speaking pidgin varieties of English all over the United States makes it plain that Gullah must have developed in such places, rather than solely in the Sea Islands and the Low Country.

This interpretation of the pidgin/interlanguage tokens, however, proceeds upon conceptions of creole genesis that have been revised since the 1960s. For one, as noted in the preceding discussion, the new "top-down" continuum model, which all evidence appears to support, no longer requires that a creole must have passed through a pidgin and then a basilectal stage. On the contrary, under the new model, we would expect that a Gullah-like mesolect would have existed from the beginning. Therefore, the pidgin citations can no longer stand as necessarily being "Ur-Gullah." Furthermore, Dillard's analysis proceeds according to a polygenetic creole genesis conception, under which Gullah is seen as developing in the United States. Along these lines, as I have noted, it is natural to assume that Gullah must have been preceded by a pidgin ancestor spoken in this country, and thus it is inevitable to see the pidgin/interlanguage tokens as that ancestor.

Later research has shown that the basic structure of Gullah did not emerge in the United States, however. Gullah is a direct offshoot of the West Indian patois that had crystallized in Barbados and other New World colonies in the mid-1600s. The founding planters of the Charleston colony were from Barbados (Cassidy 1980: 6–7), the first slaves brought to Charleston were as often as not purchased from among "seasoned" slaves in Barbados rather than directly from Africa (Wood 1974: 24), and Gullah remains partially intelligible with Jamaican and related West Indian patois varieties. These circumstances would lead us to predict that, essentially, Gullah and Bajan would be varieties of the same language, and this is, in fact, the case for these and all of the other Atlantic English-based creoles, as I have argued in chapter 8.

In his sociohistorical epilogue to the Poplack volume, Mufwene stresses instead that Gullah developed in the United States, largely independently of Caribbean English creoles. He specifies that "similarities between Gullah and Caribbean creoles need not surprise us, because the contact settings of the input varieties (African languages and British dialects) were similar in the rice and sugar-cane colonies" (245). However, Mufwene's paper includes not a single sentential example from any language, the implication being that his conclusions are linked to linguistic data not explicitly presented. In fact, his argument is quite incommensurate with the comparative data, neglecting the central observation in chapter 8 here that a crucial collection of features shared by Bajan, Gullah, and the other English-based Caribbean creoles are too idiosyncratic to be due to anything but common origin in a single, stabilized grammar. None of the features could in any logical sense have emerged in several creoles separately: in other words, they are just the kinds of features that could *not* emerge in multiple locations even when sociohistorical circumstances and mixtures of languages were similar or even identical.

The tracing of the Atlantic English-based creoles has elicited no rebuttals to date and has been adopted in general outline by other scholars of creole genesis such as Baker (1999) and Parkvall (1999). Mufwene's denial of the relationship between Bajan and Gullah, in contrast, does not take issue with these arguments but, instead, does not address them at all. Thus his introduction cannot be considered a counterargument to my analysis, for which reason in this essay I will treat my assumptions as unchallenged by Mufwene's epilogue.

Meanwhile, what locating the source of Gullah in West Indian patois means is that the distribution of the pidgin/interlanguage citations Dillard presents has little if anything to do with ascertaining where Gullah was previously spoken. Gullah was born as an import from Barbados, and thus the pidgin/interlanguage citations represent the speech of slaves imported directly from Africa, but not the source of Gullah itself. This means that the attestation of such pidgin/interlanguage in colonies like Virginia and New York can no longer be seen as supporting the Creolist Hypothesis. This speech was but one of a number of English varieties these African slaves' children would have heard. If born in the Sea Islands or the Low Country, children born to pidgin-speaking Africans would have acquired some form of West Indian patois, as this would have prevailed in the speech community. If born elsewhere, they would have acquired various gradations of Black English.

It must be recalled that when children of non-native speakers of a language are surrounded by others speaking natural-language varieties of that language, they generally do not acquire their parents' abbreviated variety, nor do they even "creolize" it—instead, they learn the full variety, especially from older peers. This is quite obvious in the case of standard languages for example, the immigrant toddler who grows up to speak indistinguishably from local peers, while his parents retain accents and evidence of incomplete acquisition of the new language—and thus would also have been true when the languages in question happened to be creoles or nonstandard dialects of the lexifier. In other words, there was no motivation for pidgin or interlanguage varieties of English to be recruited as the principal stuff of language acquisition, because representative numbers of people on any plantation were speaking full language.

## 4.3.5. The import of the historical evidence

Clearly, my assessment does not address any purported claim that *all* blacks in the United States once spoke Gullah. All advocates of the Creolist Hypothesis have been well aware that the speech competence of blacks as a whole would have formed a continuum from white standard speech to full-blown creole, accompanied by non-native pidgin varieties, with individuals' competences varying according to life circumstances. Yet these adherents have surmised that Gullah, or something related, was one pole of the general competence of black slaves outside of the Sea Islands and the Low Country. My suggestion is that general black speech did *not* include a layer that we would classify as Gullah, or in general as a creole per se, except more or less where such a layer exists today.

Nevertheless, there is evidence that in certain locations, varieties in between Gullah and Black English existed, more creole-like than any Black English apparently extant today. Kautzsch and Schneider (2000) document this in South Carolina, and Sutcliffe (2001) points to Gullah-esque depictions of black speech in the Congaree Swamp region of North Carolina, as well as to possible remnants of creole tokens in the speech of some of the WPA interviewees. This was "Black English-plus," a lightly creolized variety not distinct enough from local standards to be processed by white or black as a separate language, but different to an extent that might condition the occasional comment such as J. F. D. Smyth's (see section 4.3.3). There is also no reason to reject the possibility that "Black English-plus" might still be spoken in some remote location, nor should it surprise us to find that slivers of it are still part of the competence of some Southern blacks. This would explain Dillard's reports (e.g., 1993: 229–30) of *bin* past tense markers used by blacks he has encountered in Louisiana, for example.

However, to read such vestiges as evidence that Gullah itself was once widely spoken by people outside of Gullah territory, as Dillard and Sutcliffe do, is but one interpretation of two possible. The other is that this situation was more or less the original one. Our task is to choose which of these scenarios is best supported by the evidence. I believe that the evidence is most plausibly interpreted as supporting the latter scenario.

Obviously, there are alternate interpretations of all of the categories of evidence I have discussed when taken individually. However, what is important is that so very many things can be readily analyzed as pointing in one direction. Thus just perhaps every single transcriber of black speech outside of Gullah territory over the past 200 years "wrote up" and/or missed Gullah features. Just perhaps there is a more "creole" layer of speech on the Samaná Peninsula no researcher has found. Just perhaps ex-slave Fountain Hughes, recorded on the WPA tapes, went home after making his recording and described his day in Gullah.

But we must ask: Why would the most ready interpretation of *all* the lines of surviving evidence suggest the absence of a creole *only in the United States*, when in colonies all over the world, historical documentation readily yields concrete indications that an unequivocally creole language was widely spoken in the slave community? That is, if a creole was once widely spoken by blacks in the United States, why exactly has it been so very difficult to find concrete evidence of this in either the past or the present? Rickford (1992) clinched the mesolectal Bajan case by finding living people speaking it in Barbados; yet after thirty years, no researcher has found anything similar in this country. The Bajan case was always bolstered by historical citations; here, in contrast, our rich, well-archived and easily accessible records of slavery have failed to yield a single sentence of Gullah spoken by a black person outside of Gullah territory.

There is a "culture cult" objection one hears occasionally, that American slaves would have concealed their most intimate speech varieties from whites. But we must keep the comparative perspective in mind. If whites easily observed slaves in Jamaica speaking their in-group patois, then how likely would it have been that slaves throughout several American colonies would have so uniformly kept a creole hidden? Just what was it about slaves in this particular country that rendered them so uniquely secretive about their purported creole? In this light, although we are correct in reading historical documentation of dispossessed groups with skepticism and caution, it seems more economical to assume that in this particular case, the message the evidence offers again and again is the truth: by and large, black American slaves outside of Gullah territory did not speak Gullah.

## 5. Accounting for the "creole" features in early AAE and beyond

In the end, it remains to account for the fact that the early AAE data does, contrary to the claims of many of the Poplack volume's authors, demonstrate some features that resemble their equivalents in creoles. This not only is shown by data inconvenient to many of the authors in this volume; but also is especially clear in the case of zero-copula. For all of the correspondences between Black English and nonstandard British dialects, Black English remains all but unique among non-creole English dialects worldwide in displaying zero-copula. Even though Sali Tagliamonte (pers. comm.) has found some zero copula in Yorkshire dialect, this remains a lone exception among hundreds of Englishes that lack the feature, and we search dialect atlases in vain for any indication that sentences such as *She in the house* were at all typical of nonstandard British dialects of any region in the 1600s and 1700s or ever, for that matter. Given that Black English has shared sociohistorical space with a creole that has this feature, and was born amid conditions that have so often produced zero-copulas in myriad languages worldwide, to classify Black English's zero-copula as an "English inheritance" or as a mere diachronic accident would only be possible via infelicitous shoehorning of the data at hand.

If this and other creole-like features were due to Gullah or something similar spoken throughout the South, then at least some of the lines of evidence reviewed above would indicate this—but they do not. Where, then, did these features come from?

## 5.1. Second-language acquisition versus creole ancestry

I believe that we find our solution in noting that all of the "creole" features in early AAE, as well as its modern descendant Black English, are of a particular kind. Namely, all of them are due to ellipsis or overgeneralization of a given English feature, rather than to the calquing of *overt* structures via substrate transfer or development of same by internal innovation. Zero-copulas, unmarked plurals, a more marked dispreference for final consonant clusters than Southern white English (Wolfram and Fasold 1974: 134), morphologically unmarked possessives (*Billy book* for *Billy's book*), non-inversion in questions, use of *ain't* in the past as well as the present, and spread of negative concord all entail the *ellipsis* or *overgeneralization* of an English marker or strategy rather than its replacement by a distinct overt strategy.

Indeed, such features are typical of creoles, but here is the crucial difference: creoles are also typified by two other phenomena in comparison to their lexifiers: (1) substrate transfers such as serial verbs—absent in early AAE or Black English—and (2) internal innovations signifying a great degree of structural (and sociological) independence from the lexifier, such as multiple copulas or the grammaticalization of lexifier morphemes as tense and aspect markers. Again, neither early AAE nor Black English displays this. In other words, Black English in all of its historical layers has displayed only one *type* of creole feature, the subtractive sort.

Now, the Creolist Hypothesis advocate might propose that nevertheless, "creole" features in early AAE and Black English suggest "creole" origin, and that the lack of the other two types of creole feature simply indicates that the creole precursor to Black English was simply more upper mesolectal than modern Gullah is. However, a crucial fact is that the particular "creole" features in early AAE and Black English are also all typical features of the second-language acquisition of English. This is obviously true of elimination of morphology and simplification of phonology (cf., for example, O'Grady, Dobrovolsky, and Aronoff 1997: 483–87, 492). This is also true of failure to acquire "quirky" syntactic features such as auxiliary inversion. Lack of inversion is less a specific aspect of West African languages than a cross-linguistic commonplace: despite how much attention it receives in the linguistics literature, outside of Indo-European, *both* subject-auxiliary and subject-verb inversion are quite marked from a cross-linguistic perspective (e.g., Ultan 1978 finds it only in Europe except for Malay out of a sample of seventy-nine languages). Thus its absence in Black English is equivalent to, for example, elision of strong verb past forms in creoles, due to the tendency for second-language learners to eliminate grammar-idiosyncratic features that would be difficult for speakers of *most* languages.

Overgeneralization is a similar example: for example, the use of *ain't* in the past as well as present, which does not behave as *ain't* cognates do in mesolectal creoles, as Winford (1998: 108–9) notes.

Put another way, the particular subset of "creole"-type features adduced in Black English overlaps precisely with manifestations of a phenomenon other than creolization—second-language acquisition—whereas radical substrate transfer (as opposed to moderate and constrained transfer in second-language acquisition) and radical internal restructuring are processes diagnostic of creolization and other processes of intense language contact. This suggests that in Black English, these features are a legacy of widespread second-language acquisition in the dialect's birth.

There is a possible temptation to resist dissociating these features entirely from a hypothetical creole itself, but there are two things speaking against this: (1) So very much evidence speaks against any variety perceivable or classifiable as a creole having been spoken much beyond where Gullah is spoken now. (2) The reconstruction of this hypothetical creole is no longer, in the theoretical sense of this word, necessary: second-language acquisition explains the data just as well, but without the awkward absence of a creole from the historical record to grapple with. Creolization and second-language acquisition, for obvious reasons, overlap significantly in their manifestations on a grammar. In the case of Black English, all of the evidence—linguistic, demographic, documentary—points to second-language acquisition as the operating factor in its particular birth.

## 5.2. Parsing the "African" contribution

Thus: the non-English traits are indeed legacies of acquisition by Africans, but the manifestations of that acquisition are not transferred from African languages or West Indian-derived patois, but the same general results of *approximation* amid generally successful mastery—to use the Francophone creolists' terms—that would have resulted if Eskimos or Papuans had acquired English under the same conditions. Creolist Hypothesis advocates' designation of the non-English traits in Black English as *specifically* Niger-Congo or Caribbean would benefit from—and is technically incomplete without—checking the data in question against that in varieties of English with heavy language contact and non-native acquisition in their histories that were created by people other than Africans. In that light, the number of purportedly "African" or "Caribbean" traits that Black English shares with Singapore English (Ho and Platt 1993) or Hawaiian Creole English is of central importance in evaluating the Creolist case.

This is also the place to digress briefly to the "African" issue specifically. There is an implication in many Creolist Hypothesis advocates' work that "Niger-Congo" languages all conform to a general "West African" pattern, supposedly all roughly as akin as the Romance languages. Yet it was not for nothing that Joseph Greenberg's (1966c) taxonomy of West African languages was considered one of the signature achievements of a career. The Akan varieties (Twi, Fante, Asante, et al.) and the Gbe (Ewe, Fon, et al.) are indeed related typologically to roughly the Romance extent, but the Nigerian languages such as Yoruba and Igbo diverge significantly from these two groups on all levels. Even here, however, the likenesses are enough that all were formerly classified as "Kwa" (although now only Akan and Gbe are). In fact, it is the general typological configuration of this former "Kwa" group which is intended as "general West African" by those using this term: heavy verb serialization, multiple copulas, little inflectional morphology, lexically and syntactically contrastive tone, predicate clefting as a focus strategy, and largely CV phonotactics.

However, there is no evidence that American slave populations were significantly dominated by speakers of these languages. In the meantime, West Atlantic languages like Wolof and Fula, and Mande languages like Mandinka, Bambara, and Dyula, are as typologically distinct from the old "Kwa" group as Finno-Ugric is from Romance. Neither West Atlantic nor Mande has verb serialization; West Atlantic languages are by no means analytic; Wolof is not tonal and is as consonant-final as English; and tone plays a relatively minor contrastive role in the Mande languages listed above. Then, Bantu languages like Kikongo (quite rich inflectionally) are equally unlike all of these languages. As such, the often-encountered designation "West African pattern" has little taxonomic validity.

The "general West African" concept was frequently appealed to in earlier work on creole varieties, but since then, creole studies have come to be founded on a more rigorous approach to substrate transfer, spurred in part by Bickerton's famous charge to trace hypothetical West African contributions to people "in the right place at the right time," along with the concurrent attention to specific West African language grammars. The study of Black English has lagged behind somewhat in this methodological advance. DeBose and Faraclas's (1993) explicit linkage of Black English to Southern Nigerian languages (such as Yoruba and Igbo), treated as representative of "West African," is a particularly pointed example of a Creolist argument weakened by this tendency in terms of both linguistic and sociohistorical argumentation.

## 5.3. A useful comparison

In any case, evaluation of this appeal to general second-language acquisition tendencies must finally be seen in light of a return to my earlier observation that the study of Black English history over the past few decades has been rather unique in its focus on subtle gradations in the quantitative behaviors and conditionings of a small set of variables, rather than the grammar as a whole. To this must be added that historiographical work on Black English has been rather anomalously occasional since Dillard (1972), has been conducted mostly by scholars outside of America (cf. Schneider 1989, Ewers 1996), and tends not to occupy the center of most discussion at conferences like NWAVE where most new work on Black English is presented.

The reason for this is hardly neglect, but something more innocent: in the final analysis, in broad view, Black English simply does not resemble creoles in a definitive way very closely either in the past or the present. The surface features of the dialect are all obviously West Germanic rather than, say, West Atlantic. Recall, for instance, the general typology of the languages treated as "general West African" by some Creolist Hypothesis advocates: heavy verb serialization, multiple copulas, little inflectional morphology, lexically and syntactically contrastive tone, predicate clefting as a focus strategy, and largely CV phonotactics. Significantly, Black English evidences not a single one of these traits, whereas, for example, Saramaccan does.

The tenuousness of the African/creole characterization is especially clear when we recall that white Southern English has so very many of the same features as Black English, which in that dialect hardly give an "African" or "creole" impression.

The Creolist argument for Black English thus must appeal significantly to "underlying" African or creole features (or the hypothetical "masking" of such features with English phonetic forms). Meanwhile, historical documentation of the dialect only rarely yields tokens decisively resembling equivalents in West Indian patois. Even the ellipses and overgeneralizations we have noted, taken together, constitute a relatively minor contrast with standard English compared to the degree to which such things took place in the birth of many other contact varieties argued to have creole roots.

Réunionnais French, for example, is hardly as basilectal as its "classic creole" neighbor Mauritian Creole. Yet its roots in a partial transmission of French grammar are clear in, for example, its stark degree of monophthongization of the French vowel system, its almost total eschewal of French morphology, and its replacement of this by analytic strategies, some foreign to any French variety (such as the plural marker *bann*). Black English is a qualitatively different case altogether. Contrary to frequent assertions, Black English exhibits no particular tendency toward monophthongization: while [aj] becomes [a] and [oj] in some varieties is [ɔ], this is counterbalanced by the generally unacknowledged transformation of [ɪ] to [iə] before some consonants ([bɪl] > [biəl]) and [ɛ] to [eɪ] ([bɛd] > [beɪd]), and otherwise, the dialect is as rife with diphthongs as standard English. Claims such as Smitherman's (1977: 17) that Black English, like most West African languages, deletes "most final consonants" as a rule or even tendency are misrepresentative of a dialect that is quite comfortable with final consonants. And while creoles tend to "sound African" to Africans, Africans frequently note that Black English does not; most of the African legacy in the Black English sound system is suprasegmental. Despite the occasional phonologically conditioned omission of the past inflection and lexically restricted zero plural marking, in general, Black English is very much an inflectional dialect, which would give the same challenge to the foreign learner who spoke an analytic language as standard English would, complete with irregular strong verbs and suppletive nominal plurals.

This contrast is not an accidental one: it shows that Black English was born in a context affording a much richer transmission of the lexifier than was Réunionnais. Specifically, the evidence suggests that Black English was born as a koine of white nonstandard English dialects modified slightly by cross-linguistically typical results of widespread second-language acquisition. This is also the position of Winford (1997b, 1998), which is the most detailed, lucid, and summary Dialectologist argument to date, and ought henceforth be consulted as a foundation work by all scholars investigating Black English from a historical perspective.

## 5.4. Remaining "creole" traits

Perhaps two main areas of data could be seen as speaking against the second-language acquisition analysis and suggesting specifically creole origin. For one, the parallels in rates of copula absence and its grammatical conditioning between early AAE and Black English on the one hand and Caribbean creoles on the other may quite possibly prove to be due to a more general factor, be this prosody or another aspect of grammar-internal conditioning. For example, the high rate of zero-copula before *gonna* and V-*ing* could be attributable to the distinction that Walker in the Poplack volume suggests be attended to between auxiliary and true copula; auxiliary *be* may be inserted less readily due to the presence of the *gonna and -in(g)* markers, with lesser rates of zero copula before NP, locative, and adjectives due to its absence's greater salience because the copula does not co-occur with a second grammatical marker in such contexts (cf. Winford 1998: 12–13 for a similar and more detailed argument). As for *comparative* rates of deletion before NP, locative, and adjective, one interpretation of the lack of consensus here after thirty years is that there is no correlation between Black English and creoles strong or specific enough to indicate historical connection (cf. Winford 1998: 111). In general, the copula is an endlessly intriguing area of grammar, which was the focus of much of my early work. Nevertheless, it must be admitted that a case for a relationship between speech varieties cannot be founded primarily or even mostly or substantially on the verb *to be*, and especially on the subtopic of its rates of deletion before certain constituent types. Envisioning taxonomic arguments on such a basis for other languages Australian languages, Amazonian highlights this point usefully. We might perhaps take the weight of all of the other evidence as an argument in itself for seeking explanations beyond genetic relationship for the parallels in copula patternings.

And as for various arguments that Black English displays African or creole roots because of the role that aspect plays in its grammar (e.g., DeBose and Faraclas 1993), this issue is in fact not yet sufficiently examined to stand as an accepted fact. For one, tense plays a much more central role in Black English grammar than in creoles or the West African languages of the "Upper Guinea" region, underlyingly marking the past and future as obligatorily as any Indo-European grammar (cf. also Winford 1998: 116). Second, typical of Creolist Hypothesis advocates' generally insufficient attention to English dialects, the aspect arguments do not address the role that aspect in nonstandard British dialects may have played. This gap in argumentation alone renders the linkage of Black English aspect to Africa and creoles seriously incomplete, which is all the more significant given that there is indeed evidence that nonstandard British dialects are more aspect-focused than standard English (Trudgill and Chambers 1991).

## 6. Conclusion

*The English History of African American English*, then, is an extremely important volume, because it demonstrates in great detail and with considerable rigor a conclusion not precisely intended by its authors. On the one hand, it would be difficult to deny after reading this book that the dominant source of Black English is none other than the nonstandard Englishes spoken by white immigrants to the United States. As I have noted in McWhorter (1998b), there is not a single morphological or syntactic feature in Black English that can be responsibly traced to African languages, and very little phonological. That the only significant inheritance would be phonological is precisely what we would expect of a largely successful acquisition, as phonology is the last and most difficult level of a speech variety for a non-native to acquire perfectly.

The weight of the English inheritance in Black English has never been precisely difficult to perceive. The longevity of more extreme versions of the Africanist/Creolist Hypothesis is rooted in the fact that the position is not motivated wholly by purely linguistics-internal interests. There is an extent to which it is an outgrowth of the post–Civil Rights Act sociological trend in the United States seeking to reclaim the African component of the African American heritage (this motivating white as well as black practitioners). Combined with the essentialization of "blackness" in American racial discourse (this again typical of both races), it is perhaps surprising, awkward, and even somewhat unsavory to imagine that the dialect native to American blacks has its roots in the speech of rural and regional white Britishers. The very notion that Africans had contact intimate enough with their oppressors to acquire even the details and nuances of their speech is somewhat antithetical to an ideological tradition that has focused, quite necessarily, on segregation, violence, and disenfranchisement. To the person concerned with redressing the historiographical gaps in the African American heritage stemming from these injustices, it is perhaps natural that the speech of the scruffier characters in Dickens's work seems beside the point, in comparison to the speech of characters in Zora Neale Hurston's novels or Louise Bennett's poetry. Similarly, comparanda such as Singaporeans, French speakers from Réunion, and others, despite their necessity to a truly comprehensive address of the issue, will almost inevitably be marginalized among the "Africanist" commitment of a quest that passively but decisively discourages sustained attention to regions outside of West Africa and the Caribbean.

We must resist the admitted sociological cognitive dissonance that the truth about the origins of Black English stirs up, because we otherwise automatically saddle ourselves with a certain paradoxical and ultimately indefensible position. Most Creolist Hypothesis advocates quite readily suppose that the close likeness between Southern white English and Black English is due to blacks in the South playing a significant role in shaping white speech in that region (as Dillard [1972] notes, it could not possibly be an accident that white Southern English is spoken precisely where slaves were held in considerable numbers). This scenario is readily compatible with a commitment to tracing black Americans' impact on their country's history—but if we accept it, then it follows ineluctably that white influence on black speech was just as profound. What sociolinguistic principle could we identify, after all, that would account for the influence going only one way, and especially from the subjugated to the subjugators?

In general, I do not believe that Black English offers very much significant data to the scholar hoping to mine the dialect for specifically African or creole legacies. I believe that the interests of illuminating the dialect as a cultural inheritance would be more richly served by greater attention to aspects incidental to quantificational or diachronic interests, but integral and vibrant parts of the dialect nevertheless. This is urgent given that for all of the excellent scholarship produced as of this writing on Black English, it competes with Hawaiian Creole English for status as the nonstandard dialect for which structural description constitutes the smallest proportion of its (now massive) bibliography.

A quick example: these are sentences I have heard, which represent a construction I have encountered throughout my life, specifically in Philadelphia, Washington, D.C., San Francisco, and Oakland:

We was sittin' up at Tony's.

Don't be sittin' up in my house askin' me where's the money.

I ain't got no food up in my house.

It was buck-naked people up in my house.

Significantly, in the first two cases, the location referred to was not "up" in any literal sense; both domiciles were on the ground floor. In the case of the third sentence, I only overheard it used by a passing stranger, inviting the possibility that she lived in an upstairs unit. Yet it would be anomalous for any English speaker to specify the placement of their living space like this (consider the infelicity when we imagine this uttered in standard English, for example). These three sentences were uttered by African Americans; the fourth, however, was uttered by a white man who had many close African American friends and was given to launching into affectionate (and deft) imitations of African American speech. It was telling that he spontaneously included this usage of *up* in this case, especially since his apartment was, again, on the ground floor.

This usage of *up* is not spatial but pragmatic, by my reading conveying that the speaker has an inalienable or highly intimate relationship to the location in question; one would not say *I was up at the dentist's* (unless the dentist's office was uptown), or *I was up at that man Mr. Taylor's* (again, unless Mr. Taylor lived "up" somewhere in a spatial sense). The source of this construction (is it documented among whites?) and its possible semantic evolution (what usage of *up* is its source? Is it used in early AAE?) would be interesting to study, despite the fact that it is unlikely to trace to Africa or the Caribbean. Black English, in other words, offers a great deal of interest simply as a living speech variety regardless of its history.

Nevertheless, the authors in the Poplack volume unwittingly but quite usefully show that Black English is not solely a koine of white nonstandard dialects. To be sure, Poplack dutifully claims on the first page of the volume that the New Dialectologist position "does not of course preclude cultural, lexical, onomastic and other distinctly African and/or creole contributions to the current physiognomy of AAVE." That "other" presumably allows for the occasional non-English-derived structural feature. But there is a detectable trend in the volume toward seeking to trace each and every grammatical feature of Black English to either Merrie Old England or random internal innovation.

The Dialectologist school would be best advised to avoid this in favor of building a goodly amount of "breathing room" into their hypothesis, thereby allowing for traits attributable to second-language acquisition (zero-copula being a case where attempts to build a Dialectologist case would be particularly ill-advised). There are indeed aspects of the dialect which, while not specifically Niger-Congo or West Indian patois calques, are a legacy of its creation by Africans who acquired English as adults but transformed it into a full, living speech variety of its own, America's most fascinating and endlessly challenging English dialect.

# NOTES

## Chapter 1

1. On DeGraff's (1999a) claim that Haitian has gender inflection, see 5.1.

2. On the cline from free lexical item to affix, Negerhollands Dutch Creole plural marker *sini*, a reflex of the creole's third-person plural pronoun, was at most a clitic according to the criteria suggested by Zwicky and Pullum (1983: 503); for example, it was of optional occurrence and had no phonological effect upon the noun it followed (cf. Stolz 1986: 121–23).

Note also that my observations on Negerhollands pertain only to the *Laagkreols* ("low creole") variety indigenous to slaves, rather than the *Hoogkreols* variety used with whites and often in communications with the outside world. Hesseling (1905: 93–94) observed that the latter variety, strongly influenced by the "high" language Dutch, made great use of the Dutch plural -*s*, while *sini* (and allomorphs such as *sender*) was used in the basilectal variety.

3. In the absence of specific citations, sources are as follows: for Ndjuka: Huttar and Huttar (1994), George Huttar (pers. comm.); for Saramaccan: study by the author; for Tok Pisin: Verhaar (1995), Peter Mühlhäusler (pers. comm.); for Mauritian: Baker (1972), Philip Baker (pers. comm.); for St. Lucian: Carrington (1984); for Negerhollands: Stolz (1986), Cefas van Rossem (pers. comm.); for Angolar: Maurer (1995), Philippe Maurer (pers. comm.). There exists no grammar of Haitian Creole comprehensive enough for these purposes, and thus data on it are derived from the sources specified throughout this chapter.

I have substituted Angolar for its closely related sister creole Fa D'Ambu (Annobonese), which I used as a test case in McWhorter (1998a), because of the availability of a detailed grammar of Angolar (Maurer 1995), which will better serve the purposes of the discussion here.

4. However, it is not utterly foreign to these uses of tone to encode distinctions of meaning. In Guyanese Creole English, tonal sandhi patterns distinguish iterative from distributive reduplication: *rón-rón* "to run continuously" vs. *rôn-rón* "to run in fits and starts" (Devonish 2003: 50). Yet in broad view this remains a fillip, like the handful of minimal pairs distinguished by tone in Saramaccan: (1) this is but one construction that the grammar uses to express imperfective concepts; (2) it falls into the "expressive" subclass of construction; (3) the distinction is only operative on a subclass of verbs rather than on the category as a whole.

5. DeGraff (1999a), for example, addresses my treatment of the Mon-Khmer language Chrau by characterizing it as having "at most two affixes," but this refers only to the productive ones; several other affixes are no longer productive but are readily perceived as morphology by speakers (Thomas 1969, Thomas 1971).

6. Because only the most thorough grammars usually have occasion to make note of and exemplify noncompositional uses of derivation, in many cases it can only be identified in a language through reference to a dictionary. For example, the best available Khasi grammar (Rabel 1961) does not mention such cases, giving the preliminary impression that this language, with neither inflection nor tone, hones to the Prototype. However, Singh's (1983) dictionary immediately reveals in its preface that such cases are common, and the dictionary contains examples of several. This is also the general case with Mande grammars and many Austronesian ones.

7. Two examples:

Khmer: The meaning conveyed by these prefixes is in many instances not clearcut . . . either the partner word or the prefixed form, or both, may therefore have undergone a change of meaning (Jacob 1968: 178).

Garo (Tibeto-Burman): In some [adverbial affixes] the meaning is quite eccentric, depending on the particular base to which it is attached (Burling 1961: 13).

Statements like these are not found in the sections on derivation in creole grammars.

8. Dutch has a past inflectional suffix -te, but this merely reinforced a process for which Eastern Ijo was the driving influence. For one, while the Eastern Ijo equivalent is -tẹ́ẹ̄, the Dutch affix is realized as [də] except after voiceless consonants (Smith, Robertson, and Williamson 1987: 62). Furthermore, most creoles do not incorporate a past-marking affix from the superstrate language, and thus there is no general tendency that would explain Dutch doing so in the Berbice case. Moreover, the fact that Ijo contributed another affix and a clitic (the negator -ka[nɛ]) demonstrates that its influence was strong enough to contribute the past affix as well.

9. Scattered natural gender marking is not unheard of in other French-based plantation creoles, such as in St. Lucian, in which Carrington (1984: 46) describes it as "neither predictable nor having any syntactic repercussions."

10. DeGraff (1999a) reads McWhorter (1998a) as claiming this, based on an isolated statement in my paper noting that *pidgins* are characterized by "virtual or complete elimination" of both derivational and inflectional affixes (McWhorter 1998: 793). This statement is, first, true: some pidgins have no derivational affixes at all (complete elimination), while some have one or two (which, compared to a source language with many, is virtual elimination). Meanwhile, however, the context of the sentence, as well as the ample discussion in the paper of the derivational affixes present in creoles, makes it clear that the statement referred to pidgins rather than to creoles.

11. There are a few -s plurals in the examples in Bailey (1966), an indication of the fluid nature of the creole-lexifier continuum that English Caribbean creoles, among others, tend to manifest themselves along.

12. It is significant that Thomason and Kaufman (1988: 75) link Level Three of borrowing with the incorporation of "the addition of syllable-final consonants." Although they specify that this occurs at this level only in loanwords, the fact that a creole's lexifier was the very source of its lexicon would appear to blur this distinction in creolophone contexts.

13. Dejean (1983) questions the application of the term *diglossia* to Haiti, given that only a minority of the population speak French. Although it is true that the term technically applies only to this small elite in Haiti (and some other French creolophone countries), the

*effects* of the diglossia—the focus of this chapter—have spread throughout the population, as they regularly do in borrowing contexts in which only a minority is bilingual.

14. This figure is composed of the 550 roots that Koefoed and Tarenskeen (1996) attribute to English, plus half of the 130 that could be derived as plausibly from Dutch as from English (65), the actual figure 615 rounded back to 600 in observance of the unavoidable uncertainty regarding the actual English proportion of the 130 roots of ambiguous origin.

15. It is clear that the plural markers in Soninke are affixes, not clitics. Zwicky and Pullum (1983: 503) propose that affixes are more selective of their host than are clitics, that morphophonological idiosyncrasies are more typical of affixes than are clitics, and that semantic idiosyncrasies are also more typical of affixes. Crucially, (a) there are three allomorphs of the Soninke plural marker, and the application of a given allomorph to a given lexical item is generally arbitrary (Diagana 1995: 58–59, Girier 1996: 66–67); (b) the plural affixes often exert morphophonological changes on the root; and (c) when used with body parts, plural marking signifies a disease as well as plurality (Diagana 1995: 62–64).

16. In fact, Soninke's use of lexical and morphosyntactic tone is of the moderate extent paralleled in Saramaccan. However, the existence and number of the inflectional affixes *in addition* to this is quite unparalleled in Saramaccan or any other creole known to me, and, most important, Saramaccan is reconstructable—with an authority that I venture few would contest regardless of perspective—as having lacked all but a sliver of its (few) grammatical uses of tone when it emerged.

## Chapter 2

I would like to thank Bernard Comrie, three anonymous reviewers, Stéphane Goyette, and Mikael Parkvall for invaluable comments on the paper that this chapter is derived from, as well as the scholarly community at the Max Planck Institut für Evolutionäre Anthropologie in Leipzig for commentary and conversations that inestimably seasoned my thoughts on the issues.

1. The traits absent in the prototype creole are inflectional affixation, tone-distinguishing monosyllabic lexical items or encoding morphosyntactic distinctions, and opaque lexicalization of derivation-root combinations.

2. It also bears mentioning that even in creoles in which Kikongo is claimed to have played a significant substratal role, such as Sranan, Saramaccan, and Ndjuka, there is no such fine-grained overt subdivision of pastness. This is particularly significant in the case of Palenquero Creole Spanish, in which Kikongo was essentially the only significant substratal influence (Schwegler 1998).

3. Some creolists argue that creoles are born via the gradual "streamlining" of a lexifier language via succeeding waves of second-language acquisition, with a general implication that the end result is more a "vehicularized" version of the lexifier than a new language entirely, and with a terminological and ontological dissociation of creoles from pidgins. I argue comprehensively against this frame of reference in chapter 5; cf also McWhorter and Parkvall (2002).

For the purposes of clarity, I am oversimplifying here in a crucial respect: creolization is a cline phenomenon, and many natural languages were born via a language contact process that resulted in simplification of a degree less radical than pidginization: for example, Afrikaans, Popular Brazilian Portuguese, Réunionnais French Creole, and the English Caribbean mesolects. Furthermore, there are languages in the world in which widespread second-language acquisition has simplified their grammars to a relatively minor but perceptible extent in comparison to their close relatives for example, Swahili.

4. This assumption is, for example, the fundamental one underlying DeGraff (1999) and related writings.

5. Kihm (1980a) wrote this more as a passing speculation than as a central assertion, and in Kihm (2000) he argues provisionally that creoles are indeed closer to Universal Grammar than other languages. This chapter is an attempt to explore and support that provocative idea.

6. Whether or not a language deemed more complex by our metric would be harder to acquire as a second language is a question of limited use, given that no matter how complex a language is, speakers of a closely related one will find it easy to acquire (Polish is not hard for Russians, Ojibwe is not hard for a Cree, etc.).

7. I leave unexplored the possibility that a relatively compact phonemic inventory may entail so many allophonic distinctions overall as to encompass a larger number of possible segments than a relatively large phonemic inventory where overall allophonic variation is relatively minimal. However, by our metric, the former language's sound system would be more complex than the latter's.

8. It is also worth noting that Lahu, unlike Saramaccan or any other Prototype Creole, has a goodly component of derivation whose meaning has drifted beyond compositionality. In some cases, an original meaning is vaguely perceptible: Matisoff (1973b: 62) suggests that -qɔ "possibly involves the idea of enclosing, as a wrapper or receptacle": yàʔ-qɔ "road," mû-lòʔ=qɔ "noon, daytime," làʔ-tɔ=qɔ "palm of hand," khɨ-tɔ=qɔ "sole of the foot," mɔ̀ʔ-qɔ "mouth." Other cases have drifted beyond any recoverability, such as -ni: cɔ̀ ʔ-pɛ̄=ni "waist," kɨ-ni "sweat," pa-pa-qú-ti=ni "dragonfly," fɨ̀-kôʔ=ni "orphan" (63).

9. There does not yet exist a thorough grammar of Saramaccan, such that some machinery along these lines may have yet to be discovered. However, given how many studies of various areas of its grammar have indeed been carried out, we can be sure that Saramaccan does not have anything approaching the array of highly conventionalized modal and pragmatic particles that Lahu does; indeed, such machinery is not evidenced in recordings of running speech in the language.

10. DeGraff (1999b) misinterprets my previous observations that grammaticalization in Saramaccan and other creoles generally has yet to metaphorically extend into lexicalization as claiming that creoles lack metaphor in general. The mistake here is the misconception that opaque lexicalizations in older grammars embody metaphor in the mind of the synchronic speaker, when, in fact, the very emergence of lexicalization entails that the form is no longer generable via metaphorical inference and now requires storage as an independent form. Along these lines, in the strict sense a language with little or few lexicalized forms is richer in metaphor than one where a large subset of compounds and derivation-root combinations have drifted beyond metaphoric processibility. Metaphor is central to meaning in any human language; my point is simply that older grammars display evidence of now-defunct metaphoricizations, since replaced by the ones now living in that grammar. Moreover, the metaphoricization of compounds and derivation-root combinations is an issue largely separate from that of idiom, proverb, and word play, which the Creole Prototype hypothesis neither addresses nor entails any denial of in creole languages (contra DeGraff 2000).

11. One reviewer asks whether there is proof that these constructions resulted from evolution within the creole, as opposed to having been inherited from a substrate language. Conclusive resolution of that question must await further work on Angolar's parent creole São Tomense, as well as further work on the main serializing substrate language of this creole dialect complex, Edo (Bini). However, for Angolar to retain serials in which verbs' uses are so far abstracted from their core meanings would be unexpected. Only in cases where one substrate language had unusually heavy influence in the contact situation or persisted in use alongside the creole over a long period of time do we usually encounter transfers so specific

and extending even to the abstract level (i.e., dialects of Melanesian Pidgin English spoken alongside Melanesian languages, or Portuguese creoles in India spoken alongside Marathi or Gujarati, or Sinhala). Where a substrate language competed with others, its contribution was generally robust but of limited idiosyncrasy. A useful comparison is Saramaccan, whose substrate was about as neatly divided between a serializing language and Bantu as São Tomense's was (Fongbe vs. Kikongo in the former case, Edo vs. Kikongo and its close relative Kimbundu in the latter). The Fongbe contribution to Saramaccan is rich but largely stops at highly abstract syntactic and semantic features such as more deeply grammaticalized serials (cf. Migge 1998 and chapter 4 in this volume).

12. Nor is it accidental that all three times I have taught a seminar on the structure of Surinam creoles, the tone sandhi in Saramaccan has immediately elicited spontaneous and lasting interest from at least one student, having at this writing inspired three papers and served as a major plank in a dissertation. The sandhi is one of the few features in Saramaccan that is relatively elaborated and idiosyncratic from a cross-linguistic perspective; the paucity of such features in the language is a simple consequence of its recent origins in a pidgin and the brief period of time that has elapsed since then.

13. See chapters 3 and 4, however, for an apparent emergent alienability distinction in Saramaccan, which Bettina Migge (pers. comm.) informs me exists in Ndjuka as well. This thesis hardly rules out that creoles do not begin to accrete needless complexities as time passes; in fact, what would be unexpected is that they would not do so, as all natural languages do. However, my claim is that creoles will display fewer such features than older ones do.

14. The fundamental nature of Kabardian grammar is more to the point here than whether or not the author of the quote has actually been able to check whether or not any language happens to exceed Kabardian in this capacity.

15. Creoles that remain in contact with their lexifier, however, have a tendency to borrow liberally from its derivational (but not inflectional) morphology, as evidenced by French plantation creoles.

16. It is not insignificant in this light that Swahili displays clear evidence of heavy second-language acquisition in its history (McWhorter 1994b).

17. Dryer (1989: 85) suggests that one-third of the world's languages have articles and that 8% have both definite and indefinite articles, but his survey does not include cliticized and bound forms.

18. Subtract the last five—French creoles which have heavily borrowed from the French lexicon—and there are no lexicalized derivation-root combinations (although as in all natural languages, such combinations have developed institutionalized [idiomatized] meanings based on metaphorical and culturally-based inference; see chapter 1, 3.3.1).

## Chapter 3

I thank Jack Sidnell, Alan Baxter, Mikael Parkvall, Stéphane Goyette, Susanne Michaelis, Martin Haspelmath, Helma Pasch, Jeff Siegel, Edgar Schneider, Anthony Grant, and Bernard Comrie for invaluable comments on oral presentations of this thesis and its preliminary written drafts.

1. Indeed, during the debate in which DeGraff (2000) was presented, he quite explicitly decried "the tendency for many creolists to assume that creoles started from pidgins."

2. Lass's useful conception of the "junk" that (older) grammars are replete with (1997: 305–24) is a related but distinct concept. Lass refers to the recruitment of previously existing forms in new uses, such as the extension of the progressive construction to express present

tense in English, the use of various adpositions in Finnish to build a case system, or the reanalysis of fossilizing case marking into new paradigms in Germanic. However, where Lass refers to the fundamentally random element of what a grammar uses to build constructions, my focus is on the fundamentally random nature of the very building of many constructions at all, regardless of the material recruited to do so.

3. Wutun, a language fusing largely Mandarin Chinese and Tibetan lexicon with largely Bao'an Mongolian morphology and syntax, is ergative (Lee-Smith and Wurm 1996; cf. also Thomason and Kaufman 1988: 91–92). This, however, is an intertwined language of a class with Media Lengua and Michif. Arising not from a pidgin but from an outright mixture of two or more languages complete with their morphosyntactic idiosyncrasies, these languages do not arise from a break in language transmission and as such are developmentally distinct from pidgins and creoles (cf. Bakker and Muysken 1995), constituting examples of unusually heavy language contact (cf. Thomason and Kaufman's borrowing scale levels four and five [1988: 75–76]). (This does not, however, belie my argument in chapter 10 in this volume that creoles and intertwined languages represent points on a cline of quality of language mixture, in which the former result from speakers of several languages acquiring a single one where the latter result from speakers of one [or two closely related ones] doing so.)

4. It would apparently be typologically implausible for pidgins to express ergativity solely via syntax, because all known syntactically ergative languages also manifest ergativity through morphology (Trask 1979: 385) or, we might add, particles (with all due acknowledgment of highly marginal shades of syntactic ergativity in English and other languages).

5. Some have asked whether the failure of Korlai to recruit an ergative marker may have possibly been due to the unavailability of a ready candidate for its calquing in Portuguese. Yet creoles can depart quite sharply from lexifier behavior in such cases. The Melanesian Pidgin English transitive marker -im, calqued on Melanesian equivalents, is etymologically derived from him; surely its use was partly inspired by sentences such as Tell him, but its extension to marking transitivity in general (Mi kikim bol "I kick the ball") is starkly different from English usage: if Melanesian Pidgin happened not to have calqued the transitive marker, some might well attribute it to English having offered no suitable item. Just as often, where the lexifier lacks a ready equivalent, creoles simply borrow a substrate morpheme wholesale, such as the Saramaccan focus particle wε borrowed from Fongbe, or the Philippines Creole Spanish use of the indigenously derived mana as a plural proclitic.

6. One person in the audience at a presentation of the argument in this chapter suggested that the absence of ergative creoles may be due to the absence of marking of core grammatical relations in creoles in general. Yet Seychellois Creole French and Tayo Creole French have subject markers, while, as we have seen, there are a few creoles that mark accusativity (in animates). Thus our question is why creoles seem to only mark—when they do—a particular subset of grammatical relations .

7. Kemmer subsumes inherent reflexivity under the term "middle voice." In treatments of English, "middle voice" is generally used to refer to constructions in which the grammatical subject is a notional object while the notional agent is unexpressed (The book sells well). In many languages, these expressions and inherent reflexive ones are encoded with the same overt marker, presumably motivating Kemmer's extended use of the term "middle voice." To avoid confusion, however, I will retain the term "inherent reflexive," since Kemmer's insights apply equally, and even predominantly, to this type of verbal usage.

8. Data are currently lacking on inherent reflexive marking in St. Lucian French Creole, but its absence would be surprising.

9. See section 5, however, for a creole where one evidential marker is developing internally.

10. Thus the claim is not that creoles lack constrastive focus marking, given examples such as the Saramaccan wε.

11. In Sranan, the cognate *taki* is used in more grammaticalized functions such as to introduce subject and noun complements (*Taki Kofi no kiri Amba meki wi breyti* "That Kofi didn't kill Amba made us happy"). However, most Sranan speakers are bilingual in Dutch, and these constructions are calques on usages of the Dutch complementizer *dat,* something made particularly plain by the fact that speakers also use the Dutch-borrowed equivalent *dat* in these functions (Plag 1993: 50).

12. Many have argued that certain creoles' subject pronouns are clitics (e.g., Kouwenberg 1993, Veenstra 1996); Mauritian Creole has some long wh-movement (Adone and Vainikka 1999); Korlai Portuguese Creole has developed OV word order in convergence with Marathi (Clements 1992); if "nontopic marker" refers to subject and object markers, Seychellois Creole and some others have what can be argued to be subject markers (e.g., Seychellois' *i*).

13. DeGraff (1999b) makes ample reference to Bickerton's work *qua se,* including a paper (Bickerton 1999) written for the volume to which DeGraff (1999b) serves as an epilogue. However, DeGraff's actual discussion, in itself a worthy one, does not specifically address the specifics of what Bickerton would consider the "periphery" of grammar to be, which is important for our purposes, given that these would go far beyond the parametric and stochastic factors DeGraff concentrates on in building his model.

14. To illustrate, one creolist commenting on the CreoLIST on a discussion of McWhorter (1998a) said genially, "Now, as for whether creoles are a particular kind of grammar or not— I wouldn't want to go there." An innocent comment in itself, but also demonstrating that theory-external factors have discouraged many thinkers from investigating what is a priori one of the most intuitively intriguing reasons to study creoles. A field in which to even venture taxonomic definitions is considered vaguely gauche at best and hubristic at worst—that is, "going there," in the sense local to late 1990s American slang—is clearly one in which the world has perhaps become a bit too much with us. Repeatedly, laymen I describe my disagreement with DeGraff to spontaneously ask, "Why do those people think it's so ridiculous to propose that a creole actually *is* something?" We must ask just where these questioners are going wrong.

15. In fact, DeGraff (1999a: 525) considers children vital to creolization in transforming input received from adults into "a stable, consistent, and fully developed linguistic system"; meanwhile, I myself believe (McWhorter 2000a) that, in most cases, adults had expanded and stabilized pidgins to a considerable extent before appreciable numbers of children learned the contact language natively, such that native acquisition was not as "catastrophically" transformative as the "abrupt creolization" model proposes (this is empirically demonstrated in recent cases such as Tok Pisin and its sisters [cf. Sankoff and Laberge 1980] and Sango [cf. Samarin 1980 and later works]). Nevertheless, my view is that the input presented to children had developed to such a point *internally,* having diverged sharply from the lexifier's structure itself, while DeGraff explicitly analogizes this input to the results of second-language acquisition and stresses retentions from the lexifier (most explicitly, 1999a, 2000a). As such, Lightfoot's statement pertains usefully to the issues at hand.

## Chapter 4

1. Many creolists, especially those working on French-based creoles, question whether creoles emerge from pidgins. McWhorter and Parkvall (2002) provide an extended argument that creoles indeed display features that are clearly traceable to a degree of reduction starkly beyond that associated with either functional but incomplete second-language acquisition or uninterrupted internal change. Importantly, whether or not this sharply reduced level of competence jelled into a *conventionalized* pidgin is irrelevant. What is crucial is that a new language was built from such a reduced starting point, however long the lifespan of that starting point happened to be.

2. The one exception I know of is the Mande language Soninke, whose grammars and word lists reveal no such features. However, grammars quite often fail to mention such cases as they do not qualify as "grammar" in their very irregularity, and just as often they only become apparent in dictionaries rather than the compact word lists of the sort that Soninke has been documented by to date. It may be that Soninke refutes my hypothesis, but (1) current documentation cannot be treated as proving this, (2) noncompositional derivation is indeed documented in some of its Mande relatives (see chapter 1 in this volume), and (3) if Soninke does prove to lack this trait but few or any other languages can be shown to, then my hypothesis stands valid as a very strong tendency and, as such, vital to assessing grammars' age.

3. I might note that Ham was not concerned with a general thesis that creole languages are less complex than older ones, nor had I even developed this thesis at the time when he learned of Saramaccan tone sandhi in a seminar I taught.

4. Saramaccan's *te* is most likely derived from *tĕ* "time"; Melanesian Pidgin English varieties' grammaticalization of *taim* in a similar function suggests the plausibility of this pathway, and the denasalization would be a predictable erosion as the result of heavy usage, a process prominent in Saramaccan (agentive marker *-ma < man*; past marker *bi < ben*). As such, Fongbe offers a possible model for this recruitment of *time* in the optional use of *hwènu* "time" with past temporal subordinate clauses:

(i)  Hwènu ɖé-è      à    xá   àtín jí  ɔ́,   ùn mɔ̀ wè.
     time  NOM-3SG you climb tree on DEF I   see you
     "When you climbed up the tree, I saw you." (*Éléments de recherche* 1983: XI 2)

However, this would be an example of how creoles often incorporate substrate features in altered fashion, contrary to claims that transfer accounts are flawed unless the transferred feature's syntactic occurrence and behavior are identical to that of its source (e.g., Bickerton 1986, Veenstra 1996). Fongbe only uses *hwènu* in this function in the past, whereas in Saramaccan it is restricted to the present and future; in addition *hwènu* is usually elided in Fongbe (*Éléments de recherche* 1983: XI 2).

5. *Hɛ̃́* is cognate with the full form of the third-person singular pronoun: *hɛ̃ ku mi* "him and me," and Boretzky (1983: 110–11) notes that this otherwise highly idiosyncratic homonymy is also present in, among other West African languages, Fongbe's sister variety Ewe. However, sources on Fongbe itself reveal no such homonymy. Yet the feature is so peculiar that attributing it to Ewe speakers of which were, after all, brought to Surinam is almost unavoidable. (Just perhaps such a homonymy existed in Fongbe in the seventeenth century?) Yet once again, the Ewe item's occurrence is not conditioned by tense and aspect as the Saramaccan equivalent is.

6. This is even true of the temporal subordination marking, where speakers as often as not accept "floutings" of the rules as grammatical, although they would be unlikely to produce them, and for which exceptions occur here and there in texts. The presence of the sequential marker is also quite usual but not obligatory.

7. In reference to the possible objection that in Saramaccan reduplication serves functions often served by derivation in other languages, recall that Fongbe has these too (see section 4.1.), and more richly.

8. DeGraff's (1993) claim that Haitian has syntactic clitics has been rather decisively refuted by several authors, including Déprez (1992), Cadely (1994), and Roberts (1999).

9. Points (8) and (10) qualify as responses to Lefebvre's observation (2002: 204–5) that surface structures alone may mask complexities in terms of the multifarious semantic correlates that one surface configuration may map to. In chapter 2 I make clear that semantic distinctions are one facet of complexity according to my metric, and this instance of Fongbe-Haitian comparison reinforces my thesis that in this respect as elsewhere, older languages are more elaborated.

10. This does, however, touch on a question for further research regarding my complexity metric. In the *Linguistic Typology* issue devoted to the thesis, some linguists argue that languages typically go through cycles in which they develop, shed, and then redevelop inflection (including DeGraff 2001: 274–78). However, while shedding aspects of their overspecifications, older grammars always maintain a degree of them that surpass in their totality what creoles like Saramaccan have amassed in their short lives. English, for example, has lost most of its inflections but maintains overspecifications elsewhere that render it a much more complex language than Saramaccan by my metric.

Nevertheless, cross-linguistically this is not true of phonemic inventories. All creoles known to me have, according to documentation to date, less complex phonemic inventories than their source languages have. However, I do not know of any creole that has as small a phonemic inventory as, for example, Polynesian languages have. It appears that older languages can "decomplexify" their phonemic inventories over time far beyond what even creoles display. That this is true in this one module is something I at present have no explanation for, and it suggests decisive differences between phonology and syntax in terms of processing and evolution over time.

11. The French creoles have been influenced by French enough to have incorporated much of French's derivational apparatus, including its noncompositional instances (see chapter 1), but not enough to render them essentially "varieties of French" in the sense that Jamaican patois is "English." Evidence to date suggests that, although the derivational point pulls French creoles somewhat from the heart of the specific trifeatural Creole Prototype, they nevertheless remain less overspecified than older grammars to an extent useful to my broader thesis regarding grammatical overspecification.

12. In the appendix to chapter 2 I argue that this and other varieties of Malay/Indonesian created by acquisition among adults are, in the taxonomic sense, creoles, despite the traditional association of the "creole" label with languages born in plantations and forced labor.

## Chapter 5

This chapter is a version adapted for the purposes of this volume of "Identitfing the Creole Prototype: Vindicating a Typological Class," *Language* 1998. I thank Gerardo Lorenzino, Helma Pasch, Eric Pederson, and William Samarin for the comments and data for the original article that remain in this version.

1. It is clear from his general discussions that Chaudenson refers to relatively full acquisition, moderated only slightly by paradigmatic reductions, overgeneralization, and preference for analytic over synthetic constructions. He usually brings nonstandard regional dialects to bear for comparison, arguing that the only thing distinguishing creoles from these is a minor disruption in transmission via non-native approximation. However, a major weakness in his argument is that where the reduction or reinterpretation in a creole exceeds the boundaries of such relatively intact transmission, he refers instead to foreigner talk varieties for comparison (e.g., Chaudenson 1992: 161). The problem here is that Foreigner Talk, unlike regional dialects, is clearly a case of severely incomplete acquisition, leading to the question as to what distinguished the slaves' *"français approximatif"* from pidgin or creole French (cf. Baker 1996, McWhorter and Parkvall 2002).

2. Chaudenson allows the term *creole* somewhat more validity than Mufwene, but he concurs with Mufwene in considering creoles to differ only slightly from regional dialects and ordinary contact varieties: "This is why we can consider that the compositional and fundamental features of creolization are less linguistic structures themselves (which are found,

*for the most part* [italics mine], often in basic outline and sometimes even in identical form, in marginal or approximative French varieties in America or Africa) than in the autonomization of these usages in new systems" (Chaudenson 1992: 136; translation mine).

3. For example, regarding serial verbs, for which the substratist case is strong (Boretzky 1983, McWhorter 1992, Post 1992, Migge 1998), Mufwene prefers to treat the substrate as having acted solely in conjunction with European constructions like *go get* (Mufwene 1996a: 115–17).

4. This manuscript was discovered at the library of the University of South Carolina by Shirley Brice Heath, who brought it to the attention of J. L. Dillard, who passed it on to William Stewart, who passed it to Guy Carden and Morris Goodman. It was described in a presentation to the Society for Pidgin and Creole Linguistics in 1990, but other than in brief citation by William Jennings (1995b), it subsequently languished until its appearance here.

5. This paradigm is also found vestigially in Sierra Leone Krio (McWhorter 2000a: 89), which I have traced to a line of development that began as Sranan, was exported to Jamaica as Maroon Spirit Language, and was then brought to Sierra Leone with transplanted Jamaican maroons in 1800 to become Krio.

6. There are contemporary accounts of a mixed English-Portuguese pidgin spoken on Portuguese plantations, called "Djutongo" in one (Goodman 1987: 377–82). A word list in this Djutongo (Smith 1987a: 125–28) confirms that this was indeed the precursor to Saramaccan (for further discussion, see McWhorter 1996a: 469, 488). Meanwhile, Smith (1987a) demonstrates that, systematically, the Portuguese lexicon in Saramaccan has been phonologically reinterpreted according to different rules than the English-based component. This shows that the Saramaccan is indeed an encounter between two separately stabilized contact languages.

7. The initial settlement of Annobón was rather small in scale and vigor; it was not until the second half of the 1500s that a vital plantation system was transplanted there from São Tomé (Hodges and Newitt 1988: 18). By this time, in São Tomé, large-scale plantation agriculture had been established, conditioning the disproportion of black to white, which superstratists, along with other creolists, would expect to have led to deep restructuring of Portuguese. It is possible that São Tomense was not transplanted to Annobón until then, in which case the distance of Annobonese itself from Portuguese would not prove that its parent, São Tomense, emerged during intimate interracial contact. However, Principe, home to a closely related dialect equally distant from Portuguese, was settled from São Tomé as a thriving sister plantation economy from its outset at the turn of the 1500s, when plantation agriculture—and thus sharp black/white disproportion—on São Tomé was still embryonic.

8. Attributions of some features of Romanian (and other Balkan Sprachbund languages) to contact have been contested; however, few would question the basic validity of the Sprachbund analysis as a whole.

9. Kituba, Lingala, and Shaba Swahili have all only recently come to be spoken natively. Because in practice, creolists have tended to resist calling languages *creoles* until all of their speakers were native, in chapter 10 I propose the alternate term *semi-pidgin* as equally appropriate.

10. Some of the discomfort with the notion of semi-creole is traceable to Bickerton's proposal of a mathematically calculable "pidginization index" (1984: 176–18), ranking creoles according to degree of lexifier breakdown. Although Singler (1986) convincingly showed that the formula made too many false predictions to be maintained, this simply meant that the inherent messiness of sociohistory does not yield to rigid mathematical formulas. Bickerton's central insight was correct.

Chapter 6

1. It is assumed here that *da*, *na*, and *a* are cognates, with *da* having been the original form in languages with *na* or *a*. Two things suggest the validity of this analysis. First, the earliest Sranan

documents have *da* and show a transition over time to *na* (Arends 1989). As for *a*, it is known that in Jamaican Creole initial consonants often elide in monosyllabic grammatical morphemes undergoing heavy use such as *did> id*, *bin> in* (Rickford 1980); *a* is likely to have developed thus from *da*. This treatment differs from that of Escure (1983) who considers *a* to represent an earlier copula giving way gradually to *da*; this hypothesis seems less likely in light of the above.

2. Saramaccan material was collected by the author unless otherwise indicated.

3. These conclusions are based, first, on the my participation in an NSF-funded project investigating the copula in some 45 languages, representing a wide range of language families (BNS-8913104), and this graduate-level experience's having since lent me a perpetually "peeled eye" for copular configurations in as many languages as possible over several years.

4. The languages here considered to represent the substrate of the Caribbean English-based creoles are those which research to date suggests had the strongest influence on most of the Atlantic English-based creoles in general, based on lexical imprint (i.e., Smith 1987a), grammatical transfer (Alleyne 1980, Boretzky 1983, McWhorter 1997a, etc.), and historical evidence (LePage and DeCamp 1960, Curtin 1969). Of course, a list such as this necessarily obscures the fact that precise substrate compositions varied from location to location. However, the effectiveness of the arguments presented here do not depend on such local variations.

5. Also, some of the zero-copula sentences are grammatical in the modern language. For example,
Sranan 1796:

(i)   Hoe somma ø datty?
      which thing that
      Who is it? (Arends 1989: 152)

is paralleled in modern Sranan by *Sani ø dati?*

6. This occurrence of an oblique third-person pronoun in subject position only in equative sentences is also found in Sranan, Ndjuka, and Krio.

7. See McWhorter (1997a) for fuller argument for DA as innovation.

8. The analysis can also be seen as evidence supporting the hypothesis that the Caribbean English-based creoles have a single common ancestor (Hancock 1987, Smith 1987a, McWhorter 2000a). This is because cross-linguistically there is a wide range of items that can undergo reanalysis in the subject position of topic-comment constructions: the third-person pronoun in Hebrew, the proximal demonstrative in Chinese, an erstwhile focus marker in Swahili. The chances of a proximal demonstrative being the item to undergo this reanalysis in so very many creoles independently are nil, while the reconstruction of a common ancestor provides an elegant account of the distribution. See chapter 8 for fuller discussion.

9. An analogous argument to that presented in section 3 can be made for the locative copula *de* as well—comparative and historical analysis strongly argue that *de* is an innovation, rather than a substrate calque, as well (see chapter 8). Consequently, the alternation between *de* and zero in the upper mesolect documented by Bickerton (1973) can be addressed in the same manner as I do the equative DA in this essay.

## Chapter 7

1. Unless otherwise indicated, sentences were elicited by the author from native speakers.

2. Many sources on SM indicate *ã* (generally written *an*) rather than *á* as the predicate negator. This is due to most of Saramaccan material before the 1990s being elicited from speakers of the Upper River dialect; mine have been Lower River dialect speakers.

3. This behavior will appear particularly odd to scholars of related creoles, which do not extend the locative copula form into this domain. But the construction is readily elicited and observable in texts as well.

4. I have preserved the orthography of the missionaries, which reflected that of their native Dutch.

5. It is also possible that their informants were bilingual in Sranan and used Srananisms as a formalizing device in the presence of Europeans, Sranan having more prestige because of its association with colonial culture.

6. I have here shown the Upper River dialect form for clarity of demonstration. In actuality, Lower River speakers use the form *mê*, in which the nasality of [n] in *ná* persists as a vocalic feature.

7. Furthermore, this aspect of SM cannot be attributed to the main sociohistorical feature distinguishing SM from other Caribbean English-based creoles namely, its Portuguese element. As we have seen, related creoles have close cognates of the original predicate negator in SM. Furthermore, neither Portuguese nor creoles based on it offer models for the emergence of a predicate negator allomorphy of the SM type, particularly in topic-comment constructions.

8. My recordings, as well as textual surveys, indicate that identificational sentences are actually expressed as topic-comment constructions more often than not. By the principle of uniformity, this supports my diachronic hypothesis as to their origins, in that even today speakers exhibit a strong tendency to express identificational propositions in the topic-comment configuration.

## Chapter 8

1. Languages studied under the NSF project: Swahili, Nama, Hausa, Russian, Arabic, Chinese, Hawaiian, Yagaria, Jacaltec, Irish, West Greenlandic Eskimo, Melanesian Pidgin English, Hungarian, Vietnamese, Tagalog, Finnish, Bengali, Hindi, Nahuati, Twi, Ewe, Gã, Yoruba, Igbo, Haitian Creole, African-American Vernacular English. Other languages examined by Devitt (1990): Spanish, Portuguese, Mangarayi, Turkish, Alyawarra, Kiowa, Tamil, Zuni, Hebrew, Tigre, Kui, Kilba, Greek, Quechua, Shuswap, Lakhota, Karok.

2. The *-na* element shared by both Kikongo items is indeed indicative of their semantic relationship and may even be perceived by speakers; however, Kikongo is highly unlikely to have alone made significant impact on English-based creoles beyond the lexicon, since the British did not begin importing slaves from the Congo region until the eighteenth century, by which time most of the creoles had already stabilized (LePage and DeCamp 1960: 54–60).

3. Sources for substrate language data unless otherwise noted: Wolof: Fal, Santos, and Doneux (1990); Mandinka: Gamble (1987a); Akan: Christaller (1964[1875]); Gbe: Westermann (1928); Igbo: Welmers and Welmers (1968); Yoruba: Ogunbowale (1970[1]); Kikongo: Seidel and Struyf (1910). The languages represent the substrate languages which research to date suggests had the strongest influence on most of the Atlantic English-based creoles in general, based on lexical imprint (Hancock 1971, Mittelsdorf 1978, Cassidy 1983, Smith 1987a, etc.), grammatical transfer (Alleyne 1980, Boretsky 1983, McWhorter 1992, etc.), historical evidence (LePage and DeCamp 1960, Curtin 1969, Hancock 1986, Rickford 1987, Postma 1990, etc.), and cultural evidence (Turner 1949, Price 1983, Alleyne 1993, etc.). Specifically, they are the languages most widely spoken in the Gambian region from which the British drew many slaves (Wolof, Mandinka [representing the Manding complex]); on the

Gold and Slave coasts from which many or most of the Caribbean slaves were brought to each colony during the crucial period when the creoles were forming (Akan, Gbe, Igbo, Yoruba); and in the Congo region, from which the British brought many slaves starting in the early nineteenth century (Kikongo). See Jones (1983) for Krio; Faraclas (1988) for Nigerian; Smith (1987a) for Sranan and Saramaccan; Rickford (1987) for Guyanese; LePage and DeCamp (1960) for Jamaican, which data can also be applied broadly to Belizean and Antiguan, and Mufwene (1992) for Gullah.

While a great many other languages were represented among Caribbean slave populations and on the West African coast, evidence of the above sort suggests a preponderant influence from the preceding languages, such that we can expect that the contributions of less well-represented languages (Anyi-Baule, the Kru complex, Fula, etc.) would never have reason to predominate over those from the others except in the case of occasional lexical borrowings of African-oriented semantics (Thomason and Kaufman 1988, Thomason 1993). Of course, a list such as this necessarily obscures the fact that precise substrate compositions varied from location to location. However, the effectiveness of the arguments to be presented here will not depend on such local variations.

4. Note that the occasional occurrence of a demonstrative/copula homophony in other creoles—French Guyanais has *sa* from *ça*—is to be expected, given that such homophonies are a documented cross-linguistic diachronic tendency. Such an occurrence does not constitute counterevidence to the basic thesis presented here. What is remarkable about *da* is the uniformity of its distribution across over two dozen English-based creoles, despite the fact that the distal demonstrative is but one of several possible sources for an equative copula to be derived from. For example, while French Guyanais has *sa*, Haitian has *se* < *c 'est* and Louisiana Creole French and the Indian Ocean creoles have zero copula.

5. Mandinka also has *fó* "so that," which at first glance seems suggestive. However, it is impossible to derive the modal usage from this conjunction, and it is virtually impossible to derive the prepositional usage from it. Similarly, Yoruba has the verb *fún* "to give," which would seem relatable to the prepositional usages of *fu*. However, aside from the question as to why Yoruba would have served alone as a model (having never been even as heavily represented as Akan, Gbe, and Igbo in English-based creole substrates, according to most sources), again, the modal usage is difficult to derive from a verb "to give."

6. This is also the place for an official obituary for the grand old monogenesis hypothesis, which derived all creoles from a common Portuguese pidgin ancestor, relexified by various languages around the world. The hypothesis was motivated in part by the Portuguese lexical items in creoles of disparate lexical base and geographical location. Goodman (1987), however, exhaustively accounts for this presence on the basis of the wide-ranging migrations of Portuguese-speaking slaveholders throughout the Caribbean in the seventeenth century. Furthermore, widespread items such as *sabi* "to know" and *pikin* "small child" are attributable to the Portuguese having been first to establish a trade pidgin on the West African coast, items from this pidgin having diffused into pidgins based on other European languages established later in the same areas. Meanwhile, various conceptions of universals (bioprogram, second-language acquisition) are thought to explain many of the features the monogenesis hypothesis' promoters observed.

Textbooks continue to list the monogenesis hypothesis as one of many competing, and scholars outside of creole studies have often heard or read of it. But the reality is that no working creolist today subscribes to the monogenesis hypothesis: no serious analysis has been based on it in three decades at this writing. The hypothesis was a sensible and ingenious response to the data available in the 1950s and 1960s. But with the explosion in data collection and theorizing since then, the monogenesis hypothesis can now be considered an archival matter.

Chapter 9

1. Chaudenson first applied the concept to a hypothesis that Mauritian Creole is a direct continuation of Réunionnais French, a scenario that Baker (1996 and later works) has rather decisively argued against; however, Chaudenson makes less controversial reference to the concept in Chaudenson (2000).

2. The argument refers strictly to this modal usage; the uses of *fu* (and its cognates and allomorphs) as preposition and complementizer could easily have been incorporated from English in several separate locations and thus have no bearing on my argument for a common ancestor (cf. Bickerton's [1998: 87] misinterpretation of my reasoning).

3. The jury currently remains out on Baker's (1999) and Parkvall's (1995b) arguments that AEC traces even further back than Barbados to St. Kitts, which was settled slightly earlier. However, the importance of Barbados as a distribution point is not in question, and the actual formation of AEC on St. Kitts would have no bearing on my lines of argumentation here.

4. Schwegler (1999) traces this to a Kikongo demonstrative meaning "those," such that technically the two creoles could have incorporated the Kikongo pronoun independently. This is unlikely, however: why would both happen to choose an African etymon for the third-person plural specifically, and why would both happen to recruit a demonstrative rather than a personal pronoun in the function?

5. I do not address the Dutch creoles here because accidents of history make it difficult to draw conclusions from them. There have been only three Dutch-based plantation creoles. Berbice Creole Dutch has so heavy and deep-rooted a contribution from a single West African language, Eastern Ijo, that it, in fact, belongs more properly not to the creole but to the intertwined language class (e.g., Angloromani, Michif) (chapter 10). This leaves just Negerhollands and Skepi Dutch. This already small basis of comparison is further restricted by the fact that both are now extinct, and Skepi was only sketchily documented before its death.

6. Granda (1978: 416–17) claims that a now-extinct Spanish creole was once spoken further south in the town of Uré by descendants of slaves who escaped from gold mines. Granda gives no data and was unable to visit the town. However, if this variety was indeed a creole, then despite the fact that there is no evidence tracing it to Portuguese pidgin or creole, it nevertheless leaves intact my claim that Spanish America is crucially problematic to limited access-based creole genesis theories. My claim is not that limited access to a target language cannot drive creole genesis but that plantations (and mines) did *not* limit access to Spanish to the extent that pidgin-level competence would be passed on to future generations, in contradiction to all expectations according to creole genesis theory. In relation to Uré, it is quite natural that adult maroons, most of whom had probably spent little time in the mines, would speak only pidginized Spanish, and, if having no subsequent contact with whites, would creolize it. These, however, were conditions quite distinct from the plantation or the mine.

7. Hancock's (1969, 1986) position has been that sale slaves learned the pidgin from castle slaves tending to them before shipment, and then brought the pidgin to the New World; he also reconstructs this as a regular occurrence, such that slaves would have been bringing pidgin English to all of the colonies of the New World over centuries' time. This conception has been so well known for so long that there may be a tendency to assume that I am echoing it. In this light, I must emphasize that I suppose that *castle* slaves brought the pidgin across the Atlantic, and that they did this only once or twice during the foundation of Barbados, with AEC then disseminating from there (cf. McWhorter 2000a).

Chapter 10

The article version of this chapter included an extended section suggesting that the concept of pidgin be considered gradient just as the creole one is. However, the meat of that argument is included here in chapter 5, and I consider the argument re intertwined languages to be of more import to this volume.

Thanks to Silvia Kouwenberg, Mary Margaret Ong, Richard Rhodes, and John Wolff for sentences, and to Peter Bakker, Derek Bickerton, Chris Corne, Anthony Grant, and John Wolff for vastly helpful comments on the section of the original article that this chapter comprises. All errors are, of course, my responsibility.

1. Since pidgins and creoles are agreed to be "mixed," to restrict the term "mixed languages" to cases like Michif and Media Lengua is confusing to nonspecialists.

2. Of course, speakers may later lose competence in one or both of the languages (e.g., Angloromani speakers no longer speak Romani [Kenrick 1979]; Ma'a speakers no longer speak their ancestral Cushitic language). The important point here is the situation at the language's birth.

3. Some might object that creoles did not emerge on plantations until blacks vastly outnumbered whites, and that in the mid-1600s when French observers like Du Tertre wrote, this had yet to happen. However, like most creole theory, this view on the timing of creoles' appearance is unavoidably less an empirical observation than a deductive hypothesis, based largely on the comparison of Mauritius and Réunion by Baker and Corne (1982). Actual cross-creole documentation repeatedly suggests that creoles often emerged long before blacks outnumbered whites. A passage of indisputable creole French in Martinique has been found which dates to 1671 (Carden, Goodman, Posner, and Stewart 1990), at a time when the conversion to large sugar plantations had yet to occur. Likewise, in Suriname, Sranan arose on small farms where blacks and whites worked closely together in equal proportion (McWhorter 1996b, 2000a: 99–109). (See also Chapter 5.)

4. To be sure, the observations in this paragraph were made by the time slaves no longer controlled ancestral African languages. However, there is all reason to suppose that at least the first generation of blacks born on plantations may have often acquired reasonable competence in African languages. This was especially the case when one or two languages were strongly represented, such as Fon and Gun in French Guiana (Jennings 1995a) or Gbe and Kikongo in Suriname. Thus creoles were created and stabilized by speakers of African languages.

5. Mine is not the only argument seeking to bring creoles and intertwined languages under the same umbrella. While I argue that intertwined languages are, in a sense, creoles, Lefebvre's paradigm, summarily presented in Lefebvre (1998), can be seen as seeking to show that creoles, as products of relexification, are intertwined languages. However, by my reading, Lefebvre's schema contains too much unconstrained speculation and does not make sufficient appeal to cross-creole data, as I argue in chapter 4. For example, one would like to see why, if various syntax-internal factors blocked so much of Fongbe's structural machinery from appearing in Haitian Creole, virtually all of Quechua's grammar and morphology appears in Media Lengua, with Spanish having presented all but no barriers.

## Chapter 11

This chapter represents a longer version of the article it is based on, which had to be abbreviated for reasons of space. Short of those restrictions in book format, I judged it appropriate to preserve here the fuller outline of my argumentation. Irmengard Rauch, Anthony Grant, Stéphane Goyette, Gary Holland, James Matisoff, Peter Tiersma, Jarich Hoekstra, Andrew Garrett, Martin Haspelmath, Werner Abraham, Sally Thomason, and my once-and-future mentor Elizabeth Traugott have helped me in innumerable crucial ways in venturing this paper. Sincere thanks to all of them, none of whom are responsible, of course, for remaining flaws.

1. Page numbers refer to the following sources: Dutch: Donaldson (1997); Swedish: Holmes and Hinchliffe (1997); Danish: Thomas (1991); Norwegian: Strandskogen and Strandskogen (1986); Afrikaans: Ponelis (1993); Frisian: Tiersma (1985); Icelandic: Kress (1982); Faroese: Lockwood (1955); Yiddish: Lockwood (1995). Throughout the chapter, where not otherwise cited, the source of the data is these (e.g., in cases of negative evidence such as the absence of a feature in a grammar, which is often impossible to refer to by page).

2. Abbreviations used throughout: DAT, dative; PL, plural; IMP, imperative; OBJ, object; PART, partitive; DEF, definite determiner; ACC, accusative; 1SG, first-person singular; 3SG, third-person singular; PREP, preposition; NOM, nominative; GEN, genitive; NEG, negator; 1NF, infinitive.

3. The construction is recessive in standard Dutch; speakers accept *Men heeft zijn arm gebroken* as well.

4. Given the occasional lack of fit in languages with nominal inflection between grammatical gender and inflectional class (Spanish *mano* "hand" has masculine inflection but feminine concord), more properly, English lost inflectional class marking on nouns rather than grammatical gender marking specifically. However, the observation crucial to my thesis is that English also shed true grammatical gender marking on its articles.

5. I take the liberty of assuming that speakers of the aforementioned nonstandard dialects have generally had enough exposure to the standard one to be familiar with the concept of gender, especially in these times when dialects of this kind are so often threatened by standard varieties and geopolitically dominant languages.

6. I owe this observation to Martin Haspelmath.

7. Shortly after writing this I noticed that *thence* is used occasionally in nonfiction prose. However, the English *to*-forms *hither* and *thither* are definitely impossible in Modern English beyond the ironic or deliberately archaic.

8. Pages for data in sources listed in note 1: Dutch: 125, Yiddish: 59, Swedish: 115–16, Icelandic: 97, Faroese: 57–61; Afrikaans data from Eksteen (1997).

9. Rydén and Brorström (1987: 211) also include *change, recover, turn* (in its transformative meaning), *set* (as in *The sun is set*), and *fly*. However, as a native American English speaker I sense these as strictly archaic and suggest that *go* is indeed the only remaining form in the modern language, in concurrence with authors like Christophersen and Sandved (1969: 221).

10. To the extent that we analyze forms of this kind as clitics, we might ask why indefinite *me* could not have simply evolved into one rather than simply disappearing.

11. The term includes Low German, which some contemporary observations suggest was processed as "the same language" at the time (Peters 1987: 80).

12. If by chance any of these attestations of [i] were actually remnants of the southwestern -*y* intransitive marker (*idle chap, He'll do nothèn but fishy* [Barnes 1886: 25]), then even this—the preservation of an overt valence marker alien to English dialects northward—supports the idea that contact with Old Norse left English shorn of overspecification beyond what would have been the case during internal evolution.

13. In the Shetlands and the Orkneys, where Norse was spoken for centuries longer than in England, the *be*-perfect has been generalized to transitives (Melchers 1992) rather than contracting and disappearing. However, this cannot be taken as counterevidence that Scandinavian contact spurred the demise of the *be*-perfect in England. As Melchers and myself note, the *be*-perfect was already quite restricted in Old Norse, such that the developments in the Shetlands and Orkneys cannot be seen as a transfer. Melchers (608) suggests that the culprit may have been southwestern Norwegian dialects where the *be*-perfect has extended to the transitive in just this way, given that most settlers of the Shetlands and the Orkneys came from southwestern Norway.

14. Original German: "Die Klagen soll man zuerst aburteilen, über die man im vorigen Sommer nicht zum Urteil gelangte."

15. In both the Fiji and Riau cases, the scenario is complicated somewhat by the possible influence of pidgin varieties in the contact situations: here, Pidgin Hindustani and Bazaar Malay, respectively. However, this may be an artifact of our temporal proximity to cases such as these. It is hardly inconceivable that there was a "pidgin English" spoken by the first wave of Scandinavians, reflecting the limitations of adult language-learning capabilities. (This is especially the case given the observed fact that Old English and Old Norse were not essentially dialects of the same language as is often claimed.) It may have been the progeny of these invaders who acquired a more proficient English, nevertheless pervaded with Norse features. Our microsociolinguistic knowledge of how interference through language shift (in Thomason and Kaufman's terminology) proceeds is currently limited, most cases having occurred beyond the purview of written history. Certainly this is, and will likely remain, the case with the Norsification of English over a thousand years ago.

16. This also discourages supposing that the variability of many features in Old English was due to Celtic influence "softening up" the grammar initially, with Scandinavian contact merely reinforcing a process already begun. If other early Germanic languages unaffected by Celtic already displayed similar variability, then the Celtic explanation for English loses necessity.

17. Certainly Lightfoot's work emphasizes "catastrophic" parameter shifts. However, he makes no stipulation that the process of trigger weakening that eventually causes these parameter shifts is, itself, of such an abrupt nature. (To the extent that his earlier work claimed that such changes occurred in highly narrow time frames, in later work he has considerably tempered this tendency.)

18. As such, the contrast that English presents with its sisters in broad view suggests that it would be more elegant *not* to surmise, *contra* Thomason and Kaufman (1988: 303), that the inflectional simplifications in northerly English dialects were already taking place to a significant degree before Norse contact.

19. The latter feature is notable given that external possessive constructions can be seen as markers of inalienable possession.


## Chapter 13

This chapter began, obviously, as a book review article of Shana Poplack, ed., *The English History of African American English.* Section 3 addresses in detail each of six articles in the volume in question. I have included it here to indicate the details of my judgments on these especially thorough arguments, for the purposes of scholarship among specialists in Black English. I find this especially necessary given that in the past, most of my written statements on the dialect have been in sources aimed at a nonacademic audience (such as McWhorter 1998b), which unavoidably do not engage the issues with a scholarly level of detail. However, the issues in section 3 are so internal to this one sub-subfield that many readers outside of the community of variationist scholars of Black English might prefer to skip the section and proceed from section 4. I consider the arguments there and afterward to apply most directly to the aims of this volume.

# REFERENCES

Abraham, Roy C. 1958. *Dictionary of modern Yoruba*. London: University of London Press.

Adamson, Lilian, and Norval Smith. 1995. In Arends, Muysken, and Smith, 219–32.

———. 2003. Productive derivational predicate reduplication in Sranan. In Kouwenberg, 83–92.

Adelaar, K. Alexander, and D. J. Prentice (with Cornelis D. Grijns, Hein Steinhauer, and Aone van Engelenhoven). 1996. Malay: Its history, role and spread. In Wurm, Mühlhäusler, and Tyron, 673–93.

Adone, Dany, and Anne Vainikka. 1999. Acquisition of wh-questions in Mauritian Creole. In DeGraff, 75–94.

Ahlgren, Arthur. 1946. *On the use of the definite article with "nouns of possession" in English*. Uppsala: Appelbergs Boktryckeriaktiebolag.

Aikhenvald, Alexandra Y. 2001. Areal diffusion, genetic inheritance, and problems of subgrouping: A North Arawak case study. In *Areal diffusion and genetic inheritance*, edited by Alexandra Y. Aikhenvald and R. M. W. Dixon, 167–94. Oxford: Oxford University Press.

Alleyne, Mervyn. C. 1971. Acculturation and the cultural matrix of creolization. In Hymes, 169–86.

———. 1980. *Comparative Afro-American*. Ann Arbor: Karoma.

———. 1993. Continuity versus creativity in Afro-American language and culture. In Mufwene, 167–81.

———. 1994. Problems of standardization of creole languages. In *Language and the social construction of identity in creole situations*, edited by Marcyliena Morgan, 7–18. Los Angeles: Center for Afro-American Studies, UCLA.

———. 1998. Opposite processes in "creolization." In *Degrees of restructuring in creole languages*, edited by Ingrid Neumann-Holzschuh and Edgar Schneider, 125–33. Amsterdam: John Benjamins.

Allsopp, Richard, ed. 1996. *Dictionary of Caribbean English usage*. Oxford: Oxford University Press.

Andersen, Henning. 1988. Center and periphery: Adoption, diffusion, and spread. In *Historical dialectology: Regional and social*, edited by Jacek Fisiak, 39–83. Berlin: Mouton de Gruyter.

Andersen, Roger. 1983. *Pidginization and creolization as language acquisition*. Rowley, MA: Newbury House.

Arends, Jacques. 1989. Syntactic developments in Sranan. Dissertation, University of Nijmegen.

———. 1995a. Demographic factors in the formation of Sranan. In Arends, 233–85.

———. 2001. Simple grammars, complex languages. *Linguistic Typology* 5: 180–82.

Arends, Jacques, Pieter Muysken, and Norval Smith. 1995. *Pidgins and creoles: An introduction*. Amsterdam: John Benjamins.

Aronoff, Mark. 1976. *Word formation in generative grammar*. Cambridge, MA: MIT Press.

Aronoff, Mark, and Frank Anshen. 1998. Morphology and the lexicon: Lexicalization and productivity. In *The handbook of morphology*, edited by Andrew Spencer and Arnold M. Zwicky, 237–71. Oxford: Blackwell.

Babby, Leonard. 1975. A transformational analysis of transitive -*sja* verbs in Russian. *Lingua* 35: 297–332.

Bailey, Beryl Loftman. 1966. *Jamaican creole syntax*. Cambridge: Cambridge University Press.

Bailey, Charles-James, and Karl Maroldt. 1977. The French lineage of English. In *Pidgins-creoles-languages in contact*, edited by Jürgen Meisel, 21–53. Tübingen: Narr.

Bailey, Guy, Natalie Maynor, and Patricia Cukor-Avila, eds. 1991. *The emergence of Black English*. Amsterdam: John Benjamins.

Bailleul, Père Charles. 1981. *Petit dictionnaire Bambara–Français Français–Bambara*. Amersham, England: Avebury.

Baker, Mark C. 1996. *The polysynthesis parameter*. New York: Oxford University Press.

———. 2001. *The atoms of language*. New York: Basic Books.

Baker, Philip. 1972. *Kreol: A description of Mauritian Creole*. London: Hurst.

———. 1987. Combien y a-t-il eu de genèses créoles à base lexicale française? *Études Créoles* 10: 60–76.

———. 1990. Off target? *Journal of Pidgin and Creole Languages* 5: 107–19.

———. 1993. Australian influence on Melanesian Pidgin English. *Te Reo* 36: 3–67.

———. 1995a. Motivation in creole genesis. In Baker, 3–15.

———, ed. 1995b. *From contact to creole and beyond*. London: University of Westminster Press.

———. 1996. Review article: Pidginization, creolization, and français approximatif. *Journal of Pidgin and Creole Languages* 11: 95–120.

———. 1999. Investigating the origin and diffusion of shared features among the Atlantic English Creoles. In Baker and Bruyn, 315–64.

Baker, Philip, and Adrienne Bruyn, eds. 1999. *St. Kitts and the Atlantic creoles*. London: University of Westminster Press.

Baker, Philip, and Chris Corne. 1982. *Isle de France Creole: Affinities and origins*. Ann Arbor: Karoma.

Baker, Philip, and Vinesh Hookoomsing. 1987. *Dictionary of Mauritian Creole*. Paris: L'Harmattan.

Baker, Philip, and Anand Syea, eds. 1996. *Changing meanings, changing functions: Papers relating to grammaticalization in contact languages*. London: University of Westminster.

Bakker, Peter. 1987. Reduplications in Saramaccan. In *Studies in Saramaccan language structure*, edited by Mervyn C. Alleyne, 17–40. Amsterdam: Instituut voor Algemene Taalwetenschap.

———. 1997. *Language of our own: The genesis of Michif, the mixed Cree-French language of the Canadian Métis.* New York: Oxford University Press.

Bakker, Peter, and Maarten Mous, eds. 1994. *Mixed languages.* Amsterdam: Instituut voor Functioneel Onderzoek van Taal en Taalgebruik.

Bakker, Peter, and Pieter Muysken. 1995. Mixed languages and language intertwining. In Arends, Muysken, and Smith, 41–52.

Ball, Martin J., and Nicole Müller. 1992. *Mutation in Welsh.* London: Routledge.

Balmer, William T., and F. C. F. Grant. 1929. *A grammar of the Fante-Akan language.* London: Atlantis.

Baptista, Marlyse. 2000. Verb movement in four creole languages: A comparative analysis. In McWhorter, 1–33.

Barnes, Janet. 1990. Classifiers in Tuyuca. In *Amazonian linguistics: Studies in Lowland South American languages*, edited by Doris L. Payne, 273–92. Austin: University of Texas Press.

Barnes, Michael. 1987. Some remarks on subordinate-clause word order in Faroese. *Scripta Islandica* 38: 3–35.

Barnes, William. 1886. *A glossary of the Dorset dialect with a grammar of its word shapening and wording.* London: Trübner.

Bartens, Angela. 1999. Notes on componential diffusion in the genesis of the Kabuverdianu cluster. In McWhorter, 35–61.

Barthelemi, Georges. 1995. *Dictionnaire pratique créole guyanais–français.* Cayenne: Ibis Rouge.

Bauer, Laurie. 1988. *Introducing linguistic morphology.* Edinburgh: Edinburgh University Press.

Bauer, Winifred. 1993. *Maori.* London: Routledge.

Baugh, John. 1980. A re-examination of the Black English copula. In *Locating Language in Time and Space*, edited by William Labov, 83–106. New York: Academic Press.

Bazin, Hippolyte. 1965. Dictionnaire bambara–français. Ridgewood, NJ: Gregg Press. (Originally published 1906)

Beard, Robert. 1998. Derivation. In *The handbook of morphology*, edited by Andrew Spencer and Arnold Zwicky, 44–65. Oxford: Blackwell.

Bense, Johan F. 1939. *A dictionary of the Low-Dutch element in the English vocabulary.* The Hague: Martinus Nijhoff.

Bentley, Rev. W. Holman. 1887. *Dictionary and grammar of the Kongo language.* London: Baptist Missionary Society.

Bhattarchariya, Djiwen. 1994. Naga Pidgin: Creole or Creoloid? *California Linguistic Notes* 24: 34–50.

Bickerton, Derek. 1973. The nature of a creole continuum. *Language* 49: 640–49.

———. 1975. *Dynamics of a creole system.* Cambridge: Cambridge University Press.

———. 1977. Pidginization and creolization: Language acquisition and language universals. In *Pidgin and creole linguistics*, edited by Albert Valdman, 49–69. Bloomington : Indiana University Press.

———. 1981. *Roots of language.* Ann Arbor, MI: Karoma.

———. 1983. Notice of P. Baker and C. Corne, Isle de France Creole (Karoma, 1982). *Carrier Pidgin* 11: 8–9.

———. 1984. The Language Bioprogram Hypothesis. *Behavioral and Brain Sciences* 7: 173–88.

———. 1988. Creole languages and the bioprogram. In *Linguistics: The Cambridge survey* (Vol. 2), edited by Frederick J. Newmeyer, 268–84. Cambridge: Cambridge University Press.

————. 1990. *Language and species*. Chicago: University of Chicago Press.

————. 1995. *Language and human behavior*. Seattle: University of Washington Press.

————. 1996. The origins of variation in Guyanese. In Guy et al., 311–27.

————. 1998. A sociohistoric examination of Afrogenesis. *Journal of Pidgin and Creole Languages* 13: 63–92.

————. 1999. How to acquire language without positive evidence: What acquisitionists can learn from creoles. In DeGraff, 49–74.

Bickerton, Derek, and Aquilas Escalante. 1970. Palenquero: A Spanish-based creole of northern Colombia. *Lingua* 24: 254–67.

Bickerton, Derek, and William Wilson. 1987. Pidgin Hawaiian. In Gilbert, 61–76.

Bilby, Kenneth. 1983. How the "older heads" talk: A Jamaican Maroon Spirit possession language and its relationship to the creoles of Suriname and Sierra Leone. *Nieuwe West-Indische Gids* 57: 37–88.

————. 1992. Further observations on the Jamaican Maroon Spirit Language. Paper presented at the 1992 Annual Meeting of the Society for Pidgin and Creole Linguistics, Philadelphia.

Birmingham, John C., Jr. 1976. Papiamentu's West African cousins. In *1975 Colloquium of Hispanic Linguistics*, edited by F.M. Aid et al., 19–25. Washington, DC: Georgetown University Press.

Bobalijk, Jonathan David. 1995. Morphosyntax: The syntax of verbal inflection. PhD dissertation, MIT.

————. 2002. Realizing inflection: Why morphology does not drive syntax. Unpublished MS.

Bobalijk, Jonathan David, and Dianne Jonas. 1996. Subject positions and the roles of TP. *Linguistic Inquiry* 27: 195–236.

Bobalijk, Jonathan David, and Höskuldur Thráinnson. 1998. Two heads aren't always better than one. *Syntax* 1: 37–71.

Boretzky, Norbert. 1983. *Kreolsprachen, Substrate und Sprachwandel*. Wiesbaden: Harrassowitz.

Boretzky, Norbert, and Birgit Igla. 1994. Romani mixed dialects. In Bakker and Mous, 35–68.

Böttcher, Nikolas. 1995. *Aufstieg und Fall eines Atlantischen Handelsimperiums*. Frankfurt: Vervuert.

Boxer, Charles R. 1963. *Race relations in the Portuguese colonial empire, 1415–1825*. Oxford: Clarendon.

Brásio, Padre António. 1954. *Monumenta missionaria Africana: Africa Ocidental (1469–1599)*, Vol. 4. Lisbon: Agência Geral do Ultramar.

Brenner, Oscar. 1882. *Altnordisches Handbuch*. Leipzig: T.O. Weigel.

Bresnan, Joan. 2000. Pidgin genesis and optimality theory. In Siegel, 145–73.

Bright, William. 1957. *The Karok language* (University of California Publications in Linguistics, Vol. 13). Berkeley: University of California Press.

Brilioth, Börje. 1913. *A grammar of the dialect of Lorton (Cumberland)*. Oxford: Horace Hart.

Broch, Ingvild, and Ernst Håkon Jahr. 1984. *Russenorsk: Et pidginspråk i Norge*. Oslo: Novus.

Broeder, Peter, Guus Extra, Roeland Van Hout, and Kaarlo Voionmaa. 1993. Word formation processes in talking about entities. In *Adult language acquisition: Cross-linguistic perspectives* (Vol. 2: *The results*), edited by Clive Perdue, 1–72. Cambridge: Cambridge University Press.

Brousseau, Anne-Marie, Sandra Filipovich, and Claire Lefebvre. 1989. Morphological processes in Haitian Creole: The question of substratum and simplification. *Journal of Pidgin and Creole Languages* 4: 1–36.

Brustad, Kristen E. 2000. *The syntax of spoken Arabic*. Washington, DC: Georgetown University Press.

Bruyn, Adrienne. 1995a. *Grammaticalization in creoles: The development of determiners and relative clauses in Sranan*. Amsterdam: Instituut voor Functioneel Onderzoek van Taal en Taalgebruik.

———. 1995b. Relative clauses in early Sranan. In Arends, 149–202.

Burling, Robbins. 1961. *A Garo grammar*. Deccan College, Poona: Schools of Linguistics / Linguistic Society of India.

Byrne, Francis. 1984. *Fi* and *fu*: Origins and functions in some Caribbean English-based creoles. *Lingua* 62: 97–120.

———. 1987. *Grammatical relations in a radical creole*. Amsterdam: John Benjamins.

———. 1990. Pre-clausal forces in Saramaccan. *Linguistics* 28: 661–88.

Cabrera, Lydia. 1954. *El monte*. Paris: Gallimard.

Cadely, Jean-Robert. 1994. Aspects de la phonologie du créole haïtien. PhD dissertation, Université du Québec à Montréal.

Carden, Guy, and William A. Stewart. 1988. Binding theory, bioprogram, and creolization: Evidence from Haitian Creole. *Journal of Pidgin and Creole Languages* 3: 1–67.

Carden, Guy, Morris Goodman, Rebecca Posner, and William Stewart. 1990. A 1671 French Creole text from Martinique. Paper presented at the Society for Pidgin and Creole Linguistics meeting.

Carrington, Lawrence D. 1984. *St. Lucian creole*. Hamburg: Helmut Buske.

Carrington, Lawrence D., Dennis R. Craig, and R. Todd Dandare, eds. 1983. *Studies in Caribbean Language*. St. Augustine, Trinidad: Society for Caribbean Linguistics.

Carter, Hazel. 1987. Suprasegmentals in Guyanese: Some African comparisons. In Gilbert, 213–63.

Cassidy, Frederic G. 1980. The place of Gullah. *American Speech* 55: 3–16.

———. 1983. Sources of the African Element in Gullah. In Carrington et al., 76–81.

Castellanos, Jorge, and Isabel Castellanos. 1992. *Cultura Afrocubana* (Vol. 3). Miami: Ediciones Universal.

Cellier, Pierre. 1985. Comparaison syntactique du créole réunionnais et du français. Université de la Réunion.

Chaudenson, Robert. 1979. *Les créoles français*. Évreux: Nathan.

———. 1981. *Textes anciens en créole réunionnais et mauricien: Comparaison et essai d'analyse*. Hamburg: Buske.

———. 1992. *Des îles, des hommes, des langues*. Paris: L'Harmattan.

———. 2000. Créolisation du français et francisation du créole: Les cas de Saint-Barthélemy et de la Réunion. In Neumann-Holzschuh and Schneider, 361–81.

Christaller, Rev. Johann Gottlieb. 1933. *Dictionary of the Asante and Fante languages called Tshi*. Basel: Basel Evangelical Missionary Society.

———. 1964. *A grammar of the Asante and Fante languages called Tshi*. Ridgewood, NJ: Gregg Press. (Originally published 1875.)

Christophersen, Paul, and Arthur O. Sandved. 1969. *An advanced English grammar*. London: Macmillan.

Clements, J. Clancy. 1991. The Indo-Portuguese creoles: Languages in transition. *Hispania* 74: 637–46.

———. 1992. Elements of resistance in contact-induced language change. In *Explanation in historical linguistics*, edited by Garry W. Davis and Gregory K. Iverson, 41–58. Amsterdam: John Benjamins.

———. 1996. *The genesis of a language*. Amsterdam: John Benjamins.

Colarusso, John. 1992. *A grammar of the Kabardian language*. Calgary: University of Calgary Press.

Comrie, Bernard. 1992. Before complexity. In *The evolution of human languages*, edited by John A. Hawkins and Murray Gell-Mann, 193–211. Reading, MA: Addison-Wesley.

Comrie, Bernard, Maria Polinsky, and Ramazan Rajabov. 2000. Tsezian languages. Unpublished MS.

Corder, S. Pitt. 1978. "Simple" codes and the source of the second language learner's initial heuristic hypothesis. *Studies in Second Language Acquisition* 1: 1–10.

Corne, Chris. 1983. Review of *Theoretical orientations in creole studies*, edited by Albert Valdman and Arnold Highfield, and *Historicity and variation in creole studies*, edited by Arnold Highfield and Albert Valdman. *Language* 59: 176–90.

———. 1988. Mauritian Creole reflexives. *Journal of Pidgin and Creole Languages* 3: 69–94.

———. 1995a. A contact-induced and vernacularized language: How Melanesian is Tayo? In Baker, 121–48.

———. 1995b. Métchif, Mauritian and more: The "Creolisation" of French. The 1995 Samuel Weiner lecture delivered before the University of Manitoba. Winnepeg: Voices of Rupert's Land.

———. 1999. *From French to Creole*. London: University of Westminster Press.

———. 2000. Na pa kekan, na person: The evolution of Tayo negatives. In Siegel, 293–317.

Cornips, Leonie, and Karen Corrigan. 2002. Convergence and divergence in grammar. In *Dialect convergence and divergence in a changing Europe*, edited by P. Auer, Frans Hinskens, and P. Kerswill. Cambridge: Cambridge University Press.

Croft, William. 2000. *Explaining language change*. London: Longman.

Crowley, Terry. 1998. *An Erromangan (Sye) grammar*. Honolulu: University of Hawaii Press.

———. 2000. Simplicity, complexity, emblematicity and grammatical change. In Siegel, 175–93.

Crystal, David. 1987. *The Cambridge encyclopedia of language*. Cambridge: Cambridge University Press.

Curme, George O. 1952. *A grammar of the German language*. New York: Frederick Ungar.

Curtin, Phillip D. 1969. *The Atlantic slave trade: A census*. Madison: University of Wisconsin Press.

Da Cruz, Maxime. 1994. Les constructions sérielles du fOngbè: Approches sémantique et syntaxique. *Travaux de recherche sur le créole haïtien* 20–21: 1–154.

Daeleman, Jan. 1972. Kongo elements in Saramacca Tongo. *Journal of African Languages* 1: 1–44.

Dal, Ingerid. 1966. *Kurze Deutsche Syntax*. Tübingen: Max Niemeyer.

Dalgado, Sebastião R. 1900. *Dialecto Indo-Português de Ceylão*. Lisbon: Imprensa Nacional.

———. 1906. Dialecto Indo-portugués do Norte. *Revista Lusitana* 9: 142–66, 193–228.

Dalton-Puffer, Christiane. 1995. Middle English as a creole and its opposite: On the value of plausible speculation. In Fisiak, 35–50.

Danchev, Andrei. 1997. The Middle English creolization hypothesis revisited. In Fisiak, 79–108.

Day, Richard R. 1973. Patterns of variation in copula and tense in the Hawaiian post-creole continuum. PhD dissertation, University of Hawaii.

Deacon, Terence W. 1997. *The symbolic species: The co-evolution of language and the brain*. New York: Norton.

DeBose, Charles E. 1996. Question formation in Samaná English. Paper presented at the New Ways of Analyzing Variation conference (25), Las Vegas.

DeBose, Charles E., and Nicholas Faraclas. 1993. An Africanist approach to the linguistic study of Black English: Getting to the roots of the tense-aspectmodality and copula systems in Afro-American. In Mufwene, 364–87.

DeCamp, David. 1971. Toward a generative analysis of a post-creole speech continuum: Pidginization and creolization of languages. In Hymes, 349–70.

DeGraff, Michel 1992. The syntax of predication in Haitian. *Proceedings of the 22nd meeting of the North-Eastern Linguistics Society*, 103–17. University of Massachusetts at Amherst.

———. 1993. A riddle on negation in Haitian. *Probus* 5: 63–93.

———. 1994. To move or not to move? Placement of verbs and object pronouns in Haitian Creole and in French. In *Papers from the 30th Meeting of the Chicago Linguistic Society*, edited by Katherine Beals et al., 141–55. University of Chicago: Chicago Linguistics Society.

———. 1997. Verb syntax in, and beyond, creolization. In *The new comparative syntax*, edited by Liliane Haegeman, 64–94. London: Longmans.

———. 1999a. Morphology in creole genesis: A 20-minute (?*!"%$¡?‡!?) prolegomenon. Paper presented at the Neuvième Colloque International des Études Créoles, Aix-en-Provence.

———. 1999b. Creolization, language change, and language acquisition: An epilogue. In DeGraff, 473–543.

———, ed. 1999c. *Language creation and language change*. Cambridge, MA: MIT Press.

———. 2000. Creole speakers as a biologically definable class? Morphology in language creation. Paper presented to the Language in Society Workshop, University of Chicago, January 2000.

———. 2001. On the origin of creoles: A Cartesian critique of Neo-Darwinian linguistics. *Linguistic Typology* 5(2/3): 213–310.

DeGroot, A. 1981. *Woordregister Nederlands–Saramakaans*. Paramaribo, Suriname: A. DeGroot.

De Gruiter, Miel. 1994. Javindo, a contact-language in pre-War Semarang. In Bakker and Mous, 151–59.

Dejean, Yves. 1983. Diglossia revisited: French and creole in Haiti. *Word* 34: 189–204.

Deletant, Dennis, and Yvonne Alexandrescu. 1992. *Teach yourself Romanian*. Lincolnwood, IL: NTC Publishing Group.

Den Besten, Hans. 1983. On the interaction of root transformations and lexical deletive rules. In *On the formal syntax of the Westgermania: Papers from the Third Groningen Grammar Talks, Groningen, January 1981*, edited by Werner Abraham, 47–131. Amsterdam: John Benjamins.

Denison, David, 1993. *English historical syntax: Verbal constructions*. London: Longman.

Déprez, Viviane. 1992. Is Haitian Creole really a pro-drop language? *Travaux de recherche sur le créole haïtien* 11: 23–40.

———. 1999. The roots of negative concord in French and French-Lexicon creoles. In DeGraff, 375–427.

Derbyshire, Desmond. 1985. *Hixkaryana and linguistic typology*. Arlington, Texas: Summer Institute of Linguistics.

De Rooij, Vincent. 1995. Shaba Swahili. In Arends, Muysken, and Smith, 179–90.

Devitt, Dan. 1990. *Beingness and nothingness: Zero allomorphy in copula constructions*. SUNY Buffalo MS.

Devonish, Hubert. 2003. Reduplication as lexical and syntactic aspect marking: The case of Guyanese Creole. In Kouwenberg, 47–60.

Diagana, Ousmane Moussa. 1995. *La langue Soninkée*. Paris: L'Harmattan.

Diamond, Jared M. 1997. *Guns, germs, and steel*. New York: W.W. Norton.

Dillard, John L. 1972. *Black English: Its history and usage in the United States*. New York: Random House.

———. 1992. *A history of American English*. London: Longman.

———. 1993. The relative value of Ex-slave narratives: A discussion of Schneider's paper. In Mufwene, 222–31.

Di Sciullo, Anne-Marie, and Edwin Williams. 1987. *On the definition of word*. Cambridge, MA: MIT Press.

Dittmar, Norbert. 1984. Semantic features of pidginized learner varieties of German. In *Second languages: A cross-linguistic perspective*, edited by Roger Andersen, 243–70. Rowley, MA: Newbury House.

Dixon, Robert M.W. 1988. *A grammar of Boumaa Fijian*. Chicago: University of Chicago Press.

———. 1997. *The rise and fall of languages*. Cambridge: Cambridge University Press.

Dol, Philomena. 1999. Maybrat. PhD dissertation, University of Leiden.

Domingue, Nicole Z. 1977. Middle English: Another creole? *Journal of Creole Studies* 1: 89–100.

Donaldson, Bruce. 1997. *Dutch: A comprehensive grammar*. London: Routledge.

Drechsel, Emanuel. 1997. *Mobilian Jargon*. Oxford: Oxford University Press.

Dreyfuss, Gail Raimi, and Djoehana Oka. 1979. Chinese Indonesian: A new kind of language hybrid? *Papers in Pidgin and Creole Linguistics* (Canberra: Australian National University) 2: 247–74.

Dryer, Matthew. 1989. Article-noun order. In *Papers from the 25th Annual Regional Meeting of the Chicago Linguistic Society*, edited by Caroline Wiltshire, Randolph Graczyk, and Bradley Music, 83–97. Chicago: University of Chicago Press.

Ducoeurjoly, S. J. 1802. *Manuel des habitans de Saint-Domingue*. Paris: LeNoir.

Du Feu, Veronica. 1996. *Rapanui*. London: Routledge.

Dunbar, Robin. 1996. *Grooming, gossip and the evolution of language*. London: Faber and Faber.

Dunn, Richard S. 1972. *Sugar and slaves: The rise of the planter class in the English West Indies, 1624–1713*. Chapel Hill: University of North Carolina Press.

Du Tertre, J. B. 1667. *Histoire générale des Ant-isles de l'Amérique*. Paris: Jully.

Dutton, Tom. 1985. *Police Motu: Iena sivarai*. Port Moresby: University of Papua New Guinea Press.

———. 1997. Hiri Motu. In Thomason, 9–41.

Dzokanga, Adolphe. 1979. *Dictionnaire Lingala–Français suivi d'une grammaire Lingala*. Leipzig: VEB Verlag Enzyklopädie.

Edwards, Jay. 1974. African influence on the English of San Andres Island. In *Pidgins and creoles: Current trends and prospects*, edited by David DeCamp and Ian Hancock, 1–26. Washington, DC: Georgetown University Press.

Edwards, John. 1994. *Multilingualism*. London: Penguin.

Eksteen, Louis C. 1997. *Major dictionary / Groot woordeboek*. Cape Town: Pharos.

Ellis, Richard. 2001. *Aquagenesis: The origin and evolution of life in the sea*. New York: Viking.

Elugbe, Ben Ohi. 1989. Edoid. In *The Niger-Congo Languages*, edited by John Bendor-Samuel, 291–304. Lanham, MD: University Press of America.

Emenanjo, E. Nolue. 1978. *Elements of Modern Igbo grammar: A descriptive approach*. Ibadan: Oxford University Press.

Escure, Genevieve. 1983. The Belizean copula: A case of semantactic shift. In Carrington et al., 190–202.

———. 1997. Creole and dialect continua: Standard acquisition processes in Belize and China. Amsterdam: John Benjamins.

Ewers, Traute. 1996. The origin of American Black English: *Be*-forms in the HOODOO texts. New York: Mouton de Gruyter.

Fal, Arame, Rosine Santos, and Jean Léonce Doneux. 1990. *Dictionnaire wolof–français*. Paris: Éditions Karthala.

Faltz, Leonard M. 1985. *Reflexivization:A study in universal syntax*. New York: Garland.

Faraclas, Nicholas. 1988. Nigerian Pidgin and the languages of Southern Nigeria. *Journal of Pidgin and Creole Languages* 3: 177–97.

Fasold, Ralph. 1976. One hundred years from syntax to phonology. In *Papers from the Parasession on diachronic syntax*, edited by Sanford B. Steever, Carol A. Walker, and Salikoko S. Mufwene, 79–87. Chicago: Chicago Linguistics Society.

Fattier, Dominique. 1995. Une si proche étrangère (quelques remarques à propos de la genèse du sous-système des pronoms personnels du créole d'Haïti. *Situations du français* 33: 135–53.

Ferguson, Charles A. 1971. Absence of copula and the notion of simplicity. In Hymes, 141–50.

———. 1972. Diglossia. In *Language and social context*, edited by Pier Paolo Giglioli, 232–51. Harmondsworth, England: Penguin. (Originally published 1959)

Ferguson, Charles A., and Charles E. DeBose. 1977. Simplified registers, broken languages, and pidginization. In *Pidgin and creole linguistics*, edited by Albert Valdman, 99–125. Bloomington: Indiana University Press.

Ferraz, Luis Ivens. 1976. The origin and development of four creoles in the Gulf of Guinea. *African Studies* 35: 33–38.

———. 1979. *The creole of São Tomé*. Johannesburg: Witwatersrand University Press.

———. 1987. Portuguese creoles of West Africa and Asia. In Gilbert, 337–60.

Fiagã, Kwasi. 1976. *Grammaire Eve*. Lomé: Institut National de la Récherche Scientifique.

Finegan, Edward. 1999. Language: Its structure and use. Fort Worth: Harcourt Brace College Publishers.

Fisiak, Jacek. 1995. *Linguistic change under contact conditions*. Berlin: Mouton de Gruyter.

———. 1997. *Studies in Middle English linguistics*. Berlin: Mouton de Gruyter.

Fischer, Olga. 1992. Syntax. In *The Cambridge history of the English language*, Vol. 2, edited by Norman Blake, 207–408. Cambridge: Cambridge University Press.

———. 1997. Infinitive marking in Late Middle English: Transitivity and changes in the English system of case. In Fisiak, 109–34.

Fischer, Olga, Ans van Kemenade, Willem Koopman, and Wim van der Wurff, eds. 2000. *The syntax of early English*. Cambridge: Cambridge University Press.

Fisher, Ronald A. 1930. *The genetical theory of natural selection*. Oxford: Clarendon.

Foley, William A. 1988. Language birth: the processes of pidginization and creolization. In *Linguistics: The Cambridge survey*, Vol. 4, edited by Frederick J. Newmeyer, 162–83. Cambridge: Cambridge University Press.

Foley, William A., and Robert Van Valin. 1984. *Functional syntax and universal grammar*. Cambridge: Cambridge University Press.

Fournier, Robert. 1987. Le bioprogramme et les français créoles: Vérification d'une hypothèse. PhD dissertation, Université du Québec à Montréal.

Frake, Charles. O. 1971. Lexical origins and semantic structure in Philippine Creole Spanish. In Hymes, 223–42.

Friedemann, Nina S. de, and Carlos Patiño Roselli. 1983. *Lengua y sociedad en el Palenque de San Basilio*. Bogotá: Instututo Caro y Cuervo.

Fyle, Clifford N., and Eldred D. Jones. 1980. *A Krio-English dictionary*. Oxford: Oxford University Press.

Gamble, David P. 1987a. *Elementary Mandinka*. San Francisco: Author.

———. 1987b. *Intermediate Gambian Mandinka–English dictionary*. San Francisco: Author.

Garrett, Andrew. 1990. The origin of split ergativity. *Language* 66: 261–96.

Garrett, Paul B. 2000. "High" Kwéyòl: The emergence of a formal creole register in St. Lucia. In McWhorter, 63–101.

Gensler, Orin D. forthcoming. *The Celtic-North African linguistic link: Substrata and typological argumentation*. Oxford: Oxford University Press.

Geraty, Virginia. 1990. *Porgy: A Gullah version*. Charleston, SC: Wyrick and Co.

Gil, David. 1994. The structure of Riau Indonesian. *Nordic Journal of Linguistics* 17: 179–200.

———. 2001. Creoles, complexity, and Riau Indonesian. *Linguistic Typology* 5(2/3): 325–71.

Gilbert, Glenn G., ed. 1987. *Pidgin and creole languages*. Honolulu: University of Hawaii Press.

Gildea, Spike. 1993. The development of tense markers from demonstrative pronouns in Panare (Cariban). *Studies in Language* 17: 53–73.

Gilligan, Gary M. 1987. A cross-linguistic approach to the pro-drop parameter. PhD dissertation, University of Southern California.

Girier, Christian. 1996. *Parlons soninké*. Paris: L'Harmattan.

Givón, Talmy. 1971. Historical syntax and synchronic morphology: An archaeologist's field trip. *Chicago Linguistic Society* 7: 394–415.

———. 1975. Serial verbs and syntactic change. In Li, 47–112.

———. 1976. Topic, pronoun, and grammatical agreement. In Li, 149–88.

———. 1979. *On understanding grammar*. New York: Academic Press.

———. 1991. Serial verbs and the mental reality of "event": grammatical vs. cognitive packaging. In Traugott and Heine, 81–128.

Glock, Naomi. 1972. Clause and sentence in Saramaccan. *Journal of African Languages* 11: 45–61.

———. 1986. The use of reported speech in Saramaccan discourse. In *Pragmatics in non-Western prespective*, edited by George Huttar and Kenneth Gregerson, 35–61. Dallas: Summer Insititute in Linguistics and University of Texas at Arlington.

Goddard, Ives. 1997. Pidgin Delaware. In Thomason, 43–98.

Good, Jeff. 2003. Tonal morphology in a creole: high-tone raising in Saramaccan serial verb constructions. In *Yearbook of morphology*, edited by Geert Booij and Jaap can Marle. Dordrecht: Kluwer.

Goodman, Morris F. 1964. *A comparative study of creole French dialects*. The Hague: Mouton.

———. 1985. Review of Bickerton (1981). *International Journal of American Linguistics* 51: 109–37.

———. 1987. The Portuguese element in the American creoles. In Gilbert, 361–405.

Gordon, Eric V. 1927. *An introduction to Old Norse*. Oxford: Clarendon.

Görlach, Manfred. 1991. *Introduction to Early Modern English*. Cambridge: Cambridge University Press.

Gould, Stephen Jay, and Richard Lewontin. 1979. The spandrels of San Marco and the Panglossian paradigm: A critique of the adaptationist paradigm. *Proceedings of the Royal Society of London B* 205: 581–98.

Goulden, Richard J. 1990. *The Melanesian content in Tok Pisin*. Canberra: Australian National University.

Goyette, Stéphane. 2000. Creole wars : The prototype menace. Paper presented at the Society for Pidgin and Creole Linguistics Conference, Chicago.

Granda, German de. 1978. *Estudios lingüísticos hispánicos, afrohispánicos, y criollos*. Madrid: Editorial Gredos.

Grant, Anthony. 1996a. The evolution of functional categories in Grande Ronde Chinook Jargon: Ethnolinguistic and grammatical considerations. In Baker and Syea, 225–42.

————. 1996b. Zamboangueño, Papiamentu, and "Spanish-based Creoles." Unpublished MS, York University.

Greenberg, Joseph. 1966a. Some universals of grammar with particular reference to the order of meaningful elements. In *Universals of grammar*, edited by Joseph H. Greenberg, 73–113. Cambridge: Cambridge University Press.

————. 1966b. *Language universals, with special reference to feature hierarchies*. The Hague: Mouton.

————. 1966c. *The languages of Africa*. Bloomington: Indiana University Research Center in Anthropology, Folklore, and Linguistics.

————. 1978. How does a language acquire gender markers? In *Universals of human language* (Vol. 1), edited by Joseph H. Greenberg, 47–81. Stanford, CA: Stanford University Press.

Grimes, Charles E. 1996. Indonesian: The official language of a multilingual nation. In Wurm, Mühlhäusler, and Tyron, 719–27.

Günther, Wilfried. 1973. *Das portugiesische Kreolisch der Ilha do Príncipe*. Marburg-an-der-Lahn: H.-J. Greschat.

Haberland, Hartmut. 1994. Danish. In König and van der Auwera, 313–48.

Hagemeijer, Tjerk. 1999. Directional serial verb constructions in São-Tomense. Paper presented at the Ninth International Colloquium on Creole Studies, Aix-en-Provence.

Hagman, Roy S. 1977. *Nama Hottentot grammar*. Bloomington: Indiana University Publications.

Haiman, John. 1983. Iconic and economic motivation. *Language* 59: 781–819.

Haldane, J. B. S. 1932. *The causes of evolution*. New York: Harper and Brothers.

Hall, Joan, Nick Doane, and Dick Ringler, eds. 1992. *Old English and new: Essays in language and linguistics in honor of Frederic G. Cassidy*. New York: Garland.

Hall, Robert A. 1958. Creole languages and genetic relationships. *Word* 14: 367–73.

————. 1966. *Pidgin and creole languages*. Ithaca, NY: Cornell University Press.

Halle, Morris, and Alec Marantz. 1993. Distributed morphology and the pieces of inflection. In *The view from Building 20*, edited by Ken Hale and Samuel Jay Keyser, 111–76. Cambridge, MA: MIT Press.

Ham, William H. 1999. Tone sandhi in Saramaccan: A case of substrate transfer? *Journal of Pidgin and Creole Languages* 14: 45–91.

Hamp, Eric. 1965. The Albanian dialect of Màndres. *Sprache* 11: 137–54.

Hancock, Ian. 1969. A provisional comparison of the English-based Atlantic creoles. *African Language Review* 8: 7–72.

————. 1971. A study of the sources and development of the lexicon of Sierra Leone Krio. Dissertation, School of Oriental and African Studies, University of London.

————. 1986. The domestic hypothesis, diffusion and componentiality: An account of Atlantic Anglophone creole origins. In Muysken and Smith, 71–102.

————. 1987. A preliminary classification of the Anglophone Atlantic creoles with syntactic data from thirty-three representative dialects. In Gilbert, 264–333.

————. 1993. Creole language provenance and the African component. In Mufwene, 182–91.

————. 1994. Componentiality and the creole matrix. In *The crucible of Carolina*, edited by Michael Montgomery, 95–114. Athens: University of Georgia Press.

Handler, Jerome S. 1974. *The unappropriated people: Freedmen in the slave society of Barbados*. Baltimore: Johns Hopkins University Press.

Hannah, Dawn. 1996. Copula absence in Samaná English: Implications for research on the linguistic history of African-American Vernacular English. *American Speech* 72: 339–72.

Hansson, Inga-Lill. 1976. What we think we know about Akha grammar. Paper presented at the Ninth International Conference on Sino-Tibertan Languages and Linguistics, Copenhagen.

Harasowska, Marta. 1999. *Morphophonemic variability, productivity, and change: The case of Rusyn*. Berlin: Mouton de Gruyter.

Harris, Alice, and Lyle Campbell. 1995. *Historical syntax in cross-linguistic perspective*. Cambridge: Cambridge University Press.

Hashimoto, Anne Yue. 1969. The verb "to be" in Modern Chinese. In *The verb "be" and its synonyms: Philosophical and grammatical studies*, edited by John W.M. Verhaar, 72–111. New York: Humanities Press.

Haspelmath, Martin. 1998. "How young is Standard Average European?" *Language Sciences* 20: 271–87.

———. 1999. External possession in a European areal perspective. In *External possession*, edited by Doris L. Payne and Immanuel Barshi, 109–35. Amsterdam: John Benjamins.

Haudricourt, André-Georges. 1954. De l'origine des tons en viêtnamien. *Journal Asiatique* 242: 68–82.

Haugen, Einar. 1981. Language fragmentation in Scandinavia: Revolt of the minorities. In *Minority languages today*, edited by Einar Haugen, 100–19. Edinburgh: University Press.

Hawkins, Emily. 1982. *A pedagogical grammar of Hawaiian: Recurrent problems*. Honolulu: University Press of Hawaii.

Hawkins, John A. 1985. *A comparative typology of English and German: Unifying the contrasts*. Austin: University of Texas Press.

———. 1994. *A performance theory of order and constituency*. Cambridge: Cambridge University Press.

———. 1997. Some issues in a performance theory of word order. In *Constituent order in the languages of Europe*, edited by Anna Siewierska, 729–81. Berlin: Mouton de Gruyter.

Hazaël-Massieux, Guy. 1993. The African filter in the genesis of Guadeloupean creole: At the confluence of genetics and typology. In Mufwene, 109–22.

Heath, Jeffrey. 1975. Some functional relationships in grammar. *Language* 51: 89–104.

———. 1981. A case of intensive lexical diffusion. *Language* 57: 335–67.

Hedevind, Bertil. 1967. *The dialect of Dentdale in the West Riding of Yorkshire*. Uppsala: Appelbergs.

Heidelberger Forschungsprojekt "Pidgin Deutsch." 1975. *Sprache und Kommunikation ausländischer Arbeiter*. Kronberg: Scriptor Verlag.

Heine, Bernd. 1973. *Pidgin-Sprachen im Bantu-Bereich*. Berlin: Dietrich Riemer.

———. 1982. *The Nubi language of Kibera: An Arabic creole*. Berlin: Riemer.

———. 1997. *Possession*. Cambridge: Cambridge University Press.

Heine, Bernd, Ulrike Claudi, and Friederike Hünnemeyer. 1991. *Grammaticalization*. Chicago: University of Chicago Press.

Henry, Alison. 1995. *Belfast English and Standard English: Dialect variation and parameter setting*. New York: Oxford University Press.

Henry, Alison, and Denise Tangney. 1999. Functional categories and parameter setting in the second-language acquisition of Irish in early childhood. In DeGraff, 239–53.

Hermann, Eduard. 1895. Gab es im Indogermanischen Nebensätze? *Zeitschrift für vergleichende Sprachforschung* 33: 481–535.

Hesseling, Dirk C. 1905. *Het Negerhollands de Deense Antillen*. Leiden: A. W. Sijthoff.

Heusler, Andreas. 1950. *Altisländisches Elementarbuch*. Heidelberg: Carl Winter.

Hill, Jane. 1993. Formalism, functionalism, and the discourse of evolution. In *The role of theory in language description*, edited by William Foley, 437–55. Berlin: Mouton de Gruyter.

Hiltunen, Risto. 1983. *The decline of prefixes and the beginnings of the English phrasal verb.* Turku: Turun Yliopisto.

Hjelmslev, Louis. 1938. Études sur la notion de parenté linguistique. *Revue des Études Indo-éuropéennes* 1: 271–86.

Ho, Mian-Lian, and John T. Platt. 1993. *Dynamics of a contact continuum: Singaporean English.* Cambridge: Cambridge University Press.

Hock, Hans Heinrich. 1991. *Principles of historical linguistics.* Berlin: Mouton de Gruyter.

Hodges, Tony and Malyn Newitt. 1988. *São Tomé and Príncipe: from plantation economy to microstate.* Boulder, CO: Westview Press.

Hoff, Berend. 1994. Island Carib. In Bakker and Mous, 161–68.

Holm, John. 1984. Variability of the copula in Black English and its creole kin. *American Speech* 59: 291–309.

———. 1986. Substrate diffusion. In Muysken and Smith, 259–78.

———. 1988. *Pidgins and creoles.* Vol 1. Cambridge: Cambridge University Press.

———. 1989. *Pidgins and creoles.* Vol. 2. Cambridge: Cambridge University Press.

Holmes, Philip, and Ian Hinchliffe. 1997. *Swedish: An essential grammar.* London: Routledge.

Hook, Peter Edwin. 1991. The emergence of perfective aspect in Indo-Aryan languages. In Traugott and Heine, 59–89.

Hope, Jonathan. 1994. The use of *thou* and *you* in Early Modern spoken English: Evidence from depositions in the Durham ecclesiastical court records. In *Studies in Early Modern English*, edited by Dieter Kastovsky, 141–51. Berlin: Mouton de Gruyter.

Hopper, Paul J. 1975. *The syntax of the simple sentence in Proto-Germanic.* The Hague: Mouton.

Hopper, Paul J., and Elizabeth Closs Traugott, 1993. *Grammaticalization.* Cambridge: Cambridge University Press.

Hounkpatin, Basile B. (1985). Le verbal et le syntagme verbal du fon-gbe parlé à Massé. PhD dissertation, Université Paris III (Sorbonne Nouvelle).

Hovdhaugen, Even, Ingjerd Hoëm, Consulata Mahina Iosefo, and Arnfinn Muruvik Vonen. 1989. *A handbook of the Tokelau language.* Oslo: Norwegian University Press.

Huber, Magnus. 2000. Restructuring in vitro? Evidence from Early Krio. In Neumann-Holzschuh and Schneider, 275–307.

Hull, Alexander. 1979. On the origin and chronology of the French-based creoles. In *Readings in creole studies*, edited by Ian F. Hancock, Edgar Polomé, Morris Goodman, and Bernd Heine, 201–16. Ghent: E. Story-Scientia.

Huttar, George L. 1975. Sources of semantic structures. *Language* 51: 684–95.

Huttar, Mary, and George Huttar. 1994. *Ndjuka.* Newbury, MA: Routledge.

Hyman, Larry, and Francis X. Katamba. 1993. The augment in Luganda: Syntax or pragmatics? In *Theoretical aspects of Bantu grammar*, edited by Sam A. Mchombo, 209–56. Stanford, CA: CSLI Publications.

Hymes, Dell. 1971a. Introduction (III). in Hymes, 65–90.

Jackendoff, Ray. 2002. *Foundations of language: Brain, meaning, grammar, evolution.* New York: Oxford University Press.

Jackson, Kenneth H. 1953. *Language and history in early Britain.* Edinburgh: Edinburgh University Press.

Jacob, Judith M. 1968. *Introduction to Cambodian.* London: Oxford University Press.

Jacobsson, Bengt. 1951. *Inversion in English: With special reference to the Early Modern English period.* Uppsala: Almqvist and Wiksell.

Jelinek, Eloise. 1984. Empty categories, case, and configurationality. *Natural Language and Linguistic Theory* 2: 39–76.

Jennings, William. 1995a. The first generations of a Creole society: Cayenne 1660–1700. In Baker, 21–40.

———. 1995b. Saint-Christophe: Site of the first French creole. In Baker, 63–80.

Johnson, Kyle. 1990. On the syntax of inflectional paradigms. Unpublished MS, University of Wisconsin, Madison.

Jonas, Dianne. 1996. Clause structure, expletives and verb movement. In *Minimal ideas: Syntactic studies in the Minimalist framework*, edited by Werner Abraham, Samuel David Epstein, Höskuldur Thráinnson, and C. Jan-Wouter Zwart, 167–88. Amsterdam: John Benjamins.

Jones, Frederick C. 1983. English-derived words in Sierra Leone Krio. PhD dissertation, University of Leeds.

Joseph, Brian D. 1983. *The synchrony and diachrony of the Balkan infinitive: A study in areal, general, and historical linguistics*. Cambridge: Cambridge University Press.

Jourdan, Christine, and Roger Keesing. 1997. From Fisin to Pijin: Creolization in process in the Solomon Islands. *Language in Society* 26: 401–20.

Joyce, Patrick W. 1910. *English as we speak it in Ireland*. London: Longmans.

Kalmár, Ivan. 1985. Are there really no primitive languages? In *Literacy, language and learning*, edited by David R. Olson, Nancy Torrance, and Angela Hildyard, 148–66. Cambridge: Cambridge University Press.

Kastovsky, Dieter. 1992. Semantics and vocabulary. In *The Cambridge history of the English language* (Vol. 1), edited by Richard M. Hogg, 290–408. Cambridge: Cambridge University Press.

Kaufmann, Stuart. 1995. *At home in the universe: The search for laws of self-organization and complexity*. Oxford: Oxford University Press.

Kautzsch, Alexander, and Edgar Schneider. 2000. Differential creolization: Some evidence from earlier African American Vernacular English in South Carolina. In Neumann-Holzschuh and Edgar Schneider, 247–74.

Kay, Marvin L. M., and Lorin L. Cary. 1995: *Slavery in North Carolina, 178–1775*. Chapel Hill: University of North Carolina Press.

Kay, Paul, and Gillian Sankoff. 1974. A language-universals approach to pidgins and creoles. In *Pidgins and creoles: Current trends and prospects*, edited by David DeCamp and Ian Hancock, 61–72. Washington, DC: Georgetown University Press.

Kayne, Richard. 1994. *The antisymmetry of syntax*. Cambridge, MA: MIT Press.

Keesing, Roger. 1988. *Melanesian Pidgin and the Oceanic substrate*. Palo Alto: Stanford University Press.

Keller, Rudi. 1994. *On language change: The invisible hand in language*. London: Routledge.

Kemmer, Suzanne. 1993. *The middle voice*. Amsterdam: John Benjamins.

Kenrick, Donald. 1979. Romani English. *International Journal of the Sociology of Language* 19: 111–20.

Kihm, Alain. 1980a. Is there anything like decreolization? Some ongoing changes in Bissau Creole. In York Papers in Linguistics 11, edited by Mark Sebba and Loreto Todd, 203–14. York: University of York.

———. 1980b. Aspects d'une syntaxe historique: Études sur le créole portugais de Guiné-Bissau. Thèse de Doctorat de 3e Cycle, Université de Paris III, Sorbonne Nouvelle.

———. 1989. Lexical conflation as a basis for relexification. *Canadian Journal of Linguistics* 34: 351–76.

———. 1994. *Kriyol syntax: The Portuguese-based creole language of Guinea-Bissau*. Amsterdam: John Benjamins.

———. 2000. Are creole languages "perfect" languages? In McWhorter, 163–99.

Kilpiö, Matti. 1989. *Passive constructions in Old English translations from Latin: With special reference to the OE Bede and the "Pastoral Care."* Helsinki: Société Néophilologique.

Kimball, Geoffrey D. 1991. *Koasati grammar.* Lincoln: University of Nebraska Press.

Kiparsky, Paul. 1995. Indo-European origins of Germanic syntax. In *Clause structure and language change*, edited by Adrian Battye and Ian Roberts, 140–69. New York: Oxford University Press.

Kirby, Simon. 1999. *Function, selection and innateness: The emergence of language universals.* Oxford: Oxford University Press.

Klingler, Thomas A. 1992. A descriptive study of the Creole speech of Pointe Coupée Parish, Louisiana with focus on the lexicon (Vols. 1 and 2). PhD dissertation, Indiana University.

Koefoed, Geert, and Jacqueline Tarenskeen. 1996. The making of a language from a lexical point of view. In *Creole languages and language acquisition*, edited by Herman Wekker, 119–38. Berlin: Mouton de Gruyter.

König, Ekkehard, and Martin Haspelmath. 1997. Les constructions à possesseur externe dans les languages d'Europe. In *Actance et valence dans les languages de l'Europe*, edited by Jack Feuillet, 525–606. Berlin: Mouton de Gruyter.

Koopman, Hilda. 1984. *The syntax of verbs: From verb movement rules in the Kru languages to Universal Grammar.* Dordrecht: Foris.

Koopman, Hilda, and Claire Lefebvre. 1981. Haitian creole PU. In *Generative studies on creole languages*, edited by Pieter Muysken, 201–23. Ann Arbor: Karoma.

Kouwenberg, Silvia. 1987. Morphophonemic change in Saramaccan pronominal forms. In *Studies in Saramaccan language structure*, edited by Mervyn C. Alleyne, 1–15. Amsterdam: University of Amsterdam, Instituut voor Algemene Taalwetenschaft.

———. 1993. Cliticization of pronouns in Berbice Dutch and Eastern Ijo. In *Atlantic meets Pacific*, edited by Francis X. Byrne and John Holm, 119–32. Amsterdam: John Benjamins.

———. 1994. *A grammar of Berbice Dutch Creole.* Berlin: Mouton de Gruyter.

Kozelka, Paul R. 1980. *Ewe (for Togo): Grammar handbook.* Brattleboro, VT: Experiment in Modern Living.

Kramer, Marvin. 2002. Substrate transfer in Saramaccan creole. PhD dissertation, University of California, Berkeley.

Krapp, George P. 1924. The English of the Negro. *American Mercury* 2: 190–95.

Kress, Bruno. 1982. *Isländische Grammatik.* Munich: Max Hüber.

Kroch, Anthony. 1978. Toward a theory of dialect variation. *Language in Society* 7: 17–36.

Kroch, Anthony, and Ann Taylor. 1997. Verb movement in old and Middle English: Dialect variation and language contact. In Van Kemenade and Vincent, 297–325.

Kurath, Hans. 1949. *A word geography of the eastern United States.* Ann Arbor: University of Michigan Press.

Labov, William. 1969. Contraction, deletion, and inherent variability of the English copula. *Language* 45: 715–62.

———. 1990. On the adequacy of natural languages. In *Pidgin and creole tense-mood-aspect systems*, edited by John V. Singler, 1–58. Amsterdam: John Benjamins.

Labov, William, Paul Cohen, Clarence Robins, and John Lewis. 1968. *A study of the non-standard English of Negro and Puerto Rican speakers of New York City.* Final Report, Cooperative Research Project No. 3288, United States Office of Education. Washington, DC: U.S. Government Printing Office.

LaCroix, Pierre-François. 1967. Quelques aspects de la désintégration d'un système classificatoire (peul du sud de l'Adamawa). In *La classification nominale dans les langues négro-africaines (Colloques internationaux du Centre National de la Recherche Scientifique)*, 291–312. Paris: Éditions du Centre National de la Recherche Scientifique.

Lalla, Barbara, and Jean D'Costa. 1990. *Language in exile: Three hundred years of Jamaican Creole.* Tuscaloosa: University of Alabama Press.

Langacker, Ronald W. 1987. *Foundations of cognitive grammar: Theoretical prerequisites.* Stanford, CA: Stanford University Press.

Lardiere, Donna. 2000. Mapping features to forms in second language acquisition. In *Second language acquisition and linguistic theory*, edited by John Archibald, 102–29. Oxford: Blackwell.

Lass, Roger. 1987. *The shape of English.* London: J. M. Dent and Sons.

———. 1990. How to do things with junk: Exaptation in language evolution. *Journal of Linguistics* 26: 79–102.

———. 1992. Phonology and morphology. In *The Cambridge history of the English language* (Vol. 2), edited by Norman Blake, 23–155. Cambridge: Cambridge University Press.

———. 1997. *Historical linguistics and language change.* Cambridge: Cambridge University Press.

Lazard, Gilbert. 1990. Caractéristique actancielles de l'européen moyen type. In *Toward a typology of European languages*, edited by Johannes Bechert, Giuliano Bernini, and Claude Buridant, 241–53. Berlin: Mouton de Gruyter.

Lee-Smith, M. W. and Stephen A. Wurm. 1996. The Wutun language. In Wurm, Mühlhäusler, and Tyron, 883–97.

Lefebvre, Claire. 1993. The role of relexification and syntactic reanalysis in Haitian Creole: Methodological aspects of a research program. In Mufwene, 254–79.

———. 1998. *Creole genesis and the acquisition of grammar.* Cambridge: Cambridge University Press.

———. 2001. What you see is not always what you get: Apparent simplicity and hidden complexity in creole languages. *Linguistic Typology* 5: 186–213.

Lefebvre, Claire, and Anne-Marie Brousseau. 2002. *A grammar of Fongbe.* Berlin: Mouton de Gruyter.

Lehmann, Christian. 1985. Grammaticalization: synchronic variation and diachronic change. *Lingua e Stile* 20: 303–18.

LePage, Robert B., and David DeCamp. 1960. *Jamaican creole.* London: Macmillan.

LePage, Robert B., and André Tabouret-Keller. 1985. *Acts of identity.* Cambridge: Cambridge University Press.

Li, Charles N., and Sandra A. Thompson. 1975. A mechanism for the development of copula morphemes. In Li, 419–44.

———. 1976. Subject and topic: a new typology of language. In *Subject and topic*, edited by Charles N. Li and Sandra A. Thompson, 457–90. New York: Amsterdam Press.

Lightfoot, David. 1979. *Principles of diachronic syntax.* Cambridge: Cambridge University Press.

———. 1997. Shifting triggers and diachronic reanalyses. In van Kemenade and Vincent, 253–72.

———. 1999. *The development of language.* Oxford: Basil Blackwell.

———. 2000. The spandrels of the linguistic genotype. In Knight et al., 231–47.

Lipski, John. 1986. Sobre lingüística afroecuatoriana: el valle del Chota. *Anuario de Lingüística Hispanica* (Valladolid) 2: 153–76.

———. 1994. *Latin American Spanish.* London: Longman.

Lockwood, William B. 1955. *An introduction to Modern Faroese.* Copenhagen: Ejnar Munksgaard.

———. 1995. *Lehrbuch der modernen jiddischen Sprache.* Hamburg: Helmut Buske.

Lord, Carol. 1976. Evidence for syntactic reanalysis: from verb to complementizer in Kwa.

In *Papers from the parasession on diachronic syntax*, edited by Sanford B. Steever, Carol A. Walker, and Salikoko S. Mufwene, 179–91. Chicago: Chicago Linguistics Society.

Louden, Mark L. 1993. The evolution of prepositional complementizers: Parallels between English-based creoles and Germanic. Paper presented at the Society for Pidgin and Creole Linguistics Conference at the annual meeting of the Linguistics Society of America, Los Angeles.

Lück, Marlies, and Linda Henderson. 1993. *Gambian Mandinka*. Banjul, Gambia: WEC International.

Lumsden, John S. 1999. Language acquisition and creolization. In DeGraff, 129–57.

Luo, Cheng. 1991. Cross-categorial formal identity: A functional account. Unpublished MS, University of Manitoba.

Lyons, John. 1968. *Introduction to theoretical linguistics*. Cambridge: Cambridge University Press.

Madge, David. 1985. Temperature and sex determination in reptiles with reference to chelonians. *Testudo* 2(3).

Majerus, Michael, E. N. 1998. *Melanism: evolution in action*. New York: Oxford University Press.

Marchand, Hans. 1969. The categories and types of present-day English word formation. Munich: Beck.

Markey, Thomas L. 1982. Afrikaans: Creole or Non-creole? *Zeitschrift für Dialektologie und Linguistik* 2: 169–207.

Marshall, Margaret M. 1997. The origin and development of Louisiana Creole French. In *French and Creole in Louisiana*, edited by Albert Valdman, 333–49. New York: Plenum.

Matisoff, James A. 1973a. Tonogenesis in Southeast Asia. In *Consonant types and tone*, edited by Larry M. Hyman, 73–95. (Occasional Working Papers in Linguistics no. 1) Los Angeles: University of Southern California Linguistics Department.

———. 1973b. *The grammar of Lahu*. Berkeley: University of California Publications.

———. 1991. Areal and universal dimensions of grammaticization in Lahu. In *Approaches to grammaticalization* (Vol. 2), edited by Elizabeth Traugott and Bernd Heine, 383–453. Amsterdam: John Benjamins.

Matthews, Peter H. 1974. *Morphology*. Cambridge: Cambridge University Press.

Matthews, William K. 1956. The Livonian element in modern Latvian. In *Festschrift für Max Vasmer zur 70. Geburtstag*, edited by Margarete Woltner and Herbert Bräuer, 307–318. Berlin: Free University of Berlin. Veröffentlichungen der Abteilung für slawische Sprachen und Literaturen des Osteuropa-Instituts an der Freien Universitäts Berlin.

Maurer, Philippe. 1995. *L'angolar: Un créole afro-portugais parlé à São Tomé*. Hamburg: Helmut Buske.

———. 1998. El papiamentu de Curazao. In *América negra: Panorámica actual de los estudios lingüísticos sobre variedades hispanas, portuguesas y criollas*, edited by Matthias Perl and Armin Schwegler, 140–217. Frankfurt: Vervuert.

McDavid, Raven I., Jr., and Virginia McDavid. 1951. The relationship of the speech of American Negroes to the speech of Whites. *American Speech* 26: 3–17.

McWhorter, John H. 1992. Substratal influences on Saramaccan serial verb constructions. *Journal of Pidgin and Creole Languages* 7: 1–53.

———. 1994a. Rejoinder to Derek Bickerton's reply to McWhorter (1992) "Substratal influence in Saramaccan serial verb constructions." *Journal of Pidgin and Creole Languages* 9: 79–93.

———. 1994b. From focus marker to copula in Swahili. In *Special session on historical issues in African Languages: Proceedings of the 20th annual meeting of the Berkeley Linguistics Society*, edited by Kevin E. Moore, David A. Peterson, and Comfort Wentum, 57–66. Berkeley: Berkeley Linguistics Society.

————. 1995a. The scarcity of Spanish-based Creoles explained. *Language in Society* 24: 213–44.

————. 1995b. Sisters under the skin: A case for genetic relationship between the Atlantic English-based creoles. *Journal of Pidgin and Creole Languages* 10: 289–333.

————. 1996a. A deep breath and a second wind: Reassessing the substrate hypothesis. *Anthropological Linguistics* 38: 461–94.

————. 1996b. It happened at Cormantin: Tracing the birthplace of the Atlantic English-based creoles. *Journal of Pidgin and Creole Languages* 12: 1–44.

————. 1997a. *Towards a new model of creole genesis*. New York: Peter Lang.

————. 1997b. A creole by any other name: Streamlining the terminology in creole studies. In *Spreading the word: Proceedings of the Third Annual Westminster Creole Conference*, edited by Magnus Huber and Mikael Parkvall. Westminster: University of Westminster Press.

————. 1998a. Identifying the Creole Prototype: vindicating a typological class. *Language* 74: 788–818.

————. 1998b. *The word on the street: Fact and fable about American English*. New York: Plenum.

————. 2000a. *The missing Spanish creoles: Recovering the birth of plantation contact languages*. Berkeley: University of California Press.

————, ed. 2000b. *Language change and language contact in pidgins and creoles*. Amsterdam: John Benjamins.

————. 2001. What people ask David Gil and why: Rejoinder to the replies. *Linguistic Typology* 5(3/4): 388–412.

McWhorter, John H., and Mikael Parkvall. 2002. Pas tout à fait du français: Une étude créole. *Études Créoles* 25: 179–231.

Megenney, William W. 1985. Africa en Venezuela: Su herencia lingüística y cultura literaria. *Montalbán* 15: 3–56.

Melchers, Gunnel. 1992. "Du's no heard da last o' dis": On the use of be as a perfective auxiliary in Shetland dialect. In *History of Englishes*, edited by Matti Rissanen, Ossi Ihalainen, Terttu Nevalainen, and Irma Taavitsainen, 602–10. Berlin: Mouton de Gruyter.

Meroney, Howard M. 1945. The early history of "down" as an adverb. *Journal of English and Germanic Philology* 44: 378–86.

Mesthrie, Rajend. 1989. The origins of Fanagalo. *Journal of Pidgin and Creole Languages* 4: 211–40

Migge, Bettina M. 1998. Substrate influence in the formation of the Surinamese Plantation Creole: A consideration of the sociohistorical data and linguistic data from Ndyuka and Gbe. PhD dissertation, Ohio State University.

————. 2000. The origin of the syntax and semantics of property items in the Surinamese Plantation Creole. In McWhorter, 201–34.

————. 2003. The origin of predicate reduplication in Suriname Eastern Maroon Creole. In Kouwenberg, 61–71.

Miller, Roy Andrew. 1967. *The Japanese language*. Chicago: University of Chicago Press.

Mitchell, Bruce. 1985. *Old English syntax*, Vol. 1. Oxford: Clarendon.

Mitchell, Bruce, and Fred C. Robinson. 1986. *A guide to Old English*. Oxford: Blackwell.

Mittelsdorf, Sibylle. 1978. African retentions in Jamaican Creole: A reassessment. PhD dissertation, Northwestern University.

Mittwoch, Anita. 1990. On the distribution of bare infinitive complements in English. *Journal of Linguistics* 26: 103–31.

Moravcsik, Edith. 1969. *Determination*. Working Papers on Language Universals 1, 64–130. Palo Alto, CA: Stanford University Press.

Morrill, Charles. 1997. Sango revisited: The comparison of a creolized lingua franca to its source. Paper presented at the Society for Pidgin and Creole Linguistics Conference, Chicago.

Mous, Maarten. 1994. Ma'a or Mbugu. In Bakker and Mous, 175–200.

Mufwene, Salikoko S. 1986a. Les langues créoles peuvent-elles être définies sans allusion à leur histoire? *Études Créoles* 9: 135–50.

———. 1986b. Notes on continuous constructions in Jamaican and Guyanese creoles. In Görlach and Holm, 167–82.

———. 1989. La créolisation en bantou: Les cas du kituba, du lingala urbain, et du swahili du shaba. *Études Creoles* 12: 74–106.

———. 1990. Transfer and the substrate hypothesis in creolistics. *Studies in Second Language Acquisition* 12: 1–23.

———. 1991. Is Gullah decreolizing? A comparison of a speech sample of the 1930's with a speech sample of the 1980's. In *The emergence of Black English*, edited by Guy Bailey, Natalie Maynor, and Patricia Cukor-Avila, 213–30. Amsterdam: John Benjamins.

———. 1992. Africanisms in Gullah: A re-examination of the issues. In *Old English and new: Studies in language and linguistics in honor of Frederic G. Cassidy*, edited by Joan Hall, Nick Doane, and Dick Ringler, 156–82. New York: Garland.

———. 1994a. Creole genesis: A population genetics perspective. In *Caribbean language: Issues old and new*, edited by Pauline Christie. Mona, Jamaica: University of the West Indies Press.

———. 1994b. On decreolization: The case of Gullah. In *Language and the social construction of identity in creole situations*, edited by Marcyliena Morgan, 63–99. Los Angeles: Center for Afro-American Studies, UCLA.

———. 1994c. Restructuring, feature selection, and markedness: From Kimanyanga to Kituba. In *Proceedings of the twentieth annual meeting of the Berkeley Linguistics Society*, edited by Kevin Moore, David A. Peterson, and Comfort Wentum, 67–90. Berkeley: Berkeley Linguistics Society.

———. 1994d. Misinterpreting linguistic continuity charitably. In *The crucible of Carolina*, edited by Michael Montgomery, 38–59. Athens: University of Georgia Press.

———. 1996a. The Founder Principle in creole genesis. *Diachronica* 13: 83–134.

———. 1996b. Creolization and grammaticization: What creolistics could contribute to research on grammaticization. In Baker and Syea, 5–28.

———. 1997a. Jargons, pidgins, creoles, and koines: What are they? In Spears and Winford, 35–70.

———. 1997b. Kitúba. In Thomason, 173–208.

Mühlhäusler, Peter. 1980. Structural expansion and the process of creolization. In *Theoretical orientations in creole studies*, edited by Albert Valdman and Arnold Highfield, 19–55. New York: Academic Press.

———. 1985. The scientific study of Tok Pisin: Language planning and the Tok Pisin lexicon. In *Handbook of Tok Pisin (New Guinea Pidgin)*, edited by Stephen A. Wurm and Peter Mühlhäusler, 595–664. Canberra: Australian National University.

———. 1997. *Pidgin and creole linguistics* (expanded and revised edition). London: University of Westminster.

———. 1998. How Creoloid can you get. *Journal of Pidgin and Creole Languages* 13: 355–71.

Munford, Clarence J. 1991. *The Black ordeal of slavery and slave trading in the French West Indies, 1625–1715*, vol. 2. Lewiston, NY: Edwin Mellen.

Munro, Pamela. 1976. *Mojave syntax*. New York: Garland.

Munteanu, Dan. 1996. *El papiamento, lengua criolla hispánica*. Madrid: Gredos.

Mustanoja, Tauno F. 1960. *A Middle English syntax*, Vol. 1. Helsinki: Société Néophilologique.

Muysken, Pieter. 1981. Halfway between Quechua and Spanish: The case for relexification. In *Historicity and variation in creole studies*, edited by Arnold Highfield and Albert Valdman, 52–78. Ann Arbor, MI: Karoma.

———. 1994. Saramaccan and Haitian: A comparison. *Journal of Pidgin and Creole Languages* 9: 305–14.

———. 1997. Media Lengua. In *Contact languages: A wider perspective*, edited by Sarah G. Thomason, 365–426. Amsterdam: John Benjamins.

Muysken, Pieter, and Norval Smith. 1994. Reflexives in the creole languages: An interim report. In *Creolization and language change*, edited by Dany Adone and Ingo Plag, 45–64. Tübingen: Max Niemeyer.

Naro, Anthony J. 1978. A study on the origins of pidginization. *Language* 54: 314–47.

Neffgen, H. 1918. *Grammar and vocabulary of the Samoan language*. London: Kegan Paul, Trench, Trubner.

Nespor, Marina, and Irene Vogel. 1986. *Prosodic phonology*. Dordrecht: Foris.

Neumann, Gunter. 1966. Zur chinesisch-russischen Behelfssprache von Kjachta. *Sprache* 12: 237–51.

Neumann, Ingrid. 1985. *Le créole de Breaux Bridge, Louisiane*. Hamburg: Helmut Buske.

Nevalainen, Terttu. 1997. Recycling inversion: The case of initial adverbs and negators in Early Modern English. In *A Festschrift for Roger Lass on his sixtieth birthday* (*Studia Anglica Posnaniensa* 32), 203–14.

Newmeyer, Frederick J. 1998. *Language form and language function*. Cambridge, MA: MIT Press.

Nichols, Johanna. 1980. Pidginization and foreigner talk: Chinese Pidgin Russian. In *Papers from the Fourth International Conference on Historical Linguistics*, edited by Elizabeth Traugott, Rebecca Labrum, and Susan Shepherd, 397–407. Amsterdam: John Benjamins.

———. 1986. The bottom line: Chinese Pidgin Russian. In *Evidentialty: The linguistic encoding of epistemology*, edited by Wallace Chafe and Johanna Nichols, 239–57. Norwood, NJ: Ablex.

———. 1992. *Linguistic diversity in space and time*. Chicago: University of Chicago Press.

Nida, Eugene A., and Harold W. Fehderau. 1970. Indigenous pidgins and koinés. *International Journal of American Linguistics* 36: 146–55.

Niles, Norma A. 1980. Provincial English dialects and Barbadian English. PhD dissertation, University of Michigan.

Njie, Codu Mbassy. 1982. *Description syntaxique du wolof de Gambie*. Dakar: Nouvelles Éditions Africaines.

Nylander, Dudley K. 1983. Étude déscriptive du Krio langue créole de la Sierra-Léone: Phonologie et syntaxe. Dissertation, Université des Langues et Lettres de Grenoble.

O'Grady, William, Michael Dobrovolsky. and Mark Aronoff. 1997. *Contemporary linguistics: An introduction* (third edition). New York: St. Martin's.

Ogunbowale, P. O. 1970. *The essentials of the Yoruba language*. London: University of London Press.

Olson, Michael L. 1973. *Barai sentence structure and embedding*. Santa Ana, CA: Summer Institute of Linguistics.

O'Neil, Wayne. 1978. The evolution of the Germanic inflectional systems: A study in the causes of language change. *Orbis* 27: 248–86.

Orton, Harold, Stewart F. Sanderson, and John Widdowson, eds. 1978. *The linguistic atlas of England*. London: Croom Helm.

Pagel, Karl. 1983. *Die Hanse*. Braunschweig: Westermann.

Parkvall, Mikael. 1995a. A dual approach to creole genesis. Unpublished MS, University of Stockholm.

————. 1995b. The role of St. Kitts in a new scenario of French Creole genesis. In Baker, 41–62.

————. 1999. Feature selection and genetic relationships among Atlantic creoles. In Huber and Parkvall, 29–66.

————. 2003. Reduplication in the Atlantic creoles. In Kouwenberg, 19–36.

Pasch, Helma. 1997. Sango. In Thomason, 209–70.

Patterson, Orlando. 1967. *The sociology of slavery*. London: McGibbon and Key.

Patterson, William. 1880. *A glossary of words in use in the counties of Antrim and Down*. London: Trübner.

Paul, Hermann. 1880. *Principien der Sprachgeschichte*. Halle: Niemeyer

Peitsara, Kirsti. 1997. The development of reflexive strategies in English. In *Grammaticalization at work*, edited by Matti Rissanen, Merja Kytö, and Kirsi Heikkonen, 277–370. Berlin: Mouton de Gruyter.

Perkins, Revere. 1980. The covariation of culture and grammar. PhD dissertation, University of Michigan, Ann Arbor.

Peters, Robert. 1987. Das Mittelniederdeutsche als Sprache der Hanse. In *Sprachkontakt in der Hanse: Aspekte des Sprachausgleichs im Ostsee- und Nordseeraum*, edited by Sture Ureland, 65–88. Tübingen: Niemeyer.

Phillips, Judith Wingerd. 1982. A partial grammar of the Haitian Creole verb system. PhD dissertation, SUNY Buffalo.

Pinckard, George. 1806. *Notes on the West Indies*. London: Longman, Hurst, Rees, and Orme.

Pinker, Steven, and P. Bloom. 1990. Natural language and natural selection. *Behavioral and Brain Sciences* 13: 707–84.

————. 1994. Humans did not evolve from bats. *Behavioral and Brain Sciences* 17: 183–85.

Pintzuk, Susan. 1991. Phrase structures in competition: Variation and change in Old English word order. PhD dissertation, University of Pennsylvania.

Plag, Ingo. 1993. *Sentential complementation in Sranan*. Tübingen: Max Niemeyer,

Plank, Frans, and Edith Moravcsik. 1996. The Maltese article: Language-particulars and universals. *Rivista di Linguistica* 8: 183–212.

Platt, John T. 1975. The Singapore English speech continuum and its basilect "Singlish" as a "creoloid." *Anthropological Linguistics* 17: 363–74.

Platzack, Christer. 1986. COMP, INFL, and Germanic word order. In *Topics in Scandinavian syntax*, edited by Lars Hellan and Kirsti Koch Christensen, 185–234. Dordrecht: Reidel.

————. 1987. The Scandinavian languages and the null-subject parameter. *Natural Language and Linguistic Theory* 5: 377–401.

————. 1988. The emergence of a word order difference in Scandinavian subordinate clauses. McGill Working Papers in Linguistics (Special issue on comparative German syntax): 215–38.

Platzack, Christer, and Anders Holmberg. 1989. The role of AGR and finiteness in Germanic VO languages. *Working Papers in Scandinavian Syntax* 43: 51–76.

Polinsky, Maria. 1999. Reaching out for topics: Long-distance agreement. Paper presented at the University of California, Berkeley, October 1999.

Pollock, Jean-Yves. 1989. Verb movement, Universal Grammar and the structure of IP. *Linguistic Inquiry* 20: 365–424.

Ponelis, Fritz. 1993. *The development of Afrikaans*. Frankfurt: Peter Lang.

Poplack, Shana, ed. 2000. *The English history of African American English*. Malden, MA: Blackwell.

Poplack, Shana, and David Sankoff. 1987. The Philadelphia story in the Caribbean. *American Speech* 62: 291–314.

Poplack, Shana, and Sali Tagliamonte. 1991. African-American English in the diaspora: evidence from old-line Nova Scotians. *Language Variation and Change* 3: 301–39.

Post, Marike. 1992. The serial verb constructions in Fa d'Ambu. In *Actas do Coloquio sobre Crioulos de Base Lexical Portguesa*, edited by Ernesto D'Andrade and Alain Kihm, 153–71. Lisbon: Colibri.

———. 1995. Fa D'Ambu. In Arends, Muysken, and Smith, 191–204.

Postma, Johannes. 1990. *The Dutch in the Atlantic slave trade*. New York: Cambridge University Press.

Poullet, Hector, Sylviane Telchid, and Danièle Montbriand. 1984. *Dictionnaire des expressions du créole guadeloupéen*. Fort-de-France: Hatier Martinique.

Poussa, Patricia. 1982. The evolution of early standard English: the creolization hypothesis. *Studia Anglica Posnaniensia* 14: 69–85.

Price, Richard. 1983. *First time: The historical vision of an Afro-American people*. Baltimore: Johns Hopkins University Press.

Quint, Nicolas. 1998. Le créole de l'île de Santiago (République du Cap-Vert). PhD dissertation, University of Paris III.

Rabel, Lili. 1961. *Khasi, a language of Assam*. Baton Rouge: Louisiana State University Press.

Ramat, Paolo. 1998. The Germanic languages. In *The Indo-European languages*, edited by Anna Giacalone Ramat and Paolo Ramat, 380–414. London: Routledge.

Randt, Andreas Christoph. 1781. *Oto va oure fri Gado bi meki ko sombre*. Bambey. (Housed in the Utrecht Rijksarchief.)

Reh, Mechthild, and Christiane Simon. 1998. Experiens-Konstruktionen in Mande-Sprachen. In Experiens-Kodierung in afrikanischen Sprachen typologisch gesehen: Formen und ihre Motivierungen. Haamburg: University of Hamburg, Instuitut für Afrikanistik und Äthiopistik.

Reinecke, John E., Stanley M. Tsuzaki, David DeCamp, Ian F. Hancock, and R E. Wood, eds. 1975. *A bibliography of pidgin and creole languages*. Honolulu: University Press of Hawaii.

Rens, L. L. E. 1953. *The history and social background of Surinam's Negro English*. Amsterdam: North-Holland.

Restrepo, Vicente. 1886. *A study of the gold and silver mines of Colombia* (trans. C.W. Fisher). New York: Colombian Consulate.

Rickford, John R. 1977. The question of prior creolization in Black English. In *Pidgin and creole linguistics*, edited by Albert Valdman, 199–221. Bloomington: University of Indiana Press.

———. 1979. Variation in a creole continuum: Quantitative and implicational approaches. PhD dissertation, University of Pennsylvania.

———. 1980. How does *doz* disappear? In *Issues in English creoles: Papers from the 1975 Hawaii conference*, edited by Richard R. Day, 77–96. Heidelberg: Groos.

———. 1986. Social contact and linguistic diffusion: Hiberno-English and New World Black English. *Language* 62: 245–90.

———. 1987. *Dimensions of a creole continuum*. Stanford: Stanford University Press.

———. 1992. The creole residue in Barbados. In Hall et al., 183–201.

———. 1996. Copula variability in Jamaican Creole and African American Vernacular English: A reanalysis of DeCamp's texts. In Guy et al., 357–72.

———. 1997. Prior creolization of AAVE? Sociohistorical and textual evidence from the 17th and 18th centuries. *Journal of Sociolinguistics* 1: 315–36.

———. 1998. The creole origins of African-American Vernacular English: Evidence from copula absence. In *African American English: structure, history, use*, edited by Salikoko Mufwene, John R. Rickford, Guy Bailey, and John Baugh, 154–200. London: Routledge.

Rickford, John R., and Jerome S. Handler. 1994. Textual evidence on the nature of early Barbadian speech, 1676–1835. *Journal of Pidgin and Creole languages* 9: 221–55.

Rickford, John R., and Christine Théberge. 1996. Preterit HAD + V-ed in the narratives of African American preadolescents. *American Speech* 71: 227–52.

Rissanen, Matti. 1987. Whatever happened to the Middle English indefinite pronouns? In Fisiak, 513–29.

Rizzi, Luigi. 1982. *Issues in Italian syntax.* Dordrecht: Foris.

Roberts, Ian. 1985. Agreement parameters and the development of English auxiliaries. *Natural Language and Linguistic Theory* 3: 21–58.

———. 1992. *Verbs and diachronic syntax.* Dordrecht: Kluwer.

———. 1993. A formal account of grammaticalization in the history of Romance futures. *Folia Linguistica Historica* 13: 219–58.

———. 1999. Verb movement and markedness. In DeGraff, 287–327.

Roberts, Sarah J. 1995. Pidgin Hawaiian: a sociohistorical study. *Journal of Pidgin and Creole Languages* 10: 1–56.

———. 1998. The genesis of Hawaiian Creole and diffusion. *Language* 74: 1–39.

———. 2000. Nativization and the genesis of Hawaiian Creole. In McWhorter, 257–300.

Rohrbacher, Bernhard. 1999. *Morphology-driven syntax: A theory of V to I raising and pro-drop.* Amsterdam: John Benjamins.

Romaine, Suzanne. 1988. *Pidgin and creole languages.* London: Longman.

———. 1992. *Language, education and development: Urban and rural Tok Pisin in Papua New Guinea.* Oxford: Clarendon.

Rongier, Jacques. 1988. *Apprenons l'ewe.* Paris: Éditions l'Harmattan.

Ross, Alan S. C., and A. W. Moverley. 1964. *The Pitcairnese language.* New York: Oxford University Press.

Rottet, Kevin. 1992. Functional categories and verb movement in Louisiana Creole. *Probus* 2: 261–89.

Rountree, Catharine S. 1972. Saramaccan tone in relation to intonation and grammar. *Lingua* 29: 308–25.

———. 1992. *Saramaccan grammar sketch.* Paramaribo, Suriname: Summer Institute of Linguistics.

Rountree, Catherine S., and Naomi Glock. 1976. *Lesi buku a Saamaka tongo, Deel I.* Paramaribo, Suriname: Summer Institute of Linguistics.

———. 1977. *Saramaccan for beginners.* Paramaribo, Suriname: Summer Institute of Linguistics.

Rout, Leslie B. 1976. *The African experience in Spanish America: 1502 to the present day.* Cambridge: Cambridge University Press.

Rowlands, Evan C. 1969. *Teach yourself Yoruba.* New York: David McKay.

Roy, John D. 1986. The structure of tense and aspect in Barbadian English Creole. In Görlach and Holm, 141–56.

Rydén, Mats, and Sverker Brorström. 1987. *The 'be/have' variation with intransitives in English: with special reference to the Late Modern period.* Stockholm: Almqvist and Wiksell International.

Sadler, Wesley. 1964. *Untangled CiBemba.* Kitwe, N. Rhodesia: United Church of Central Africa in Rhodesia.

Safir, Kenneth J. 1985. *Syntactic chains.* Cambridge: Cambridge University Press.

Samarin, William. 1967. *A grammar of Sango.* The Hague: Mouton.

———. 1980. Creolizing lag in Creole Sango. *Ba Shiru* 11: 3–20.

———. 1990. The origins of Kituba and Lingala. *Journal of African Languages and Linguistics* 12: 47–77.

———. 1997. The creolization of pidgin morphophonology. In Spears and Winford, 175–216.

———. 2000. The status of Sango in fact and fiction. In McWhorter, 301–33.

Sankoff, Gillian, and Suzanne Laberge. 1980. On the acquisition of native speakers by a language. In *The social life of language*, edited by G. Sankoff, 195–209. Philadelphia: University of Pennsylvania Press.

Sapir, David J. 1971. West Atlantic: an inventory of the languages, their noun class systems and consonant alternation. In *Current trends in linguistics* (Vol. 7), edited by T. A. Sebeok, 45–112. The Hague: Mouton.

Sapir, Edward. 1921. *Language: An introduction to the study of speech*. New York: Harcourt Brace.

Sawyer, Peter H. 1971. *The age of the Vikings*. London: Edward Arnold.

Scalise, Sergio. 1984. *Generative morphology*. Dordrecht: Foris.

Schachter, Paul. 1990. Tagalog. In *The world's major languages*, edited by B. Comrie, 936–58. New York: Oxford University Press.

Schneider, Edgar W. 1989. *Earlier American Black English*. Tuscaloosa: University of Alabama Press.

Schuchardt, Hugo. 1888. Kreolische Studien VIII. Über das Annamito-französische. *Sitzungsberichte der kaiserlichen Akademie der Wissenschaften zu Wien* 116: 227–34.

———. 1914. *Die Sprache der Saramakkaneger in Suriname*. Amsterdam: Johannes Müller.

———. 1980. Notes on the English of American Indians: Cheyenne, Kiowa, Pawnee, Pueblo, Sioux and Wyandot. In *Pidgin and creole languages: Selected essays*, edited and translated by Glenn G. Gilbert, 30–37. Cambridge: Cambridge University Press.

Schwegler, Armin. 1991. El habla cotidiana del Chocó (Colombia). *América Negra* 2: 85–119.

———. 1993. Rasgos (afro-)portugueses en el criollo del Palenque de San Basilio (Colombia). In *Homenaje a José Perez Vidal*, edited by Carmen Díaz D. Alayón, 667–96. La Laguna, Tenerife: A. Romero.

———. 1996a. *Chi ma nkongo, chi ma ri Luango: Cantos ancestrales afrohispanos del Palenque de San Basilio (Colombia)*. Frankfurt: Vervuert.

———. 1996b. La doble negación dominicana y la génesis del español caribeño. *Hispanic Linguistics* 8: 246–315.

———. 1998. El palenquero. In *América negra: Panorámica actual de los estudios lingüísticos sobre variedades criollas y afrohispanas*, edited by Matthias Perl and Armin Schwegler, 219–91. Frankfurt: Vervuert.

———. 1999. El vocabulario africano de Palenque (Colombia). Part II: Compendio de palabras (con etimologías). In *El Caribe hispánico: Perspectivas lingüísticas actuales (Homenaje a Manuel Alvarez Nazario)*, edited by Luis Ortiz, 171–253. Frankfurt: Vervuert.

———. 2000. The myth of decreolization: the anomalous case of Palenquero. In Neumann-Holzschuh and Schneider, 409–36.

Sebba, Mark. 1997. *Contact languages: Pidgins and creoles*. New York: St. Martin's.

Seidel, August, and Ivon Struyf. 1910. *La langue congolaise*. Paris: Jules Groos.

Selkirk, Elisabeth O. 1982. *The syntax of words*. Cambridge, MA: MIT Press.

———. 1984. *Phonology and syntax: The relation between sound and structure*. Cambridge: MIT Press.

———. 1986. On derived domains in sentence phonology. *Phonology* 3: 371–405.

Seuren, Pieter, and Herman Wekker. 1986. Semantic transparency as a factor in creole genesis. In Muysken and Smith, 57–70.

Shanks, Louis. 1994. *A buku fu okanisi anga ingiisi wowtu (Aukan–English Dictionary)*. Paramaribo, Suriname: Summer Institute of Linguistics.

Sharp, William Frederick. 1976. *Slavery on the Spanish frontier*. Norman: University of Oklahoma Press.

Sherzer, Joel. 1976. *An areal-typological study of American Indian languages north of Mexico*. Amsterdam: North-Holland.

Shibatani, Masayoshi. 1991. Grammaticization of topic into subject. In Traugott and Heine, 93–133.

Siegel, Jeff. 1987. *Language contact in a plantation environment*. Cambridge: Cambridge University Press.

———, ed. 2000. *Processes of language contact: studies from Australia and the South Pacific*. Quebec: AGMV Marquis.

Siegel, Jeff, Barbara Sandeman, and Chris Corne. 2000. Predicting substrate influence: tense-modality-aspect marking in Tayo. In Siegel, 75–97.

Singh, U. Nissor. 1983. *Khasi–English dictionary*. Delhi: Cultural Publishing House.

Singler, John V. 1981. *An introduction to Liberian English*. East Lansing: Michigan State University, African Studies Center / Peace Corps.

———. 1986. Short note. *Journal of Pidgin and Creole Languages* 1: 141–45.

———. 1988. The homogeneity of the substrate as a factor in pidgin/creole genesis. *Language* 64: 27–51.

———. 1989. Plural marking in Liberian Standard English, 1829–1980. *American Speech* 64: 40–64.

———. 1991. Liberian settler English and the ex-slave recordings: A comparative study. In Bailey et al., 249–74.

———. 1993. African influence upon Afro-American language varieties: A consideration of sociohistorical factors. In Mufwene, 235–53.

———. 1995. The demographics of creole genesis in the Caribbean: A comparison of Martinique and Haiti. In Arends, 203–32.

———. 2000. Optimality theory, the minimal-word constraint, and the historical sequencing of substrate influence in pidgin/creole genesis. In McWhorter, 336–51.

———, ed. 1990. *Pidgin and creole tense-mood-aspect systems*. Amsterdam: John Benjamins.

Smith, Henry. 1992. "Dative sickness" and abstractness. In *On Germanic linguistics: Issues and methods*, edited by Irmengard Rauch, Gerald F. Carr, and Robert L. Kyes, 283–97. Berlin: Mouton de Gruyter.

Smith, Ian R. 1984. The development of morphosyntax in Sri Lanka Portuguese. In *York Papers in linguistics 11*, edited by Mark Sebba and Loreto Todd, 291–301. York: University of York.

Smith, Norval J. 1987a. The genesis of the creole languages of Surinam. Dissertation, University of Amsterdam.

———. 1987b. Gbe words in the creole languages of Surinam. Paper presented at the Workshop on Creoles, University of Amsterdam.

———. 2001. Voodoo Chile: Differential substrate effects in Saramaccan and Haitian. In *Creolization and contact*, edited by Norval Smith and Tonjes Veenstra, 43–80. Amsterdam: John Benjamins.

Smith, Norval J., Ian E. Robertson, and Kay Williamson. 1987. The Ijo element in Berbice Dutch. *Language in Society* 16: 49–90.

Smitherman, Geneva. 1977. *Talkin and testifyin*. Detroit: Wayne State University Press.

Sorace, Antonella. 2000. Gradients in auxiliary selection with intransitive verbs. *Language* 76: 859–90.

Sordam, Max, and Hein Eersel. 1985. *Sranantongo / Surinaamse Taal*. Baarn, Netherlands: Bosch and Keuning.

Spears, Richard A. 1973. Elementary Maninka-kan. Unpublished MS, Northwestern University.

Speedy, Karin. 1995. Mississippi and Tèche Creole: Two separate starting points for Creole in Louisiana. In Baker, 97–114.

Spencer, Andrew. 1998. Morphophonological operations. In Spencer and Zwicky, 123–43.

Sreedhar, M. V. 1985. *Standardized grammar of Naga Pidgin*. Mysore: Central Institute of Indian Languages.

Stahlke, Herbert F. 1970. Serial verbs. *Studies in African Linguistics* 1: 60–99.

Staudacher-Valliameé, Gilette. 1994. Eine synchron dynamische Phologie des Réunion Créole als Ausgangspunkt zur Annäherung an Kreolisierung und Sprachwandel. In *Creolization and language change*, edited by Dany Adone and Ingo Plag, 139–60. Tübingen: Max Niemeyer.

Stein, Peter. 1995. Early creole writing and its effects on the discovery of creole language structure. In Arends, 43–61.

Stenson, Nancy. 1981. *Studies in Irish syntax*. Tübingen: Günter Narr.

Stewart, William A. 1967. Sociolinguistic factors in the history of American Negro dialects. *Florida FL Reporter* 5: 11.

———. 1969. Historical and structural aspects of sociolinguistic variation: The copula in Black English. In *Georgetown University Roundtable on Languages and Linguistics*, edited by James E. Alatis, 215–33. Washington, DC: Georgetown University Press.

———. 1971. Sociolinguistic factors in the history of American negro dialects. In *Black-white speech relationships*, edited by Walt Wolfram and N. Clarke, 74–89. Washington, DC: Center for Applied Linguistics.

Stolz, Thomas. 1986. Gibt es das Kreolische Sprachwandelmodell? Vergleichende Grammatik des Negerholländischen. Frankfurt: Peter Lang.

Strandskogen, Åse-Berit, and Rolf Strandskogen. 1986. *Norwegian: An essential grammar*. London: Routledge.

Strang, Barbara M. H. 1970. *A history of English*. London: Methuen.

Streitberg, Wilhelm. 1906. *Gotisches Elementarbuch*. Heidelberg: Carl Winter.

Summer Institute of Linguistics. 1982. *Saamaka Nongo*. Paramaribo, Suriname: Summer Institute of Linguistics.

Sutcliffe, David. 2001. The voice of the ancestors: New evidence on 19th-century precursors to 20th-century African American English. In *Sociocultural and Historical Contexts of African American English*, edited by Sonja Lanehart, 129–68. Amsterdam: John Benjamins.

Swartenbroeckx, S. J. Pierre. 1973. *Dictionnaire Kikongo et Kituba–Français*. Banbundu, Zaire: Ceeba.

Sweetser, Eve. 1988. Grammaticalization and semantic bleaching. In *Berkeley Linguistics Society: General session and parasession on grammaticalization* (Berkeley Linguistics Society 14), edited by Shelley Axmaker, Annie Jaisser and Helen Singmaster, 389–405. Berkeley: University of California, Berkeley.

Talmy, Leonard. 1972. Semantic structures in English and Atsugewi. PhD dissertation, University of California, Berkeley.

———. 1985. Lexicalization patterns. In *Language typology and syntactic description*. Vol. 3: *Grammatical categories and the lexicon*, edited by Timothy Shopen, 57–149. Cambridge: Cambridge University Press.

Tchekhoff, Claude. 1979. From ergative to accusative in Tongan: An example of synchronic dynamics. In Plank, 407–18.

Thomas, Dorothy M. 1969. *Chrau affixes*. (Mon-Khmer Studies III), 90–107. Saigon: Summer Institute of Linguistics.

Thomas, David D. 1971. *Chrau grammar*. Honolulu: University of Hawaii Press.

Thomas, E. J. 1911. *Danish conversation-grammar*. Heidelberg: Julius Groos.

Thomas, P. W. 1990. The Brythonic consonant shift and the development of consonant mutation. *Bulletin of the Board of Celtic Studies* 37: 1–42.

Thomason, Sarah G. 1982. Chinook Jargon in areal and historical context. *Language* 59: 820–70.

———. 1993. On identifying the sources of creole structures. In Mufwene, 280–95.

———. 1997a. A typology of contact languages. In Spears and Winford, eds, 71–88.

———. 1997b, ed. *Contact languages: A wider perspective.* Amsterdam: John Benjamins.

Thomason, Sarah G., and Terence Kaufman. 1988. *Language contact, creolization, and genetic linguistics.* Berkeley: University of California Press.

Thompson, Laurence C. 1965. *A Vietnamese grammar.* Seattle: University of Washington Press.

Tiersma, Pieter M. 1985. *Frisian reference grammar.* Dordrecht: Foris.

Tinker, Edward L. 1936. *Gombo: The creole dialect of Louisiana.* Worcester, MA: Proceedings of the American Antiquarian Society.

Trask, R. Larry. 1979. On the origins of ergativity. In Plank, 385–404.

Traugott, Elizabeth C. 1972. *A history of English syntax: A transformational approach to the history of English sentence structure.* New York: Holt, Rinehart and Winston.

Travis, Lisa. 1984. Parameters and effects of word order variation. PhD dissertation, MIT.

———. 1989. Parameters of phrase structure. In *Alternative conceptions of phrase structure*, edited by Mark R. Baltin and Anthony S. Kroch, 263–79. Chicago: University of Chicago Press.

Trubetskoy, Nicholas. 1931. Die phonologischen Systeme. *Travaux du Cercle Linguistique de Prague* 4: 96–116.

Trudgill, Peter. 1989. Contact and evolution in linguistic change. In *Language change: Contributions to the study of its causes*, edited by Leiv Egil Brevik and Ernst Håkon Jahr, 227–37. Berlin: Mouton de Gruyter.

———. 1996. Dialect typology: isolation, social network and phonological structure. In *Towards a social science of language.* Vol. 1: *Variation and change in language and society*, edited by Gregory Guy, Crawford Feagin, Deborah Schiffrin, and John Baugh, 3–21. Amsterdam: John Benjamins.

———. 1999. Language contact and the function of linguistic gender. *Posnan Studies in Contemporary Linguistics* 35: 133–52.

———. 2001. Contact and simplification: Historical baggage and directionality in linguistic change. *Linguistic Typology* 5: 371–73.

Trudgill, Peter, and Jack Chambers. 1991. Aspect in English dialects. In *Dialects of English*, edited by Peter Trudgill and Jack Chambers, 145–47. London: Longmans.

Turner, Lorenzo D. 1949. *Africanisms in the Gullah dialect.* Ann Arbor: University of Michigan Press.

Ultan, Russell. 1978. Some general characteristics of interrogative systems. In *Universals of human language* (Vol. 4), edited by Joseph H. Greenberg, 211–48. Palo Alto, CA: Stanford University Press.

Upton, Clive, David Parry, and John D. A. Widdowson, eds. 1994. *Survey of English dialects: The dictionary and grammar.* London: Routledge.

Valdman, Albert, Thomas Klingler, Margaret Marshall, and Kevin Rottet. 1998. *Dictionary of Louisiana Creole.* Bloomington: Indiana University Press.

Van der Voort, Hein. 1995. Eskimo Pidgin. In Arends, Muysken, and Smith, 137–51.

Van der Voort, Hein, and Pieter Muysken. 1995. Eighteenth-century Negerhollands reflexives revisited. In Arends, 25–61.

van Kemenade, Ans. 1987. *Syntactic case and morphological case in the history of English.* Dordrecht: Foris.

van Kemenade, Ans, and Nigel Vincent. 1997. *Parameters of morphosyntactic change.* Cambridge: Cambridge University Press.

Van Ness, Silke. 1994. Pennsylvania German. In König and van der Auwera, 420–38.

Van Rheeden, Hadewych. 1994. Petjo: the mixed language of Batavia. In Bakker and Mous, 223–37.

Veenstra, Tonjes. 1996. *Serial verbs in Saramaccan*. The Hague: Holland Academic Graphics.

Vennemann, Theo. 2001. Atlantis semitica: Structural contact features in Celtic and English. In *Historical linguistics 1999*, edited by Laurel J. Brinton, 351–69. Amsterdam: John Benjamins.

Vergnaud, Jean-Roger, and Marie-Louise Zubizarreta. 1992. The definite determiner and the inalienable constructions in French and English. *Linguistic Inquiry* 23: 595–652.

Verhaar, John. W. M. 1995. *Toward a reference grammar of Tok Pisin: An experiment in corpus linguistics*. Honolulu: University of Hawaii Press.

Viereck, Wolfgang. 1993. The medieval European common market and its impact on Middle English. *Neuphilologische Mitteilungen* 94: 69–78.

Vikner, Sten. 1995. V°-to-I° movement and inflection for person in all tenses. *Working Papers in Scandinavian Syntax* 55: 1–27.

Visser, Fredericus T. 1963. *An historical syntax of the English language*, Vol. 1. Leiden: E. J. Brill.

Volker, Craig A. 1998. *The Nalik language of New Ireland, Papua New Guinea*. New York: Peter Lang.

Voorhoeve, Jan. 1964. *Creole languages and communication: Symposium on multilingualism* (Publication 87). London: Commission de coopération technique en Afrique.

———. 1985. A note on epenthetic transitive /m/ in Sranan Tongo. In Hancock, 89–93.

Voss, Manfred. 1995. Kent and the Low Countries revisited. In Fisiak, 327–63.

Voyles, Joseph B. 1992. *Early Germanic grammar*. New York: Academic Press.

Wakelin, Martyn. 1972. *English dialects: An introduction*. London: Athlone.

Wakeman, Canon C. W. 1979. *A dictionary of the Yoruba language*. Ibadan: University Press.

Washabaugh, William. 1975. On the development of complementizers in creolization. *Stanford University Working Papers on Language Universals* 17: 109–40.

Watkins, Calvert. 1962. *Indo-European origins of the Celtic verb*. Dublin: Dublin Institute for Advanced Studies.

———, ed. 1985. *The American heritage dictionary of Indo-European roots*. Boston: Houghton Mifflin.

Watters, J. R. 1979. Focus in Aghem. In *Aghem Grammatical Structure*, edited by Larry Hyman, 137–97. Los Angeles: Southern California Occasional Papers in Linguistics.

WEC International. 1992. *Wolof learning manual*. Banjul, Gambia: WEC International.

Weldon, Tracy. 1996. Copula variability in Gullah: Implications of the Creolist hypothesis. Paper presented at the New Ways of Analyzing Variation Conference, Las Vegas.

Welmers, Beatrice F., and William E. Welmers. 1968. *Igbo: A learner's dictionary*. Los Angeles: African Studies Center.

Welmers, William E. 1973. *African language structures*. Berkeley: University of California Press.

West, Robert C. 1957. *The Pacific lowlands of Colombia*. Baton Rouge: Louisiana State University Press.

Westermann, Diedrich. 1928. *Ewe–English / English–Ewe dictionary*. Berlin: Dietrich Riemer.

———. 1930. *A study of the Ewe language*. London: Oxford University Press.

Whinnom, Keith. 1956. *Spanish contact vernaculars in the Philippine Islands*. Hong Kong: Hong Kong University Press.

Wierzbicka, Anna. 1992. *Semantics, culture and cognition: Universal human concepts in culture-specific configurations*. Oxford: Oxford University Press.

Wiesemann, Ursula. 1991. Tone and intonational features in Fon. *Linguistique Africaine* 7: 65–90.

Wietz, Br. 1805. *Die Apostelgeschichte in die Saramakka Negersprache*. (Housed in the Utrecht Rijksarchief.)

Winford, Donald. 1985. The syntax of fi complements in Caribbean English Creole. *Language* 61: 588–624.

———. 1992. Another look at Black English and Caribbean creoles. *American Speech* 67: 21–60.

———. 1993. *Predication in Caribbean English creoles*. Amsterdam: John Benjamins.

———. 1997a. Property items and predication in Sranan. *Journal of Pidgin and Creole Languages* 12: 237–301.

———. 1997b. On the origins of African American Vernacular English: A creolist perspective. Part I: The sociohistorical background. *Diachronica* 14: 305–44.

———. 1998. On the origins of African American Vernacular English: A creolist perspective. Part II: The linguistic features. *Diachronica* 15: 99–154.

———. 2000. Tense and aspect in Sranan and the creole prototype. In McWhorter, 383–442.

Wolfenden, Elmer. 1975. *A description of Hiligaynon syntax*. Norman, OK: Summer Institute of Linguistics.

Wolfram, Walt, and Ralph Fasold. 1974. *The study of social dialects in American English*. Englewood Cliffs, NJ: Prentice Hall.

Wood, Peter. 1974. *Black majority*. New York: Knopf.

Wright, Joseph. 1892. *A grammar of the dialect of Windhill in the West Riding of Yorkshire*. London: Kegan Paul.

Wylie, Jonathan. 1995. The origins of Lesser Antillean French Creole: Some literary and lexical evidence. *Journal of Pidgin and Creole Languages* 10: 77–126.

Zobl, Helmut, and Juana Liceras. 1994. Functional categories and acquisition orders. *Language Learning* 44: 159–80.

Zwicky, Arnold M., and Geoffrey K. Pullum. 1983. Cliticization vs. inflection: English *n't*. *Language* 59: 502–13.

# INDEX